ASCENT
CENTER FOR TECHNICAL KNOWLEDGE

Autodesk® Inventor® 2017 (R1) Sheet Metal Design

Student Guide
Mixed Units - 1ˢᵗ Edition

AUTODESK.
Authorized Publisher

ASCENT - Center for Technical Knowledge®
Autodesk® Inventor® 2017 (R1)
Sheet Metal Design
1st Edition

Prepared and produced by:

ASCENT Center for Technical Knowledge
630 Peter Jefferson Parkway, Suite 175
Charlottesville, VA 22911

866-527-2368
www.ASCENTed.com

Lead Contributor: Jennifer MacMillan

ASCENT - Center for Technical Knowledge is a division of Rand Worldwide, Inc., providing custom developed knowledge products and services for leading engineering software applications. ASCENT is focused on specializing in the creation of education programs that incorporate the best of classroom learning and technology-based training offerings.

We welcome any comments you may have regarding this student guide, or any of our products. To contact us please email: feedback@ASCENTed.com.

The following are registered trademarks or trademarks of Autodesk, Inc., and/or its subsidiaries and/or affiliates in the USA and other countries: 123D, 3ds Max, Alias, ATC, AutoCAD LT, AutoCAD, Autodesk, the Autodesk logo, Autodesk 123D, Autodesk Homestyler, Autodesk Inventor, Autodesk MapGuide, Autodesk Streamline, AutoLISP, AutoSketch, AutoSnap, AutoTrack, Backburner, Backdraft, Beast, BIM 360, Burn, Buzzsaw, CADmep, CAiCE, CAMduct, Civil 3D, Combustion, Communication Specification, Configurator 360, Constructware, Content Explorer, Creative Bridge, Dancing Baby (image), DesignCenter, DesignKids, DesignStudio, Discreet, DWF, DWG, DWG (design/logo), DWG Extreme, DWG TrueConvert, DWG TrueView, DWGX, DXF, Ecotect, Ember, ESTmep, FABmep, Face Robot, FBX, Fempro, Fire, Flame, Flare, Flint, ForceEffect, FormIt 360, Freewheel, Fusion 360, Glue, Green Building Studio, Heidi, Homestyler, HumanIK, i-drop, ImageModeler, Incinerator, Inferno, InfraWorks, Instructables, Instructables (stylized robot design/logo), Inventor, Inventor HSM, Inventor LT, Lustre, Maya, Maya LT, MIMI, Mockup 360, Moldflow Plastics Advisers, Moldflow Plastics Insight, Moldflow, Moondust, MotionBuilder, Movimento, MPA (design/logo), MPA, MPI (design/logo), MPX (design/logo), MPX, Mudbox, Navisworks, ObjectARX, ObjectDBX, Opticore, P9, Pier 9, Pixlr, Pixlr-o-matic, Productstream, Publisher 360, RasterDWG, RealDWG, ReCap, ReCap 360, Remote, Revit LT, Revit, RiverCAD, Robot, Scaleform, Showcase, Showcase 360, SketchBook, Smoke, Socialcam, Softimage, Spark & Design, Spark Logo, Sparks, SteeringWheels, Stitcher, Stone, StormNET, TinkerBox, Tinkercad, Tinkerplay, ToolClip, Topobase, Toxik, TrustedDWG, T-Splines, ViewCube, Visual LISP, Visual, VRED, Wire, Wiretap, WiretapCentral, XSI.

NASTRAN is a registered trademark of the National Aeronautics Space Administration.

All other brand names, product names, or trademarks belong to their respective holders.

General Disclaimer:

Notwithstanding any language to the contrary, nothing contained herein constitutes nor is intended to constitute an offer, inducement, promise, or contract of any kind. The data contained herein is for informational purposes only and is not represented to be error free. ASCENT, its agents and employees, expressly disclaim any liability for any damages, losses or other expenses arising in connection with the use of its materials or in connection with any failure of performance, error, omission even if ASCENT, or its representatives, are advised of the possibility of such damages, losses or other expenses. No consequential damages can be sought against ASCENT or Rand Worldwide, Inc. for the use of these materials by any third parties or for any direct or indirect result of that use.

The information contained herein is intended to be of general interest to you and is provided "as is", and it does not address the circumstances of any particular individual or entity. Nothing herein constitutes professional advice, nor does it constitute a comprehensive or complete statement of the issues discussed thereto. ASCENT does not warrant that the document or information will be error free or will meet any particular criteria of performance or quality. In particular (but without limitation) information may be rendered inaccurate by changes made to the subject of the materials (i.e. applicable software). Rand Worldwide, Inc. specifically disclaims any warranty, either expressed or implied, including the warranty of fitness for a particular purpose.

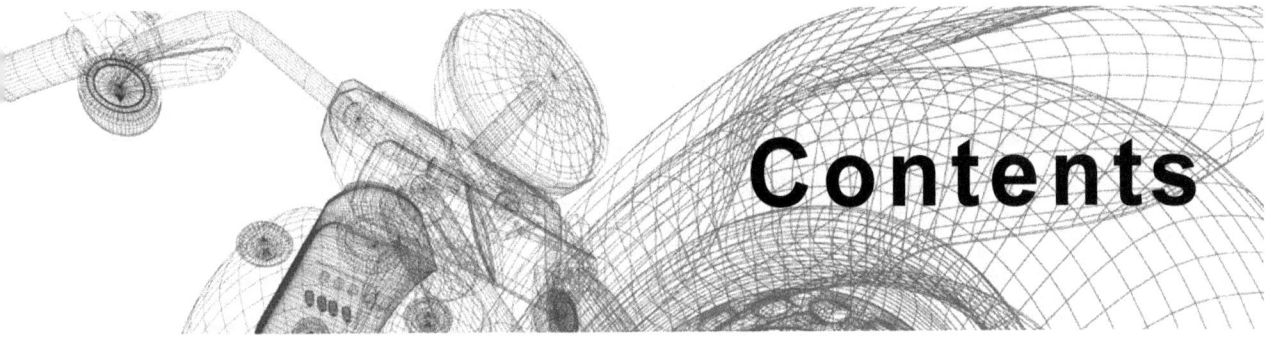

Contents

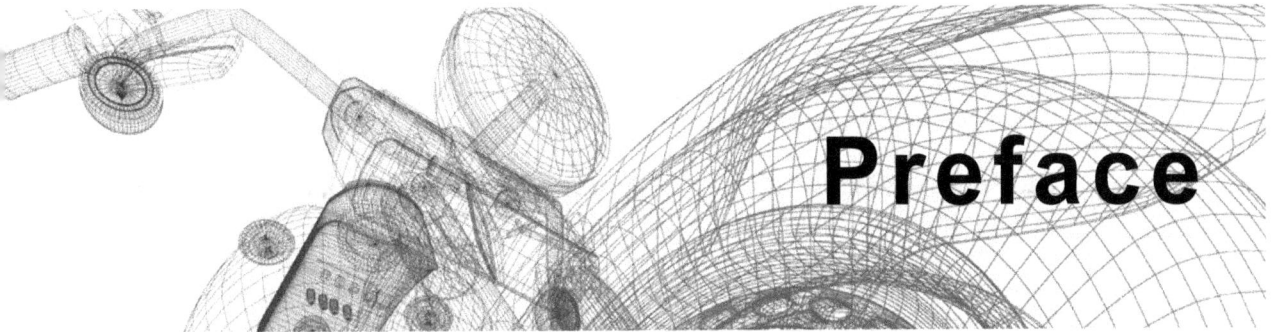

Preface

The *Autodesk® Inventor® 2017 (R1) Sheet Metal Design* student guide introduces the concepts and techniques of sheet metal modeling with the Autodesk Inventor software.

The structure of the student guide follows the typical stages of using the Autodesk Inventor software. That is, to create and edit sheet metal parts, generate flat patterns, and document the designs in drawings.

Topics Covered

- Autodesk Inventor Sheet Metal interface
- Sheet metal design process
- Creating base Faces, Contour Flanges, and Contour Rolls
- Creating secondary Faces, Contour Flanges, and Contour Rolls
- Sheet metal parameters
- Creating Flanges
- Creating Hems, Folds, and Bends
- Corner Rounds and Chamfers
- Sheet Metal Cuts (Holes, Cuts, and Punch Features)
- Corner Seams (Seams and Miters)
- Generating Flat Patterns
- Lofted Flanges
- Rips
- Unfolding and Refolding
- Multi-Body Sheet Metal Modeling
- Documentation and Annotation of drawings
- Converting solid models to sheet metal models
- Sheet Metal Styles

Note on Software Setup

This student guide assumes a standard installation of the software using the default preferences during installation. Lectures and practices use the standard software templates and default options for the Content Libraries.

Students and Educators can Access Free Autodesk Software and Resources

Autodesk challenges you to get started with free educational licenses for professional software and creativity apps used by millions of architects, engineers, designers, and hobbyists today. Bring Autodesk software into your classroom, studio, or workshop to learn, teach, and explore real-world design challenges the way professionals do.

Get started today - register at the Autodesk Education Community and download one of the many Autodesk software applications available.

Visit www.autodesk.com/joinedu/

Note: Free products are subject to the terms and conditions of the end-user license and services agreement that accompanies the software. The software is for personal use for education purposes and is not intended for classroom or lab use.

Lead Contributor: Jennifer MacMillan

With a dedication for engineering and education, Jennifer has spent over 20 years at ASCENT managing courseware development for various CAD products. Trained in Instructional Design, Jennifer uses her skills to develop instructor-led and web-based training products as well as knowledge profiling tools.

Jennifer has achieved the Autodesk Certified Professional certification for Inventor and is also recognized as an Autodesk Certified Instructor (ACI). She enjoys teaching the training courses that she authors and is also very skilled in providing technical support to end-users.

Jennifer holds a Bachelor of Engineering Degree as well as a Bachelor of Science in Mathematics from Dalhousie University, Nova Scotia, Canada.

Jennifer MacMillan has been the Lead Contributor for *Autodesk Inventor Sheet Metal Design* since 2008.

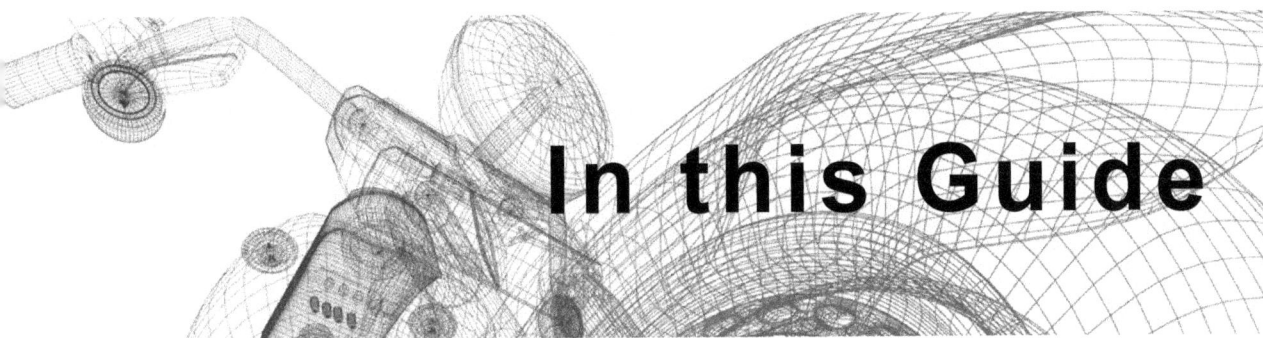

In this Guide

The following images highlight some of the features that can be found in this Student Guide.

Practice Files

To download the practice files for this student guide, use the following steps

1. Type the URL shown below into the address bar of your Internet browser. The URL must be typed **exactly as shown**. If you are using an ASCENT ebook, you can click on the link to download the file.

        Address bar
   http://www.ASCENTed.com/getfile?id=xxxxxxxx

   File Edit View Favorites Tools Help

2. Press <Enter> to download the .ZIP file that contains the Practice Files

3. Once the download is complete, unzip the file to a local folder. The unzipped file contains an .EXE file.

4. Double-click on the .EXE file and follow the instructions to automatically install the Practice Files on the C:\ drive of your computer.

   Do not change the location in which the Practice Files folder is installed. Doing so can cause errors when completing the practices in this student guide

http://www.ASCENTed.com/getfile?id=xxxxxxxx

Stay Informed!
Interested in receiving information about upcoming promotional offers, educational events, invitations to complimentary webcasts, and discounts? If so, please visit www.ASCENTed.com/updates/

Help us improve our product by completing the following survey:
www.ASCENTed.com/feedback
You can also contact us at: feedback@ASCENTed.com

FTP link for practice files

Practice Files

The Practice Files page tells you how to download and install the practice files that are provided with this student guide.

Chapter

1

Getting Started

In this chapter you learn how to start the AutoCAD® software, become familiar with the basic layout of the AutoCAD screen, how to access commands, use your pointing device, and understand the AutoCAD Cartesian workspace. You also learn how to open an existing drawing, view a drawing by zooming and panning, and save your work in the AutoCAD software

Learning Objectives in this Chapter

- Launch the AutoCAD software and complete a basic initial setup of the drawing environment.
- Identify the basic layout and features of AutoCAD interface including the Ribbon, Drawing Window, and Application Menu
- Locate commands and launch them using the Ribbon, shortcut menus, Application Menu, and Quick Access Toolbar.
- Locate points in the AutoCAD Cartesian workspace.
- Open and close existing drawings and navigate to file locations.
- Move around a drawing using the mouse, the **Zoom** and **Pan** commands, and the Navigation Bar.
- Save drawings in various formats and set the automatic save options using the **Save** commands.

Learning Objectives for the chapter

Chapters

Each chapter begins with a brief introduction and a list of the chapter's Learning Objectives.

Side notes

Side notes are hints or additional information for the current topic.

Practice Objectives

Instructional Content

Each chapter is split into a series of sections of instructional content on specific topics. These lectures include the descriptions, step-by-step procedures, figures, hints, and information you need to achieve the chapter's Learning Objectives.

Practices

Practices enable you to use the software to perform a hands-on review of a topic.

Some practices require you to use prepared practice files, which can be downloaded from the link found on the Practice Files page.

Chapter Review Questions

Chapter review questions, located at the end of each chapter, enable you to review the key concepts and learning objectives of the chapter.

Command Summary

The Command Summary is located at the end of each chapter. It contains a list of the software commands that are used throughout the chapter, and provides information on where the command is found in the software.

Autodesk Certification Exam Appendix

This appendix includes a list of the topics and objectives for the Autodesk Certification exams, and the chapter and section in which the relevant content can be found.

Icons in this Student Guide

The following icons are used to help you quickly and easily find helpful information.

New in 2017	Indicates items that are new in the Autodesk Inventor 2017 (R1) software.
Enhanced in 2017	Indicates items that have been enhanced in the Autodesk Inventor 2017 (R1) software.

Practice Files

To download the practice files for this student guide, use the following steps:

1. Type the URL shown below into the address bar of your Internet browser. The URL must be typed **exactly as shown**. If you are using an ASCENT ebook, you can click on the link to download the file.

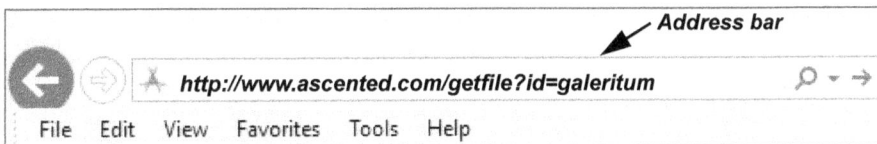

Address bar

http://www.ascented.com/getfile?id=galeritum

File   Edit   View   Favorites   Tools   Help

2. Press <Enter> to download the .ZIP file that contains the Practice Files.

3. Once the download is complete, unzip the file to a local folder. The unzipped file contains an .EXE file.

4. Double-click on the .EXE file and follow the instructions to automatically install the Practice Files on the C:\ drive of your computer.

   Do not change the location in which the Practice Files folder is installed. Doing so can cause errors when completing the practices in this student guide.

http://www.ascented.com/getfile?id=galeritum

Stay Informed!

Interested in receiving information about upcoming promotional offers, educational events, invitations to complimentary webcasts, and discounts? If so, please visit:

www.ASCENTed.com/updates/

Help us improve our product by completing the following survey:

www.ASCENTed.com/feedback

You can also contact us at: *feedback@ASCENTed.com*

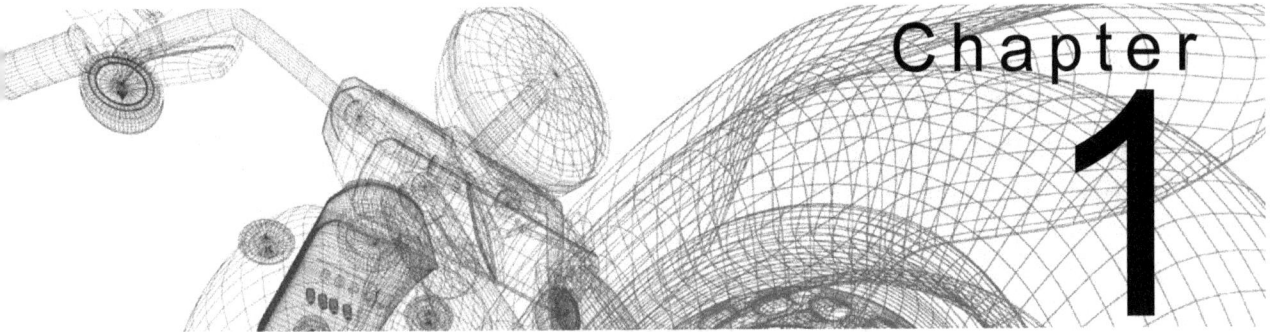

Introduction to Sheet Metal Modeling

The Autodesk® Inventor® sheet metal environment enables you to create features that are specific to the sheet metal modeling process. This chapter introduces you to some of the tools and terminology that are used to create these types of parts and are covered throughout this student guide.

Learning Objectives in this Chapter

- Identify the differences between solid and sheet metal models.
- Gain an understanding of the sheet metal terminology that is used in this student guide.
- Recognize the Sheet Metal interface that is used to create and work in a sheet metal model.
- Understand the overall workflow that is used to create a sheet metal model in the Autodesk Inventor software.
- Start the creation of a new sheet metal model using a provided template.

1.1 Sheet Metal Concepts

Uses for Sheet Metal Components

The sheet metal application in the Autodesk Inventor software enables you to effectively capture design intent while creating sheet metal parts in the sheet metal environment. An example is shown in Figure 1–1.

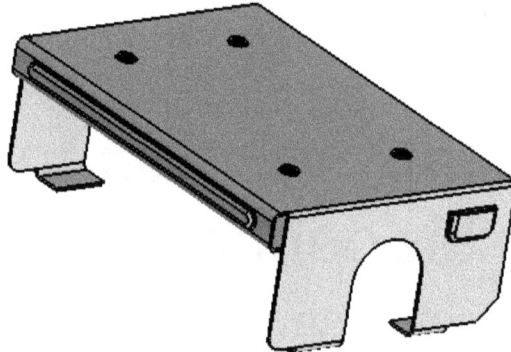

Figure 1–1

The Autodesk Inventor Sheet Metal environment enables you to do the following:

- Create features specific to the sheet metal manufacturing process.

- Design a sheet metal model within the context of an assembly so that all 3D information is present.

- Create different instances of the model to use at different times or for varied situations.

- Extract information and establish dimensional and geometric controls that are beneficial to the manufacturing process.

- Generate views and information to document the design of sheet metal parts.

Similarities to Solid Models

Considering the order in which the part is bent or cut during fabrication is equally important to considering the design intent in sheet metal.

The creation of a sheet metal model is similar to the creation of a solid part in the following ways:

- Sheet metal models are feature-based.

- Sheet metal parts can include sketched and placed features.

- Individual sheet metal features (e.g., faces, flanges, bends, cuts, and holes) are created in sequence and reference one another, resulting in parent-child feature relationships.

- Reference geometry can be created when adding certain types of features, such as flanges or holes, just as extrusions and cuts can reference other features on solid parts.

- Sheet metal parts can use named parameters and equations.

- A sheet metal model can be designed using multi-body modeling.

Differences from Solid Models

The creation of a sheet metal model is different from the creation of a solid part in the following ways:

- Sheet metal parts have a constant thickness.

- Radii and bend relief sizes are generally consistent in a part.

- Flat patterns can be created for manufacturing drawings.

- Features can be added to a flat pattern but do not display on the model in the folded state.

Several simple sheet metal parts are shown in Figure 1–2.

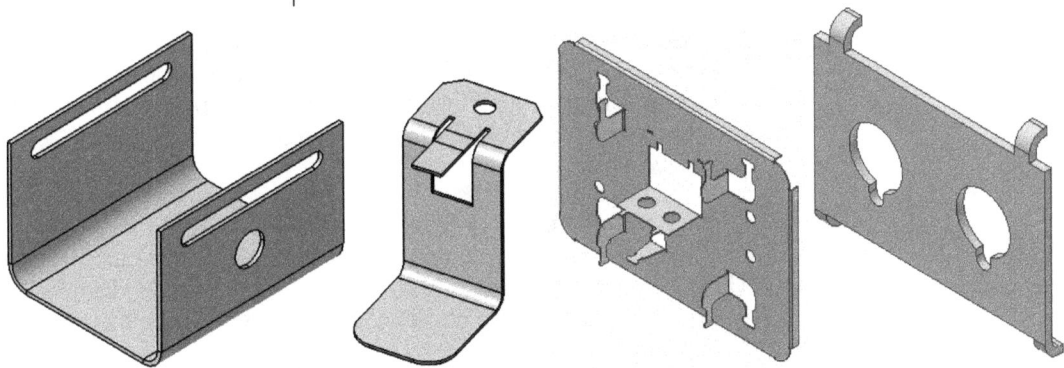

Figure 1–2

1.2 Sheet Metal Terminology

It is helpful to become familiar with some of the standard terminology used in sheet metal design. Figure 1–3 shows a part with a few of the features labeled.

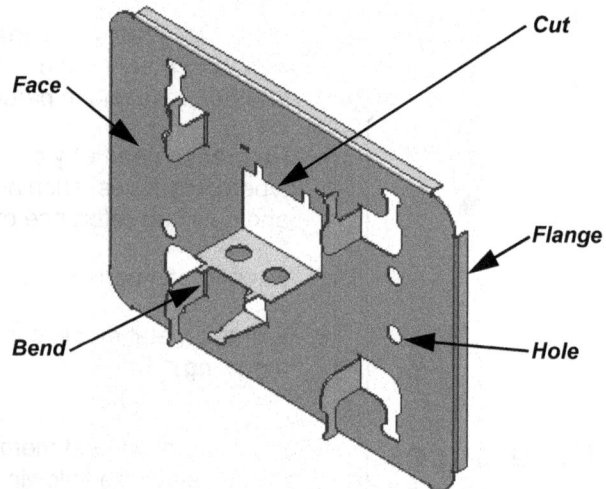

Figure 1–3

Sheet Metal Features

Various sheet metal features can be produced (such as a hems, flanges, cut-outs, holes, and punches).

Styles

Sheet metal styles include settings, such as material thickness, default bend radius, and type of bend relief for a part. Most of the style information is stored in standard parameters.

Face

A sheet metal Face feature is a flat area of the sheet metal model. It is created from a closed loop sketch profile with thickness added. Its final shape is controlled by the shape of the closed sketch and other features that are attached to (or removed from) it.

The **Face** command creates planar (flat) sheet metal features, which are often the building blocks for sheet metal parts. Faces can have a simple rectangular profile, as shown on the left in Figure 1–4, or a more complex profile as shown on the right.

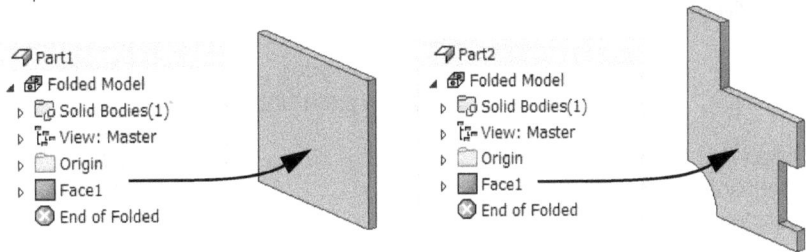

Figure 1–4

Flange

A standard Flange feature is a type of secondary planar feature added to a sheet metal part. When you create a flange, a Bend feature is also created between the flange and the face feature on which the flange is built. A flange can be added to a single edge of a face or to an edge loop on a face. Figure 1–5 shows a face with two flanges added.

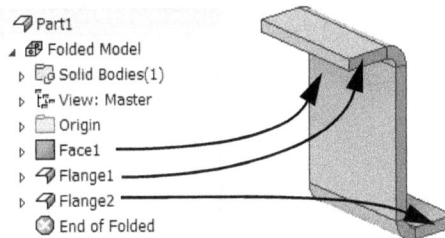

Figure 1–5

Contour Flange

A Contour Flange feature is a feature created from an open loop sketched profile. The profile is extruded to create a surface and then adds thickness to turn it into a sheet metal feature. Contour flanges can be used as base features or secondary features. They are often used to create a rolled feature or multiple flanges on a sheet metal part.

A part made from an open loop sketch is shown on the left in Figure 1–6. It is turned into a contour flange as shown on the right.

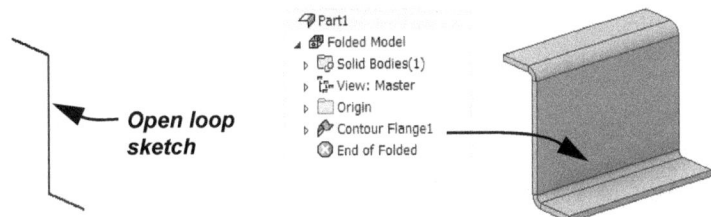

***Open loop
sketch***

Figure 1–6

Lofted Flange

Lofted flanges are most commonly used with duct design.

A Lofted Flange feature creates transitional sheet metal geometry that is blended between two profile sketches, as shown in Figure 1–7. Lofted flanges can be used as base or secondary features.

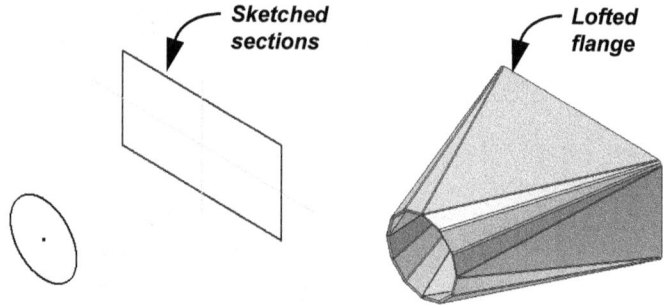

Figure 1–7

Contour Roll

A Contour Roll feature creates sheet metal geometry that supports the roll forming sheet metal manufacturing process. Similar to contour flanges, a contour roll feature requires an open loop sketch profile that is revolved to create the required geometry, as shown in Figure 1–8. Contour rolls can be used as base or secondary features.

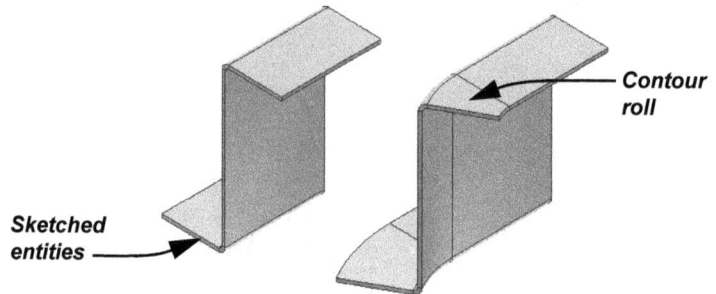

Figure 1–8

Hem

Adding a Hem feature creates a folded edge along sheet metal edges to strengthen the part, and/or to eliminate sharp edges. Four standard hem styles are shown in Figure 1–9.

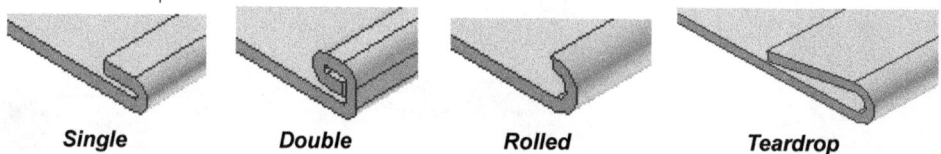

Single *Double* *Rolled* *Teardrop*

Figure 1–9

Bend

You can add a Bend feature between two sheet metal faces that are parallel or at an angle to each other. A bend is a feature that is dependent on two existing faces. It alters the length of a face, if required, so that the two faces can meet at the bend, as shown in Figure 1–10.

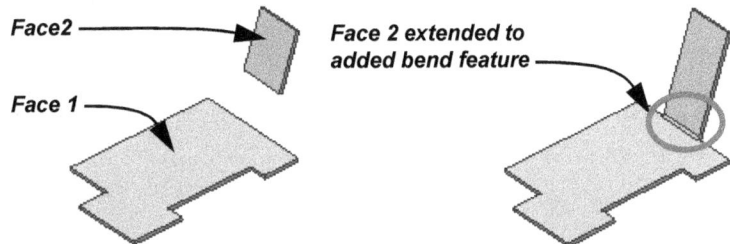

Figure 1–10

Bend Radius

Bend features can be added between existing features or incorporated during the creation of a feature. They are added to accommodate the fabrication of the sheet metal part when it is formed from a flat sheet to create a folded shape. If an appropriate radius is not used, the part can split along a sharp corner. In general, the radius used for a bend is determined by the type and thickness of the material. However, a zero bend radius can also be applied, as required. Bend radius values can be assigned to the model using the Sheet Metal Rule or entered individually as you create features.

Bend Relief

Bend Relief features are defined to enable bends to be fabricated. In some cases, they remove material to enable clearance between edges. Figure 1–11 shows straight, round, and tear style bend reliefs applied on the three flanges from left to right.

Figure 1–11

Fold

A Fold bends a sheet metal face by folding it along a sketched line. The sketched line must terminate at the edges of the face, as shown in Figure 1–12. The fold becomes a dependent feature on the face.

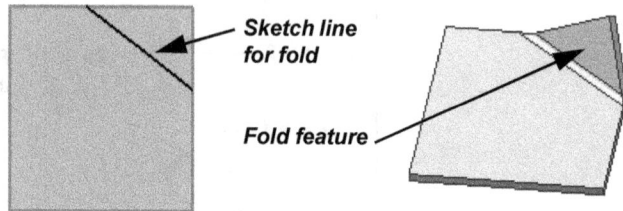

Sketch line
for fold

Fold feature

Figure 1–12

Holes and Cuts

Hole and Cut features remove material, similar to the methods used in solid models, as shown in Figure 1–13. Cuts require a closed loop sketch to define the profile of the cut.

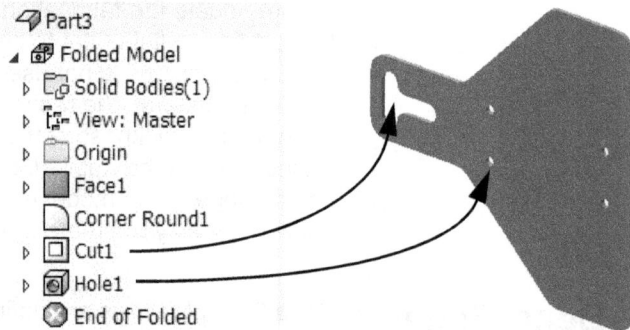

Part3
Folded Model
Solid Bodies(1)
View: Master
Origin
Face1
Corner Round1
Cut1
Hole1
End of Folded

Figure 1–13

Corner Seam

Corner Seam features create an overlap or gap at the intersection of two or three faces. Examples with a gap and overlap are shown in Figure 1–14.

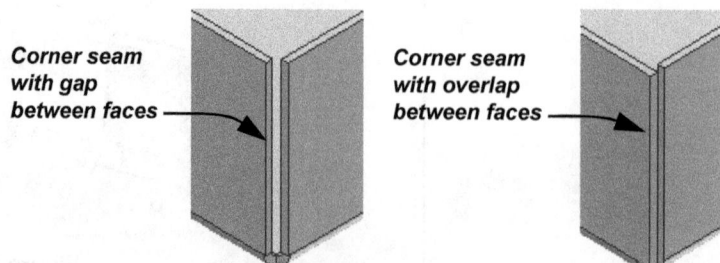

Corner seam
with gap
between faces

Corner seam
with overlap
between faces

Figure 1–14

Rip

A Rip feature enables you to create an open gap (rip) in geometry that is closed, similar to that shown in Figure 1–15. Adding a rip to a closed shape enables you to generate a flat pattern. Rips are not affected by cut-outs, emboss, or other formed features.

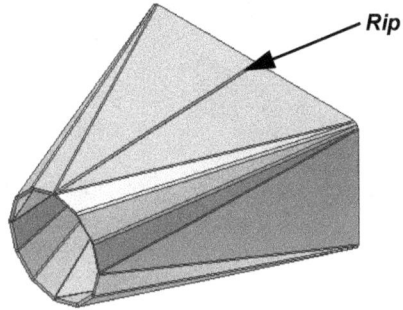

Rip

Figure 1–15

Unfold/Refold

The Unfold and Refold features enable you to unfold a model at any point in the its design, and then refold the geometry at any point thereafter, as shown in Figure 1–16. Any features created between the unfolding and refolding are maintained on the model geometry as it was created when unfolded.

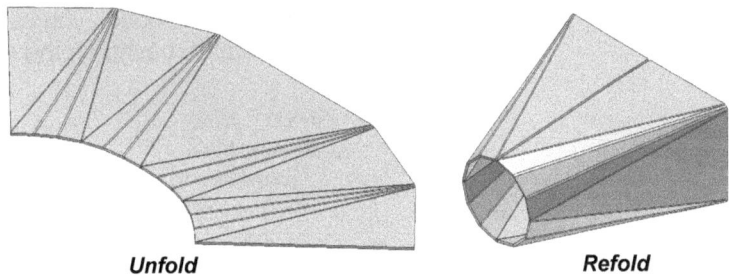

Unfold *Refold*

Figure 1–16

Flat Pattern

Flat Pattern features are used to provide information about a part before bending and other manufacturing processes as shown in Figure 1–17.

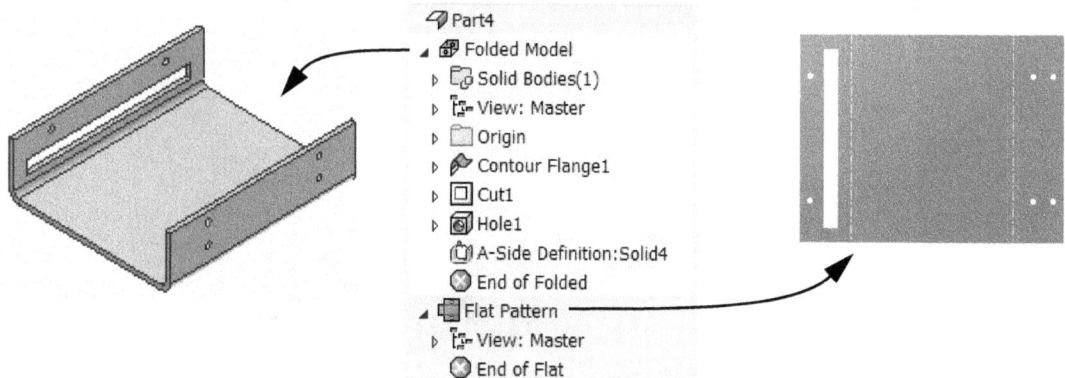

Figure 1–17

Punch

When modeling sheet metal components, you might place the same feature(s) multiple times for use in the same part or different parts. The **Punch Tool** command enables you to place a saved feature or group of features in one command, as shown in Figure 1–18. Common uses for punch tools include keyways, slots, and cuts for specific shape connectors. When placing a Punch feature in a model, you can control the placement and size of the feature based on the definition of the Punch.

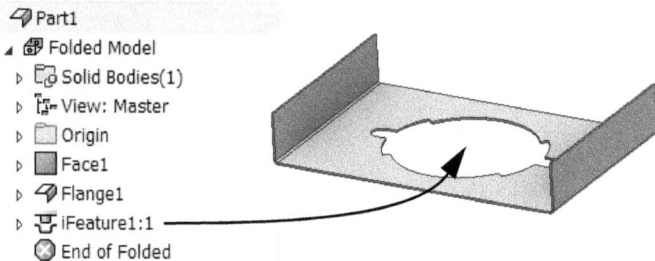

Figure 1–18

1.3 Sheet Metal Environment

Autodesk Inventor sheet metal tools are specifically designed for creating sheet metal parts. Figure 1–19 shows the user interface with the *Sheet Metal* tab active. After creating a sketch for your base feature, you can add faces, contour flanges, cuts, folds, and other features.

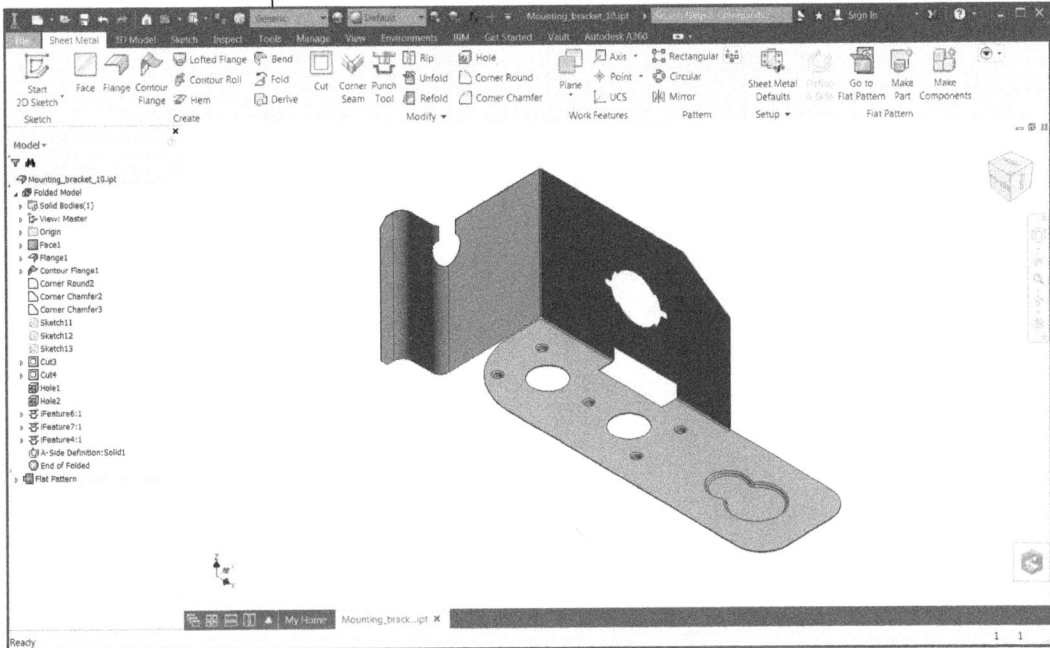

Figure 1–19

Sheet Metal Tools

The Sheet Metal tab (shown in Figure 1–20) provides access to the available tools that you can use to design sheet metal models.

Figure 1–20

The sheet metal application includes several tools that should be familiar from working with solid parts (e.g., **Hole**, **Work Plane**, and **Pattern**). Also included are tools specific to sheet metal fabrication (e,g.,**Face**, **Flange**, **Fold**, and **Corner Seam**).

Model Display

As with solid models, you can display sheet metal models in shaded, hidden edges displayed, or wireframe display. You also have access to the same model orientation tools as when orienting a solid model.

1.4 Sheet Metal Design Process

The process of creating sheet metal models is similar to the process of creating solid part models. Individual features are created in sequence and reference one another, resulting in parent-child relationships.

When modeling a sheet metal part, remember that the part always has a consistent wall thickness.

To start a new sheet metal part, use of the following methods:

New in 2017

- On the *Get Started* tab>Launch panel, click ☐ (New).

- Click ☐ (New) in the Quick Access Toolbar.

- In the **File** menu, select **New**.

When you use any of these three methods, the Create New File dialog box opens, which enables you to select a template to use as the basis for a new sheet metal model. Select a sheet metal template from those available in the *English* and *Metric* folders.

> **Hint: Starting a Sheet Metal Model from the My Home tab.**
>
> You can start a new sheet metal model on the *My Home* tab by selecting the **Advanced** option in the *New* area and selecting a sheet metal template for use. There is no button in the *New* area to quickly create a new sheet metal model with the default template.

Use the following steps as the general workflow for creating new sheet metal models:

You can also convert a solid part into a sheet metal part by clicking

(Convert to Sheetmetal) in the Model tab>Convert panel.

1. Start a new part using a sheet metal template (.IPT) file.
2. Define the sheet metal style parameters, as required.
3. Create the base feature.
4. Add secondary features (such as flanges, hems, and cut-outs).
5. Create the flat pattern, if required.
6. Create the deliverables (drawings).

Practice 1a

Opening a Sheet Metal Model

Practice Objectives

- Assign a project file for use in the Autodesk Inventor software.
- Open existing sheet metal models and review their features and the relationships between features using the Model Browser.
- Manipulate the visual display style and orientation of the sheet metal model.

In this practice, you will use the sheet metal environment and tools to identify sheet metal features and manipulate the model's display.

Task 1 - Set up a Project folder.

1. In the *Get Started* tab>Launch panel, click ⬚ (Projects) to open the Projects dialog box. Project files identify folders that contain the required Autodesk Inventor models.

2. Click **Browse** and find and select **C:\Autodesk Inventor 2017 Sheet Metal Practice Files\Sheet Metal.ipj** (or the directory of the installation files if you changed the default directory). Click **Open**. The Projects dialog box updates and a checkmark displays next to the new project name, indicating that it is the active project. The project file tells the system where your files are stored. As an alternative, you can select **Browse** from the Project drop-down list on the My Home dashboard and find and select the project file.

3. Click **Done**.

Task 2 - Open a sheet metal model.

1. Open **sm_door_bell_base.ipt**. The part displays as shown in Figure 1–21. The **End of Folded** icon is placed just below **Flange1**.

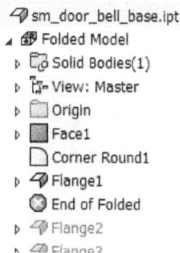

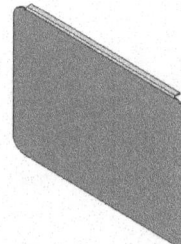

This project file is used for the entire student guide.

Figure 1–21

Task 3 - Identify sheet metal features in the Model Browser.

1. Drag the **End of Folded** icon through the individual features in the Model Browser, stopping under each feature to see how the sheet metal part was created (you might need to rotate the model to display the features).

2. When the **End of Folded** icon is at the bottom of all of the features, the part displays a variety of bends, folds, cuts, and faces, as shown in Figure 1–22.

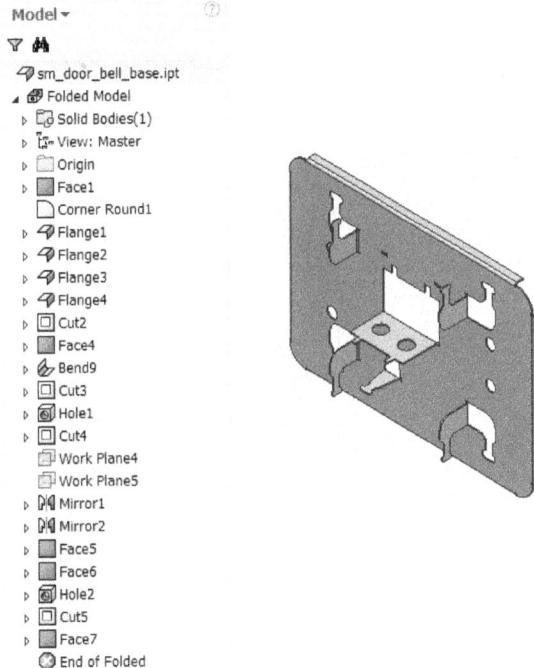

Figure 1–22

3. Expand **Face1** in the Model Browser and select the sketch to display its sketch dimensions.

4. Expand each of the four Flange features and note that each one has a Bend feature as a dependent (child) feature.

5. Hover the cursor over **Face5** in the Model Browser and note that the corresponding feature highlights in the model.

Task 4 - Identify parent-child feature relationships.

1. Right-click on **Flange2** in the Model Browser and select **Suppress Features**. Click **Accept** in the Warning dialog box. **Bend2** is automatically suppressed because it is a child feature of **Flange2**.

2. Unsuppress **Flange2**.

3. Suppress **Bend9** in the Model Browser. Click **Accept** in the Warning dialog box. The part is still displayed but the bend feature between **Face4** and **Cut3** is suppressed.

4. Unsuppress **Bend9**.

Task 5 - Manipulate the model's display style and orientation.

1. Use the viewing tools to spin the model to the approximate position shown in Figure 1–23. Zoom in to the area shown in Figure 1–23.

Orient the model and zoom in on this area

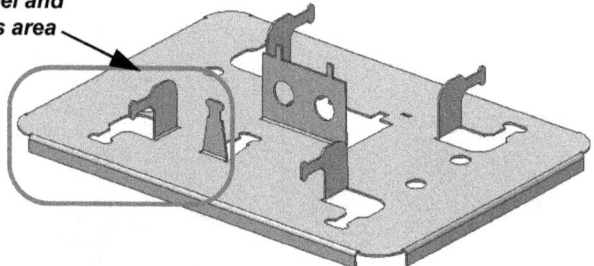

Figure 1–23

2. Select the *View* tab. Using the Visual Style drop-down list in the Appearance panel, change the display to **Shaded with Hidden Edges** and **Wireframe**. The wireframe model is shown in Figure 1–24.

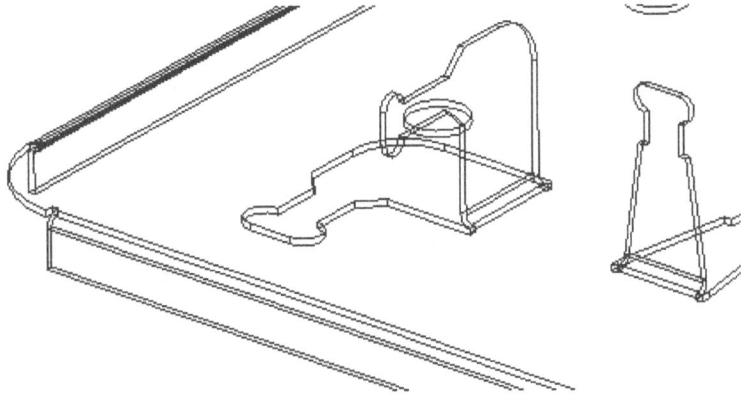

Figure 1–24

*The **Fixed Distance** option enables you to store the zoom level of the view. The **Fit to View** option maintains the orientation and always refits the view in the main window.*

3. Move the cursor over the ViewCube, right-click on

   (Home) in the top-left corner of the ViewCube and select **Set Current View as Home>Fixed Distance**. This sets the rotated view as the isometric home view for the model.

4. Practice using the ViewCube to orient the model by selecting the sides of the ViewCube or its corners. You can also rotate the model by selecting the clockwise or counter-clockwise arrows that display when the cursor is positioned over the ViewCube.

5. Move the cursor over the ViewCube and click (Home) in the top-left corner of the ViewCube to orient the model into its isometric Home view (3D). You can also right-click on the ViewCube and select **Go Home** to orient the model in the same way.

6. Save and close the file.

Task 6 - Review a second simple model.

1. Open **sm_endplate.ipt**, as shown in Figure 1–25. Review the features in the Model Browser.

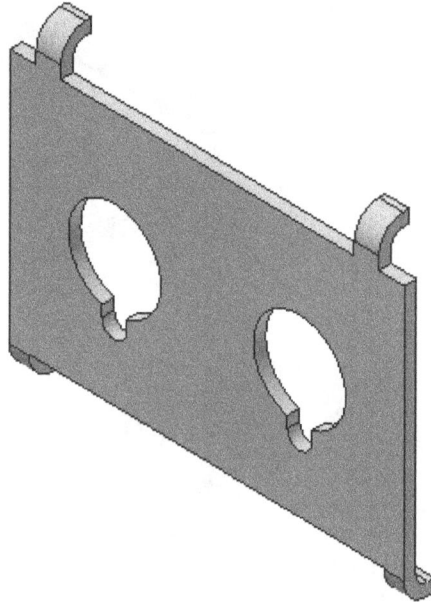

Figure 1–25

2. Rotate the part. Change the view to **Wireframe**.

3. Close the part without saving.

Chapter Review Questions

1. Which of the following describes valid methods for creating a sheet metal part? (Select all that apply.)

   a. Convert an existing solid model to sheet metal.

   b. Start a new part using a standard part.ipt template file and assign all of the sheet metal parameters in the Parameters dialog box.

   c. Start a new part using a **sheet metal.ipt** template file.

2. Which of the following statements is true regarding a sheet metal model? (Select all that apply.)

   a. Sheet metal parts can include sketches and placed features to create its geometry.

   b. Unlike solid part models, parent-child relationships are not established between the features in a sheet metal model.

   c. Unlike solid part models, sheet metal models have a constant thickness.

   d. The model display and orientation settings for a sheet metal model are the same as those available in a solid part model.

3. Which of the following are valid sheet metal features? (Select all that apply.)

   a. Extrude

   b. Face

   c. Contour Flange

   d. Bend

   e. Rip

   f. Tear

   g. Hole

4. Which sheet metal feature was used to create the geometry shown in Figure 1–26?

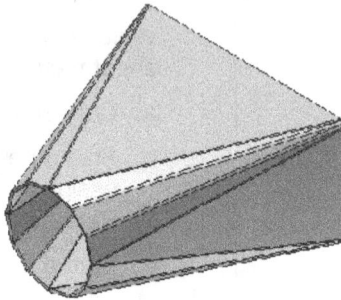

Figure 1–26

a. Face

b. Flange

c. Contour Flange

d. Lofted Flange

5. Which sheet metal feature was used to create the geometry shown in Figure 1–27?

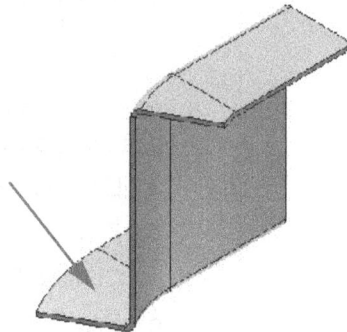

Figure 1–27

a. Face

b. Flange

c. Contour Flange

d. Contour Roll

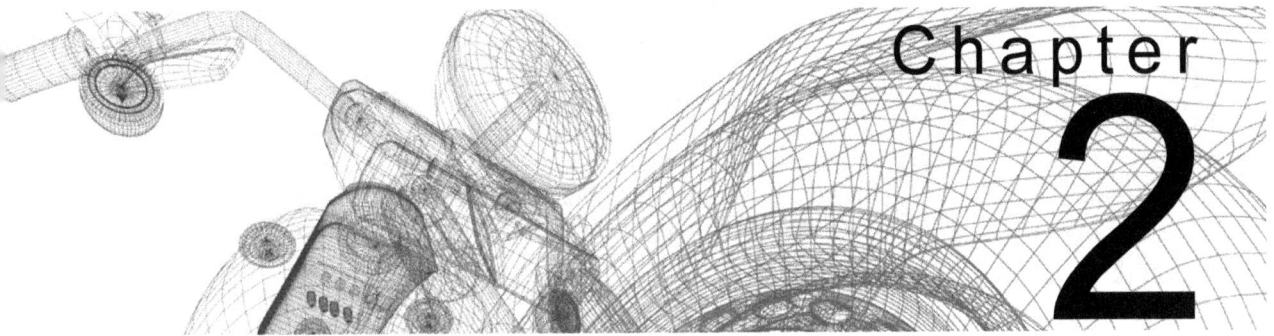

Sheet Metal Base Features

The process of creating sheet metal parts is similar to the creation of solid models. Individual features are built in sequence and reference one another, resulting in parent-child relationships. Every sheet metal model starts with a base feature. The base feature is the first feature to be created. It forms the foundation on which all other features are built. Each sheet metal part needs to have defaults set that define material type and thickness, as well as other parameters.

Learning Objectives in this Chapter

- Assign master rules for sheet metal models using the Sheet Metal Defaults dialog box.
- Use the Style and Standards Editor to make changes to the Sheet Metal rules that exist in a sheet metal file.
- Sketch the appropriate geometry and use it to create a Face, Contour Flange, and Contour Roll feature that represents the base feature in a sheet metal model.

2.1 Applying Existing Sheet Metal Defaults

A sheet metal part is a type of part file (.IPT), the same as solid part models. One difference is that when you start a new part from a sheet metal template, a different set of application tools are displayed compared to those that are displayed for regular (solid) parts. Another difference is that sheet metal parts have uniform material thickness. Figure 2–1 shows the same part in thin copper and thicker stainless steel material styles.

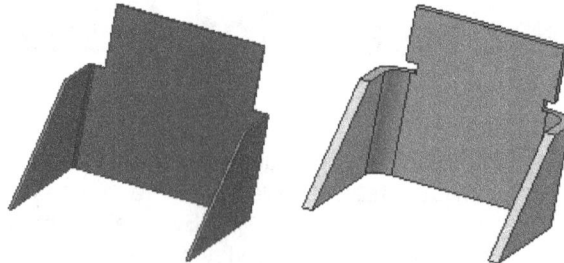

Figure 2–1

One of the first steps in creating a new sheet metal part is to select and apply sheet metal defaults. These define a master rule for the model or specific material or unfolding rules by which the model is created. Sheet metal rules include information, such as the material, thickness, bend relief shape, and unfold method. These property settings can be changed as the design progresses, along with many other style settings. However, you should assign a default when you first create the part, which can be changed as required throughout the design process.

Predefined rules are set based on the templates used or by creating your own defaults that are saved in template files. For example, material and bend radii information should be defined early in the design process. This is easily done by initially assigning the required default with the proper parameters.

Note the following about sheet metal rules:

- Rules are defined in individual sheet metal (.IPT) files.

- A default rule is available in sheet metal templates. You can edit this or create more rules, as required.

- To make a rule available in new parts, place the file that contains that style in the *C:\Users\Public\Public Documents\ Autodesk\Inventor 2017\Templates* folder.

- **Unfold** and **Bend Relief** options can be set in individual feature dialog boxes, but other style options must be set with the Sheet Metal Rule.

General Steps

Use the following general steps to apply an existing sheet metal style:

1. Open the Sheet Metal Defaults dialog box.
2. Select or define a Sheet Metal Rule.
3. Update the Sheet Metal Defaults, as required.

Step 1 - Open the Sheet Metal Defaults dialog box.

In the *Sheet Metal* tab>Setup panel, click ![icon] (Sheet Metal Defaults). The Sheet Metal Defaults dialog box opens as shown in Figure 2–2.

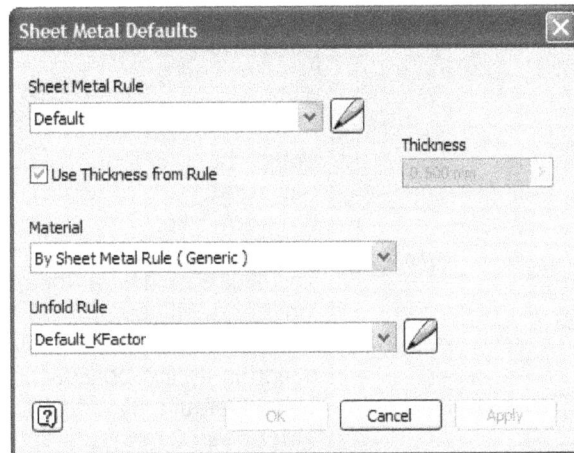

Figure 2–2

Step 2 - Select or define a Sheet Metal Rule.

The Sheet Metal Defaults dialog box enables you to assign a rule that defines default parameters values for such items as material, thickness, unfolding rule, bend relief, and corner information. You can select a default rule supplied with the selected template or you can create your own rules.

Typically, the creation of standard Sheet Metal Rules and Unfold Methods is done in a Template or Styles Library.

To create a rule, click ✐ next to the Sheet Metal Rule drop-down list. The Style and Standard Editor opens. In the *Sheet*, *Bend*, and *Corner* tabs you can review the default settings and make any changes. You can save the existing rule or create a new one using **Save** and **New** respectively. All rules are stored in the left column of the Style and Standard Editor under the Sheet Metal Rule heading, as shown in Figure 2–3.

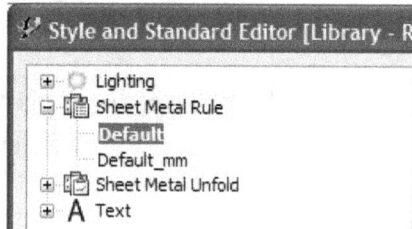

Figure 2–3

Click **Done** when the rule has been fully defined to close the Style and Standard Editor.

Step 3 - Update the Sheet Metal Defaults, as required.

Make changes to the assigned Sheet Metal Rule as required. If new rules were previously created they are available in the drop-down list.

The entire model can be driven by a single rule or you can independently control the *Material* style, *Unfold Rule* as well as the *Thickness*. To control the *Material* and *Unfold Rule*, select an option in their drop-down lists in the lower portion of the Sheet Metal Defaults dialog box. To control *Thickness*, clear the **Use Thickness from Rule** option and enter a value.

2.2 Creating a Face as a Base Feature

Face features are the building blocks for many sheet metal parts. A Face feature is planar and extrudes a 2D sketched profile to the thickness set in the sheet metal defaults for the part. You cannot change the face thickness in the Face Feature dialog box.

The primary Face feature can be as simple as a sketched rectangle or a more complex shape, as shown in Figure 2–4. The sketch must contain a closed loop.

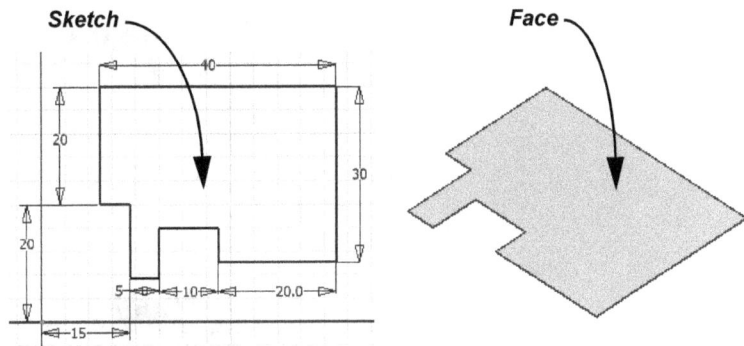

Figure 2–4

Note the following about sketching the profile for the Face feature:

- Simple sketches are generally best for creating faces. Holes and cuts are added later as separate sheet metal features.

- For a sketch with multiple closed loops, you need to specify which loop(s) to include in the solid area of the face.

General Steps

Use the following general steps to create a face as the base feature:

1. Create a closed sketch for the face.
2. Start the creation of the Face feature.
3. Select the profile and specify options.
4. Complete the feature.

Step 1 - Create a closed sketch for the face.

A face sketch that is used to create a base feature is defined by sketching a closed loop on a work plane. The base feature stays in place when the model is unfolded to create a flat pattern. Once a base feature has been added, face sketches can also be added to existing planar faces, not just to work planes.

Some sheet metal parts are designed to be created in automated fixtures. It is good design practice to project the origin planes and/or origin point into your initial sketch when starting a new sheet metal part. You can then use any of these as references to locate entities in the sketch.

Step 2 - Start the creation of the Face feature.

Once the face geometry has been sketched, click ⬜ (Face) in the *Sheet Metal* tab>Create panel. The Face dialog box opens as shown in Figure 2–5.

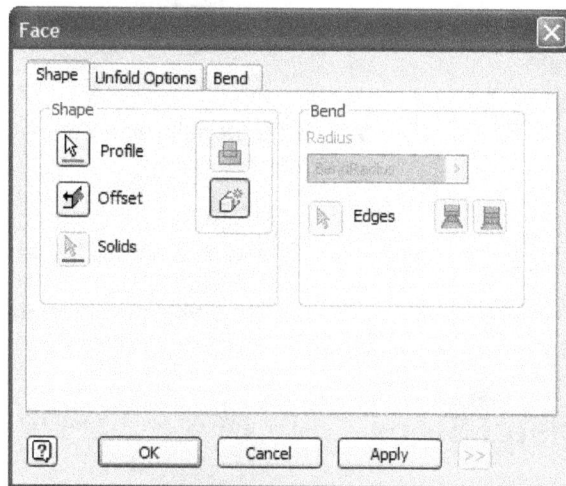

Figure 2–5

Step 3 - Select the profile and specify options.

If the sketch only contains a single closed loop, that loop is selected automatically. If it contains multiple sketched loops (such as circles in a rectangle), ensure that 🔲 (Profile) is selected and select a point inside the closed loop(s) that defines the required face. Figure 2–6 shows a single closed loop on the left and multiple simple closed loops on the right.

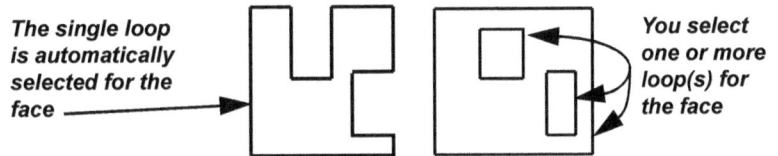

The single loop is automatically selected for the face ────────▶

You select one or more loop(s) for the face

Figure 2–6

If there are multiple loops in a sketch consider sharing the sketch so that it can be used later to create secondary features (such as cuts).

Click 🔧 (Offset) to determine the direction of the face thickness, as shown in Figure 2–7.

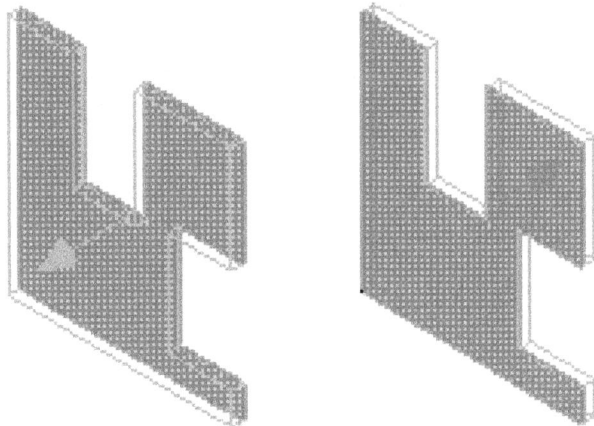

Figure 2–7

Bend and *Edge* options
are not available for the
base feature.

Step 4 - Complete the feature.

Click **OK** to complete the feature. Alternatively, you can
right-click and select **OK (Enter)** or press <Enter> to complete
the feature. Figure 2–8 shows a Face feature and its resulting
Model Browser.

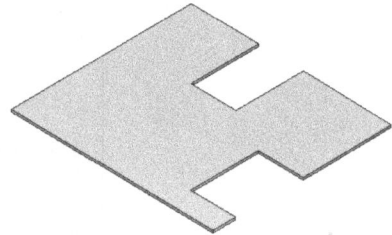

Part1
⊿ Folded Model
  ▷ Solid Bodies(1)
  ▷ View: Master
  ▷ Origin
  ▷ Face1
    End of Folded

Figure 2–8

2.3 Creating a Contour Flange as a Base Feature

A Contour Flange feature is a feature created from an open loop sketched profile. The profile is extruded and the default sheet metal thickness value is added to turn it into a sheet metal feature.

- Bend radii are added automatically to the sketch when created.

- Contour flanges can be used as base features or secondary features.

- Contour flanges are often used to create a rolled feature or multiple flanges on a sheet metal part.

Figure 2–9 shows a profile on the left and the contour flange created from it on the right.

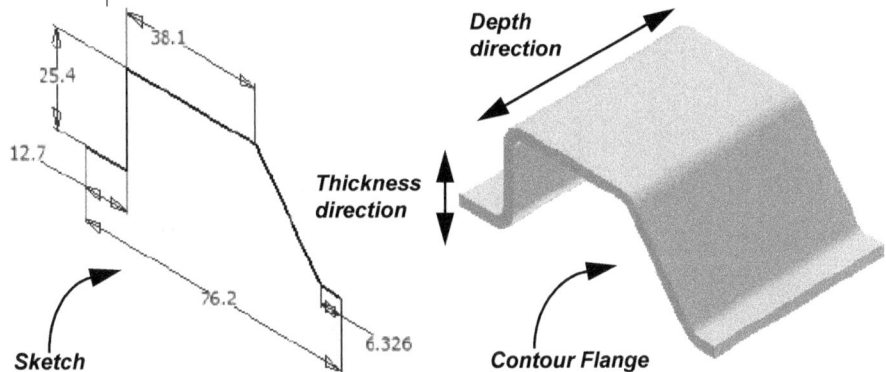

Figure 2–9

A variety of part shapes can be created from contour flanges, such as those shown in Figure 2–10.

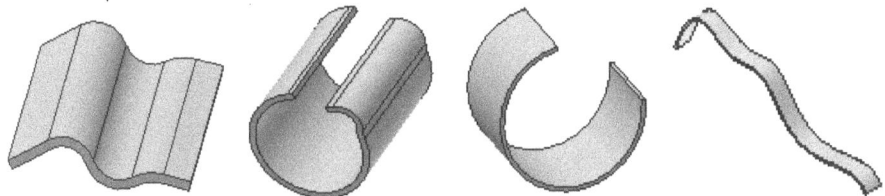

Figure 2–10

General Steps

Use the following general steps to create a contour flange as a base feature.

1. Sketch an open loop profile for the contour flange.
2. Start the creation of the Contour Flange feature.
3. Select the profile and specify options.
4. Complete the feature.

Step 1 - Sketch an open loop profile for the contour flange.

Select a sketch plane, sketch, and dimension an open loop profile. An example of an open loop profile is shown in Figure 2–11.

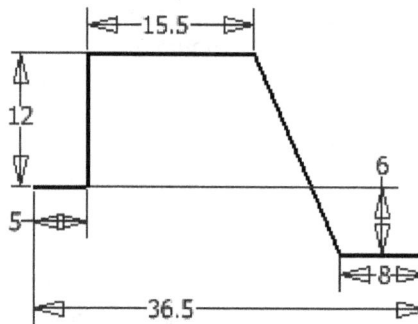

Figure 2–11

Step 2 - Start the creation of the Contour Flange feature.

In the *Sheet Metal* tab>Create panel, click (Contour Flange). The Contour Flange dialog box opens as shown in Figure 2–12.

Figure 2–12

Step 3 - Select the profile and specify options.

Select the sketch for the contour flange. This is the open loop profile that was created in Step 1. The options available in the Contour Flange dialog box enable you to do the following:

- In the *Offset Direction* area, click ⊠, ⊠, or ⊠ to determine the direction in which the material thickness is applied (inside, outside, or on both sides of the profile).

- Accept the default value for the *Bend Radius* field or enter a new value. The default is based on the settings for the assigned Sheet Metal Rule. A zero bend radius value can be assigned, if required.

- The **Edge Select** and **Loop Select** options are not applicable for the first feature in a part.

- The two *Bend Extension* options are not applicable, because this is the first feature in the part.

- If the expanded options are not displayed, click [>>] and set the *Distance* value for extruding the section. Select a Distance Direction for extruding using [⟋], [⟍], or [⟋] in the *Width Extents* area.

Step 4 - Complete the feature.

Click **OK** to complete the feature, as shown in Figure 2–13. Alternatively, you can right-click and select **OK (Enter)** to complete the feature.

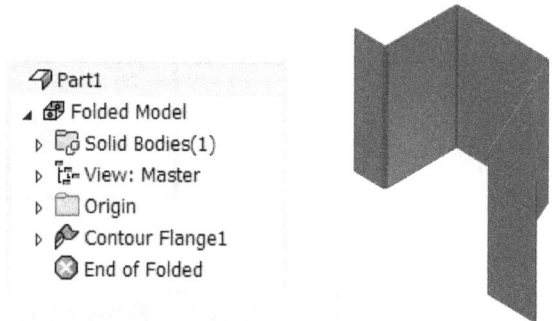

Figure 2–13

2.4 Creating a Contour Roll as a Base Feature

A Contour Roll feature creates sheet metal geometry that supports the roll forming sheet metal manufacturing process. Similar to contour flanges, a contour roll feature requires an open loop sketch profile that is revolved to create the required geometry. Figure 2–14 shows completed contour roll geometry and the profile sketch and axis.

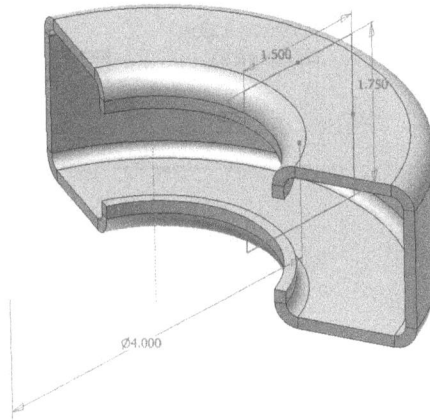

Figure 2–14

General Steps

Use the following general steps to create a contour roll as a base feature:

1. Sketch an open loop profile and axis for the contour roll.
2. Start the creation of the feature.
3. Select the profile and axis and specify the options.
4. Complete the feature.

Step 1 - Sketch an open loop profile and axis for the contour roll.

Select a sketch plane, sketch, and dimension an open loop profile. The axis around which the contour roll is going to rotate must also be included in the sketch. An open loop profile and construction line are shown in Figure 2–15.

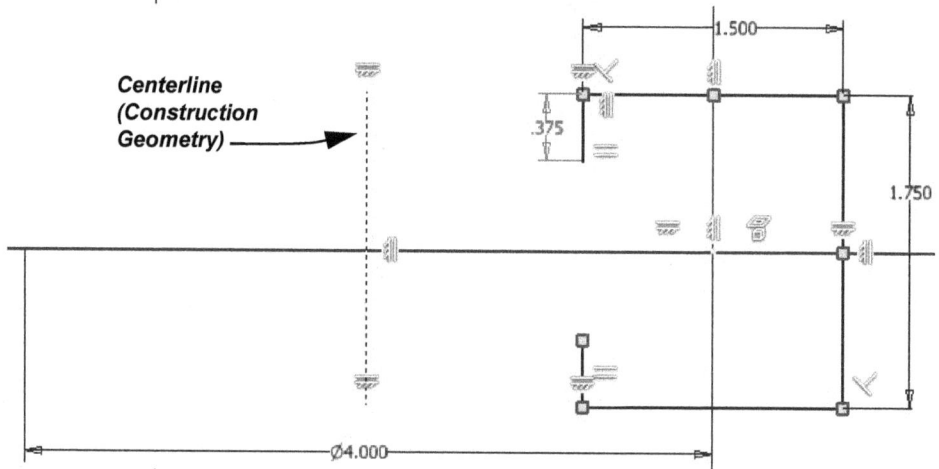

Figure 2–15

Step 2 - Start the creation of the feature.

In the *Sheet Metal* tab>Create panel, click 🗲 (Contour Roll). The Contour Roll dialog box opens as shown in Figure 2–16.

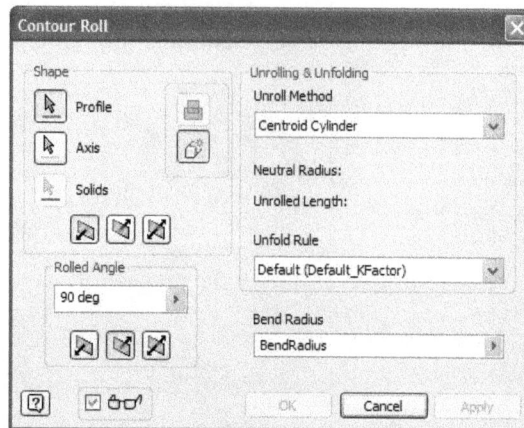

Figure 2–16

Step 3 - Select the profile and axis and specify the options.

Select the profile to define the section to be rolled. The sketched profile must exist in the model before you create the contour roll feature and must be an open profile. Select the axis around which the sketched profile is going to be rotated. The axis geometry must exist in the same sketch as the profile geometry.

- In the *Shape* area, click ▨, ▨, or ▨ to determine the direction in which the material thickness is applied (inside, outside, or on both sides of the profile).

- Define the *Rolled Angle* value. This value can be between 0 and 360 degrees, depending on the profile. For profiles with multiple segments, you cannot roll a profile a full 360 degrees. Only single line segments can be rolled 360 degrees. The ▨, ▨, or ▨ options can be selected to define the direction in which rotation is measured relative to the sketch.

- Select the *Unroll Method* for this feature. The option selected defines how the developed length is calculated. Once an option has been selected, the dialog box updates to reflect any additional required input. The information included here provides the designer with relevant manufacturing information on the neutral radius and unrolled length.

- (Optional) Select the *Unfold Rule* for this feature. The default value uses the **Default (Default_KFactor)** parameter value that is assigned by the Sheet Metal Rule. You can enter a different rule if required.

- Accept the default value for the *Bend Radius* field or enter a new value. The default is based on the settings for the assigned Sheet Metal Rule. A zero bend radius value can be assigned, if required.

Step 4 - Select the profile and axis and specify the options.

Once you have fully defined the contour roll, click **OK** to complete the feature. Alternatively, you can right-click and select **OK (Enter)** to complete the feature.

Practice 2a

Creating Base Features I

Practice Objectives

- Create new sheet metal part files using a provided sheet metal template file.
- Sketch the appropriate geometry and use it to create both a Face and Contour Flange base feature in the new sheet metal part files.
- Edit the default parameter values that are provided in the sheet metal template file.

In this practice, you will create a new sheet metal part from a sheet metal template, set the material thickness, and create a face as a base feature. You will then create a second model that uses a contour flange as its base feature.

Task 1 - Create a new part from a sheet metal template.

1. In the Quick Access Toolbar, click ☐. The Create New File dialog box opens displaying the default templates.

2. Select the *Metric* folder and in the *Part - Create 2D and 3D objects* area, select **Sheet Metal(mm).ipt**.

3. Click **Create**. A new part file is created and the *Sheet Metal* tab is active.

4. In the *Sheet Metal* tab>Sketch panel, click 🗗 (Start 2D Sketch). The Origin planes are temporarily displayed in the graphics window, as shown in Figure 2–17, so that you can select the sketch plane.

You can click ▷ next to Origin in the Model Browser to expand it and review the Origin features. Rolling the cursor over any of the feature names temporarily highlights them with their name in the graphics window.

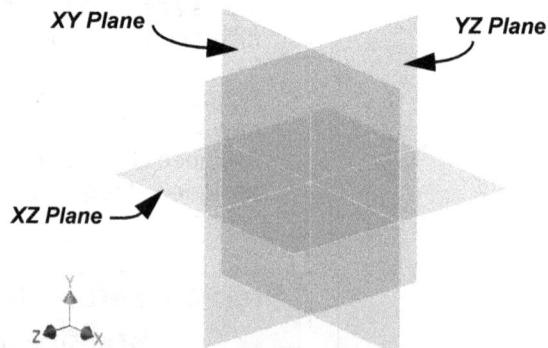

XY Plane

YZ Plane

XZ Plane

Figure 2–17

*Alternatively, you can right-click on the plane name in the Model Browser or right-click and select **New Sketch** in the graphics window.*

5. Select the XY Plane in the graphics window (as shown in Figure 2–17) to start a new sketch on the XY Plane. You are now placed in the sketch environment. The XY Plane is the current sketch plane and the *Sketch* tab is active.

6. In the Create panel, click ▱ (Project Geometry). In the Model Browser, in the *Origin* folder, select the **YZ** and **XZ** planes.

7. Sketch and dimension a rectangle, as shown in Figure 2–18.

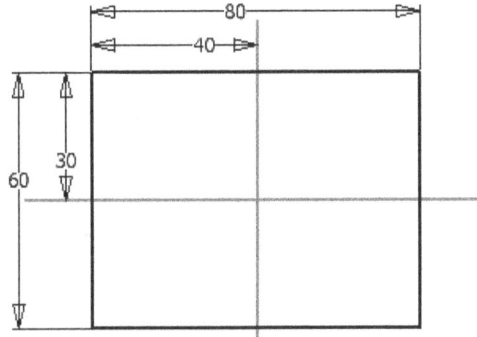

Figure 2–18

8. In the Exit panel, click ✔ (Finish Sketch).

9. The *Sheet Metal* tab becomes the active tab. In the Create panel, click ▱ (Face) to open the Face dialog box, as shown in Figure 2–19.

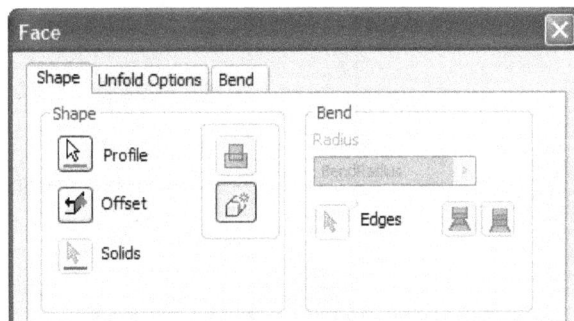

Figure 2–19

- The sketched rectangle is automatically selected as the profile because it is the only closed loop.

10. Click [icon] (Offset) to flip the direction in which the face will be extruded. Set the offset direction upwards when the model is in its Home View.

11. Click **OK** to complete the face. The model displays as shown in Figure 2–20.

Figure 2–20

Task 2 - Edit the default parameters for material and thickness.

1. In the Setup panel, click [icon] (Sheet Metal Defaults) to open the Sheet Metal Defaults dialog box, as shown in Figure 2–21. Based on the template that was used to create the part, there are two Sheet Metal Rules. By default, the **Default_mm** rule is set.

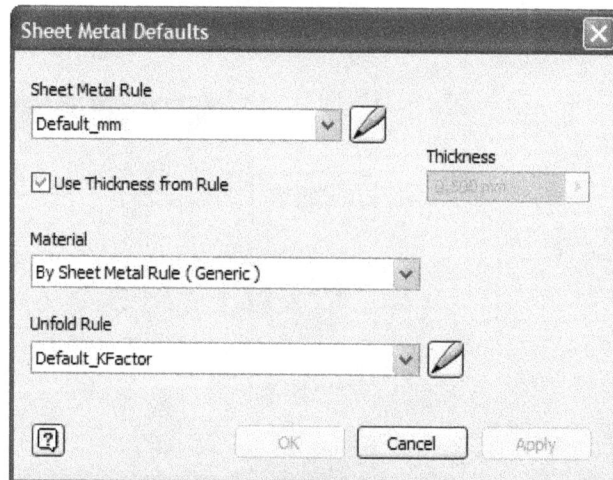

Figure 2–21

2. Click [icon] next to the Sheet Metal Rule drop-down list. The Style and Standard Editor opens. In the *Sheet*, *Bend*, and *Corner* tabs you can review the default settings. The *Material* is **Generic**, and the *Thickness* is **0.500mm**.

3. In the Material list, select **Copper**.

4. In the *Thickness* field, enter **1.0mm**.

5. Click **Save** at the top of the Style and Standard Editor.

6. Click **Save and Close** at the bottom of the Style and Standard Editor. The model displays as shown in Figure 2–22. You might need to zoom in to see the change in thickness, but you should see the color change.

Figure 2–22

7. Click **Cancel** to close the Sheet Metal Defaults dialog box.

8. Save the model as **base_face.ipt**.

9. Close the file.

Task 3 - Create a contour flange as a base feature.

1. In the Quick Access Toolbar, click [icon]. The Create New File dialog box opens displaying the default templates.

2. Select the *Metric* folder. In the *Part - Create 2D and 3D objects* area, select **Sheet Metal (mm).ipt**.

3. Click **Create**. A new part file is created and the *Sheet Metal* tab is active.

4. In the *Sheet Metal* tab>Sketch panel, click (Start 2D Sketch). The Origin planes are temporarily displayed in the graphics window (as shown in Figure 2–23) so that you can select the sketch plane.

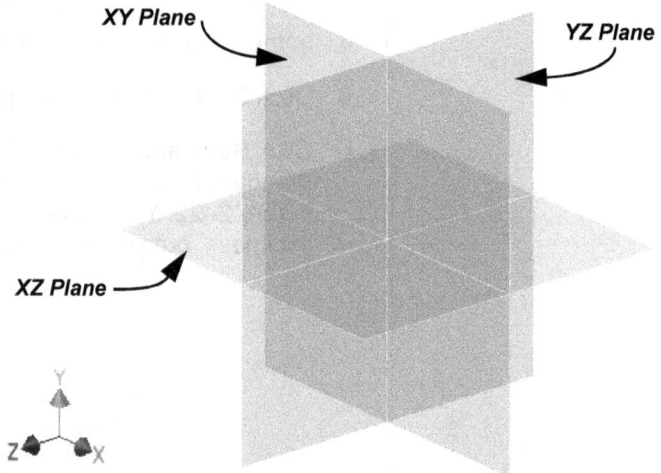

You can click ▷ next to Origin in the Model Browser to expand it and review the Origin features. Rolling the cursor over any of the feature names temporarily highlights them in the graphics window.

Figure 2–23

5. Select the XY Plane in the graphics window (as was shown in Figure 2–17) to start a new sketch on the XY Plane. You are now placed in the sketch environment. The XY Plane is the current sketch plane and the *Sketch* tab is active.

*Alternatively, you can right-click on the plane name in the Model Browser or right-click and select **New Sketch** in the graphics window.*

6. In the Create panel, click (Project Geometry). In the Model Browser, in the *Origin* folder, select the **YZ** and **XZ** planes.

7. Sketch and dimension the open loop shown in Figure 2–24. (Note that the dimensions are in millimeters.) Start the sketch with the lower left end point at the intersection of the projected planes.

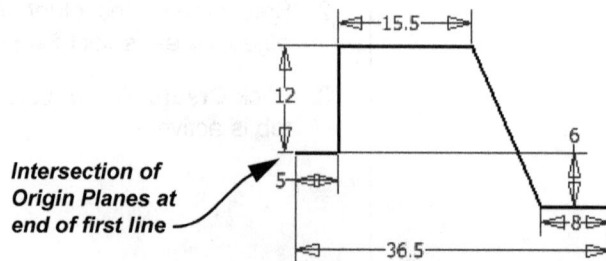

Figure 2–24

8. In the Exit panel, click ✔ (Finish Sketch).

9. In the Create panel, click 🏴 (Contour Flange) to open the Contour Flange dialog box, as shown in Figure 2–25.

Figure 2–25

10. Select your sketch as the profile.

11. Click the offset icon to apply the offset (thickness) toward the inside of the sketched profile, if it is not already set.

12. If it is not already open, click >> to open the expanded options area in the dialog box.

13. In the *Distance* field, enter **20**. (You do not have to type **mm**.)

14. Accept the default Distance direction (upward in the Home View).

15. Click **OK** to complete the feature. The model displays as shown in Figure 2–26.

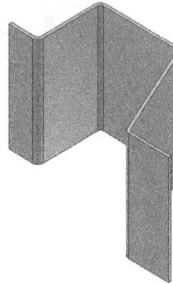

Figure 2–26

Task 4 - Edit the parameters for material and thickness.

1. In the Setup panel, click ![icon] (Sheet Metal Defaults) to open the Sheet Metal Defaults dialog box.

2. Click ![icon] next to the Sheet Metal Rule drop-down list. The Style and Standard Editor opens.

3. In the Material list, select **Brass, Soft Yellow**.

4. In the *Thickness* field, enter **0.2 mm**.

5. Click **Save** at the top of the Style and Standard Editor.

6. Click **Save and Close** at the bottom of the Style and Standard Editor. Close the Sheet Metal Defaults dialog box. The part displays as shown in Figure 2–27.

Figure 2–27

7. Save the model as **base_contour.ipt** and close the file.

Practice 2b

Creating Base Features II

Practice Objectives

- Create new sheet metal part files using a provided sheet metal template file.
- Sketch the appropriate geometry and use it to create both a Face and Contour Flange base feature in the new sheet metal part files.

In this practice, you will create two new sheet metal parts and change their thicknesses. One part is a face and the other is a contour flange.

Task 1 - Create a base feature face.

1. In the Quick Access Toolbar, click ▢.

2. Select **Sheet Metal (mm).ipt** and click **Create**. A new part file is created and the *Sheet Metal* tab is active.

3. In the *Sheet Metal* tab>Sketch panel, click ▱ (Start 2D Sketch).

4. Select the XY Plane in the graphics window as the sketch plane. You are now placed in the sketch environment. The XY Plane is the current sketch plane and the *Sketch* tab is active.

5. The Origin Center Point should be projected into the sketch by default, as indicated by the yellow dot at the center of the sketch. If not, click ▱ (Project Geometry) in the Create panel and select the Center Point in the *Origin* folder in the Model Browser.

6. Sketch and dimension the profile shown in Figure 2–28. Note that its lower left is coincident with the projected origin point.

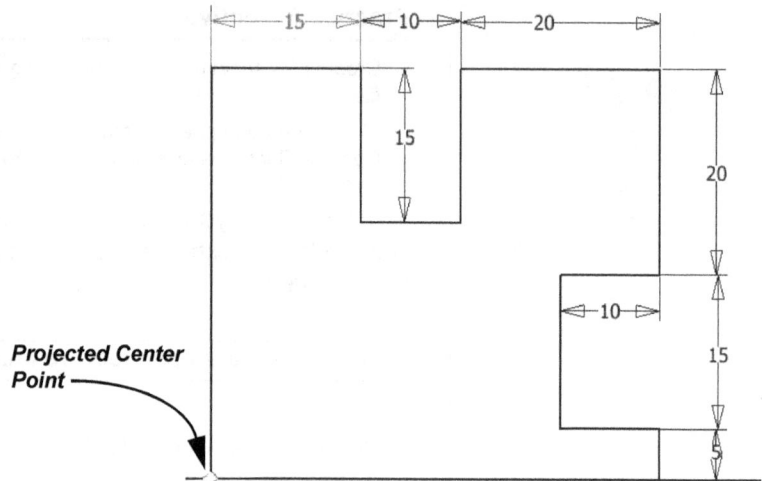

Projected Center Point

Figure 2–28

7. In the Exit panel, click ✔ (Finish Sketch).

8. In the Create panel, click ⬜ (Face) to open the Face dialog box. The sketch is automatically selected because the closed loop sketch is the only profile available.

9. Click 🔄 (Offset) to flip the direction in which the face will be extruded. When it is flipped to add the thickness upwards, click **OK**. **Face1** is created as shown in Figure 2–29.

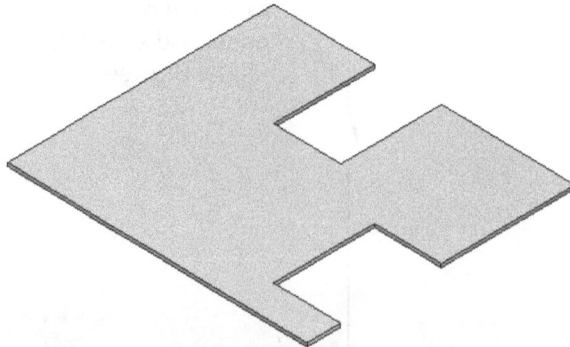

Figure 2–29

10. Save the model as **base_face2.ipt** and close the file.

Task 2 - Create a base feature contour flange.

1. In the Quick Access Toolbar, click ⬜.

2. Select **Sheet Metal (mm).ipt** and click **Create**. A new part file is created and the *Sheet Metal* tab is active.

3. In the *Sheet Metal* tab>Sketch panel, click 🗗 (Start 2D Sketch).

4. Select the XY Plane in the graphics window as the sketch plane. You are now placed in the sketch environment. The XY Plane is the current sketch plane and the *Sketch* tab is active.

5. The Origin Center Point should be projected onto the sketch by default, as indicated by the yellow dot at the center of the sketch. If not, click 🖾 (Project Geometry) in the Create panel and select the Center Point in the *Origin* folder in the Model Browser.

6. Sketch the open loop profile shown in Figure 2–30.

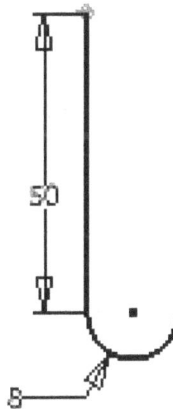

Figure 2–30

7. In the Create panel, click 🏴 (Contour Flange). Select the sketched profile and enter **10 mm** for the distance.

8. Switch to the Home View as shown in Figure 2–31, if it is not already displayed.

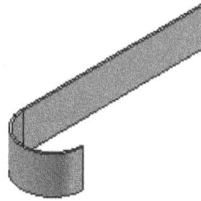

Figure 2–31

9. Press and hold <F4> and spin the part (or select and drag the ViewCube), as shown in Figure 2–32.

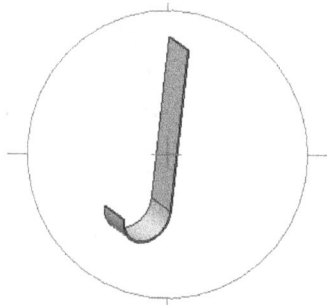

Figure 2–32

10. Move the cursor over the ViewCube, right-click on ⌂ in the top-left corner of the ViewCube and select **Set Current View as Home>Fixed Distance**. This sets the rotated view as the new isometric Home View for the model.

11. Rotate the model again and use the ViewCube to return to the newly defined Home View.

12. Save the model as **J_hook_contour.ipt** and close the file.

Practice 2c

Creating Base Features III

Practice Objectives

- Create a new sheet metal part file using a provided sheet metal template file.
- Sketch the appropriate geometry and use it to create a Contour Roll base feature in the new sheet metal part file.
- Vary the unroll, unfold, and bend radius options that can be used to create a Contour Roll to compare the resulting geometry.

In this practice, you will create a new sheet metal part using a contour roll.

Task 1 - Create a base feature contour roll.

1. In the Quick Access Toolbar, click ▢.

2. In the *English* folder, select **Sheet Metal(in).ipt** and click **Create**. A new part file is created and the *Sheet Metal* tab is active.

3. In the *Sheet Metal* tab>Sketch panel, click ▱ (Start 2D Sketch).

4. Select the XY Plane as the sketch plane.

5. Ensure that the Origin Center Point is projected onto the sketch.

6. Sketch and dimension the profile and centerline in Figure 2–33. The projected Center Point is located in the center and locates the mid points of the top horizontal and right vertical lines.

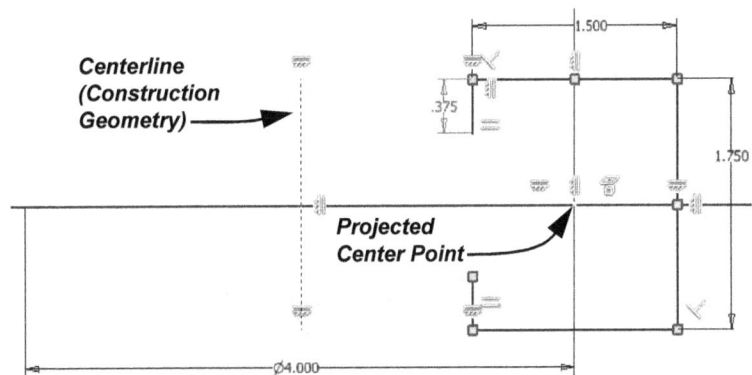

Figure 2–33

7. In the Exit panel, click ✓ (Finish Sketch).

8. In the Create panel, click (Contour Roll) to open the Contour Roll dialog box. Select the sketch if it is not automatically selected as the profile.

9. Select the construction line that was added to the sketch as the axis around which the sketched profile will be rotated. A preview of the geometry displays as shown in Figure 2–34.

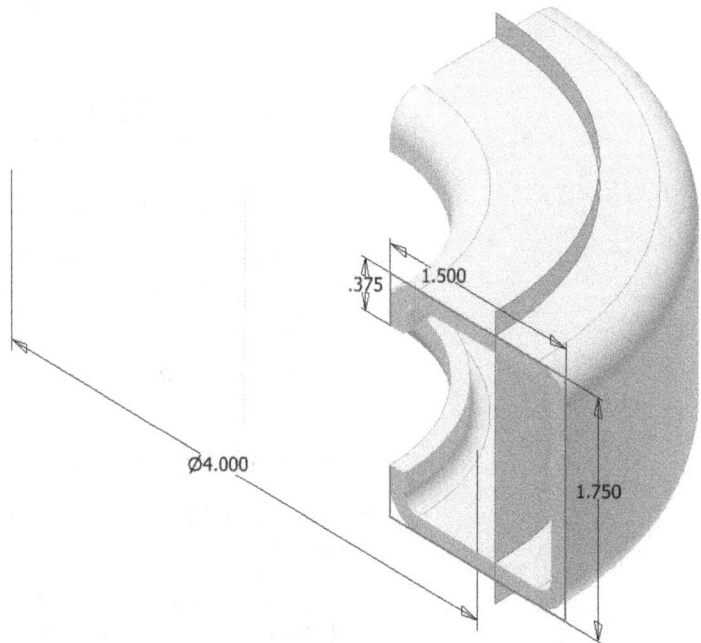

.375   1.500

Ø4.000

1.750

Figure 2–34

10. Change the default material thickness direction by clicking in the *Shape* area.

11. Set the *Rolled Angle* value to **135**, and click so that the direction for the rolled angle value is divided on both sides of the profile sketch plane. The preview updates.

12. Rotate the model to display the end sections of the geometry.

13. By default, the *Bend Radius* value is set using the **BendRadius** parameter, which sets it equal to the part's thickness value. Set the *Bend Radius* value to **0.2**. Figure 2–35 shows the effect on the completed geometry.

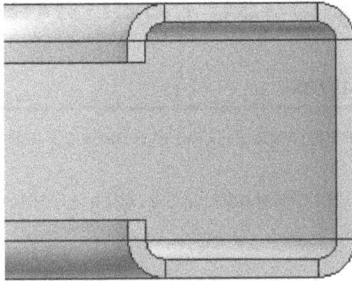

**Bend Radius value set using
BendRadius parameter (1.2)**

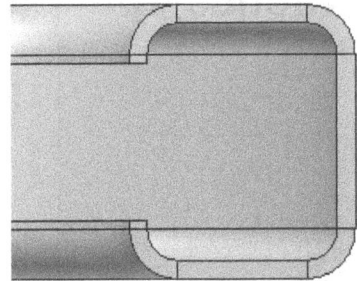

Bend Radius value set to 0.2

Figure 2–35

14. Return the *Bend Radius* to its default value of **BendRadius**.

15. In the *Unroll Method* drop-down list, select **Developed Length** and set the value to **7**. Note how the preview geometry updates.

16. In the *Unroll Method* drop-down list, select **Neutral Radius** and set the value to **1.25**. Note how the preview geometry updates.

17. Return the *Unroll Method* to the **Developed Length** option. Note that the value of the developed length updates to reflect the last change made to the Neutral Axis value.

18. Return to the **Centroid Cylinder** Unroll Method.

19. Click **OK** to complete the feature. The model displays as shown in Figure 2–36.

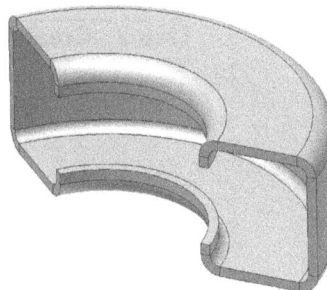

Figure 2–36

20. Save the model as **base_contour_roll.ipt** and close the file.

Practice 2d

Creating Base Features IV

Practice Objectives

- Create a new sheet metal part file that uses a Face feature as its base feature.
- Create a new sheet metal part file that uses a Contour Flange feature as its base feature.

In this practice, you will create Face and Contour Flange features without step-by-step instructions. Estimate the dimensions required to create the shapes.

Task 1 - Create a Face feature.

Create the Face feature shown in Figure 2–37.

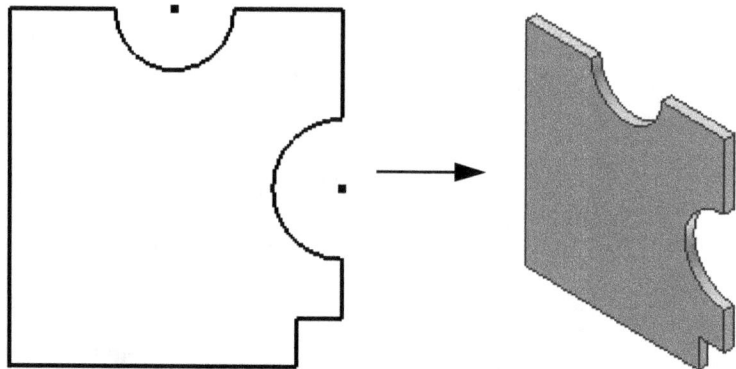

Figure 2–37

Task 2 - Create a Contour Flange feature.

Create the Contour Flange feature shown in Figure 2–38.

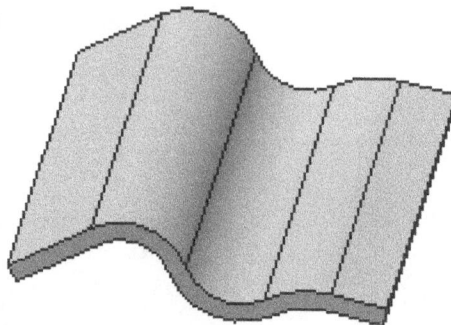

Figure 2–38

Chapter Review Questions

1. What initially determines the default Sheet Metal Rule that is set in a new sheet metal model?

   a. A rule is not initially set in a new sheet metal model. In the *Sheet Metal* tab>Setup panel, click (Sheet Metal Defaults) and set the rule before creating any geometry.

   b. A rule is not initially set in a new sheet metal model. In the *Manage* tab>Styles and Standards panel, click (Sheet Metal Defaults) and set the rule before creating any geometry.

   c. A rule is not initially set in a new sheet metal model. When you create each feature you assign a rule for that feature.

   d. The initial default rule is the rule that was set in the sheet metal template file that was used to create the sheet metal model.

2. How is the thickness of a sheet metal face determined? (Select all that apply.)

   a. The thickness of the face is determined by the thickness value that is entered in the Face dialog box that is used to create the feature.

   b. The thickness of the face is determined by the assigned Sheet Metal Rule in the Sheet Metal Defaults dialog box.

   c. The thickness of the face can be overridden to be driven independent of the assigned rule in the Sheet Metal Defaults dialog box.

   d. The thickness for all faces that are created are set as 1.0 mm or 1 in.

3. Which of the following statements is true regarding creating a Face feature as a base feature in a sheet metal model? (Select all that apply.)

    a. The sketch for a Face feature must be an open loop.

    b. Multiple closed loop sections can be selected at the same time to create the Face feature.

    c. The offset direction of a Face feature can be on either side of the profile's sketch plane or set so that the depth is divided evenly on both sides of the profile's sketch plane.

    d. The depth of the Face feature is determined based on the default rule that is set for the sheet metal model.

4. How is the profile for a face different from the profile for a contour flange or contour roll?

    a. The profile for the face, contour flange, or contour roll feature must be one or more closed loop(s).

    b. The profile for the face, contour flange, or contour roll feature must be a single closed loop.

    c. The profile for a face must be one or more closed loop(s). The profile for a contour flange and contour roll must be a single open loop.

    d. The profile for a face must be one or more open loop(s). The profile for a contour flange and contour roll must be a single closed loop.

5. Which of the following options in the Contour Flange and Contour Roll dialog boxes enable you to set the material thickness so that the sketch is at the mid-plane when the thickness is added?

    a.

    b.

    c.

    d. None of the above.

Command Summary

Button	Command	Location
	Contour Flange	• **Ribbon**: *Sheet Metal* tab>Create panel
	Contour Roll	• **Ribbon**: *Sheet Metal* tab>Create panel
	Face	• **Ribbon**: *Sheet Metal* tab>Create panel
	Sheet Metal Defaults	• **Ribbon**: *Sheet Metal* tab>Setup panel

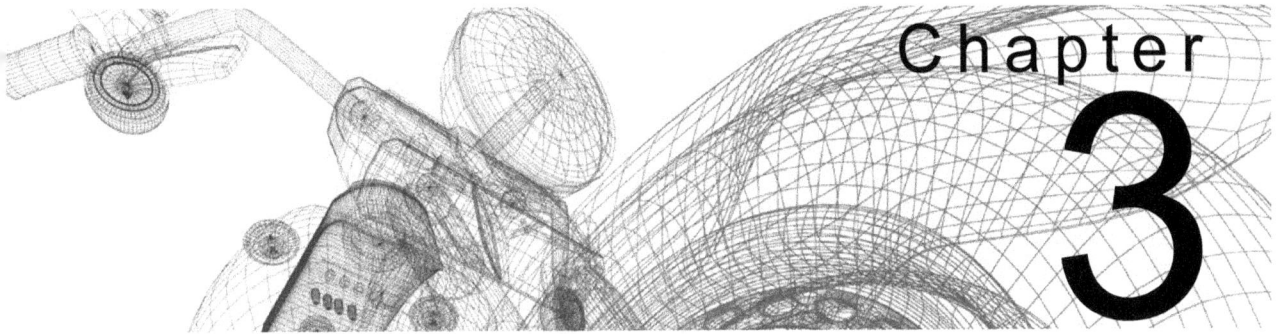

Sheet Metal Secondary Features

After creating the base feature for a sheet metal model, you add features that are dependent on that base feature. These are referred to as secondary features. As with solid models, secondary features are built by referencing existing features. The Face, Contour Flange, and Contour Roll commands can be used to create secondary features that add material to a part.

Learning Objectives in this Chapter

- Set the rule to be used in a sheet metal model to specify the default parameters that drive the resulting model's geometry.
- Use the Sheet Metal Defaults dialog box to control a model's thickness independent of the thickness value in the rule.
- Set the Bend Relief shape using the default rule or using the feature override so that the required shape is used in the geometry.
- Create secondary face geometry that uses a sketch, an existing model edge reference, and appropriate options to create the geometry.
- Create secondary contour flange geometry that uses a sketch, an existing model edge reference, and appropriate options to create the geometry.
- Create secondary contour roll geometry that uses a sketched profile, a centerline, and appropriate options to create the geometry through a specified angle.

3.1 Sheet Metal Parameters

The Autodesk® Inventor® software provides default Sheet Metal rules in each sheet metal template. Setting an Active Rule assigns the default options for such things as material type, thickness, bend radii, unfold, and bend relief shapes. The rule also sets the defaults for the corner options, and even markings that represent punched features on Flat Patterns. Rules can be edited and new rules created directly in a sheet metal file. To make the rule available for reuse, use the file as a template and store it in the template folder. The Styles and Standard Editor used to define rules is shown in Figure 3–1. All available rules are listed in the left column in the *Sheet Metal Rule* area.

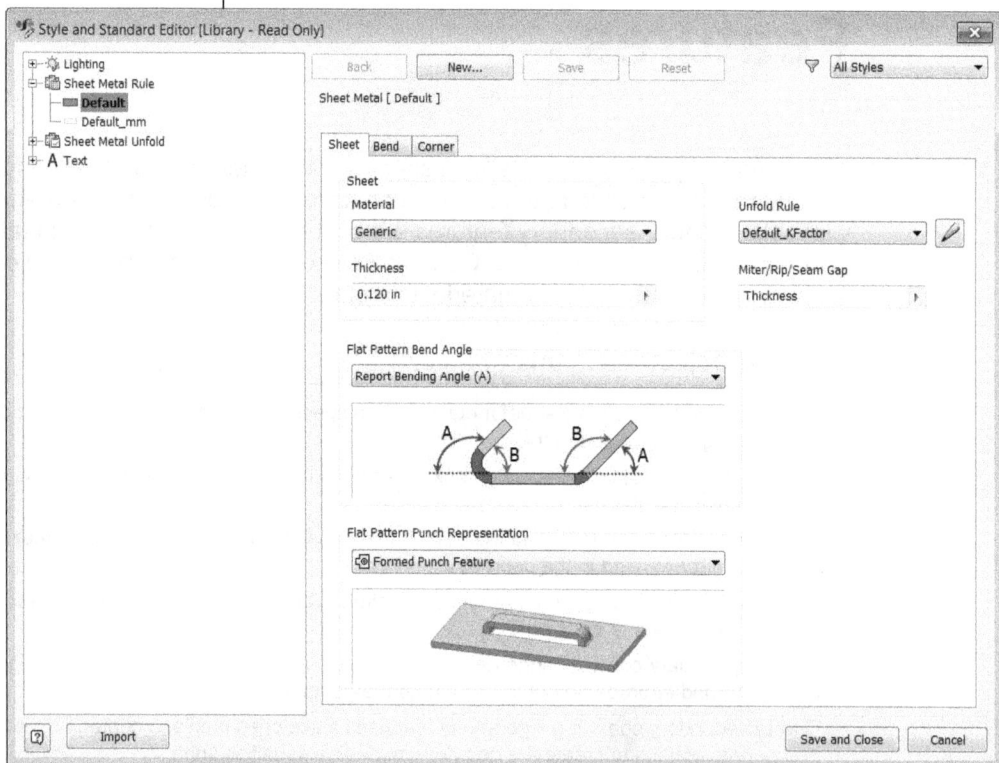

Figure 3–1

Some settings in a Rule can be overridden in individual feature dialog boxes. These include the *Unfold*, *Bend*, and *Corner* options. However, in most cases this is not required. For example, the *Thickness* setting stays consistent throughout the sheet metal part and would not be overridden. However, the default rule setting of **BendRadius** for the *Bend Radius* might need to be altered to fabricate a specific component.

Parameters

The Sheet Metal Rule for each part uses defined parameters. Parameters are named values and equations set up for values (such as **Thickness** of the material, **BendRadius**, and **MinimumRemnant**). Parameters are applied to the part as it is created. An example of a default set of parameters is shown in Figure 3–2.

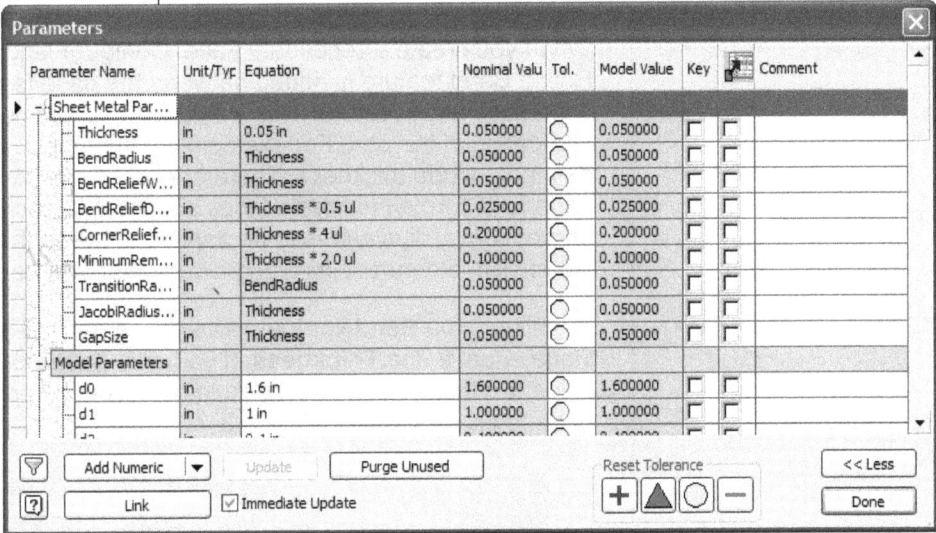

Figure 3–2

Thickness Parameter

The Sheet Metal Defaults dialog box (⬚) enables you to determine whether the Sheet Metal Rule drives the part thickness or whether it is controlled independently. For example, in Figure 3–3 the thickness value of 0.5mm is defined independent of the Rule and drives the **Thickness** parameter for the part. To control the thickness using the Rule, select **Use Thickness from Rule** and define the required thickness in the Styles and Standard Editor.

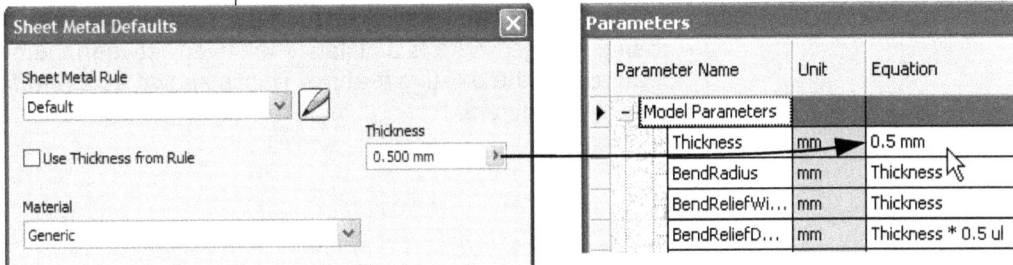

Figure 3–3

If you change the **Thickness** value in either the Sheet Metal Defaults dialog box or the Styles and Standard Editor, it updates the value of the parameter in the Parameters dialog box. However, you can only edit the value in the Parameters dialog box if the **Thickness** is independent of the Rule.

BendRadius Parameter

When you create a secondary Face, Contour Flange, or Contour Roll, a Bend feature is added between the base feature and each secondary feature. This is added to accommodate the fabrication of the part. For example, a sheet metal part has a defined uniform thickness. Therefore, when the flat sheet metal material is formed to create faces at angles to each other, an appropriate radius needs to be applied between the two faces. Otherwise, the part splits along a very sharp corner.

By default, the **BendRadius** parameter is defined as having a value equal to the **Thickness**. If you change the **BendRadius** value to **Thickness * 3** in the Rule definition, it applies to the parameter, as shown in Figure 3–4.

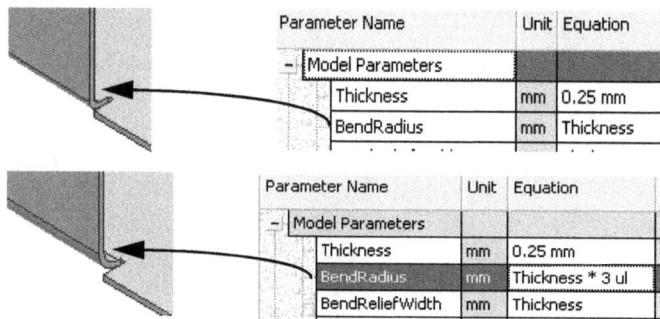

Parameter Name	Unit	Equation
Model Parameters		
Thickness	mm	0.25 mm
BendRadius	mm	Thickness

Parameter Name	Unit	Equation
Model Parameters		
Thickness	mm	0.25 mm
BendRadius	mm	Thickness * 3 ul
BendReliefWidth	mm	Thickness

Figure 3–4

Minimum Remnant Parameter

When a secondary feature is added, it might not run along the entire length of an existing edge. If the new feature is shorter than the edge, there is a distance left over between the new feature and the existing feature. This is known as a *remnant*, as shown in Figure 3–5.

When the remnant is too small, it is likely to break off or bend, in an undesirable way. The **MinimumRemnant** parameter, defined with the Sheet Metal Rule, is set to a value so that when the remnant is less than that value, it is simply removed, as if you had cut it off when making the part. By default, the **MinimumRemnant** is set to **Thickness *2.0 ul**, as shown in the Parameters dialog box in Figure 3–5.

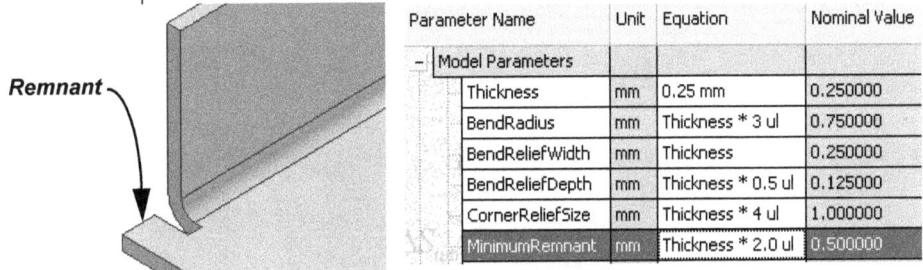

Parameter Name	Unit	Equation	Nominal Value
− Model Parameters			
Thickness	mm	0.25 mm	0.250000
BendRadius	mm	Thickness * 3 ul	0.750000
BendReliefWidth	mm	Thickness	0.250000
BendReliefDepth	mm	Thickness * 0.5 ul	0.125000
CornerReliefSize	mm	Thickness * 4 ul	1.000000
MinimumRemnant	mm	Thickness * 2.0 ul	0.500000

Figure 3–5

In the example on the left in Figure 3–6, a part is shown with a remnant that is larger than the required **MinimumRemnant**. The example on the right shows that the secondary Face has been edited and is closer to the edge of the base Face then the value for **MinimumRemnant**. Therefore, the remnant has automatically been cut away to avoid leaving a small area of metal sticking out.

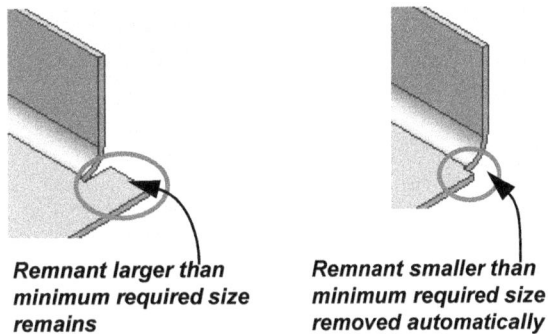

Remnant larger than minimum required size remains

Remnant smaller than minimum required size removed automatically

Figure 3–6

GapSize Parameter

The **GapSize** parameter defines the gap size value that is used in feature creation. By entering the parameter name as the value, the parameter's current value is used. If a change is required, the **GapSize** parameter value can be modified in the Parameters dialog box (as shown in Figure 3–7), and all features in the model that reference it update.

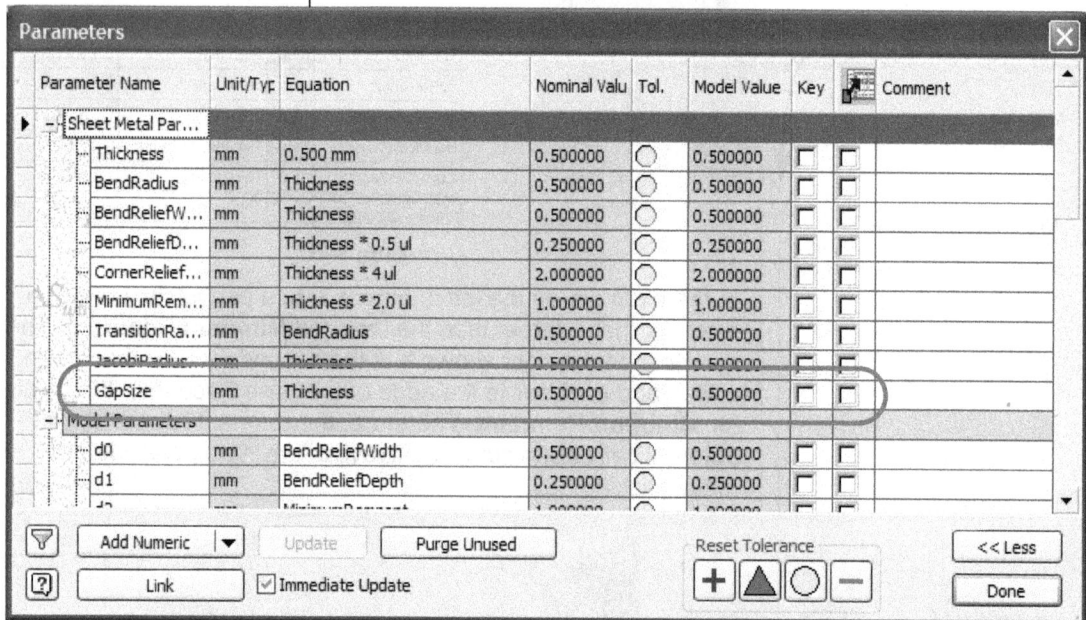

Figure 3–7

Hint: Sheet Metal iParts

iParts use one design to create multiple parts that vary by size, material, or other parameters as shown in Figure 3–8. They link a table to a part file, with each row in the table representing a different configuration.

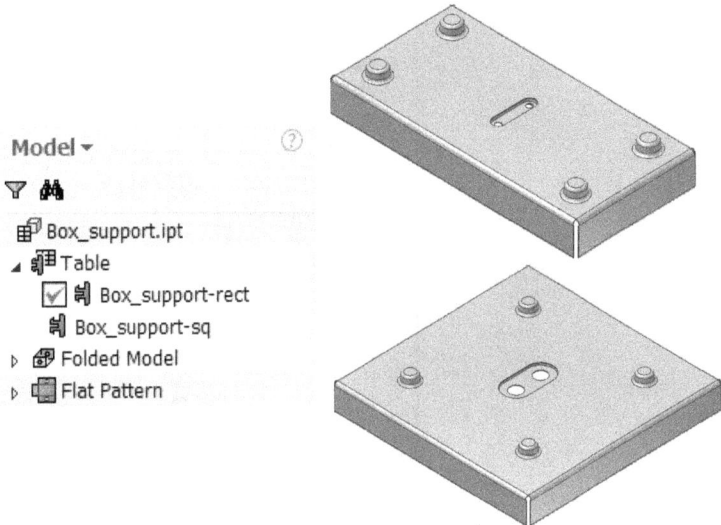

Figure 3–8

Sheet metal parts are converted to iParts by selecting the

Manage tab>Author panel and clicking [i] (Create iPart). This opens the iPart Author in which you can modify the table to add rows or configure iPart instances. For example, features in the folded model or flat pattern can be suppressed, parameter values can be modified, and property values can be changed. If the iPart is a sheet metal part, there is an additional tab in the iPart author that provides access to the sheet metal rule, sheet metal unfold method, and flat pattern orientation as shown in Figure 3–9.

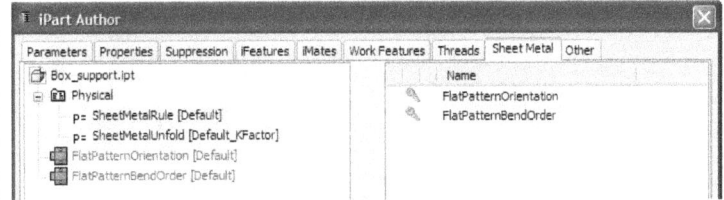

Figure 3–9

3.2 Bend Relief Shapes

When a sheet metal part is bent to create a secondary feature, a small amount of material is often removed to enable clearance between the edges of the new feature and the existing feature as they are folded. This is called *Bend Relief*.

The default bend relief shape, relief width, and relief depth, are assigned in the Sheet Metal Rule and are listed as parameter values in the Parameter dialog box (**BendReliefWidth** and **BendReliefDepth**). These values can be overridden in the *Bend* tab for individual features. Figure 3–10 shows the options for Bend Relief shapes that are supported: **Tear**, **Round**, and **Straight**.

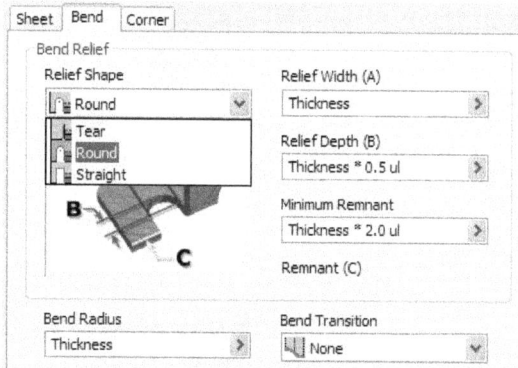

Figure 3–10

The same part can often be created with any of the three bend relief shapes. A **Straight** (square) bend relief is shown in Figure 3–11.

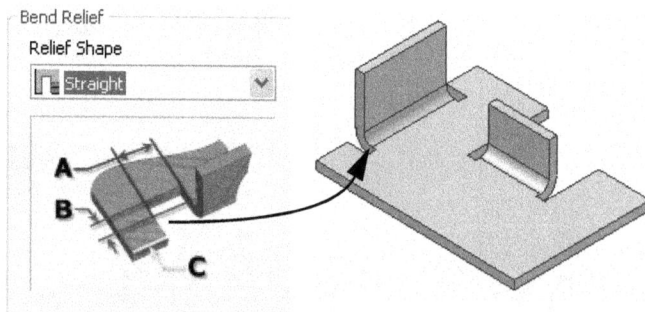

Figure 3–11

The **Round** bend relief shape has a full radius curve cut at its end, as shown in Figure 3–12.

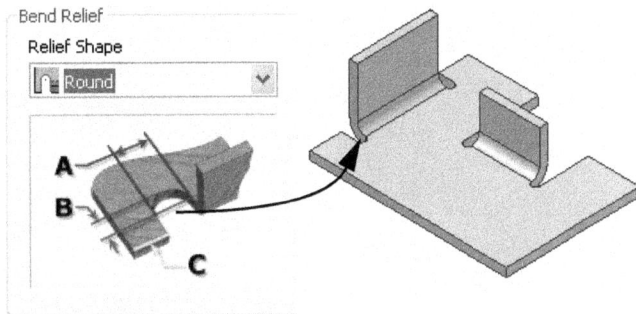

Figure 3–12

Material has not been removed from the **Tear** bend relief shape. It is created by a material failure when the bend is created, as shown in Figure 3–13.

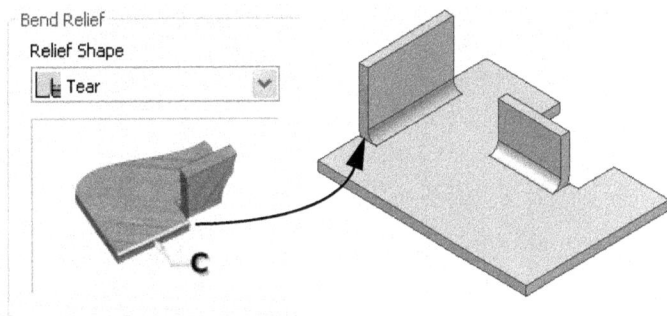

Figure 3–13

3.3 Faces as Secondary Features

A secondary face can be created on a new sketch plane at an angle from a base feature. Secondary faces can also be created from new sketches that are parallel but not coplanar, to existing planar faces or Work Planes. Several different *Bend* and *Double Bend* options are available to attach secondary faces to existing features, depending on how you create them.

General Steps

Use the following general steps to create a secondary Face feature:

1. Define a sketch plane.
2. Create the sketch.
3. Start the creation of the secondary Face.
4. Define the Shape options.
5. Define the Bend options.
6. Apply Double Bend options.
7. Complete the feature.

Step 1 - Define a sketch plane.

As with any sketched feature, you must select a sketch plane. This can be a Work Plane or a planar face on an existing feature.

The common method is to select the surface of an existing face if you want to create a new sketch that is going to be perpendicular to the existing Face, as shown at the top in Figure 3–14. A sketch plane at an angle, and a sketch plane parallel to a base Face are also shown as two other common options.

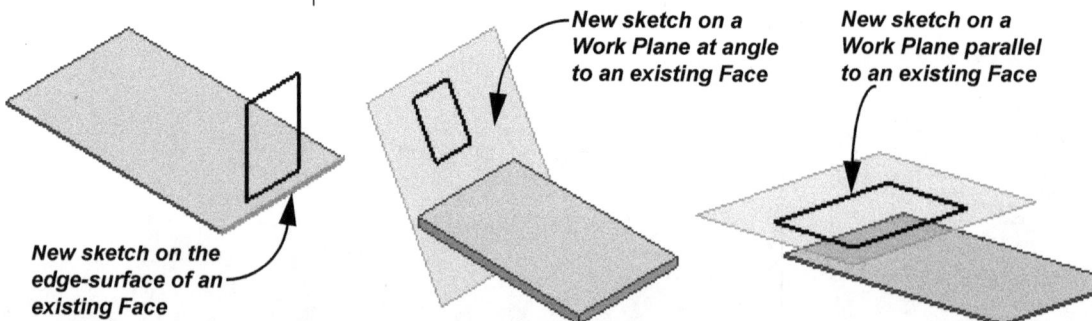

New sketch on a Work Plane at angle to an existing Face

New sketch on a Work Plane parallel to an existing Face

New sketch on the edge-surface of an existing Face

Figure 3–14

Step 2 - Create the sketch.

Draw the geometry for the sketch. You can also use projected edges of the part to sketch geometry, or to dimension and locate the sketch for your secondary Face.

An example of a sketch for a secondary Face at a perpendicular angle to the existing Face is shown on the left in Figure 3–15. The new sketch has been created by selecting the planar surface (which is actually created by the thickness of the existing Face) as a new sketch plane.

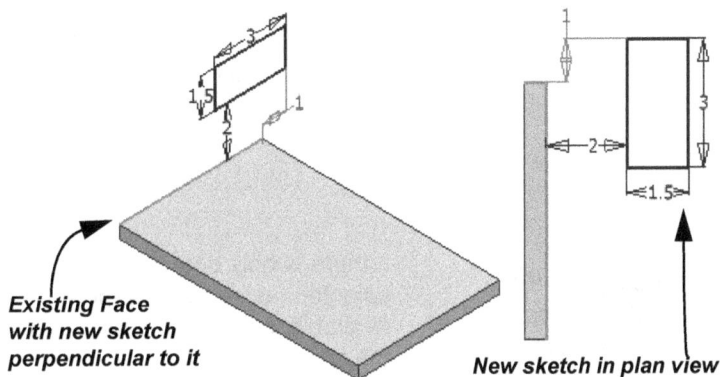

Existing Face with new sketch perpendicular to it

New sketch in plan view

Figure 3–15

Using projected edges as part of your sketch geometry creates a feature relationship between the projected and sketched geometry. If the referenced geometry (projected geometry) changes, the sketched geometry updates.

Step 3 - Start the creation of the secondary Face.

Once the sketch has been dimensioned and constrained, click

▱ (Face) in the *Sheet Metal* tab>Create panel. The Face dialog box opens as shown in Figure 3–16.

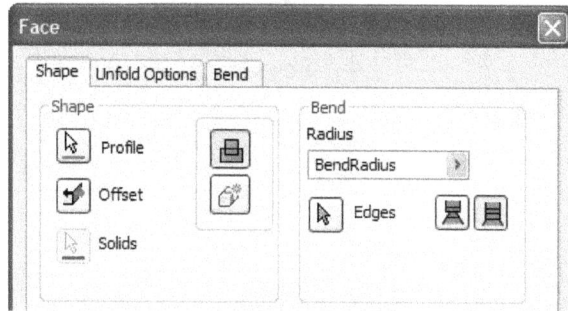

Figure 3–16

If ⊞ displays at the bottom of the Face dialog box it could indicate that there are open loops in the sketch. This can be ignored if the selected profile is a closed loop.

If there is only one closed loop, the profile is automatically selected, as shown in Figure 3–17. If multiple loops are available, select the loop(s) that you want to use as the profile for the new Face.

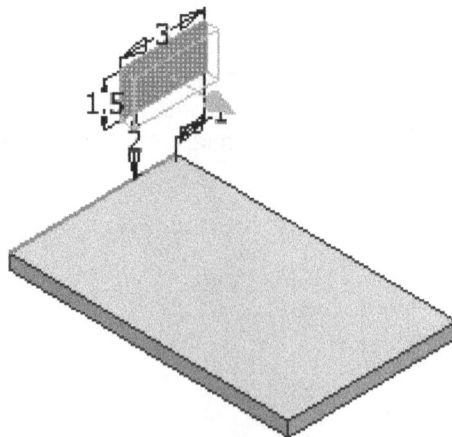

Figure 3–17

Step 4 - Define the Shape options.

Determine the direction for the creation of the face using

🖋 (Offset), as shown in Figure 3–18.

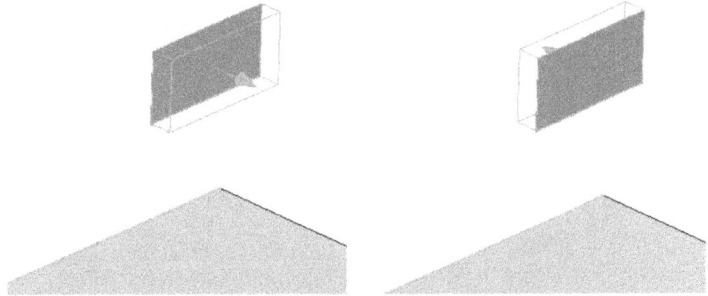

Figure 3–18

Step 5 - Define the Bend options.

The default value for the bend radius of the new Face feature is set to the **BendRadius** parameter. This is set based on the Sheet Metal Rule. Accept the default value and select an edge on the existing part to use as the attachment edge, as shown in Figure 3–19.

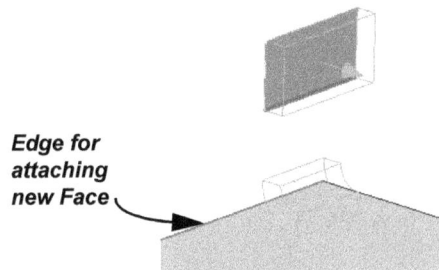

Edge for attaching new Face

Figure 3–19

Click (Extend Bend Aligned to Side Faces), as shown in

Figure 3–20. Alternatively, click (Extend Bend Perpendicular to Side Faces), as shown in Figure 3–21. This option only applies when the edge of the new Face extends beyond the width of the edge to which it is going to join.

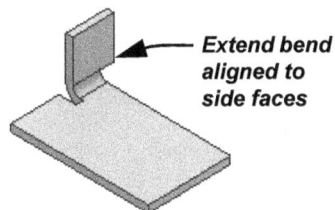

Extend bend aligned to side faces

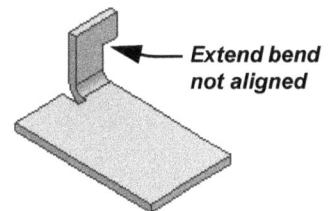

Extend bend not aligned

Figure 3–20

Figure 3–21

Step 6 - Apply Double Bend options.

When a secondary Face is created parallel, but not coplanar, to an existing Face (as shown in Figure 3–22), two Bends can be created between the Faces. If required, a new (third) Face is also created between those two Bends and the two Faces.

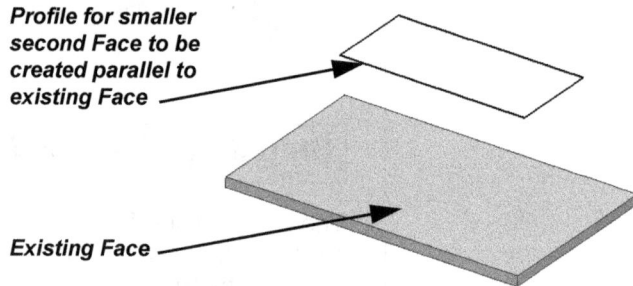

Profile for smaller second Face to be created parallel to existing Face

Existing Face

Figure 3–22

After you click (Edges) and select one edge of an existing Face to which to attach the new Face feature, the Face dialog box displays the *Double Bend* area. If it is not already expanded,

click >> to expand the Face dialog box, as shown in Figure 3–23.

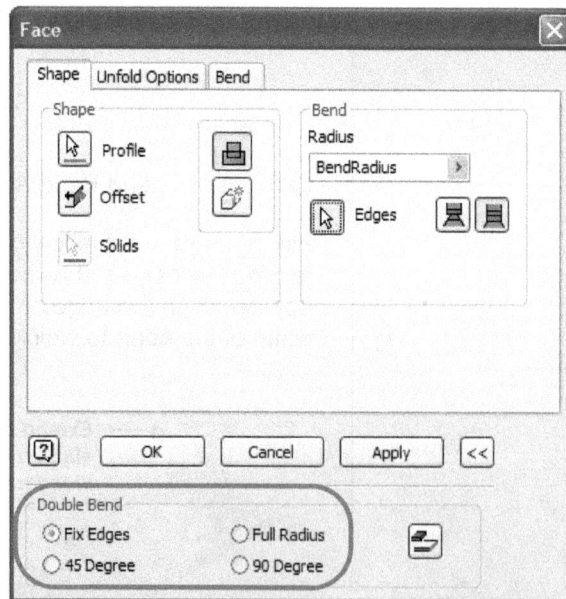

Figure 3–23

Results for the new Face feature and its *Double Bend* setting can vary widely, depending on the Offset direction of the new Face, which edge you select on the existing face, and the specified type of *Double Bend*. The four *Double Bend* options are **Fix Edges**, **45 Degree**, **Full Radius**, and **90 Degree**.

Fix Edges

The **Fix Edges** option maintains the location of the new sketched profile, and the edge that you select on an existing Face, in their original positions.

*(Flip Fixed Edge) does not apply to the **Fix Edges** option.*

A new Bend feature is created as a child of the new Face. This single Bend feature consists of a planar surface (when required) and two bend radii with equal bend angles applied at the two fixed edges. Figure 3–24 shows the **Bend1** feature attaching the newly created **Face2** to the previously existing **Face1**.

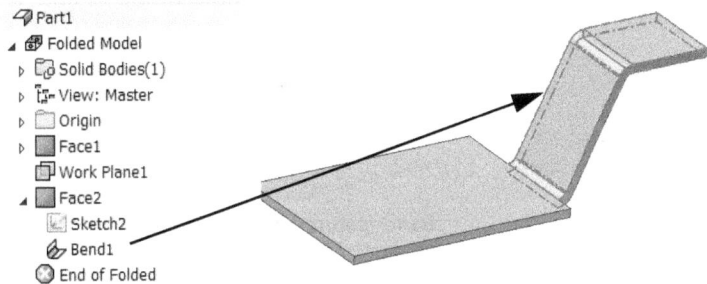

Figure 3–24

Different possible results are shown in Figure 3–25. On the left (from top to bottom), a model is shown with the short edge of an existing Face selected as an attachment edge. On the right, the same model and sketch is shown with an alternate attachment edge. For both, the new (smaller) Face is completely above the existing Face.

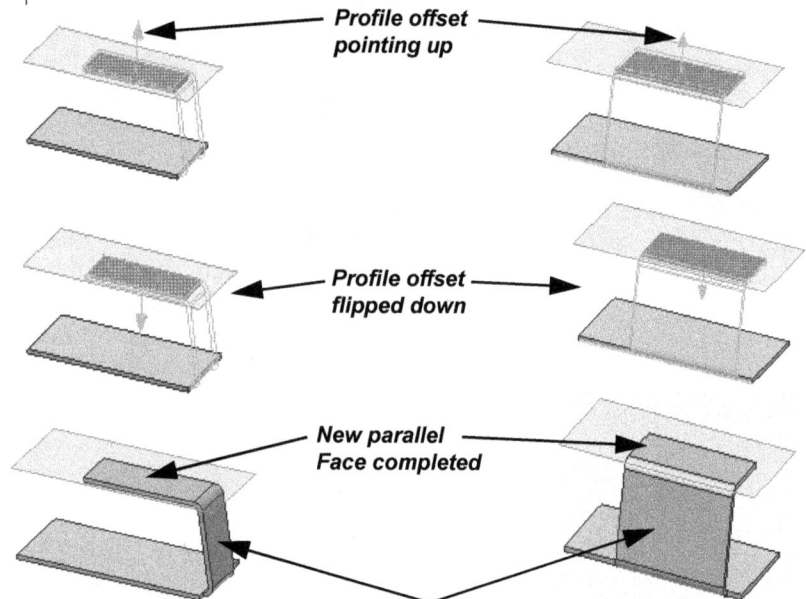

Profile offset pointing up

Profile offset flipped down

New parallel Face completed

Bend feature between fixed edges (The planar face and two bend angles are all part of the Bend feature; they are not three separate features.)

Figure 3–25

45 Degree

When you select the **45 Degree** option, a new Bend is created between the existing Face and the new Face. In this option, the Bend angles are both set to 45 degrees. In many cases, this results in needing to extend or shorten one of the two Faces so that they both meet at the ends of the Bend. Clicking ⬛ (Flip Fixed Edge) enables you to toggle between the Face to be lengthened or shortened, as shown in Figure 3–26.

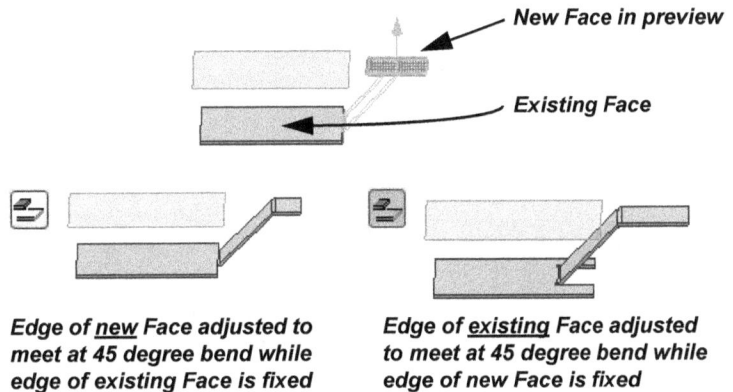

New Face in preview

Existing Face

Edge of <u>new</u> Face adjusted to meet at 45 degree bend while edge of existing Face is fixed

Edge of <u>existing</u> Face adjusted to meet at 45 degree bend while edge of new Face is fixed

Figure 3–26

90 Degree

The **90 Degree** option applies a Bend with a planar surface and two 90 degree bend angles between the new Face feature and an existing Face.

The **90 Degree** option is similar to the **45 Degree** option in that you can toggle ⬛ (Flip Fixed Edge) to adjust the edge of the new Face or the existing Face to meet the Bend feature.

This option is different from the **45 Degree** option in that when you apply this option, the new Face and the existing Face end up on the same side of the Bend feature, as shown in Figure 3–27 (even when you use the ⬀ toggle).

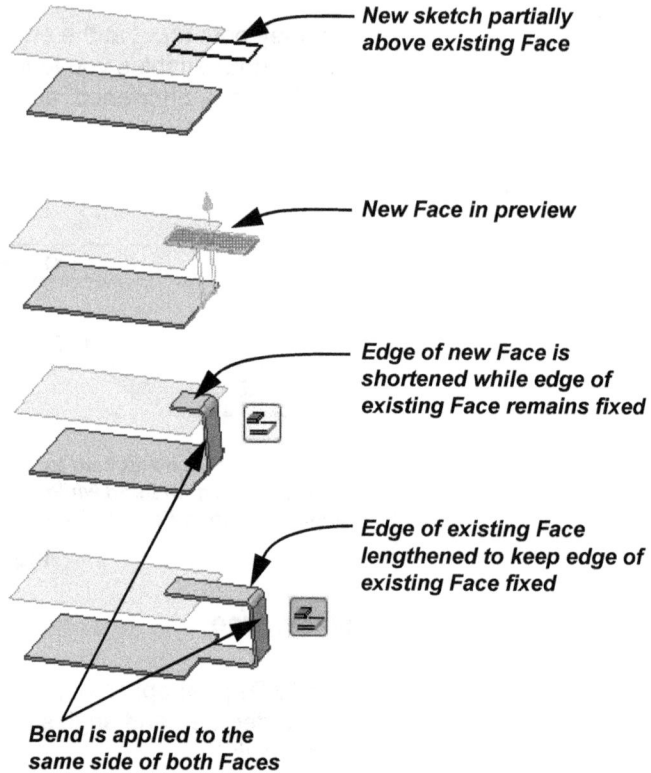

New sketch partially above existing Face

New Face in preview

Edge of new Face is shortened while edge of existing Face remains fixed

Edge of existing Face lengthened to keep edge of existing Face fixed

Bend is applied to the same side of both Faces

Figure 3–27

Full Radius

The **Fix Edges**, **45 Degree**, and **90 Degree** options each require a planar surface and two bend angles/radii be created between an existing Face and the new Face. The fourth option, **Full Radius**, only creates a semi-circular (180 degree) Bend feature.

Depending on the sizes and location of the sketch for the new Face and the existing Face, the features are trimmed or extended to create the Bend.

Click (Flip Fixed Edge) to select which face is shortened or lengthened to add the Bends, as shown in Figure 3–28. On the top, the new (upper) Face is shortened. This is because the edge of the existing (lower) Face maintains its original position. On the bottom, the existing Face is lengthened. This is because the sketched edge of the new (upper) Face maintains its position.

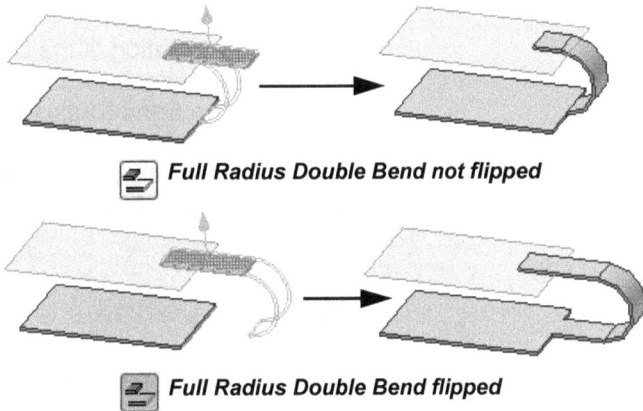

Full Radius Double Bend not flipped

Full Radius Double Bend flipped

Figure 3–28

Step 7 - Complete the feature.

Click **OK** to complete the secondary Face. Alternatively, you can right-click and select **OK (Enter)** or press <Enter> to complete the feature.

When you add a secondary face, a single Bend feature is created to attach the secondary Face to the existing Face, as shown in the Model Browser in Figure 3–29.

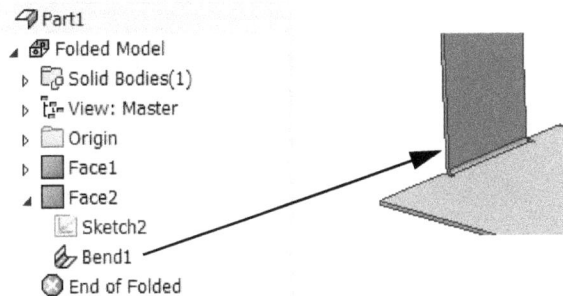

Figure 3–29

3.4 Contour Flanges as Secondary Features

General Steps

Use the following general steps to create a secondary Contour Flange feature:

1. Define a sketch plane.
2. Create the sketch.
3. Start the creation of the Contour Flange.
4. Define the profile and edges.
5. Define the Bend Radius and Bend Extension options.
6. Define the Width Extents options.
7. Edit the Unfold, Bend, and Corner options (optional).
8. Complete the feature.

Step 1 - Define a sketch plane.

Select a sketch plane for the secondary Contour Flange. This can be a Work Plane or planar face on the part.

Step 2 - Create the sketch.

Sketch, dimension, and constrain an open loop for the Contour Flange. Figure 3–30 shows a simple contour profile with two straight line segments and two arc segments, sketched to the right of the existing Face. Once created the Contour Flange is extended automatically to join to the selected edge with a bend.

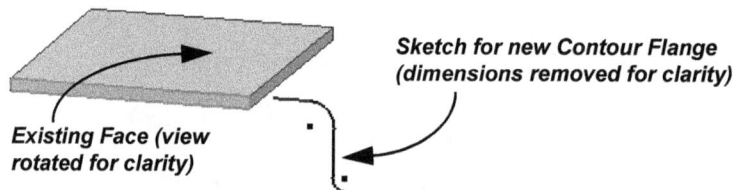

Existing Face (view rotated for clarity)

Sketch for new Contour Flange (dimensions removed for clarity)

Figure 3–30

Step 3 - Start the creation of the Contour Flange.

In the *Sheet Metal* tab>Create panel, click (Contour Flange) to open the Contour Flange dialog box, as shown in Figure 3–31.

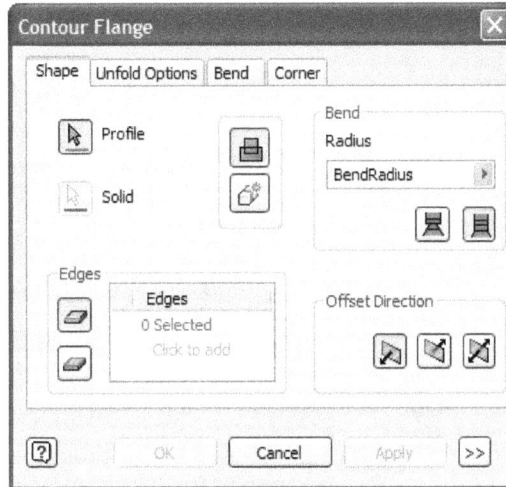

Figure 3–31

Step 4 - Define the profile and edges.

Select the open loop to use as the profile for the Contour Flange. Select an edge that is perpendicular to the sketch plane, as shown in Figure 3–32.

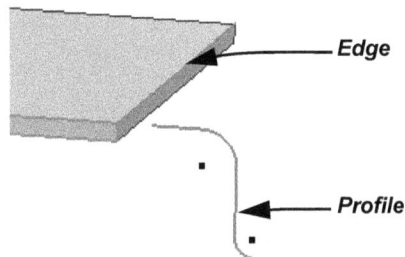

Figure 3–32

Step 5 - Define the Bend Radius and Bend Extension options.

The default value for the bend radius of the new Contour Flange feature is set to the **BendRadius** parameter. This is set based on the Sheet Metal Rule. Accept the default value or enter a new value and select the appropriate **Bend** option.

Step 6 - Define the Width Extents options.

Five types of *Width Extents* settings are available for secondary Contour Flanges. They are **Edge**, **Width**, **Offset**, **From To**, and **Distance**.

The options vary depending on the type of width extent you select. You can access these options by clicking [>>] to expand the dialog box if it is not already.

Edge | Creates the Contour Flange along the full length of a selected edge. The selected edge must be perpendicular to the sketch plane, as shown in Figure 3–33.

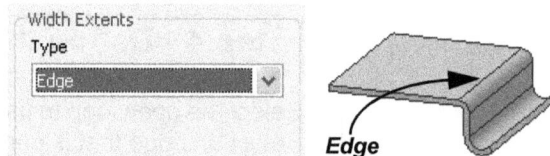

Figure 3–33

Width | The following options are available when the **Width** type is selected:

* **Centered** creates the Contour Flange at the middle of the selected edge using the value in the *Width* field, as shown in Figure 3–34.

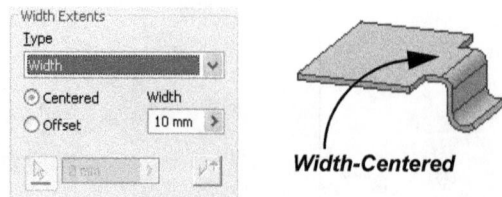

Figure 3–34

- **Offset** creates the Contour Flange starting at a specified distance offset from a single point that you select. The *Width* value determines the overall length of Contour Flange.

  - (Offset) enables you to select a point from which to start measuring the offset, as shown in Figure 3–35.

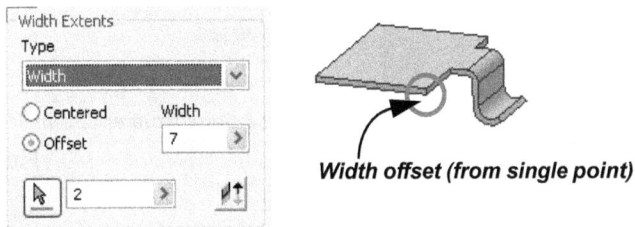

Width offset (from single point)

Figure 3–35

  - (Offset Flip) switches the location of the Contour Flange from one side of a locating plane to the other, as shown in Figure 3–36.

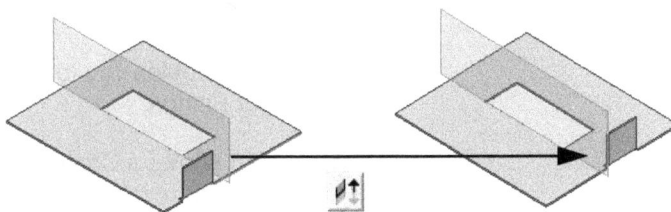

Figure 3–36

Offset

The following options are available when the **Offset** type is selected:

- (Offset1) enables you to select a point and enter a distance from that point to begin the contour flange.

- (Offset2) enables you to select a point and enter a distance away from that point to end the contour flange.

Figure 3–37 shows a Contour Flange that is offset 2 units from one end point and 10 units from the other end point of an edge.

Offset 2 units from endpoint 1   *Offset 10 mm from endpoint 2*

Figure 3–37

From To

The following options are available when the **From To** type is selected:

- 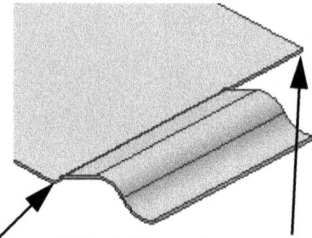 enables you to select a point at which to begin the Contour Flange.

- 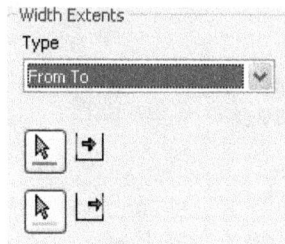 enables you to select a point at which to end the Contour Flange.

Figure 3–38 shows a Contour Flange that starts at one point and ends at another point on a different feature.

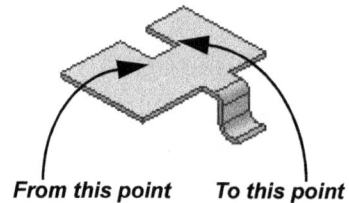

From this point   *To this point*

Figure 3–38

Distance

The following options are available when the **Distance** type is selected:

- The *Distance* field enables you to specify a distance (length) for the contour flange.

- ⬈ (Distance Direction), ◩ (Distance Flip), and ⬈ (Distance Midplane) enable you to specify the side of the sketch plane on which to create the Contour Flange, as shown in Figure 3–39. The sketch profile for the Contour Flange is on a Work Plane that is centered in the part.

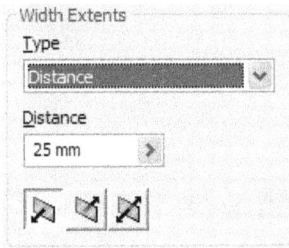

Width Extents
Type
Distance
Distance
25 mm

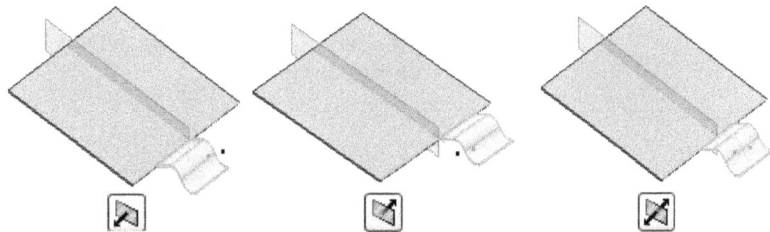

Figure 3–39

Width Extents for Multiple Flanges

When multiple edges are selected as reference edges to create a flange, you can define the width extent on each edge separately. Click the 🔩 glyph that is associated with each bend to open its Bend Edit dialog box, as shown in Figure 3–40. You can activate and select an extent type, as required.

*To edit the width extent once the feature has been created, right-click on the Bend node under the feature in the Model Browser and select **Bend Edit**, or edit the feature and click the 🔩 glyph on the model.*

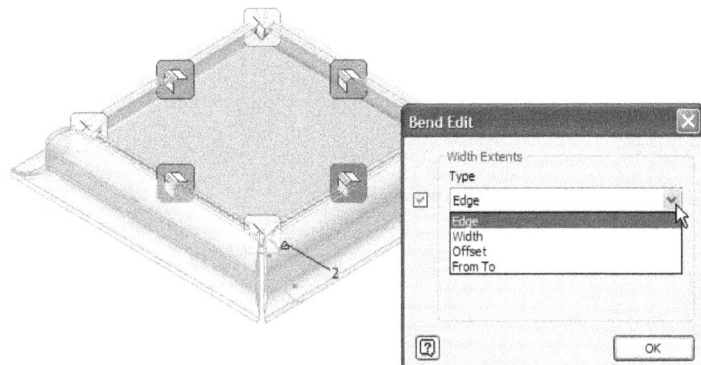

Figure 3–40

The extent type for each bend can be different (as shown in Figure 3–41), even though all flanges exist as one feature in the model.

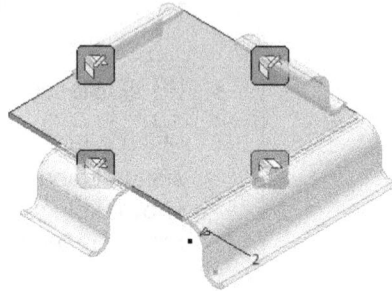

Figure 3–41

The Width Extents options in the expanded dialog box are not available once multiple reference edges have been selected.

The Bend Edit dialog box is also available for individual edges created for a Flange.

Step 7 - Edit the Unfold, Bend, and Corner options (optional).

You can also edit the unfold, bend, and corner settings on their respective tabs. The default values for these options are predefined in the Default Rule.

Step 8 - Complete the feature.

Click **OK** to complete the feature. Alternatively, you can right-click and select **OK (Enter)** to complete the feature.

3.5 Contour Rolls as Secondary Features

A Contour Roll feature creates sheet metal geometry that supports the roll forming sheet metal manufacturing process. Similar to contour flanges, a contour roll feature requires an open loop sketch profile that is revolved to create the required geometry, as shown in Figure 3–42.

Contour rolls can be used as base or secondary features.

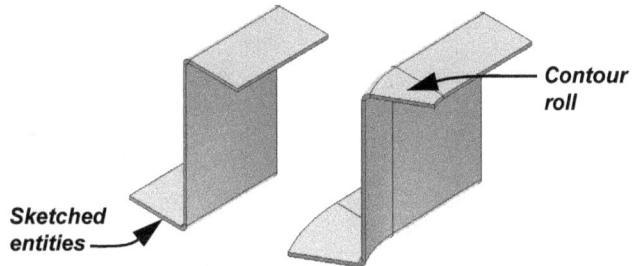

Figure 3–42

General Steps

Use the following general steps to create a secondary Contour Roll feature:

1. Define a sketch plane.
2. Create the sketch.
3. Start the creation of the Contour Roll.
4. Define the Shape options.
5. Define the Rolled Angle options.
6. Define the Unrolling and Unfolding options.
7. Define the Bend Radius option (optional).
8. Complete the feature.

Step 1 - Define a sketch plane.

Select a sketch plane for the secondary Contour Flange. This can be a Work Plane or planar face on the part.

Step 2 - Create the sketch.

Sketch and dimension an open loop profile. The axis around which the contour roll rotates must also be included in the sketch. To create the contour roll as a secondary feature that is adjacent to another feature, you should consider using faces as sketching planes and projecting existing geometry to create the profile. The sketch in Figure 3–43 shows sketched entities that represent the profile (edge projections) and axis for the contour roll.

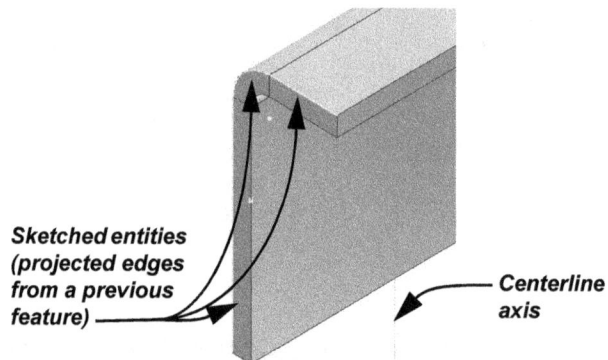

Sketched entities (projected edges from a previous feature)

Centerline axis

Figure 3–43

Step 3 - Start the creation of the Contour Roll.

In the *Sheet Metal* tab>Create panel, click 🔲 (Contour Roll). The Contour Roll dialog box opens as shown in Figure 3–44.

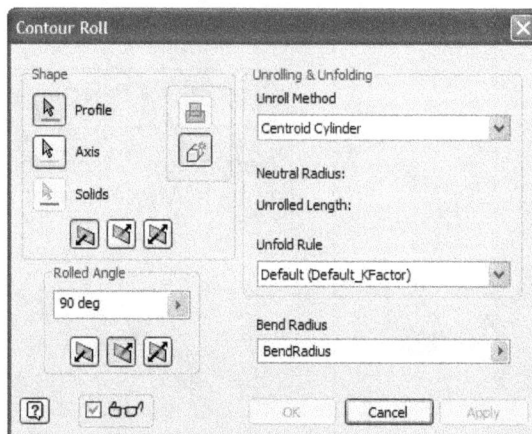

Figure 3–44

Step 4 - Define the Shape options.

Select the profile to define the section that is going to be rolled. The sketched profile must exist in the model before you create the contour roll feature and must be an open section. Select the axis around which the sketched profile is going to be rotated. The axis geometry must exist in the same sketch as the profile geometry.

Select the side of the profile to add the material thickness using the side options in the *Shape* area. The material can be added to the inside ([⊠]), outside ([⊠]), or divided evenly on both sides ([⊠]).

Step 5 - Define the Rolled Angle options.

Define the *Rolled Angle* value. It can be between 0 and 360 degrees, depending on the profile. For profiles with multiple segments, you cannot roll a profile a full 360 degrees. Only single line segments can be rolled 360 degrees. The [⊠] and [⊠] options can be selected to define the direction in which rotation is measured relative to the sketch. The [⊠] option enables you to divide the rotation equally on both sides of the sketch.

Step 6 - Define the Unrolling and Unfolding options.

Select the *Unroll Method* for this feature. The selected option defines how the developed length is calculated. Once an option has been selected, the dialog box updates to reflect any additional required input. The information included here provides the designer with relevant manufacturing information on the neutral radius and unrolled length.

Select the Unfold Rule for this feature. The default value uses the **Default (Default_KFactor)** parameter value that is assigned by the Sheet Metal Rule. You can enter a different rule if required.

Step 7 - Define the Bend Radius option (optional).

Define the *Bend Radius*. The default value uses the **BendRadius** parameter value that is assigned by the Sheet Metal Rule. You can enter a different bend radius if required.

Step 8 - Complete the feature.

Once you have fully defined the contour roll, click **OK** to complete the feature. Alternatively, you can right-click and select **OK (Enter)** to complete the feature. The contour roll shown in Figure 3–45 was created as a secondary feature and references the initial feature that was created as a contour flange.

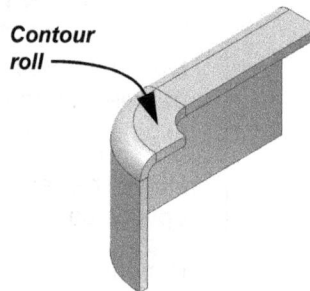

Contour roll

Figure 3–45

Practice 3a | Creating Secondary Faces

Practice Objectives

- Create secondary face geometry that uses a sketch and an existing edge in the model to create the geometry.
- Edit the minimum remnant size that is created when a face does not extend to the end of the selected reference edge.
- Change the bend relief shape that is used when a face does not extend to the end of the selected reference edge.

In this practice, you will open a sheet metal part that consists of a single face, and then create secondary Faces joined with bends. You will also edit minimum remnant and bend relief shapes, as shown in Figure 3–46.

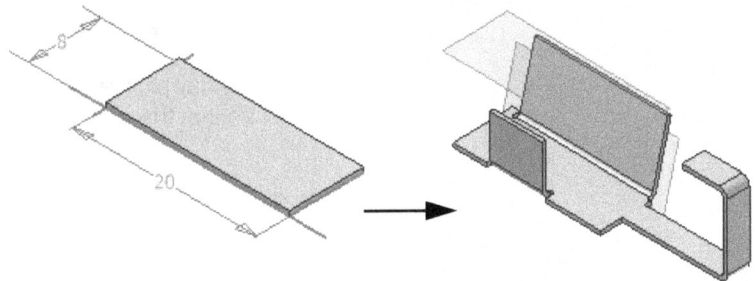

Figure 3–46

Task 1 - Create a face perpendicular to existing geometry.

1. Open **Faces.ipt**.

2. Expand **Face1** in the Model Browser. Hover the cursor over **Sketch1** to display the sketch, as shown in Figure 3–47.

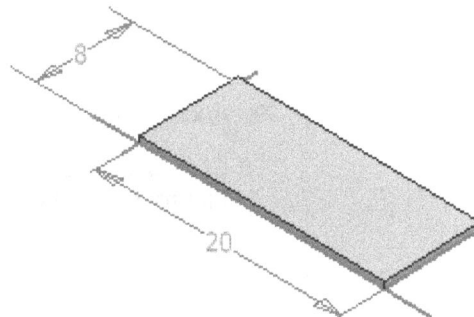

Figure 3–47

3. Create a new sketch. Draw and dimension the profile on the edge surface of the part, as shown in Figure 3–48.

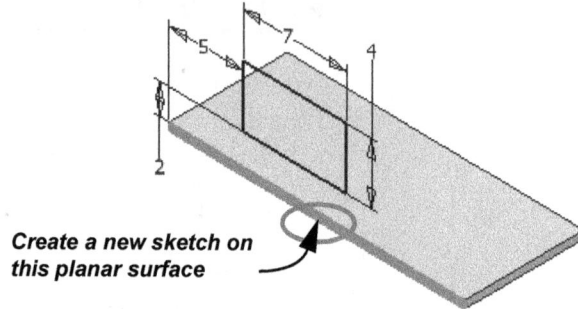

Create a new sketch on this planar surface

Figure 3–48

4. Finish the sketch.

5. In the Create panel, click ☐ (Face).

6. The rectangular profile that you created is automatically selected as it is the only closed profile in the sketch.

7. In the dialog box, click 🛠 (Offset), if required, to set the thickness to the side of the sketch plane pointing away from you.

8. Click ▟ next to **Edges**. Select the edge at the top of the Face, as shown in Figure 3–49.

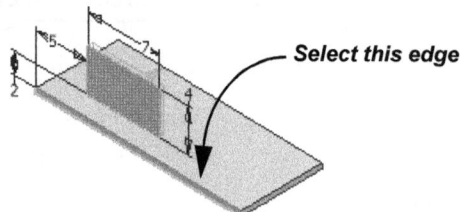

Select this edge

Figure 3–49

9. Accept the defaults options in the *Bend* area.

10. Click **OK** to complete the new Face, as shown in Figure 3–50. The Bend and Bend Relief are created automatically.

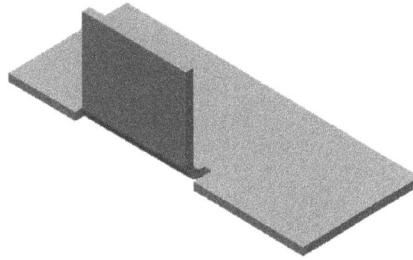

Figure 3–50

Task 2 - Create a Face at an angle to another Face.

1. Create a new Work Plane at a 75 degree angle to the top surface of **Face1**, as shown in Figure 3–51.

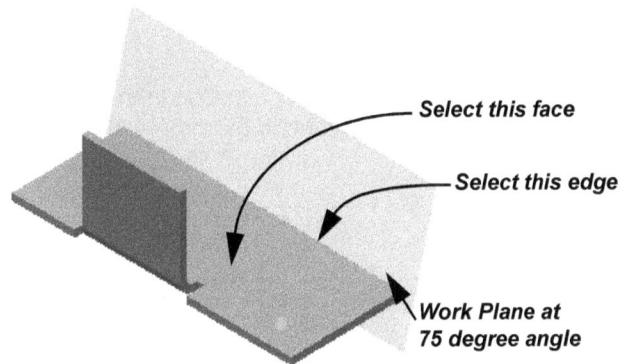

Select this face

Select this edge

Work Plane at 75 degree angle

Figure 3–51

2. In the Navigation Bar, click ⛶ (View Face) and select **WorkPlane1**, which you just created.

3. Create a new sketch and dimension it, as shown in Figure 3–52.

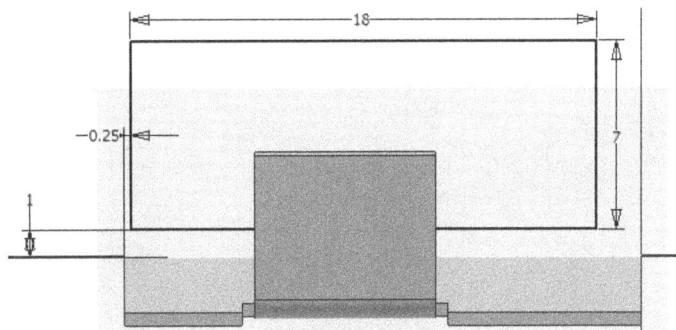

Figure 3–52

4. Finish the sketch.

5. Create a new Face with the thickness set toward you. Click

   [cursor icon] (Edges) and select the edge nearest the sketch. Click **OK** to create the face as shown in Figure 3–53.

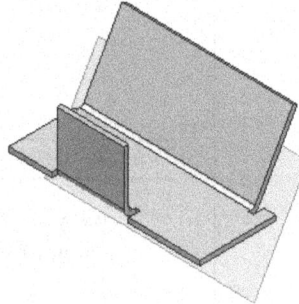

Figure 3–53

If [+] displays in the dialog box, it indicates that there is an open loop in the profile. For this practice, you can safely ignore the warning. The open loop is caused by the reference geometry that was projected as you dimensioned the sketch to existing edges.

Task 3 - Change the minimum remnant.

1. Zoom in to where the right end of the new Face meets the part. A remnant now displays on the right end of the new Face.

2. Zoom to the left end (rotate if required) and note that a remnant does not display at that end.

3. In the Model Browser, in the **Face3** feature, double-click on **Sketch3** to edit it. Change the *0.25* dimension to **1.5**, as shown in Figure 3–54.

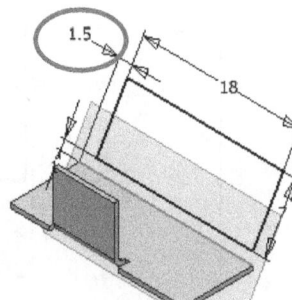

Figure 3–54

4. Finish the sketch. The part updates as shown in Figure 3–55.

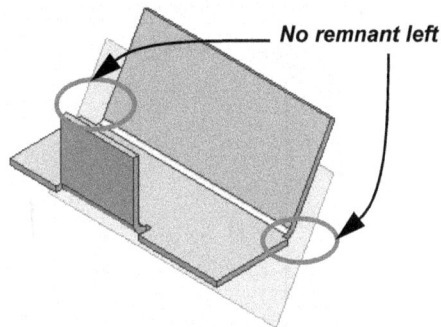
No remnant left

Figure 3–55

A remnant is not left over at either end of **Face3** because the setting for a minimum remnant is set to twice the current thickness. The current thickness set in the Sheet Metal Style is 0.5mm. Therefore, any remnant less than 1mm is removed.

5. In the *Manage* tab>Parameters panel, click

   f_x (Parameters). Try to edit the **MinimumRemnant** to **Thickness*0.5ul**. The parameter value is driven by the rule and must be edited within the rule to make the change. Close the Parameters dialog box.

6. In the *Sheet Metal* tab>Setup panel, click (Sheet Metal Defaults). Click next to the Sheet Metal Rule drop-down list. The Style and Standard Editor opens.

7. Select the *Bend* tab. Change the equation for *MinimumRemnant* to **Thickness*0.5ul**, as shown in Figure 3–56.

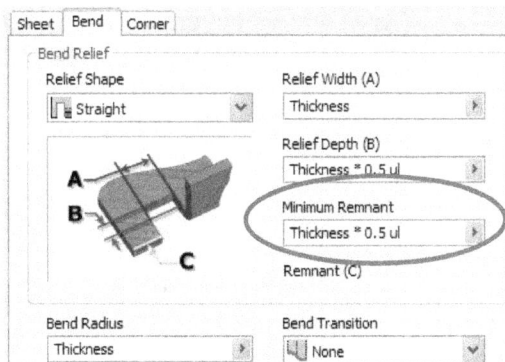

Figure 3–56

8. Click **Save and Close**. Close the Sheet Metal Defaults dialog box. If required, update the part. The model now has a remnant of material at the left end, as shown in Figure 3–57 (the view is rotated for clarity).

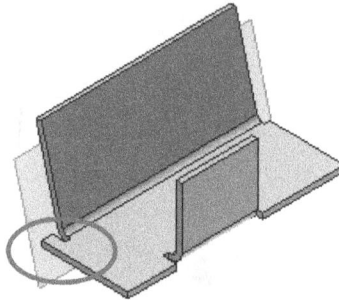

Figure 3–57

Task 4 - Create a Face parallel to another Face.

1. Suppress **Face2** and **Face3** to clarify the display for the next steps. Toggle off the visibility of **WorkPlane1** as well.

2. Create a new Work Plane offset **10mm** from the top surface of **Face1**, as shown in Figure 3–58.

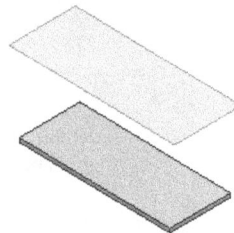

Figure 3–58

3. Create a new sketch on **WorkPlane2**. Draw and dimension the profile for an offset Face, as shown in Figure 3–59 (rotate the sketch to display it directly).

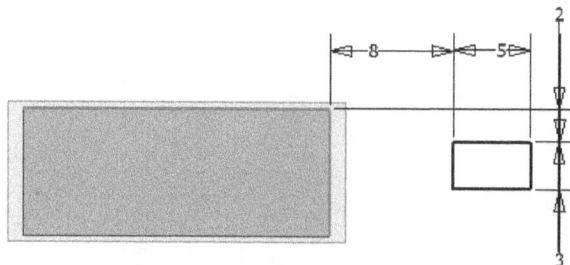

Figure 3–59

4. Finish the sketch.

5. In the Create panel, click ☐ (Face). The closed loop rectangle is selected as the profile.

6. In the dialog box, toggle 🔧 (Offset) as required to apply the thickness away from the existing part.

7. Accept the default **BendRadius** as the *Radius* option.

8. Select the edge shown in Figure 3–60 as the edge for attaching the new Face to the part.

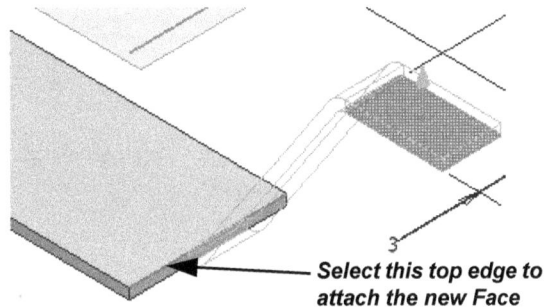

Select this top edge to attach the new Face

Figure 3–60

9. If not already displayed, click >> to display the *Double Bend* area in the expanded Face dialog box.

10. Select **Fix Edges**.

11. Click **OK** to complete the new Face, as shown in Figure 3–61.

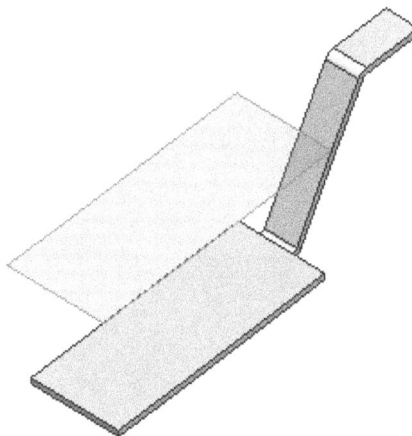

Figure 3–61

Task 5 - Edit the Double Bend options.

1. Double-click on **Face4** in the Model Browser to open the feature editing dialog box.

2. Select **45 Degree** and display the preview, as shown on the left in Figure 3–62. Click ⬦ (Flip Fixed Edge) to display the preview shown on the right.

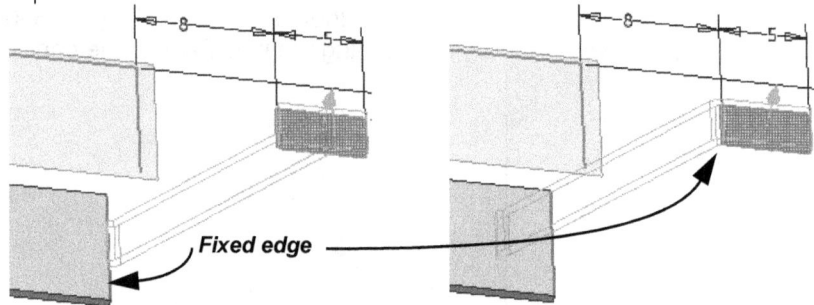

Figure 3–62

3. Click **OK** to complete the Face.

Task 6 - Change the Bend options.

1. Edit **Face4** again and set the *Double Bend* to **Full Radius**. Flip the fixed edge as required to achieve the result shown in Figure 3–63.

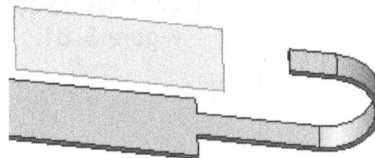

Figure 3–63

2. Edit **Face4** again and set *Double Bend* to **90 Degree**. Flip the fixed edge as required to achieve the result shown in Figure 3–64.

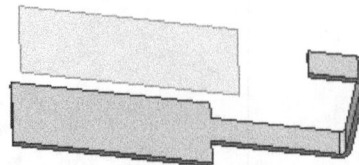

Figure 3–64

Task 7 - Edit the bend relief shape for the default rule.

1. Unsuppress **Face2** and **Face3**.

2. Toggle on the visibility of **WorkPlane1**.

3. Rotate the model so that it is similar to the view shown in Figure 3–65.

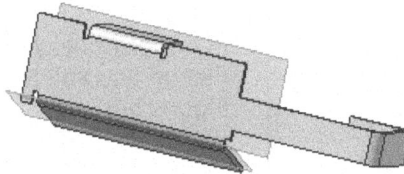

Figure 3–65

4. In the *Sheet Metal* tab>Setup panel, click ⬚ (Sheet Metal Defaults).

5. Click ▱ next to the Sheet Metal Rule drop-down list. The Style and Standard Editor opens.

6. Select the *Bend* tab.

7. Change the *Relief Shape* option of the bend to **Round**.

8. Click **Save and Close**. The model displays as shown in Figure 3–66.

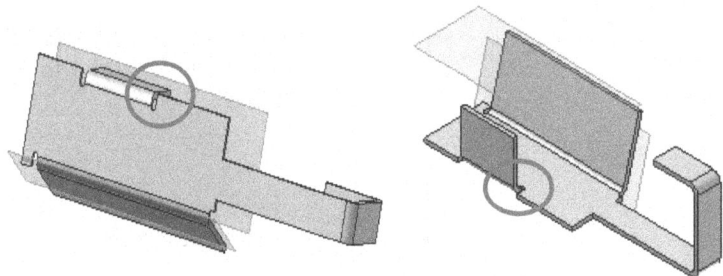

Figure 3–66

9. Zoom in to review the round bend relief shape.

10. Save and close the file.

Practice 3b

Creating Secondary Contour Flanges

Practice Objective

*   Create contour flange geometry that uses a sketch as the profile and an existing edge as the placement reference to attach the contour flange to existing geometry.

In this practice, you will open a part with an existing Contour Flange and add two secondary Contour Flanges, as shown in Figure 3–67.

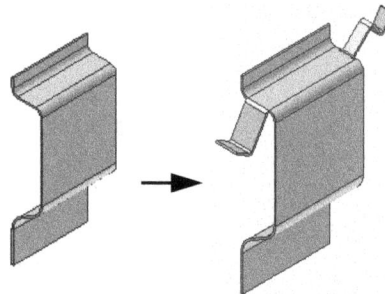

Figure 3–67

Task 1 - Create a secondary Contour Flange using the default feature options.

1. Open **Contours.ipt**.

2. In the Model Browser, expand **Contour Flange1** and hover the cursor over **Sketch1** to display the sketch, as shown in Figure 3–68.

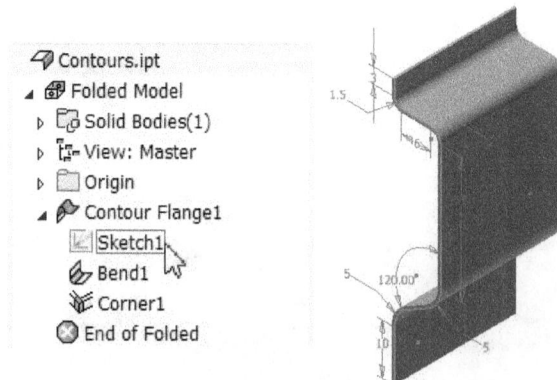

Figure 3–68

3. Create a new sketch on the largest planar face of the existing Contour Flange. It is the face with a 25mm height.

4. Project the edge shown in Figure 3–69 to create a point on the sketch.

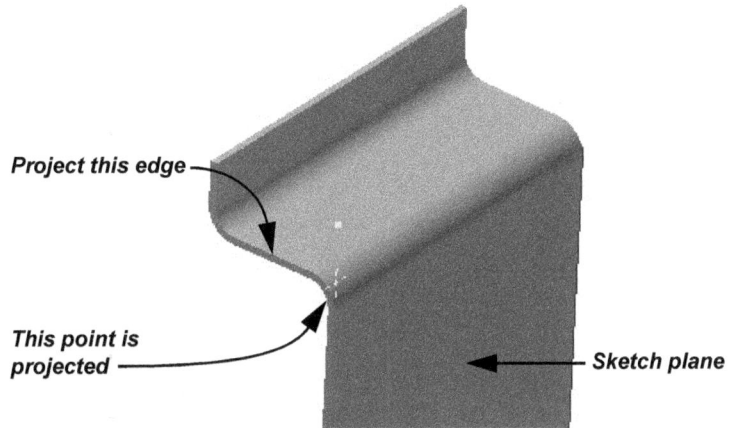

Figure 3–69

5. Sketch and dimension a profile for the new Contour Flange, as shown in Figure 3–70. The sketch consists of only two lines and three dimensions. Ensure that the top end point of the 10mm line is coincident with the point that was created in Step 2.

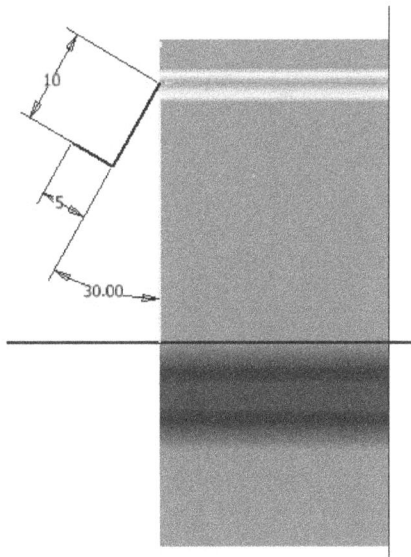

Figure 3–70

6. Finish the sketch.

7. In the *Sheet Metal* tab>Create panel, click ⚑ (Contour Flange). Select the sketch as the *Profile*, and select the edge that you just projected as the edge reference for the Contour Flange to follow. The preview is shown in Figure 3–71.

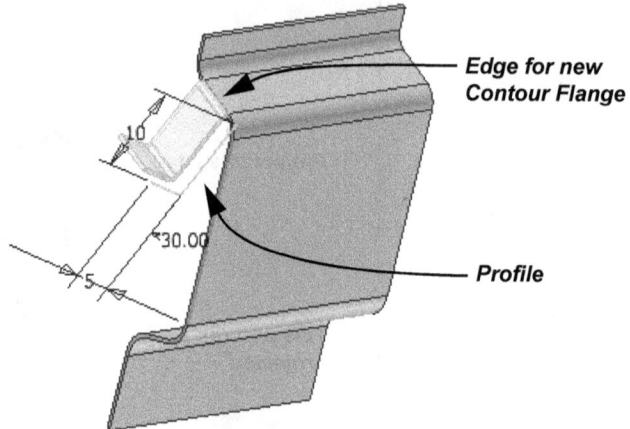

Figure 3–71

8. Click **OK** to complete the secondary Contour Flange.

Task 2 - Create a Contour Flange with an offset.

1. Rotate the model and create a new sketch on the face that was used for the previous sketch.

2. Sketch and dimension a profile as shown in Figure 3–72.

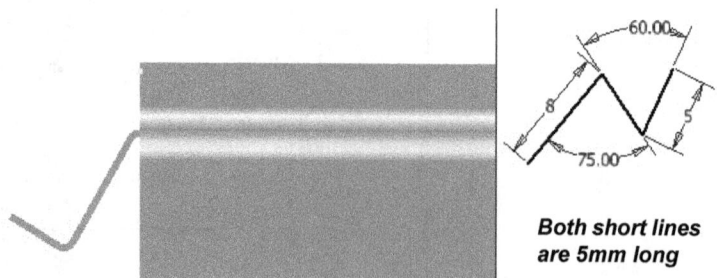

Both short lines are 5mm long

Figure 3–72

3. Rotate the model as shown in Figure 3–73. Project the edge of the face that is perpendicular to the sketch. This creates a point in the sketch.

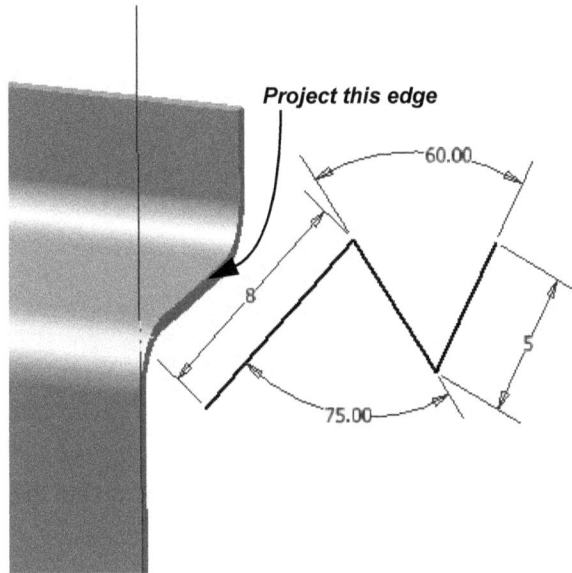

Figure 3–73

4. Add a **Coincident** constraint between the projected point and the end of the sketch profile to locate the Contour Flange.

5. The sketch is not fully constrained; the 8mm line can still be dragged to different angles. Leave it under-constrained for now.

6. Finish the Sketch.

7. In the *Sheet Metal* tab>Create panel, click (Contour Flange).

8. Select the sketch as the *Profile* and the edge you projected as the edge reference for the Contour Flange to follow.

9. Click >> to expand the dialog box to display the *Width Extents* area. Apply the settings shown on the left in Figure 3–74. The preview of the Contour Flange is shown on the right. For *Offset1*, ensure that the front end of the edge you projected is selected. For *Offset2*, ensure that the back end of the edge you projected is selected.

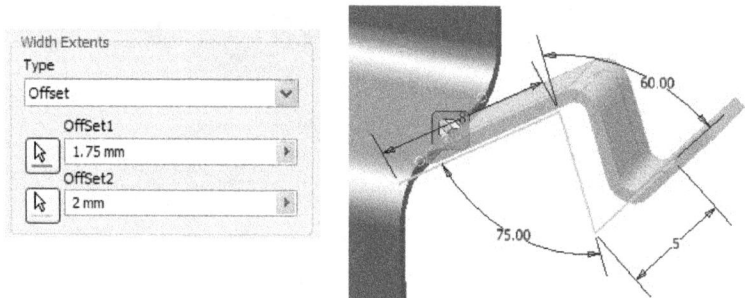

Figure 3–74

10. Click **OK** to complete the feature. The finished part is shown in Figure 3–75.

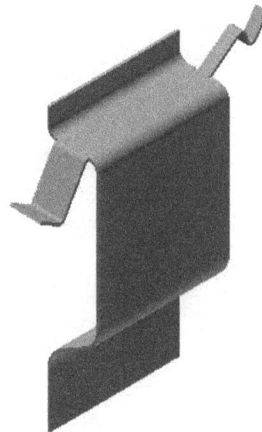

Figure 3–75

11. Save and close the model.

Practice 3c

Creating Secondary Contour Rolls

Practice Objective

- Create contour roll geometry that uses the edge of existing geometry as the profile and a sketched centerline to create the geometry for the feature.

In this practice, you will add a Contour Roll feature to existing geometry. The completed model is shown in Figure 3–76.

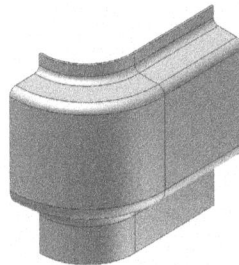

Figure 3–76

Task 1 - Define the profile and centerline for a contour roll.

1. Open **ContourRoll.ipt**. A single Contour Flange feature is provided in the model.

2. In the Sketch panel, click ⃞ (Start 2D Sketch). Select the face shown in Figure 3–77 as the sketch plane.

The model has been rotated in Figure 3–77.

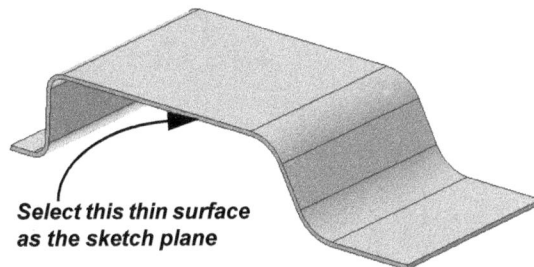

Select this thin surface as the sketch plane

Figure 3–77

3. Project the edges and sketch the centerline shown
   Figure 3–78.

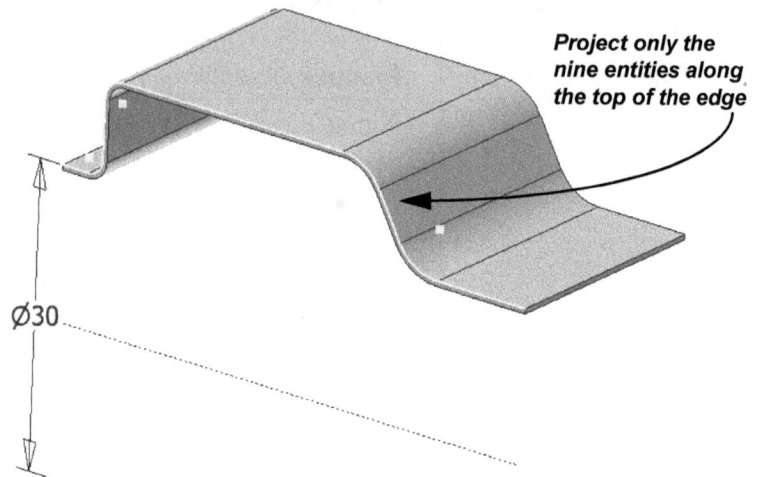

Project only the nine entities along the top of the edge

Ø30

Figure 3–78

4. In the Exit panel, click ✔ (Finish Sketch).

Task 2 - Create a contour roll.

---

1. In the *Sheet Metal* tab>Create panel, click 🖑 (Contour Roll).
   The Contour Roll dialog box opens as shown in Figure 3–79.

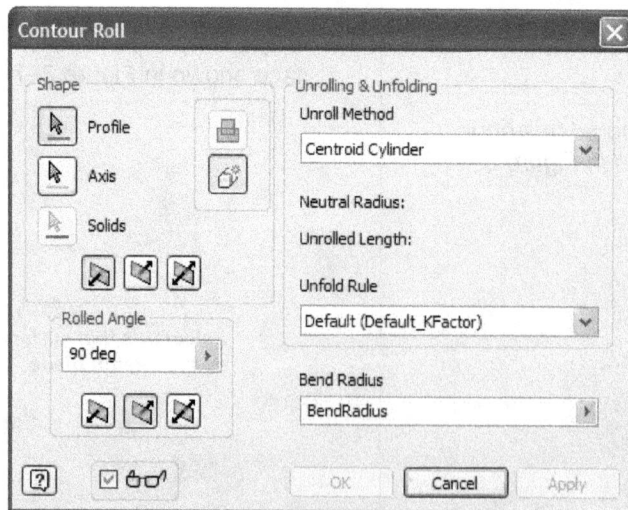

Figure 3–79

Since the sketch that was just created is the only unconsumed open sketch in the model, it is automatically selected as the *Profile* reference for the contour roll.

2. Select the centerline as the *Axis* reference around which the sketched profile will be rotated.

3. Keep 🔲 selected as the side to which to add the material thickness.

The Rolled Angle value can be between 0 and 360 degrees, depending on the profile. For profiles with multiple segments, you cannot roll a profile a full 360 degrees. Only single line segments can be rolled 360 degrees.

4. Enter **90 deg** for the *Rolled Angle*. Keep 🔲 selected as the default direction, so that the material is created as an extension to the existing geometry.

5. Keep the remaining defaults in the Contour Roll dialog box and click **OK** to complete the feature. The model displays as shown in Figure 3–80.

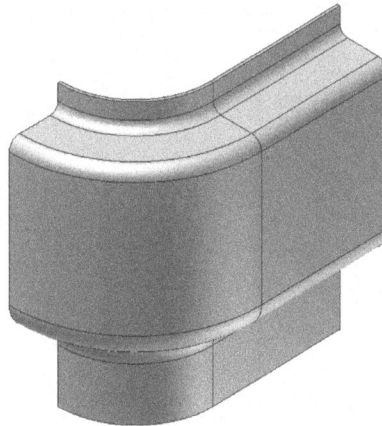

Figure 3–80

6. Save the model and close the window.

Chapter Review Questions

1. Which of the following are sheet metal parameters that are used to drive the geometry in a sheet metal model? (Select all that apply.)

   a. **d0**

   b. **Thickness**

   c. **Depth**

   d. **BendRadius**

   e. **Radius**

   f. **MinimumRemnant**

   g. **GapSize**

2. Which of the following bend relief shapes was used in the model shown in Figure 3–81?

   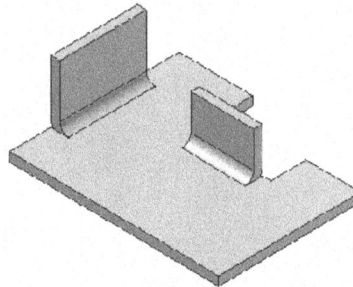

   Figure 3–81

   a. Tear

   b. Round

   c. Straight

3. Which of the following statements is true regarding secondary Face features? (Select all that apply.)

   a. A secondary Face feature can be created on a sketch plane that is positioned at any angle relative to a base feature.

   b. A secondary Face feature can be created on a sketch plane that is parallel but not coplanar to an existing planar face or work plane.

   c. A separate Bend feature must be used to join a secondary face feature to a base feature.

   d. The Double Bend options in the expanded Face dialog box are always available when creating a Face feature as either a base or secondary feature.

4. Which of the following Double Bend types was used to create the secondary Face feature shown in Figure 3–82?

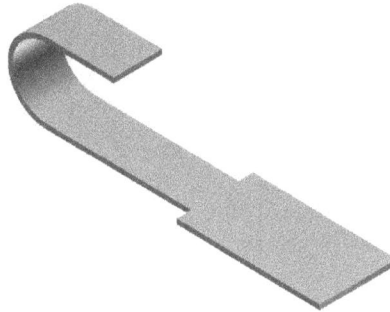

Figure 3–82

   a. Fix Edges

   b. 45 Degrees

   c. Full Radius

   d. 90 Degrees

5. Which of the following is the best *Width Extent* option to use to create the Contour Flange feature highlighted in Figure 3–83?

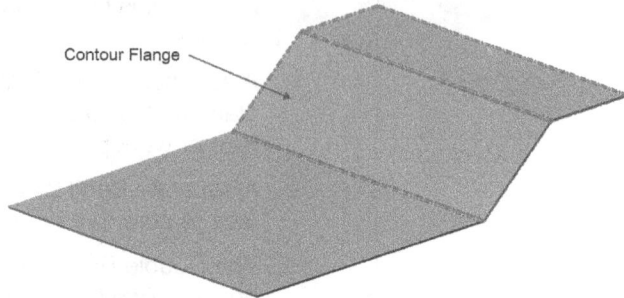

Contour Flange

Figure 3–83

a. Edge

b. Width

c. Offset

d. From To

e. Distance

6. Which of the following statements is true regarding the Contour Roll feature? (Select all that apply.)

a. The profile for a Contour Roll feature must be a closed loop.

b. The Axis that is selected as the rotational reference can exist in another sketch as long as it is planar with the Profile sketch.

c. The unroll method that is defined when the Contour Roll feature is created defines how the developed length is calculated when the feature is unrolled.

d. The default Bend Radius value is assigned through the Sheet Metal Rule.

Command Summary

Button	Command	Location
	Contour Flange	• **Ribbon**: *Sheet Metal* tab>Create panel
	Contour Roll	• **Ribbon**: *Sheet Metal* tab>Create panel
	Face	• **Ribbon**: *Sheet Metal* tab>Create panel
f_x	**Parameters**	• **Ribbon**: *Manage* tab>Parameters panel • **Quick Access Toolbar**
	Sheet Metal Defaults	• **Ribbon**: *Sheet Metal* tab>Setup panel
	Styles Editor	• **Ribbon**: *Manage* tab>Styles and Standards panel • *Click* next to the Sheet Metal Rule in the Sheet Metal Defaults dialog box.

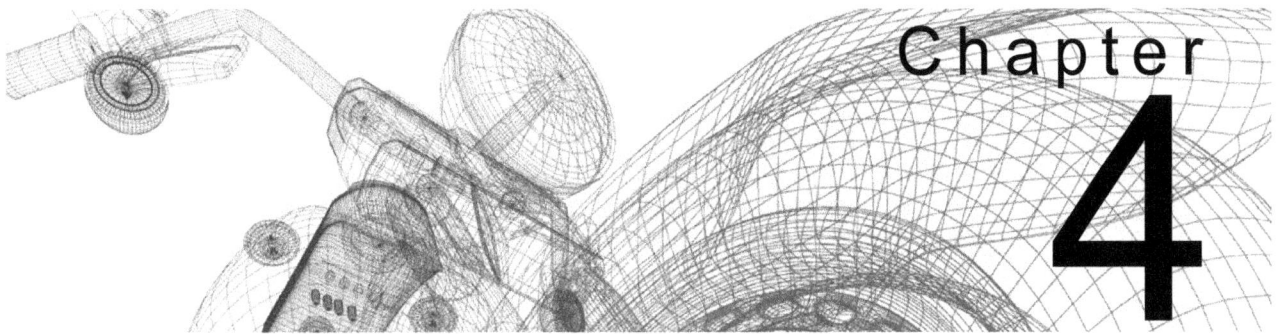

Flanges

A Flange is a projecting rim that is attached at the edge of a Face. It is formed to give additional strength, stiffness, or support to an area of a part. A Flange can also be used to provide a place for attaching other objects.

Learning Objectives in this Chapter

- Use the various selection type options to locate a Flange feature on single edges, multiple edges, or a loop of edges.
- Edit the Flange creation, width extent, and corner relief options to vary the resulting flange geometry.
- Set the default Corner Relief setting in the Sheet Metal rule that drives the sheet metal model.
- Control the Corner Relief setting for all corners and individual corners in a Flange feature, independent of the Sheet Metal rule.
- Control the corner mitering of adjacent flanged geometry.

4.1 Creating Flanges

While you can add secondary Faces or Contour Flanges to create a rim on the edge of a sheet metal part, a **Flange** command is specifically designed to create this type of feature. Creating a Flange is simpler than creating a secondary Face for two reasons. First, it creates *a placed feature,* which by definition, does not require a sketch and is usually quicker to create. Second, if you want to create a rim that is at any angle other than 90 degrees to a face, you can do so without having to create a Work Plane for the new feature.

The **Flange** command also has options for assigning the position of the Bend feature, which in some cases, might be more difficult to locate when adding a secondary Face. Figure 4–1 shows three separate Flange features added to the edges of an existing Face.

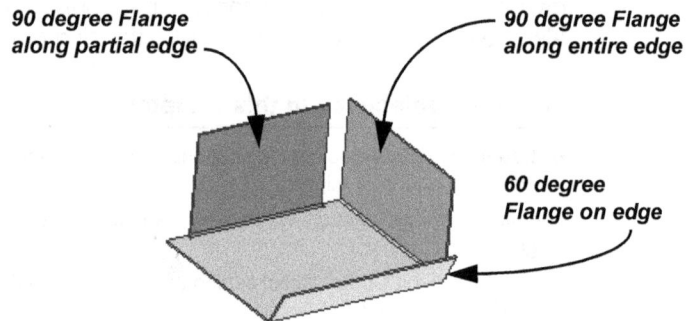

90 degree Flange along partial edge

90 degree Flange along entire edge

60 degree Flange on edge

Figure 4–1

General Steps

Use the following general steps to create a Flange feature:

1. Start the creation of the Flange.
2. Select the placement references.
3. Set the offset direction.
4. Define the Height Extents.
5. Define the Flange Angle.
6. Apply the Bend Radius.
7. Define the Height Datum.
8. Define the Bend Position.
9. Define the Width Extents.
10. Set the Design Method (optional).
11. Edit the Bend, Corner, and Unfold options (optional).
12. Complete the feature.

Step 1 - Start the creation of the Flange.

In the *Sheet Metal* tab>Create panel, click (Flange). The Flange dialog box opens as shown in Figure 4–2.

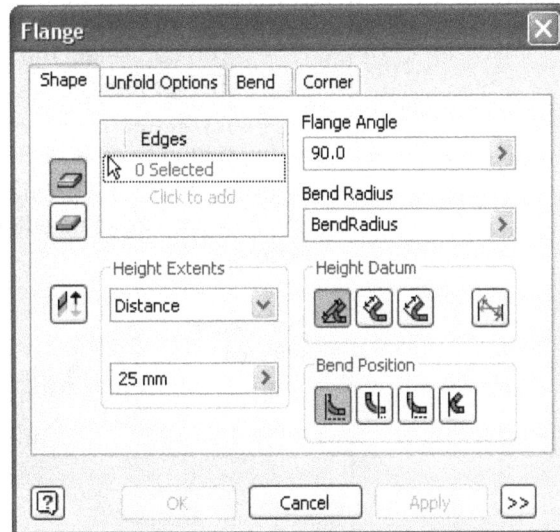

Figure 4–2

Step 2 - Select the placement references.

There are two options for selecting the placement of a Flange: **Edge Select Mode** and **Loop Select Mode**, as shown in Figure 4–3.

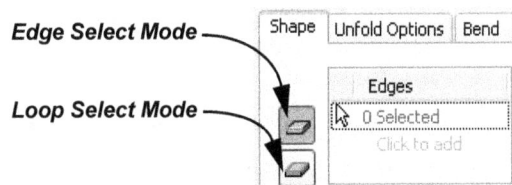

Figure 4–3

Edge Flanges

Using **Edge Select Mode** enables you to select one or more individual edges on which to build a single Flange feature.

How To: Create a Flange using Edge Select Mode

1. In the *Shape* tab, click 🖻 (Edge Select Mode).
2. Select the edge(s) of a Face to attach the Flange.
   - You can select multiple individual edges to build a single Flange feature.
   - If you need to clear an edge, use <Ctrl> + the left mouse button to clear it.

Figure 4–4 shows a preview of a single edge selected on the left, and multiple edges selected on the right to create a new Flange feature.

Single edge selected   *Multiple edges selected*

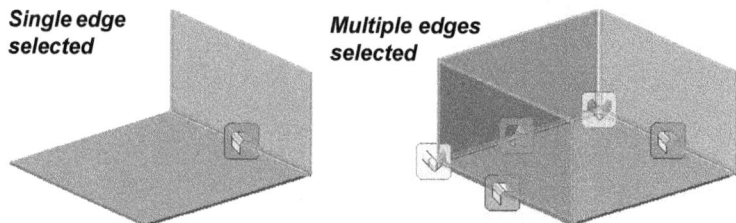

Figure 4–4

Loop Flanges

Using **Loop Select Mode** enables you to create a single Flange feature with appropriate Bends and Corners. The Flange is created on a loop that follows the edges of an existing Face.

A loop must have at least one straight edge to create a Flange. Loop Flanges are not able to form along curves. The Flange skips curved edges on the loop and continues creating the feature on all straight edges for that loop.

How To: Create a Flange Using Loop Select Mode

1. In the *Shape* tab, click 🖻 (Loop Select Mode).
2. Select the edge of a Face to highlight the Loop. Three examples of Flanges formed along loops with straight and curved edges are shown in Figure 4–5.

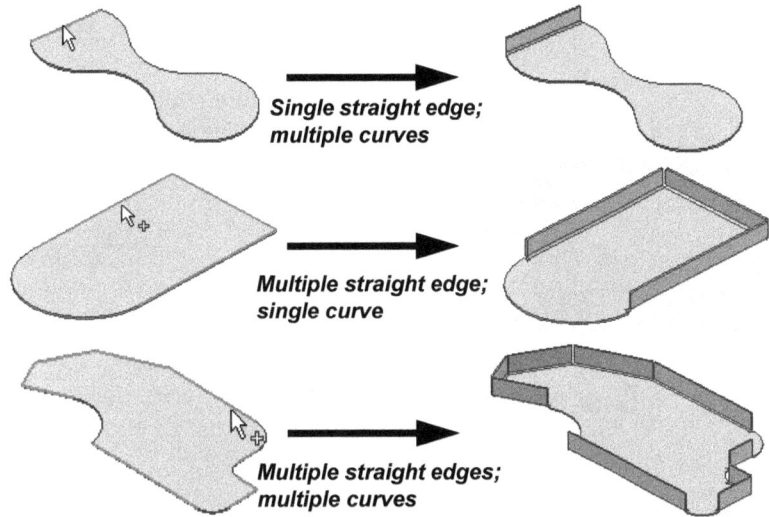

Single straight edge;
multiple curves

Multiple straight edge;
single curve

Multiple straight edges;
multiple curves

Figure 4–5

If no curves are on the loop, a Flange that continues all of the way around the profile of the Face is created, as shown in Figure 4–6.

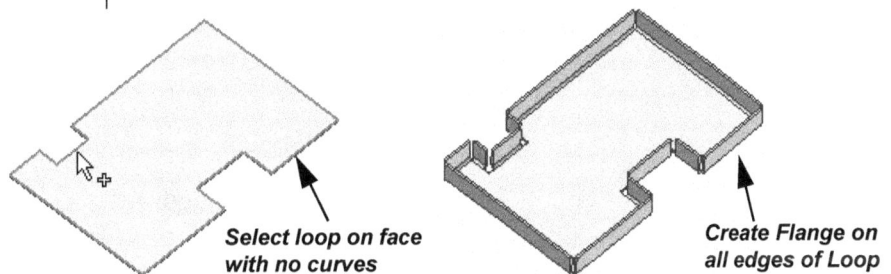

Select loop on face
with no curves

Create Flange on
all edges of Loop

Figure 4–6

Step 3 - Set the offset direction.

Click ▣ (Flip direction) to apply the Flange height in one of two opposing directions, as shown in Figure 4–7.

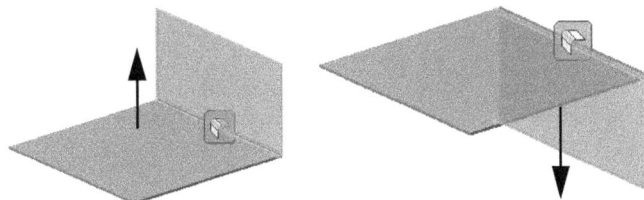

Figure 4–7

Step 4 - Define the Height Extents.

Two *Height Extents* options are available: **Distance** and **To**, as shown in Figure 4–8.

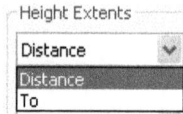

Figure 4–8

Distance

The **Distance** option enables you to enter an exact value for the height of the Flange, as shown in Figure 4–9.

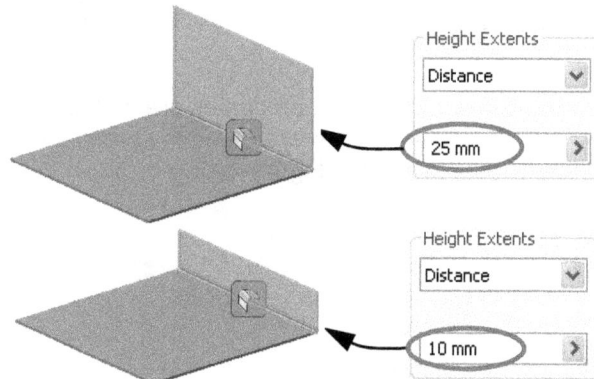

Figure 4–9

To

The **To** option enables you select an edge to set the termination location for the new Flange, as shown in Figure 4–10.

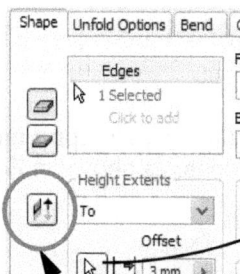

Flip option cannot be used for the To style

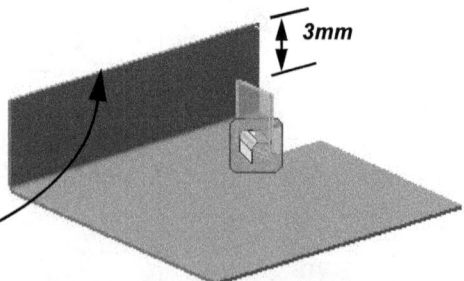

Height of new Flange is offset so it is lower than top edge of existing Flange by 3.

Figure 4–10

Step 5 - Define the Flange Angle.

Enter the number of degrees for the *Flange Angle*, as shown in Figure 4–11.

Flange Angle
90.0 deg

Figure 4–11

Figure 4–12 shows how the *Flange angle* is applied relative to the position of the *Flange* area (before folding during fabrication).

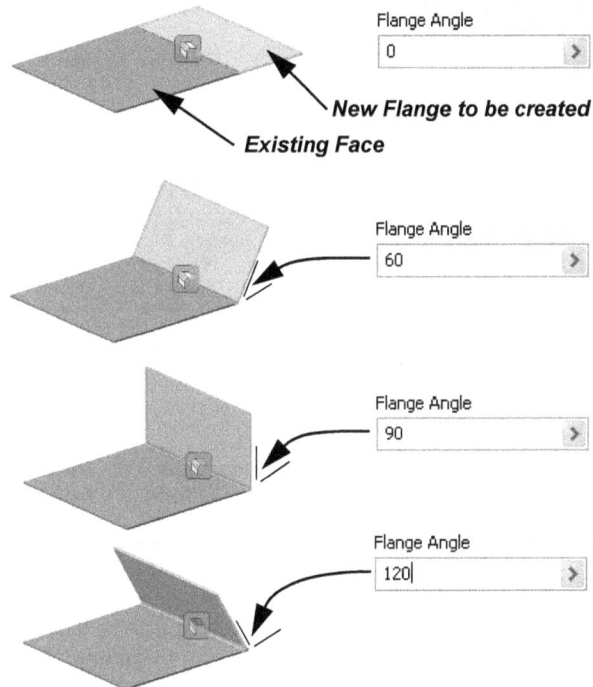

Flange Angle
0

New Flange to be created

Existing Face

Flange Angle
60

Flange Angle
90

Flange Angle
120

Figure 4–12

Step 6 - Apply the Bend Radius.

Accept the default value for the *Bend Radius*. The default is based on the Sheet Metal Rule that was assigned for the model. You can enter a different bend radius, if required.

Step 7 - Define the Height Datum.

Select the *Height Datum* options as required. The first three options enable you to assign the faces used to measure the height of the Flange. The three options (shown in Figure 4–13) include:

- ⬛ (Bend from the intersection of the two outer faces),

- ⬛ (Bend from the intersection of the two inner faces), and

- ⬛ (Parallel to flange termination detail face).

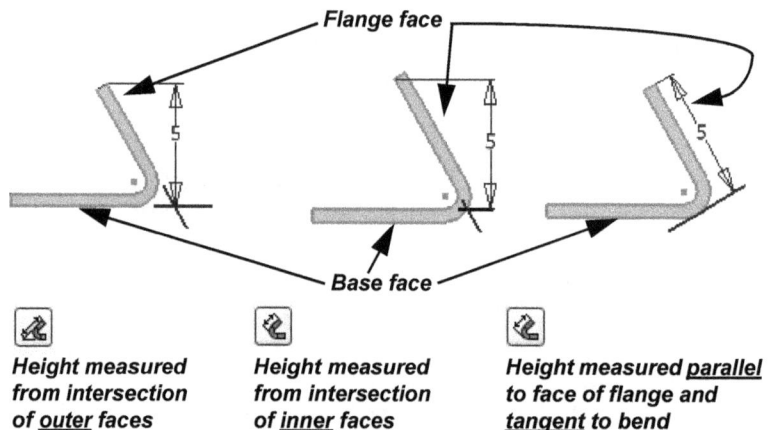

Figure 4–13

⬛	⬛	⬛
Height measured from intersection of _outer_ faces	**Height measured from intersection of _inner_ faces**	**Height measured _parallel_ to face of flange and _tangent_ to bend**

The fourth option is ⬛ (Aligned vs. Orthogonal). This option enables you to select whether the Flange is measured aligned (parallel) to the Flange, or orthogonal (90 degrees) to the base Face. This option is shown in Figure 4–14.

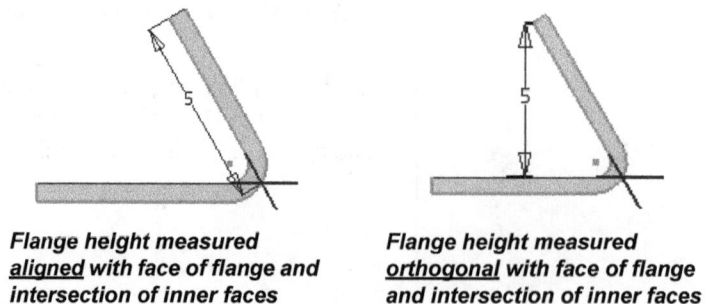

Flange height measured _aligned_ with face of flange and intersection of inner faces	**Flange height measured _orthogonal_ with face of flange and intersection of inner faces**

Figure 4–14

Step 8 - Define the Bend Position.

Select the *Bend Position* option. The setting applies to the faces of the newly created Flange. The four options include:

- (Inside of Base Face Extents) applies the position of the Flange's Bend feature so that the outside face of the new Flange remains inside the face extent from the placement edge, as shown in Figure 4–15.

Selected edge of existing Face feature

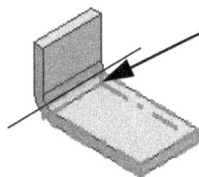

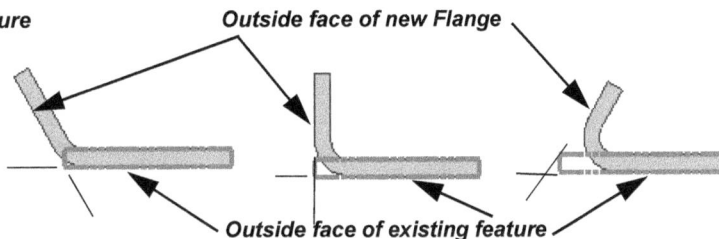

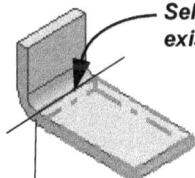

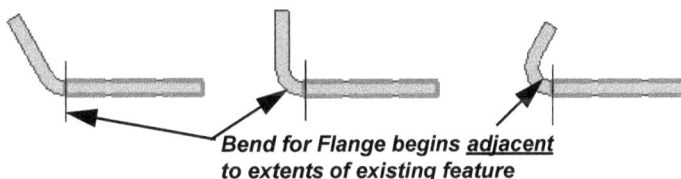

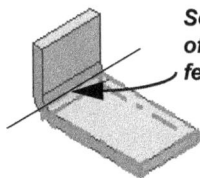

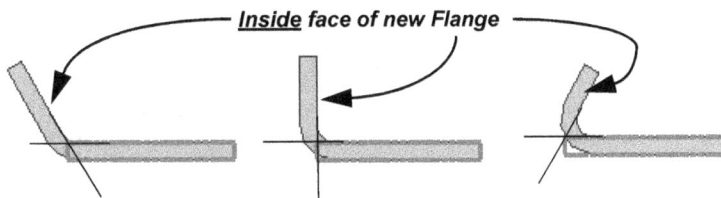

Outside face of new Flange

Outside face of existing feature

Figure 4–15

- (Bend from the Adjacent Face) applies the position of the Flange's Bend feature so that it starts adjacent to the face at the extents of the original base Face feature, as shown in Figure 4–16.

Selected edge of existing feature

Bend for Flange begins adjacent to extents of existing feature

Figure 4–16

- (Outside of the Base Face Extents) applies the position of the Flange's Bend feature so that the inside face of the new Flange remains outside the face extent from the placement edge, as shown in Figure 4–17.

Selected edge of existing Face feature

Inside face of new Flange

Figure 4–17

- (Bend Tangent to Side Face) applies the position of the Flange's Bend feature so that the outside of the Bend is tangent to the outer extents of the original base Face feature, as shown in Figure 4–18.

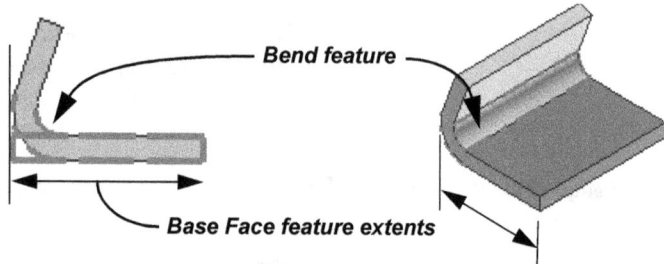

Bend feature is <u>tangent</u> (left side) to base face extents

Figure 4–18

Step 9 - Define the Width Extents.

The method for defining the width extents of a flange depends on the number of edge references that are selected for flange placement. If a single edge is selected, click in the Flange dialog box to display the *Width Extents* area. The options are available in the Type drop-down list, as shown Figure 4–19. If there are multiple edge references, the options in the expanded dialog box are not available and you must select individual glyphs () in the feature preview. Selecting each glyph opens the Bend Edit dialog box that provides the Type drop-down list shown in Figure 4–19.

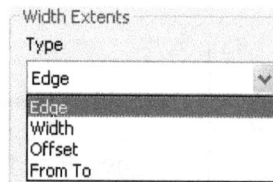

Figure 4–19

The following width extent types are available:

- **Edge** creates a Flange that runs the full length of each edge you select, as shown in Figure 4–20. You can select a single edge or multiple individual edges for this type of Flange.

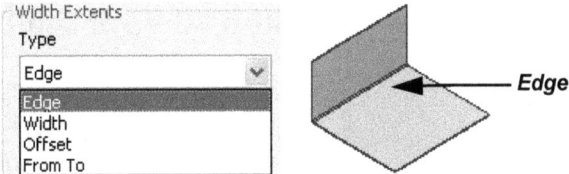

Figure 4–20

- **Width** can be used to make a Centered Flange that has a specified width distance, or an Offset Flange that has a width and one point specified, from which it is going to be offset. Examples of Width-Centered and Width-Offset Flanges are shown in Figure 4–21.

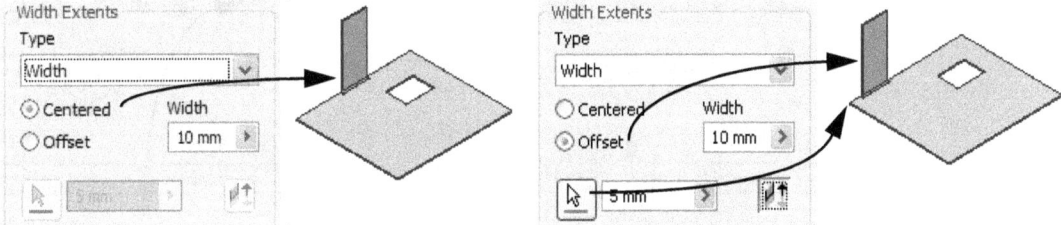

Figure 4–21

- **Offset** creates a Flange with offset distances specified from two points that you select, as shown in Figure 4–22.

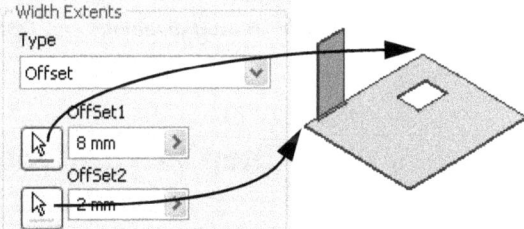

Figure 4–22

- **From To** creates a Flange that starts and ends at two points on one or more features. Figure 4–23 shows a Flange with its offset points located on an existing Cut feature. If the Cut changes size or position, the Flange updates.

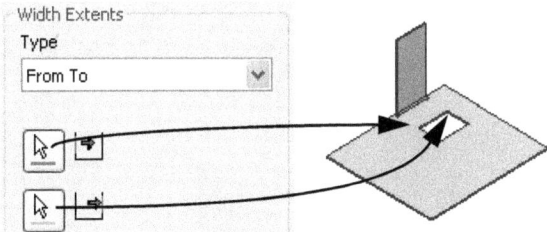

Figure 4–23

Step 10 - Set the Design Method (optional).

This option is automatically enabled for parts created in versions earlier than the Autodesk® Inventor® 2009 software. When enabled, some of the *Height Extents*, *Height Datum*, and *Bend Position* options are grayed out.

For new parts that are created with the Autodesk Inventor 2009 software or later, the **Old Method** option is disabled by default, as shown in Figure 4–24.

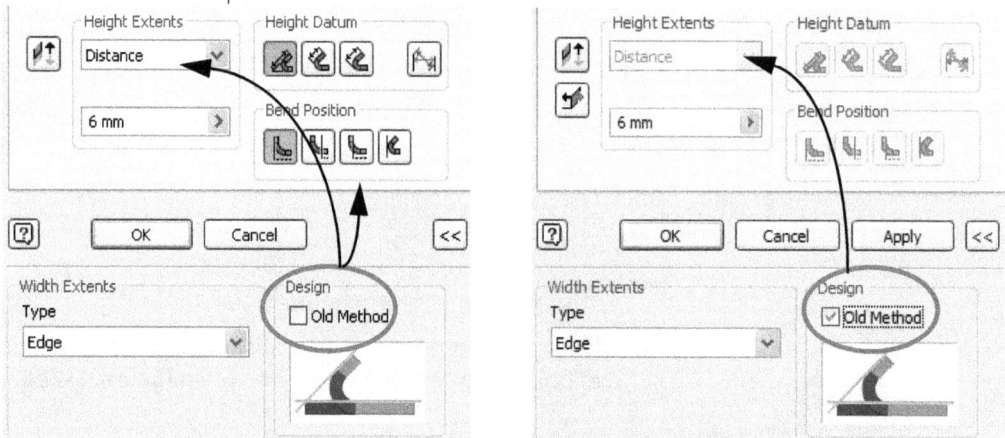

Options available with Old Method disabled   **Options not available with Old Method enabled**

Figure 4–24

Step 11 - Edit the Bend, Corner, and Unfold options (optional).

Use the *Bend*, *Corner*, and *Unfold* tabs to define the associated options. The defaults are based on the settings from the assigned Sheet Metal Rule.

When two or more non-tangent edges are selected to create a Flange you are provided with individual controls to edit the default corner relief. These controls are in the form of a button, displayed when the feature is previewed. The button is located at the corner near the selected placement edge, as shown in Figure 4–25. Once a button has been selected to edit the corner the Corner Edit dialog box opens.

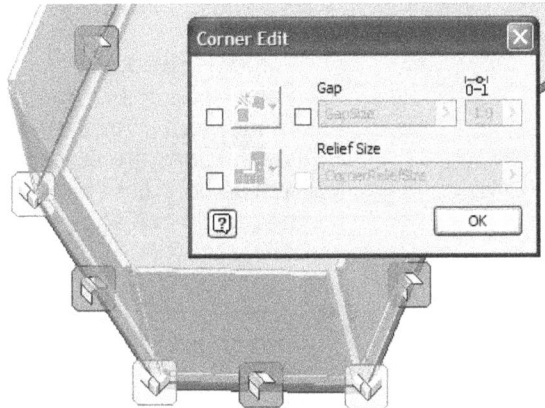

Figure 4–25

The Corner Edit dialog box enables you to edit the corner relief Gap type and size as well as the Relief type and its size. This is done on a corner by corner basis. It provides much more flexibility then editing using the *Corner* tab that controls all corners in the feature at the same time. To enable any of the editing options in the Corner Edit dialog box you must select the appropriate check box.

Step 12 - Complete the feature.

Once you have fully defined the options, click **OK** to complete the feature. Alternatively, you can right-click and select **OK (Enter)** to complete the feature.

4.2 Corner Relief Options

If multiple Flanges are created on a flat sheet of metal where two edges meet, Corner Relief is often incorporated into the flat sheet of material before it is formed. The Corner Relief is a cut out shape that removes material. This prevents excess material at the intersection of the folded areas from intersecting and causing a bulge.

Corner Relief options are applied by default based on the Sheet Metal Rule. In the Style and Standard Editor dialog box, options for the Corner Relief shape at both the 2 Bend and 3 Bend intersections are provided, as shown in Figure 4–26. This section only discusses the *2 Bend Intersection* Corner Reliefs as they apply to Flanges.

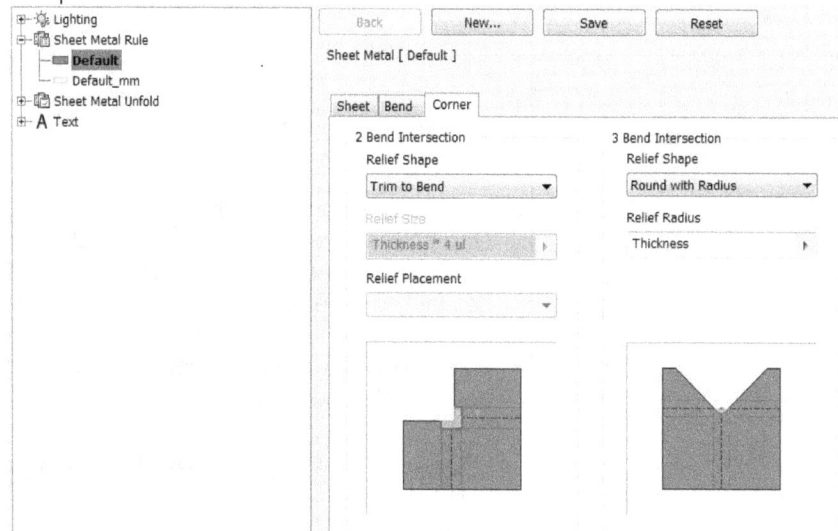

Figure 4–26

Corner Relief Shapes for 2 Bend Intersections

When an intersection occurs between 2 Bends, you can apply one of six Corner Relief shapes. Each option defines the shape of the material that needs to be removed, while the sheet metal part is still flat. The six shapes are **Trim to Bend**, **Round**, **Square**, **Tear**, **Linear Weld**, and **Arc Weld**. You can override the default Corner Relief that was assigned in the Rule (**Trim to Bend**) using the *Corner* tab in the Flange dialog box, as shown in Figure 4–27.

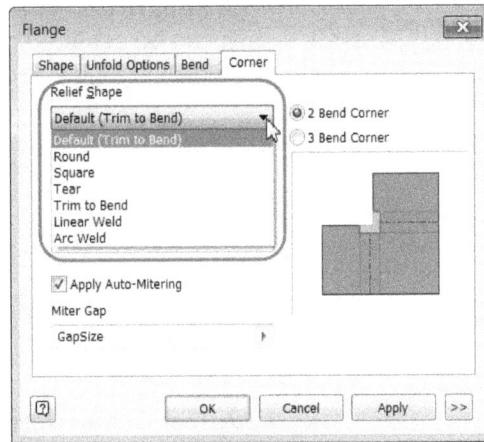

Figure 4–27

- **Trim to Bend** is the default Corner Relief shape for 2 Bend Intersections (based on whether the default Rule is assigned). In the flat layout, this option is a polygonal cut out that is bounded by the bending zone lines, as shown in Figure 4–28.

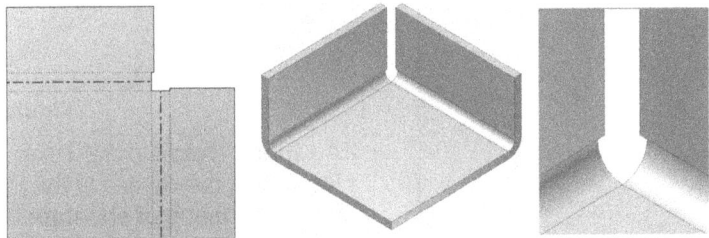

Figure 4–28

Enhanced in 2017

- A **Round** Corner Relief is a circular cut out in the flat pattern It can be centered at the intersection of the bend lines (as shown in Figure 4–29), tangent to the adjacent flange edges, or positioned with its circumferences on the vertex.

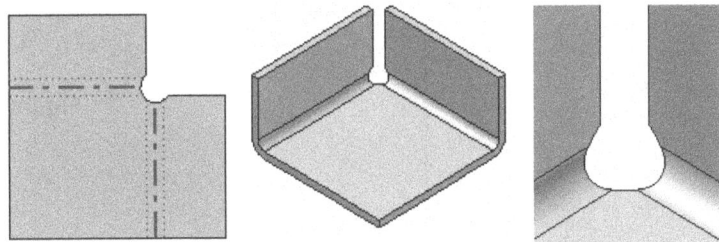

Figure 4–29

Enhanced
in 2017

- A **Square** Corner Relief is a square cut out in the flat pattern. It can be centered of the intersection of the bend lines (as shown in Figure 4–30), or positioned on the vertex.

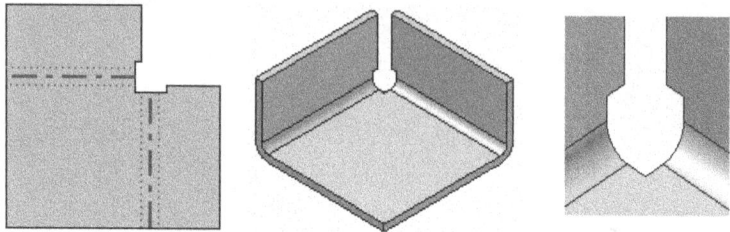

Figure 4–30

- A **Tear** Corner Relief is actually not a relief cut at all. It is simply that the material is torn at the intersection of the two bend lines, as shown in Figure 4–31.

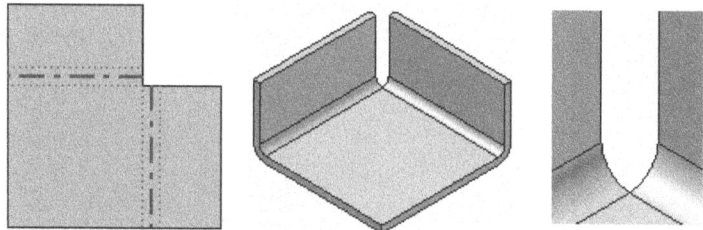

Figure 4–31

- A **Linear Weld** Corner Relief is a V-shaped cut out. It is located at the center of the intersection of the two bend lines when the piece of sheet metal is flat before bending, as shown in Figure 4–32.

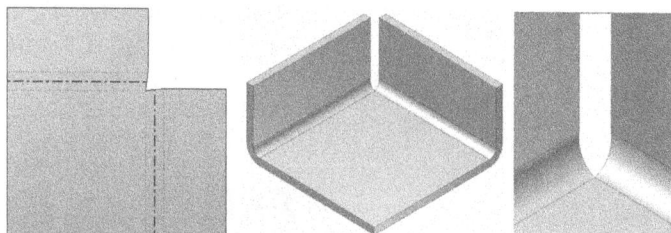

Figure 4–32

- An **Arc Weld** Corner Relief is an arc-shaped cutout. It is defined by curves tangent to the flange edges on the outer edge. The curves continue to a depth where the distance between the curves on each side is equal to the Miter Gap value when the piece of sheet metal is flat before bending, as shown in Figure 4–33. This corner relief facilitates large radius bends.

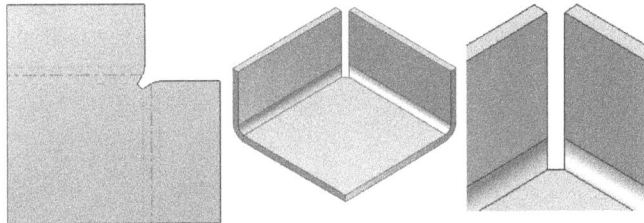

Figure 4–33

Corner Relief Size

When any two Flanges or Contour Flanges meet at a 2 Bend corner, a parameter called **CornerReliefSize** is applied. This parameter sets the space between the Flanges and is defined by the Sheet Metal Rule. The default setting is four times the **Thickness** parameter, as shown in Figure 4–34.

Parameter Name	Unit	Equation
— Model Parameters		
Thickness	mm	0.500 mm
BendRadius	mm	Thickness
BendReliefWidth	mm	Thickness
BendReliefDepth	mm	Thickness * 0.5 ul
CornerReliefSize	mm	Thickness * 4 ul
MinimumRemnant	mm	Thickness * 2.0 ul

Figure 4–34

In Figure 4–35 a part is shown with the default **CornerReliefSize** on the left, and a value on the right that is two times the default.

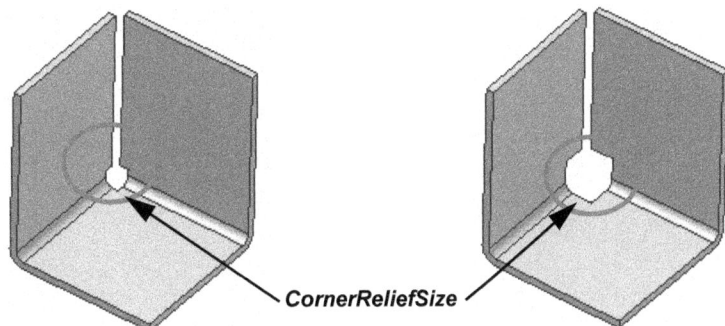

CornerReliefSize

Figure 4–35

Corner Mitering

Auto-Mitering adds or removes material from adjacent Flanges or Contour Flanges that are created from multiple edges. This is done so that Flange edges at corners meet at a specified Miter Gap distance, as shown in Figure 4–36.

In parts with two adjacent Flanges, a gap is normally created between the Flanges when they are formed at a 90 degree angle. This is due to the bend radius at the fold. Turning on Auto-Mitering extends each Flange slightly so that the space between them is adjusted to the value set for the **MiterGap** parameter. In 90 degree Flanges, the difference between toggling Auto-Mitering on and off can be very slight, as shown in Figure 4–36.

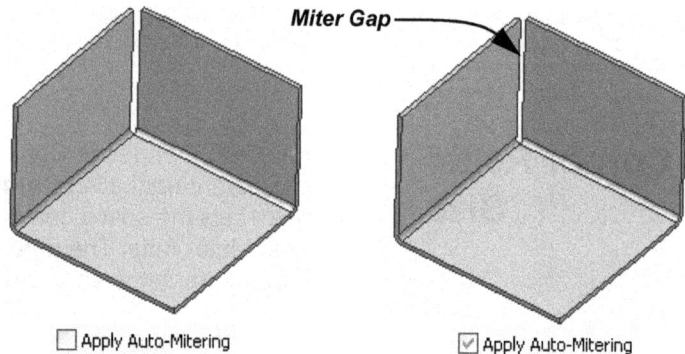

Figure 4–36

For adjacent Flanges that have an angle of less than 90 degrees, the **Apply Auto-Mitering** option adds material so that the Flanges meet with the **MiterGap** distance applied between them, as shown in Figure 4–37.

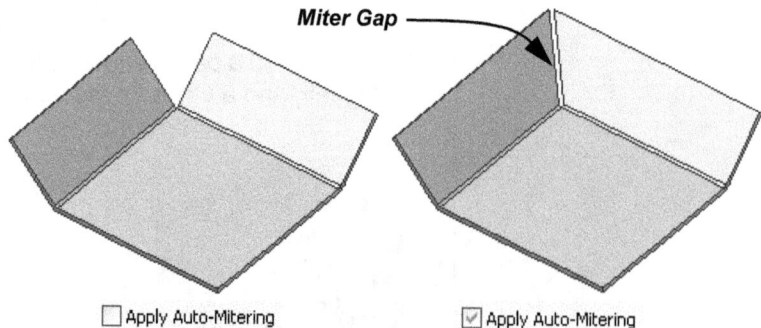

Figure 4–37

For adjacent Flanges that have an angle greater than 90 degrees, the **Apply Auto-Mitering** option removes material so that the faces meet with the **MiterGap** distance applied between them. If Auto-Mitering is not applied, the Flange edges intersect. For angles of more than 90 degrees, the change between toggling Auto-Mitering on and off might influence whether or not the part can be fabricated, as shown in Figure 4–38.

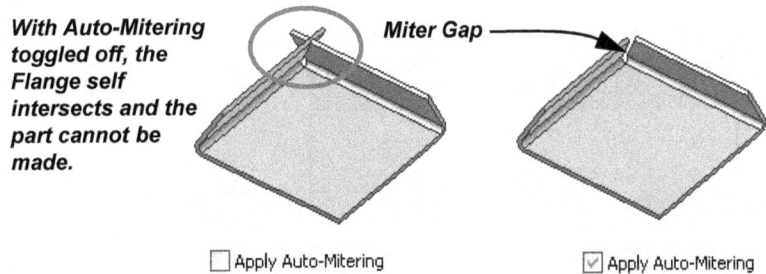

With Auto-Mitering toggled off, the Flange self intersects and the part cannot be made.

Miter Gap

☐ Apply Auto-Mitering   ☑ Apply Auto-Mitering

Figure 4–38

Corner Editing

At any time during or after the creation you can edit how corners are created. This can be done in one of two ways:

*   Edit the corner options for all corners in the feature using the *Corner* tab in the Flange dialog box.

*   Edit the corner options for individual corners using the button associated with the corner the requires editing, as shown in Figure 4–39.

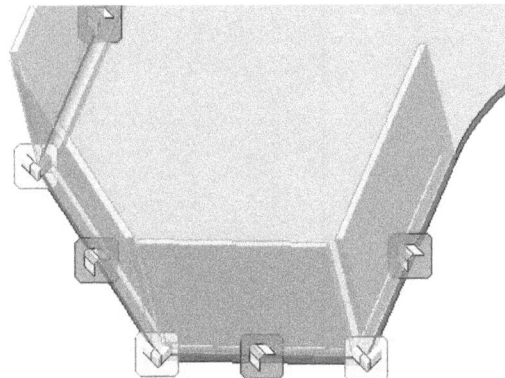

Figure 4–39

Once a button has been selected to edit the corner, the Corner Edit dialog box opens. To enable any of the editing options in the Corner Edit dialog box, select the appropriate check box, as shown in Figure 4–40. Once enabled you can edit the corner relief options as required independent of the other corners, as shown in Figure 4–41.

To enable the options in the Corner Edit dialog box, select the appropriate check boxes.

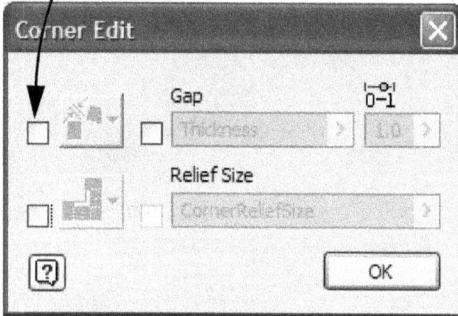

Figure 4–40

Gap Type *Gap Size*

Relief Shape

Relief Size

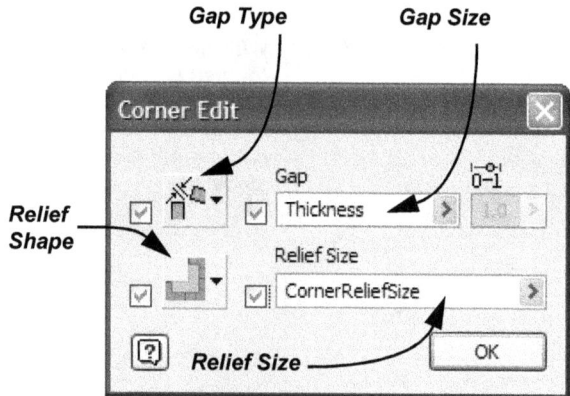

Figure 4–41

Practice 4a

Creating Flanges

Practice Objectives

- Use the various selection type options to locate a Flange feature on single edges, multiple edges, or a loop of edges in a model.
- Set the height and angle options to vary the resulting flange geometry in a model.
- Use the Width Extent options to vary width of a flange feature along an edge.
- Control corner relief settings independent of the model's overall corner settings.

In this practice, you will practice creating Flanges on individual edges and loops. You will also create a Flange offset from points on a Cut feature, as shown in Figure 4–42.

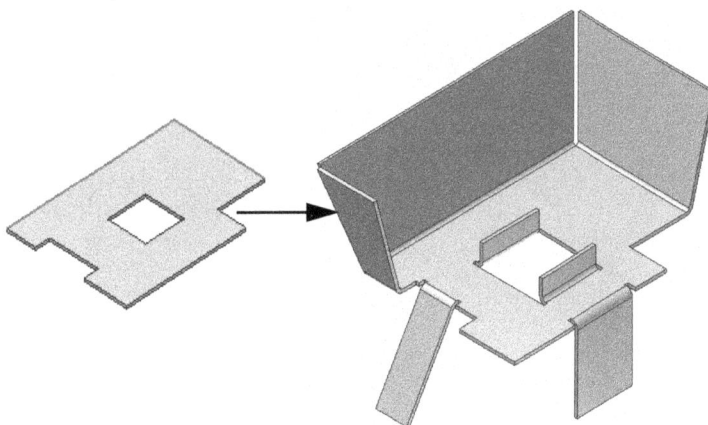

Figure 4–42

Task 1 - Create an Edge Flange.

1. Open **Flange_m.ipt**.

2. In the *Sheet Metal* tab>Create panel, click (Flange).

3. Verify that (Edge Select Mode) is active and select the two edges of the face, as shown in Figure 4–43.

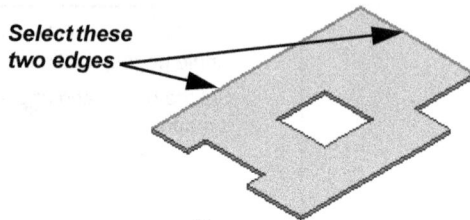

Select these two edges

Figure 4–43

4. Set the *Height Extents* to **Distance** and enter **10mm** in the field below.

5. If required, toggle (Flip Direction) to create the Flanges directing upward, as shown in Figure 4–44.

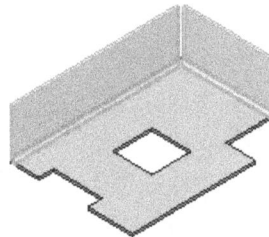

Figure 4–44

6. In the *Flange Angle* field, enter **45.0** for the number of degrees.

7. Accept the defaults in the *Bend Radius*, *Height Datum*, and *Bend Position* areas.

8. Click **OK** to create the Flange feature, as shown in Figure 4–45.

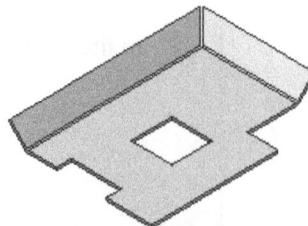

When the feature is previewed an icon is displayed in the Corner where the two edges meet. This enables you to edit the corner's gap and relief size for each individual corner.

Figure 4–45

9. Expand **Flange1** in the Model Browser and note that a Bend and a Corner have been created as children of the **Flange1** feature, as shown in Figure 4–46.

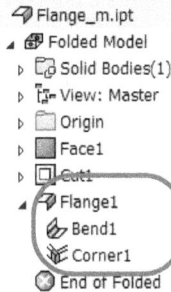

Figure 4–46

Task 2 - Create and edit a Width Extents Flange.

1. Restart the **Flange** command and select the edge shown in Figure 4–47.

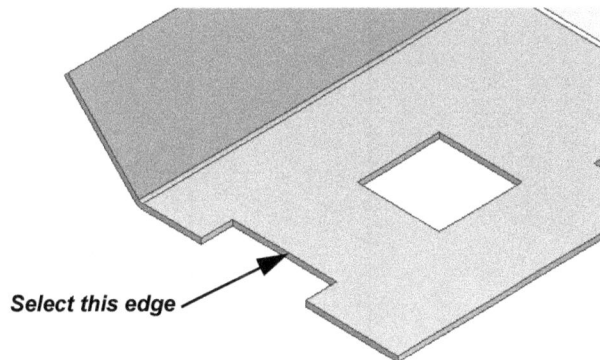

Select this edge

Figure 4–47

2. Enter **20** in the *Flange Angle* field.

3. Enter **10 mm** for the distance in the *Height Extents* area.

4. Click so that the flange is created downwards.

5. Click to expand the dialog box.

6. In the *Width Extents* area, select **Width** in the Type drop-down list.

7. Select **Offset** and select the end point of the edge, as shown in Figure 4–48.

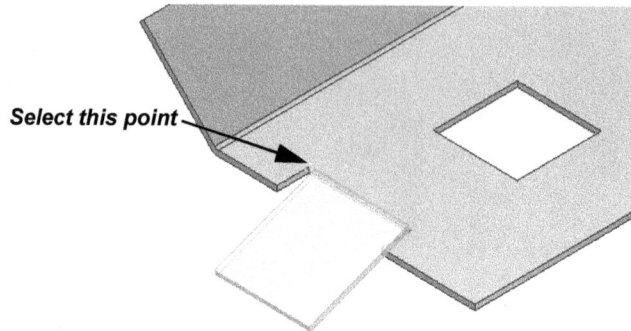

Figure 4–48

8. Enter **5 mm** in the *Width* field and **1 mm** in the *Offset* field, as shown in Figure 4–49.

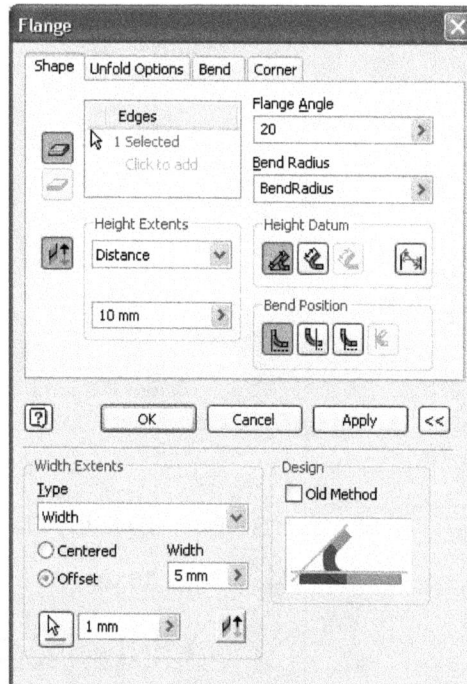

Figure 4–49

9. Click **OK** to create the new Flange, as shown in Figure 4–50.

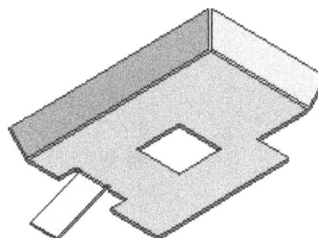

Figure 4–50

Task 3 - Add a Loop Flange.

1. Start the **Flange** command.

2. Activate ▨ (Loop Select Mode) and select the loop on the top surface of the square cut out, as shown in Figure 4–51. The dialog box displays **4 Selected** in the *Edges* field.

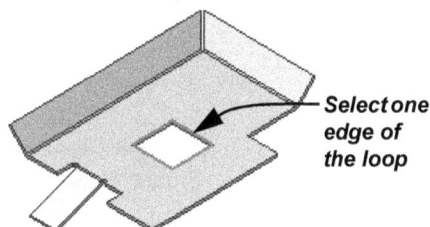

Select one edge of the loop

Figure 4–51

3. Set the *Height Extents* to **Distance** and enter **3mm**. Enter **90 deg** for the *Flange Angle*.

In this practice, the Width Extent for the four flanges is maintained. To modify each width extent separately, you can select the ▨ glyph that is associated with each bend to open its own Bend Edit dialog box.

4. Accept the defaults for the other options and click **OK** to create **Flange3** on the loop, as shown in Figure 4–52.

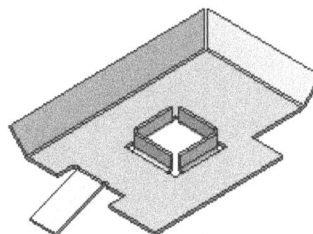

Figure 4–52

Task 4 - Add an Offset Flange.

1. Start the **Flange** command.

2. Select the longest edge that does not have a Flange, as shown in Figure 4–53. Set the *Height Extents* to **To** and select the point shown in Figure 4–53.

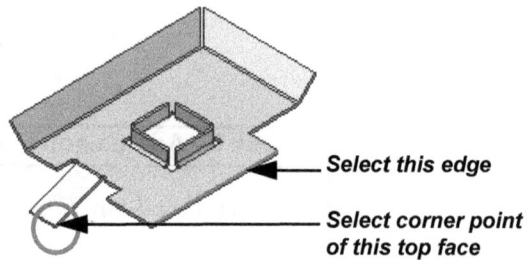

Select this edge

Select corner point of this top face

Figure 4–53

3. Verify that the *Offset* distance is **0** and the *Flange Angle* is **90**.

4. If it is not already expanded, click [>>] to display the expanded options area in the Flange dialog box.

5. Set the *Width Extents Type* to **From To**. Select the two end points shown in Figure 4–54 as the From and To points for the new Flange. The preview should display as shown in Figure 4–54.

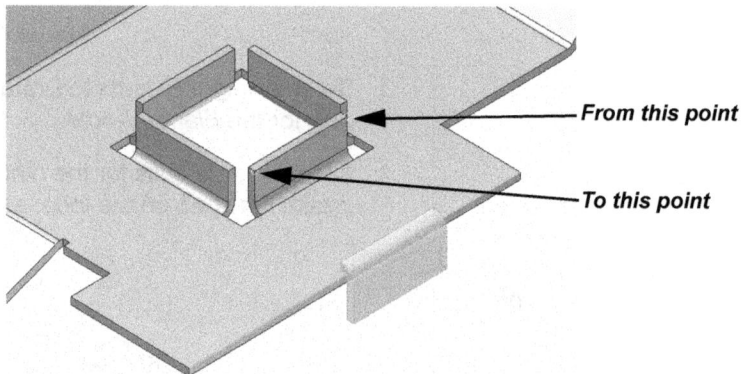

From this point

To this point

Figure 4–54

6. Click **OK** to create **Flange4**, as shown in Figure 4–55.

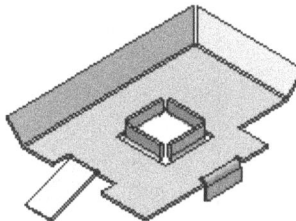

Figure 4–55

Task 5 - Edit the Cut feature and its dependent Flange.

1. Right-click on **Cut1** in the Model Browser and select **Edit Sketch**.

2. Change both 8 mm dimensions to **10 mm**. Finish the sketch. The length of the flanged edges increases to match the new size of the Cut feature.

Task 6 - Edit Flanges.

1. Right-click on **Flange1** in the Model Browser and select **Edit Feature**. Select the edge shown in Figure 4–56 to add another Flange.

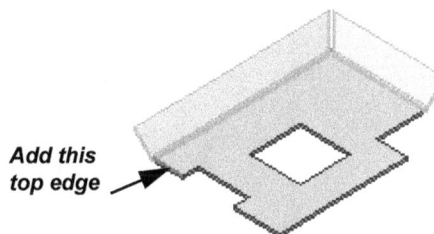

Add this
top edge

Figure 4–56

2. Change the *Height Extents* to **15 mm**, and the *Flange Angle* to **75 deg**. Click **OK**. The model displays as shown in Figure 4–57.

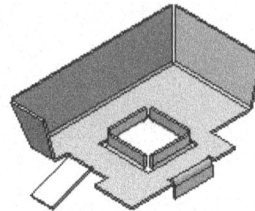

Figure 4–57

3. Right-click on **Flange2** in the browser and select **Edit Feature**. Change the *Height Extents* to **15 mm** and its *Flange Angle* to **60 deg**. Click **OK**. **Flange4** also updates because it has a parent-child relationship with **Flange2**, as shown in Figure 4–58.

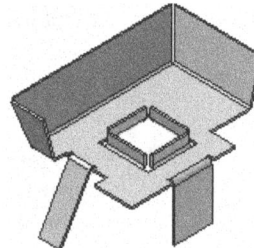

Figure 4–58

4. Edit **Flange3**. Press <Shift> and select the two edges shown in Figure 4–59 to remove the two Flanges.

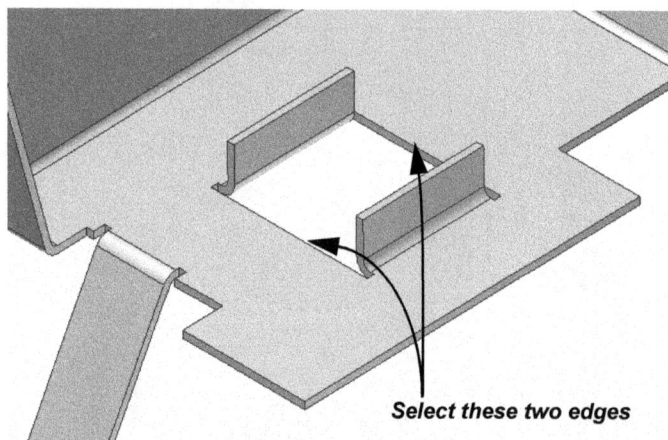

Select these two edges

Figure 4–59

5. In the *Height Datum* area, click ⬚ (Bend from the intersection of the two inner faces).

6. In the *Bend Position* area, click ⬚ (Outside of base face extents).

7. Click **OK** to complete the changes. Click **Accept** in the message box. You will resolve the error in Step 8.

8. Right-click on **Flange4** and select **Edit Feature**. Because of the change to **Flange3**, the references for the *Width Extents* in **Flange4** must be redefined.

9. Click ⬚ to expand the dialog box. Reselect both offset points in the *Width Extents* area and ensure that the Offset value is set to **0 mm** in the *Height Extents* area. Click **OK**. The model displays as shown in Figure 4–60.

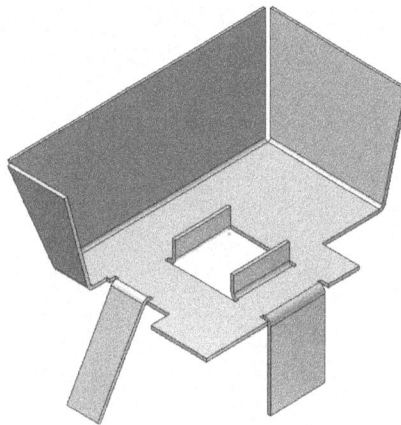

Figure 4–60

10. Save and close the file.

Practice 4b | Loop Flange

Practice Objectives

- Use the Loop Select mode to locate a Flange feature on a series of adjacent edges.
- Edit the edges that were selected for inclusion in a Flange feature.
- Set the height and angle options to vary the resulting flange geometry in a model.
- Control whether automatic mitering is incorporated for the corners of Flange geometry.
- Control corner relief settings independent of the model's overall corner settings.
- Control width extent settings for edges independent of the model's overall width extent settings.

In this practice, you will create a Loop Flange. You will also edit the Corner Relief, Auto-Mitering, and Width Extent settings. The initial and final model geometry are shown in Figure 4–61.

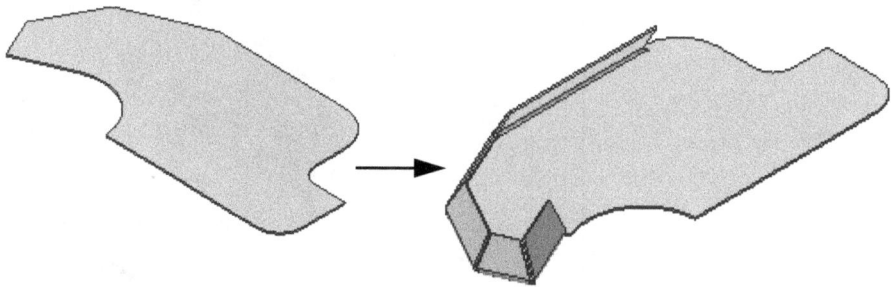

Figure 4–61

Task 1 - Create a Loop Flange.

1. Open **Flange_loop_m.ipt**.

2. In the *Sheet Metal* tab>Create panel, click ⬦ (Flange).

3. Click ⬠ (Loop Select Mode) and select the edge of the Face, as shown in Figure 4–62. Only the straight edges highlight.

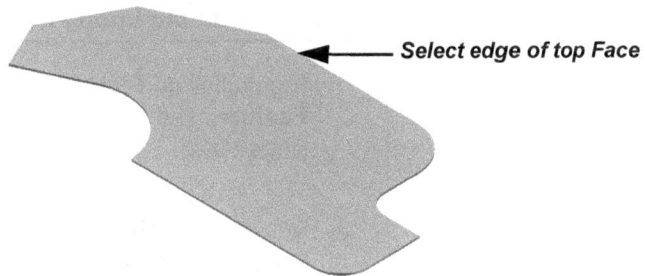

Figure 4–62

4. Enter **9 mm** in the *Distance* field and accept the defaults for all other options and complete the feature. The model displays as shown in Figure 4–63.

When the feature is previewed, icons are displayed in the Corner where the two edges meet and along each edge. These enable you to edit the corner's gap and relief size (for each corner) and the width extent for each edge, respectively.

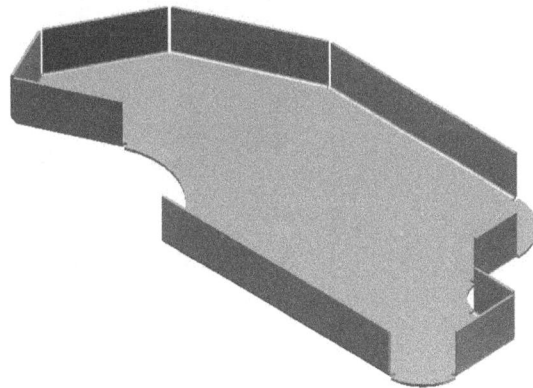

Figure 4–63

5. Zoom and rotate to see that there are gaps in the model. They are in the corners between the five adjacent faces of the Flange feature.

6. Rotate the model to the position shown in Figure 4–64.

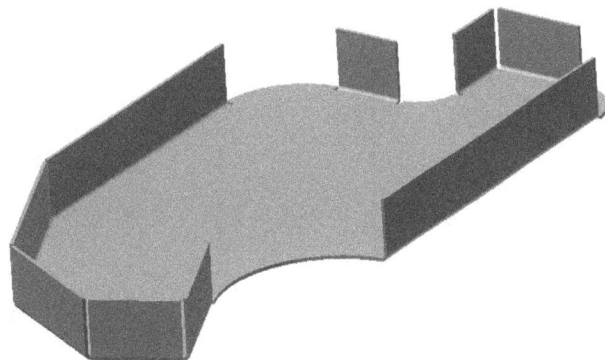

Figure 4–64

Task 2 - Edit the Loop Flange edges.

1. Right-click on **Flange1** in the Model Browser and select **Edit Feature**. The Flange dialog box displays **9 Selected** in the *Edges* field.

2. Activate ⬛(Edge Select) and press <Ctrl> + the left mouse button to clear the four edges shown in Figure 4–65.

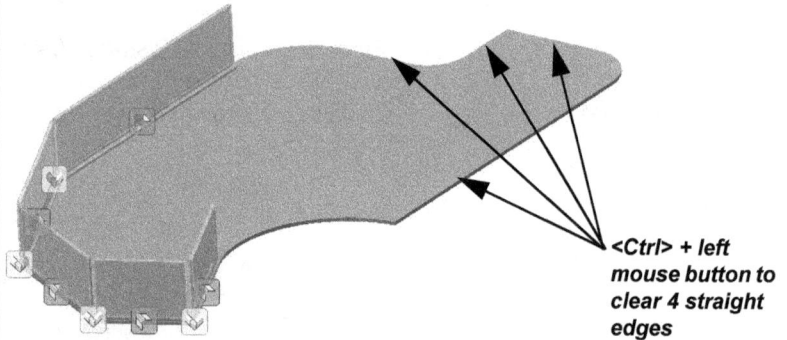

<Ctrl> + left mouse button to clear 4 straight edges

Figure 4–65

3. Click **OK** to complete the editing.

Task 3 - Edit Height and Angle settings for a Loop Flange.

1. Right-click on **Flange1** in the Model Browser and select **Edit Feature**.

2. Toggle ⬛ (Flip Direction) to change the Flange direction.

3. Change the *Flange Angle* to **50**.

4. Click **OK**. The model displays as shown in Figure 4–66.

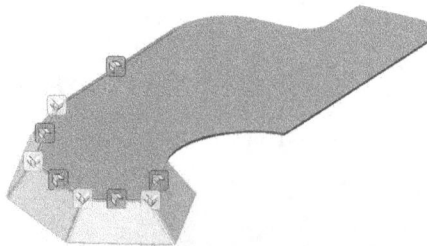

Figure 4–66

Task 4 - Edit Auto-Mitering option.

1. Right-click on **Flange1** in the Model Browser and select **Edit Feature**.

2. Select the *Corner* tab.

3. Clear the **Apply Auto-Mitering** option. (Do not click **OK** yet.) The preview displays as shown in Figure 4–67.

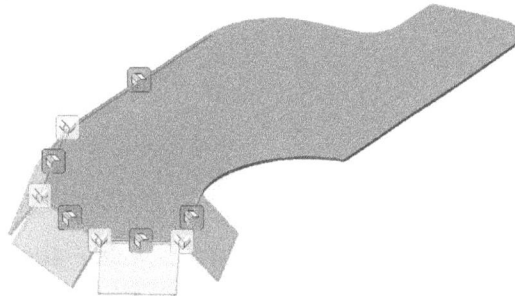

Figure 4–67

4. Switch back to the *Shape* tab. Flip the Flange again so it is directed upwards. Change the **Flange Angle** to **120 deg**. Note that in the preview the adjacent Flange faces overlap, as shown in Figure 4–68.

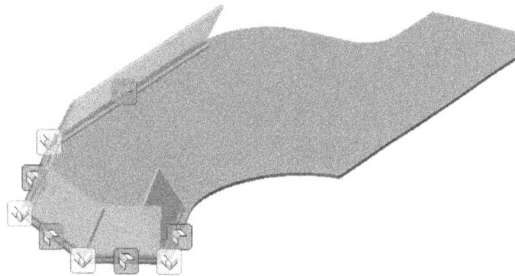

Figure 4–68

5. Click **OK**. A Warning dialog box opens as shown in Figure 4–69.

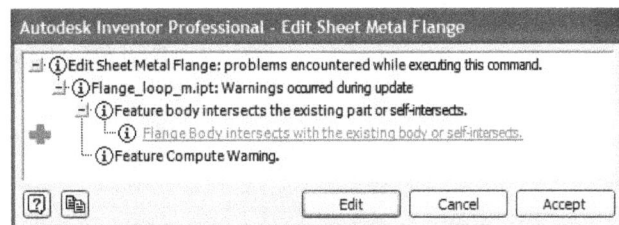

Figure 4–69

6. Click **Edit**. The Flange Edit dialog box opens.

7. In the *Corner* tab, toggle on **Apply Auto-Mitering**.

8. Click **OK**. The model displays as shown in Figure 4–70.

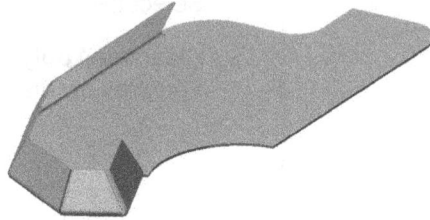

Figure 4–70

Task 5 - Edit individual corner settings.

1. Right-click on **Flange1** in the Model Browser and select **Edit Feature**.

2. In the preview display of the model, click 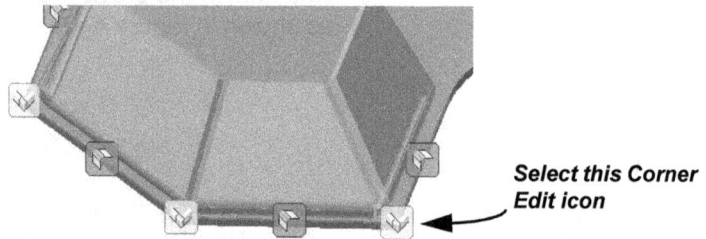 for the corner shown in Figure 4–71. The Corner Edit dialog box opens.

Select this Corner Edit icon

Figure 4–71

3. Enable the Relief Type check box and click ⬛ (Square (Intersection)) relief in the drop-down list, as shown in Figure 4–72.

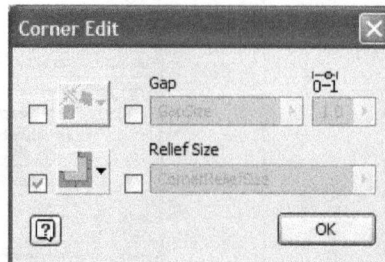

Figure 4–72

4. Click **OK**. Note that the corner editing icon has changed to
   ![icon] instead of ![icon], indicating that this corner relief is
   independent of the relief set for the entire feature.

5. (Optional) Return to the Corner Edit dialog box and make
   additional changes to other corners in the model.

Task 6 - Edit individual width extent settings.

1. In the preview display of the model, click ![icon] for the edge
   shown in Figure 4–73. The Bend Edit dialog box opens.

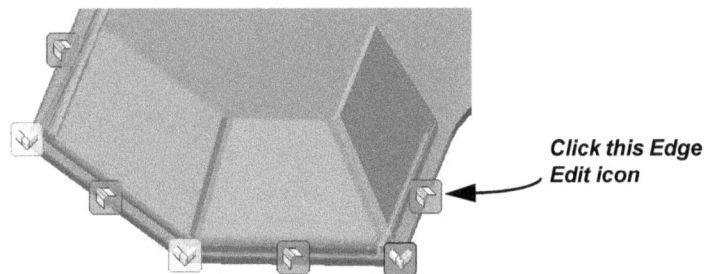

Click this Edge
Edit icon

Figure 4–73

2. Select the Width Extents check box to display the Type
   drop-down list options.

3. Select **Width** in the Type drop-down list.

4. By default, the **Centered** option is enabled and centers the
   flange on the wall. Enter **15mm** for the value.

5. Click **OK**. Note that the corner editing icon has changed to
   ![icon] instead of ![icon], indicating that this width extent is
   independent from the other flanges.

6. (Optional) Click ![icon] for any of the other edges and modify
   their widths.

7. Click **OK** to complete the feature.

8. Save and close the file.

Practice 4c | Flanges

Practice Objective

- Add Flange features to an existing model to create the required geometry.

In this practice, you will create Flange features on the edges of a model. The initial and final model geometry are shown in Figure 4–74.

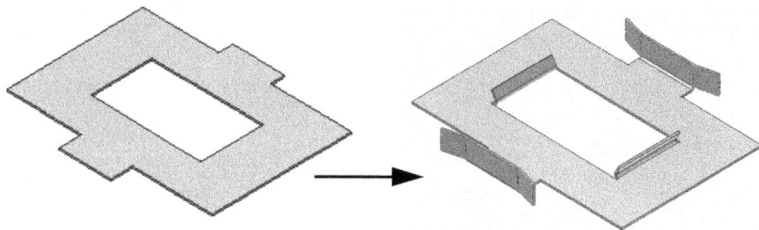

Figure 4–74

Task 1 - Create a Flange to an enclosed area.

1. Open **Flange_practice.ipt**.

2. Create a Flange on the open space in the part. You can select individual edges or use loop selection and clear edges. Use a *Height Extent* of **4 mm** and a *Flange Angle* of **120 deg**, as shown in Figure 4–75.

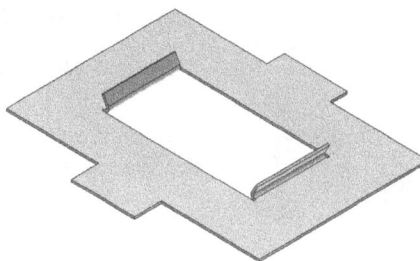

Figure 4–75

Task 2 - Add Flanges to the edges of other Flanges.

1. Add Flanges to the two short edges shown in Figure 4–76. Use a *Height Extent* of **6 mm** and a *Flange Angle* of **90 deg**.

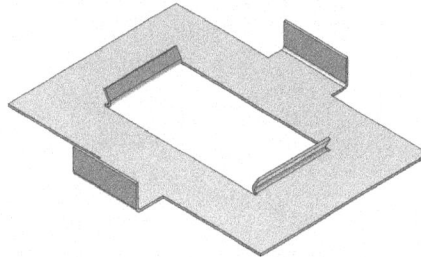

Figure 4–76

Task 3 - Add a Flange to Existing Flange Edges.

1. Add another Flange feature to the edges of **Flange2** that you just created. Select the outside edges of the existing **Flange2**.

2. Use a *Height Extent* of **6 mm** and a *Flange Angle* of **15 deg**. The model displays as shown in Figure 4–77.

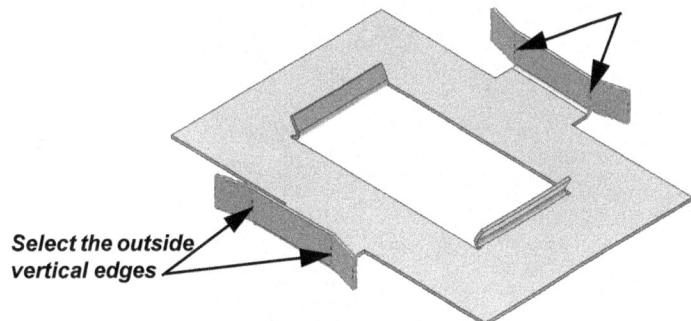

Select the outside vertical edges

Figure 4–77

3. Save and close the file.

Chapter Review Questions

1. Which of the following best describes a Flange sheet metal feature?

   a. A Flange is a flat area of geometry created from a closed loop sketch profile.

   b. A Flange is a projecting rim attached at the edge of a Face.

   c. A Flange is transitional sheet metal geometry that is blended between two profile sketches.

   d. A Flange is the geometry between two sheet metal faces that are at an angle to each other.

2. How many edges are going to be affected when a flange is added to the Face feature shown in Figure 4–78 using the **Loop Select mode selection** option?

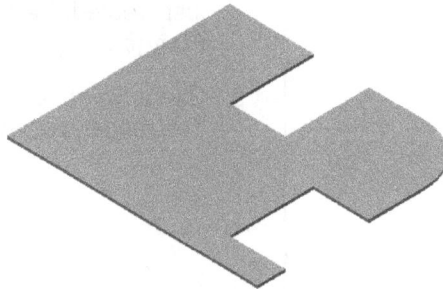

Figure 4–78

   a. 2

   b. 6

   c. 8

   d. 12

3. Why might the *Width Extents* options be grayed out in the expanded Flange dialog box?

   a. The *Width Extents* options are grayed out if a single edge is selected to place a Flange feature.

   b. The *Width Extents* options are grayed out if the Height Extents option is set as To.

   c. The *Width Extents* options are grayed out if you select more than one edge to place a Flange feature.

   d. All of the above.

4. Which of the following **Width Extents** options would best be used to create the Flange shown in Figure 4–79 ? The width references geometry in the Face feature.

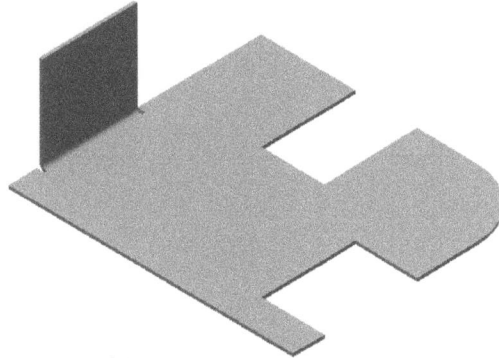

Figure 4–79

  a. Edge

  b. Width - Offset

  c. Offset

  d. From To

5. Which of the following are true statements regarding adding corner relief between adjacent flanges?

  a. The default Corner Relief setting is set in the Sheet Metal rule.

  b. Corner Relief for all corners in a Flange feature can be controlled independently of the Sheet Metal rule.

  c. Corner Relief for individual corners can be controlled independently of the feature and Sheet Metal rule settings.

  d. All of the above.

6. Which of the following types of Corner Relief was used to create the corner relief geometry shown in Figure 4–80 ?

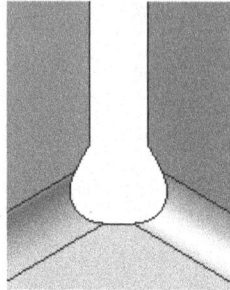

Figure 4–80

a. Trim to Bend

b. Round (Intersection)

c. Square (Intersection)

d. Tear

e. Linear Weld

f. Arc Weld

Command Summary

Button	Command	Location
	Flange	• **Ribbon:** *Sheet Metal* tab>Create panel
	Styles and Standards	• **Ribbon:** *Manage* tab>Styles and Standards panel • (*Click* ▱ *next to the Sheet Metal Rule in the Sheet Metal Defaults dialog box.*)

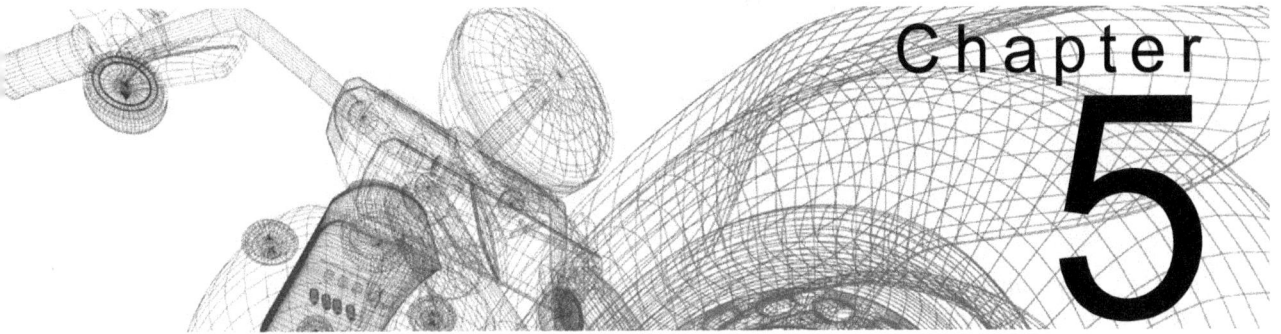

Bending Sheet Metal

Bending sheet metal parts can be accomplished using many different processes. Among these are hemming, folding, and bending. In the Autodesk® Inventor® software, Hems and Bends are placed features, while Folds are sketched features.

Learning Objectives in this Chapter

- Create Hem geometry in a model that is folded or rolled back on itself to strengthen it or cover sharp edges.
- Create geometry that folds existing sheet metal geometry along a sketched line.
- Create geometry that joins two disconnected non-planar faces to one another using the Bend feature.

5.1 Hems

A Hem is sheet metal geometry that is folded back on itself or rolled around a radius. Hems are added to strengthen a part and to cover rough or sharp edges. Each Hem is a placed feature that can only be applied to one edge per instance of the feature. To add Hems to multiple edges you must apply one Hem to each edge.

For a real sheet metal part, folding the edge of a part to create a Hem shortens the part's overall size. But in the Autodesk Inventor software, Hem features add material to an existing edge.

Figure 5–1 shows four separate Hem features. Each one is applied to a different edge of the sheet metal part. **Hem1** and **Hem4** are added to the outside edge of a Face. **Hem2** and are added to the edges of a Cut feature. If the Cut is later suppressed, the Hems that are dependent on it are suppressed as well. Hems cannot be applied to a loop in the way Flanges and Contour Flanges are applied.

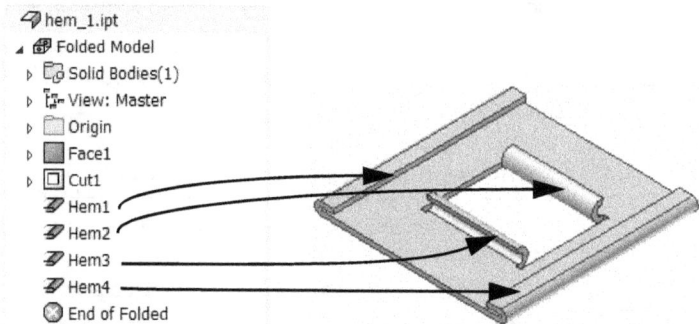

Figure 5–1

General Steps

Use the following general steps to create a Hem feature:

1. Start the creation of the Hem feature.
2. Select the Hem shape.
3. Define the Shape options.
4. Define the Width Extents.
5. (Optional) Edit the Unfold and Bend options.
6. Complete the feature.

Step 1 - Start the creation of the Hem feature.

In the *Sheet Metal* tab>Create panel, click (Hem). The Hem dialog box opens as shown in Figure 5–2.

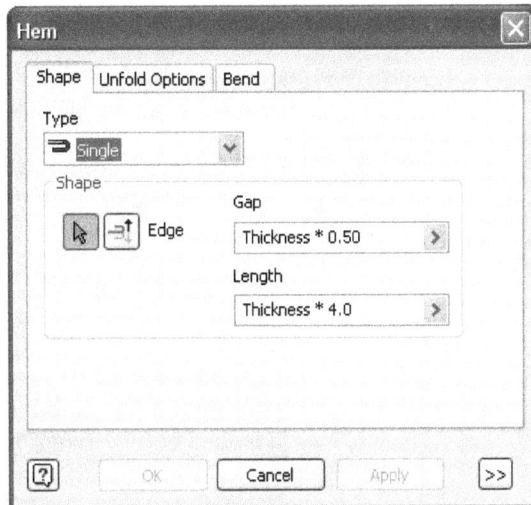

Figure 5–2

Step 2 - Select the Hem shape.

Four Hem shapes are available in the Type drop-down list ( ), as shown in Figure 5–3.

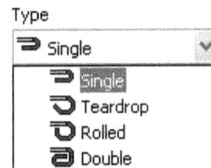

Figure 5–3

For each Hem shape, the overall height of the original face does not change. The Bend is added tangent to the selected edge. Examples of the four Hem shapes are shown in Figure 5–4.

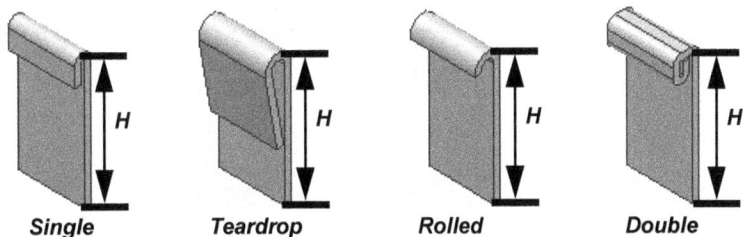

Single   *Teardrop*   *Rolled*   *Double*

Figure 5–4

Single Hem

A Single Hem is created by adding a face parallel to the existing face with a bend between them. The **Thickness** parameter defined in the Sheet Metal Rule is used to define the *Gap* and *Length* values of a Single Hem.

- The *Gap* defines the distance between the two inner faces of the completed single Hem, as shown in Figure 5–5.

- The *Length* specifies the distance from the end of the sheet metal material to the outside tangency on the folded over Hem, as shown in Figure 5–5.

By default, the *Gap* is set to half the **Thickness** parameter and the *Length* is set to four times the **Thickness** parameter. These distances can be overridden, if required.

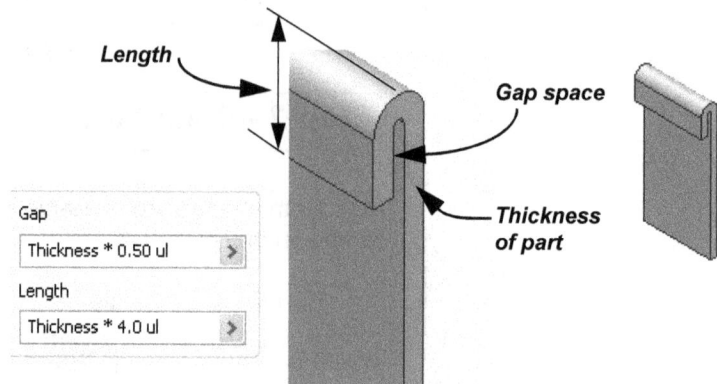

Length

Gap space

Gap

Thickness * 0.50 ul

Length

Thickness * 4.0 ul

Thickness of part

Figure 5–5

Teardrop Hem

A Teardrop Hem is created by rolling the edge of a sheet metal face around a specified radius, until the outer face of the new Hem reaches a specified angle from its original position. The **BendRadius** parameter defined in the Sheet Metal Rule is used to define the inside *Radius* of the curved section. An *Angle* for the finished position of the Teardrop's flat plane is specified in the Hem dialog box, as shown in Figure 5–6.

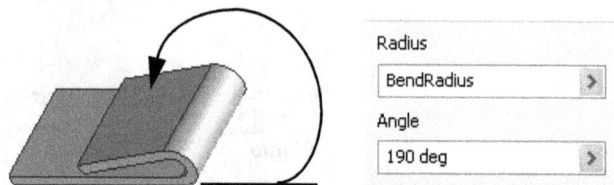

Radius

BendRadius

Angle

190 deg

Face of Hem is 190 degrees from original position

Figure 5–6

The minimum angle for the Teardrop Hem needs to be greater than 180°. The maximum angle depends on the part's Thickness and the Radius of the Hem. Generally, this requires an angle of less than 300° to avoid a self-intersecting feature.

The flat portion of the Teardrop Hem is lengthened or shortened, depending on the angle of the bend, to obtain a distance that is 1/4 of the Thickness between the existing face and the flat portion of the hem. A small change in angle can significantly alter the length of the flat surface on the Teardrop, as shown in Figure 5–7. In this example, as the angle of the Teardrop Hem increases from 187° to 215°, the length of the flat portion decreases to avoid interference with the existing face that it is folded towards.

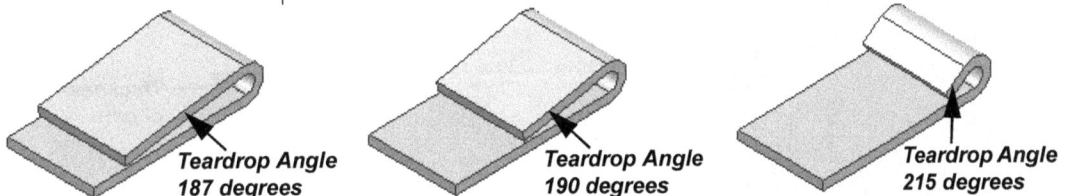

Teardrop Angle 187 degrees   *Teardrop Angle 190 degrees*   *Teardrop Angle 215 degrees*

Figure 5–7

Rolled Hem

A Rolled Hem is created by curling a sheet metal face around a radius and back towards itself. The *Radius* for the Rolled Hem is set by default to the **BendRadius** parameter defined in the Sheet Metal Rule. It can be overridden in the Hem dialog box.

The *Angle* of the Rolled Hem is defined in the Hem dialog box rather than by a parameter. To understand the *Angle* setting, imagine a vector tangent to the end point of the Rolled Hem. The Angle sets the number of degrees in the angle formed between this tangent vector and the original position of the face before bending, as shown in Figure 5–8.

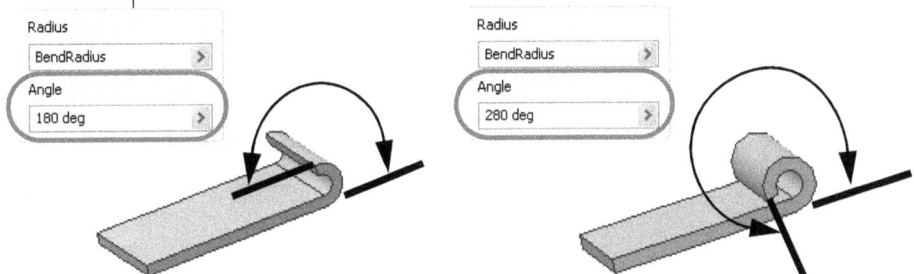

Figure 5–8

Double Hem

A Double Hem is created by adding two faces parallel to the existing face. Its settings are the same as those used for a Single Hem. The **Thickness** parameter defined in the Sheet Metal Rule is used to define the *Gap* and *Length* of a Double Hem as is done for a Single Hem. These distances can be overridden in the Hem dialog box if required.

Similar to the Single Hem, the *Length* of the Double Hem is measured between tangency at both ends of the folded over portions, as shown in Figure 5–9.

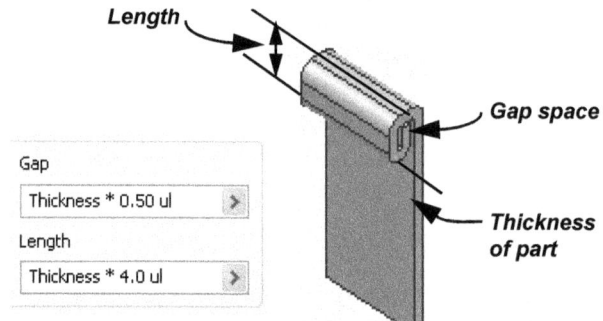

Figure 5–9

Step 3 - Define the Shape options.

If you have changed the Hem shape, verify that (Select Edge) is ready (red arrow) and select a single edge for the new Hem feature. You can only place a Hem on one edge at a time.

Toggle (Flip Direction) to set the direction of the Hem, as shown in Figure 5–10.

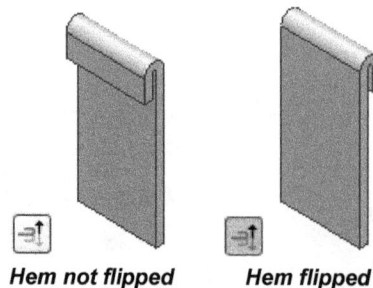

Hem not flipped   *Hem flipped*

Figure 5–10

Change the dimensional values associated with each Hem type, as required. The provided defaults are based on those assigned in the Sheet Metal Rule.

Step 4 - Define the Width Extents.

Click [>>] to display the *Width Extents* area in the Hem dialog box. Click [v] in the Type drop-down list to display the options shown in Figure 5–11.

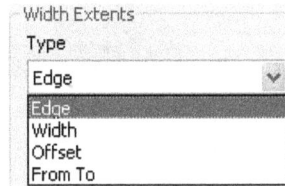

Figure 5–11

Edge

Edge creates a Hem along the full length of a selected edge, as shown in Figure 5–12.

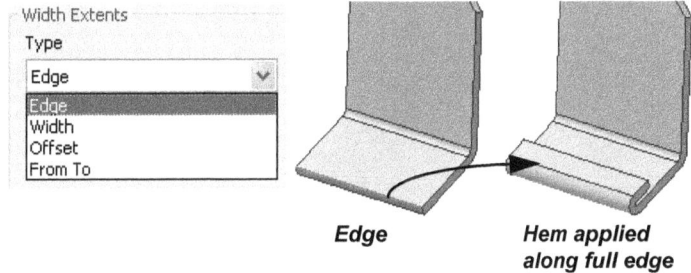

Edge   *Hem applied along full edge*

Figure 5–12

Width

Width can be used to make either a **Centered** Hem that has a specified width distance, or an **Offset** Hem that has a width and one point specified, from which it is offset. Examples of Width-Centered and Width-Offset Hems are shown in Figure 5–13.

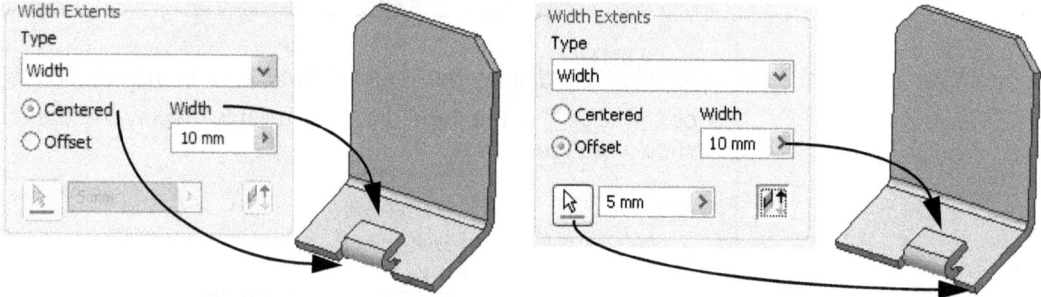

Figure 5–13

Offset

Offset creates a Hem with offset distances specified from two points that you select, as shown in Figure 5–14.

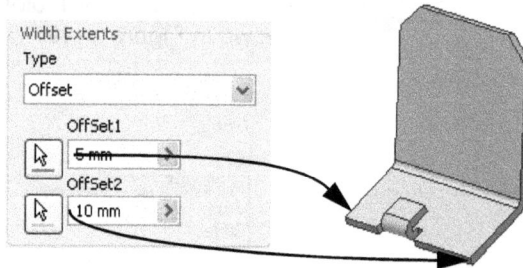

Figure 5–14

From To

From To creates a Hem that starts and ends at two points that you select on one or more features, as shown referencing a cut in Figure 5–15.

If the Cut changes size or position, the Hem updates as well.

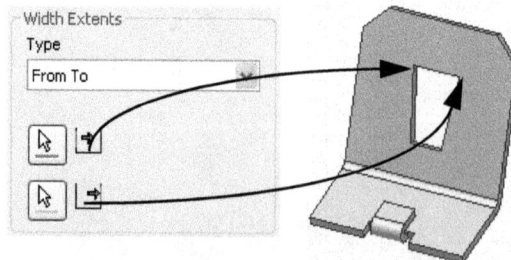

Figure 5–15

Step 5 - (Optional) Edit the Unfold and Bend options.

Accept the default values for the *Bend* and *Unfold* options in their associated tabs. The defaults are based on the settings in the Sheet Metal Rule. You can change these settings if required.

Step 6 - Complete the feature.

Once you have fully defined the Hem, click **OK** to complete the feature. Alternatively, you can right-click and select **OK (Enter)** to complete the feature.

If you want to continue to add Hem features on other edges using the same options, you can click **Apply** and select an alternate edge to create another feature.

5.2 Folds

Folds are sketched features in the Autodesk Inventor software. A single sketched line is required when creating each Fold feature. When you fold a face along the sketched line, the face displays as if it becomes two separate faces at an angle to each other and joined by a separate Bend feature. However, no new features are added as dependents of the fold, and no material is added in this process. Figure 5–16 shows a part to which three Fold features have been added. Each Fold has its own sketched line.

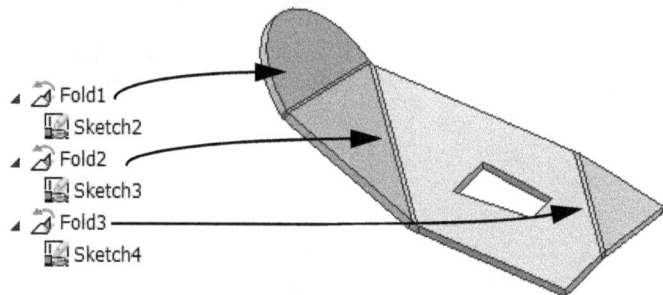

Figure 5–16

General Steps

Use the following general steps to create a Fold feature:

1. Create a sketch with a straight line.
2. Start the creation of the Fold feature.
3. Select the Bend Line.
4. Apply Flip Controls.
5. Set the Fold Location.
6. Enter a Fold Angle.
7. Set the Bend Radius (optional).
8. Edit the Unfold and Bend Relief options (optional).
9. Complete the feature.

Step 1 - Create a sketch with a straight line.

On an existing planar face, create a new sketch with a line. This line is used as the Bend Line. It must be a single straight segment and be coincident with the edges of the planar face that is being bent. Dimensions can be added if required. An example is shown in Figure 5–17.

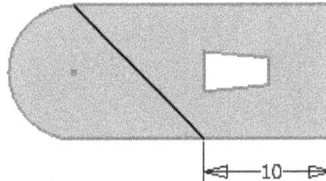

Figure 5–17

Step 2 - Start the creation of the Fold feature.

In the *Sheet Metal* tab>Create panel, click ⟋ (Fold). The Fold dialog box opens as shown in Figure 5–18.

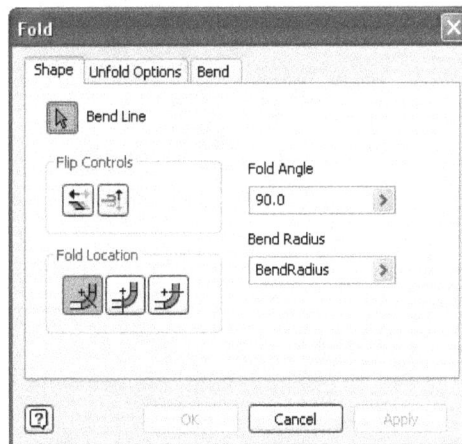

Figure 5–18

Step 3 - Select the Bend Line.

Select the sketched line as the *Bend Line* reference, as shown in Figure 5–19.

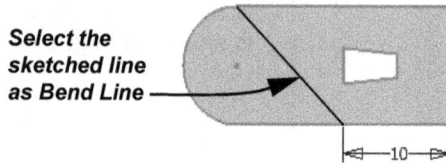

Select the sketched line as Bend Line ⟶

Figure 5–19

A preview with two green arrows displays on the planar face near the bend line, as shown in Figure 5–20. These arrows determine the side of the bend line that the Autodesk Inventor software selects to edit and the direction in which it is folded.

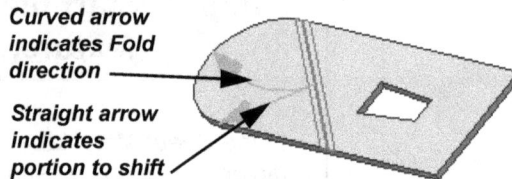

Curved arrow indicates Fold direction ⟶

Straight arrow indicates portion to shift ⟶

Figure 5–20

Step 4 - Apply Flip Controls.

Use (Flip Side) to determine which portion of the part the software repositions when folding, as shown in Figure 5–21.

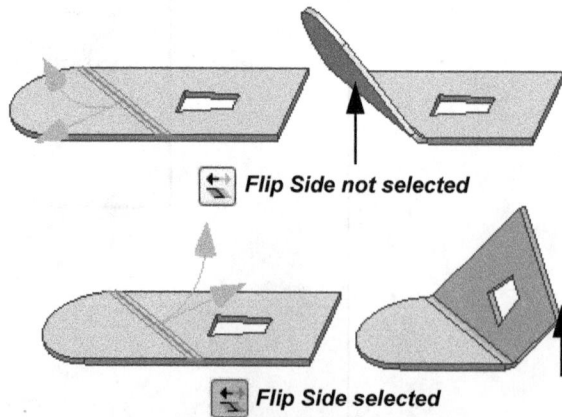

 Flip Side not selected

 Flip Side selected

Figure 5–21

Use ⊟↑ (Flip Direction) to determine the direction of the fold, as shown in Figure 5–22.

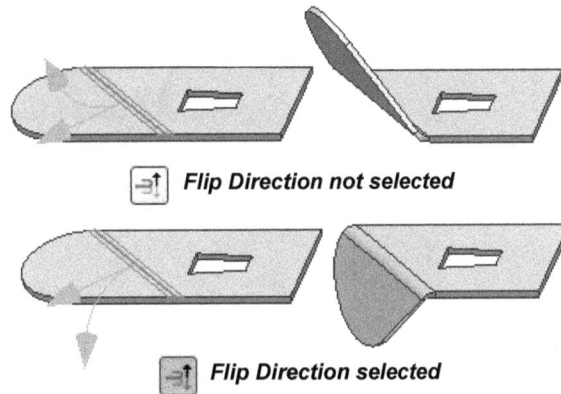

⊟↑ *Flip Direction not selected*

⊟↑ *Flip Direction selected*

Figure 5–22

Step 5 - Set the Fold Location.

The *Fold Location* (as shown in Figure 5–23) controls the position of the Fold's centerline, starting location, or ending location relative to the sketched bend line.

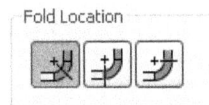

Fold Location

Figure 5–23

⊟↲ (Centerline of Bend) creates the Fold feature with the sketched bend line positioned at the centerline of the bend, as shown in Figure 5–24.

Sketched line is positioned at centerline of bend

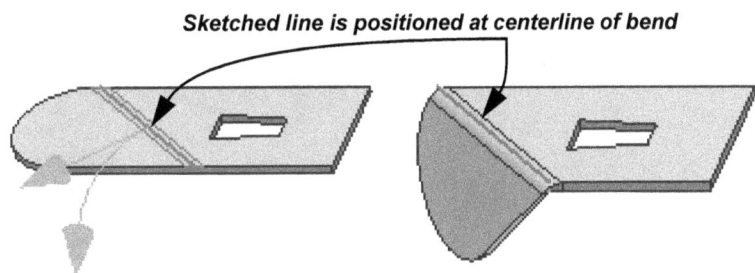

Figure 5–24

(Start of Bend) creates the Fold feature with the sketched bend line positioned at the start of the bend, as shown in Figure 5–25.

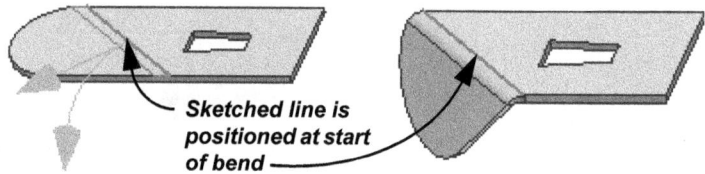

Figure 5–25

Sketched line is positioned at start of bend

(End of Bend) creates the Fold feature with the sketched bend line positioned at the end of the bend, as shown in Figure 5–26.

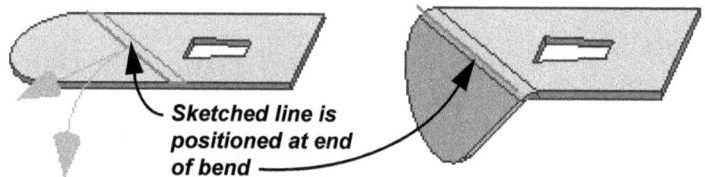

Figure 5–26

Sketched line is positioned at end of bend

Step 6 - Enter a Fold Angle.

Enter the degrees by which to fold the part in the *Fold Angle* field, as shown in Figure 5–27. This is the angle between the original planar face and the new angled surface created by the Fold feature.

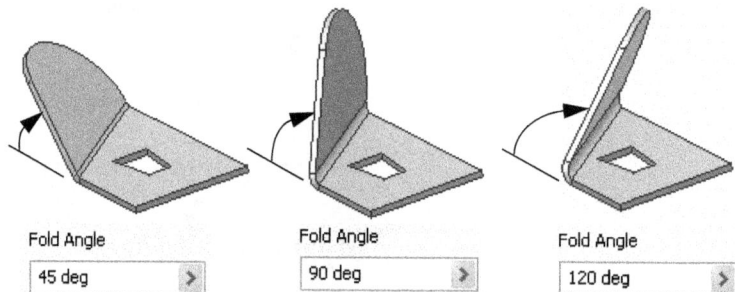

Fold Angle
45 deg

Fold Angle
90 deg

Fold Angle
120 deg

Figure 5–27

Step 7 - Set the Bend Radius (optional).

Accept the default values for the *Bend Radius*. The defaults are based on the settings in the Sheet Metal Rule. You can change these settings if required.

Step 8 - Edit the Unfold and Bend Relief options (optional).

Accept the default values for the *Bend* and *Unfold* options in their associated tabs. The defaults are based on the settings in the Sheet Metal Rule. You can change these settings if required.

Step 9 - Complete the feature.

Once you have fully defined the Fold, click **OK** to complete the feature. Alternatively, you can right-click and select **OK (Enter)** to complete the feature.

If you want to continue to add Fold features on other sketched lines using the same options, you can click **Apply** and select an alternate bend line to create another feature.

5.3 Bends

A Bend feature is a placed feature added between two existing faces. You do not have to set an angle as is done for a Fold feature because the angle already exists between the two faces. The faces can be either parallel or at an angle to each other. However, if the faces are parallel but not coplanar, you must specify the type of Double Bend to use.

General Steps

Use the following general steps to create a Bend feature:

1. Start the creation of the Bend feature.
2. Select the Bend options.
3. Set the Bend Extension.
4. Select the Double Bend options (optional).
5. Edit the Unfold and Bend options (optional).
6. Complete the feature.

Step 1 - Start the creation of the Bend feature.

In the *Sheet Metal* tab>Create panel, click ⬚ (Bend). The Bend dialog box opens as shown in Figure 5–28.

Figure 5–28

Step 2 - Select the Bend options.

Select one edge on each of two faces to connect with a Bend feature, as shown in Figure 5–29. Accept the default **BendRadius** or enter a new value, as required.

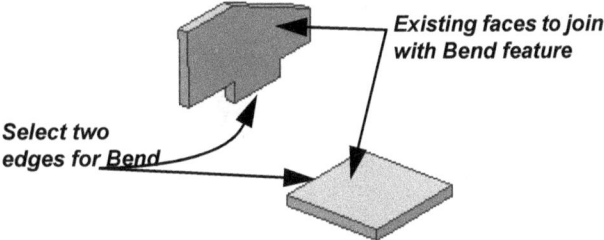

Existing faces to join with Bend feature

Select two edges for Bend

Figure 5–29

Step 3 - Set the Bend Extension.

The ⬛ (Extend Bend Aligned to Side Faces) and ⬛ (Extend Bend Perpendicular to Side Faces) options determine how material is extended to create the Bend feature.

- The ⬛ option enables you to extend the Bend aligned to side faces. With this option, the Autodesk Inventor software extends material perpendicular to the axis of the Bend feature. In the example shown on the left in Figure 5–30, **Face1** is created above and to the left of **Face2**. On the right in Figure 5–30, a Bend is added and the edge of **Face1** has been extended to meet the Bend feature.

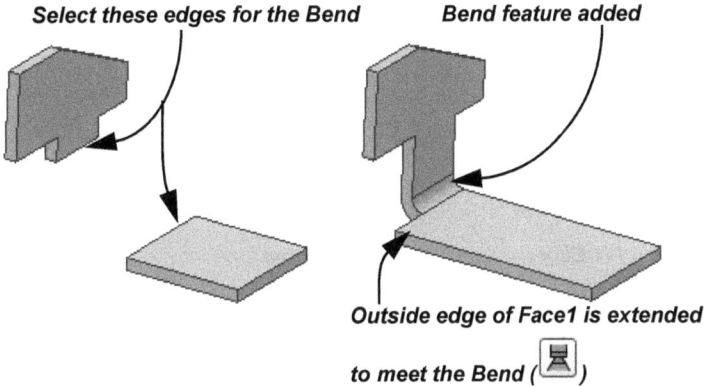

Select these edges for the Bend   *Bend feature added*

Outside edge of Face1 is extended

to meet the Bend (⬛)

Figure 5–30

- The 🖳 option enables you to extend the bend. With this
  option, the Autodesk Inventor software only adds the material
  required to attach the Bend to both faces. In Figure 5–31, the
  outside edge of **Face1** is not extended across its entire width,
  but only across the distance required to attach the shorter
  edge that is selected on **Face2**.

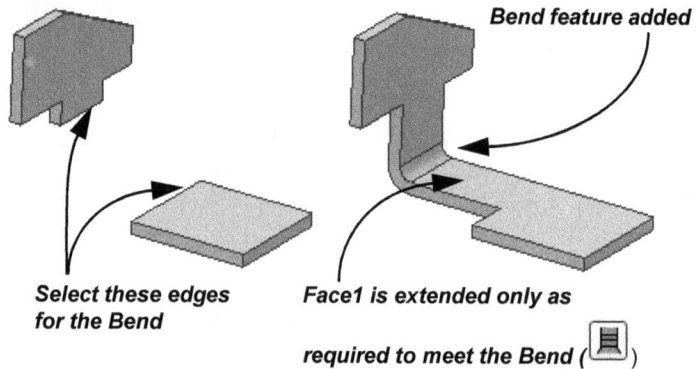

Bend feature added

*Select these edges
for the Bend*

*Face1 is extended only as
required to meet the Bend (🖳)*

Figure 5–31

Step 4 - Select the Double Bend options (optional).

When a Bend feature is applied between parallel faces that are
not coplanar, you can specify the *Double Bend* options, as
shown in Figure 5–32. The faces are trimmed or extended as
required to apply **45 Degree**, **90 Degree**, and **Full Radius**
bends. If the **Fix Edges** option is selected, the **BendRadius** is
applied to the existing edges.

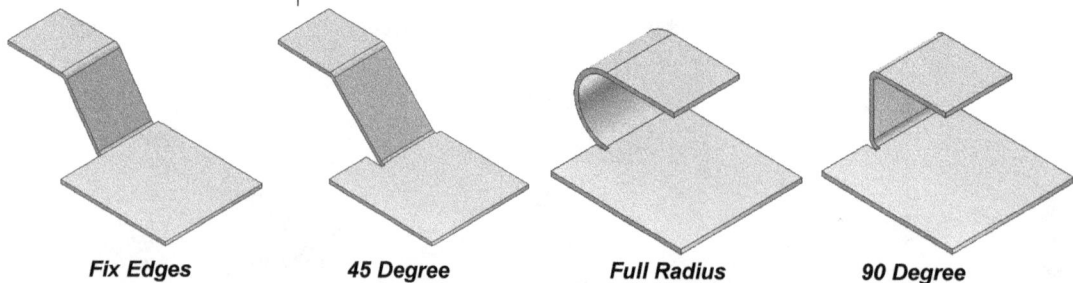

Fix Edges   *45 Degree*   *Full Radius*   *90 Degree*

Figure 5–32

Step 5 - Edit the Unfold and Bend options (optional).

Accept the default values for the *Bend* and *Unfold* options in their associated tabs. The defaults are based on the settings in the Sheet Metal Rule. You can change these settings if required.

Step 6 - Complete the feature.

Once you have fully defined the Bend, click **OK** to complete the feature. Alternatively, you can right-click and select **OK (Enter)** to complete the feature.

If you want to continue to add Bend features using the same options, you can click **Apply** and select alternate edges to create another feature.

Practice 5a

Hems, Folds, and Bends

Practice Objectives

- Create geometry in a model that is folded or rolled back on itself using the Hem feature.
- Create geometry that folds existing sheet metal geometry along a sketched line.
- Create geometry that joins two disconnected non-planar faces to one another using a Bend feature.

In this practice, you will add Hem, Fold, and Bend features to an existing part, as shown in Figure 5–33.

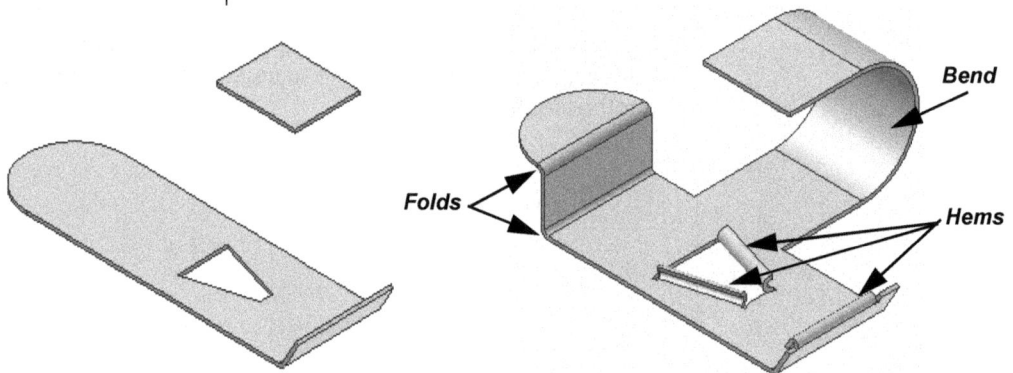

Figure 5–33

Task 1 - Add a Hem.

1. Open **Holder.ipt**. The part consists of two faces.

2. In the *Sheet Metal* tab>Create panel, click ✐ (Hem). The Hem dialog box opens, as shown in Figure 5–34.

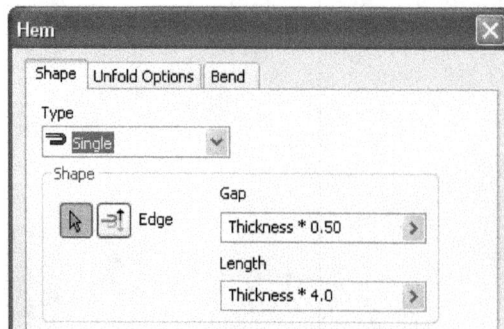

Figure 5–34

3. Select the edge shown in Figure 5–35.

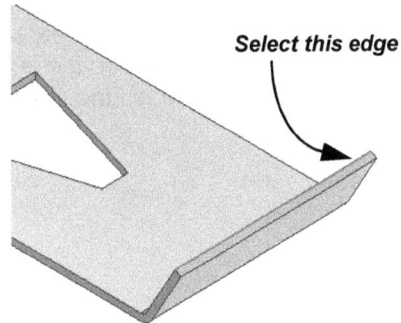

Select this edge

Figure 5–35

4. Click ⬆ (Flip Direction) to place the Hem toward the outside of the part.

5. Click >> to expand the dialog box.

6. Select **Width** in the Type drop-down list and verify that the **Centered** option is selected.

7. Enter **8 mm** in the *Width* field.

8. Click **OK**. The features display as shown in Figure 5–36. Reliefs are added automatically according to the Sheet Metal style set for the default rule.

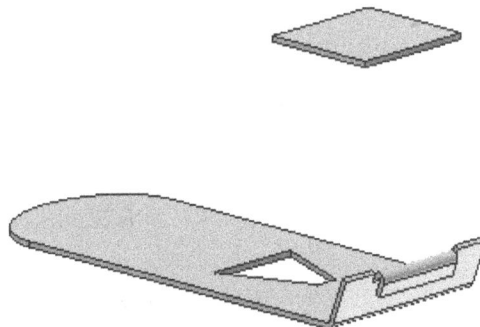

Figure 5–36

Task 2 - Create a Fold.

1. Create a new sketch on the large face and sketch a line between the end points of the arc, as shown in Figure 5–37. Finish the sketch.

Ensure that the end points of the sketched line are constrained to be coincident with the endpoints of the arc edge.

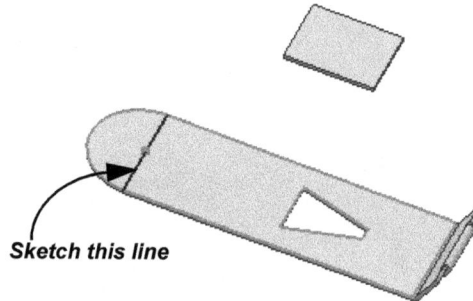

Sketch this line

Figure 5–37

2. In the *Sheet Metal* tab>Create panel, click (Fold). The Fold dialog box opens as shown in Figure 5–38.

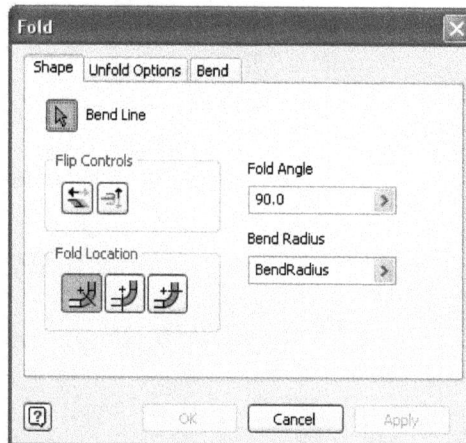

Figure 5–38

3. Select the line that you just sketched as the **Bend Line**.

4. If required, click (Flip Side) and (Flip Direction) so that the curved portion of the existing face folds down, as shown in Figure 5–39.

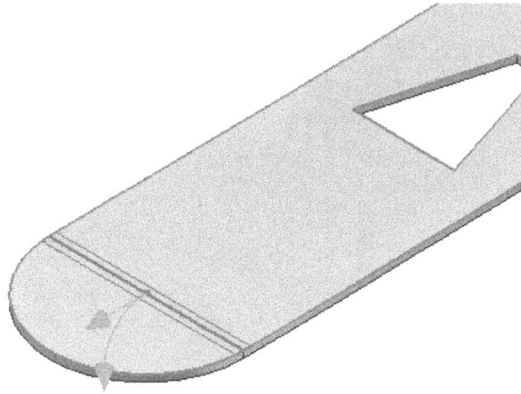

Figure 5–39

5. Verify that the *Fold Angle* is set to **90 deg**. Click **OK**.

Task 3 - Create a second Fold.

---

1. Create another sketch on the same plane as before and sketch a line **12 mm** from the end of the Cut feature, as shown in Figure 5–40. The line must be coincident to the edges of the face and parallel to the edge of the Cut feature.

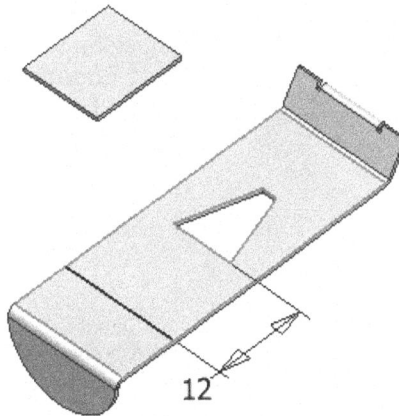

Figure 5–40

2. Finish the sketch.

3. In the *Sheet Metal* tab>Create panel, click (Fold). Select the bend line that you just sketched.

4. If required, click ⬒ to fold the end closest to the curve upwards, as shown in Figure 5–41. Verify that the *Fold Angle* is set to **90 deg** and click **OK**.

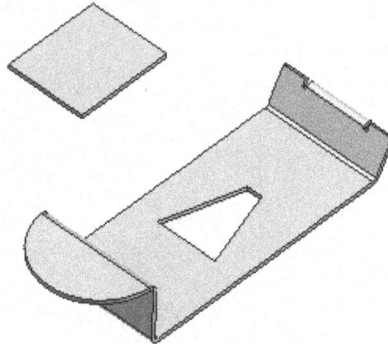

Figure 5–41

Task 4 - Add a Bend between parallel faces.

1. In the *Sheet Metal* tab>Create panel, click 🪶 (Bend). The Bend dialog box opens.

2. Select the two edges shown in Figure 5–42. Click 🗂 (Flip Fixed Edge) as required, so that the preview displays on the selected edge.

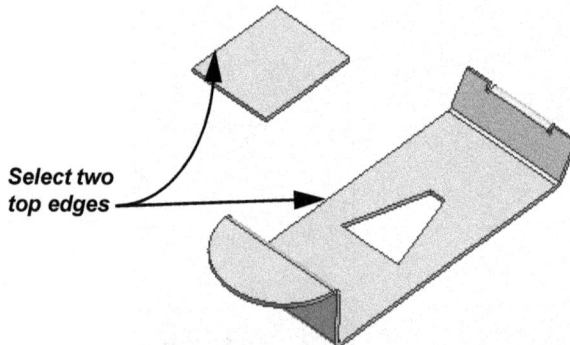

Select two top edges

Figure 5–42

3. Click **OK** to complete the feature. The model displays as shown in Figure 5–43.

*The same geometry
could also be created
using a Face or Contour
Flange.*

Figure 5–43

Task 5 - Edit a Bend.

1. Right-click on **Bend4** in the Model Browser and select **Edit Feature**. The Bend dialog box opens.

2. Select **Full Radius** in the *Double Bend* area in the Bend dialog box. Click **OK**. The model displays as shown in Figure 5–44.

Figure 5–44

Task 6 - Add Hems to a Cut feature.

1. In the *Sheet Metal* tab>Create panel, click ✏ (Hem). The Hem dialog box opens.

2. Select the edge shown in Figure 5–45.

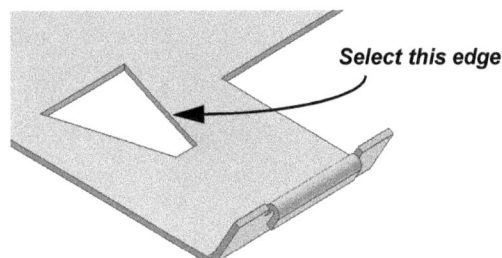

Select this edge

Figure 5–45

3. Select **Rolled** in the Type drop-down list. Verify the other settings as shown in Figure 5–46. Click **Apply**.

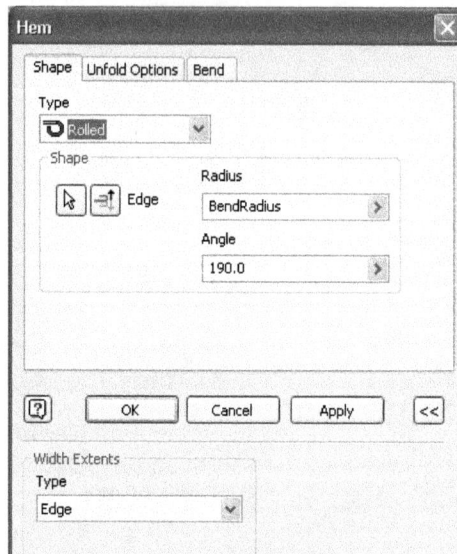

Figure 5–46

4. Repeat for the opposite edge of the Cut feature. The model displays as shown in Figure 5–47. Reliefs are added automatically according to the Sheet Metal Rule.

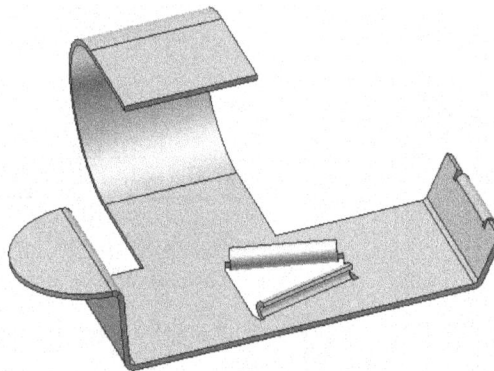

Figure 5–47

Task 7 - Edit features.

1. Right-click on **Hem6** in the Model Browser and select **Edit Feature**. The Hem dialog box opens.

2. Click [↗] (Flip Direction) to create the Hem on the opposite side of the face.

3. Click [>>] to expand the dialog box. Select **Offset** in the Type drop-down list. Set the offset distances shown in Figure 5–48.

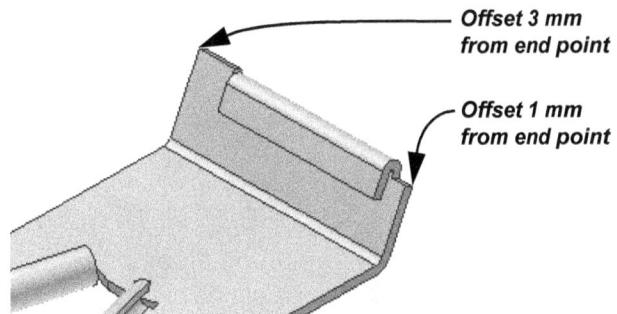

Offset 3 mm from end point

Offset 1 mm from end point

Figure 5–48

4. Click **OK** to complete the feature. The Hem is adjusted, as shown in Figure 5–49. The remnant on the 1 mm side is less than the **MinimumRemnant** set in the Sheet Metal Rule, so the remnant is only removed on that side.

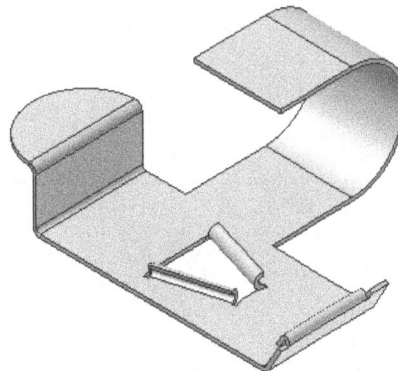

Figure 5–49

5. Save and close the file.

Practice 5b | Bending Sheet Metal

Practice Objectives

- Create geometry in a model that is folded or rolled back on itself using the Hem feature.
- Create geometry that folds existing sheet metal geometry along a sketched line using the Fold feature.
- Create geometry that joins two disconnected non-planar faces to one another using the Bend feature.

In this practice, you will practice adding Hem, Fold, and Bend features to multiple parts. The finished models are shown in Figure 5–50.

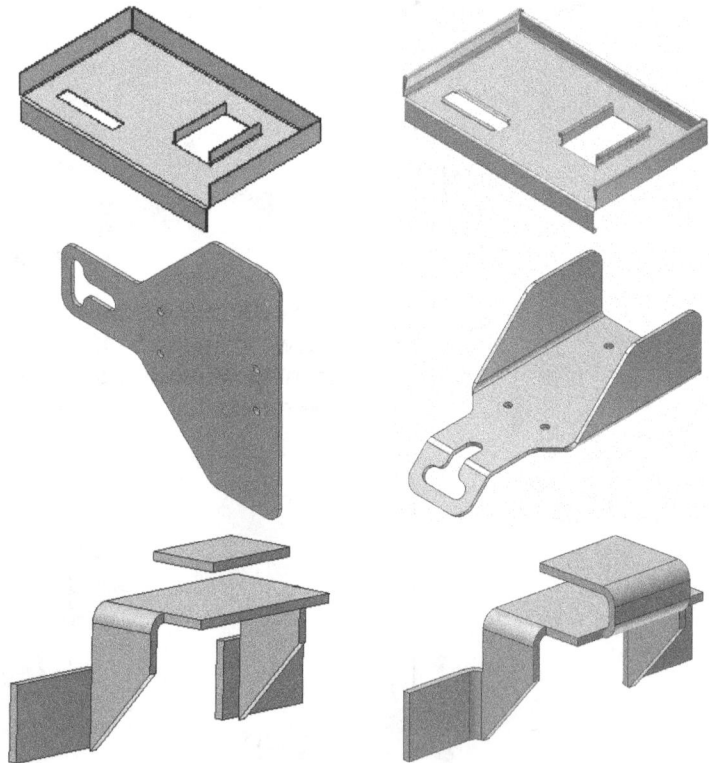

Figure 5–50

Task 1 - Create single hems.

1. Open **Hem.ipt**.

2. In the *Sheet Metal* tab>Create panel, click 🖉 (Hem).

3. Select one of the long edges of the rectangular cut out without flanges.

4. Click [>>] to display the *Width Extents* area. Select **Offset** in the Type drop-down list and verify that the offset values are set to **5 mm**.

5. Click **Apply**. The model displays as shown in Figure 5–51.

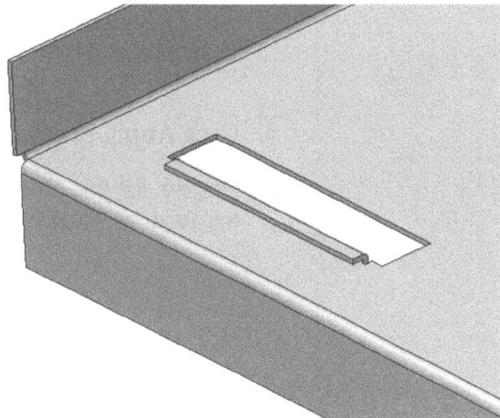

Figure 5–51

6. Repeat for the opposite edge of the cut out. Click **OK** to complete the feature and close the Hem dialog box, or click **Cancel** to close the dialog box.

Task 2 - Create Double Hems.

1. In the *Sheet Metal* tab>Create panel, click 🖉 (Hem).

2. Select **Double** in the Type drop-down list.

3. Select the outside edge on one of the flanges of the cut out, as shown in Figure 5–52.

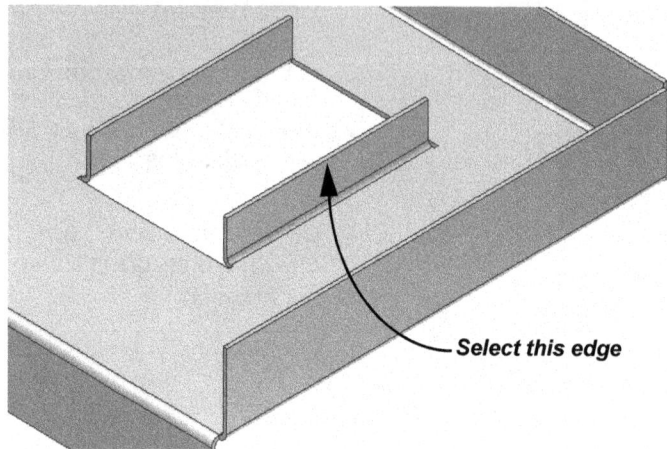

Select this edge

Figure 5–52

4. Click **Apply** to create the feature.

5. Repeat for the other flange on the cut out. The model displays as shown in Figure 5–53.

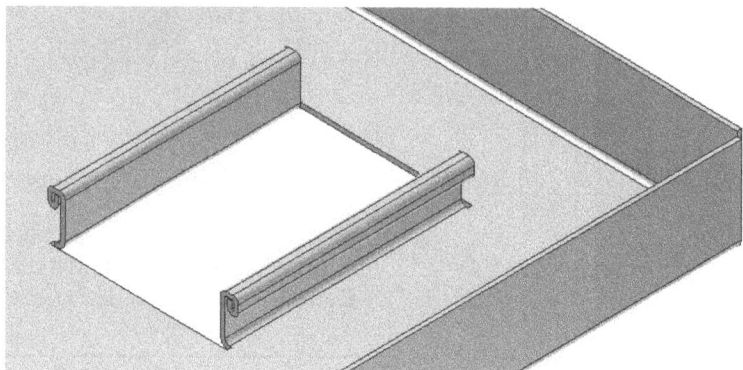

Figure 5–53

Task 3 - Create a Rolled Hem.

1. In the *Sheet Metal* tab>Create panel, click (Hem).

2. Select **Rolled** in the Type drop-down list.

3. Select the inside edge of the flange that is in the opposite direction to the other flanges.

4. Enter **270 deg** in the *Angle* field.

5. Click **OK** to create the Hem. The model displays as shown in Figure 5–54.

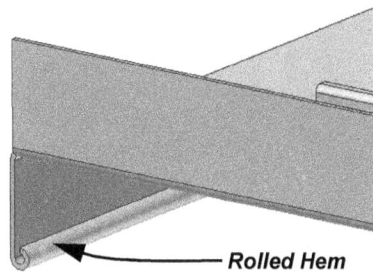

Rolled Hem

Figure 5–54

Task 4 - Create Teardrop Hems.

1. In the *Sheet Metal* tab>Create panel, click ✐ (Hem).

2. Select **Teardrop** in the Type drop-down list.

3. Select the inside edge of one of the shorter flanges.

4. Enter **190 deg** in the *Angle* field.

5. Click **Apply** to create the feature.

6. Repeat for the other short flange.

7. While still in the Hem dialog box, select the inside edge of the long flange (the only one without a hem) and verify that the Type is set to **Teardrop**.

8. Click **Apply**. A warning dialog box opens prompting you that the Hem Body intersects the existing body. The Hem that you are trying to create intersects the Hems created in the previous steps. To resolve this, you will offset the Hem edges. Click **Cancel** to return to the Hem dialog box.

9. Click ⟩⟩ to display the *Width Extents* area.

10. Select **Offset** in the Type drop-down list. Verify that the offset values are set to **5 mm**. Click **OK**. The model displays as shown in Figure 5–55.

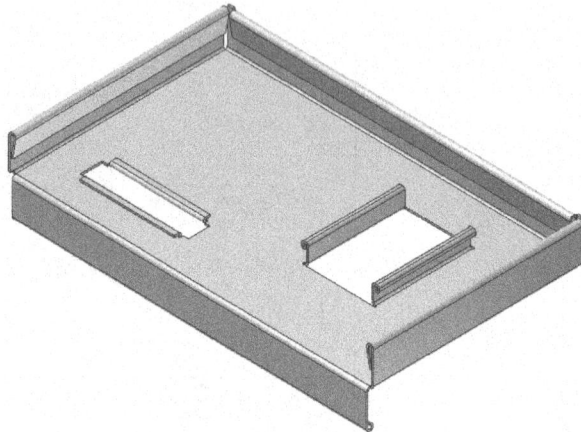

Figure 5–55

11. Save and close the file.

Task 5 - Create Folds.

1. Open the file **Fold.ipt**.

2. Create a sketched line on one face of the part, as shown in Figure 5–56. Verify that the line is coincident to the edges of the face and parallel to the horizontal edges. Finish the sketch.

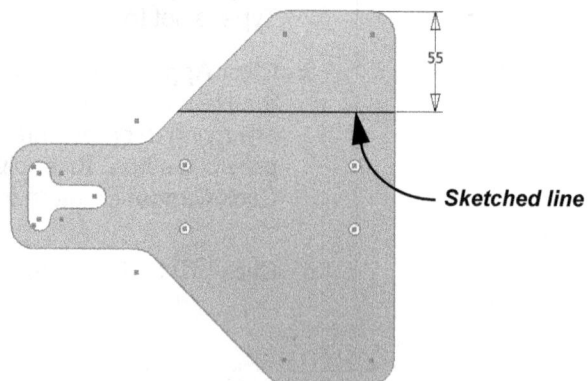

Figure 5–56

3. In the *Sheet Metal* tab>Create panel, click ✍ (Fold). The Fold dialog box opens.

4. Select the line that you just created as the *Bend Line*.

5. Verify that *Fold Angle* is set to **90 deg** and adjust the *Flip Controls* to create the Fold shown on the left in Figure 5–57.

6. Repeat to create the same Fold on the opposite side of the part, as shown on the right in Figure 5–57.

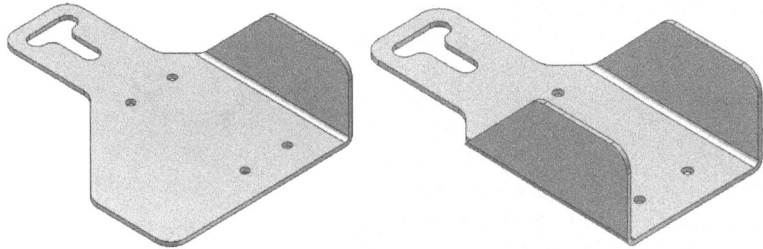

Figure 5–57

7. Create a sketch on one face of the part, as shown in Figure 5–58. Verify that the line is coincident to the edges of the face and parallel to the horizontal edges. Finish the sketch.

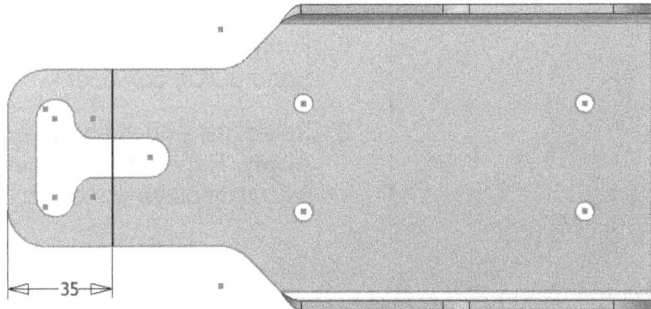

Figure 5–58

8. In the *Sheet Metal* tab>Create panel, click ✍ (Fold).

9. Select the line that you just created as the *Bend Line*.

10. Enter **45 deg** for the *Bend Angle* and adjust the *Flip Controls* to create the Bend shown in Figure 5–59.

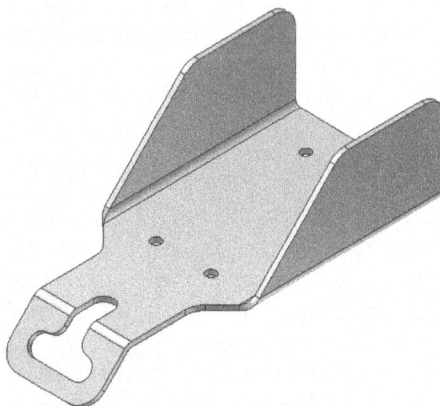

Figure 5–59

11. Save and close the file.

Task 6 - Create Bends.

1. Open the file **Bend.ipt**. The part contains four disjointed faces. You will use the **Bend** command to join the faces into a single body.

2. In the *Sheet Metal* tab>Create panel, click ⌐ (Bend). The Bend dialog box opens.

3. Select the edges shown on the left in Figure 5–60 and click **Apply**. Repeat for the short flange on the other side. The model displays as shown on the right.

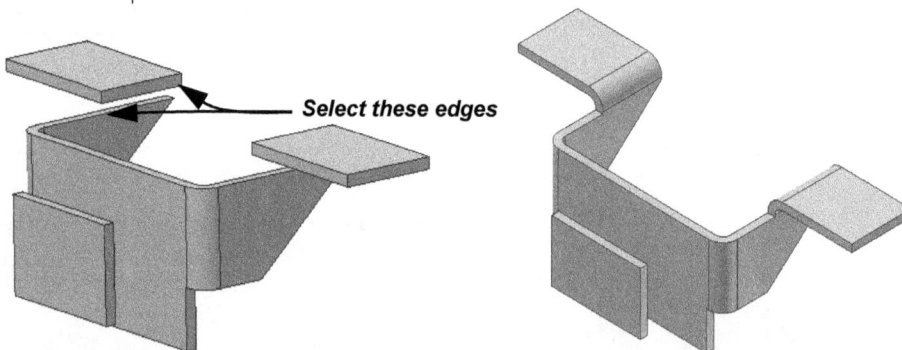

Select these edges

Figure 5–60

4. In the *Sheet Metal* tab>Create panel, click (Bend), if not already available. Select the edges shown in Figure 5–61.

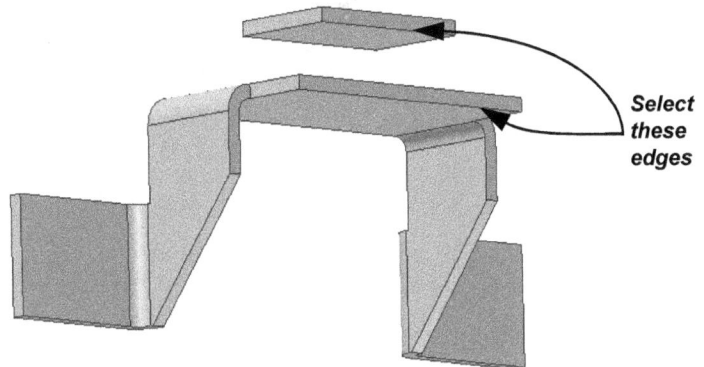

Figure 5–61

5. Verify that the **90 Degree** option is selected in the *Double Bend* area. Click (Extend Bend Aligned to Side Faces) and click **OK**. The model displays as shown in Figure 5–62.

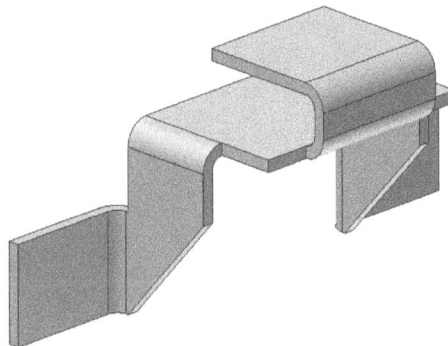

Figure 5–62

6. Save and close the file.

Practice 5c	**Bracket**

Practice Objectives

- Create geometry in a model that is folded or rolled back on itself using the Hem feature.
- Create geometry that folds existing sheet metal geometry along a sketched line using the Fold feature.
- Create geometry that joins two disconnected non-planar faces to one another using the Bend feature.

In this practice, you will create Hem, Fold, and Bend features on a Bracket part, as shown in Figure 5–63.

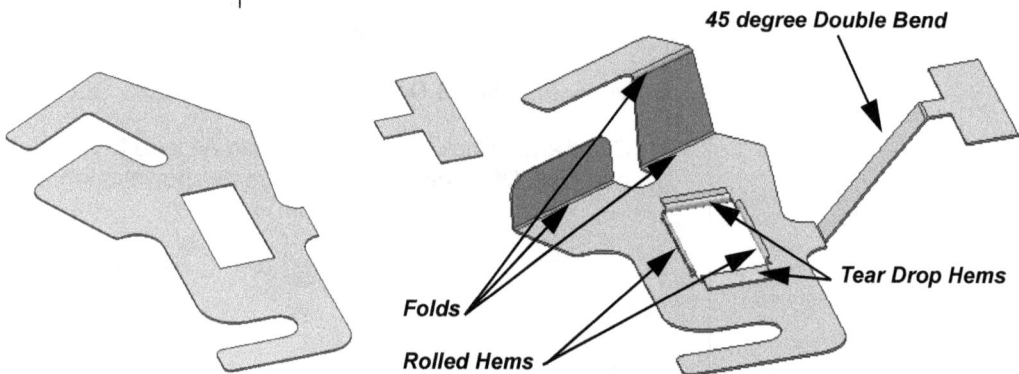

45 degree Double Bend

Tear Drop Hems

Folds

Rolled Hems

Figure 5–63

Task 1 - Add a Fold.

1. Open **Bracket.ipt**. **Face1** is the larger face and **Face2** is the smaller face parallel to **Face1** on a workplane.

2. Create a sketch on the large face, as shown in Figure 5–64.

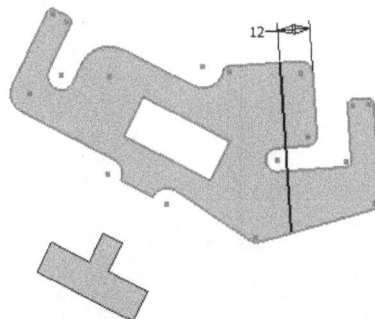

Figure 5–64

3. Create a **90 degree** Fold, as shown in Figure 5–65. If required, use ⬅️ and ➡️ to control the direction of the Fold.

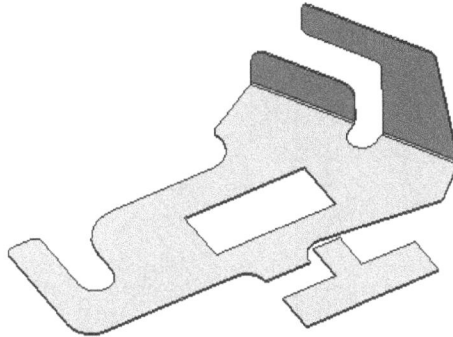

Figure 5–65

Task 2 - Add a second Fold.

1. Create the sketch shown in Figure 5–66. The line is aligned with the center of the arc.

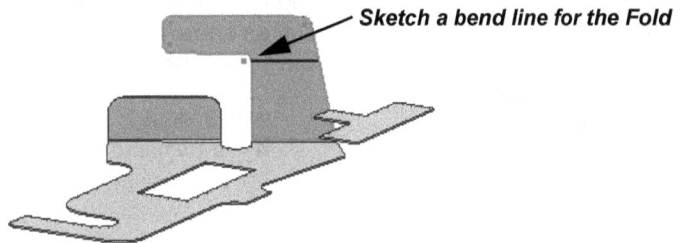

Sketch a bend line for the Fold

Figure 5–66

2. Fold the model 90 degrees, as shown in Figure 5–67.

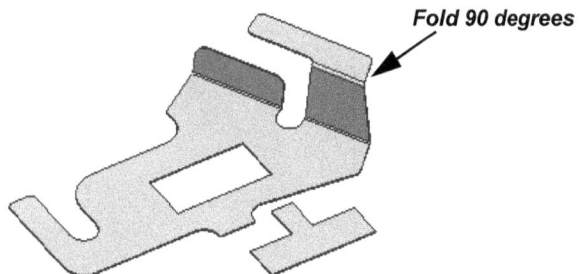

Fold 90 degrees

Figure 5–67

Task 3 - Add two Teardrop Hems.

1. Add two Teardrop Hems to the short edges of the rectangular Cut, as shown in Figure 5–68. Set the *Width Extents* to **Edge**.

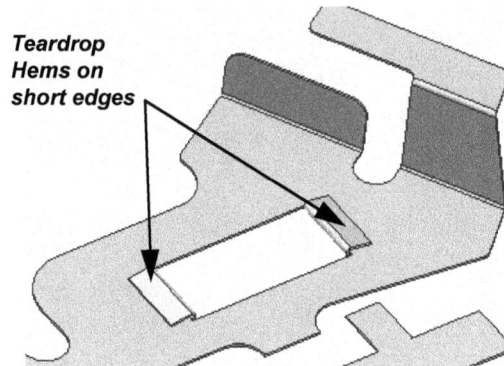

Teardrop Hems on short edges

Figure 5–68

Task 4 - Add two Rolled Hems.

Sheet metal features can be mirrored to maintain design intent instead of creating individual features.

1. Add two Rolled Hems to the long sides of the rectangular Cut, as shown in Figure 5–69. Set the *Width Extents* to **Width** and select the **Centered** option. Set the *Width* to **30 mm**.

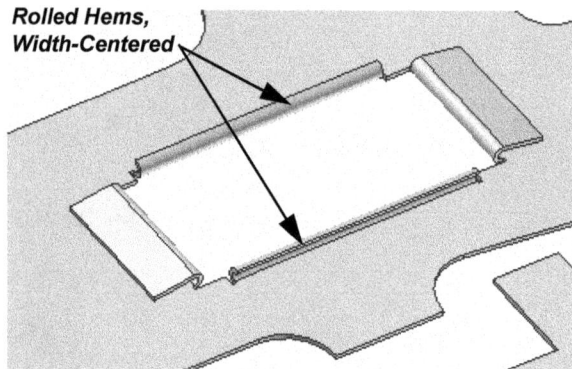

Rolled Hems, Width-Centered

Figure 5–69

Task 5 - Add a Bend.

1. Add a 45 degree Bend between **Face2** and **Face1**, as shown in Figure 5–70. Click [icon] (Flip Fixed Edge), if required, to shorten **Face2**.

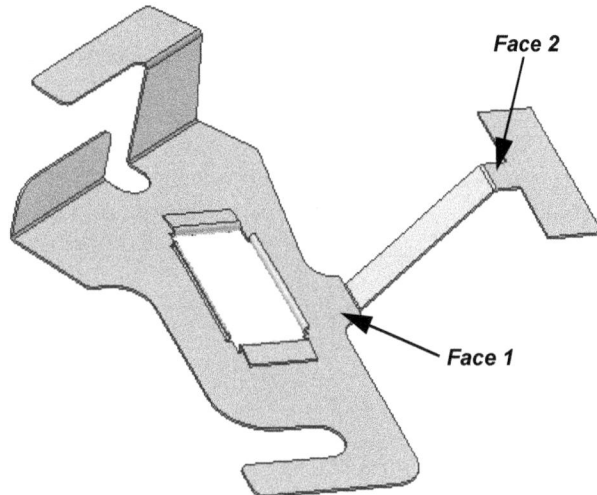

Figure 5–70

2. Save and close the file.

Practice 5d | Working in an Assembly

Practice Objectives

- Create a new sheet metal component in the context of a top-level assembly model.
- Add a Face feature in a new sheet metal component by referencing geometry in another component.
- Add Flange and Bend features to a sheet metal component.

In this practice, you will practice working in an assembly file to create a sheet metal component. To create the component, you will reference geometry in another assembly component and use the **Face**, **Flange**, and **Bend** options to create the geometry. The finished model is shown in Figure 5–71.

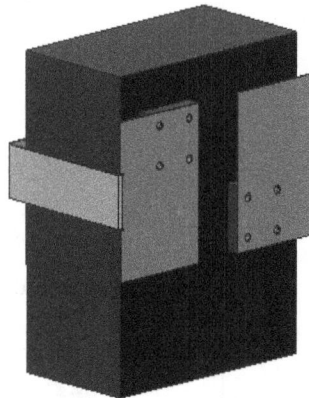

Figure 5–71

Task 1 - Create a new component in the assembly.

1. Open **Cabinet Enclosure.iam**.

2. In the *Assemble* tab>Component panel, click (Create).

3. In the Create In-Place Component dialog box, enter **Covering** for the new component name and select the **Sheet Metal (in).ipt** template. Select **Constrain sketch plane to selected face or plane**. Click **OK** to create the component.

4. Select the face shown in Figure 5–72 as the sketch plane for the base feature. You can select either this face or the other that also has four holes.

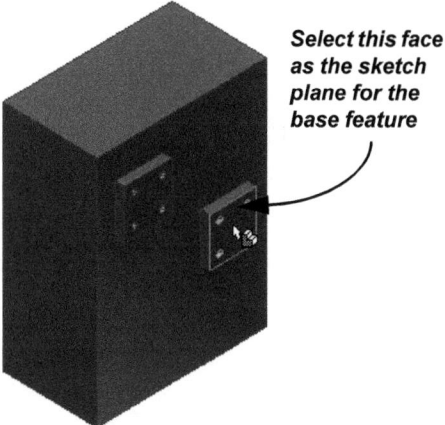

Select this face as the sketch plane for the base feature

Figure 5–72

5. Create a sketch on the XY plane of the new component. Project the geometry shown in Figure 5–73. Depending on your application option settings, the projected entities might vary.

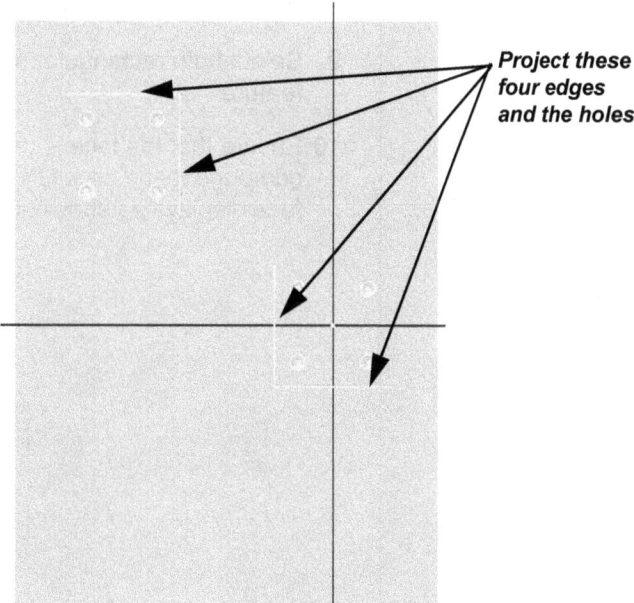

Project these four edges and the holes

Figure 5–73

6. Sketch the geometry shown in Figure 5–74. Constrain the rectangular sketches to the projected edges of the Cabinet's lifted faces.

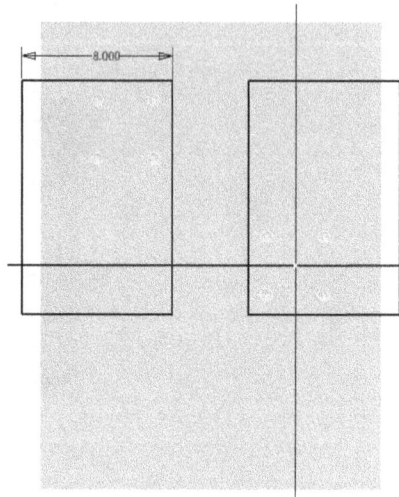

Figure 5–74

7. Finish the sketch.

8. In the *Sheet Metal* tab>Create panel, click (Face).

9. Select both rectangular sections as the profiles for the face feature.

10. Ensure that the face is created away from the Cabinet component and click **OK** to complete the component. The face displays as shown in Figure 5–75.

Figure 5–75

Task 2 - Create two flanges on the Covering.ipt component.

1. Ensure that the **Covering.ipt** component is still active in the assembly.

2. In the *Sheet Metal* tab>Create panel, click ⬗ (Flange).

3. Select the two edges that form the flanges shown in Figure 5–76. Extend the height of the flanges to **12in**.

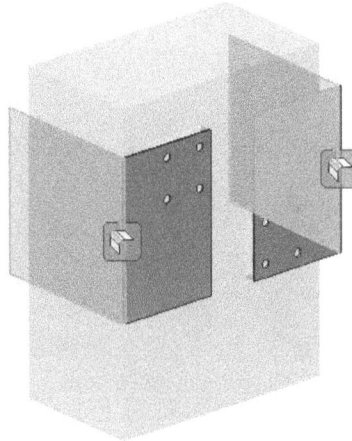

Figure 5–76

4. In the preview display of the model, click ▣ on either of the edges. The Bend Edit dialog box opens.

5. Select the **Width Extents** option to enable the Type drop-down list options.

6. Select **Width** in the Type drop-down list.

7. By default, the **Centered** option is enabled and centers the flange on the wall. Enter **4in** for the value.

8. Click **OK**. Note that the corner editing icon has changed to ▣ instead of ▣, indicating that this width extent is independent from the other flanges.

9. Click ▣ for the other edge and modify its width using the same value.

10. Click **OK** to complete the feature. The model displays as shown in shown in Figure 5–77.

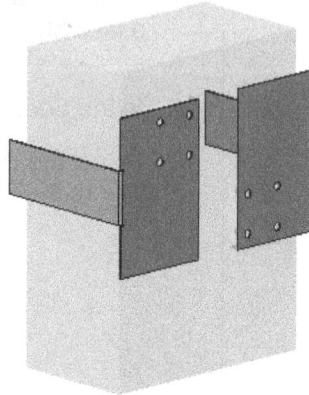

Figure 5–77

Task 3 - Complete the component by closing the geometry using a Bend.

1. Ensure that the **Covering.ipt** component is still active in the assembly.

2. In the *Sheet Metal* tab>Create panel, click 🔨 (Bend).

3. Select the two edges that form the bend. The model displays as shown in Figure 5–78.

Create this bend to close the geometry for the created component

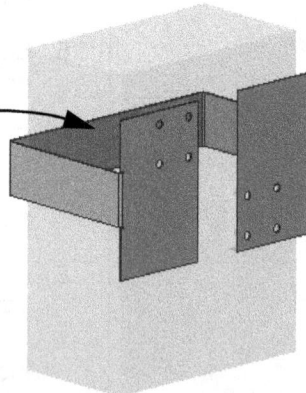

Figure 5–78

4. Double-click on **Cabinet Enclosure.iam** at the top of the Model Browser to activate the top-level assembly.

5. Save the assembly and close the files.

Chapter Review Questions

1. Which of the following best describes a Hem sheet metal feature?

   a. A Hem creates geometry that folds existing sheet metal geometry along a sketched line.

   b. A Hem creates a smooth radius on the corners of a sheet metal part.

   c. A Hem creates geometry that is folded or rolled back on itself.

   d. A Hem creates geometry that joins two disconnected non-planar faces to one another using the Bend feature.

2. Which of the following Hem types was used to create the Hem features shown in Figure 5–79?

Figure 5–79

   a. Single

   b. Teardrop

   c. Rolled

   d. Double

3. Which of the following best describes a Fold sheet metal feature?

   a. A Fold creates geometry that folds existing sheet metal geometry along a sketched line.

   b. A Fold creates a smooth radius on the corners of a sheet metal part.

   c. A Fold creates geometry that is folded or rolled back on itself.

   d. A Fold creates geometry that joins two disconnected non-planar faces to one another using the Bend feature.

4. You can only create one Fold feature per instance of the command.

   a. True

   b. False

5. Which of the following previews produces the Fold feature shown in Figure 5–80?

Figure 5–80

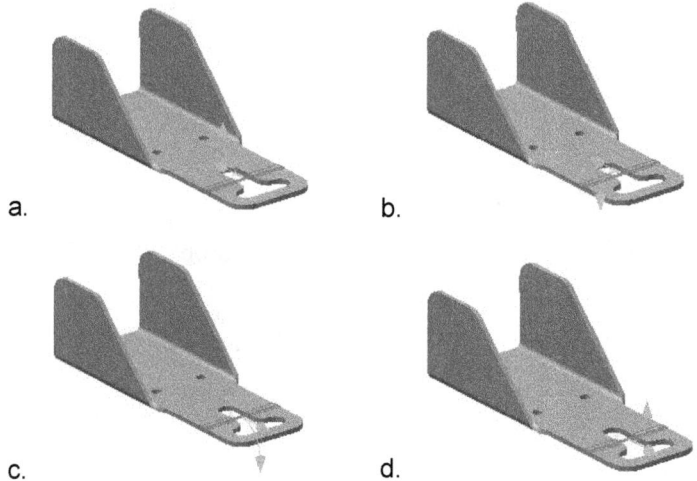

a.   b.

c.   d.

6. Which of the following best describes a Bend sheet metal feature?

   a. A Bend creates geometry that folds existing sheet metal geometry along a sketched line.

   b. A Bend creates a smooth radius on the corners of a sheet metal part.

   c. A Bend creates geometry that is folded or rolled back on itself.

   d. A Bend creates geometry that joins two disconnected non-planar faces to one another using the Bend feature.

7. You can only create one Bend feature per instance of the command.

   a. True

   b. False

Command Summary

Button	Command	Location
	Bend	• **Ribbon:** *Sheet Metal* tab>Create panel
	Fold	• **Ribbon:** *Sheet Metal* tab>Create panel
	Hem	• **Ribbon:** *Sheet Metal* tab>Create panel

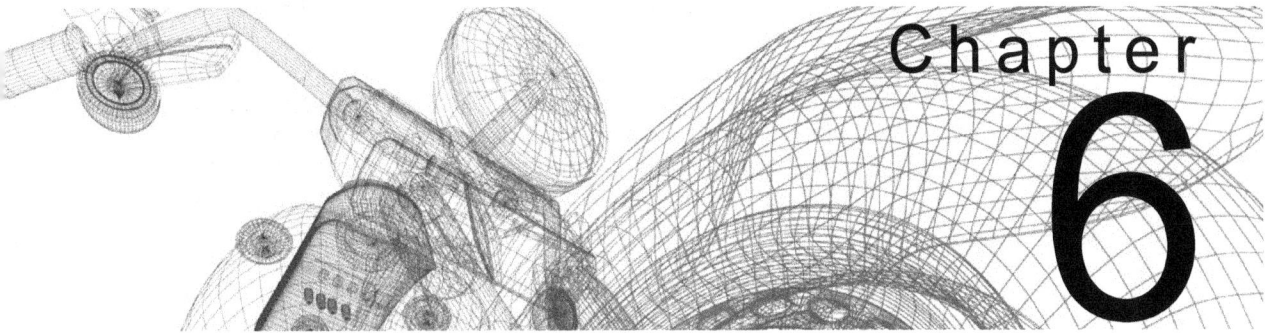

Chapter 6

Corner Rounds and Chamfers

The corners of a sheet metal part can be rounded or chamfered using Corner Round and Corner Chamfer*s*. These features can be used to shape a sheet metal part or to remove sharp corners.

Learning Objectives in this Chapter

- Create corner rounds by selecting individual corners or an entire feature to place the geometry.
- Create a corner chamfer by entering a single distance value that defines the size of the chamfered corner.
- Create a corner chamfer by entering a distance value and angle to define the size of the chamfered corner.
- Create a corner chamfer by entering two distance values to define the size of the chamfered corner.

6.1 Creating Corner Rounds

A Corner Round is a placed feature. You can apply a single radius to multiple corners or to an entire feature on a sheet metal part. Corner Rounds on exterior corners are used to prevent chipping and to remove dangerous sharp edges. In addition, applying them to interior corners can help strengthen a part.

The Corner Round is similar to the Fillet, except that you are limited to selecting the corners on geometry. Figure 6–1 shows an example of a Corner Round on two different corners of a Flange.

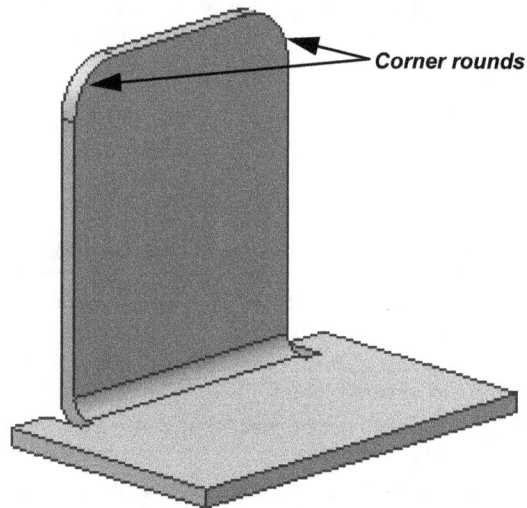

Corner rounds

Figure 6–1

General Steps

Use the following general steps to create a Corner Round feature:

1. Start the creation of the Corner Round feature.
2. Select a Selection Mode.
3. Select the corner(s) of the part.
4. Define the radius.
5. Complete the feature.

Step 1 - Start the creation of the Corner Round feature.

In the *Sheet Metal* tab>Modify panel, click ⬜ (Corner Round). The Corner Round dialog box opens as shown in Figure 6–2.

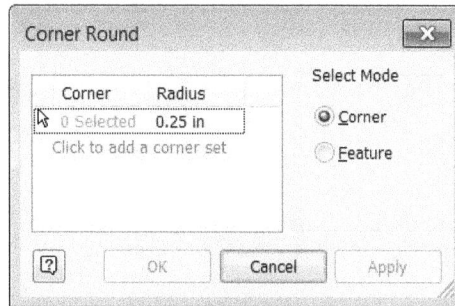

Figure 6–2

Step 2 - Select a Selection Mode.

Two selection modes are available for selecting the placement references for a corner round: **Corner** and **Feature**.

The **Corner** option enables you to select as many individual corners as required for each radius. The **Feature** option automatically applies the radius to all corners on the selected feature. Figure 6–3 shows a part in which Feature select mode is used. A Face with a flange added is shown on the left. A single Corner Round feature applied to all corners of the Face is shown on the right.

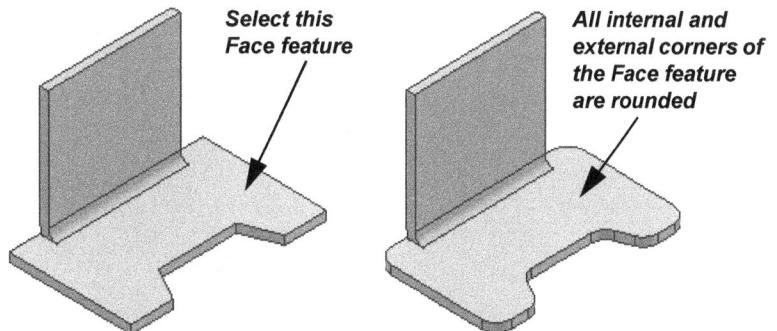

Select this Face feature

All internal and external corners of the Face feature are rounded

Figure 6–3

Step 3 - Select the corner(s) of the part.

Select the corner(s) that you want to round, as shown in Figure 6–4.

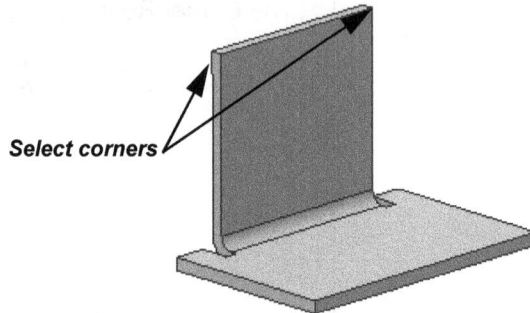

Select corners

Figure 6–4

Step 4 - Define the radius.

Enter a size in the *Radius* field, as shown in Figure 6–5.

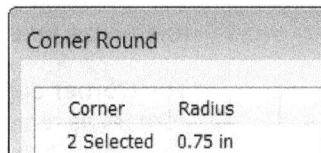

Corner Round

Corner	Radius
2 Selected	0.75 in

Figure 6–5

A preview of the rounded corners displays similar to that shown in Figure 6–6.

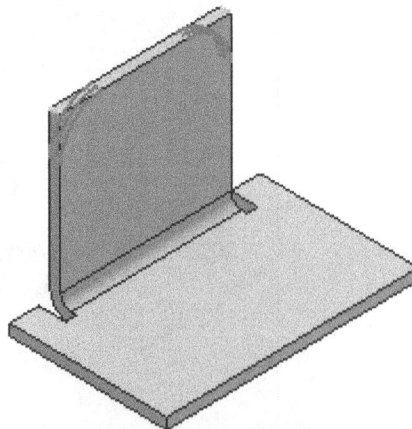

Figure 6–6

You can add multiple radii to the part with a single Corner Round feature. To do so, enter the first radius and select the corners to which to apply that radius. Next, select **Click to add a corner set**, enter a new radius, and select the corner(s) to which you want to apply the second radius.

Using this method, all corners in multiple sets are part of the same Corner Round feature. This can make it easier to suppress or edit the feature, and reduces the number of features in the Model Browser. Figure 6–7 shows a part with two corner sets being applied in one feature.

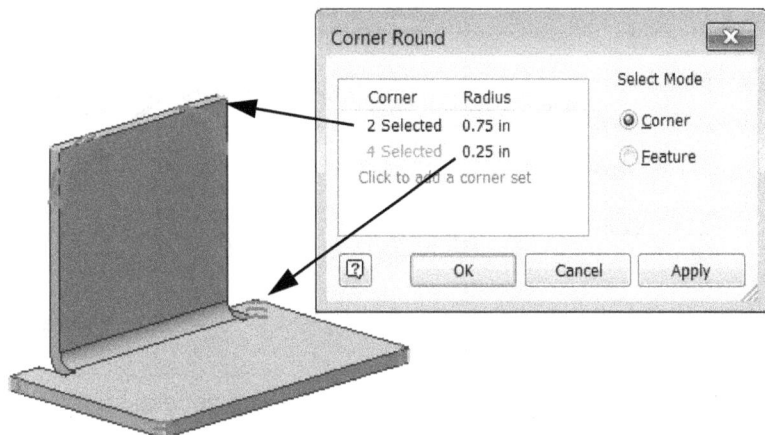

Figure 6–7

Step 5 - Complete the feature.

Click **OK** to complete the Corner Round feature. Alternatively, you can right-click and select **OK (Enter)** to complete the feature.

6.2 Creating Corner Chamfers

A Corner Chamfer is a placed feature that creates a beveled edge on the corners of a sheet metal part. Like Corner Rounds, the Corner Chamfer can add strength to an area of a part or remove sharp edges. Several options enable you to control the distance and angle of a Corner Chamfer. You can apply the same style to multiple corners on a sheet metal part.

The Corner Chamfer is similar to the Chamfer except that you are limited to selecting the corners on geometry. Figure 6–8 shows an example of a Corner Chamfer on the four corners of a model.

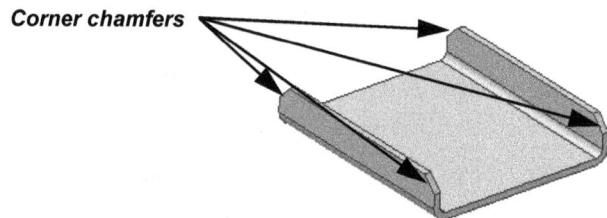

Corner chamfers

Figure 6–8

General Steps

Use the following general steps to create a Corner Chamfer feature:

1. Start the creation of the Corner Chamfer feature.
2. Select a creation method.
3. Select corners and edges.
4. Enter *Distance* and *Angle* values.
5. Complete the feature.

Step 1 - Start the creation of the Corner Chamfer feature.

In the *Sheet Metal* tab>Modify panel, click ☐ (Corner Chamfer). The Corner Chamfer dialog box opens as shown in Figure 6–9.

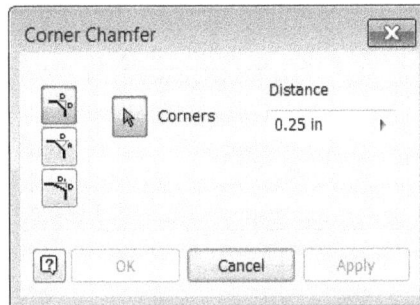

Figure 6–9

Step 2 - Select a creation method.

Three dimensioning methods are available to define Corner Chamfers. Each method requires different types of input, as described below.

- (One Distance) removes the same specified distance from both edges of the part at a selected corner, as shown in Figure 6–10.

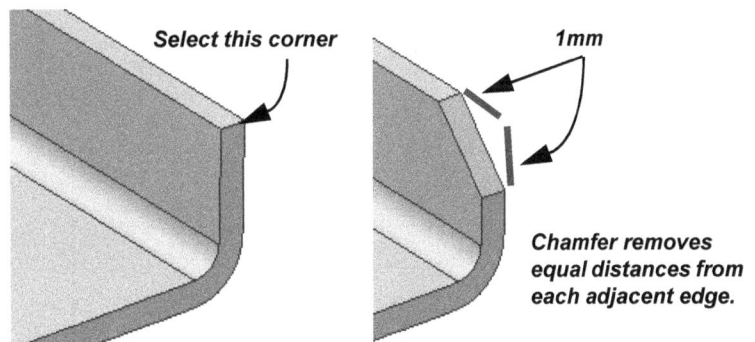

Select this corner

1mm

Chamfer removes equal distances from each adjacent edge.

Figure 6–10

- ⬚ (Distance and Angle) measures the specified distance from the corner along one edge of part. An angle is then applied from that location, as shown in Figure 6–11.

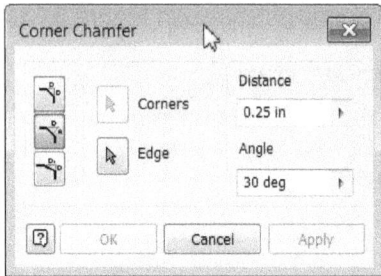

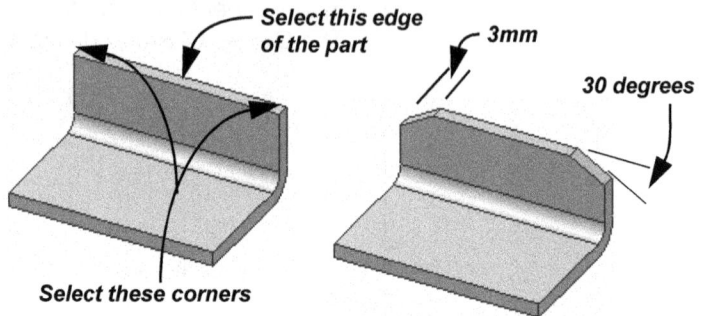

Corner Chamfer dialog box with **Corners** and **Edge** selection options, **Distance** 0.25 in, **Angle** 30 deg.

Select this edge of the part
3mm
30 degrees
Select these corners

Figure 6–11

- ⬚ (Two Distances) removes two distance values from the edges of the part at a selected corner, as shown in

Figure 6–12. Clicking ⬚ (Flip) enables you to reverse the edges used to apply *Distance1* and *Distance2*.

Step 3 - Select corners and edges.

Depending on the method you select for the Corner Chamfer measurements, you can select one or more edges. The **One Distance** and **Distance Angle** options enable you to select multiple edges. The **Two Distances** option enables you to select only one edge.

Unlike a **Corner Round**, the **Corner Chamfer** does not have a Feature select mode, so you need to select each edge individually.

Step 4 - Enter Distance and Angle values.

Entering *Distance* and *Angle* values can be done before or after selecting corners and edges. In many cases, you might prefer to wait until after selecting corners and edges before specifying the values. This enables you to display a preview of the resulting feature as you edit the sizes for the Corner Chamfer.

Figure 6–12 shows a Chamfer with two distances and the Flip selection applied. A Two Distance chamfer enables you to select only one corner per feature.

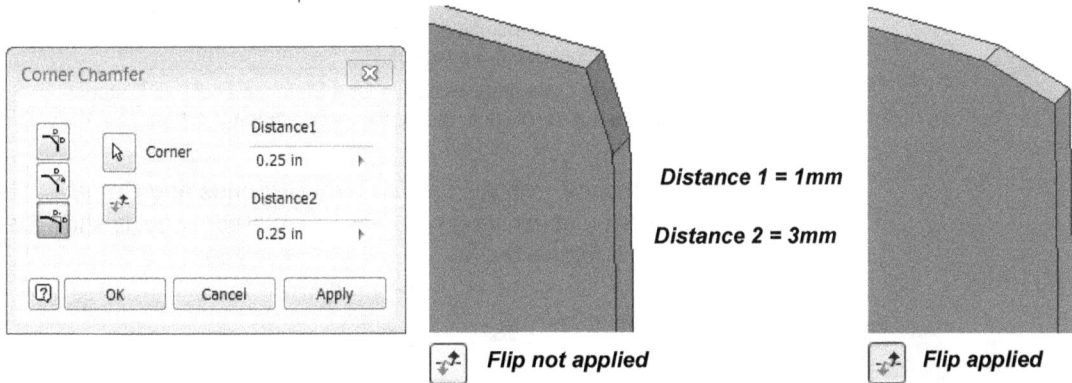

Distance 1 = 1mm

Distance 2 = 3mm

Flip not applied   Flip applied

Figure 6–12

Step 5 - Complete the feature.

Click **OK** to complete the Corner Chamfer feature. Alternatively, you can right-click and select **OK (Enter)** to complete the feature.

Practice 6a

Corner Rounds and Chamfers I

Practice Objectives

- Create corner rounds using the corner and feature selection methods to place the geometry in the model.
- Create corner chamfers using the One Distance and Two Distance dimensioning methods to locate the geometry on a corner.

In this practice, you will create Corner Rounds and Corner Chamfers on an existing part. The completed model is shown on the right in Figure 6–13.

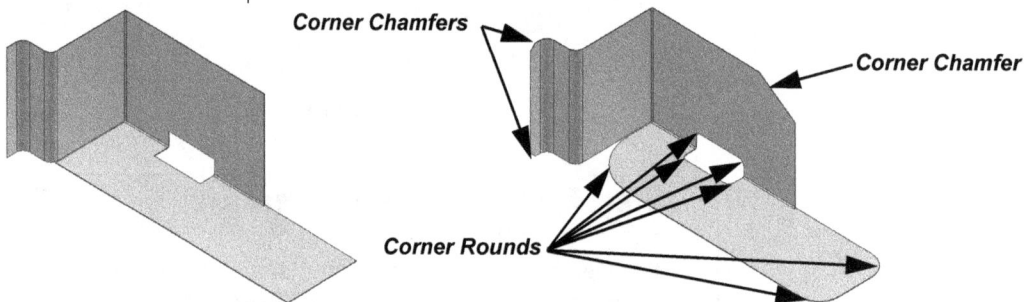

Corner Chamfers

Corner Chamfer

Corner Rounds

Figure 6–13

Task 1 - Create Corner Rounds on selected edges.

1. Open **Mounting_bracket_6.ipt**.

2. In the *Sheet Metal* tab>Modify panel, click ☐ (Corner Round). The Corner Round dialog box opens as shown in Figure 6–14.

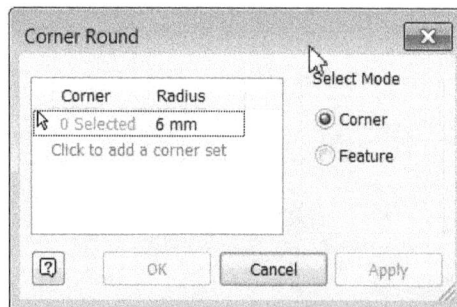

Figure 6–14

3. Select the corner shown in Figure 6–15.

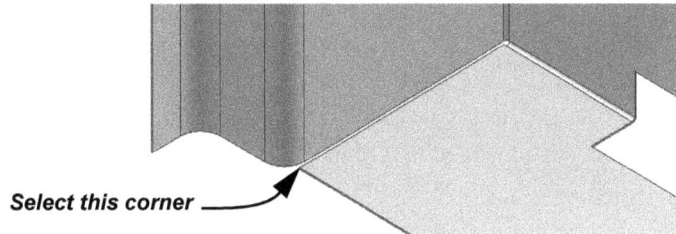

Figure 6–15

4. Change the *Radius* to **100 mm**.

5. Select **Click to add a corner set** in the dialog box.

6. Select the corners shown in Figure 6–16.

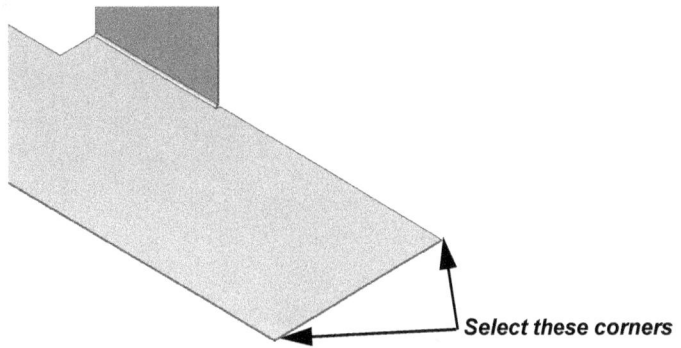

Figure 6–16

7. Change the *Radius* to **40 mm** for this second set.

8. Click **OK**. The model displays as shown in Figure 6–17.

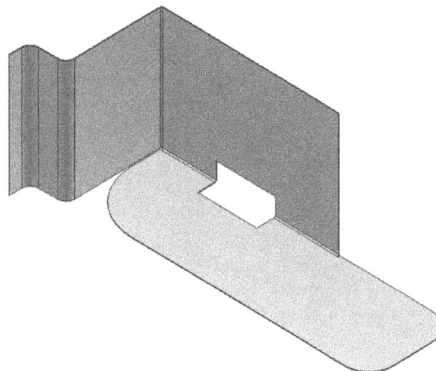

Figure 6–17

Task 2 - Create Corner Rounds on an entire feature.

1. In the *Sheet Metal* tab>Modify panel, click ⬜ (Corner Round). The Corner Round dialog box opens.

2. Select **Feature** as the *Select Mode*.

3. Select the cut out as shown in Figure 6–18. (**Cut2** can be selected in the Model Browser instead of selecting it in the graphics window.)

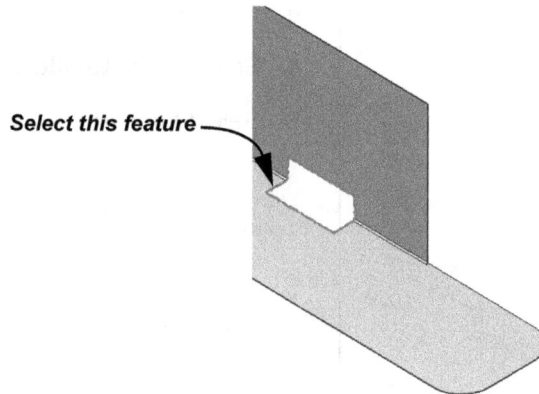

Select this feature

Figure 6–18

4. Change the *Radius* to **10 mm**.

5. Click **OK**. The model displays as shown in Figure 6–19.

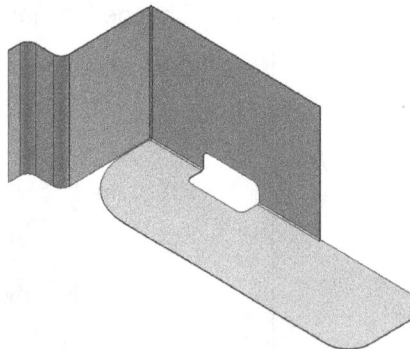

Figure 6–19

Task 3 - Add Corner Chamfers with one distance.

1. In the *Sheet Metal* tab>Modify panel, click ◻ (Corner Chamfer). The Corner Chamfer dialog box opens as shown in Figure 6–20.

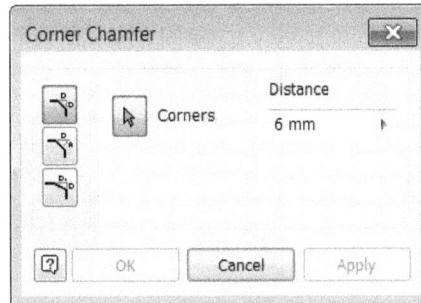

Figure 6–20

2. Select the corners shown in Figure 6–21.

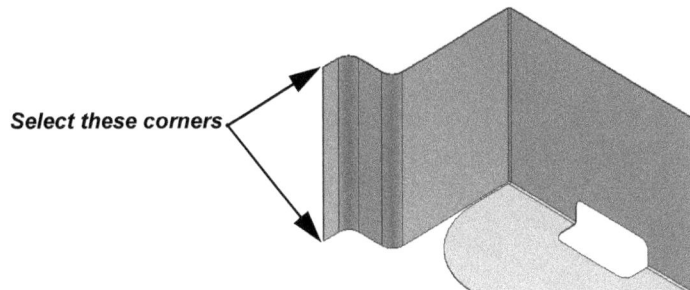

Select these corners

Figure 6–21

3. Change the *Distance* to **10 mm** and click **OK**. The model displays as shown in Figure 6–22.

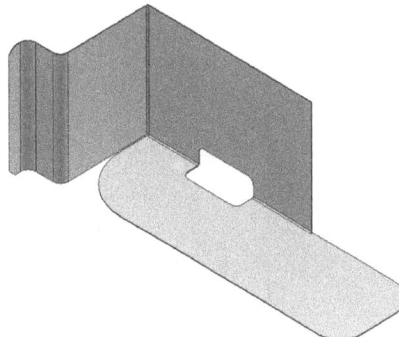

Figure 6–22

Task 4 - Create a Corner Chamfer with two distances.

1. In the *Sheet Metal* tab>Modify panel, click ⬜ (Corner Chamfer). The Corner Chamfer dialog box opens.

2. Click 🔲 (Two Distances) in the Corner Chamfer dialog box and select the corner shown in Figure 6–23.

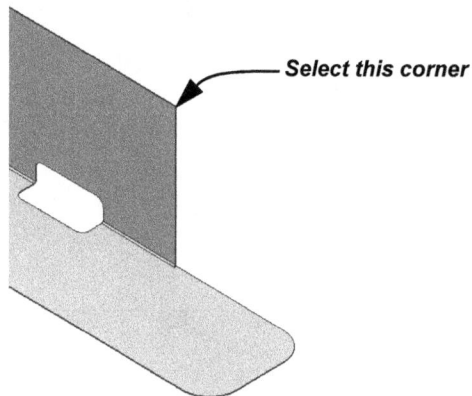

Select this corner

Figure 6–23

3. Enter **75 mm** for *Distance1* and **50 mm** for *Distance2*.

4. Click **OK**. The model displays as shown in Figure 6–24.

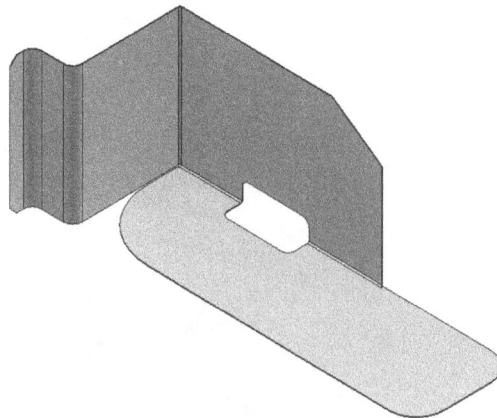

Figure 6–24

5. Save and close the file.

Practice 6b

Corner Rounds and Chamfers II

Practice Objectives

- Create corner rounds using the corner selection method to place the geometry in the model.
- Create corner chamfers using the Two Distance dimensioning method to locate the geometry on a corner.

In this practice, you will add Corner Rounds to the outside and inside corners of a sheet metal part. You will also add a Corner Chamfer using the Two Distances method. The completed model is shown on the right in Figure 6–25.

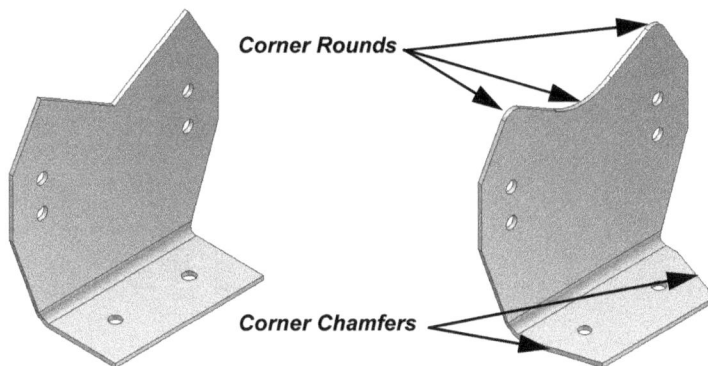

Corner Rounds

Corner Chamfers

Figure 6–25

Task 1 - Create Corner Rounds.

1. Open **Bracket_chamfer_round.ipt**.

2. Add **3 mm** radius corner rounds to the corners shown in Figure 6–26.

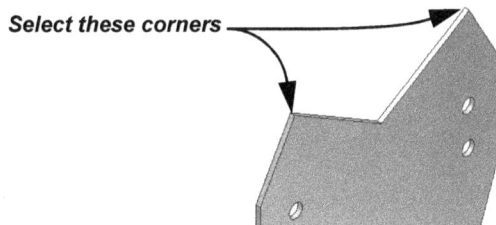

Select these corners

Figure 6–26

3. Add a **15 mm** corner round to the inside corner shown in Figure 6–27.

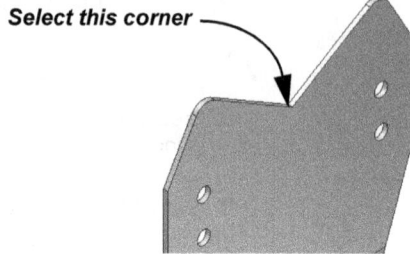

Select this corner

Figure 6–27

Task 2 - Add Corner Chamfers.

1. Add a ⬚ (Two Distances) Corner Chamfer to the corner shown in Figure 6–28. Enter **5 mm** and **15 mm** for the distances. Click ⬚ if required, to apply the 15 mm distance to the shorter edge.

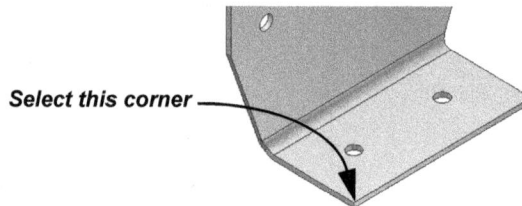

Select this corner

Figure 6–28

2. Add a Corner Chamfer to the other corner using the same distances. The model displays as shown in Figure 6–29.

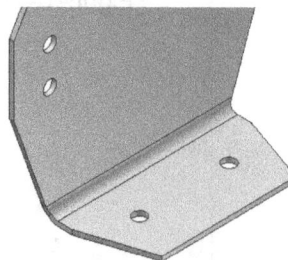

Figure 6–29

3. Save and close the file.

Practice 6c

Corner Rounds and Chamfers III

Practice Objectives

- Create corner rounds using the feature selection method to place the geometry in the model.
- Create corner chamfers using the One Distance and Two Distance dimensioning methods to locate the geometry on a corner.

In this practice, you will add Corner Rounds to a cut out using the Feature select mode. You will then add Corner Chamfers using the One Distance and Two Distances methods. The completed model is shown on the right in Figure 6–30.

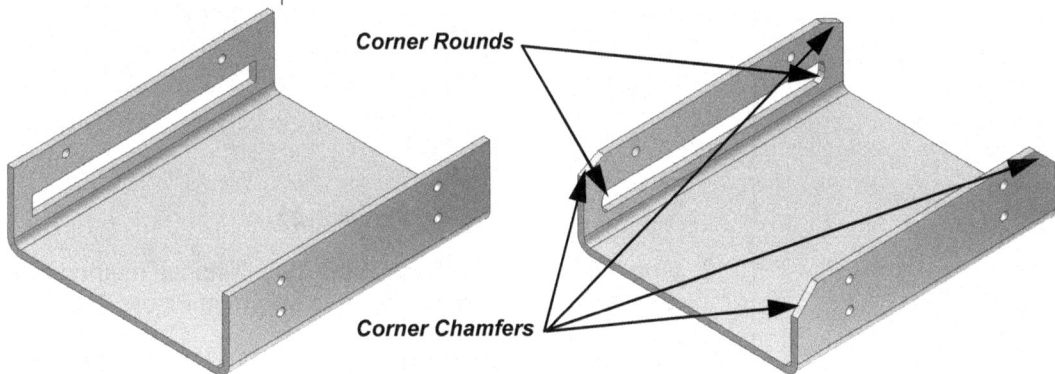

Corner Rounds

Corner Chamfers

Figure 6–30

Task 1 - Create Corner Rounds.

1. Open **Chamfer_round_6.ipt**.

2. Add **3 mm** radius corner rounds to the corners of **Cut1**, shown in Figure 6–31.

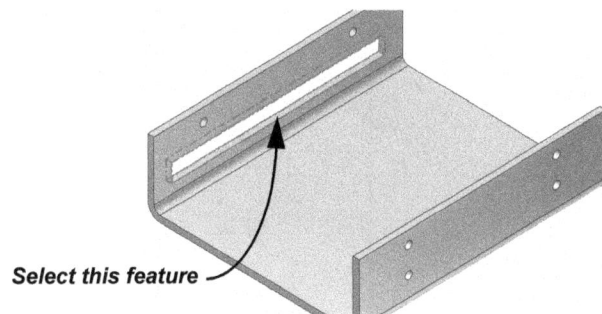

Select this feature

Figure 6–31

Task 2 - Create Corner Chamfers.

1. Add a Corner Chamfer with the One Distance method to add **10 mm** Corner Chamfers to the corners shown in Figure 6–32.

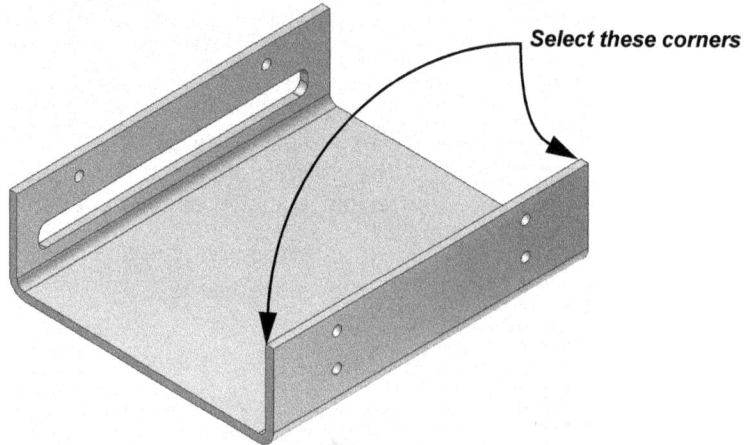

Select these corners

Figure 6–32

2. Add a Corner Chamfer with the Two Distance method to add Corner Chamfers to the corners shown in Figure 6–33. Use

   10 mm and **5 mm** for the distances. Click [icon] if required, to apply the 10 mm distance to the top edge.

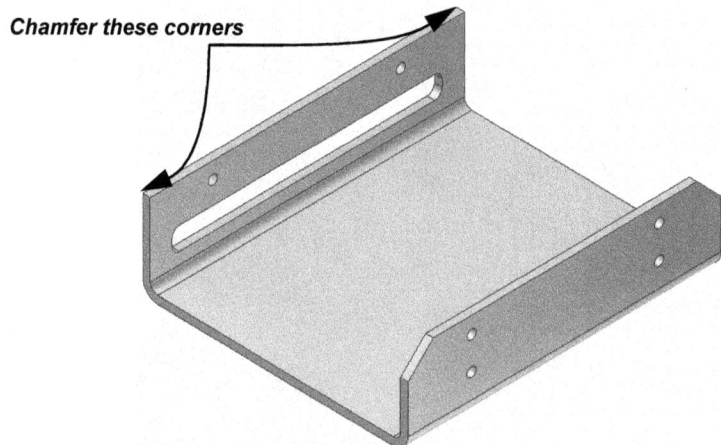

Chamfer these corners

Figure 6–33

The model displays as shown in Figure 6–34.

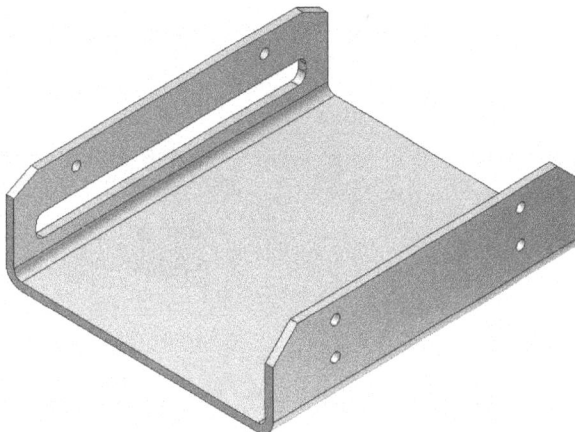

Figure 6–34

3. Save and close the file.

Chapter Review Questions

1. Which of the following best describes a Corner Round sheet metal feature?

   a. A Corner Round is transitional sheet metal geometry that is blended between two profile sketches.

   b. A Corner Round creates a smooth radius on the corners of a sheet metal part.

   c. A Corner Round creates a beveled edge on the corners of a sheet metal part.

   d. A Corner Round creates geometry between two sheet metal faces that are at an angle to each other.

2. Which of the following statements is true of a Corner Round sheet metal feature? (Select all that apply.)

   a. A corner round adds material to a corner.

   b. A corner round removes material from a corner.

   c. Only a single corner can be rounded in the model per corner round feature.

   d. Multiple corners can be rounded in the model per corner round feature.

3. Based on the Corner Round dialog box shown in Figure 6–35, how many Corner Round features are going to be created in the model?

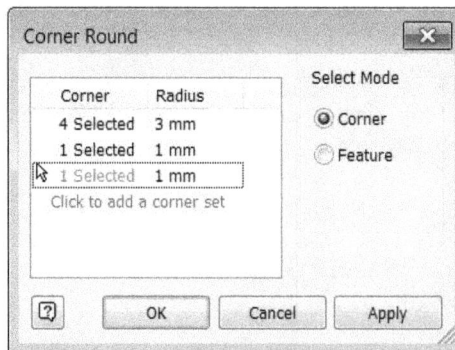

Figure 6–35

   a. 1

   b. 3

   c. 6

4. Which Corner Round selection mode is used to add a radius to all of the edges of a Flange or Face at the same time?

   a. Corner

   b. Feature

   c. All of the above.

5. Which of the following best describes a Corner Chamfer sheet metal feature?

   a. A Corner Chamfer is transitional sheet metal geometry that is blended between two profile sketches.

   b. A Corner Chamfer creates a smooth radius on the corners of a sheet metal part.

   c. A Corner Chamfer creates a beveled edge on the corners of a sheet metal part.

   d. A Corner Chamfer creates geometry between two sheet metal faces that are at an angle to each other.

6. Which Corner Chamfer dimensioning option was used to create the corner chamfer geometry shown in Figure 6–36?

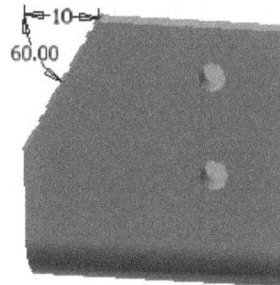

Figure 6–36

   a.

   b.

   c.

Command Summary

Button	Command	Location
	Corner Chamfer	• **Ribbon:** *Sheet Metal* tab>Modify panel
	Corner Round	• **Ribbon:** *Sheet Metal* tab>Modify panel

Sheet Metal Cuts

During fabrication, sheet metal parts often need to have material removed. The Autodesk® Inventor® software provides tools to create Cuts, Holes, and Punches. Each of these features can remove material through the entire thickness of the face, leaving a void in the material. Each type can also remove material partially through a face by setting a specified distance. This creates a recess without deforming the face. Punches can be used to create complex-shaped cuts that can go through the entire thickness of the face, or deform it, leaving an embossed area.

Learning Objectives in this Chapter

- Remove material from a sheet metal model using a sketched profile.
- Create a straight hole that removes material from a sheet metal model.
- Use a punch tool file to remove material from a sheet metal model.
- Create geometry and customizable parameters that represent a punch tool for use in a sheet metal model.
- Remove material from a sheet metal model by splitting solid geometry where it intersects an extruded surface.

7.1 Creating Cut Features

Cut features for sheet metal are similar to extruded cuts for solid parts where they begin with a sketched profile. You draw and constrain a closed loop, and then use the **Cut** command to remove material. Cuts can be created in the Folded or Unfolded view of the model. Typically, Cut features use the Thickness parameter value as their depth. Figure 7–1 shows a sheet metal part with two Cut features. Each Cut has its own sketched profile, but you can have multiple sketches on the same plane or use a shared sketch, as you would for solid models.

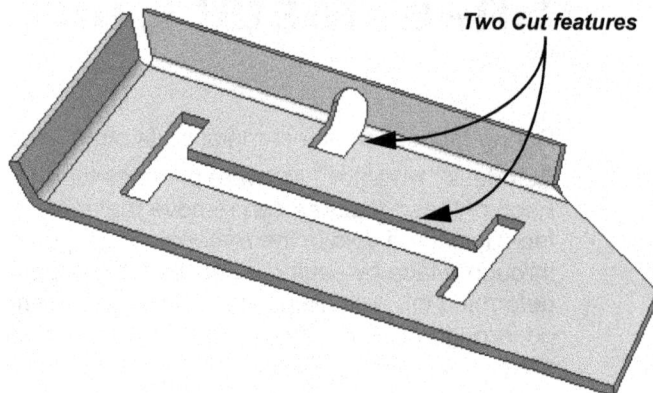

Two Cut features

Figure 7–1

General Steps

Use the following general steps to create a Cut feature:

1. Create a sketch for the Cut feature.
2. Start the creation of the feature.
3. Select the Shape options.
4. Select the Extents options.
5. Complete the feature.

Step 1 - Create a sketch for the Cut feature.

Create a closed loop sketch to use as the profile of the Cut, as shown in Figure 7–2. Add dimensions and constraints as required.

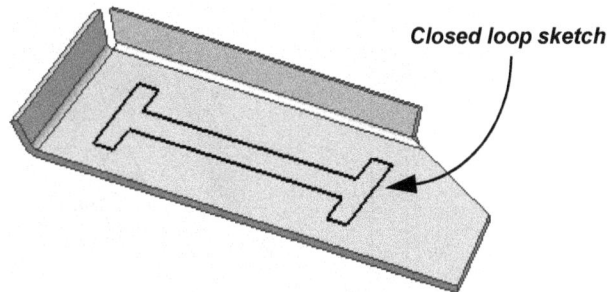

Closed loop sketch

Figure 7–2

Step 2 - Start the creation of the feature.

In the *Sheet Metal* tab>Modify panel, click ▢ (Cut). The Cut dialog box opens as shown in Figure 7–3.

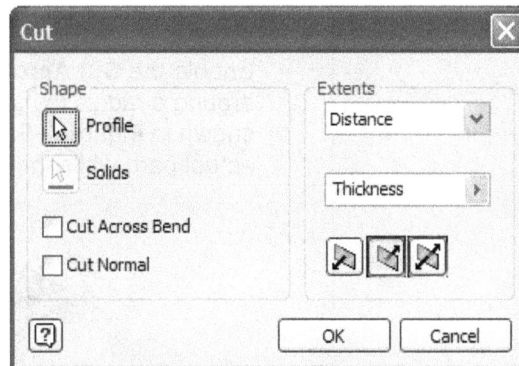

Figure 7–3

Step 3 - Select the Shape options.

Select a Profile for the Cut. Ensure that [cursor icon] (Profile) is active and select the area of the profile to use for the Cut's shape, as shown in Figure 7–4.

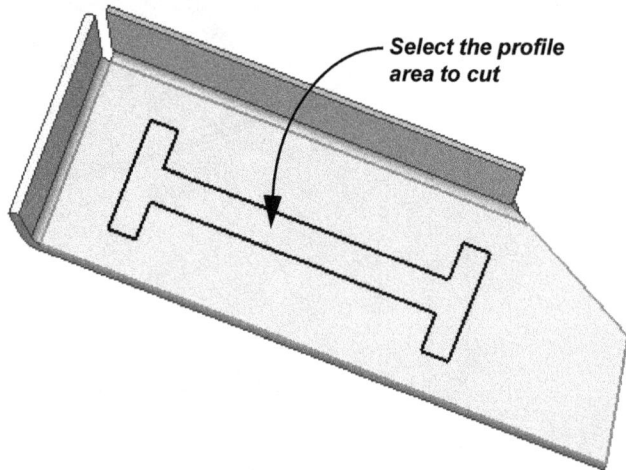

Select the profile area to cut

Figure 7–4

If the profile can be wrapped around a bend to cut through more than one face, consider the following:

- Enable the **Cut Across Bend** option to wrap the profile around a radius to the next face and cut through that face, as shown in Figure 7–5. This type of cut would be made on an actual part, while the sheet metal is still flat before bending.

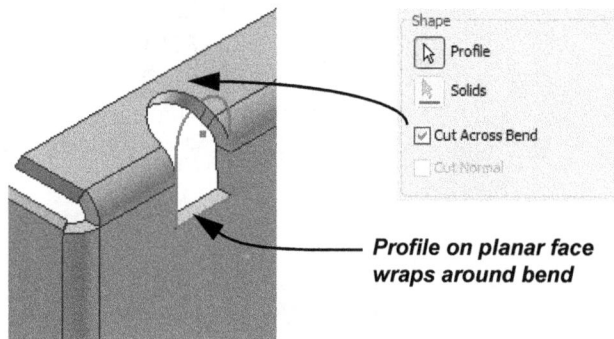

Profile on planar face wraps around bend

Figure 7–5

- Disable the **Cut Across Bend** option to extrude the feature normal to the sketch plane, as shown in Figure 7–6. The resulting shape only matches the profile as far as the depth of the Cut feature (dependent on the *Extent* option that is used).

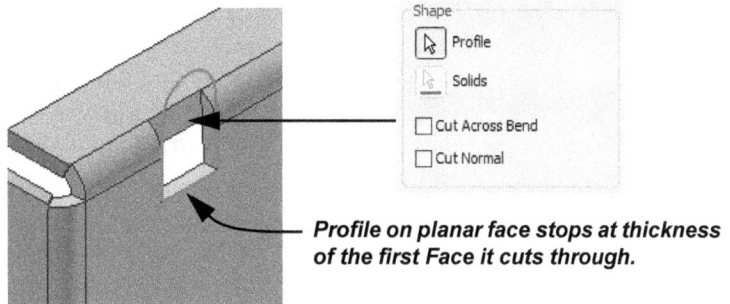

Profile on planar face stops at thickness of the first Face it cuts through.

Figure 7–6

To customize how a cut is extruded through sheet metal geometry over bent geometry (as shown in Figure 7–7), use the **Cut Normal** option.

- When **Cut Normal** is disabled, the cut is created normal to the sketch plane, as shown in Figure 7–8.

- When **Cut Normal** is enabled, the cut is created normal to the face of the geometry, not just the sketch plane, as shown on the right of Figure 7–9.

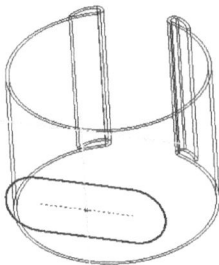

Slot shaped sketch for use as a Cut feature.

Figure 7–7

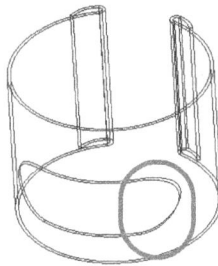

Cut created normal to the sketch plane.

Figure 7–8

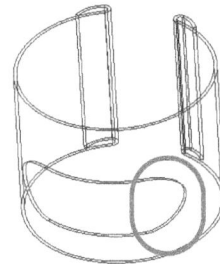

Cut created using the Cut Normal option to cut normal to the face of the geometry.

Figure 7–9

> ## Step 4 - Select the Extents options.

Extent Options When not Cutting Across Bends

When the **Cut Across Bend** option is not selected, five Extents options are available to control the depth of the Cut. These are the same options that are available for the **Extrude** command. Each option requires different input. The types include **Distance**, **To Next**, **To**, **From To**, and **All**.

Distance

The **Distance** option is the default. It requires a value for the depth and a direction and is perpendicular to the sketch plane. Using the **Thickness** parameter as the depth, this option cuts through the face on which the sketch is created to the specified depth, as shown in Figure 7–10.

*Using a value smaller then the **Thickness** parameter enables you to create a cut that does not go through the entire part.*

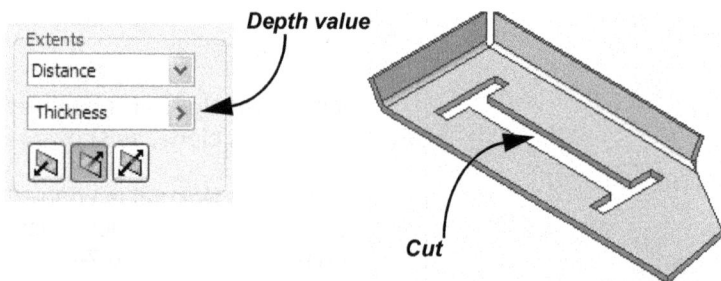

Figure 7–10

There are three options for selecting the direction of the Cut: (Direction), (Flip Direction), and (Both Directions).

To Next

The **To Next** option cuts the material toward the next face in the direction you specify, as shown in Figure 7–11. This is useful for a Cut that does not need to go all of the way through a part.

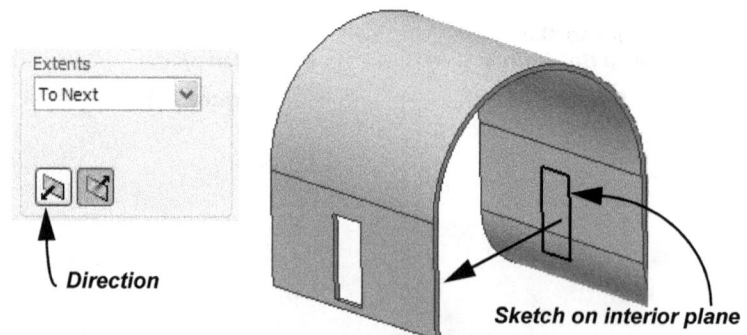

Figure 7–11

To

The **To** option projects the profile toward a selected plane or face. The Cut passes through the part until it reaches the selected termination plane, as shown in Figure 7–12.

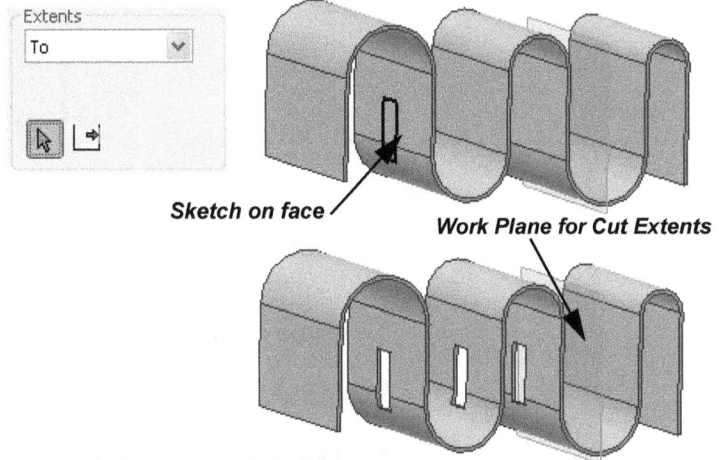

Figure 7–12

From To

The **From To** option removes material between two selected faces or planes, as shown in Figure 7–13.

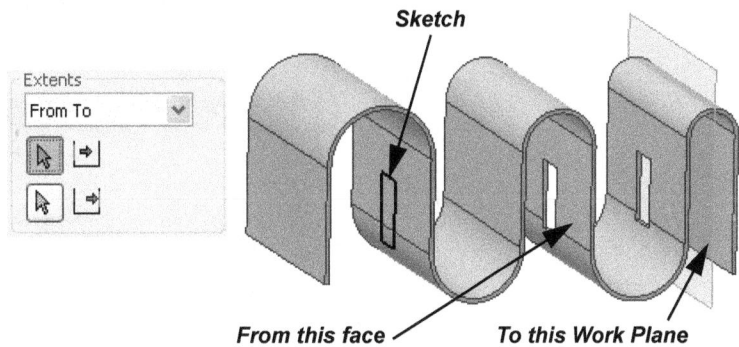

Figure 7–13

All

The **All** option removes all material through the entire part in the specified direction, as shown in Figure 7–14.

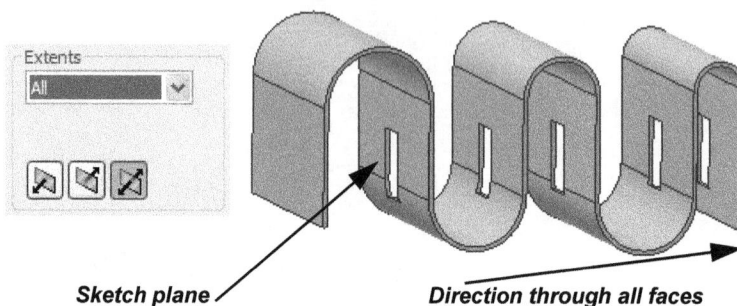

Sketch plane   **Direction through all faces**

Figure 7–14

The three options for selecting the direction of the Cut include:

⬈ (Direction), ⬈ (Flip Direction), and ⬈ (Both Directions).

Distance Options for Cutting Across Bends

The *Extents* options are not available if you select the **Cut Across Bend** option. In this case, **Distance** becomes the default option and **Thickness** the value. The cut applies across a Bend.

You can accept the default value, enter a new value, or click ⬈ to display the list of *Distance* values, as shown in Figure 7–15.

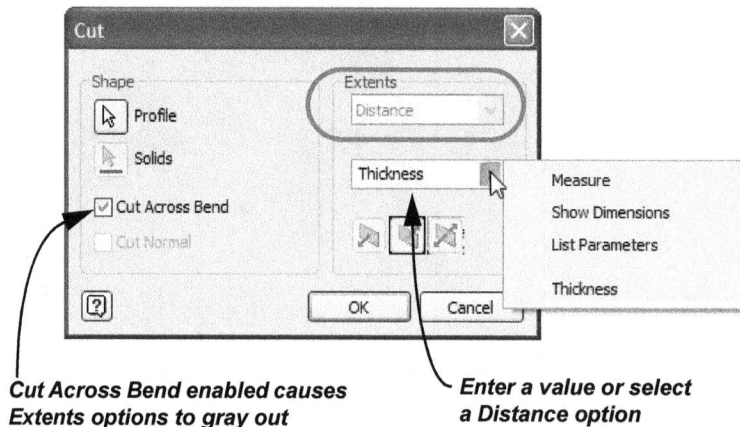

Cut Across Bend enabled causes   *Enter a value or select*
Extents options to gray out   *a Distance option*

Figure 7–15

Two examples of *Distance* settings are shown in Figure 7–16.

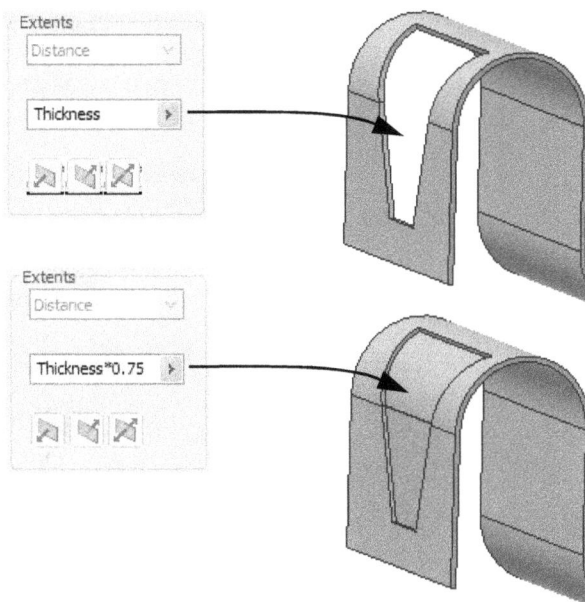

Figure 7–16

Step 5 - Complete the feature.

Click **OK** to complete the Cut feature. Alternatively, you can right-click and select **OK (Enter)** to complete the feature

Hint: Projecting Folded Geometry

During the design process, you might need to create another
sketch to use when creating a Cut with the **Cut Across Bend**
option. Positioning sketch geometry for the Cut might require
you to reference areas on the part that have already been
folded away from the sketch plane.

The **Project Flat Pattern** command enables you to create an
unfolded representation of flanges or other features and project
them into the sketch, as shown in Figure 7–17. This enables
you to dimension to the edges of a feature as if they were
unfolded, while the features remain in their folded position.

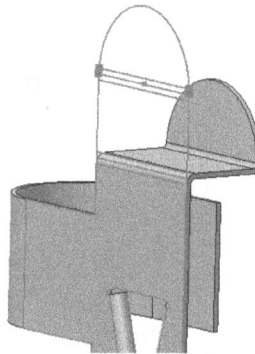

Figure 7–17

The **Project Flat Pattern** command is found in the Project
Geometry drop-down list in the Create panel, as shown in
Figure 7–18.

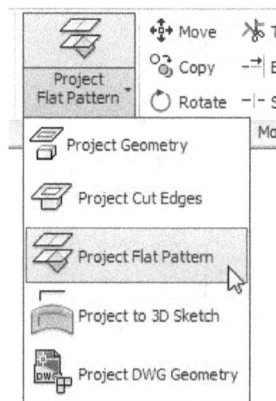

Figure 7–18

7.2 Creating Straight Holes

Holes remove material from the model. To create holes in sheet metal you can use the **Hole** option. The **Hole** option in the sheet metal environment includes the same options as in the solid modeling environment.

General Steps

Use the following general steps to create a Straight Hole feature:

1. Create a sketch (optional).
2. Start the creation of the Hole feature.
3. Select placement references.
4. Define the type of Hole.
5. Define the dimensions of the feature.
6. Define the depth of the feature.
7. Complete the feature.

Step 1 - Create a sketch (optional).

If you plan to use the **From Sketch** placement method to place the hole in your model, a sketch with selectable points is required. However, a work point is required for the **From Point** placement method. No sketch or work point is required for the **Concentric** or **Linear** placement method.

Step 2 - Start the creation of the Hole feature.

In the *Sheet Metal* tab>Modify panel, click (Hole). The Hole dialog box opens as shown in Figure 7–19.

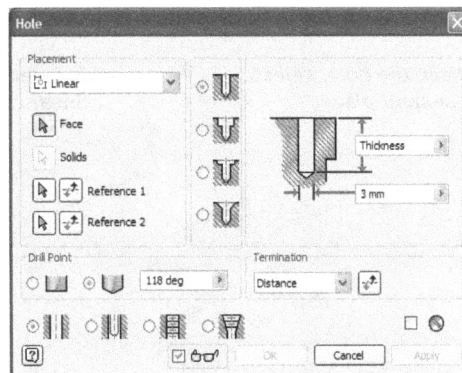

Figure 7–19

Step 3 - Select placement references.

Holes are placed on the model by referencing existing features using one of the following four placement methods: **From Sketch**, **Linear**, **Concentric**, or **On Point**. Examples are shown in Figure 7–20.

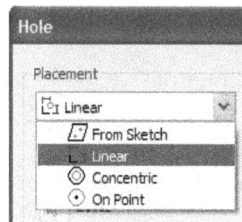

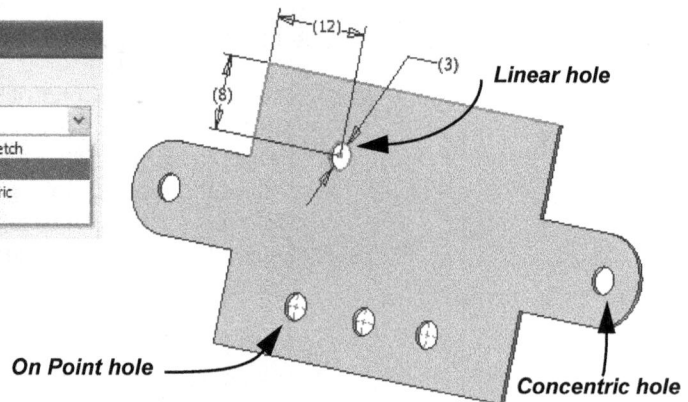

Figure 7–20

Linear Placement

How To: Select Placement References for Linear Hole Placement

1. Select **Linear** in the Placement drop-down list.

2. Click ⬚ (Face) and select a planar face or Work Plane as the placement plane for the Hole, as shown in Figure 7–21. Once selected, the hole is automatically placed.

3. Click ⬚ (Reference 1) and select the first linear edge to locate the Hole on the model, as shown in Figure 7–21.

4. Click ⬚ (Reference 2) and select the second linear edge to locate the Hole on the model, as shown in Figure 7–21.

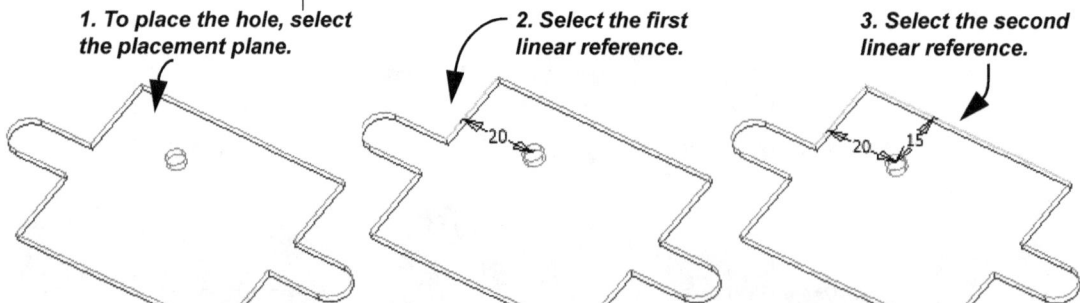

1. To place the hole, select the placement plane.

2. Select the first linear reference.

3. Select the second linear reference.

Figure 7–21

Concentric Placement

How To: Select Placement References for Concentric Hole Placement

1. Select **Concentric** in the Placement drop-down list as shown in Figure 7–22.

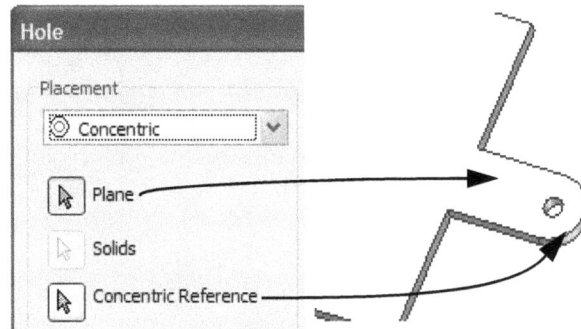

Figure 7–22

2. Click ⬚ (Plane) and select a planar face or Work Plane as the placement plane for the Hole. Once selected, the hole automatically placed.

3. Click ⬚ (Concentric Reference) to select a circular edge or a cylindrical face to reference the Hole center.

From Sketch Placement

To create a hole with the **From Sketch** placement option, the hole's center must already exist in the model. The hole center is defined in a sketch with a point, or with sketched entities where the end points or centers of an existing sketch can be used, as shown in Figure 7–23.

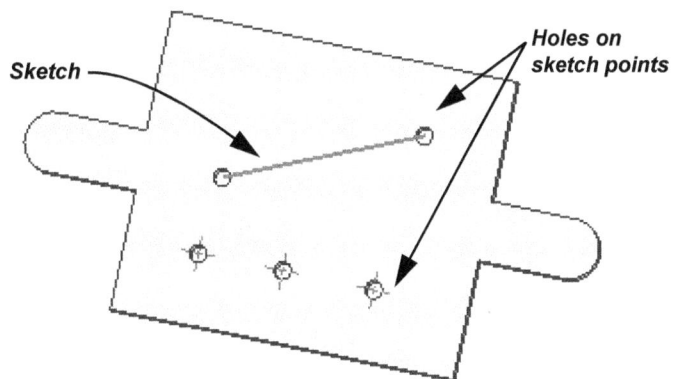

Figure 7–23

How To: Select Placement References for From Sketch Hole Placement

1. Select **From Sketch** in the Placement drop-down list as shown in Figure 7–24.

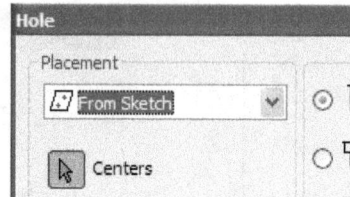

Figure 7–24

2. Click ⬚ (Centers) to select the location for the centers of the Holes. You can select sketch points, end points of lines and arcs, and centers of arcs and circles, etc.

On Point Placement

The **On Point** option places a Hole coincident with a Work Point and is located with respect to an Axis, edge, or Work Plane.

How To: Select Placement References for On Point Hole Placement

1. Select **On Point** in the Placement drop-down list as shown in Figure 7–25.

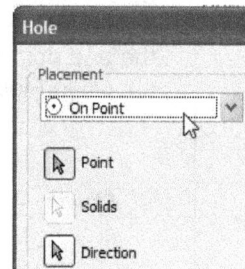

Figure 7–25

2. Click ⬚ (Point) to select a Work Point to set as the center of the hole.

3. Click ⬚ (Direction) to specify the direction of the axis of the hole. If you select a planar face or Work Plane, the hole axis is perpendicular to it. If you select an edge or Axis, the hole axis is parallel to it.

In the example shown in Figure 7–26, the center of the hole is placed on the Work Point, and the hole axis is perpendicular to the face of the model.

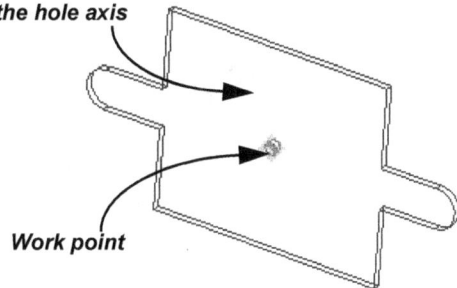

Figure 7–26

Step 4 - Define the type of Hole.

Four types of holes can be created. Since sheet metal material is typically thin, the **Drilled** type of hole is commonly used and you probably do not need to create holes with counterbores, countersinks, or spotfaces. The 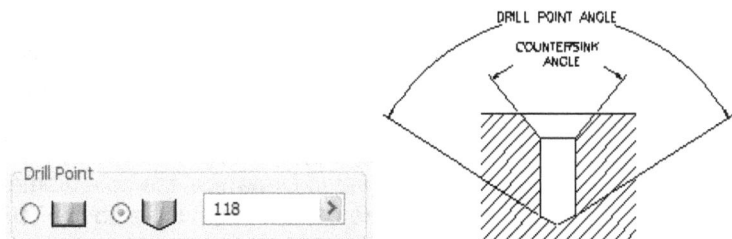 (Drilled) option is the default hole type. Based on the type of hole that is selected, the options in the dialog box update. You can create a hole with a flat or angled drill point, as shown in Figure 7–27. In the case of sheet metal, where holes are cut through the entire part, either option is appropriate.

Figure 7–27

You can define the following hole properties: **Simple**, **Clearance**, **Tapped**, and **Taper Tapped**. Only Simple and Clearance holes apply to sheet metal fabrication.

Simple Hole

To create a Simple hole, click [icon] at the bottom of the Hole dialog box. No additional options need to be defined for Simple holes.

Clearance Hole

To create a Clearance hole that fits a selected fastener, click

[icon] in the Holes dialog box. In the *Fastener* area, select the *Standard*, *Fastener Type*, *Size*, and *Fit*, as shown in Figure 7–28.

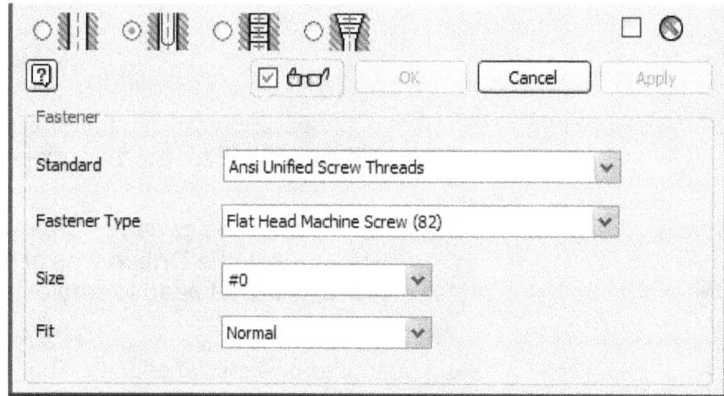

Figure 7–28

Step 5 - Define the dimensions of the feature.

To set the dimensions of the hole, enter values on the right side in the dialog box, as shown in Figure 7–29. The values available depend on the type of hole. If the *Termination* is set to **Through All**, only the hole diameter option is available. If the *Termination* is set to **Distance**, the hole diameter and hole depth is available. The default depth is set to the **Thickness** parameter.

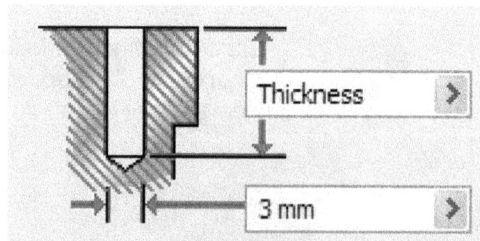

Figure 7–29

Step 6 - Define the depth of the feature.

The *Termination* options are as follows:

Distance	Creates a blind hole at a specified depth.
Through All	Creates a hole through the entire model.
To	Creates a blind hole that terminates at a selected plane or at the extension of the selected plane.

Step 7 - Complete the feature.

Once the references have been defined, click **OK** in the dialog box to complete the Hole feature. Alternatively, you can right-click and select **OK (Enter)** or press <Enter> to complete the feature.

7.3 Using Punch Tool Features

When modeling sheet metal components, you might place the same feature(s) multiple times, either in the same part or different parts. The **Punch Tool** command enables you to place a saved feature or a group of features in one command. Common uses for punch tools include keyways, slots, and cuts for specific shape connectors. When placing a Punch feature in a model, you can control the placement and size of the feature based on the definition of the Punch.

Punch Tools use iFeatures to store and place geometry. The difference between iFeatures and Punches is that Punches require a sketch with a point or selectable point (end point of line, center point of circle, etc.) to place the feature. Both use a file with an IDE extension to store the geometry. The Autodesk Inventor software includes a sample library of iFeatures and Punches.

Figure 7–30 shows a sheet metal part with an iFeature (**D-Sub connector.ide**) added with the Punch Tool.

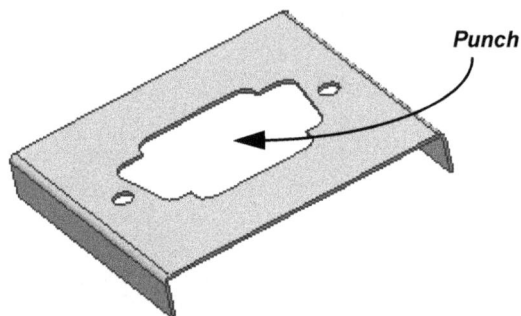

Figure 7–30

General Steps

Use the following general steps to place a Punch feature:

1. Create a sketch to place the punch.
2. Start the creation of the Punch feature.
3. Select Preview, Geometry, and Size options.
4. Complete the feature.

Step 1 - Create a sketch to place the punch.

Create a sketch that has geometry for locating the Punch. Add dimensions and constraints, as required. The sketch can include one or more points, or other geometry. End points, center points, and midpoints can all be used as shown in Figure 7–31. If a point is included in the sketch, it is selected automatically when placing a punch.

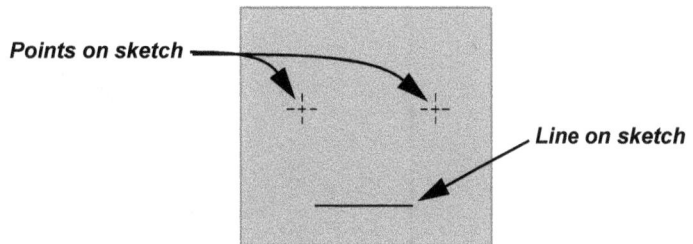

Points on sketch

Line on sketch

Figure 7–31

Step 2 - Start the creation of the Punch feature.

In the *Sheet Metal* tab>Modify panel, click ⊔ (Punch Tool). The PunchTool Directory opens as shown in Figure 7–32.

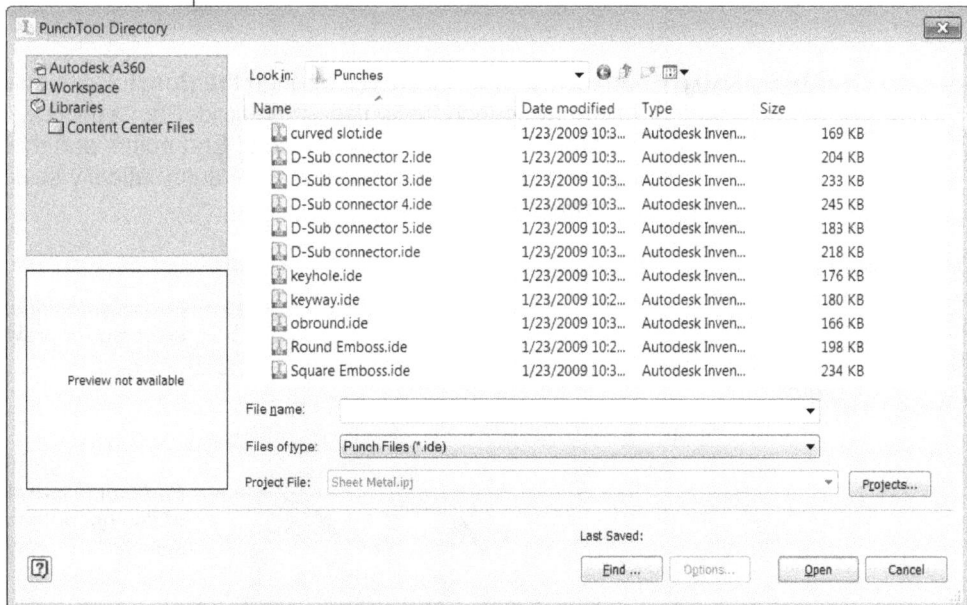

Figure 7–32

Select a Punch File (IDE) to use and click **Open**. The PunchTool dialog box opens as shown in Figure 7–33. The Punch file contains the geometry to use, the parameters to control the size of the feature, the Punch ID, and the representation to use in the flat pattern.

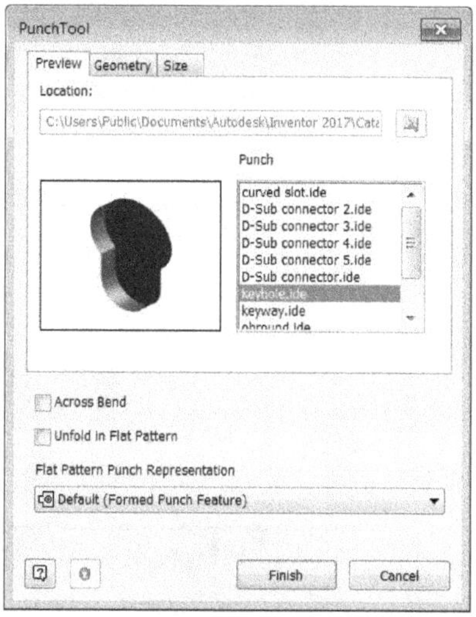

Figure 7–33

Step 3 - Select Preview, Geometry, and Size options.

Preview

In the *Preview* tab, scroll through the Punch list to select an alternate punch file to use, if required. Points included in the sketch are automatically selected. End points and midpoints of geometry can be used, but are not automatically selected, as shown in Figure 7–34.

Drag the PunchTool dialog box to the side if required, to display a preview of the Punch using your sketch.

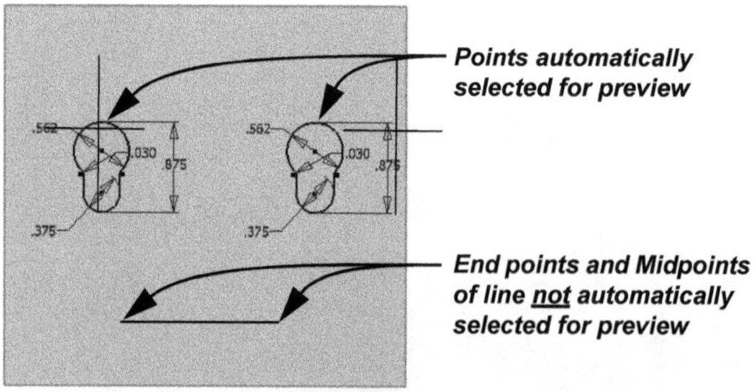

Figure 7–34

Punch features can also be applied across a bend. To create the punch across a bend, select **Across Bend** in the *Preview* tab, as shown in Figure 7–35. The models shown on the right display a punch feature that was created with and without the **Across Bend** option selected.

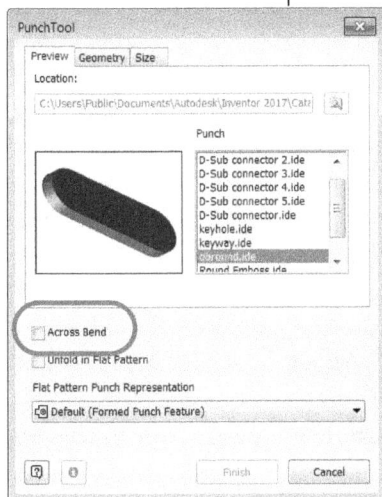

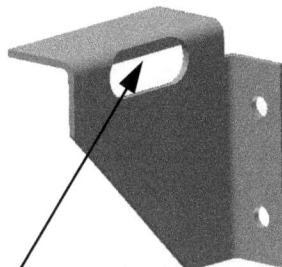

Clear the Across Bend option to ensure that the punch does not continue across a bend.

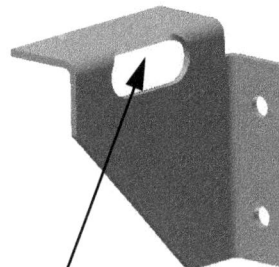

The punch was created across the bend using the Across Bend option.

Figure 7–35

Geometry

Flat Pattern options will be covered later in this student guide.

In the *Geometry* tab, click (Centers) to add or remove locations for the Punch. The number of Centers selected is displayed in brackets adjacent to the Centers selection button.

- Click on an end point or midpoint to add the Punch to that point.

- Drag the selection window from right to left to include all of the entities that touch any part of the selection box.

- Drag from right to left to only include the entities that are completely within the selection box.

• To remove points from the punch selection set, hold <Ctrl> and select the points to be removed. Alternatively, you can drag windows around any previously selected points to clear them, as shown in Figure 7–36.

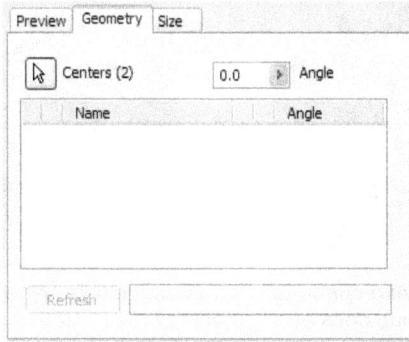

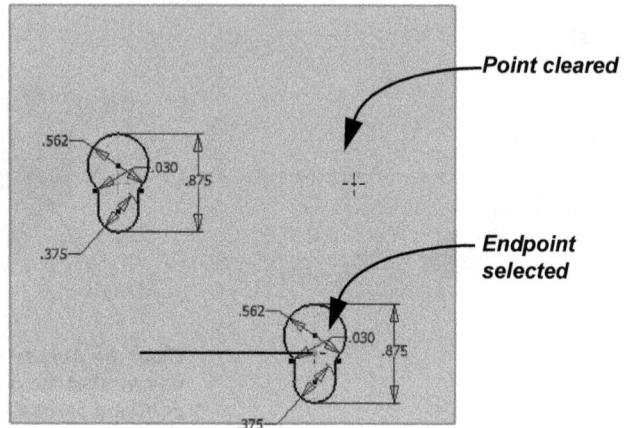

Figure 7–36

Enter a value in the *Angle* field to rotate the Punch position, as required. If more than one location exists for the same instance of the Punch, all locations are assigned the same angle.

Size

The *Size* tab in the PunchTool dialog box (shown in Figure 7–37), enables you to edit the size values, as required. The parameters available are determined when the Punch file is created.

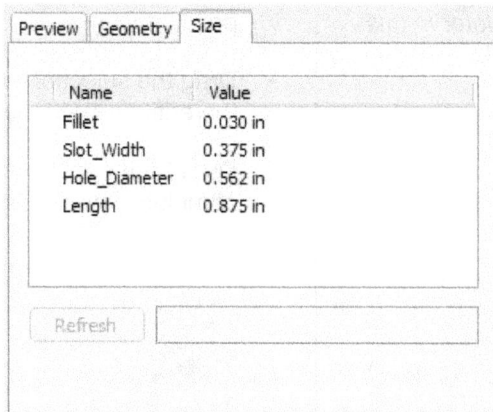

Figure 7–37

Step 4 - Complete the feature.

Click **Finish** to complete the Punch feature. Alternatively, you can right-click and select **OK (Enter)** to complete the feature. The part displays as shown in Figure 7–38. The Punch is listed an iFeature in the Model Browser.

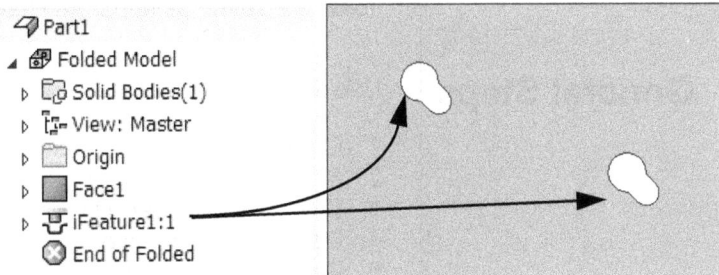

Figure 7–38

7.4 Creating a Punch Tool

To create your own Punch Tool file, use the **Extract iFeature** command. The features used for a Punch Tool should be created in a sheet metal file and must contain a sketched point. Renamed parameters are useful to help you identify the dimensions you want to include in the Punch Tool file. Punch Tools are saved as separate files with the .IDE extension.

General Steps

Use the following general steps to create Punch Tool file:

1. Create feature(s) and parameters.
2. Start the creation of the Punch Tool file.
3. Select the feature(s) in the Model Browser.
4. Define the Punch file.
5. Save the Punch file.

Step 1 - Create feature(s) and parameters.

In a sheet metal file, create a face and the features required for the Punch Tool. You can also use an existing part that contains the required features. You can use a combination of sheet metal features and standard features. An example of a feature used to create a Punch Tool is shown in Figure 7–39.

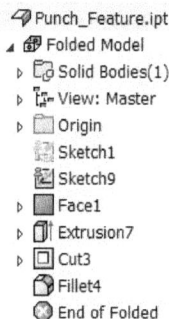

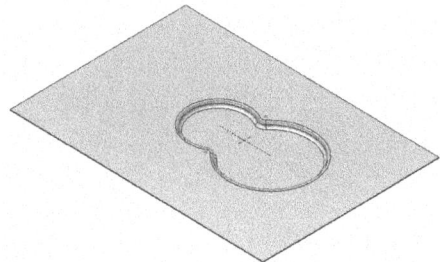

Figure 7–39

The sketch for the first feature included must include a point. This point is used to position the Punch geometry when the feature is placed using the Punch Tool.

It is recommended that you rename any parameters that you plan to include in the Punch. This makes it easier to identify the parameters in the Extract iFeature dialog box.

Step 2 - Start the creation of the Punch Tool file.

In the *Manage* tab>Author panel, click (Extract iFeature). The Extract iFeature dialog box opens.

Step 3 - Select the feature(s) in the Model Browser.

Select the feature(s) in the Model Browser that you want to include in the new Punch Tool. The selected features are listed in the *Selected Features* area in the Extract iFeature dialog box, as shown in Figure 7–40. Reference geometry and parameters are listed below each feature.

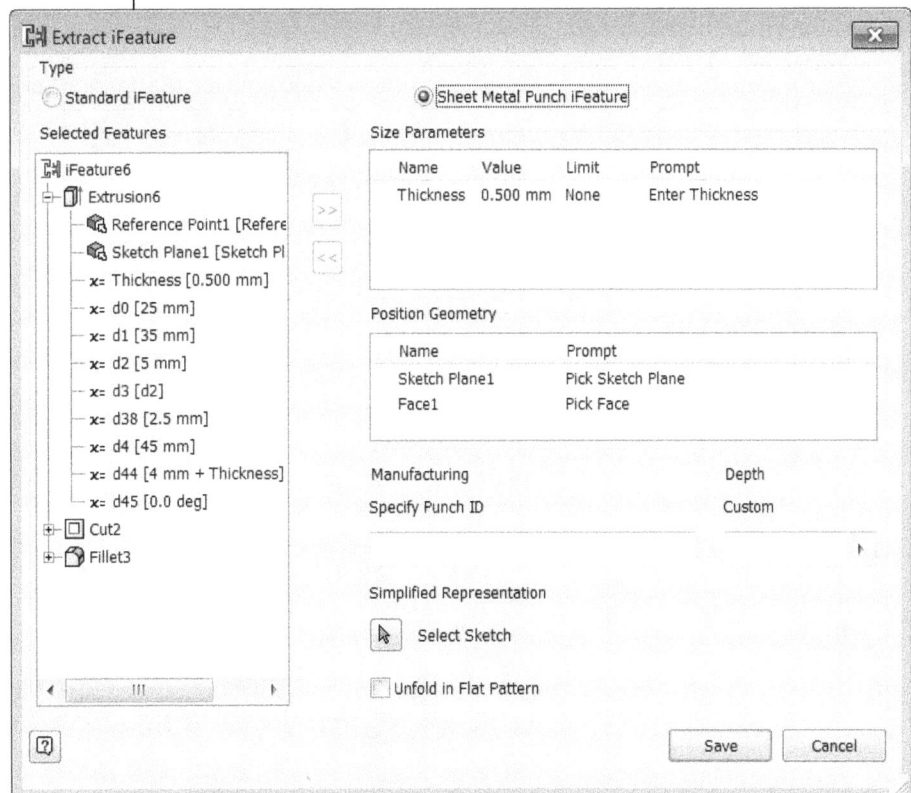

Figure 7–40

Step 4 - Define the Punch file.

Select the **Sheet Metal Punch iFeature** option in the *Type* area in the dialog box. This indicates that the iFeature file (IDE) that is created is used with the Sheet Metal Punch Tool. It also activates the *Manufacturing* and *Depth* areas in the dialog box. These areas are only used for Punch Tools.

Parameters listed in the *Size Parameters* area can be modified when the Punch Tool is used in a model. Any parameters that were renamed are automatically added to the *Size Parameters* area as shown in Figure 7–41.

Size Parameters			
Name	Value	Limit	Prompt
Thickness	0.500 mm	None	Enter Thickness

Figure 7–41

You can add any parameters used in the creation of selected features. In the *Selected Features* area, select the required parameter and click ⬚ (Add) to move them to the Size Parameters list on the right. Click ⬚ (Remove) to delete parameters in the Size Parameters list.

- The *Name* field controls the name of the parameter.

- The *Value* field controls the default value of the parameter.

- The *Limit* field controls the acceptable values for the parameter. **None** enables any numeric value for the parameter. **Range** places an upper and lower limit for the value of the parameter. **List** limits the values to a user-specified list of values.

- The *Prompt* field displays the text that you will be prompted when placing the iFeature. Each parameter can have a unique prompt. Ensure that a descriptive prompt is used to help identify the parameter's intent.

Planes or faces used to position the selected features are listed in the *Position Geometry* area, as shown in Figure 7–42.

Position Geometry	
Name	Prompt
Sketch Plane1	Pick Sketch Plane
Face1	Pick Face

Figure 7–42

You can add other reference geometry to the list or combine reference geometry. The *Position Geometry* area controls the placement of the features in the model.

The *Manufacturing* area specifies the *Punch ID* and *Simplified Representation* for the Punch, as shown in Figure 7–43.

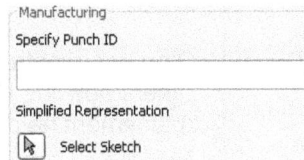

Figure 7–43

- The Punch ID is used in drawing tables and annotations.

- The Simplified Representation is used in the flat pattern of

  the model. To specify a Simplified Representation, click and select a sketch. The sketch must contain a point.

The *Depth* area, as shown in Figure 7–44, defines a depth. Depth does not affect geometry, but is used in drawing tables and annotations.

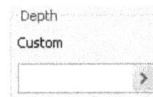

Figure 7–44

New
in **2017**

The **Unfold in Flat Pattern** checkbox enables you to specify that the punch should be unfolded in the Flat Pattern as long as it meets the following criteria:

- The punch geometry could be unfolded if it were created as standard sheet metal features.

- The punch geometry does not result in deformed shapes (e.g., louver geometry results in deformation and cannot be unfolded).

- The **Unfold in Flat Pattern** checkbox is also selected in the Punch Tool dialog box when placing the punch feature.

Step 5 - Save the Punch file.

Click **Save** in the Extract iFeature dialog box, or right-click and select **Save**. The Save As dialog box opens. Browse to the folder in which you want to store the Punch file, enter a name for the file, and click **Save**.

Placement Help

You can create a separate document to help describe to future users how the Punch is to be placed and used. To attach a placement help file, open the Punch's .IDE file and in the *Tools* tab>Insert panel, click (Insert Object). Select the **Create from File** option and click **Browse** to browse to the document. Click **Open** when you have selected the required document.

7.5 Cuts Using Surfaces

When modeling sheet metal geometry, closed section cuts can be used. However, there might be situations in which a sheet metal cut feature does not provide the required result. In these situations, consider using the **Cut** tool in the *3D Model* tab to create an extruded surface and use that surface to cut the model.

The model shown on the left in Figure 7–45 was created using sheet metal model features. The model on the right shows the resulting geometry that is required. To create this curved cut, a surface and split feature must be added to the sheet metal model.

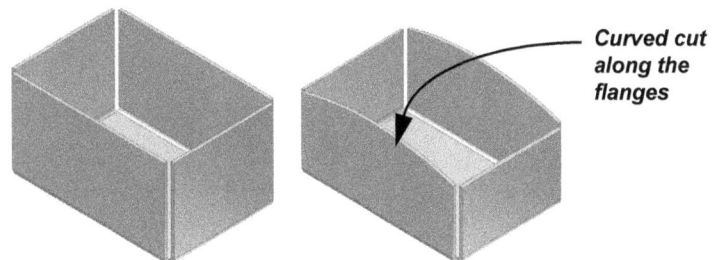

Curved cut along the flanges

Figure 7–45

General Steps

Use the following general steps to create a cut using a surface in a sheet metal model:

1. Create a sketch to represent the required cut.
2. Create an extruded surface.
3. Split the sheet metal model.
4. Complete the feature.

Step 1 - Create a sketch to represent the required cut.

Create a sketch in the sheet metal model that represents the cut to be made through the sheet metal model. To create the section for the cut, you use the standard sketching tools. The section can be open or closed, unlike a sheet metal cut, which must be a closed section. The sketch shown in Figure 7–46 was created on an origin plane through the center of the sheet metal model.

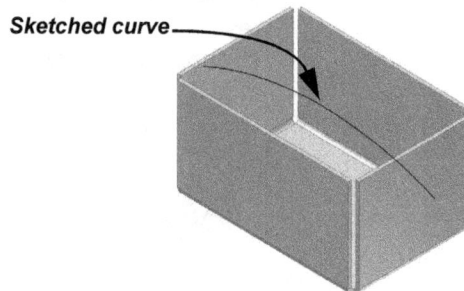

Sketched curve

Figure 7–46

Step 2 - Create an extruded surface.

Once the sketch has been created, select the *3D Model* tab> Create panel and click (Extrude). In the Extrude dialog box, set the *Output* option to (Surface) and select the sketch for the profile. The extrude should extend through all surfaces of the model that are to be removed. The surface shown in Figure 7–47 was extruded on both sides of the sketch plane and extended using the **Between** option.

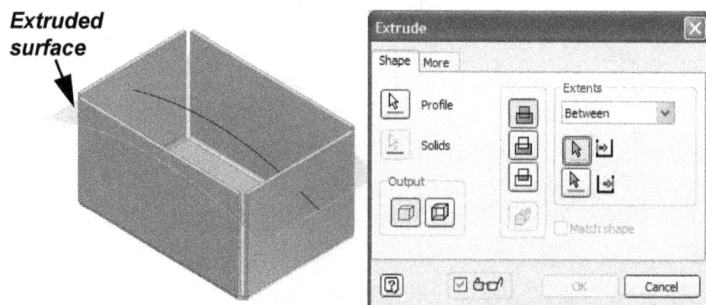

Extruded surface

Figure 7–47

Step 3 - Split the sheet metal model.

To complete the geometry, split the sheet metal geometry using the extruded surface. In the *3D Model* tab>Modify panel, click

(Split). Click (Trim Solid) for the split method. The Split dialog box opens as shown in Figure 7–48.

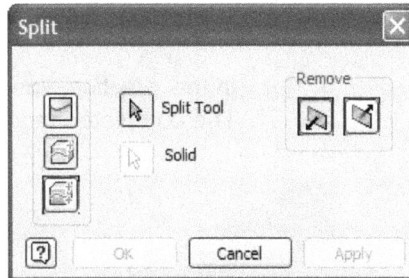

Figure 7–48

Select the extruded surface as the **Split Tool** to define where the split occurs and toggle the sides to remove, as required.

Step 4 - Complete the feature.

Click **OK** to complete the split. Alternatively, you can right-click and select **OK (Enter)** to complete the feature. The model in Figure 7–49 shows the completed sheet metal geometry.

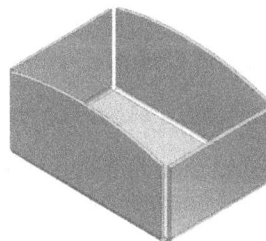

*Extruded surface has
been removed for clarity*

Figure 7–49

Practice 7a | Creating Cut Features I

Practice Objectives

- Locate a hole feature on a sheet metal model based on the location of a sketched point.
- Remove material from a sheet metal model using a sketched profile.
- Use the **Cut Across Bend** cut option to vary the geometry that results when a cut feature is added across bend geometry.

In this practice, you will place a Hole and several Cut features. The completed model is shown on the right in Figure 7–50.

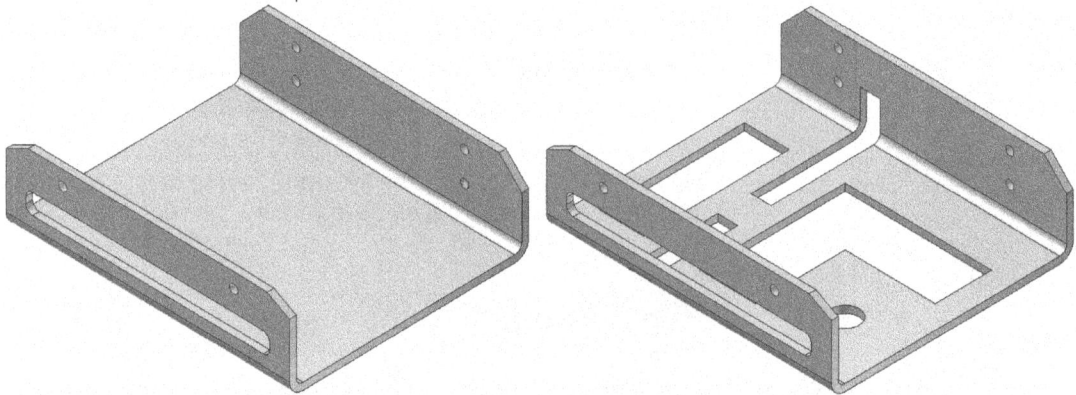

Figure 7–50

Task 1 - Create a Hole feature.

1. Open **Chamfer_round_7.ipt**.

2. Create a sketch on the large flat surface inside the part.

3. Add a point to the sketch and dimension it **25 mm** from the two nearest edges (use the inside of the bend). Finish the sketch.

4. In the *Sheet Metal* tab>Modify panel, click 🔲 (Hole). The point is automatically selected. Set the *Termination* to **Through All** and the diameter to **12.5 mm**. Click **OK**.

Task 2 - Create cut Features.

1. Create a new sketch on the same face. Sketch and constrain the profile as shown in Figure 7–51. Finish the sketch.

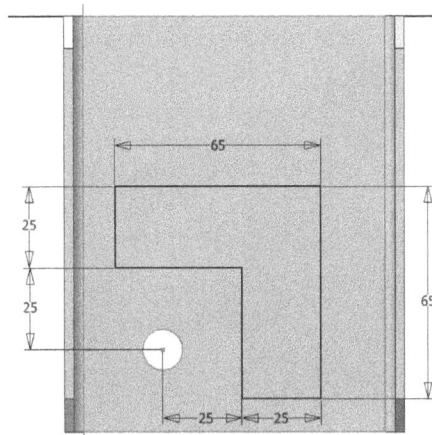

Figure 7–51

2. In the *Sheet Metal* tab>Modify panel, click ▢ (Cut). Select the shape that you just sketched as the profile. Select **All** in the Extents drop-down list. Click **OK**.

3. Create a new sketch on the same face. Sketch and constrain the profile as shown in Figure 7–52. (**Hint:** Add a Colinear constraint between one of the vertical segments of the rectangle and the corresponding vertical segment of the polygon below it.) Finish the sketch.

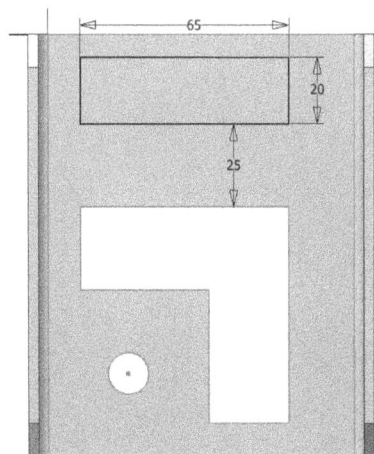

Figure 7–52

4. In the *Sheet Metal* tab>Modify panel, click ☐ (Cut). Select the shape that you just sketched as the profile. Select **Distance** as the *Extents* option and set the *Depth* to **Thickness**. Click **OK**.

Task 3 - Redefine Cut1 and change the Extent option.

Consider using the **All** extent option if the intent is for the cut to remove material from multiple faces instead of just the thickness of the metal on which it is originally located. In Task 2 you did not see a difference, but for **Cut1** (created for you) you would see a difference depending on the *Extents* option used.

1. Right-click on **Cut1** in the Model Browser and select **Edit Feature**.

2. In the *Extents* area, select **All** in the drop-down list. Because of the sketching plane that was selected you must click ⊠ to extend the cut through all surfaces on both sides of the sketching plane.

3. Complete the feature. Note how **Cut1** cuts through all material. Undo the change to return **Cut1** to its original extent option (**Distance** with a value of **Thickness**).

Task 4 - Create Cuts across a bend.

1. Create a new sketch on the same face. Sketch and constrain the profile, as shown in Figure 7–53. Finish the sketch.

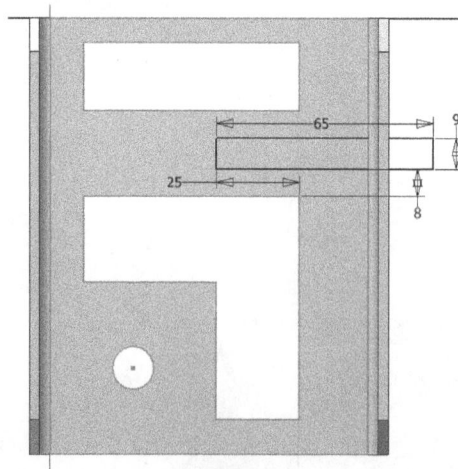

Figure 7–53

2. In the *Sheet Metal* tab>Modify panel, click ⬜ (Cut). Select the shape that you just sketched as the profile. Select the **Cut Across Bend** option and click **OK**.

3. Create a new sketch on the same face. Sketch and constrain the profile, as shown in Figure 7–54. Finish the sketch.

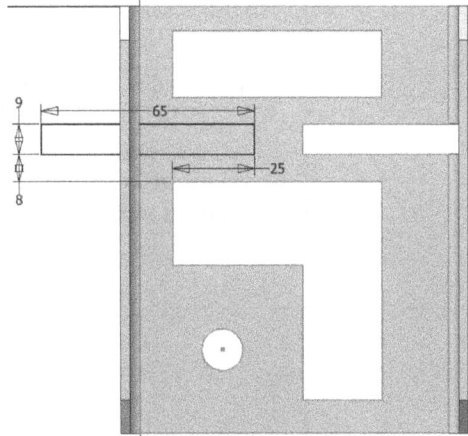

Figure 7–54

4. In the *Sheet Metal* tab>Modify panel, click ⬜ (Cut). Select the shape that you just sketched as the profile. Verify that the **Cut Across Bend** option is not selected. Select **All** for *Extents* and click **OK**.

5. Rotate the part and examine the difference between the two features, as shown in Figure 7–55. The second cut does not take into account the bend, even with the **All** option selected.

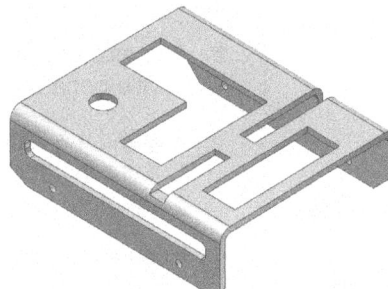

Figure 7–55

6. Save and close the file.

Practice 7b | Creating Cut Features II

Practice Objective

- Create a cut that is normal to the sheet metal geometry.

In this practice, you will create a cut feature that remains normal to the sheet metal geometry instead of to the sketch plane.

Task 1 - Create a new part file.

1. Open **Band_Cut_Normal.ipt**. The model opens as shown in Figure 7–56. It consists of a Contour Flange, work features, and a slot shaped sketch.

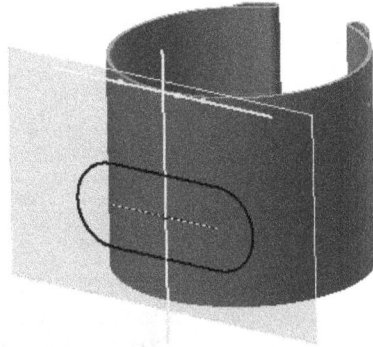

Figure 7–56

Task 2 - Create a cut through the Contour Flange.

1. In the *Sheet Metal* tab>Modify panel, click ☐ (Cut).

2. The slot shaped sketch is automatically selected as the cut profile because it is in the only sketch in the model.

3. Expand the Extents drop-down list and select **To Next**. Ensure that the cut is cutting toward the sheet metal geometry.

4. Ensure that the **Cut Normal** option is not selected. Click **OK**.

5. Clear the visibility of the **Sketch Plane** plane.

6. Zoom in on the cut and hover the cursor over the new cut in the Model Browser. The feature highlights in red as shown in Figure 7–57. Note that the cut remains normal to the sketching plane through the thickness of the sheet metal model.

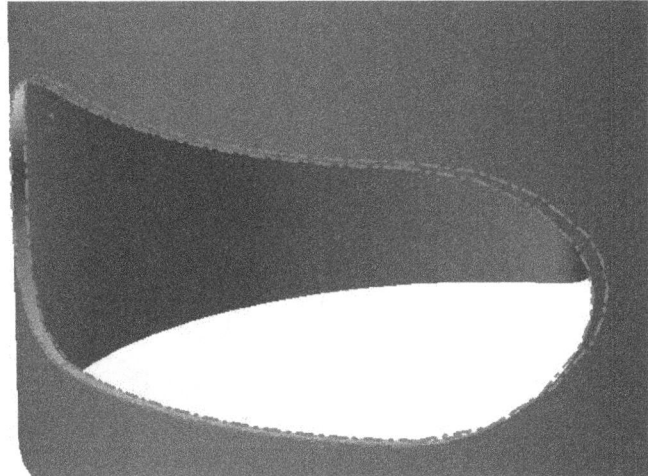

Figure 7–57

Task 3 - Edit the Cut.

1. Right-click on the Cut feature in the Model Browser and select **Edit Feature**.

2. In the dialog box, select the **Cut Normal** option, as shown in Figure 7–58. Click **OK**.

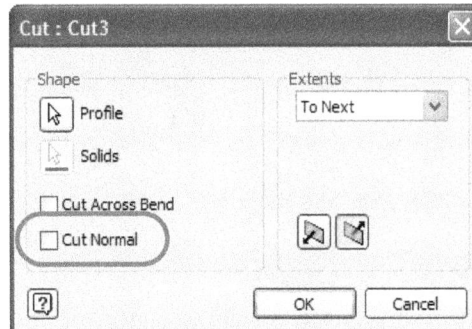

Figure 7–58

3. Hover the cursor over the edited cut in the Model Browser. The feature highlights in red, as shown in Figure 7–59. Note that the cut now remains normal to the sheet metal geometry, not the sketching plane.

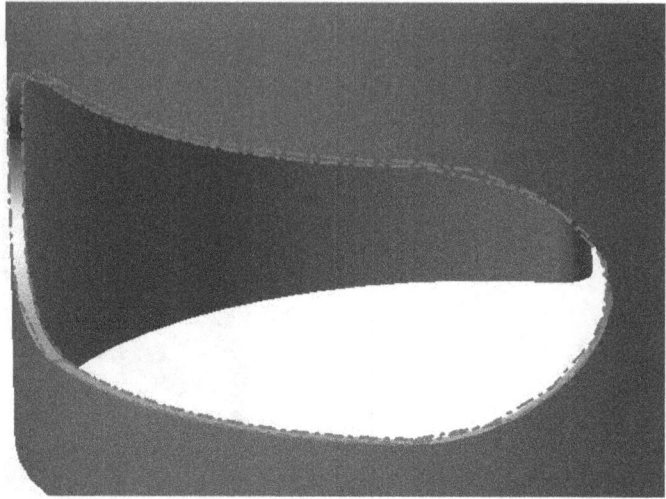

Figure 7–59

4. Save the model and close the window.

Practice 7c

Punch Tool, Holes, and Cut Features

Practice Objectives

- Create a punch tool file that is stored locally for reuse when adding punches to a sheet metal model.
- Use a punch tool file to remove material from a sheet metal model.
- Remove material from a sheet metal model using a sketched profile.
- Establish sketch references by projecting edges into a sketch that would exist when the model is in a flat pattern state.
- Use the **Cut Across Bend** cut option to vary the geometry that results when a cut feature is added across bend geometry.
- Locate holes on a sheet metal model relative to existing edges in the model.

In this practice, you will create a Sheet Metal Punch file. You will then use the Punch file in another model. To complete the design, you will place additional Punch features, Cuts, and Holes. The completed model is shown on the right in Figure 7–60.

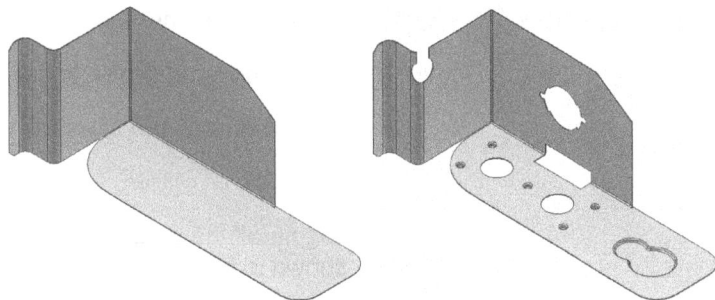

Figure 7–60

Task 1 - Create features for the Punch file.

1. Open **Punch_Feature.ipt**.

2. Enter **E** to start the **Extrude** command. Select the outer and inner profiles to extrude. By selecting the shortcut key to initiate the command, you do not have to switch to the *3D Model* tab to access the command.

3. Select both the inner and outer profiles to extrude.

4. Enter **4 mm + Thickness** as the *Distance* value. Flip the direction down to add material below the sketch plane. The preview displays as shown in Figure 7–61. Click **OK**.

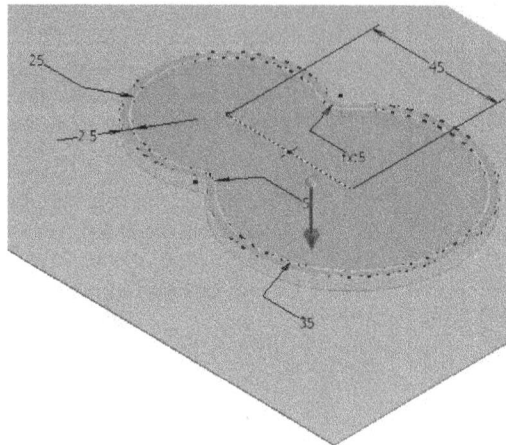

Figure 7–61

5. Toggle on the visibility of **Sketch1**.

6. In the *Sheet Metal* tab>Modify panel, click ⬜ (Cut). The Cut dialog box opens.

7. Select the inner profile to cut.

8. Enter **4 mm** as the *Distance* value.

9. Click **OK**.

10. Toggle off the visibility of **Sketch1**. The model displays as shown in Figure 7–62.

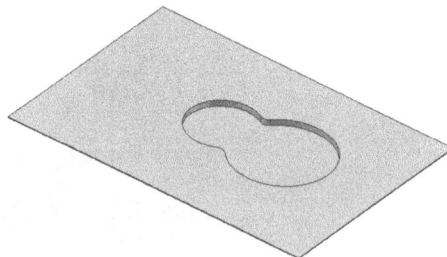

Figure 7–62

11. Enter **F** to start the **Fillet** command. Select the top and bottom edges of the interior part of the extrusion and of the exterior part of the extrusion on the underside of the feature. The dialog box should indicate that the 16 edges are selected.

12. Enter **2 mm** for the *Radius* and click **OK**. The model displays as shown in Figure 7–63.

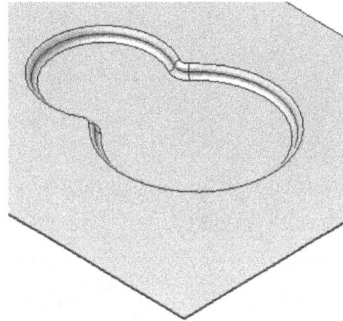

Figure 7–63

Task 2 - Create a Punch file.

1. Toggle on the visibility of **Sketch9**. This sketch contains the profile for the inner part of the feature and a point. It will be used as the Simplified Representation of the Punch.

2. In the *Manage* tab>Author panel, click (Extract iFeature). The Extract iFeature dialog box opens.

3. Select **Extrusion7** and **Cut3** in the Model Browser. **Fillet4** is automatically selected, as it is dependent on **Extrusion7**. The features and parameters are added to the Selected Features list.

4. Select **Sheet Metal Punch iFeature** in the *Type* area in the dialog box.

5. Enter **ID-1234** in the *Specify Punch ID* field.

6. Click (Select Sketch) and select **Sketch9** in the Model Browser.

7. Right-click on Face1 in the *Position Geometry* area and select **Combine Geometry**. Select **Sketch Plane1** in the *Position Geometry* area. This combines the placement of the two faces into one selection. The Extract iFeature dialog box displays as shown in Figure 7–64.

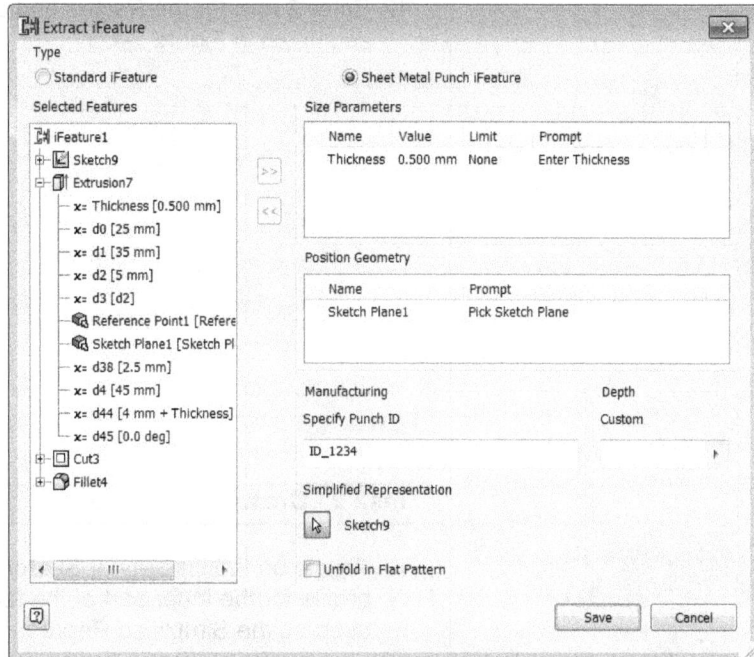

Figure 7–64

8. Click **Save**. The Save As dialog box opens.

9. Browse to your practice files folder. Enter **ID-1234** in the *Name* field and click **Save**. The Punch iFeature file is saved. This Punch will be used in a different part file.

10. Save and close the file.

Task 3 - Open the part called Mounting_bracket_7.ipt.

1. Open the file **Mounting_bracket_7.ipt**. The file displays as shown in Figure 7–65.

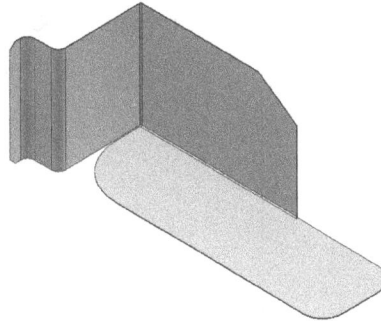

Figure 7–65

Task 4 - Place a Punch feature.

1. Create a sketch on the face shown in Figure 7–66.

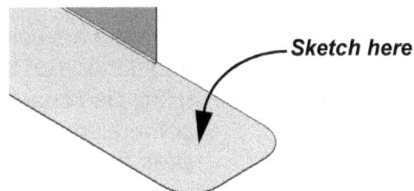

Sketch here

Figure 7–66

2. Place a point and dimension it as shown in Figure 7–67. Finish the sketch.

74   105

Figure 7–67

3. In the *Sheet Metal* tab>Modify panel, click (Punch Tool). The PunchTool Directory dialog box opens.

4. Browse to your practice folder, select **ID-1234.ide**, and click **Open**. You can select **ID-1234_Done.ide** if you did not complete Task 3. The PunchTool dialog box opens.

5. The Punch feature is automatically placed on the point. Click **Finish** to complete the feature. The model displays as shown in Figure 7–68.

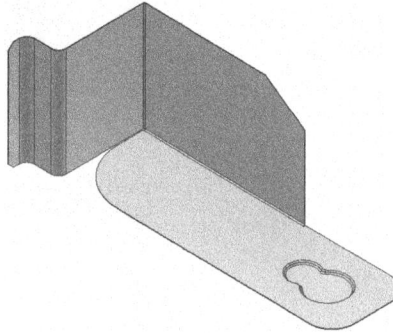

Figure 7–68

Task 5 - Place Punch features on sketched points.

1. Create a new sketch on the same face as in Task 5. Sketch and dimension the point and rectangle shown in Figure 7–69. (Hint: Use constraints and/or construction lines to position the point relative to the midpoints of the rectangle.) Finish the sketch.

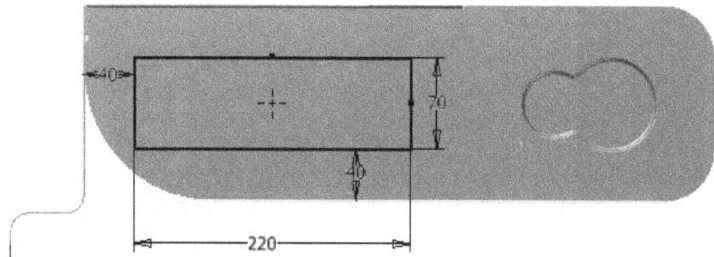

Figure 7–69

2. In the *Sheet Metal* tab>Modify panel, click (Punch Tool). The PunchTool Directory dialog box opens.

3. Browse to your practice folder, select **ID-5678.ide**, and click **Open**. The PunchTool dialog box opens.

4. The point is selected automatically. Select the *Geometry* tab and ensure that the ⬚ (Centers) button is active. Select the four corners of the rectangle that you sketched. As an alternative you can also drag a selection box around the sketch to automatically select all endpoints of entities or referenced points. Note that the sketched point clears if you use the selection box - if this occurs, reselect it. If unwanted points are selected, press <Ctrl> and select the point to clear it. A total of 5 *Centers* should be selected.

5. Click **Finish** to create the features. The model displays as shown in Figure 7–70.

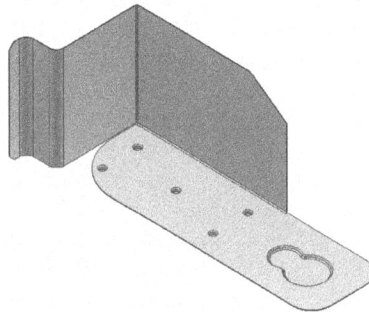

Figure 7–70

Task 6 - Place Punch features.

1. Create a sketch on the face shown in Figure 7–71. Create a point that is centered on the face. (Hint: Use constraints and/or construction lines to position the point.) Finish the sketch.

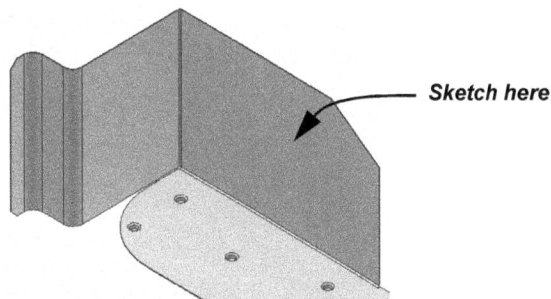

Sketch here

Figure 7–71

2. In the *Sheet Metal* tab>Modify panel, click 🔧 (Punch Tool). The PunchTool Directory dialog box opens.

3. Browse to the practice files folder, select **ID-4567.ide**, and click **Open**. The PunchTool dialog box opens.

4. The point is automatically selected. Click **Finish** to create the feature. The model displays as shown in Figure 7–72.

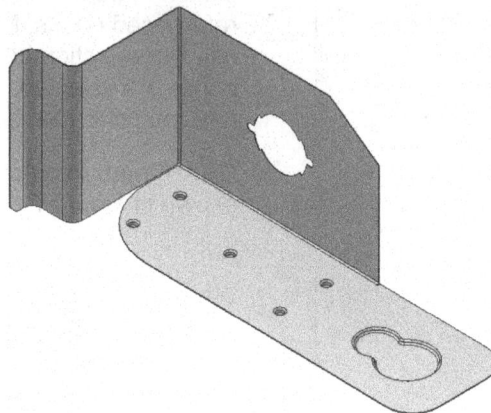

Figure 7–72

Task 7 - Create and edit a Cut feature.

1. Create a new sketch on the face shown in Figure 7–73 (back face of the part).

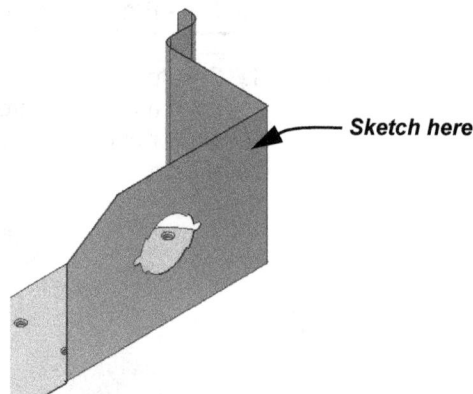

Sketch here

Figure 7–73

2. In the *Sketch* tab>Create panel, click ⬦ (Project Flat Pattern) in the expanded drop-down list for the *Project* options.

3. Select the face that contains the five round Punches. The flat pattern for that Flange is projected to the sketch. Note the projected entities are shown in green in Figure 7–74 for clarity. The projected entities display in yellow in the sketch.

4. Sketch and dimension the rectangle shown in Figure 7–74. Finish the sketch.

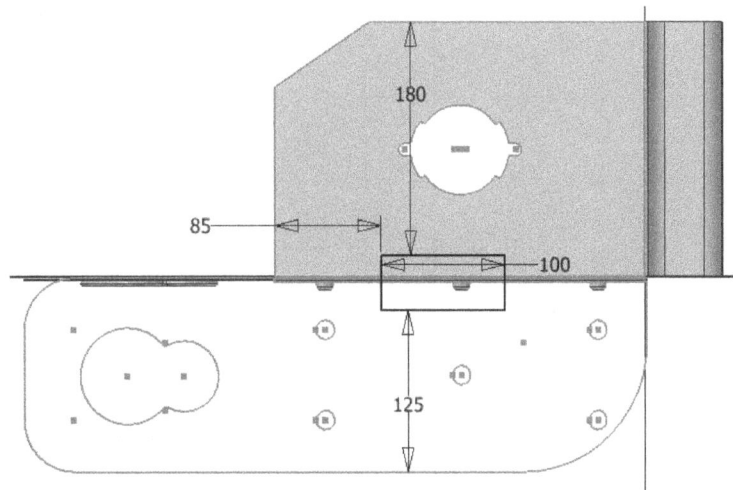

Figure 7–74

5. In the *Sheet Metal* tab>Modify panel, click ⬜ (Cut). The Cut dialog box opens.

6. Select the rectangle that you just created for the profile of the Cut.

7. Click **OK**. The Cut feature only removes material to the depth specified by the **Thickness** parameter in the sheet metal part, as shown in Figure 7–75.

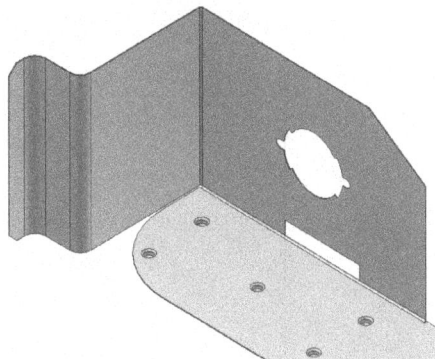

Figure 7–75

8. Right-click on **Cut3** in the Model Browser and select **Edit Feature**.

9. Select **Cut Across Bend** and click **OK**. The Cut feature is wrapped around the Flange, as shown in Figure 7–76.

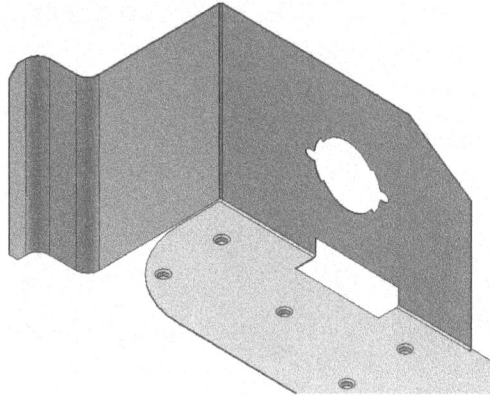

Figure 7–76

Task 8 - Create a Cut around a bend.

1. Create a new sketch on the face shown in Figure 7–77. Sketch the profile shown in Figure 7–77. Finish the sketch.

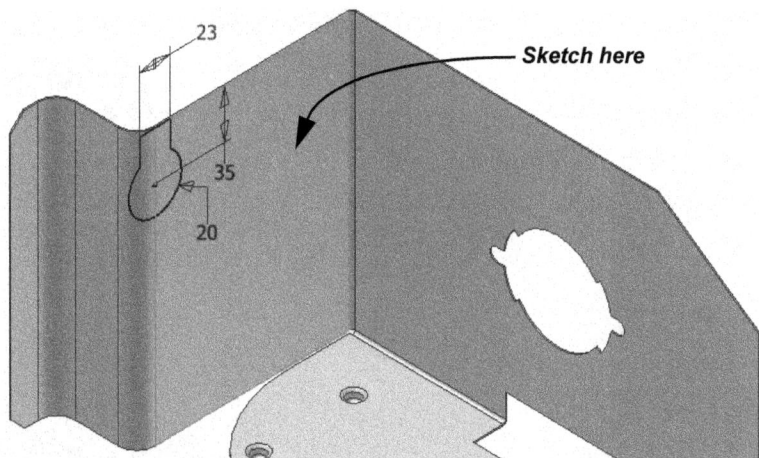

Figure 7–77

2. In the *Sheet Metal* tab>Modify panel, click ▢ (Cut). The Cut dialog box opens.

3. Select the sketch that you just created for the Cut profile.

4. Select the **Cut Across Bend** option and click **OK**. The model displays as shown in Figure 7–78.

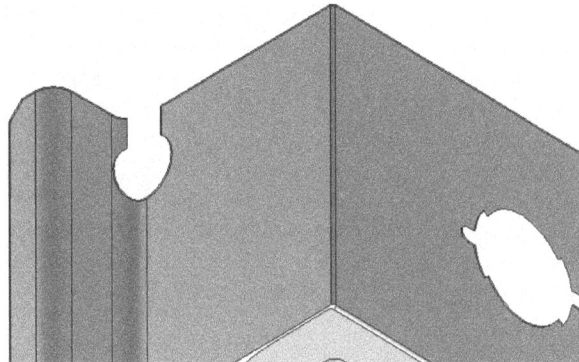

Figure 7–78

Task 9 - Create Holes.

1. In the *Sheet Metal* tab>Modify panel, click 🔘 (Hole). Use the **Linear** placement method to place the 50 mm diameter Hole shown in Figure 7–79. Set the *Termination* as **Distance** and leave the *Depth* as the default **Thickness** parameter.

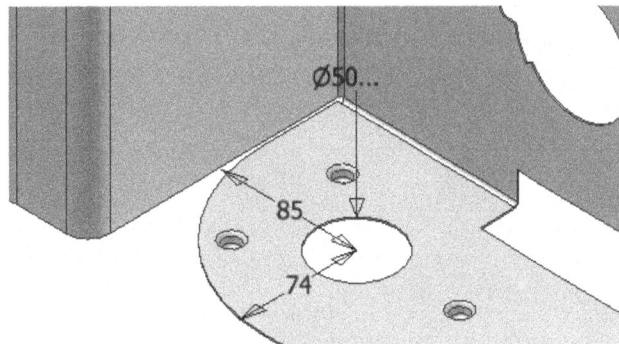

Figure 7–79

2. Repeat the process to place the Hole shown in Figure 7–80.

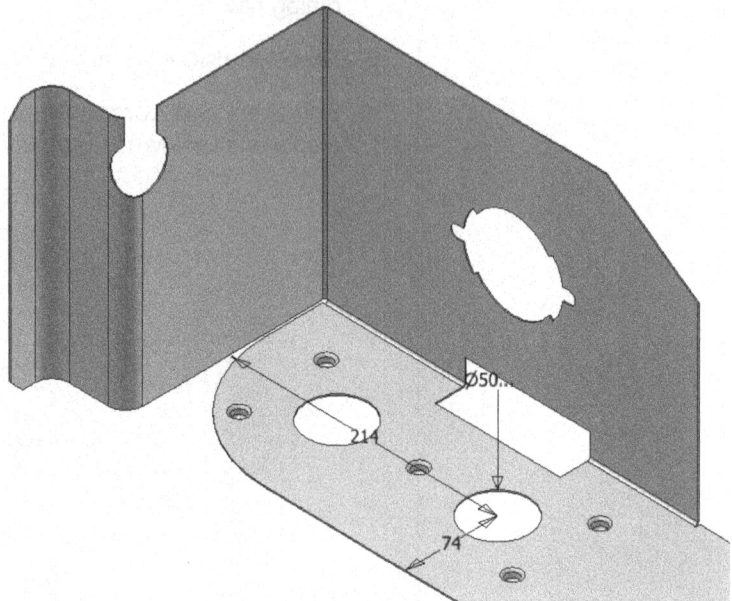

Figure 7–80

3. Save and close the file.

Practice 7d

Create and Insert a Punch Feature

Practice Objectives

- Open an existing model that has been created to represent a required punch that is to be removed from a sheet metal model.
- Create a punch tool file that is stored locally for reuse when adding punches to a sheet metal model.
- Use a punch tool file to remove material from a sheet metal model.

In this practice, you will create a Sheet Metal Punch file that includes parameters. You will then place the Punch in another model, rotating the features and changing the parameters. You will also place a Punch from the sample library. The completed model is shown on the right in Figure 7–81.

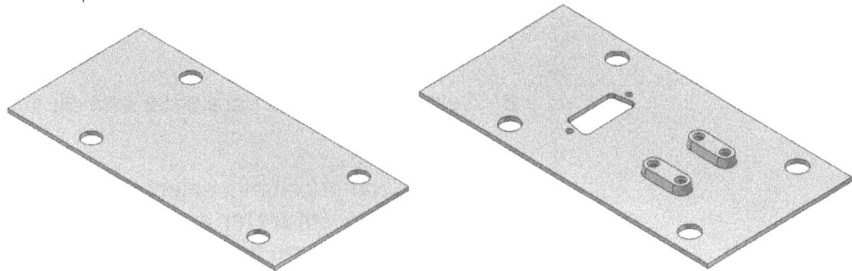

Figure 7–81

Task 1 - Create a Punch file.

1. Open **Support.ipt**. The model displays as shown in Figure 7–82. The model contains features that are used to create the Punch file.

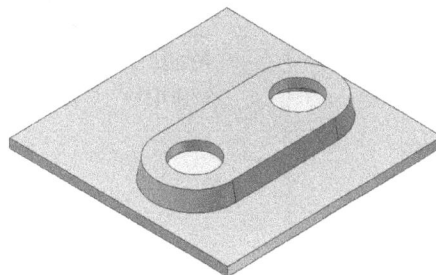

Figure 7–82

2. In the *Manage* tab>Parameters panel, click

   f_x (Parameters). The Parameters dialog box opens.

3. Scroll down to the **User Parameters** node. The part contains several user-defined parameters that are used in the equations of model dimensions.

4. Click **Done** to close the Parameters dialog box.

5. In the *Manage* tab>Author panel, click (Extract iFeature). The Extract iFeature dialog box opens.

6. Select **Extrusion1** in the Model Browser. **Extrusion1** and its dependent features are added to the Selected Features list. The user-defined parameters for these features are added to the Size Parameters list.

7. Select the **Angle** parameter and click [<<] to remove it from the list.

8. Select the **Radius** parameter and click [<<] to remove it from the list.

9. In the *Prompt* column, select **Enter Extrusiondist** and change it to **Enter Depth**. Be sure to change the *Prompt* field and not the *Name* field.

10. Select **Sheet Metal Punch iFeature** in the *Type* area in the dialog box.

11. Enter **ID-7890** in the *Specify Punch ID* field.

12. Click (Select Sketch) in the *Simplified Representation* area and select **Sketch4** in the Model Browser.

13. Enter **Extrusiondist** in the Custom drop-down list. This is a user-defined parameter that controls the height of the Punch feature. The Extract iFeature dialog box displays as shown in Figure 7–83.

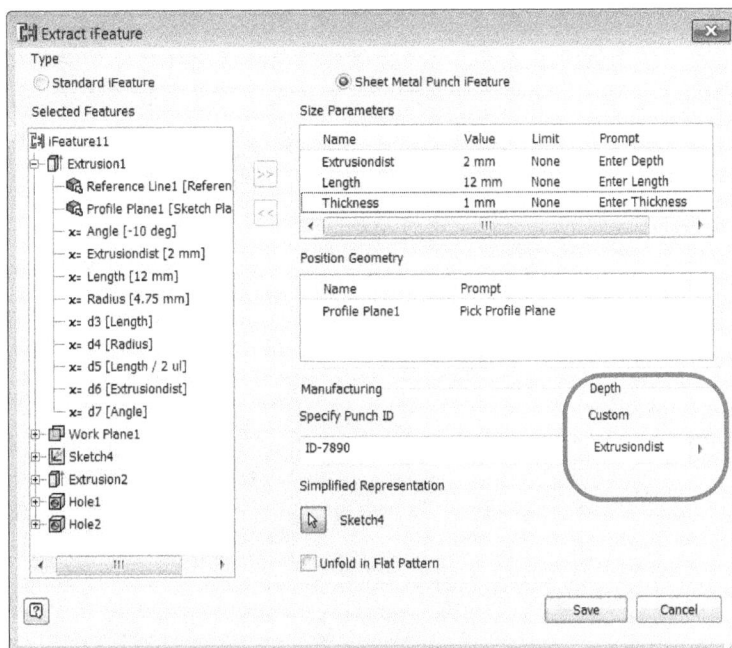

Figure 7–83

14. Click **Save**. The Save As dialog box opens.

15. Browse to your practice files folder. Name the file **ID-7890** and click **Save**.

16. Close the **Support.ipt** file.

Task 2 - Open the part called Punch.ipt.

---

1. Open the file **Punch.ipt**. The model displays as shown in Figure 7–84.

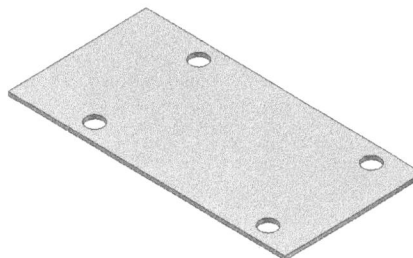

Figure 7–84

Task 3 - Place a Punch from the punch library.

1. Create a new sketch on the top face.

2. Sketch and constrain a point, as shown in Figure 7–85. Finish the sketch.

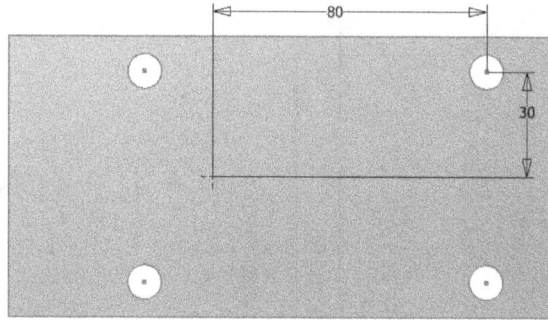

Figure 7–85

3. In the *Sheet Metal* tab>Modify panel, click (Punch Tool) and select **D-Sub Connector.ide**. Click **Open**. This punch is located in the punch library. In your work environment you might also want to add your punches to this directory.

4. Select the *Geometry* tab and change the *Angle* to **270**.

5. Click **Finish** to place the Punch feature. The model displays as shown in Figure 7–86.

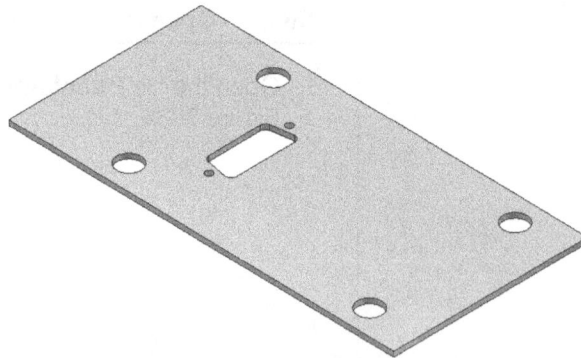

Figure 7–86

Task 4 - Place a user-defined Punch.

1. Create a new sketch on the top face.

2. Sketch and constrain a line, as shown in Figure 7–87. Finish the sketch.

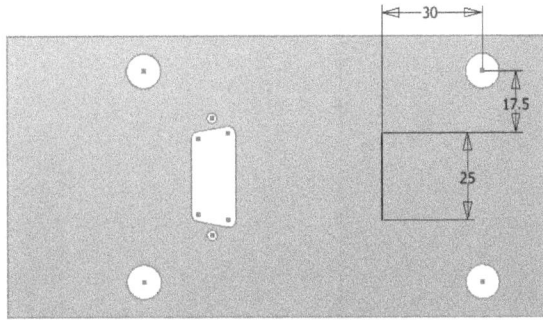

Figure 7–87

3. In the *Sheet Metal* tab>Modify panel, click (Punch Tool). Browse to your practice files folder and select **ID-7890.ide**. Click **Open**. You can open **ID-7890_Done.ide** if you did not complete the creation of the Punch file earlier.

4. Select the two end points of the line you sketched, or draw a bounding box around the entity.

5. Select the *Geometry* tab and enter **90** in the *Angle* field.

6. Select the *Size* tab. Enter **4 mm** for the *Extrusiondist* and **15 mm** for the *Length*.

7. Click **Finish** to place the Punch feature. The model displays as shown in Figure 7–88.

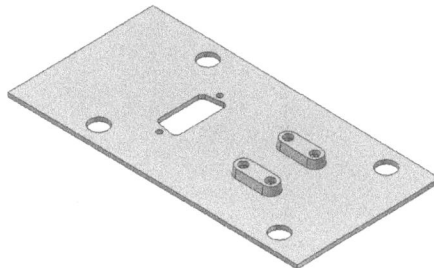

Figure 7–88

8. Save and close the file.

Chapter Review Questions

1. In Figure 7–89, the **Cut Across Bend** option was disabled when the sheet metal cut shown was created.

Figure 7–89

   a. True

   b. False

2. Which of the following statements best describes why **Distance** is the only available option in the Extents drop-down list when you are creating a sheet metal Cut feature?

   a. All sheet metal cuts, regardless of any selected options, can only be extended the *Thickness* of the sheet metal model.

   b. The **Cut Across Bend** option has been enabled.

   c. The **Cut Across Bend** option has been disabled.

   d. The profile was sketched on a work plane.

3. Which of the following *Projection* options can be used to project the edges onto a sketch plane shown in Figure 7–90?

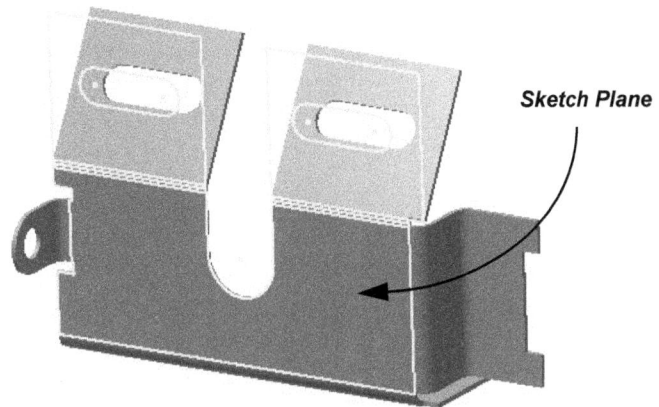

Figure 7–90

a. **Project Geometry**

b. **Project Cut Edges**

c. **Project Flat Pattern**

d. **Project to 3D Sketch**

4. All sheet metal holes require a sketch.

a. True

b. False

5. What type of feature is added to the Model Browser when you use the Punch Tool?

a. Punch

b. Bend

c. iFeature

d. Extrude

6. Which of the following commands must be used to create the punch across the bend shown in Figure 7–91.

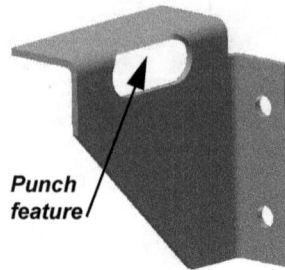

Punch
feature

Figure 7–91

a. **Across Bend**

b. **Cut Across Bend**

7. What sketched geometry does a Punch Tool automatically select to create the feature?

a. Work Points

b. Work Axis

c. Construction Lines

d. Points

8. Which command is used to create a Punch Tool .IDE file for use in your sheet metal models?

a.   (Punch Tool)

b.   (Extract iFeature)

c.   (Cut)

d.   (Extrude)

Command Summary

Button	Command	Location
	Cut	• **Ribbon:** *Sheet Metal* tab>Modify panel
	Extract iFeature	• **Ribbon:** *Manage* tab>Author panel
	Extrude	• **Ribbon:** *3D Model* tab>Create panel
	Hole	• **Ribbon:** *Sheet Metal* tab>Modify panel
f_x	**Parameters**	• **Ribbon:** *Manage* tab>Parameters panel • **Quick Access Toolbar**
	Punch Tool	• **Ribbon:** *Sheet Metal* tab>Modify panel
	Start 2D Sketch	• **Ribbon:** *Sheet Metal* tab>Sketch panel • **Ribbon:** *3D Model* tab>Sketch panel • **Ribbon:** *Sketch* tab>Sketch panel

Corner Seams

When two sheet metal faces form a corner that is not joined by a bend, you can control how they come together with the Corner Seam tool. This enables you to control the size of the space between the faces and the way they overlap. In some cases, material needs to be added or trimmed. In other cases, you might need to reverse the overlap between the faces.

Learning Objectives in this Chapter

- Control the geometry that results when two edges come together using a Corner Seam feature.
- Control the geometry that results when two edges that are coplanar are mitered using a Corner Seam feature.
- Create an open corner where faces were previously joined using the Corner Seam feature.
- Convert an existing Bend feature to a Corner feature to change the design intent of a sheet metal model.
- Convert an existing Corner feature to a Bend feature to change the design intent of a sheet metal model.

8.1 Creating Corner Seams and Miters

A Corner Seam is a placed feature. It creates a small space with a specified Gap distance between folded areas of the part. Although the gap can be set to be very small, Corner Seam features cannot create a completely closed joint between the faces, because they represent the location where separate faces meet. If the gap needs to be sealed during fabrication, it is done by adding a weld, or appropriate fasteners. Depending on the faces used to create a corner, overlap options are provided for seams or miters.

Overlap Options

Corner Seams

Where two faces come together at an angle to each other, the **Corner Seam** tool creates a space. This is referred to as a *Seam* between the faces.

Figure 8–1 shows an example of a part that has been folded to create two vertical faces on the left. On the right, an Overlap style Corner Seam is added so that there is still a small gap, but one face overlaps the other.

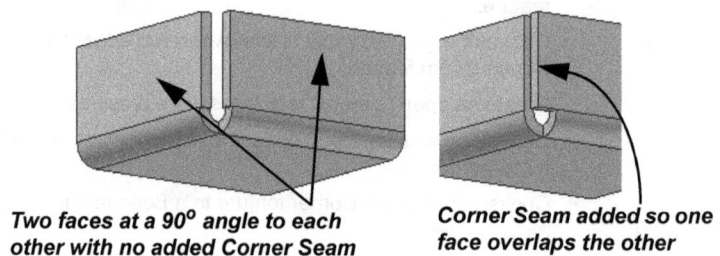

Two faces at a 90° angle to each other with no added Corner Seam

Corner Seam added so one face overlaps the other

Figure 8–1

Corner Miters

Where two faces meet and are coplanar, the **Corner Seam** tool creates a space between them. This is referred to as a *Miter*. Figure 8–2 shows the **45 Degree Miter** option. The two faces have been extended toward each other.

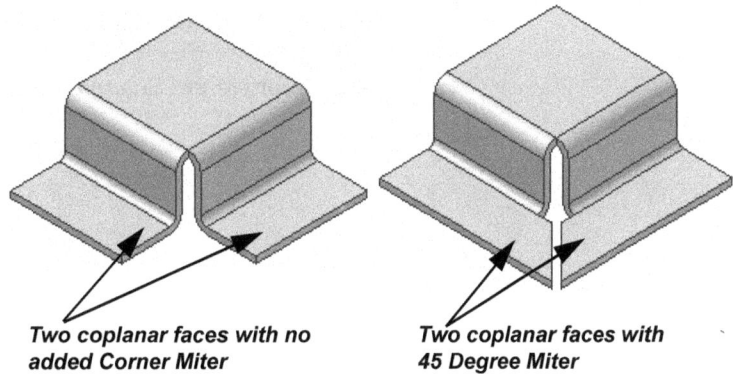

**Two coplanar faces with no
added Corner Miter**

**Two coplanar faces with
45 Degree Miter**

Figure 8–2

General Steps

Use the following general steps to create Corner Seams and
Miters:

1. Start the Corner Seam tool.
2. Select the Seam Shape Mode.
3. Select Placement Edges.
4. Set the Seam/Miter options.
5. Set the Extend Corner options (optional).
6. Set the Bend Tab options (optional).
7. Set the Corner Tab options (optional).
8. Complete the Feature.

Step 1 - Start the Corner Seam tool.

In the *Sheet Metal* tab>Modify panel, click 🔲 (Corner Seam).
The Corner Seam dialog box opens as shown in Figure 8–3.

Figure 8–3

Step 2 - Select the Seam Shape Mode.

Select **Seam** in the *Shape* area as shown in Figure 8–4.

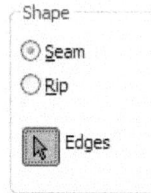

Figure 8–4

The Seam Shape mode enables you to create a new Corner Seam feature between two existing faces that are either at angles to each other or coplanar. Both Corner Seams and Corner Miters are listed as Corner features in the Model Browser.

Figure 8–5 shows a typical example of an Overlap Corner Seam.

Seams between faces that are at an angle are referred to as Corner Seams.

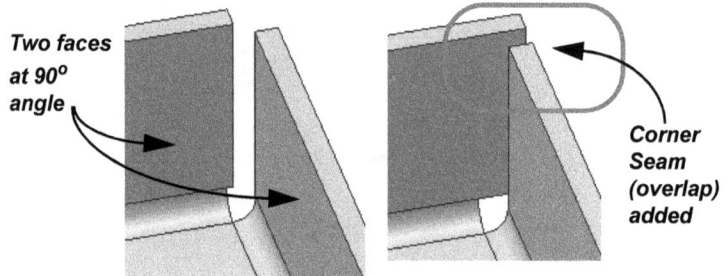

Figure 8–5

Seams between faces that are coplanar are referred to as Corner Miters.

Figure 8–6 shows a typical example of a 45 Degree Miter applied between two coplanar faces.

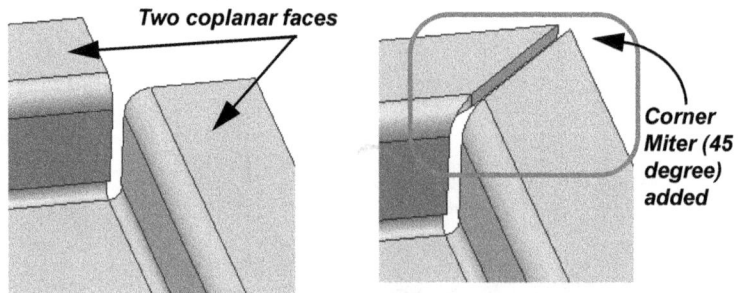

Figure 8–6

Step 3 - Select Placement Edges.

Select the edges that you want to use for the creation of the Corner Seam feature. In Figure 8–7 the placement edges for a Corner Seam are shown on the left, while a Corner Miter is shown on the right.

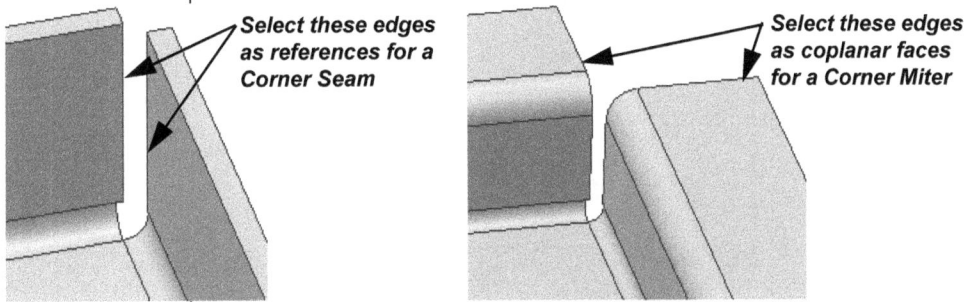

Select these edges as references for a Corner Seam

Select these edges as coplanar faces for a Corner Miter

Figure 8–7

Step 4 - Set the Seam/Miter options.

Depending on whether or not the selected edges are coplanar, the options in the *Seam* or *Miter* area vary slightly. If the selected edges are coplanar you are presented with *Miter* options, otherwise the *Seam* options are displayed. The gap distance measurement option also affects the options available in the *Seam/Miter* areas. These options include the following:

- **Maximum Gap Distance:** Creates a corner seam in which the gap value is measured consistent with the manufacturing inspection process. The gap value is constant along the seam.

The Face/Edge Distance option produces corner seams similar to those created before Autodesk® Inventor® 2009.

- **Face/Edge Distance:** Creates a corner seam in which the gap is measured from the face adjacent to the first selected edge to the second selected edge.

All of the Corner Seam dialog box options are shown in Figure 8–8.

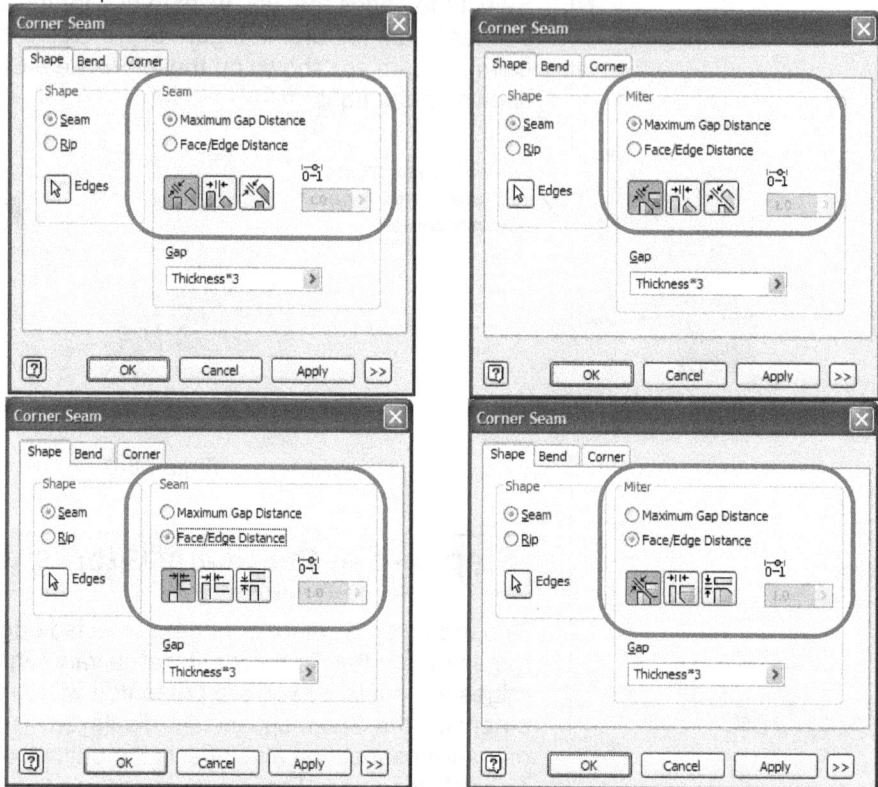

Figure 8–8

Overlap Options for Seams Between Intersecting Faces

When faces are not coplanar they are referred to as intersecting faces. This is the case even if they do not physically intersect, but instead might have a gap between them. Depending on the selected gap measurement method the overlap options might vary.

The **Maximum Gap Distance** method creates a gap that can be measured using an inspection gauge. If this method is selected the following options are available (displayed in blue):

- (**Symmetric Gap**): Creates a Corner Seam between two edges. The Gap is measured across the shortest distance between the edges. Material is added or removed from each face to create the Gap space, as shown in Figure 8–9.

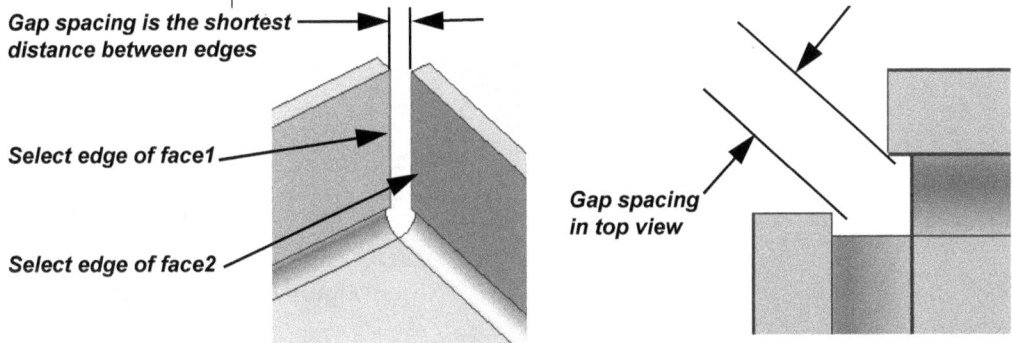

Gap spacing is the shortest distance between edges

Select edge of face1

Select edge of face2

Gap spacing in top view

Figure 8–9

Increasing or decreasing the Gap distance setting adjusts the space between the faces, as shown in Figure 8–10.

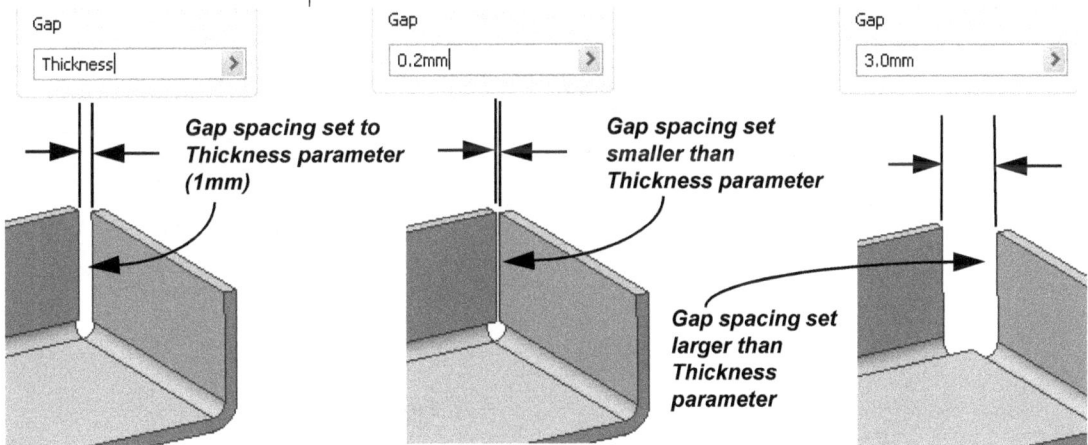

Gap

| Thickness | > |

Gap spacing set to Thickness parameter (1mm)

Gap

| 0.2mm | > |

Gap spacing set smaller than Thickness parameter

Gap

| 3.0mm | > |

Gap spacing set larger than Thickness parameter

Figure 8–10

*With the **Overlap** or **Reverse Overlap** option you can specify the overlap as a percentage of the flange thickness, ranging from 0 to 1.*

- (**Overlap**): Extends the first selected edge so that it overlaps the face of the second selected edge, as shown in Figure 8–11.

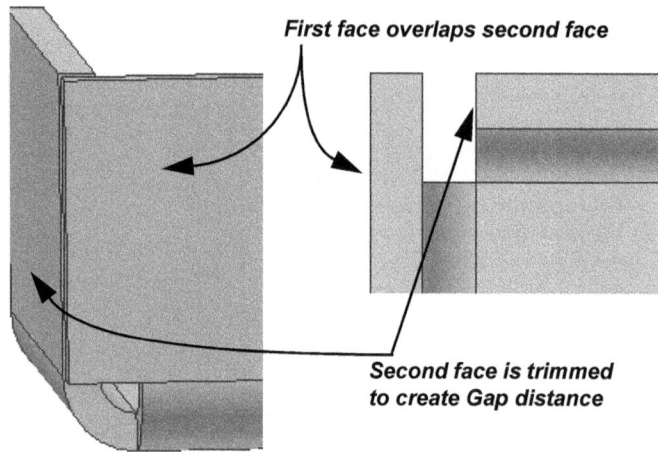

First face overlaps second face

Second face is trimmed to create Gap distance

Figure 8–11

*With the **Overlap** or **Reverse Overlap** option you can specify the overlap as a percentage of the flange thickness, ranging from 0 to 1.*

- (**Reverse Overlap**): Extends the second selected edge so that its face overlaps the edge of the first selected face. An example is shown in Figure 8–12.

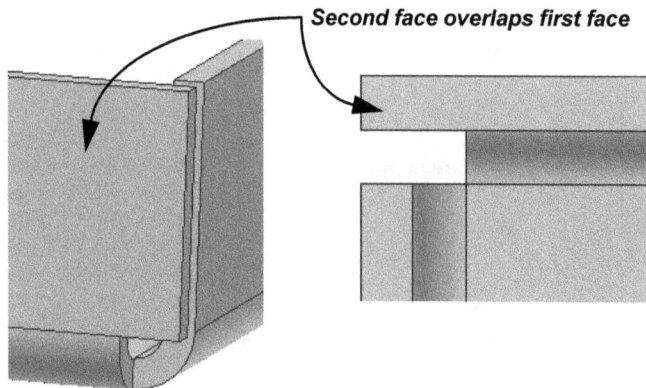

Second face overlaps first face

Figure 8–12

The **Face/Edge Distance** method creates a gap that is measured from the face adjacent to the first selected edge to the second selected edge. If this method is selected the following options are available (displayed in yellow):

- (**No Overlap**): Creates a Corner Seam between two intersecting faces with the gap being measured parallel to the edges of each face, as shown in Figure 8–13.

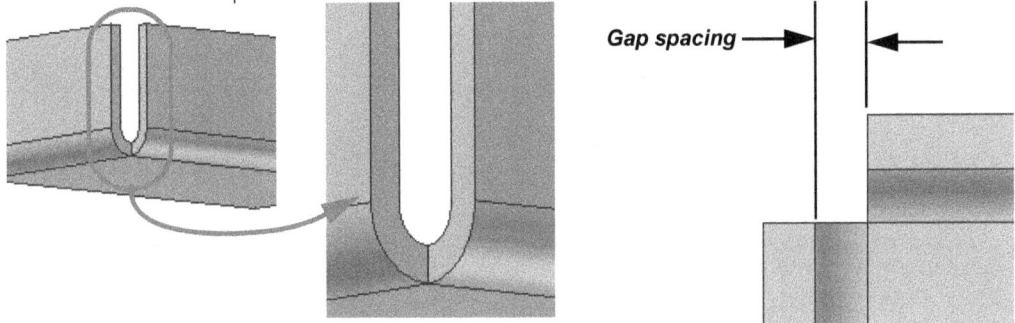

Gap spacing

Figure 8–13

With the Overlap or Reverse Overlap option you can specify the overlap as a percentage of the flange thickness, ranging from 0 to 1.

- (**Overlap**): Extends the first selected edge so that it overlaps the face of the second selected edge, as shown in Figure 8–14.

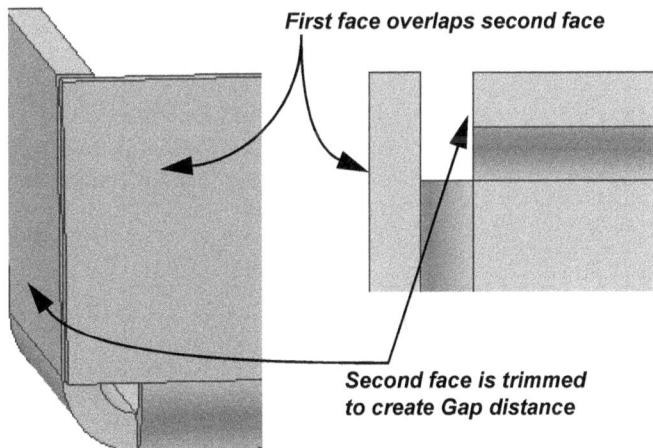

First face overlaps second face

Second face is trimmed to create Gap distance

Figure 8–14

*With the **Overlap** or **Reverse Overlap** option you can specify the overlap as a percentage of the flange thickness, ranging from 0 to 1.*

- ⊡ (**Reverse Overlap**): Extends the second selected edge so that its face overlaps the edge of the first selected face. An example is shown in Figure 8–15.

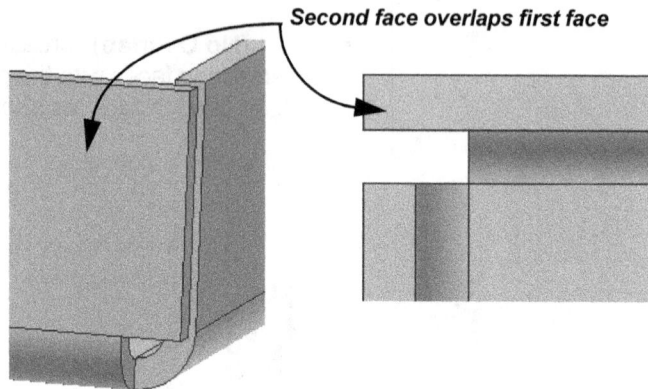

Second face overlaps first face

Figure 8–15

Overlap Options for Miters between Coplanar Faces

When faces lie in the same plane in space and are not at an angle to each other, they are referred to as Coplanar and seams created between edges that are coplanar create a Miter. Depending on the gap measurement method selected the overlap options might vary.

If the **Maximum Gap Distance** measurement method is selected the following options are available (displayed in blue):

- ⊡ (**45 Degree**): Creates a 45 degree miter between the two faces. A Gap distance is specified to control the distance between the two faces, as shown in Figure 8–16.

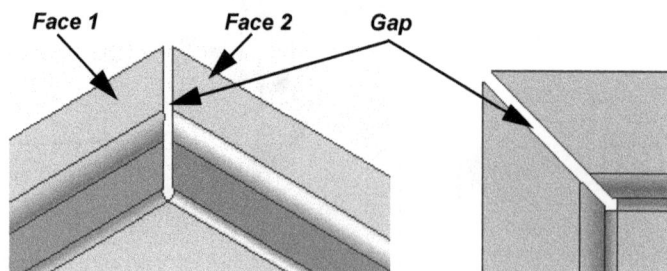

Face 1   Face 2   Gap

Figure 8–16

The **45 Degree** miter enables you to associate the Gap distance to the distance between two selected edges. If edges are selected using **Measure Gap**, the value in the *Gap* field is ignored. To access it, click [>>] to open the expanded *Options* area in the Corner Seam dialog box. Click [↖] (Measure Gap) and select two edges that form a corner (edges of flanges or corners) as shown in Figure 8–17. The distance between the edges of the mitered corner is associated with the distance between the selected edges. If the distance between the selected edges is changed, the corner updates.

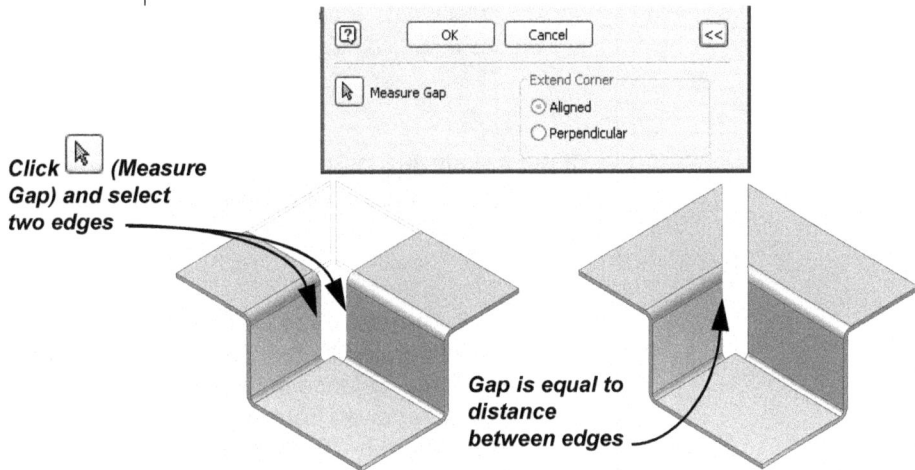

Click [↖] (Measure Gap) and select two edges

Gap is equal to distance between edges

Figure 8–17

- [⊹‖⊹] (**Overlap**): Creates a 90 degree Corner Miter between the two faces with the first face extending to reach the farthest edge of the second face. The gap is measured parallel to the edges of each face, as shown in Figure 8–18.

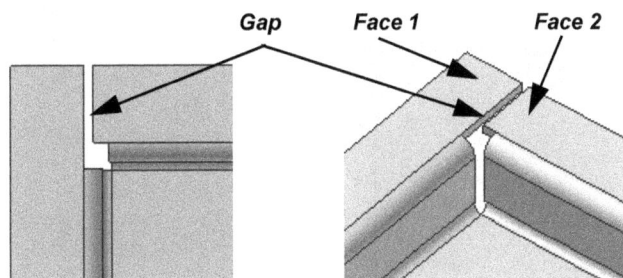

Gap   **Face 1**   **Face 2**

Figure 8–18

- (**Reverse Overlap**): Creates a 90 degree Corner Miter between the two faces with the second face selected, extending to the farthest edge of the first face. The Gap is measured parallel to the edges of each face, as shown in Figure 8–19.

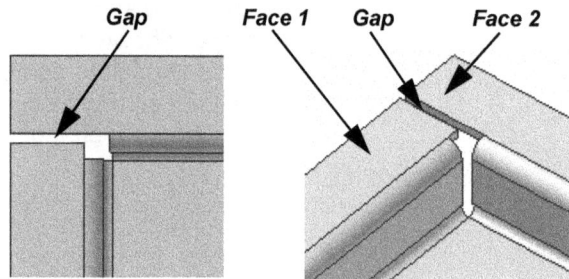

Figure 8–19

If the **Face/Edge Distance** gap distance measurement method is selected the following options are available (displayed in yellow):

- (**Symmetric Gap**): Creates a Corner Miter between two edges separated by the Gap value. The Gap is measured as the shortest distance between the two edges. Material is added or removed from each face to create the assigned Gap space. Figure 8–20 shows the added Symmetric Corner Miter between two coplanar faces.

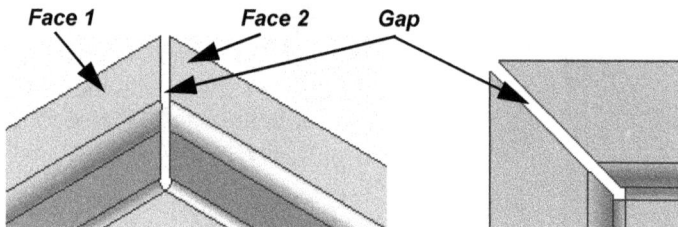

Figure 8–20

- ⊞ (**Overlap**): Creates a 90 degree Corner Miter between the two faces with the first face extending to reach the farthest edge of the second face. The gap is measured parallel to the edges of each face, as shown in Figure 8–21.

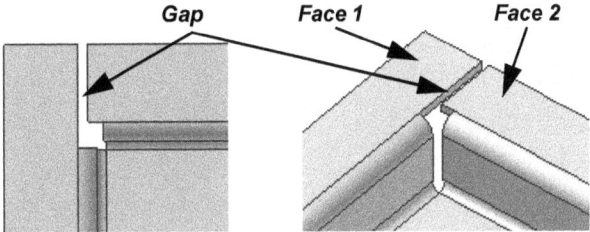

Gap   *Face 1*   *Face 2*

Figure 8–21

- ⊞ (**Reverse Overlap**): Creates a 90 degree Corner Miter between the two faces with the second face selected, extending to the farthest edge of the first face. The Gap is measured parallel to the edges of each face, as shown in Figure 8–22.

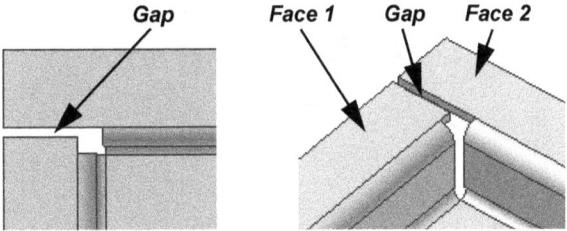

Gap   *Face 1*   *Gap*   *Face 2*

Figure 8–22

Step 5 - Set the Extend Corner options (optional).

Click ⊞ in the Corner Seam dialog box to display the *Extend Corner* options, as shown in Figure 8–23.

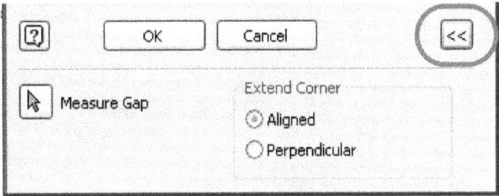

Figure 8–23

The *Extend Corner* options are **Aligned** and **Perpendicular**. These are used when a face with an angled edge needs to be projected toward another face to create a Corner Seam. In the following examples a Corner Seam is required to narrow the gap between the two faces so that they can be welded together. One of the faces is inclined.

- **Aligned:** Extends the first face along its angle to meet the second face and create a Corner Seam, as shown in Figure 8–24.

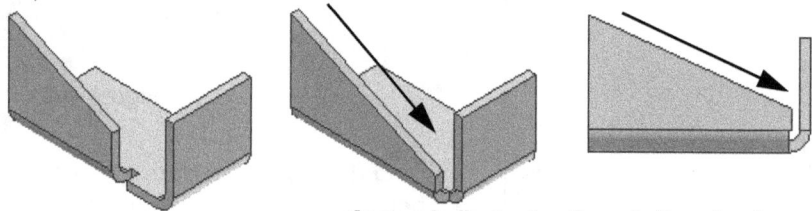

Arrows indicate direction of aligned path for extending face to create Corner Seam

Figure 8–24

- **Perpendicular:** Extends the first face starting at an endpoint that you select. It is projected perpendicular to the second face, as shown in Figure 8–25.

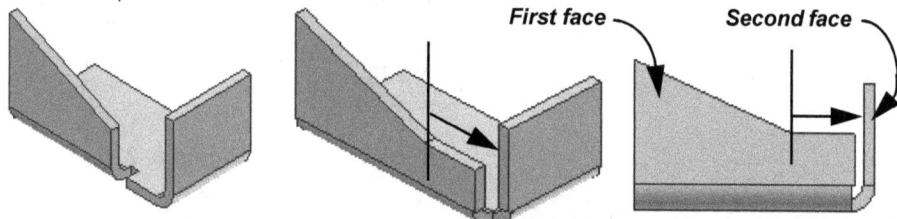

First face — Second face —

First face is projected from end point of its angled edge in a direction perpendicular to second face

Figure 8–25

Step 6 - Set the Bend Tab options (optional).

By default, the *Bend* tab options are set based on the Sheet Metal Rule. You can override them in the Corner Seam dialog box, as required.

Step 7 - Set the Corner Tab options (optional).

By default, the *Corner* tab options are set based on the Sheet Metal Rule. You can override them in the Corner Seam dialog box, as required.

Step 8 - Complete the Feature.

Click **OK** to complete the Corner Seam feature. Alternatively, you can right-click and select **OK (Enter)** to complete the feature. Click **Apply** to create the Corner Seam and leave the Corner Seam dialog box open to create additional corner seams in the model.

8.2 Creating Corner Rips

The **Corner Seam** tool is not only used for closing gaps between separate faces, it can also be used to create rips. Rips are created using the **Rip** option in the *Shape* area, as shown in Figure 8–26.

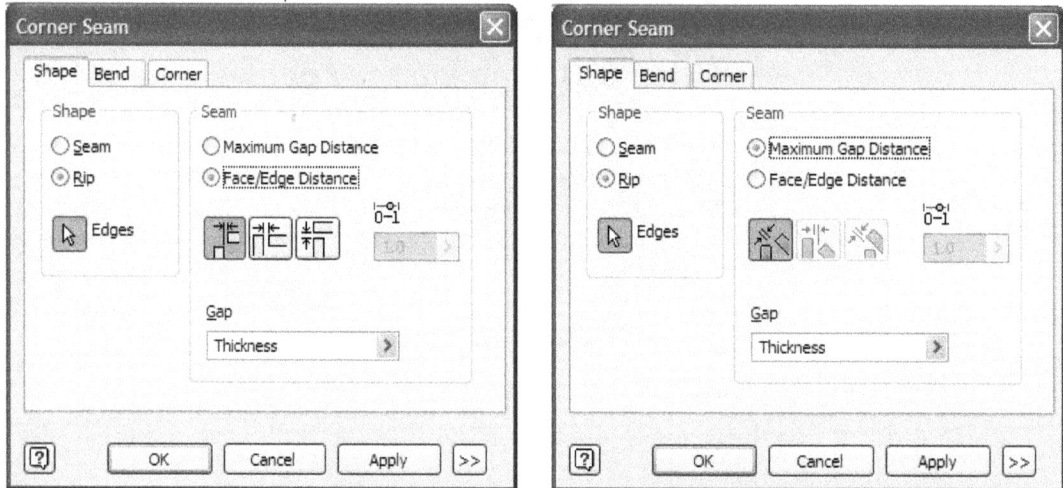

Figure 8–26

Rip mode enables you to create an open corner where faces had previously been joined. This is useful when you have a part that was originally created as a solid and was converted to a sheet metal part. When using **Rip**, you have the *Seam* controls that were also available for Seams. Figure 8–27 shows a model that was originally created as a solid cube. It was then shelled and converted to sheet metal. The **Rip** opens a corner where edges would be folded in fabrication.

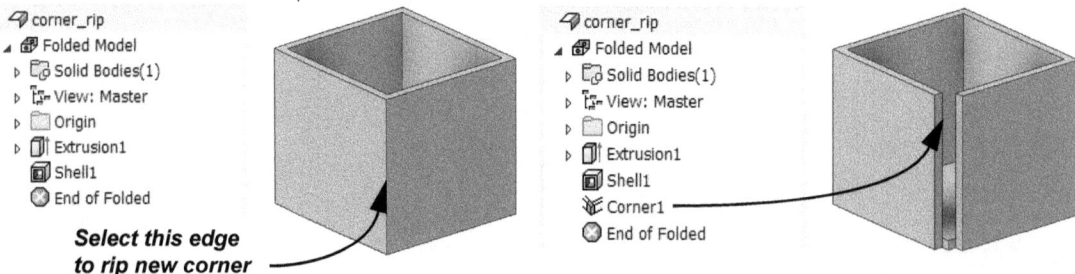

Select this edge to rip new corner

Figure 8–27

8.3 Converting Corner Seams and Bends

Once you have created Corner Seams, you might discover that an opening on the corner of the part needs to be closed with a bend to alter the folding sequence during manufacturing. You can change an open Corner Seam to a closed Bend by right-clicking on a Corner feature in the Model Browser and selecting **Change to Bend**. The part shown in Figure 8–28 is a sheet metal model containing one added Bend feature and one Corner feature.

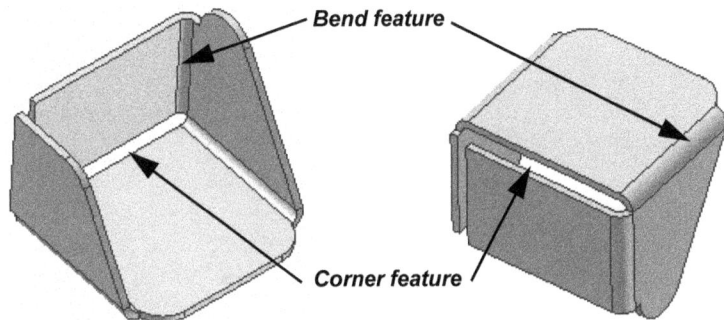

Bend feature

Corner feature

Figure 8–28

Before it is folded, it is marked out on a flat sheet of metal and then cut to shape. Lines are marked to indicate fold locations. Its current flat pattern (unfolded view) would display as shown in Figure 8–29.

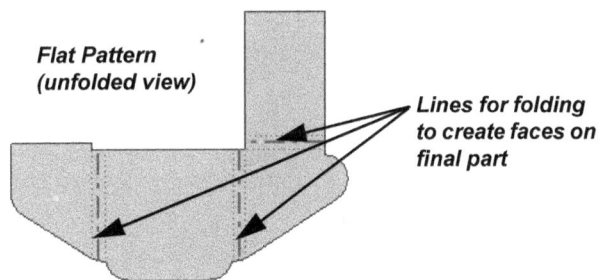

Flat Pattern (unfolded view)

Lines for folding to create faces on final part

Figure 8–29

The flat pattern shown in Figure 8–29 might not be the layout that the designer wants to use. To alter the fold locations, the final part can be re-designed so that its flat layout would start differently. The designer might want to have three folds made from the same original face, rather than having to reposition the part to make the three folds. In this case, a better layout might be that shown in Figure 8–30.

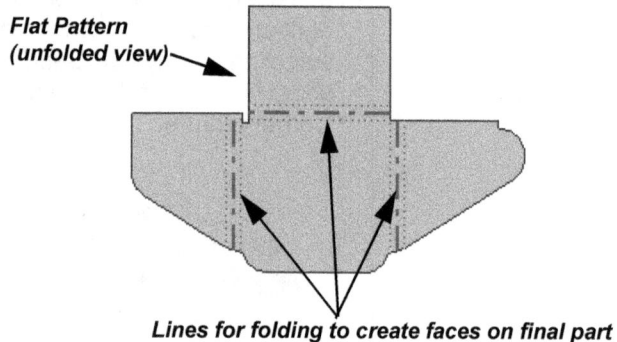

Flat Pattern (unfolded view)

Lines for folding to create faces on final part

Figure 8–30

Remember that Bend features form closed corners while Corner Seam features form open corners. To change the final part so that a different layout can be used on the sheet metal, you can convert Bend features into Corner Seams and also convert Corner Seams into Bends.

To convert a Bend, right-click on a Bend feature in the Model Browser and select **Change to Corner**, as shown in Figure 8–31.

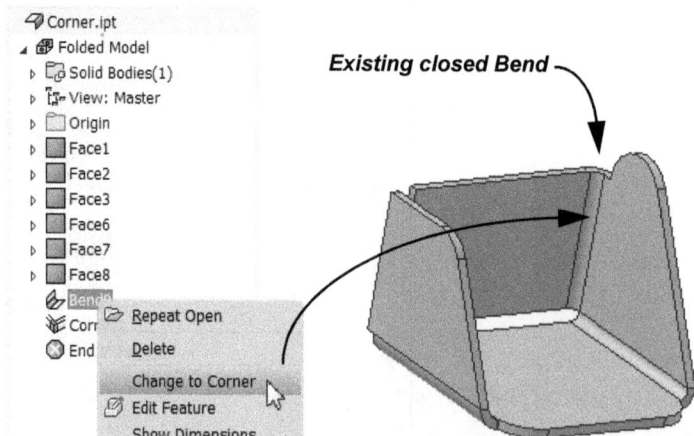

Existing closed Bend

Figure 8–31

Select the *Shape* and *Seam* options in the Corner Seam dialog box and click **OK** to complete the conversion, as shown in Figure 8–32.

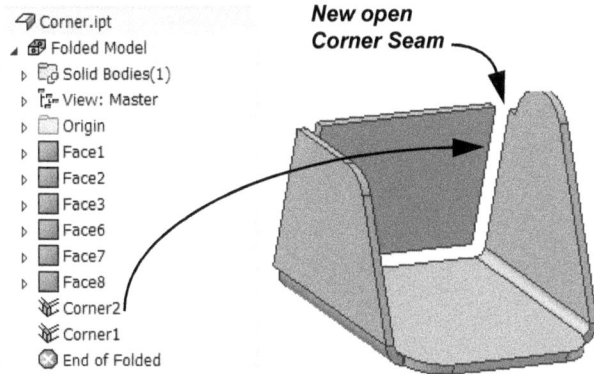

Figure 8–32

If you need to close an open Corner, right-click on the Corner feature in the Model Browser and select **Change to Bend**, as shown in Figure 8–33.

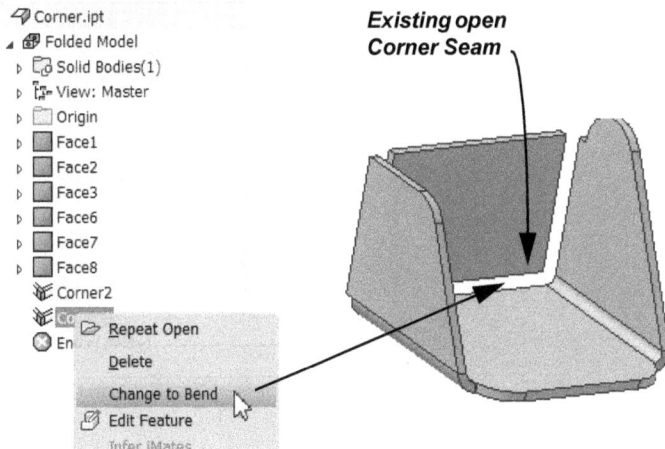

Figure 8–33

Select the *Bend*, *Double Bend*, and *Bend Extension* options in the Bend dialog box and click **OK** to complete the conversion. The new Bend feature displays as shown in Figure 8–34.

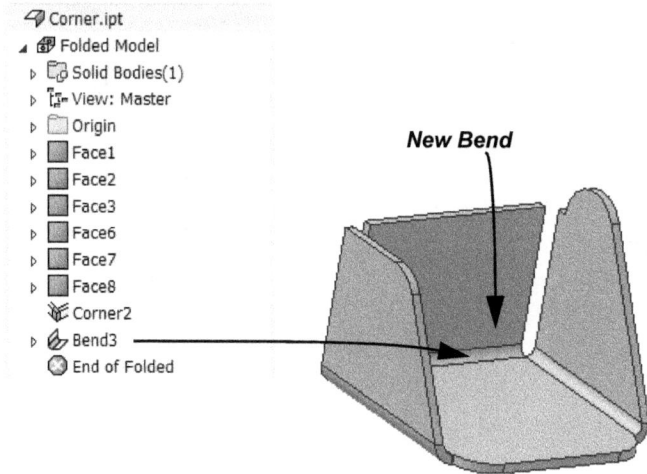

Figure 8–34

Practice 8a

Corner Seams and Miters I

Practice Objectives

- Control how two edges come together using a Corner Seam feature.
- Control how two edges meet that are coplanar using a Corner Miter feature
- Convert an existing Bend feature to a Corner feature and a Corner feature to a Bend feature to change the design intent of a sheet metal model.

In this practice, you will add Corner Seams to a part, convert a bend to a corner, and convert a corner to a bend as shown in Figure 8–35. You will start by adding a corner seam to two edges to control their alignment. You will then miter two edges and change a bend to a corner to open the edges of the part. This creates a disjointed face on the part. To reconnect the part, you will convert a corner to a bend.

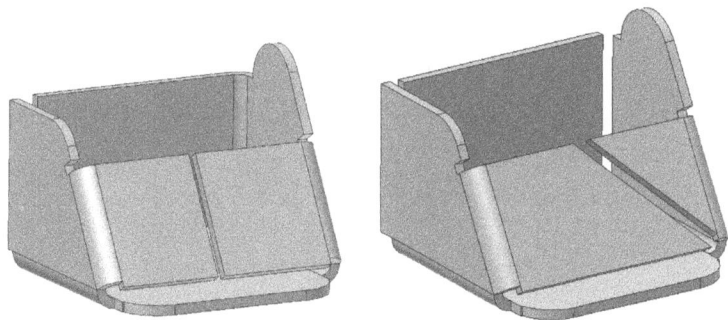

Figure 8–35

Task 1 - Add a Corner Seam.

1. Open **Corner.ipt**.

2. In the *Sheet Metal* tab>Modify panel, click ⚝ (Corner Seam). The Corner Seam dialog box opens.

3. Select the edges shown in Figure 8–36.

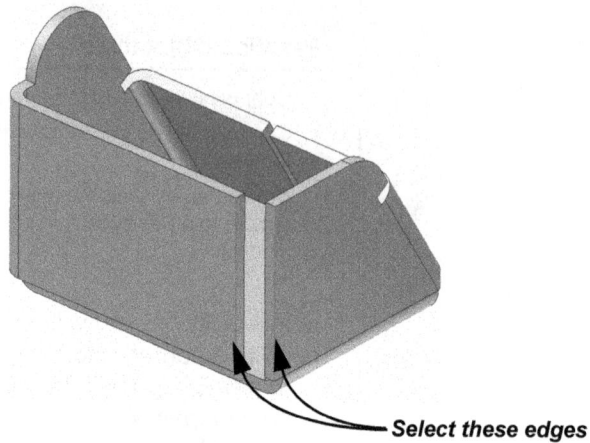

Select these edges

Figure 8–36

4. Ensure that the **Maximum Gap Distance** option is selected.

5. Click ⬛ (Overlap) or ⬛ (Reverse Overlap) so that the trapezoidal face overlaps the rectangular face. The order in which you select the edges affects which option you use.

6. Click **Apply** to create the Corner Seam feature shown in Figure 8–37.

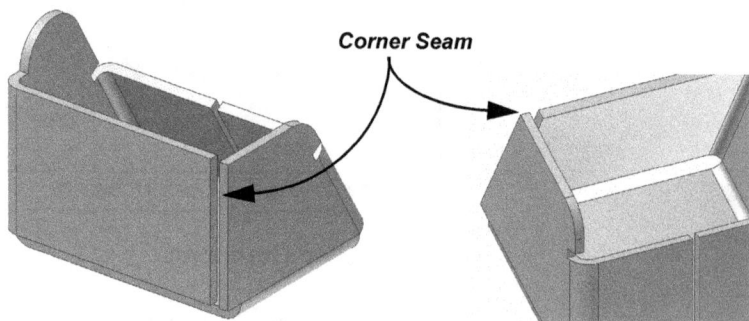

Corner Seam

Figure 8–37

Task 2 - Create a Miter.

1. Leave the Corner Seam dialog box open and select the edges shown in Figure 8–38.

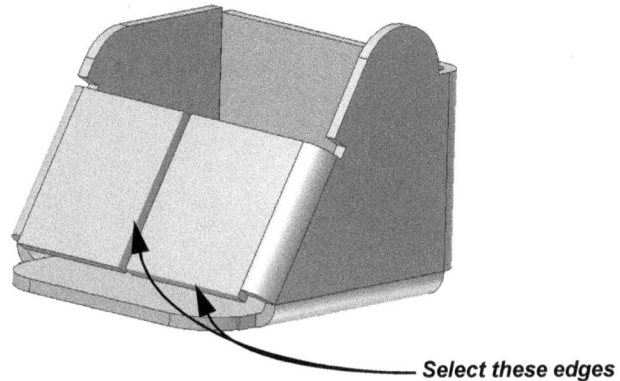

— *Select these edges*

Figure 8–38

2. The options in the Corner Seam dialog box change to **Miter** options (instead of **Seam**) because the faces are coplanar. Click ⬛ (45 Degree Miter).

3. Enter **Thickness * 1.5** in the *Gap* field and click **OK** to create the Corner Seam feature, as shown in Figure 8–39.

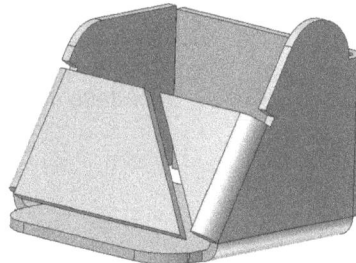

Figure 8–39

Task 3 - Change a corner to a bend.

1. In the Model Browser, right-click on **Corner1** and select **Change to Bend**. The Bend dialog box opens.

2. Click **OK** to create the bend. The face is connected to the part with two bends as shown in Figure 8–40. **Bend9** is converted to a corner in the next task.

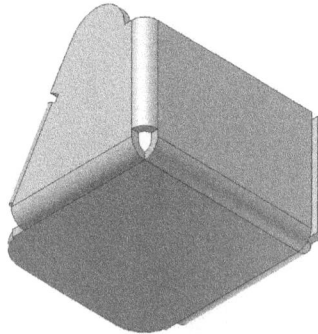

Figure 8–40

Task 4 - Change a bend to a corner.

1. In the Model Browser, right-click on **Bend9** and select **Change to Corner**. The Corner Seam dialog box opens.

2. Click (Symmetric Gap) and click **OK** to create the Corner feature. The part displays as shown in Figure 8–41. The face in the back is now connected properly.

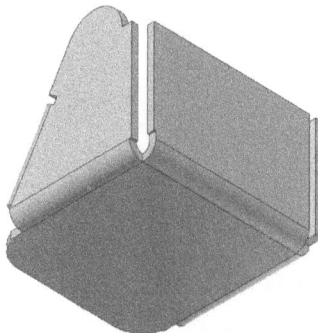

Figure 8–41

3. Save and close the file.

Practice 8b

Corner Seams and Miters II

Practice Objectives

- Control how two edges come together using a Corner Seam feature.
- Control how two faces meet that are coplanar using a Corner Miter feature.
- Control the gap of the miter using the gap value of the Corner Seam to ensure that values remain the same if changes are made to the sheet metal model.
- Edit existing Corner Seam features to capture an alternate design intent.

In this practice, you will use Corner Seams to align intersecting faces and miter coplanar faces as shown in Figure 8–42. For one corner, you will use (Symmetric Gap) with the **Measure Gap** option to set the Gap distance. For another corner, you will use (Symmetric Gap) and set the Gap manually. You will then edit the Corner Seams to see how the miter corners adjust. The miter using the **Measure Gap** option will adjust with the corner seam and the other will not. You will edit the second miter to use **Measure Gap**. Finally, you will add Corner Seams to the remaining corners of the model.

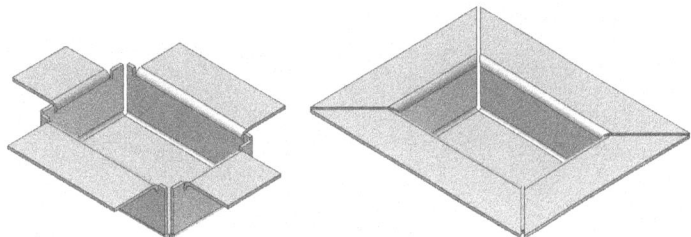

Figure 8–42

Task 1 - Create a flat pattern.

1. Open **Box.ipt**.

2. In the *Sheet Metal* tab>Modify panel, click (Corner Seam). The Corner Seam dialog box opens.

3. Select the edges shown in Figure 8–43.

Select these edges

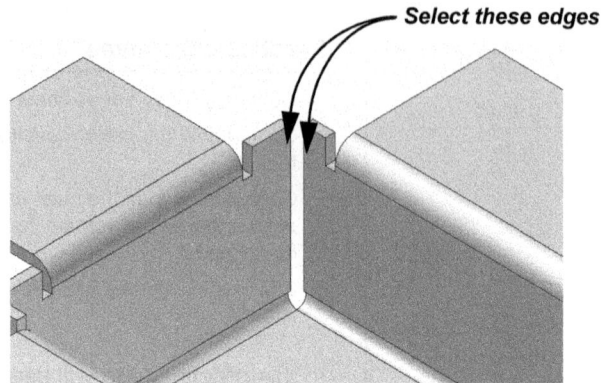

Figure 8–43

4. Click ⬚ (Symmetric Gap) and enter **Thickness * 3** in the *Gap* field.

5. Click **Apply** to create the Corner feature as shown in Figure 8–44.

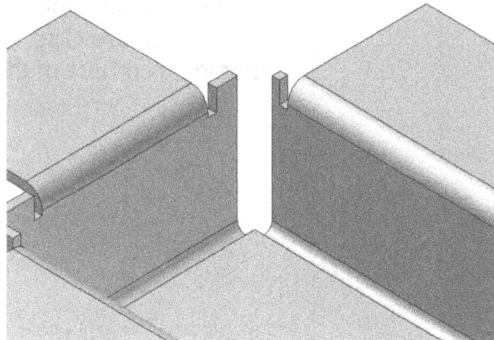

Figure 8–44

Task 2 - Create a miter corner.

1. Leave the Corner Seam dialog box open and select the edges shown in Figure 8–45. The options in the dialog box change to Miter options because the faces are coplanar.

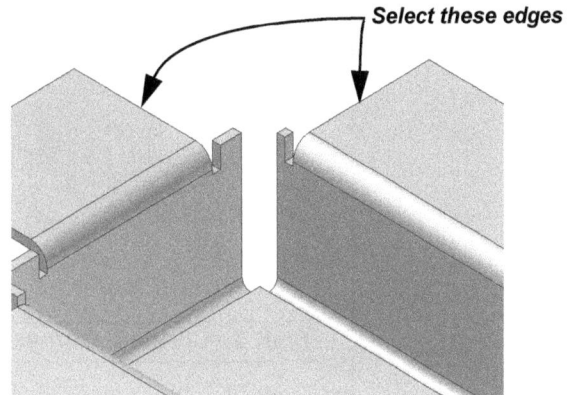

Select these edges

Figure 8–45

2. Select **Face/Edge Distance**.

3. Click ⬚ (Symmetric Gap).

4. Click ⬚ to expand the dialog box.

5. Click ⬚ (Measure Gap) and select the edges shown in Figure 8–46.

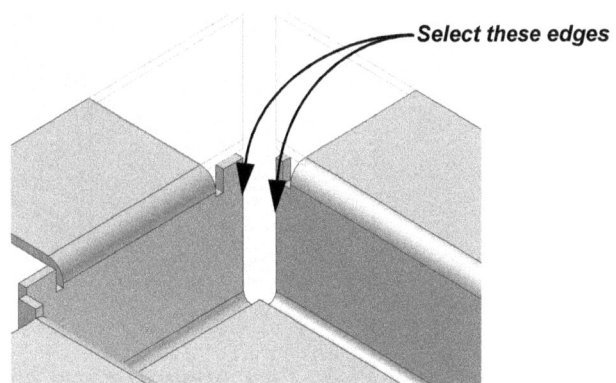

Select these edges

Figure 8–46

6. Click **OK**. The part displays as shown in Figure 8–47.

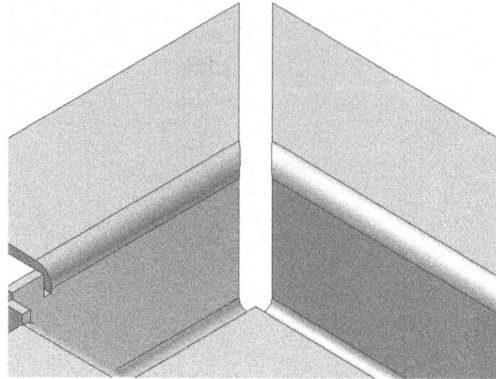

Figure 8–47

Task 3 - Create a Corner Seam.

---

1. Rotate the view to display one of the other corners of the box.

2. In the *Sheet Metal* tab>Modify panel, click ⬙ (Corner Seam). Create a corner seam on the edges shown in Figure 8–48. Use **Maximum Gap Distance** and

   ⬙ (Symmetric Gap) and enter **Thickness * 3** in the *Gap* field.

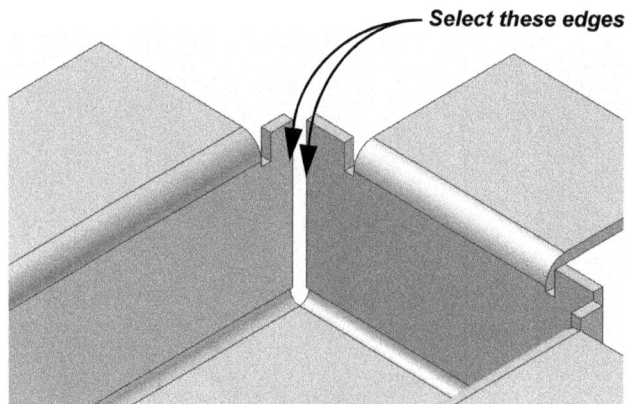

Select these edges

Figure 8–48

3. Click **Apply** to create the Corner Seam.

Task 4 - Create a Miter Corner Seam.

1. Create a miter corner seam on the edges shown in

   Figure 8–49. Use **Face/Edge Distance** and ⬛ (Symmetric Gap) and enter **Thickness * 3** in the *Gap* field.

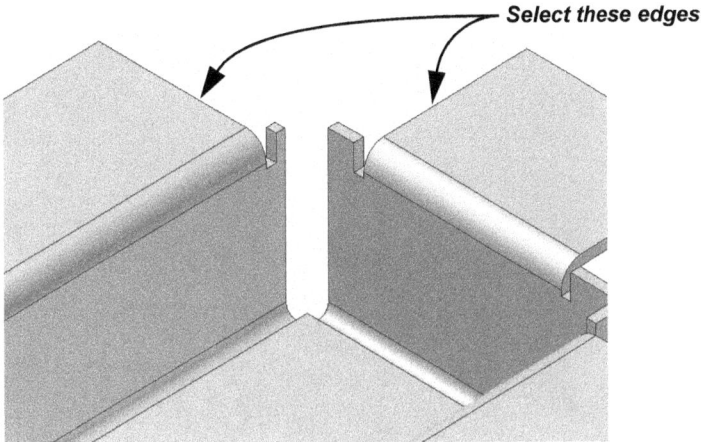

Figure 8–49

2. Click **OK** to create the corner seam shown in Figure 8–50.

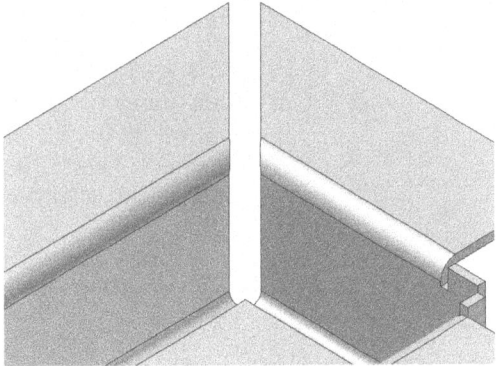

Figure 8–50

The miters created in Task 2 and Task 4 were created differently in terms of how the Gap value is calculated. One was created referencing the measured gap of its associated seam and the other was created by explicitly entering a value. In the next task you will edit the seam gap values and see how the miters update.

Task 5 - Edit the Gap value of the Corner Seams.

1. In the Model Browser, right-click on **Corner6** and select **Edit Feature**. The Corner Seam dialog box opens.

2. Change the *Gap* value to **Thickness** and click **OK**. The gap between the miter edges also changes because it was created using the **Measure Gap** option, as shown in Figure 8–51.

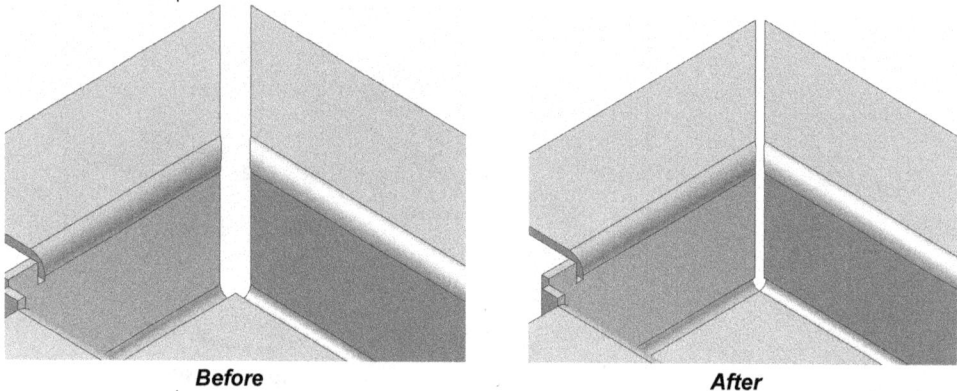

Before   *After*

Figure 8–51

3. In the Model Browser, right-click on **Corner8** and select **Edit Feature**. The Corner Seam dialog box opens.

4. Change the *Gap* value to **Thickness** and click **OK**. The gap between the intersecting edges is updated, but the gap between the miter edges is maintained at Thickness * 3 because it was created with an entered *Gap* value. The before and after models are shown in Figure 8–52.

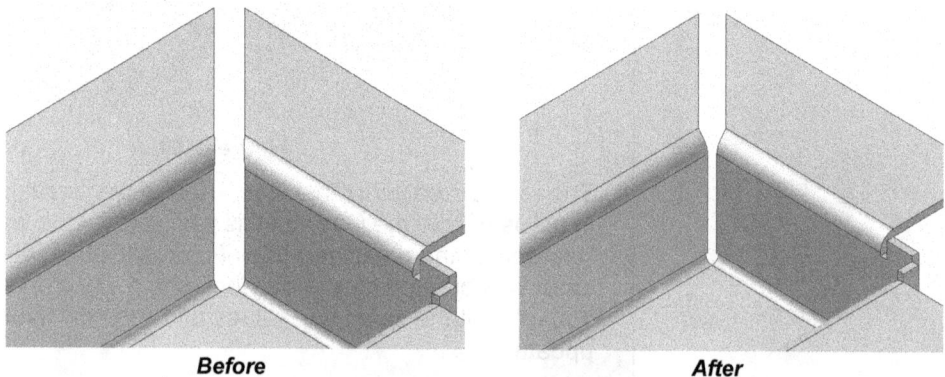

Before   *After*

Figure 8–52

5. In the Model Browser, right-click on **Corner9** and select **Edit Feature**. The Corner Seam dialog box opens.

6. Verify that **Face/Edge Distance** and ⬚ (Symmetric Gap) are selected.

7. Click ⬚ to expand the dialog box.

8. Click ⬚ (Measure Gap) and select the edges as shown in Figure 8–53.

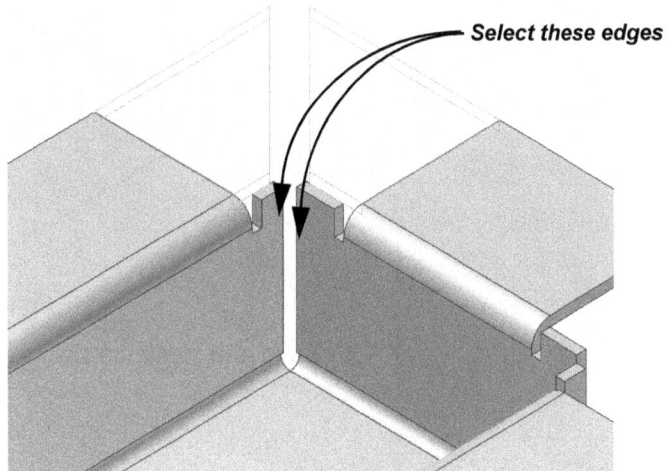

Select these edges

Figure 8–53

9. Click **OK** to accept the changes. The part displays as shown in Figure 8–54.

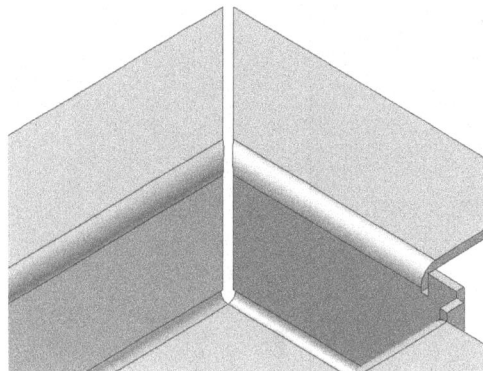

Figure 8–54

Task 6 - Add Corner Seams to the other corners of the part.

1. Add corner seams to the other corners of the part. For the intersecting faces, use **Maximum Gap Distance** with

   ⬚ (Symmetric Gap) and a *Gap* of **Thickness**. For the coplanar faces, use **Face/Edge Distance** with

   ⬚ (Symmetric Gap) and the **Measure Gap** option to align the faces to the adjacent corner seam. The model displays as shown in Figure 8–55.

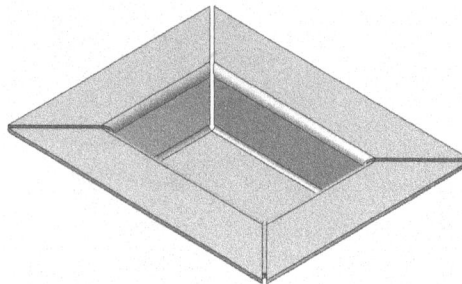

Figure 8–55

2. Save and close the file.

Chapter Review Questions

1. What is the main purpose of the **Corner Seam** tool? (Select all that apply.)

   a. Where two faces come together at an angle to each other, the Corner Seam tool creates the required space.

   b. Creates an opening where two adjacent faces were previously joined.

   c. Converts a Bend feature to a Corner feature that is open.

   d. Joins two adjacent faces that are non-planar to one another.

2. The corner seam is added to the model, followed by a corner miter as shown in Figure 8–56. How do you ensure that the corner miter gap value and the corner seam gap value reference one another?

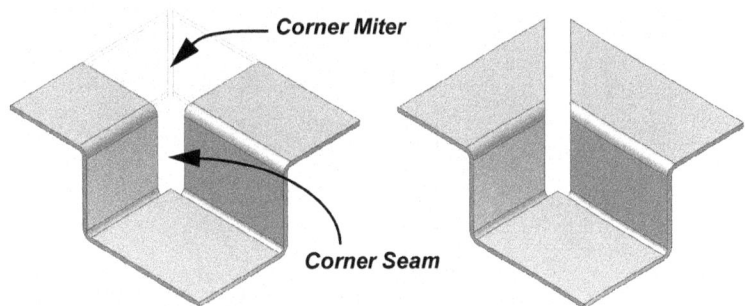

Corner Miter

Corner Seam

Figure 8–56

   a. In the Corner seam feature, expand the additional options and use the Measure Gap value to measure the distance between the mitered edges.

   b. In the Corner miter feature, expand the additional options and use the Measure Gap value to measure the distance between the edges used in the Corner seam feature.

   c. Either of the above achieves the required result.

3. Which of the following options can be used to convert an existing Bend to a Corner Seam?

   a. Change to Bend

   b. Change to Seam

   c. Change to Corner

   d. Edit Feature

4. The **Corner Seam - Rip** option is most commonly used after a solid model has been converted to a sheet metal model to open corners?

   a. True

   b. False

5. The **Maximum Gap Distance** measuring option creates a corner seam in which the gap value is measured consistent with the manufacturing inspection process. The **Face/Edge Distance** measuring option creates a corner seam in which the gap is measured from the face adjacent to the first selected edge to the second selected edge. Which measuring option (shown in Figure 8–57) was used if the following Seam measuring types are available?

Figure 8–57

   a. Maximum Gap Distance

   b. Face/Edge Distance

Command Summary

Button	Command	Location
N/A	**Change to Bend**	• *(Context menu with Corner feature selected.)*
N/A	**Change to Corner**	• *(Context menu with Bend feature selected.)*
	Corner Seam	• **Ribbon:** *Sheet Metal* tab>Modify panel

Flat Pattern Environment

One of the final stages of designing sheet metal parts is creating a flat pattern. Flat patterns describe the part in an unfolded state. Manufacturing drawings then use views of the flat pattern for fabrication. The unfolded view can also be used to construct additional features that are not displayed on the folded part, such as custom-shaped corner reliefs, or center locations for punches.

Learning Objectives in this Chapter

- Flatten planar and non-planar folded sheet metal geometry to provide flattened details for manufacturing.
- Manipulate the horizontal or vertical orientation of the flattened sheet metal geometry to permit proper nesting of the metal and grain direction.
- Save a manipulated orientation as the default view or as a user-defined orientation.
- Specify how punch features are represented in a flat pattern by customizing either the Default Rule or the Flat Pattern feature.
- Specify whether the bend angle is measured from the inside or outside of the sheet metal model.
- Add features to the flattened sheet metal model to include geometry that is not required in the folded model.
- Export the flat pattern of a sheet metal model in a .DWG, .DWF, or .SAT file format for review in another software application.
- Export the face of a sheet metal model in a .DWG or .DWF file format for review in another software application.

9.1 Creating Flat Patterns

A flat pattern is an unfolded view of the model that exists in the sheet metal file. The flat pattern displays information about the folded model including bend lines, bend zones, locations for punches, and the overall extents of the part before any bends are created. Flat patterns are typically used to create drawing views or for export for manufacturing processes.

Figure 9–1 shows a sheet metal part in its Folded state on the left and in its flat pattern state on the right.

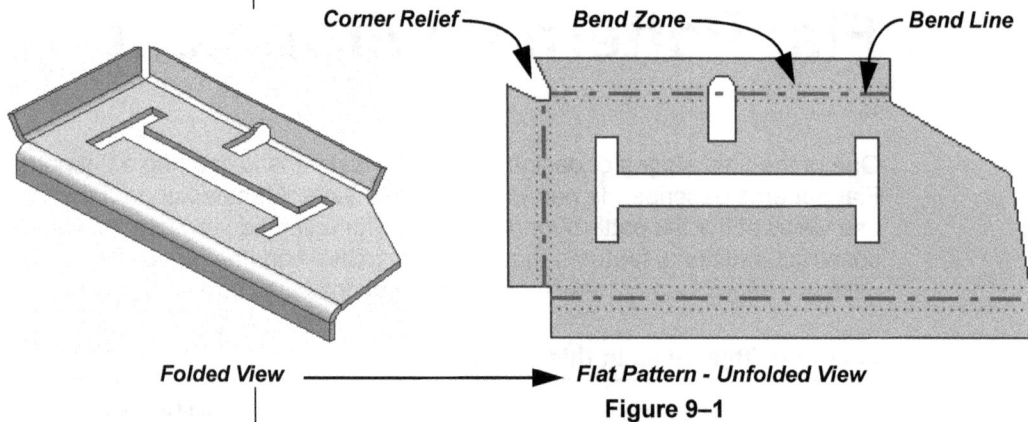

Figure 9–1

General Steps

Use the following general steps to create a Flat Pattern feature:

1. Create a sheet metal part with bends.
2. Activate the **Flat Pattern** command.

Step 1 - Create a sheet metal part with bends.

Create a sheet metal part with folds, bends, punches, or other sheet metal features that need to be on the final model, as shown in Figure 9–2.

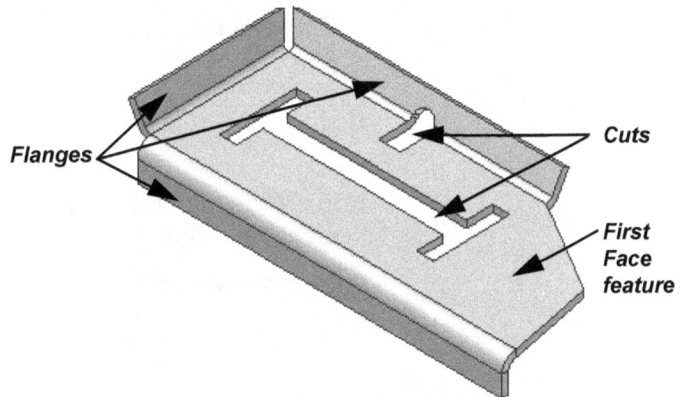

Figure 9–2

Step 2 - Activate the Flat Pattern command.

In the *Sheet Metal* tab>Flat Pattern panel, click [icon] (Create Flat Pattern). The flat pattern of the model displays in the graphics window, as shown in Figure 9–3.

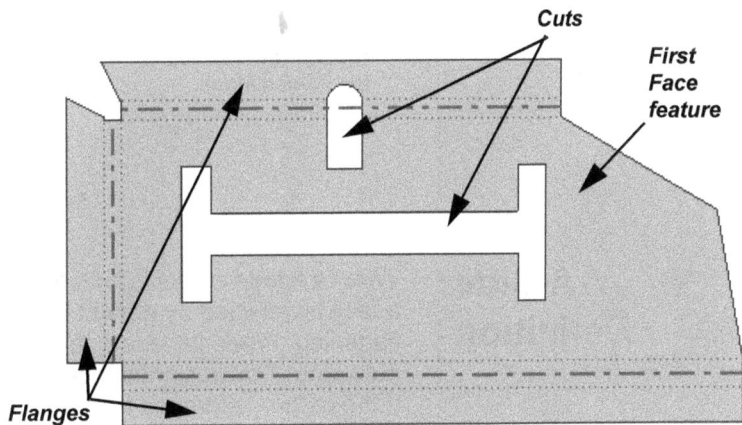

Figure 9–3

When you first create a flat pattern, a **Flat Pattern** node is added to the Model Browser, as shown in Figure 9–4. The node automatically becomes active enabling you to work in the flat pattern environment.

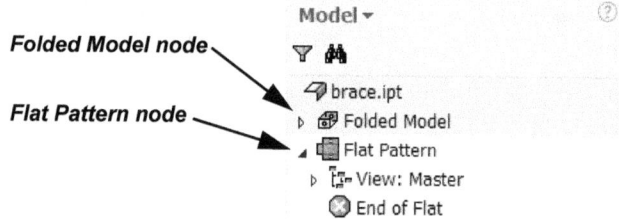

Folded Model node

Flat Pattern node

Figure 9–4

In the Model Browser, when the flat pattern is initially created, the features in the **Folded Model** are collapsed. To expand the

Folded Model node, click ▷ (Arrow) in the Model Browser, as shown in Figure 9–5.

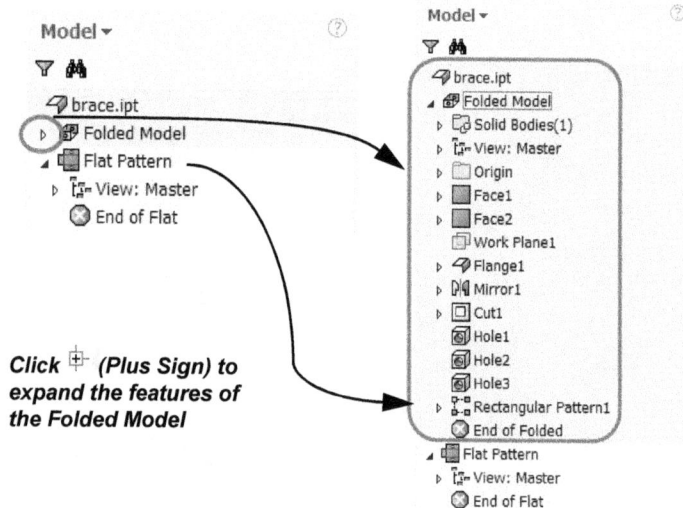

Click ⊞ (Plus Sign) to expand the features of the Folded Model

Figure 9–5

A-Side Definition

When a folded model is flatted using the **Flat Pattern** command, a face is selected by default to be used as the reference for flattening. When flattened, the assigned face is oriented to face outwards. This assigned face is known as the A-Side reference. If the default reference for flattening is incorrect or needs to be changed, you can manually assign this reference.

To manually assign the A-Side reference, in the Flat Pattern panel, click (Define A-Side), shown in Figure 9–6.

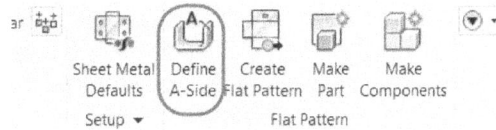

Figure 9–6

Once the command has been selected, select the face on the model that is to face upward when the flat pattern is created. An A Side Definition node is added to the Model Browser, as shown in Figure 9–7.

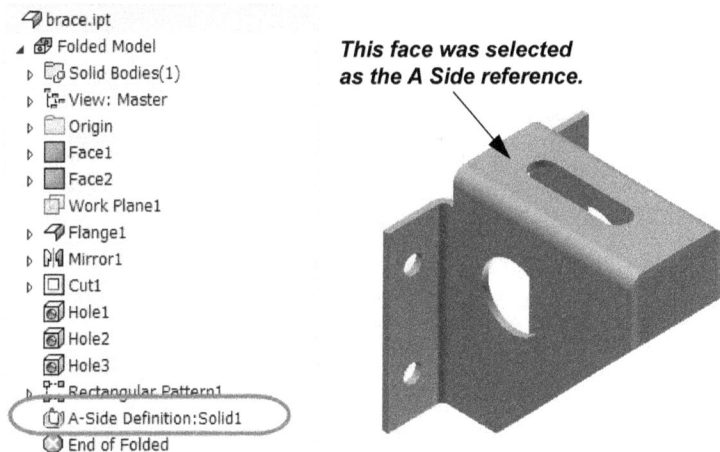

This face was selected as the A Side reference.

Figure 9–7

Consider the following when working with the A-Side Definition node:

• To review the A-Side Definition in the model, right-click on the **A-Side Definition** node in the Model Browser and select **Highlight A-Side**. When highlighted, the faces are added to the currently active selection set and are displayed in blue.

• The **A-Side Definition** node can be deleted from the model if a flat pattern does not exist in the model. To delete the reference, right-click on the **A-Side Definition** node in the Model Browser and select **Delete**.

- If a change to the flat pattern orientation causes the A-Side to fail, right-click on the **A-Side Definition** node in the Model Browser and select a new face.

- To redefine the default A-Side reference assignment, you must delete the Flat Pattern and explicitly assign the A-Side Definition reference, using the **Define A-Side** option to assign a new face.

Switching Between the Folded and Flat Environments

You can add features to the Folded Model view or Flat Pattern view by switching between them. Switching is similar to switching between active parts in an assembly, or active sheets in a drawing file. To activate the Folded Model or Flat Pattern view, double-click on the associated node in the Model Browser, as shown in Figure 9–8.

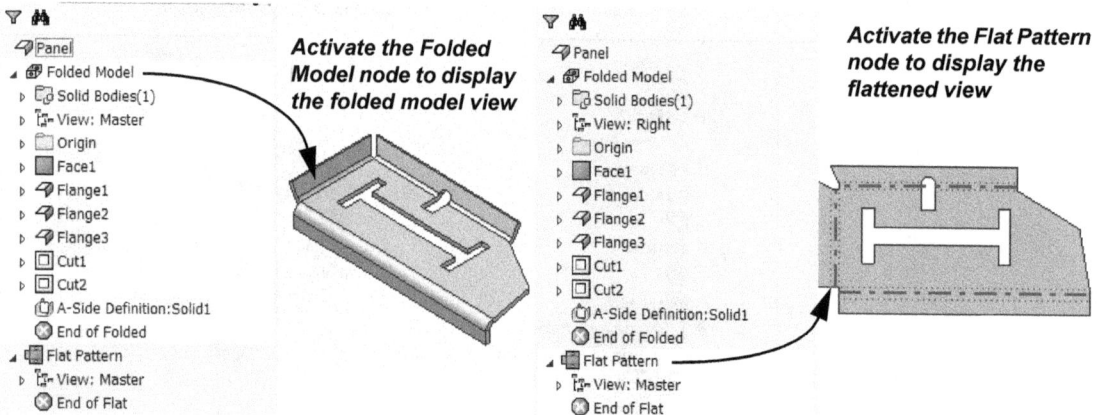

Activate the Folded Model node to display the folded model view

Activate the Flat Pattern node to display the flattened view

Figure 9–8

Defer Update

New in 2017

Right-click on the **Flat Pattern** node in the Model Browser and select **Defer Update**, as shown in Figure 9–9. If this option is activated, the flat pattern will not update with changes to the folded model until it is deactivated. The icon on the **Flat Pattern** node in the Model Browser will change to ⚡, indicating that changed to the folded model were made and that the defer status should be changed to update the flat pattern definition.

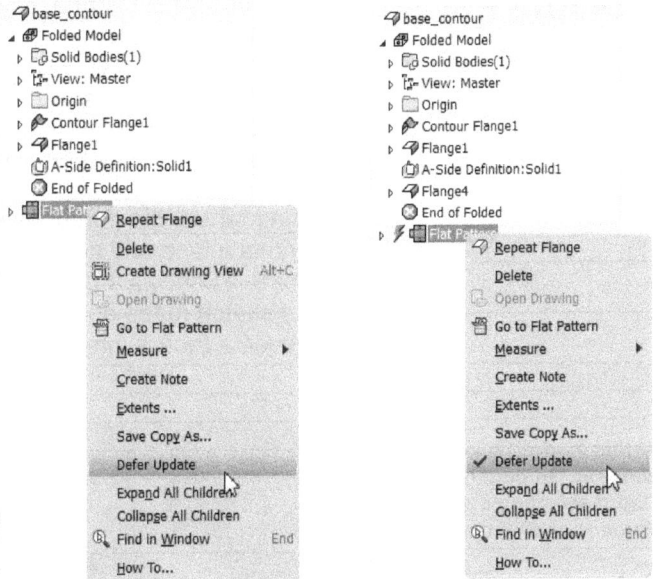

base_contour
⊿ Folded Model
  ▷ Solid Bodies(1)
  ▷ View: Master
  ▷ Origin
  ▷ Contour Flange1
  ▷ Flange1
    A-Side Definition:Solid1
    End of Folded
  ▷ Flat Pat...

    Repeat Flange
    Delete
    Create Drawing View   Alt+C
    Open Drawing
    Go to Flat Pattern
    Measure   ▸
    Create Note
    Extents ...
    Save Copy As...
    Defer Update
    Expand All Children
    Collapse All Children
    Find in Window   End
    How To...

base_contour
⊿ Folded Model
  ▷ Solid Bodies(1)
  ▷ View: Master
  ▷ Origin
  ▷ Contour Flange1
  ▷ Flange1
    A-Side Definition:Solid1
  ▷ Flange4
    End of Folded
  ▷ Flat Pat...

    Repeat Flange
    Delete
    Open Drawing
    Go to Flat Pattern
    Measure   ▸
    Create Note
    Extents ...
    Save Copy As...
  ✓ Defer Update
    Expand All Children
    Collapse All Children
    Find in Window   End
    How To...

Figure 9–9

Unfolding the Flat Pattern

The A-Side reference is the face of the part that is selected as the primary face to display in the flat pattern. This face is oriented orthographically to face the screen in a plan-view. Other faces and features are unfolded from it, as shown in Figure 9–10.

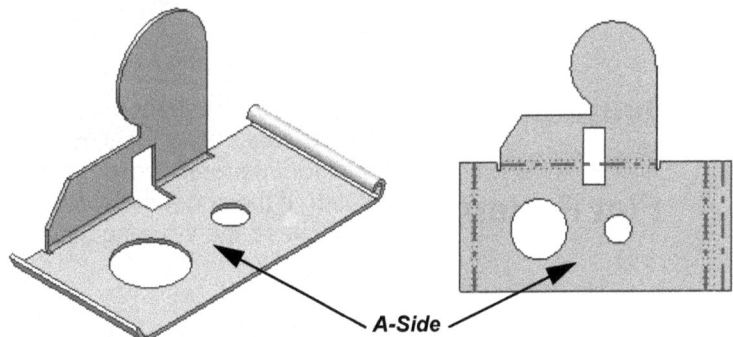

A-Side

Figure 9–10

Unfolding Parts Without a Planar Face

Sheet metal parts might or might not have a planar face to select as a default for creating the flat pattern. This situation can occur if the part is created as a Contour Flange without linear segments. In some cases, parts that have been converted from a non-sheet metal part, or imported from other software, might not have a feature history from which to select a face.

In cases where the part does not have a flat face, the software interprets a face and generates the flat pattern on its own. Figure 9–11 shows a part created as a single Contour Flange with a sketch made only of arcs. There is no planar face. However, a face is interpreted to unfold the flat pattern.

For this model, you can create the flat pattern without selecting a surface reference on the model.

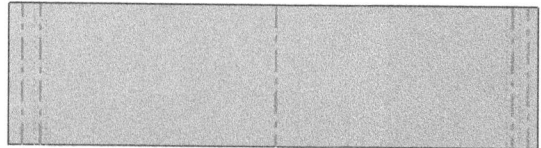

Figure 9–11

If the face that was automatically selected is not correct, you can define your own. To change the face, right-click on any existing **Flat Pattern** node and select **Delete**. A Warning dialog box might open, indicating that any drawing views associated with the flat pattern are going to be deleted. Accept the warning so that you can recreate a correct Flat Pattern. Using the **Define A-Side** option, select the required face and recreate the flat pattern.

Overlapping Features in Flat Pattern

When creating a sheet metal part, interferences are monitored between features of the folded model. However, it does not check for interferences in the flat pattern until the flat pattern is created. If the sheet metal component cannot be created from a single sheet, the Warning dialog box opens as shown in Figure 9–12.

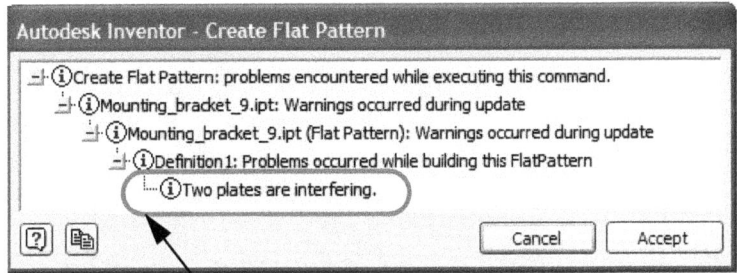

Autodesk Inventor - Create Flat Pattern

- (i) Create Flat Pattern: problems encountered while executing this command.
  - (i) Mounting_bracket_9.ipt: Warnings occurred during update
    - (i) Mounting_bracket_9.ipt (Flat Pattern): Warnings occurred during update
      - (i) Definition 1: Problems occurred while building this FlatPattern
        - (i) Two plates are interfering.

Cancel   Accept

Warning indicates interference

Figure 9–12

If you click **Cancel**, the flat pattern is not created and you are returned to the folded model. If you click **Accept**, the flat pattern displays with the overlapping features, as shown in Figure 9–13. In either case, you should modify the folded model to eliminate interference in the flat pattern.

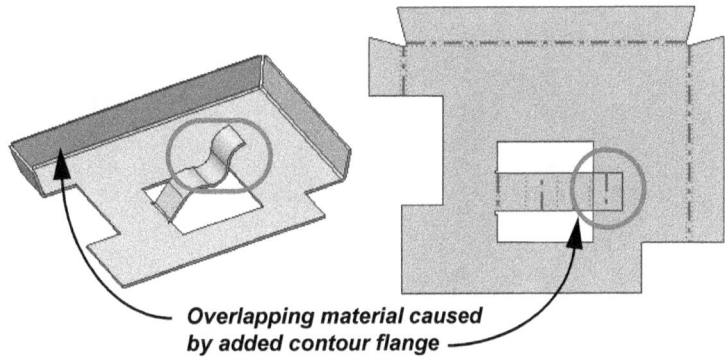

Overlapping material caused by added contour flange

Figure 9–13

9.2 Orienting Flat Patterns

The default orientation of the flat pattern might not be required for nesting of the metal and setting grain direction. You can reorient a flat pattern to be displayed as required for documentation, as shown in Figure 9–14.

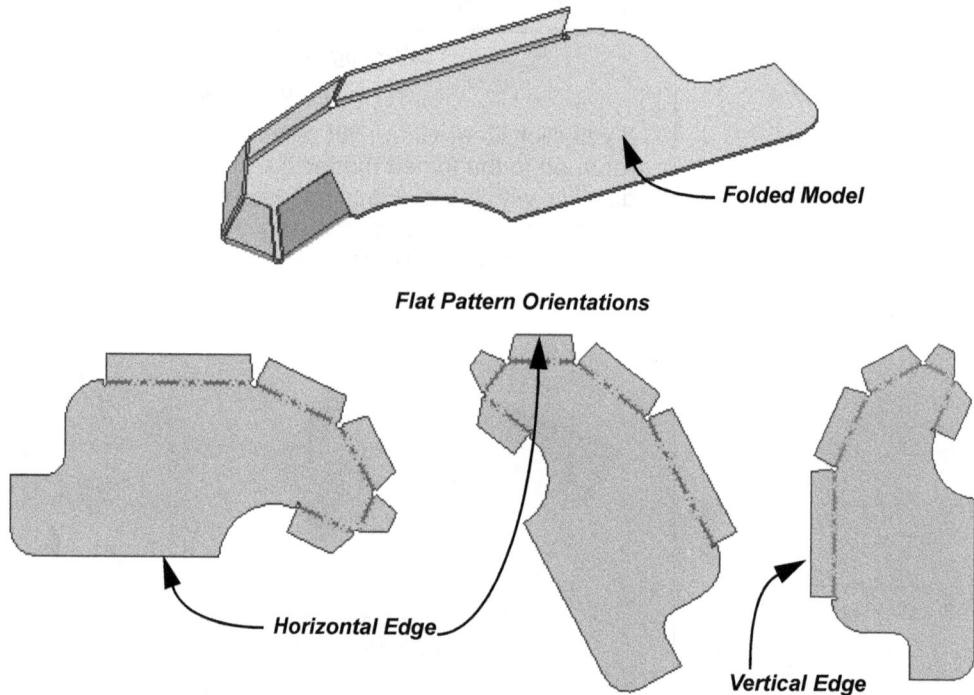

Folded Model

Flat Pattern Orientations

Horizontal Edge

Vertical Edge

Figure 9–14

General Steps

Use the following general steps to orient a Flat Pattern feature:

1. Activate the Flat Pattern.
2. Open the Edit Flat Pattern Definition dialog box.
3. Set the Alignment options.
4. Flip the Base Face (optional).
5. Save the Orientations (optional).
6. Complete the command.

Step 1 - Activate the Flat Pattern.

Double-click on the **Flat Pattern** node in the Model Browser. The Flat Pattern view of the model displays similar to that shown in Figure 9–15.

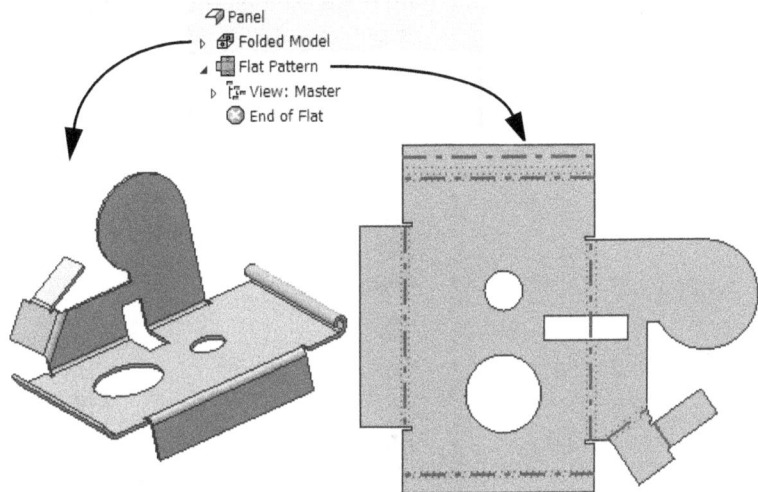

Figure 9–15

Step 2 - Open the Edit Flat Pattern Definition dialog box.

Right-click on the **Flat Pattern** node in the Model Browser and select **Edit Flat Pattern Definition**. The Flat Pattern dialog box opens as shown in Figure 9–16.

If the Flat Pattern feature was created before Autodesk® Inventor® 2009 you might need to delete and recreate the flat pattern to use the orientation when editing the flat pattern.

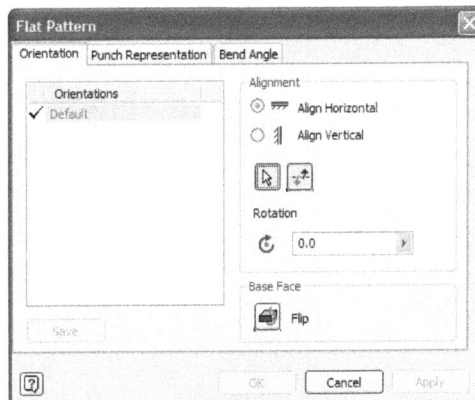

Figure 9–16

Step 3 - Set the Alignment options.

In the *Orientation* tab, click 〃 (Align Horizontal) or ∦ (Align Vertical). Verify that ⬚ (Alignment Axis) is selected and select an edge on the part that you want to follow the selected alignment option, as shown in Figure 9–17.

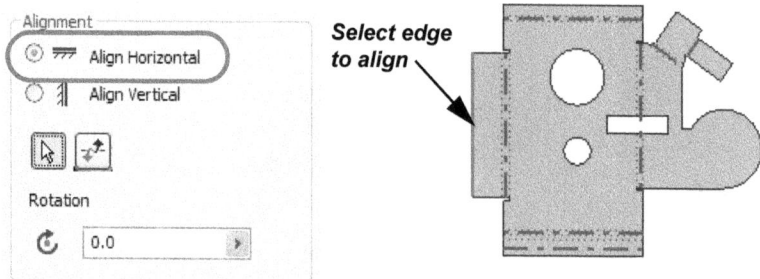

Figure 9–17

An *alignment indicator* displays a set of red and green arrows indicating the direction of the coordinate system. The longer arrow indicates the horizontal axis (red). The shorter arrow indicates the vertical axis (green). When the **Align Horizontal** option is selected, the horizontal arrow is red, as shown in Figure 9–18. When the **Align Vertical** option is selected, the vertical arrow is red. These arrows help determine the resulting orientation of the flat pattern. When you select an edge, the alignment indicator moves to that edge to preview the new alignment.

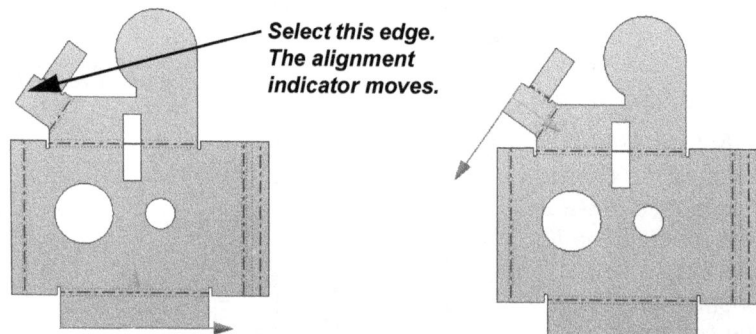

Figure 9–18

Select the edge to which to align and click **Apply**. The selected edge becomes horizontal, as shown in Figure 9–19.

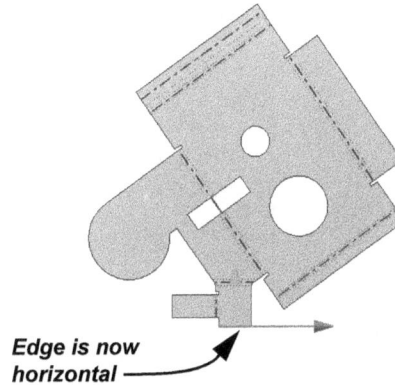

Edge is now horizontal

Figure 9–19

Rotational control can also be incorporated as part of the *Alignment* options to reorient a sheet metal flat pattern. Enter a rotational value for additional control when defining the flat pattern's orientation. Figure 9–20 shows the *Rotation* field in the Flat Pattern dialog box. The sheet metal model shown on the right indicates that a 12 degree rotation was applied to the model.

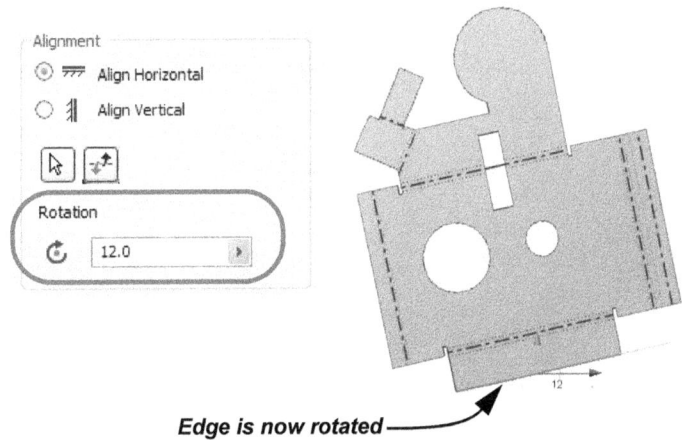

Edge is now rotated

Figure 9–20

Step 4 - Flip the Base Face (optional).

![Flip icon] (Flip) reverses the direction of the Y-Axis. As with the *Alignment* options described in Step 3, the new alignment is previewed first. After clicking ![Flip icon] (Flip), click **Apply** to reorient the flat pattern. An example of possible results is shown in Figure 9–21.

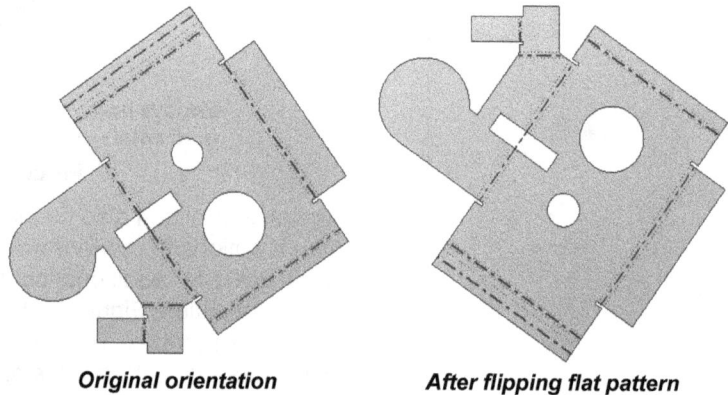

Original orientation   *After flipping flat pattern*

Figure 9–21

Step 5 - Save the Orientations (optional).

When you initially edit the orientation of the flat pattern you are editing the default orientation, as indicated by **Default** in the *Orientations* area, as shown in Figure 9–22.

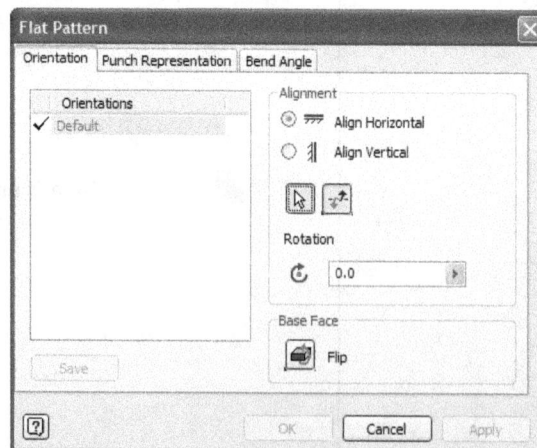

Figure 9–22

You can create additional user-defined orientations as required. These saved orientations can be used to quickly reorient the model or in a Sheet Metal iPart, to define the flat pattern orientation for each iPart member.

How To: Save a User-Defined Orientation for Use with an iPart Factory

1. Right-click on the Default orientation or on a user-defined orientation if one exists, and select **New**.
2. Define the *Alignment* settings as described in Steps 3 and 4.
3. Click **Apply** to reorient the flat pattern.

How To: Activate a User-Defined Orientation

1. Double-click on the required Orientation in the Flat Pattern dialog box to activate it. A checkmark displays next to the active orientation. The alignment arrows display on the model.
2. Click **Apply** to reorient the flat pattern.

Step 6 - Complete the command.

Click **OK** to reorient the flat pattern and close the Flat Pattern dialog box. Alternatively, you can right-click and select **OK (Enter)** to complete the feature.

If you have already clicked **Apply** to reorient the flat pattern, click **Cancel** to close the Flat Pattern dialog box.

9.3 Punch Representations

Punches Through a Feature

Punch features can be displayed in different representations in the Flat Pattern view. The available representation options depend on whether the Punch has a thickness setting that punches completely through a face or not. For Punches that do not go all of the way through or Punches that are formed, such as louvers, the available representation options are reduced.

The default style is set with the Sheet Metal Rule. You can edit the rule or edit the flat pattern to change the display. Figure 9–23 shows the dialog boxes and available options for setting the Punch representation.

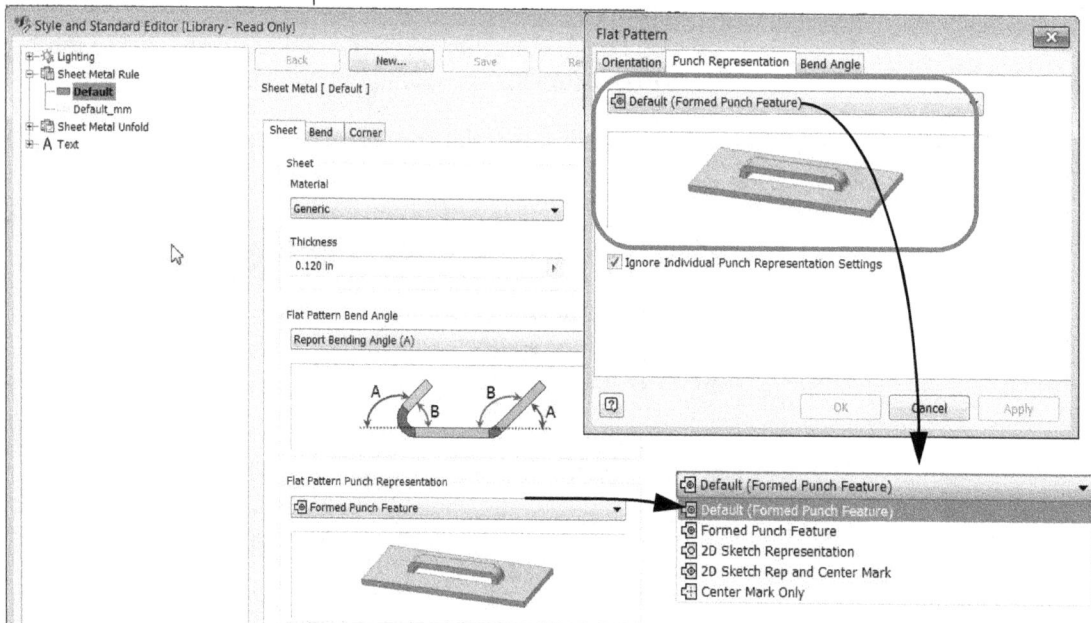

Figure 9–23

Enhanced in 2017

When placing a punch feature in a model, the Punch Tool dialog box includes the **Flat Pattern Punch Representation** menu. This enables you to select different representations for individual punch features. However, to enable this in a flat pattern, the **Ignore Individual Punch Representation Settings** checkbox on the *Punch Representation* tab, in the Flat Pattern dialog box must be cleared.

The four styles of flat pattern punch representations include:

- **Formed Punch Feature:** Displays Sheet Metal Punch iFeatures in the flat pattern as 3D features. An example is shown in Figure 9–24.

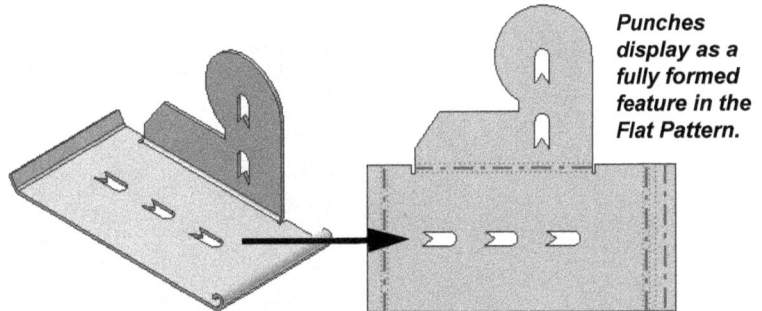

Punches display as a fully formed feature in the Flat Pattern.

Figure 9–24

- **2D Sketch Representation:** Enables the display of Sheet Metal Punch iFeatures in the flat pattern as a 2D sketch of the feature. The 2D sketch must have been defined in the Sheet Metal Punch iFeature. An example is shown in Figure 9–25 using a simple rectangular sketch that was assigned when the iFeature definition was created.

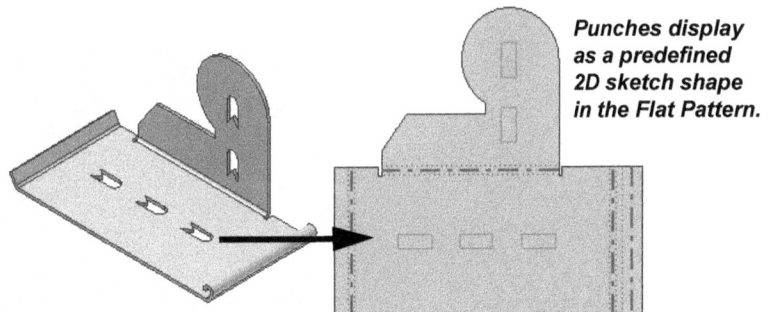

Punches display as a predefined 2D sketch shape in the Flat Pattern.

Figure 9–25

- ⊡ **2D Sketch Rep and Center Mark:** Displays Sheet Metal Punch iFeatures in the flat pattern as a previously defined 2D sketch and center mark. An example is shown in Figure 9–26.

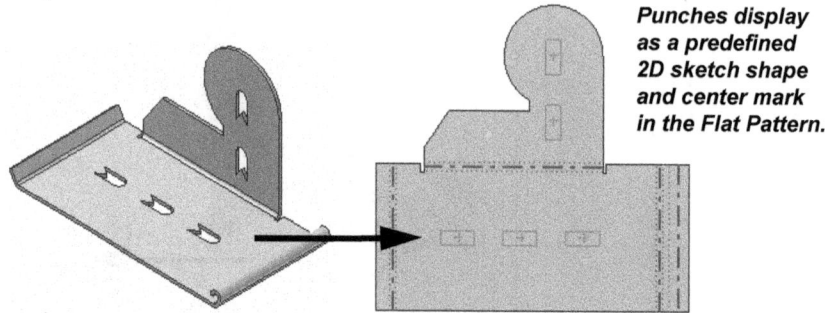

Punches display as a predefined 2D sketch shape and center mark in the Flat Pattern.

Figure 9–26

- ⊞ **Center Mark Only:** Displays Sheet Metal Punch iFeatures in the flat pattern only as a sketched center mark. An example is shown in Figure 9–27.

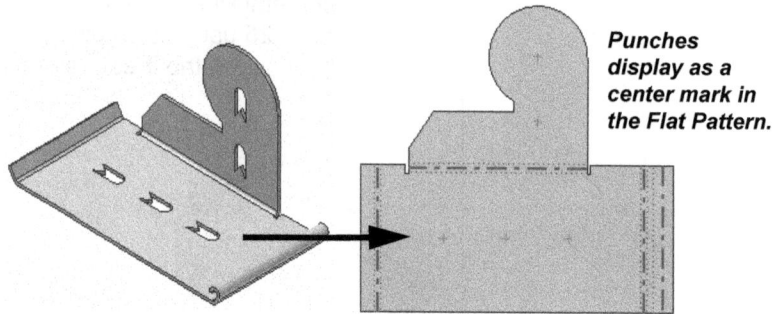

Punches display as a center mark in the Flat Pattern.

Figure 9–27

Embossed Features

Some punched features require material deformation, but do not cut fully through a part, as shown in Figure 9–28. They result in embossed areas, such as dimples or louvers. The Autodesk Inventor software is not able to flatten this type of feature.

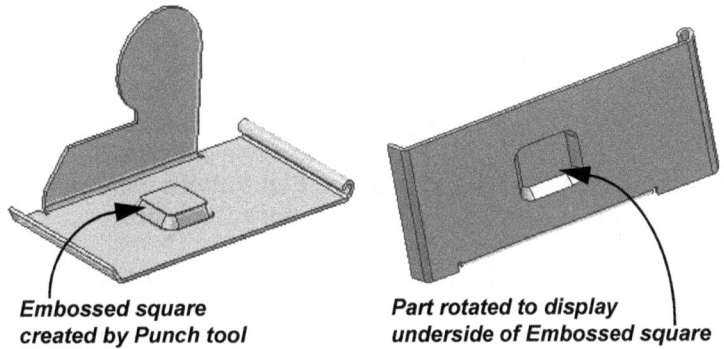

**Embossed square
created by Punch tool**

**Part rotated to display
underside of Embossed square**

Figure 9–28

When the flat pattern displays, the embossed feature is not
flattened. The Punch feature is displayed according to the
Punch Representation settings in the Flat Pattern dialog box or
Punch Tool dialog box. Figure 9–29 shows a formed Punch
feature in a flat pattern.

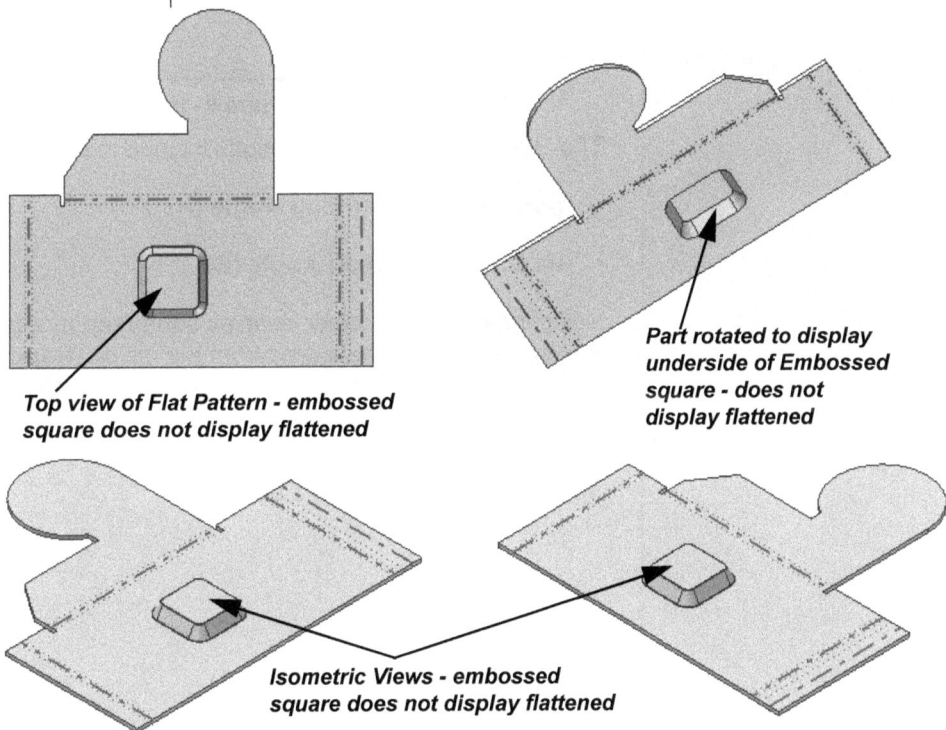

**Top view of Flat Pattern - embossed
square does not display flattened**

**Part rotated to display
underside of Embossed
square - does not
display flattened**

**Isometric Views - embossed
square does not display flattened**

Figure 9–29

9.4 Bend Angle

The Bend Angles reporting method for a drawing can be controlled using the *Bend Angle* tab in the Flat Pattern dialog box, as shown in Figure 9–30. To open this dialog box, right-click on the **Flat Pattern** node in the Model Browser and select **Edit Flat Pattern Definition**.

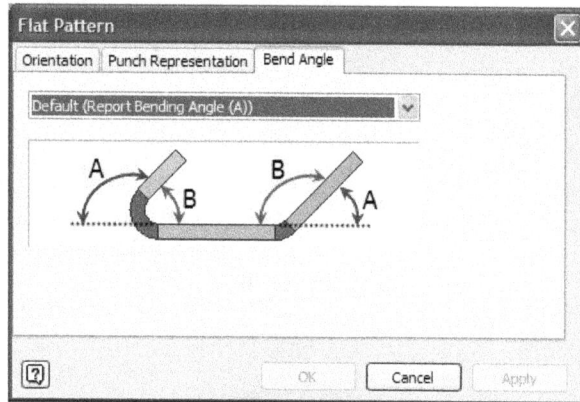

Figure 9–30

The Bend Angle reporting options include the following:

- **Reporting on Bending Angle (A)**

- **Reporting on Open Angle (B)**

Selecting one or the other enables you to report a bend angle in the drawing that is measured from the inside (**Reporting on Bending Angle (A)**) or outside (**Reporting on Open Angle (B)**).

9.5 Flat Pattern Cleanup

To cleanup flat patterns from previous releases, delete the flat pattern, recreate it in the current version, and use the cleanup commands.

Most sheet metal feature creation and editing is done in the Folded Model environment. Features that are added to, removed from, or edited in a folded model update and display in the flat pattern.

Adding Features to a Flat Pattern

Some features do not need to be displayed on the folded model, although they do need to be created during fabrication. This is done to keep the folded model as simple as possible. Sometimes this is done for cosmetic reasons. In other cases, the geometry cannot be generated in the folded model. This often involves removing material in the flat pattern for bend reliefs, but not in the folded model. This could also include punches, corner chamfers, corner rounds, extrusions, revolves, and other features.

Adding features to a flat pattern is called *Flat Pattern Cleanup*. Figure 9–31 shows a model with a Punch Feature added to the flat pattern. The Folded Model view is on the left. The flat pattern of the model with a single sketch, which includes two Center Points for locating a Punch feature is on the right.

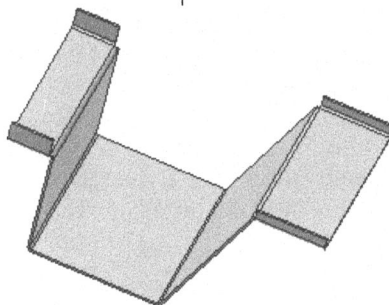

Folded Model

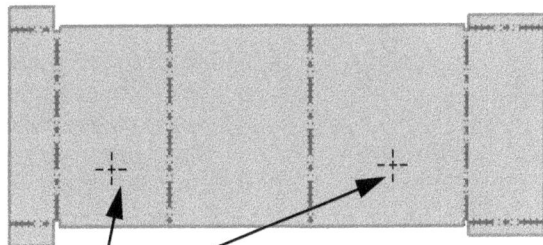

New sketch with two Center Points for a Punch feature to be created in the Flat Pattern

Figure 9–31

Punch features added to the flat pattern cannot be displayed with alternative 2D Punch Representations.

In Figure 9–32 the Punch feature is completed and only exists in the flat pattern. In the Model Browser in the example, there is a Punch (iFeature) in the Flat Pattern environment, but no Punch in the Folded Model environment.

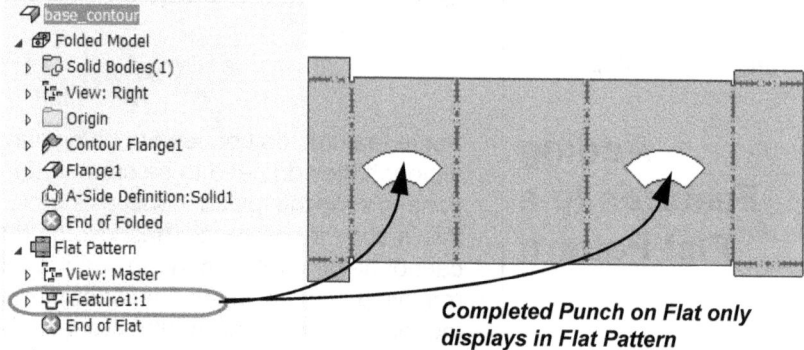

Completed Punch on Flat only displays in Flat Pattern

Figure 9–32

Copy to Flat Pattern

Unconsumed sketches that are created in a folded model are not automatically copied to the flat pattern. To copy the sketch so that it displays in the flat pattern and maintains an associative link to the folded model, right-click on the unconsumed sketch and select **Copy to Flat Pattern**. If the sketch is used in the folded model to create a feature, it becomes consumed. However, you can still right-click on the sketch that is nested in its feature and select **Copy to Flat Pattern** to display it in the Flat Model. Because of the associative nature of this command, any changes made to the sketch in the Folded Model environment reflect in the Flat Pattern environment. Once in the flat pattern, you can control the sketch's visibility in the same way as other features, and it is available to be controlled with layers when exporting.

Flat Pattern Features Panel

The Flat Pattern environment includes tools for sketched features (such as **Cut** and **Punch**) and tools for placed features (such as **Corner Chamfer**). All tools in the *Flat Pattern* tab work the same as in the Folded Model or Solid Modeling environment. The *Flat Pattern* tab is shown in Figure 9–33.

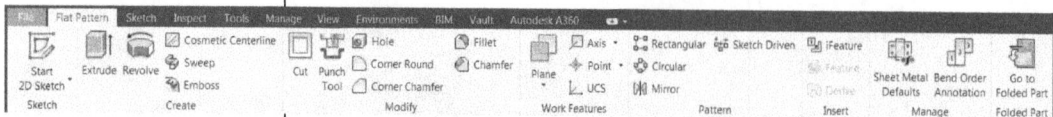

Figure 9–33

General Steps

Use the following general steps to create features on a flat pattern:

1. Activate the Flat Pattern environment.
2. Create a new sketch (optional).
3. Create the feature.
4. Complete the feature.
5. Complete additional cleanup (optional).

Step 1 - Activate the Flat Pattern environment.

If not already active, double-click on the **Flat Pattern** node in the Model Browser to switch to the Flat Pattern environment. The Flat Pattern displays as shown in Figure 9–34.

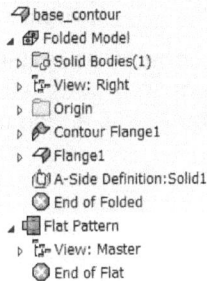

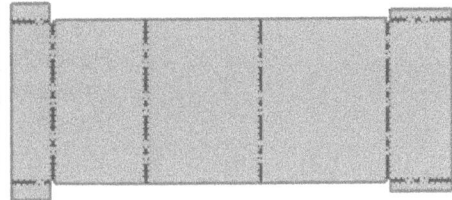

Figure 9–34

Step 2 - Create a new sketch (optional).

When working with solid models or in the folded models, some features require a sketch. The same is true for features when added to flat patterns. For example, cuts and punches always require a sketch, holes sometimes do (depending on the selected options), and Corner Chamfers do not require a sketch.

In the *Flat Pattern* tab>Sketch panel, click (Start 2D Sketch) and select a sketch plane to create a new sketch in the **Flat Pattern** node. A Warning dialog box opens indicating that any editing is not going to display in the folded model, as shown in Figure 9–35. Click **OK** to confirm the warning and continue.

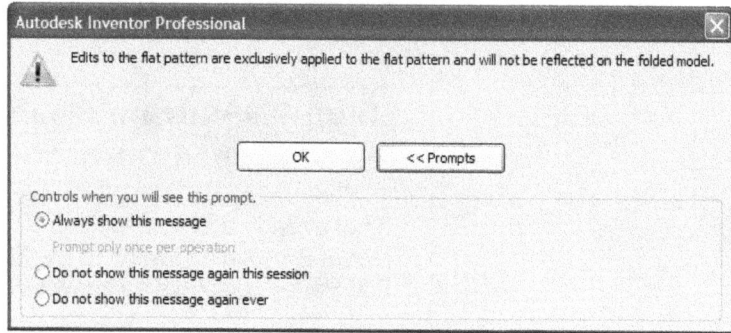

*The expanded **Prompts** options enable you to control when you see this prompt in the future.*

Autodesk Inventor Professional

Edits to the flat pattern are exclusively applied to the flat pattern and will not be reflected on the folded model.

OK   << Prompts

Controls when you will see this prompt.
◉ Always show this message
   Prompt only once per operation
○ Do not show this message again this session
○ Do not show this message again ever

Figure 9–35

Create sketch geometry as required, including center points for Punch features, or lines, arcs, etc. for Cut features. Figure 9–36 shows two Center Points added to the sketch for creating a Punch.

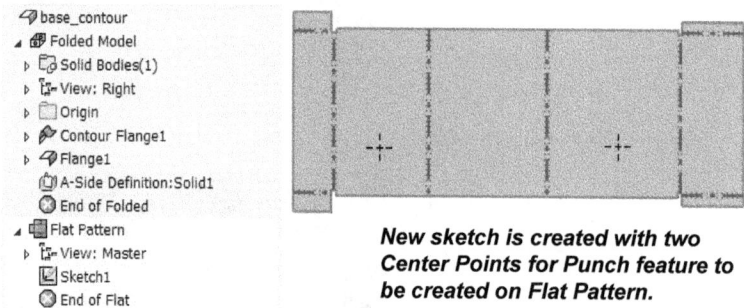

New sketch is created with two Center Points for Punch feature to be created on Flat Pattern.

Figure 9–36

Step 3 - Create the feature.

After completing any necessary sketches, select the tool that you want to use. This example uses the **Punch** tool to create a curved slot on each point. Apply the options required for the feature, as required.

Step 4 - Complete the feature.

The finished flat pattern displays with the new completed feature. Figure 9–37 shows the Curved Slot added on each Center Point.

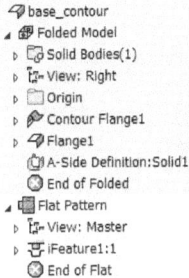

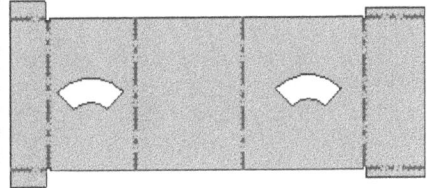

base_contour
Folded Model
  Solid Bodies(1)
  View: Right
  Origin
  Contour Flange1
  Flange1
  A-Side Definition:Solid1
  End of Folded
Flat Pattern
  View: Master
  iFeature1:1
  End of Flat

Figure 9–37

Step 5 - Complete additional cleanup (optional).

You can continue to add features to the flat pattern, as required. Figure 9–38 shows a folded view of a model with two flanges, which have sharp corners that need to be removed. In the Flat Pattern environment a Corner Round feature can be added to each of these sharp corners. You can rotate a part while in the flat pattern and select corners, as shown in Figure 9–38.

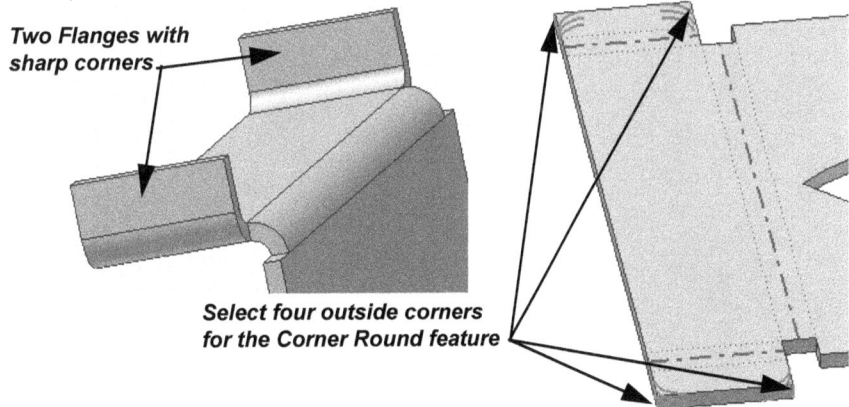

Two Flanges with sharp corners

Select four outside corners for the Corner Round feature

Figure 9–38

Once complete, the Corner Round displays in the Flat Pattern environment, but not in the Folded Model one, as shown in Figure 9–39.

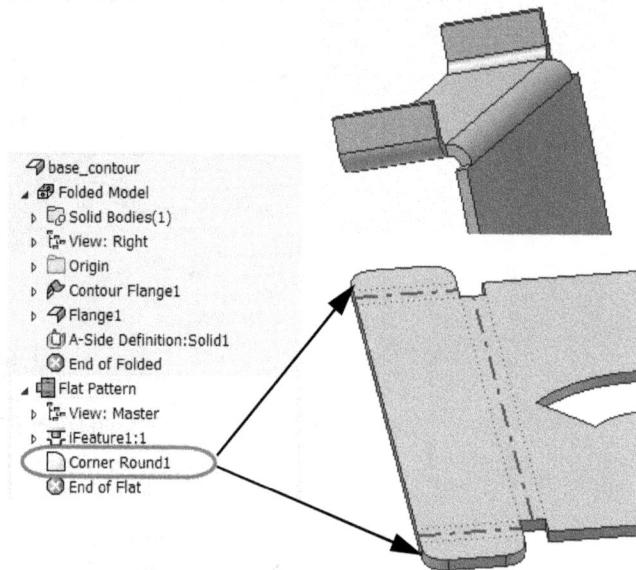

Figure 9–39

9.6 Exporting to DXF/DWG

You can export the flat pattern or a face of the model to an external file. These files can be used for manufacturing operations (such as laser cutting or wire-burning) or used with computer controlled machinery to create sheet metal parts. The files created by exporting are not linked to the model as an .IDW file is. They do not update if you edit the folded or flat views of the sheet metal part.

Exporting Flat Patterns

Exporting a flat pattern creates a non-associative 2D file as a .DWG or .DWF or a non-associative 3D file for .SAT. When saving as .DWG or .DXF, you can control file version, layers, and geometry simplification.

General Steps

Use the following general steps to export a flat pattern:

1. Start the **Save Copy As** command.
2. Specify the file format, location, and name.
3. Set the options.
4. Complete the command.

Step 1 - Start the Save Copy As command.

To export a flat pattern, right-click on **Flat Pattern** in the Model Browser and select **Save Copy As**, as shown in Figure 9–40. The Save Copy As dialog box opens.

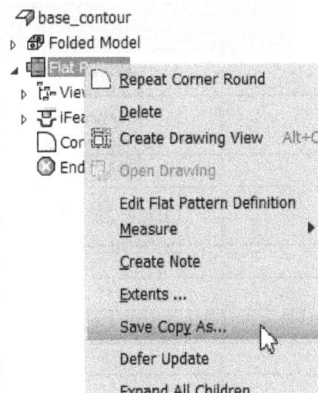

Figure 9–40

Step 2 - Specify the file format, location, and name.

In the Save Copy As dialog box, select a location in which to save the file. Enter a name, and select a file format, as shown in Figure 9–41.

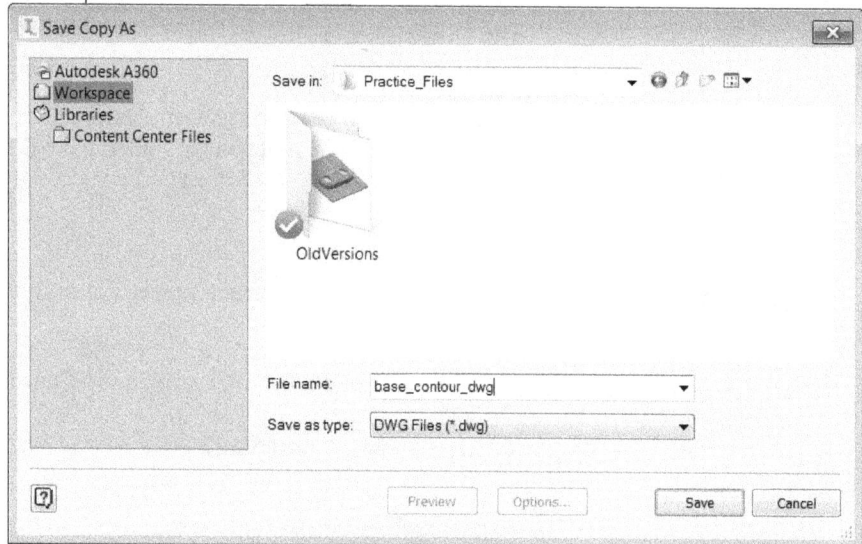

Figure 9–41

The three available file types include:

- **SAT Files:** The standard text format for exchanging information with 3D ACIS geometry definitions stored in ASCII files.

- **DWG Files:** Creates an AutoCAD® DWG file format.

- **DXF Files:** Creates an AutoCAD DXF file that many CNC applications can read.

Once all of the information has been specified, click **Save** to continue.

Step 3 - Set the options.

If saving to a .DWG or .DXF, the Flat Pattern DWG (DXF) Export Options dialog box opens. In the *General* tab you can select the file version to save to. You can also select a post process file to modify the file after it has been saved. The *General* tab is shown in Figure 9–42.

You can save the settings using

| Save Configuration ... |

.

These settings can be used the next time you export a flat pattern.

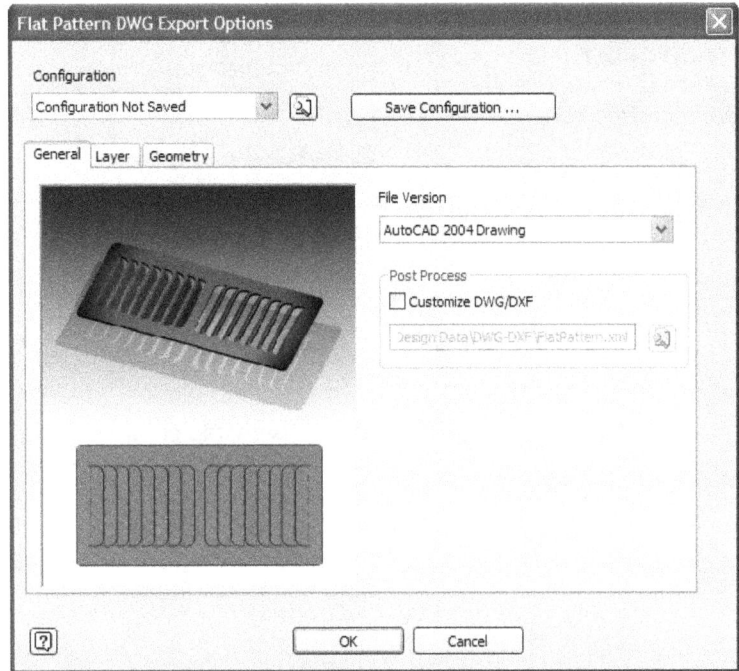

Figure 9–42

In the *Layer* tab you can change the layer names that are created in the file and toggle them on/off. Each layer contains objects from the flat pattern. The *Layer* tab is shown in Figure 9–43.

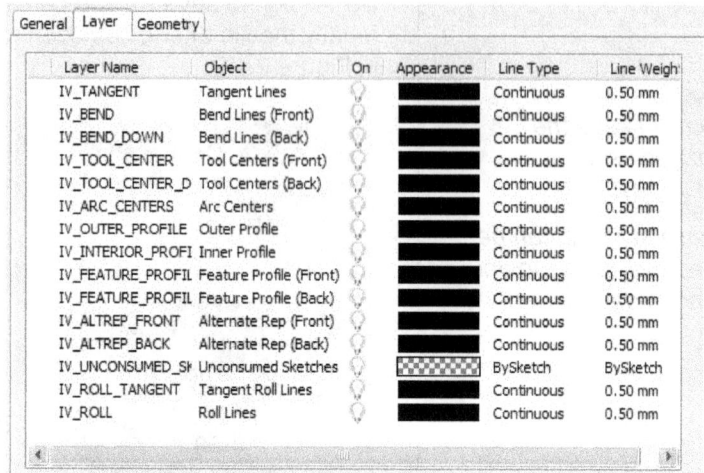

When exporting to .DWG or .DXF, you can control the line types, line colors, and line weights for each exported layer in the Layer tab in the Export Options dialog box.

Layer Name	Object	On	Appearance	Line Type	Line Weigh
IV_TANGENT	Tangent Lines			Continuous	0.50 mm
IV_BEND	Bend Lines (Front)			Continuous	0.50 mm
IV_BEND_DOWN	Bend Lines (Back)			Continuous	0.50 mm
IV_TOOL_CENTER	Tool Centers (Front)			Continuous	0.50 mm
IV_TOOL_CENTER_D	Tool Centers (Back)			Continuous	0.50 mm
IV_ARC_CENTERS	Arc Centers			Continuous	0.50 mm
IV_OUTER_PROFILE	Outer Profile			Continuous	0.50 mm
IV_INTERIOR_PROFI	Inner Profile			Continuous	0.50 mm
IV_FEATURE_PROFIL	Feature Profile (Front)			Continuous	0.50 mm
IV_FEATURE_PROFIL	Feature Profile (Back)			Continuous	0.50 mm
IV_ALTREP_FRONT	Alternate Rep (Front)			Continuous	0.50 mm
IV_ALTREP_BACK	Alternate Rep (Back)			Continuous	0.50 mm
IV_UNCONSUMED_SK	Unconsumed Sketches			BySketch	BySketch
IV_ROLL_TANGENT	Tangent Roll Lines			Continuous	0.50 mm
IV_ROLL	Roll Lines			Continuous	0.50 mm

Figure 9–43

The *Geometry* tab controls options for simplifying the geometry in the file. Splines can be replaced with straight lines, contours can be merged into a single spline, and all geometry can be moved to positive X- and Y-coordinates. This simplifies the file for manufacturing processes. The *Geometry* tab is shown in Figure 9–44.

If saving to an .SAT file, the SAT Save Options dialog box opens. It controls the version of .SAT to which to save.

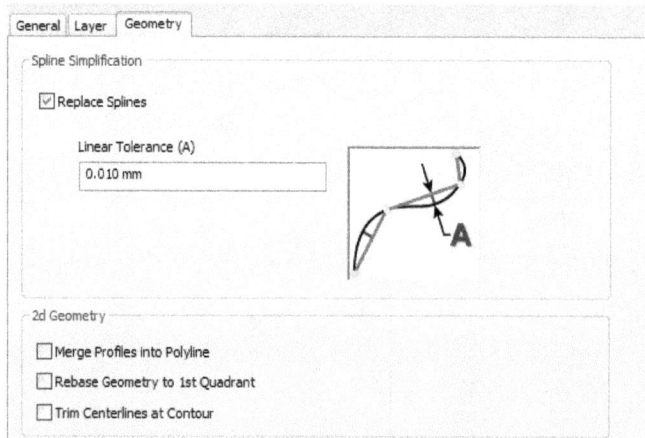

Figure 9–44

Step 4 - Complete the command.

Once all of the options have been configured, click **OK** to create the file. Figure 9–45 shows an example of how a folded model with its flat pattern, is displayed in the Autodesk Inventor software and the AutoCAD software.

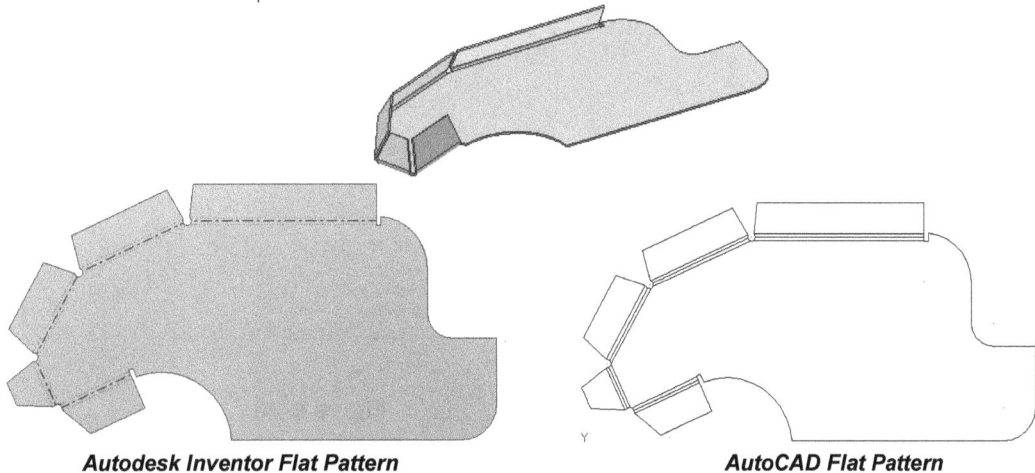

Autodesk Inventor Flat Pattern   *AutoCAD Flat Pattern*

Figure 9–45

Exporting Faces

You can also export only the face of a sheet metal flat pattern. This is limited to creating a non-associative 2D .DWG or .DXF file. While providing fewer options than using **Save Copy As**, this is a quick way of exporting only the cutting profile that would be used for manufacturing operations.

General Steps

Use the following steps to export a face of a flat pattern:

1. Export the face.
2. Specify the file format, location, and name.
3. Set the options.
4. Complete the command.

Step 1 - Export the face.

Right-click on the face of the flat pattern and select **Export Face As** as shown in Figure 9–46. The Save Copy As dialog box opens.

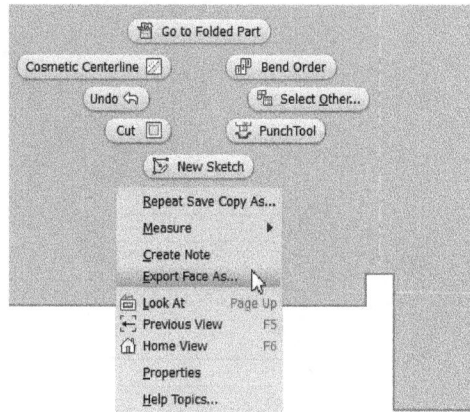

Figure 9–46

Step 2 - Specify the file format, location, and name.

In the Save Copy As dialog box, select a location in which to save the file. Enter a name and select a file format as shown in Figure 9–47.

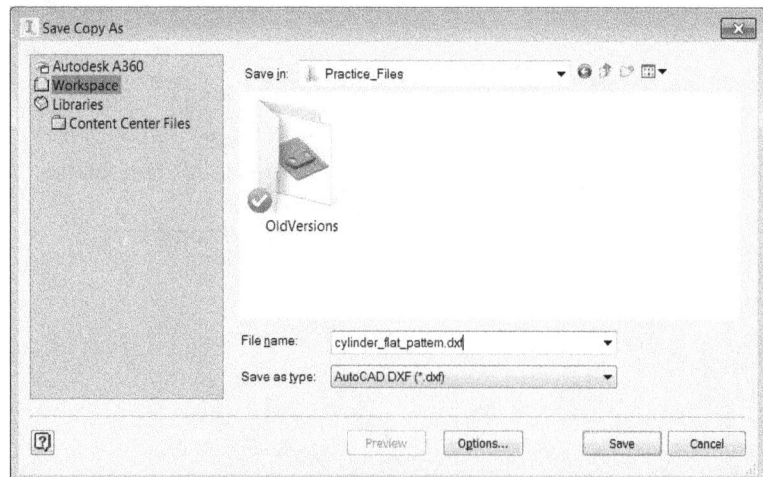

Figure 9–47

The available file types are:

- **DWG Files:** Creates an AutoCAD .DWG file format.

- **DXF Files:** Creates an AutoCAD .DXF file, which many CNC applications can read.

Step 3 - Set the options.

Click **Options** to open the DWG (DXF) File Export Options dialog box. In it, you can select the configuration and set the file version. Click **Next** to continue to customize the export options. Click **Finish**.

Step 4 - Complete the command.

Once all of the information has been specified, click **Save** to create the file.

Practice 9a | Flat Pattern I

Practice Objectives

- Flatten a folded sheet metal model to provide flattened details for manufacturing.
- Add features to the flattened sheet metal model to include geometry that is not required in the folded model.
- Control how punch feature geometry is represented in a flattened model.
- Export the face of a flattened sheet metal model in a .DWG format.

In this practice, you will generate the flat pattern of a folded model as shown in Figure 9–48. Initially, a Warning dialog box will open indicating that there are interfering plates. You will modify a flange to resolve the interference and then clean up the flat pattern by removing material for a corner relief. In this case, the relief could be created in the folded model, but to keep the model simple you will only display the relief in the flat pattern. Finally, you will export the face of the flat pattern to a .DWG file.

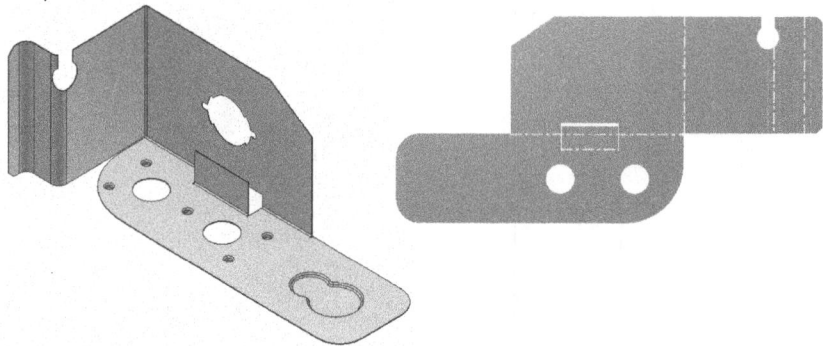

Figure 9–48

Task 1 - Create a flat pattern.

1. Open **Mounting_bracket_9.ipt**.

2. In the *Sheet Metal* tab>Flat Pattern panel, click ⬚ (Create Flat Pattern). Expand the error messages in the dialog box as shown in Figure 9–49.

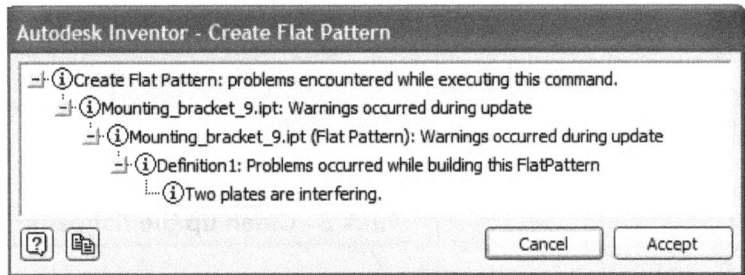

Figure 9–49

3. Click **Accept** to display the flat pattern. There is interference between the cut out and the flange attached to it as shown in Figure 9–50.

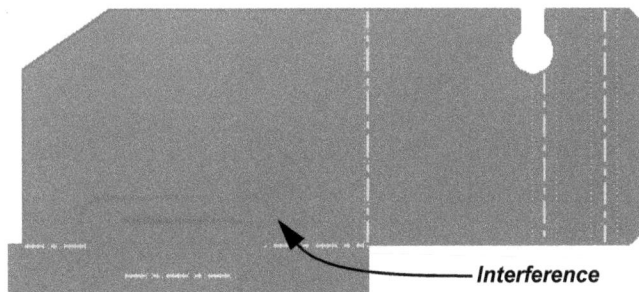

Figure 9–50

4. In the Model Browser, double-click on **Folded Model** to display the folded model.

5. In the Model Browser, right-click on **Flange2** and select **Edit Feature**. The Flange: Flange2 dialog box opens.

6. In the *Height Extents* area, change the value to **40 mm**. Click **OK**.

7. In the Model Browser, double-click on **Flat Pattern** to display the flat pattern. Changing the height of **Flange2** eliminated the interference in the flat pattern, as shown in Figure 9–51.

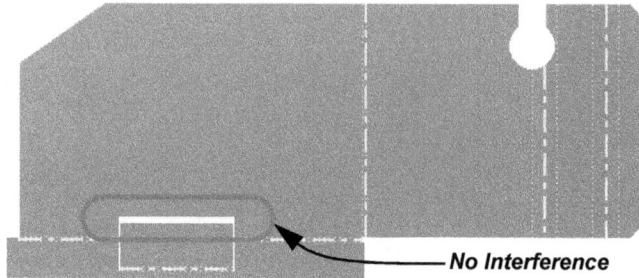

No Interference

Figure 9–51

Task 2 - Clean up the flat pattern.

1. Zoom to the area shown in Figure 9–52. You will clean up the flat pattern by adding a round relief where there are straight edges.

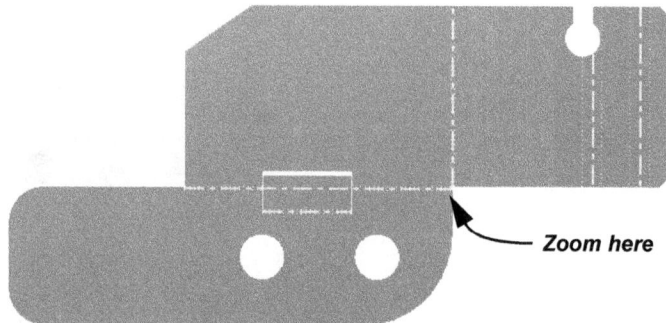

Zoom here

Figure 9–52

2. Create a new sketch on the front face of the flat pattern. Click **OK** in the Message dialog box that indicates that features added to the flat pattern are not reflected in the folded model.

3. Sketch and constrain the arc shown in Figure 9–53. The center point of the arc is coincident to the corner of the existing relief. Project additional entities on the edges of the sheet metal model to ensure that the arc is closed.

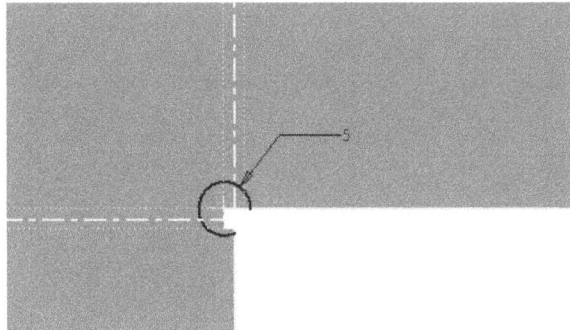

Figure 9–53

4. Finish the sketch.

5. Create a Cut feature using the sketch you just created. Set the depth to **Thickness**. The flat pattern displays as shown in Figure 9–54.

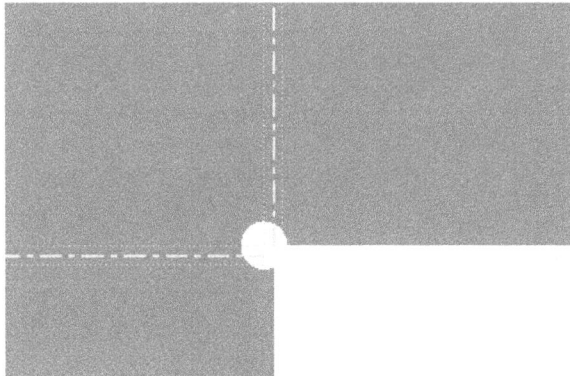

Figure 9–54

6. In the Model Browser, double-click on **Folded Model**.

7. Zoom to the corner you modified in the flat pattern. The relief has straight edges as shown in Figure 9–55. This is because features added to the flat pattern are not reflected in the folded model. This is done to simplify the model.

Figure 9–55

Task 3 - Change the punch representation.

1. In the Model Browser, double-click on **Flat Pattern** to display the flat pattern. Orient the model to display the punch features (Back view). They are displayed with yellow outlines instead of displaying the formed punch feature.

2. In the *Flat Pattern* tab>Manage panel, click (Sheet Metal Defaults). The Sheet Metal Defaults dialog box opens.

3. Click next to the assigned Sheet Metal Rule. The Style and Standard dialog box opens.

4. In the *Flat Pattern Punch Representation* area, select **Formed Punch Feature**.

5. Click **Save and Close** to accept the changes. The punch features are displayed as 3D features as shown in Figure 9–56.

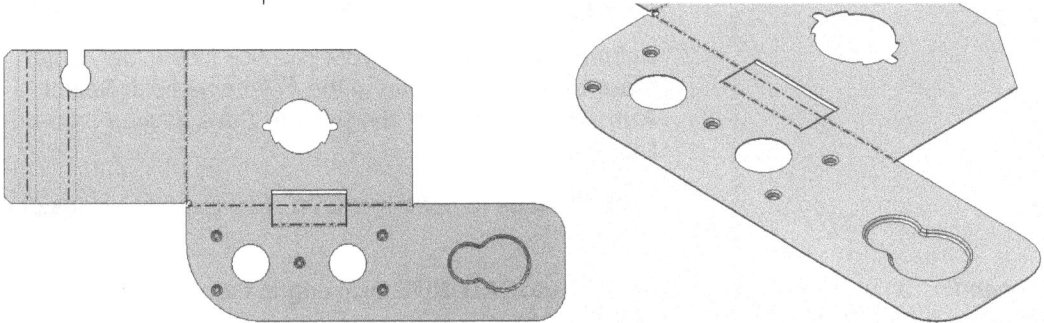

Figure 9–56

6. Click ⬜ next to the assigned Sheet Metal Rule.

7. In the *Flat Pattern Punch Representation* area, select **2D Sketch Rep and Center Mark**.

For punch features to display as 2D sketch reps, the sketch must be defined in the punch .IDE file used to create the feature.

8. Click **Save and Close** to accept the changes. The Punch features are displayed as 2D simplified representations with the center mark for the punch, as shown in Figure 9–57. The holes do not change because they are Hole features and not Punch features. If you want to have holes displayed similar to Punch features, you have to create a Punch feature with the required geometry.

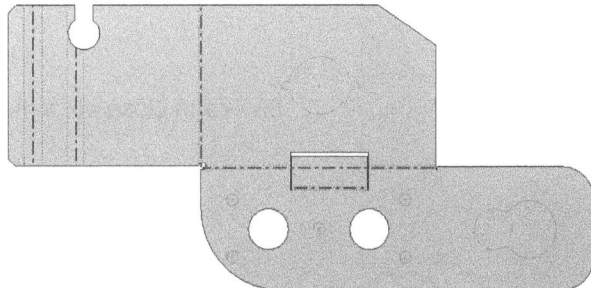

Figure 9–57

If you do not want to edit the Sheet Metal Rule you can also edit the flat pattern punch representation by right-clicking on **Flat Pattern** in the Model Browser and selecting **Edit Flat Pattern Definition**. The Punch Representation can be changed in its associated tab.

Task 4 - Export face of flat pattern.

1. Right-click on the back face of the flat pattern and select **Export Face As**. The Save Copy As dialog box opens.

2. Set the Save location to your practice files folder. Enter **Mounting_bracket_flat** in the *File name* field. Select **AutoCAD Drawing (*.dwg)** in the *Save as type* drop-down list.

3. Click **Options** to open the .DWG File Export Options dialog box.

Depending on where the data is sent, it is safest to save it back to the oldest version so that vendor shops or tool rooms can work with the data without having to resend an older version.

4. Select **AutoCAD 2013 Drawing** in the *File Version* area and click **Finish**.

5. Click **Save** to create the file.

6. Open the .DWG file in the Autodesk Inventor software (or the AutoCAD software). Only the cutting edges of the flat pattern were exported as shown in Figure 9–58.

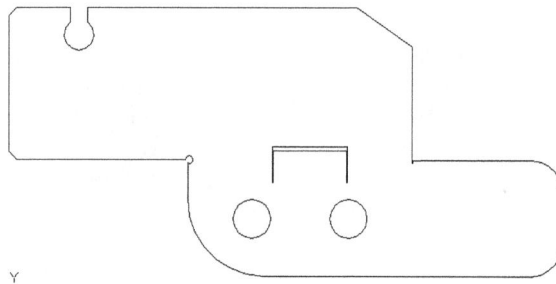

Figure 9–58

7. Save and close all of the files.

Practice 9b | Flat Pattern II

Practice Objectives

- Flatten a folded sheet metal model to provide flattened details for manufacturing.
- Manipulate the orientation of the flattened sheet metal geometry to permit proper nesting of the metal and grain direction.
- Control how punch feature geometry is represented in a flattened model.
- Export the face of a flattened sheet metal model in a .DWG format.

In this practice, you will generate the flat pattern of a folded model as shown in Figure 9–59. You will then change the orientation of the flat pattern; first by rotating the flat pattern and then by flipping the front face. You will then change the Punch Representation to only display the center marks for the punches. Finally, you will export the flat pattern to a .DWG file.

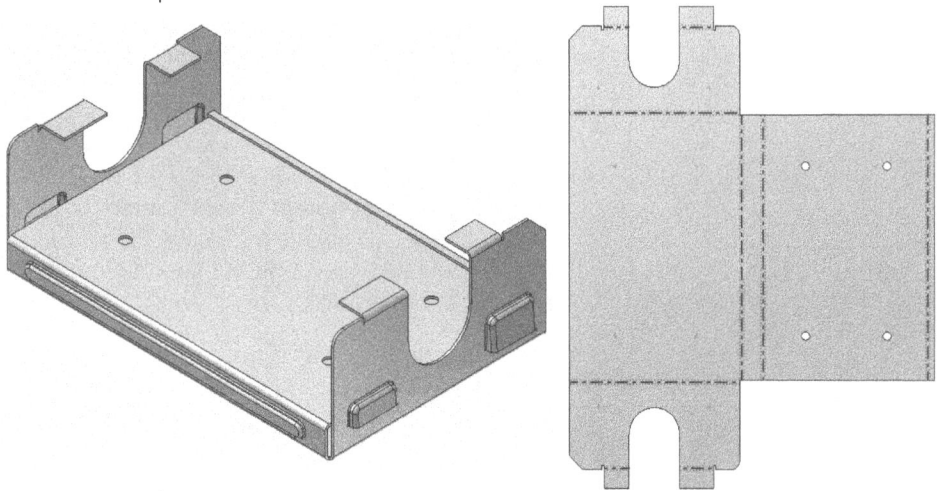

Figure 9–59

Task 1 - Create a flat pattern.

1. Open **Mount.ipt**.

2. In the *Sheet Metal* tab>Flat Pattern panel, click ⬛ (Define A-Side) and select the face shown in Figure 9–60 to assign the **A-Side Definition** node to the Folded Model environment. This assigns the A-Side reference that will be used when the flat pattern is created.

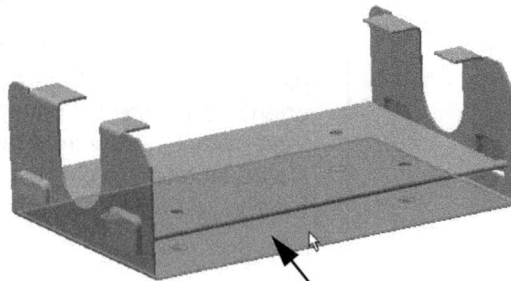

Select this face as the A-Side.

Figure 9–60

3. In the *Sheet Metal* tab>Flat Pattern panel, click ⬛ (Create Flat Pattern) to generate the flat pattern of the folded model. The flat pattern displays as shown in Figure 9–61. The Front view should be facing you but you might have to rotate it to achieve the orientation.

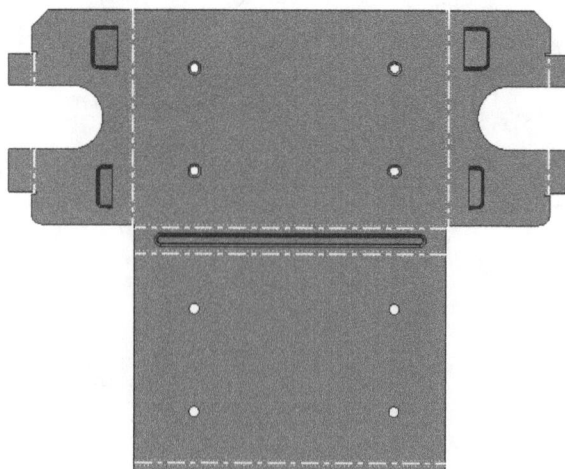

Figure 9–61

Task 2 - Change the orientation of the flat pattern.

1. In the Model Browser, right-click on **Flat Pattern** and select **Edit Flat Pattern Definition**. The Flat Pattern dialog box opens as shown in Figure 9–62.

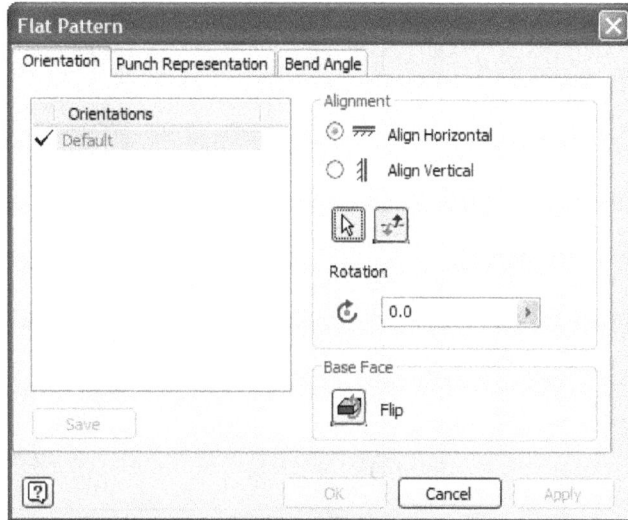

Figure 9–62

2. Verify that **Align Horizontal** and (Alignment Axis) are selected.

3. Select the long vertical edge on the left and click **Apply**. The flat pattern is rotated similar to that shown in Figure 9–63. The Front view should still be facing you.

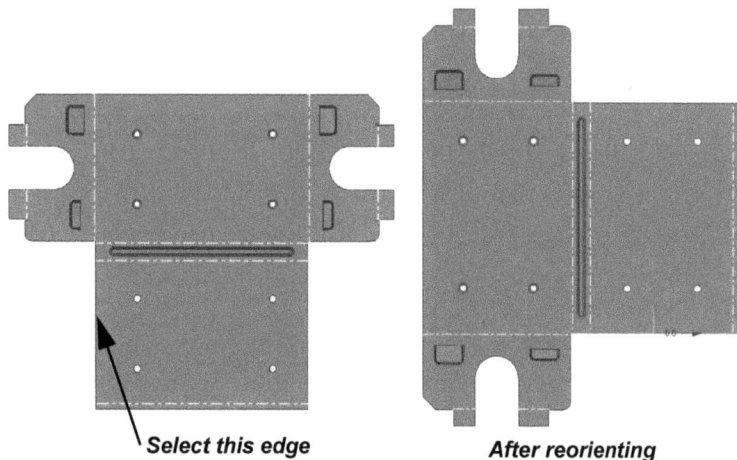

Select this edge   *After reorienting*

Figure 9–63

4. Click (Flip Base Face) and click **Apply** to rotate the flat pattern 180° so that the Punch features are facing you. The Punch features should appear to be raised toward you. If required, rotate the view to verify this. The flat pattern displays similar to that shown in Figure 9–64.

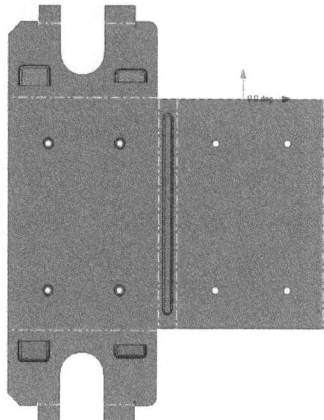

Figure 9–64

Task 3 - Change the Punch Representation.

You can also change the flat pattern punch representation in the Sheet Metal Rule.

1. Select the *Punch Representation* tab. The dialog box displays as shown in Figure 9–65.

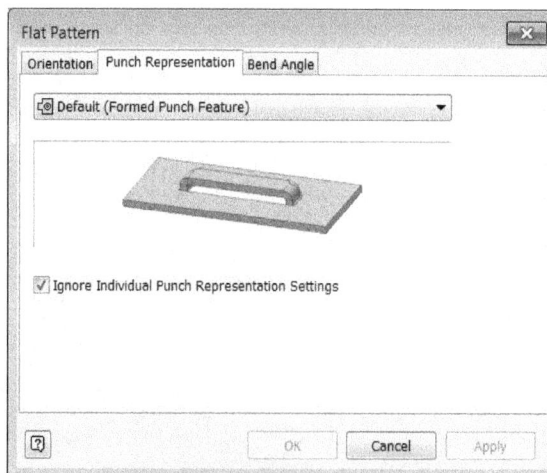

Figure 9–65

2. Select **Center Mark Only** and click **OK**. The Punch features change to only display the center mark. The holes do not change because they are Hole features, not Punch features. The flat pattern displays as shown in Figure 9–66.

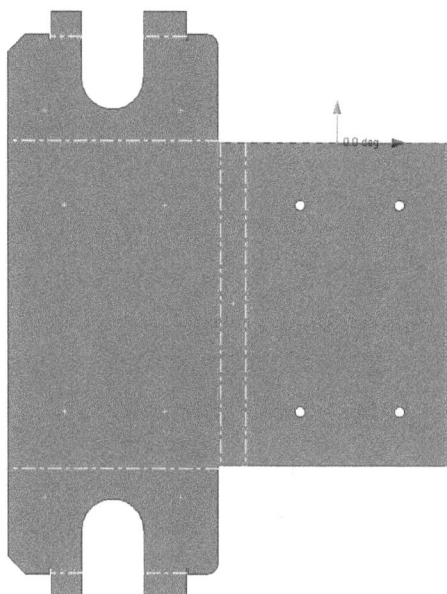

Figure 9–66

3. Close the Flat Pattern dialog box.

Task 4 - Export the flat pattern using Save Copy As.

1. In the Model Browser, right-click on **Flat Pattern** and select **Save Copy As**. The Save Copy As dialog box opens.

2. Set the Save location as your practice files folder. Enter **Mount_flat** in the *File name* field. Select **Drawing files(*.dwg)** in the *Save as type* drop-down list.

3. Click **Save** to save the file. The Flat Pattern DWG Export Options dialog box opens.

4. Select the *Layer* tab and note the layer names that are assigned to the objects. Click **OK** to create the file.

5. Open the .DWG file in the Autodesk Inventor software (or the AutoCAD software). Only layers that contain objects are created in the file. The file displays as shown in Figure 9–67.

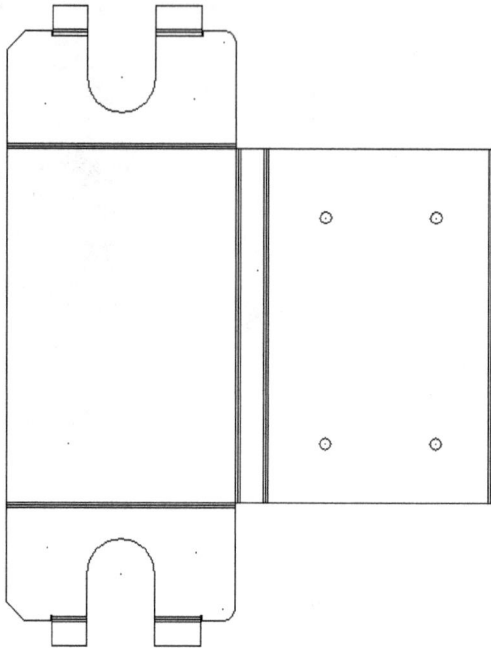

Figure 9–67

6. Save and close all of the files.

Practice 9c

Flat Pattern of Curved Parts

Practice Objectives

- Flatten a curved sheet metal model to provide flattened details for manufacturing.
- Export the face of a flattened sheet metal model in a .DXF format.

In this practice, you will generate a flat pattern for the two folded models shown in Figure 9–68. You will unfold the models by simply unfolding them, because the software makes assumptions as to what the unfolded surface reference should be. You then save a .DXF file from the flat pattern.

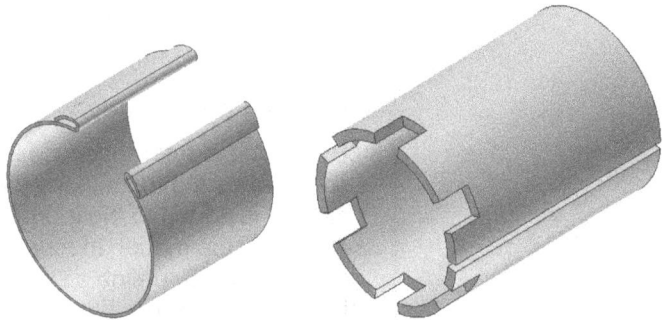

Figure 9–68

Task 1 - Create a flat patterns.

1. Open **Band.ipt**.

2. In the *Sheet Metal* tab>Flat Pattern panel, click ![icon] (Create Flat Pattern) to generate the flat pattern. The flat pattern is created immediately, as shown in Figure 9–69.

Figure 9–69

3. Open the file **Cylinder_flat_pattern.ipt**.

4. In the *Sheet Metal* tab>Flat Pattern panel, click (Create Flat Pattern) to generate the flat pattern as shown in Figure 9–70.

Figure 9–70

Hint: A-Side Definition

By default, a reference face is automatically selected by the software as the model face that will be face-up when the flat pattern is added to the model. The face is assigned as the A-Side of the model. In most cases, the default assignment is appropriate. To define a specific face prior to flattening, use the **Define A-Side** option in the Flat Pattern panel to assign a face.

Task 2 - Export a flat pattern.

1. Using either of the two models, right-click on **Flat Pattern** in the Model Browser and select **Save Copy As**. The Save Copy As dialog box opens.

2. Set the Save location as your practice files folder. Enter **Flat_pattern** in the *File name* field. Select **DXF files(*.dxf)** in the *Save as type* drop-down list.

3. Click **Save**. The Flat Pattern DXF Export Options dialog box opens.

4. Select **AutoCAD 2013 DXF** in the *File Version* area.

5. Click **OK** to create the file.

6. If time permits, open the .DXF file in AutoCAD. The file displays similar to the flat pattern shown in the Autodesk Inventor software.

7. Save and close all of the files.

Depending on where the data is to be sent, it is safest to save back to the oldest version so that vendor shops or tool rooms can work with the data without having to resend an older version.

Chapter Review Questions

1. Which of the following Model Browsers accurately describes the state of the model shown in Figure 9–71?

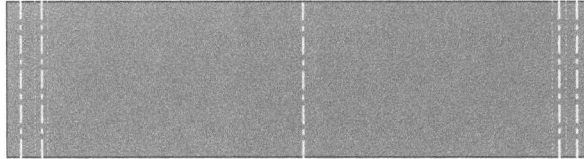

Figure 9–71

a.
```
 Band.ipt
 ▲ Folded Model
   ▷ Solid Bodies(1)
   ▷ View: Master
   ▷ Origin
   ▷ Contour Flange2
     End of Folded
 ▲ Flat Pattern
   ▷ View: Master
     End of Flat
```

b.
```
 Band.ipt
 ▲ Folded Model
   ▷ Solid Bodies(1)
   ▷ View: Master
   ▷ Origin
   ▷ Contour Flange2
     End of Folded
 ▲ Flat Pattern
   ▷ View: Master
     End of Flat
```

2. Which of the following best describes the sheet metal modeling situation that causes the dialog box shown in Figure 9–72 to open?

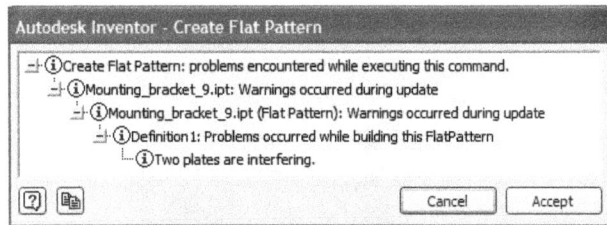

Figure 9–72

a. The model is incorrectly oriented and must be reoriented before flattening is permitted.

b. The geometry being flattened was imported and the default face feature that is used for flattening cannot be identified.

c. Geometry in the flattened model has been identified as overlapping.

d. The model already contains a flattened feature and a second cannot be created.

3. The flat pattern shown in Figure 9–73 is being reoriented. Which of the examples correctly displays the new orientation?

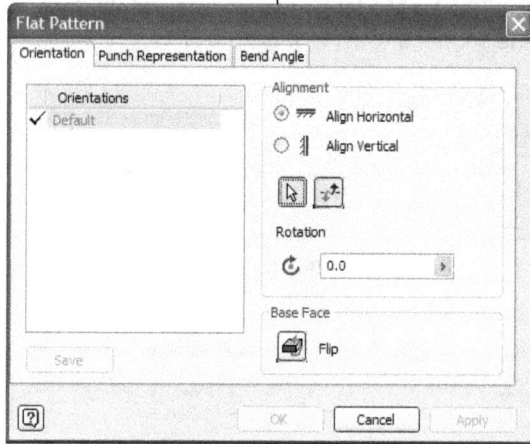

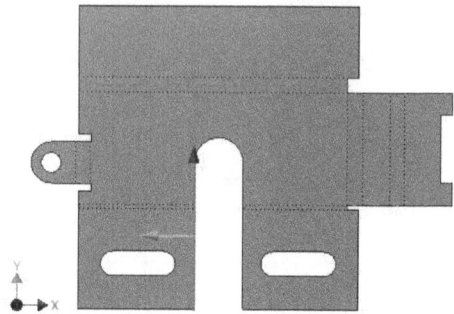

Figure 9–73

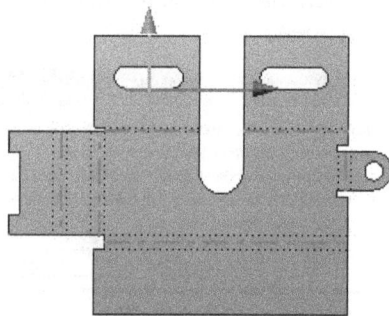

a.

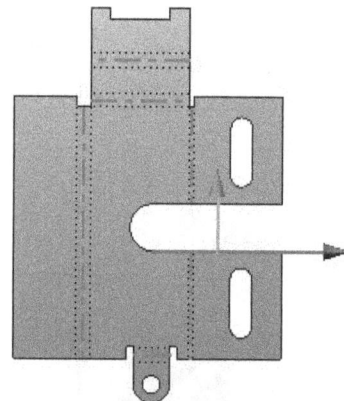

b.

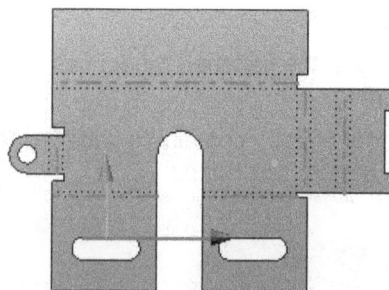

c.

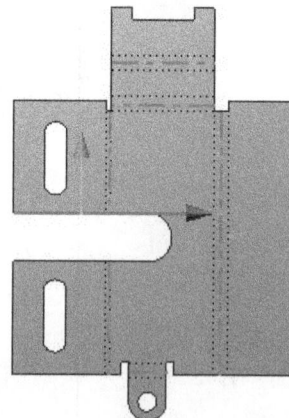

d.

4. The model shown in Figure 9–74 has three Punch features. It is displayed in its flat pattern state. Which Punch Representation is currently being used for this flat pattern display?

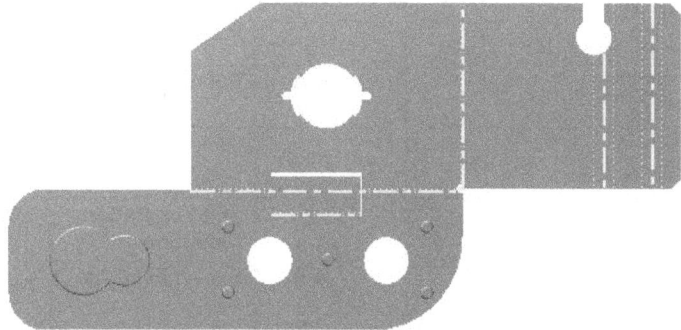

Figure 9–74

   a. Formed Punch Feature

   b. 2D Sketch Representation

   c. 2D Sketch Representation with Center Mark

   d. Center Mark Only

5. Features created in the flat pattern translate back to the Folded stated of the model.

   a. True

   b. False

6. Which of the following sheet metal commands enables you to copy a sketch that was created in the folded model onto the flat pattern?

   a. Create Flat Pattern

   b. Go To Flat Pattern

   c. Copy to Flat Pattern

   d. Create 2D Sketch>Project Flat Pattern

Command Summary

Button	Command	Location
	**Create Flat Pattern**	• **Ribbon**: *Sheet Metal* tab>Flat Pattern panel
N/A	**Defer Update**	• *(Context menu with Flat Pattern node selected in Model Browser.)*
	**Define A-Side**	• **Ribbon**: *Sheet Metal* tab>Flat Pattern panel
N/A	**Edit Flat Pattern Definition**	• *(Context menu with Flat Pattern node selected in Model Browser.)*
N/A	**Export Face As**	• *(Context menu with a face selected in the graphics window.)*
N/A	**Save Copy As**	• *(Context menu with Flat Pattern node selected in Model Browser.)*
	Sheet Metal Defaults	• **Ribbon**: *Sheet Metal* tab>Setup panel
	**Start 2D Sketch**	• **Ribbon**: *Sheet Metal* tab>Sketch panel • **Ribbon**: *Flat Pattern* tab>Sketch panel • **Ribbon**: *3D Model* tab>Sketch panel • **Ribbon**: *Sketch* tab>Sketch panel

Lofted Flange and Rips

The Lofted Flange and Rip features are advanced tools that enable you to create complex geometry shapes and provide a rip that will permit flattening. A Lofted Flange creates transitional sheet metal geometry that blends between two profile sketches. A Rip enables you to create an open gap (rip) in geometry that is closed, such as a Lofted Flange.

Learning Objectives in this Chapter

*   Create sheet metal geometry that blends between two profile sketches.
*   Create a rip feature on a surface to permit the flattening of the sheet metal geometry.

10.1 Lofted Flange

A Lofted Flange feature creates transitional sheet metal geometry that is blended between two profile sketches, as shown in Figure 10–1. Lofted flanges can be used as base or secondary features.

Lofted flanges are most commonly used with duct design.

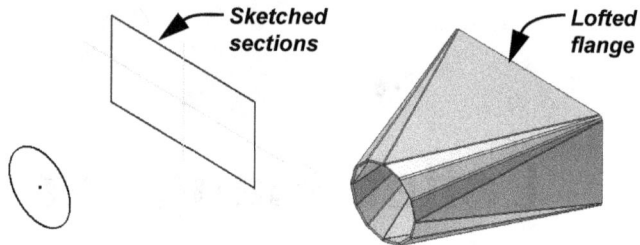

Figure 10–1

The sketches that are selected as references for a lofted flange must exist in the model before you create the feature.

The profiles for lofted flanges can be open or closed. However, when selected for use both profiles must be either open or closed. One profile cannot be open and the other closed.

How To: Create a Flange Feature

1. In the *Sheet Metal* tab>Create panel, click ⬛ (Lofted Flange). The Lofted Flange dialog box opens as shown in Figure 10–2.

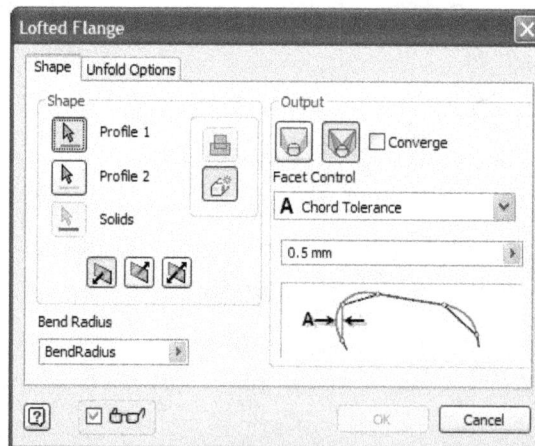

Figure 10–2

2. Select the profiles to define the lofted flange. By default, **Profile 1** is active, enabling you to select the first sketched profile. Once selected, **Profile 2** is activated for you to select the second sketched profile. A preview of the feature displays when you have selected profiles, similar to that shown in Figure 10–3.

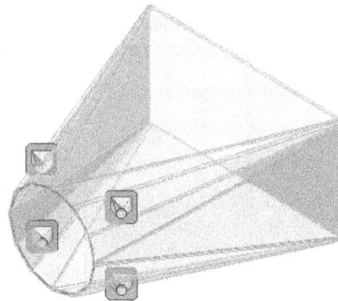

Figure 10–3

3. Select the side of the profiles to which to add the material thickness using the options in the *Shape* area. The material can be added to the inside (⬜), outside (⬜), or it can be evenly divided on both sides (⬜) of the profile.

4. Define the *Bend Radius*. The default value for the bend radius uses the **BendRadius** parameter value that is assigned by the Sheet Metal Rule. You can enter a different bend radius if required.

5. Refine the geometry between the sections of the lofted flange using the options in the *Output* area in the dialog box. The available options are as follows:

(Die Formed)	Generates a smooth die formed lofted flange. If this option is selected, the remaining options in the *Output* area are disabled.	
(Press Brake)	Generates a faceted press brake lofted flange. If this option is selected, you can continue to define the remaining options in the *Output* area to further control the geometry.	
Converge	Converges the bends of the flattened faceted section to a point.	n/a

Facet Control	Defines the method of obtaining the size of the faceted face. The options include **A Chord Tolerance**, **B Facet Angle**, and **C Facet Distance**. The Lofted Flange dialog box provides the following diagrams to show how the option values are measured:	

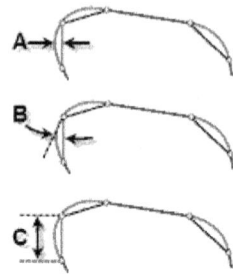

Deciding on the Output type for a lofted flange depends on how you are going to manufacture the component and the resulting shape that is required:

- **Press Break** is more commonly used because it is cheaper to manufacture. It does not provide a smooth finish, but is suitable for many types of designs.

- **Die Formed** provides a smoother result, because it manufactures directly from a die.

6. If the **Press Brake** Output type is used, you can further redefine the *Facet Control* method for each faceted zone in the model. For example, four faceted zones are in the model shown in Figure 10–4. Select the glyph that is associated with the faceted zone. You can open the Bend Zone Edit dialog box to control the sections' specific facets.

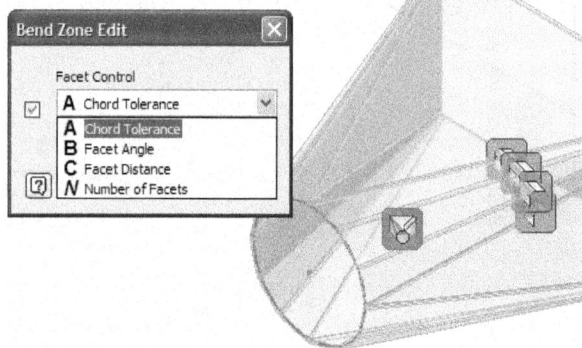

Figure 10–4

The **A Chord Tolerance**, **B Facet Angle**, and **C Facet Distance** options are the same as those used to define the model's overall facet control. You can also select the **N Number of Facets** option to assign a specific number of required facets for the section, as shown in Figure 10–5.

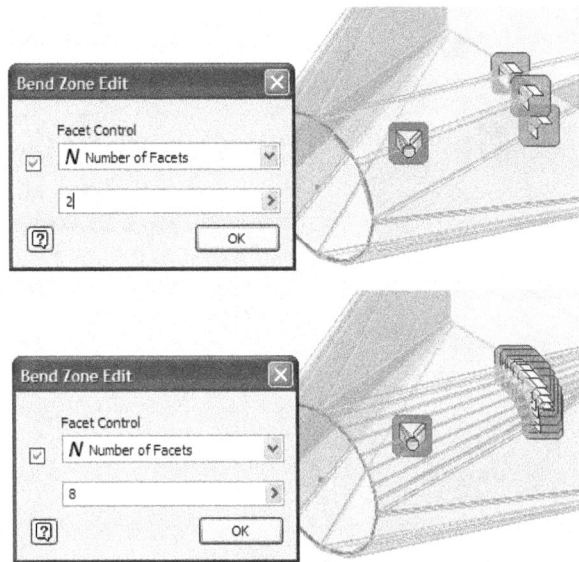

Figure 10–5

In addition to the facet control settings that can be specified for each faceted zone, you can control the *Bend Radius* and *Unfold Rule* for each bend in a bend zone. To control a bend,

select the ⬚ glyph that is associated with the bend and edit the values in the Bend Edit dialog box, as shown in Figure 10–6.

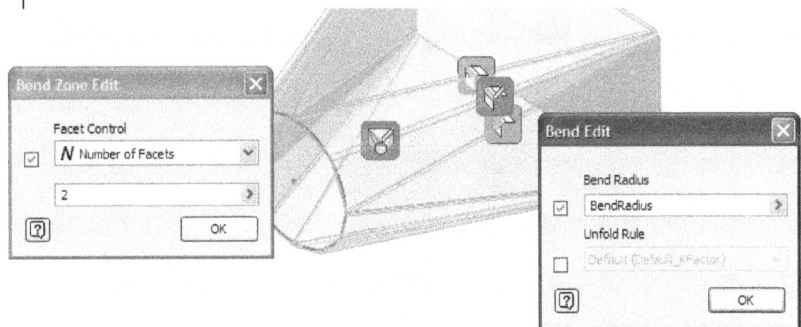

Figure 10–6

7. (Optional) The model's default unfold rule is specified as the unfold rule for this feature. To change the rule, select the *Unfold Options* tab and select a new rule. Remember that the unfold rule can also be individually specified for each bend in a faceted zone, as explained in Step 6.

Lofted flanges can be flattened by adding a Rip feature before flattening.

8. Once you have fully defined the lofted flange, click **OK** to complete the feature. Alternatively, you can right-click and select **OK (Enter)** to complete the feature.

Hint: Changing the Output Type

Once the feature has been completed, the Output type (**Die Formed/Press Brake**) cannot be changed. You must delete and recreate the lofted flange to switch between these types. If you created a **Press Brake** lofted flange, you can still redefine the other output options for this type.

10.2 Rip

A Rip feature enables you to create an open gap (rip) in geometry that is closed, similar to that shown in Figure 10–7. Adding a rip to a closed shape enables you to generate a flat pattern. Rips are not affected by cut-outs, emboss, or other formed features.

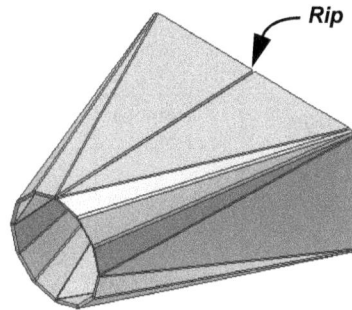

Figure 10–7

How To: Create a Rip Feature

1. In the *Sheet Metal* tab>Modify panel, click [icon] (Rip). The Rip dialog box opens as shown in Figure 10–8.

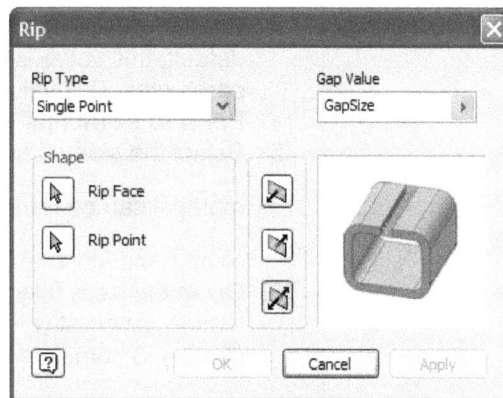

Figure 10–8

2. Select the type of rip in the *Rip Type* drop-down list.

Any point selected as a reference in defining a rip must lie on the face that is being ripped. Therefore, in the case of a lofted flange, the point must be sketched once the lofted flange geometry has been generated. The rip point reference cannot exist in the sections used to create the lofted flange.

3. Define the references for placing the rip. The required *Shape* references vary depending on the selected rip type. The rip options and their required shape references are described in the following table. The images shown for each rip type are displayed in the dialog box when the option is selected.

Single Point		Defines the rip feature based on a sketched point and the face to be ripped. To define: • Select a rip face. • Select a rip point (work points, sketch points, midpoints on edges, or end points).
Point to Point		Defines the rip feature between two points on the face that is to be ripped. To define: • Select a rip face. • Select a start point. • Select an end point. The start and end points can be work points, sketch points, midpoints on edges, or end points.
Face Extents		Defines the rip feature by removing a face. To define: • Select a rip face to fully remove.

4. Enter a gap value for the rip in the *Gap Value* field. By default, this value is driven by the **GapSize** system parameter. This value is only available for **Single Point**, and **Point to Point** rips.
5. Select the side of the rip from which to remove material. The material can be removed from the inside (⧄), outside (⧄), or be removed evenly from both sides (⧄).
6. Once you have fully defined the rip, click **OK** to complete the feature. Alternatively, you can right-click and select **OK (Enter)** to complete the feature.

Practice 10a | Lofted Flanges and Rips

Practice Objectives

- Create sheet metal geometry that transitions between sections on two parallel planes.
- Create a single point rip that permits the flattening of sheet metal geometry.
- Flatten a folded sheet metal model.
- Independently control the faceting along the bend line of a flattened sheet metal model.

In this practice, you will create a lofted flange feature that blends between two sketched profiles. Once created, you will create a rip so that the model can be flattened. To complete the model, you will create a lap seam to cover the rip. The completed model is shown in Figure 10–9.

Figure 10–9

Task 1 - Create a new sheet metal model.

1. Create a new model using the **Sheet Metal(mm).ipt** Metric template.

2. In the *Sheet Metal* tab>Setup panel, click (Sheet Metal Defaults).

3. Clear the **Use Thickness from Rule** option.

4. Enter **2.667mm** for the new *Thickness* value.

5. Click **OK**.

Task 2 - Review a custom equation for unfolding.

Before the Autodesk® Inventor® 2009 version of the software, you could define the deformation between the folded and the flat model with a linear approximation or with a bend table. Since the Autodesk Inventor 2010 software, you can define an unfold rule with a custom equation. The default templates already contain a custom bend compensation equation.

1. Select the *Manage* tab>Style and Standard panel and click

    ✐ (Styles Editor).

2. Expand the *Sheet Metal Unfold* area.

3. Select **Bend Compensation** for the equation type. The Style and Standard Editor updates as shown in Figure 10–10. Note the *Custom Equation* that has been written to define this unfold rule.

Sheet Metal Unfold [BendCompensation]

Unfold Method

ꓳ Custom Equation ▽	β - Angle	L = L1 + L2 + v
Equation Type	μ - Thickness	
V Bend Compensation ▽	ρ - Radius, Inner	
Angular Reference(β)	π - Pi	
Open Angle ▽	γ - Neutral Surface	
	L - Developed Length	

	Custom Equation	Bounding Condition
v =	π * ((180deg - β)/180deg) * (ρ + (μ/2ul) * (0.65ul + 0.5ul * log (ρ/μ))) - 2ul * (ρ + μ)	0 deg < β ≤90 deg
v =	π * ((180deg - β)/180deg) * (ρ + (μ/2ul) * (0.65ul + 0.5ul * log (ρ/μ))) - 2ul * (ρ + μ) * tan((180 deg - β)/2ul)	90 deg < β ≤165 deg
v =	0 in	165 deg < β ≤180 deg

Figure 10–10

4. Click **Done** to close the Style and Standard Editor without making any changes.

The Bend Compensation unfold rule is not the current active rule. However, it was shown to highlight the possibilities for creating custom unfold equations.

Task 3 - Sketch the profiles that will be used to create a lofted flange.

1. In the *Sheet Metal* tab>Sketch panel, click ⬚ (Start 2D Sketch). Select the XY plane as the sketch plane.

2. Sketch the section shown in Figure 10–11 using the **Rectangle** and **Fillet** commands.

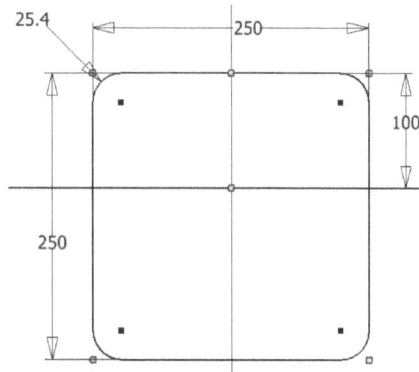

Figure 10–11

3. In the *Sketch* tab>Exit panel, click ✔ (Finish Sketch).

4. Expand the **Origin** node in the Model Browser, right-click on the XY Plane, and select **Visibility** to toggle on its display.

5. To create the sketch plane for the second profile of the lofted flange, you will create an offset work plane. In the *Sheet Metal* tab>Work Features panel, click ⬚ (Plane). Select the XY Origin Plane and drag the cursor to create a new offset work plane. Release the mouse button, enter **200mm** for the offset value, and click ✔.

6. In the *Sheet Metal* tab>Sketch panel, click (Start 2D Sketch). Select the new work plane that you just created. Sketch the section shown in Figure 10–12.

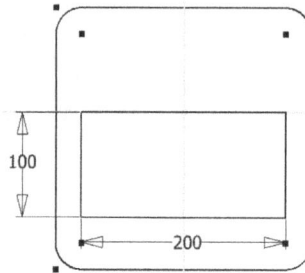

Figure 10–12

7. In the *Sketch* tab>Exit panel, click (Finish Sketch).

8. Turn off the visibility of the two work planes.

Task 4 - Create a lofted flange.

---

1. In the *Sheet Metal* tab>Create panel, click (Lofted Flange). The Lofted Flange dialog box opens as shown in Figure 10–13.

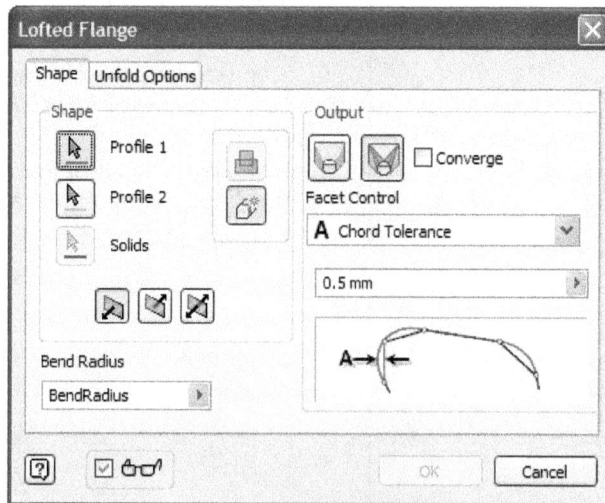

Figure 10–13

2. Select the two profiles that you previously sketched. A preview of the feature displays when you finish selecting the profiles, as shown in Figure 10–14.

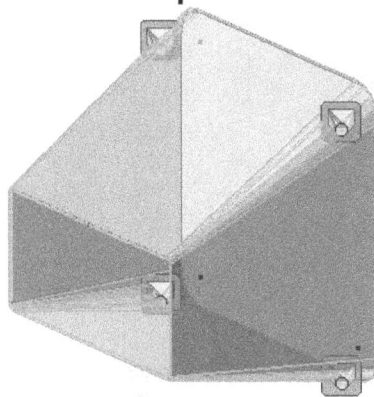

Figure 10–14

3. Add the material thickness to the default side (⬛).

4. Keep the **BendRadius** parameter as the value for the *Bend Radius*. This creates the feature with a bend radius that is equal to the model's thickness.

5. By default, the *Output* type for the lofted flange is ⬛ (Press Brake). This generates a faceted result over the bend zone.

6. Click ⬛ (Die Formed) in the *Output* area. Note how the preview updates as a smooth bend, as shown in Figure 10–15.

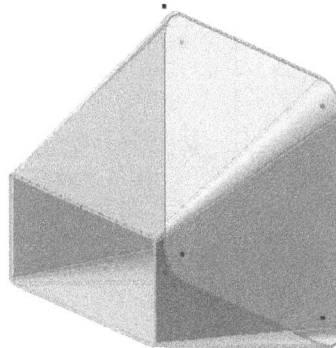

Figure 10–15

Deciding on the *Output* option for a lofted flange depends on how you are going to manufacture the component and the resulting shape that is required. **Press Break** is more commonly used, because it is cheaper to manufacture. It does not provide a smooth finish, but is suitable for many types of designs. **Die Formed** provides a smoother result, because it manufactures directly from a die. Once an *Output* option has been selected, it cannot be redefined to the other type without having to delete and recreate the feature. When you redefine a **Press Brake** lofted flange, you can still manipulate the facet control options, but you cannot change it to a die formed lofted flange.

7. Return the *Output* type to [icon] (Press Brake).

8. Keep the remaining default options for the facet control of the lofted flange and click **OK** to complete the feature.

Task 5 - Create a rip feature.

1. In the *Sheet Metal* tab>Modify panel, click [icon] (Rip). The Rip dialog box opens as shown in Figure 10–16.

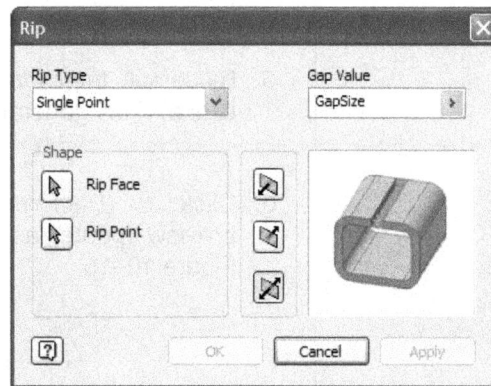

Figure 10–16

2. Keep **Single Point** as the type of rip in the *Rip Type* drop-down list. Single Point defines the rip feature based on a sketched point and the face that is to be ripped.

3. Select the face shown in Figure 10–17 as the **Rip Face** reference.

4. Select the midpoint of the edge shown in Figure 10–17 as the **Rip Point**.

Select this face as the Rip Face

Select the midpoint of this edge

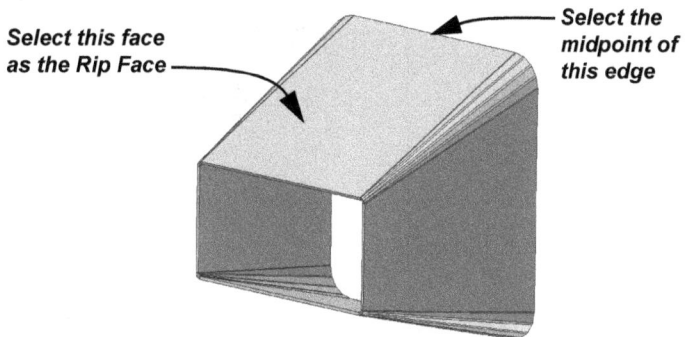

Figure 10–17

5. Click ⊠ to remove material evenly from both sides of the gap.

6. Override the **GapSize** parameter by manually entering **12.5mm** for the *Gap Value*.

7. Click **OK** to complete the feature. The rip displays in the model as shown in Figure 10–18.

Figure 10–18

Task 6 - Create a lap seam flange.

1. In the *Sheet Metal* tab>Create panel, click (Flange).

2. Select the edge shown in Figure 10–19 as the reference edge for the flange.

Select this edge to place the flange

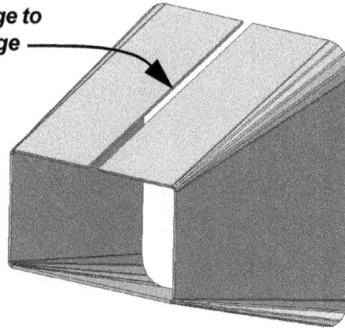

Figure 10–19

3. Enter **0.0** for the **Flange Angle**.

4. Click >> at the bottom of the Flange dialog box to display additional options.

5. Select **Old Method**. Once selected, many options are no longer available in the upper portion of the Flange dialog box.

6. Click **OK** to complete the feature. The model displays as shown in Figure 10–20 with the lap seam covering the rip.

Figure 10–20

Task 7 - Create a flat pattern.

1. In the *Sheet Metal* tab>Flat Pattern panel, click (Create Flat Pattern). The model displays as shown in Figure 10–21. The bends formed by the lofted flange are identified in the flat pattern state.

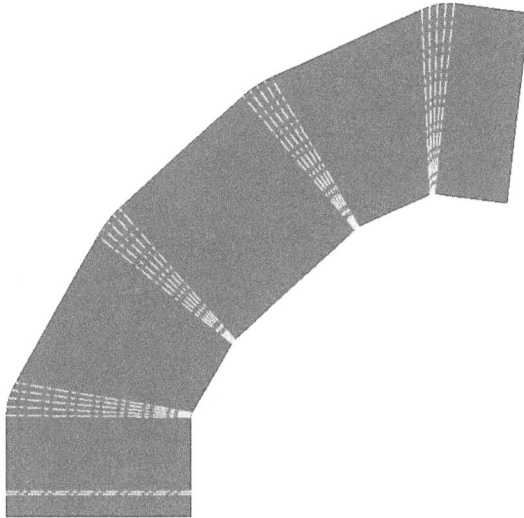

Figure 10–21

Task 8 - (Optional) Modify the facet control of the lofted flange.

1. In the *Flat Pattern* tab>Folded Part panel, click (Go to Folded Part).

2. Double-click on **Lofted Flange1** in the Model Browser. The

   Lofted Flange dialog box opens. Note that (Die Formed) is no longer available. To change the feature so that it is die formed, you must delete and recreate the feature.

The *Facet Control* options help refine the shape of the resulting lofted flange by customizing the size of the faceted face. The options include **A Chord Tolerance**, **B Facet Angle**, and **C Facet Distance**. The diagrams in the Lofted Flange dialog box, shown in Figure 10–22, help to show how the values are measured.

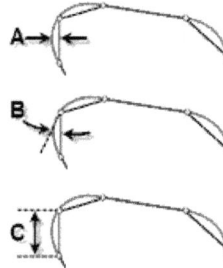

Figure 10–22

3. Keep the **A Chord Tolerance** option selected in the Lofted Flange dialog box. This defines the facet control for the entire feature. You can also individually control the facets in each zone.

4. Click the glyph that is associated with the faceted zone shown in Figure 10–23. The Bend Zone Edit dialog box opens.

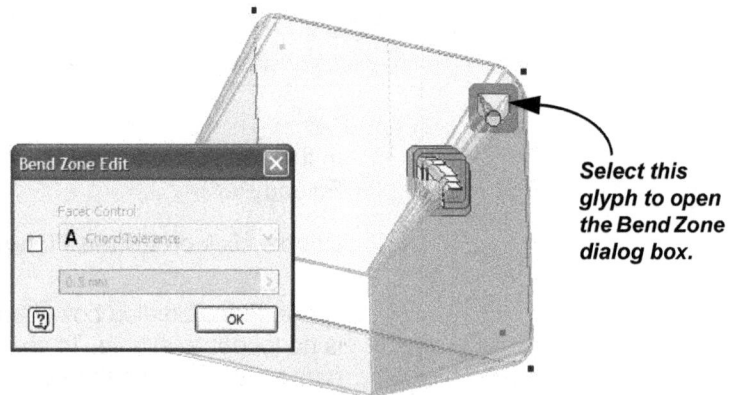

Select this glyph to open the Bend Zone dialog box.

Figure 10–23

You can change the bend radius on each facet, if required. For this practice, keep the default bend radius.

5. Select the check box to enable **Facet Control** and select **N Number of Facets** in the drop-down list. This option enables you to assign the number of facets for the zone. Enter **8** for the number of facets. Click **OK**.

6. Change the number of facets in the opposite bend zone to **8**, as shown in Figure 10–24.

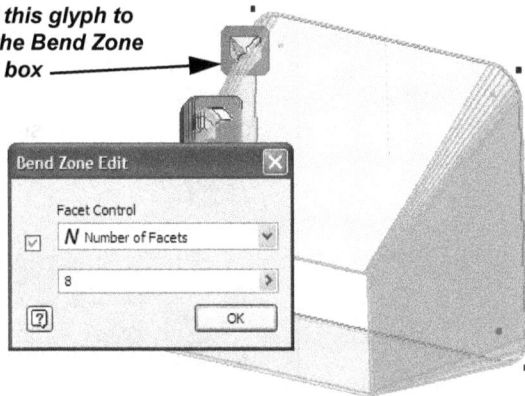

Select this glyph to open the Bend Zone dialog box

Figure 10–24

7. Click **OK** in the Bend Zone Edit and the Lofted Flange dialog boxes to complete the feature.

8. Double-click on **Flat Pattern** in the Model Browser. Review the changes to the flat pattern.

9. Save the model and close the window.

Practice 10b | Point to Point Rip

Practice Objectives

- Create a rip feature that is created on a surface between two selected points to permit the flattening of the sheet metal geometry.
- Flatten a folded sheet metal model.

In this practice, you will create a rip on a cylindrical surface so that it rips between two selected points. You will then create a flat pattern of the model to complete it. The completed flat and folded models are shown in Figure 10–25.

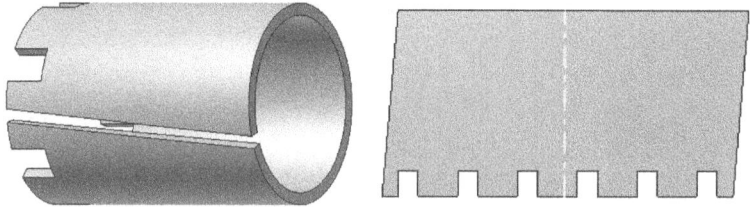

Figure 10–25

Task 1 - Open a sheet metal model.

1. Open **Point to Point Rip.ipt**. The model displays as shown in Figure 10–26. The points required to create the rip have been sketched for you.

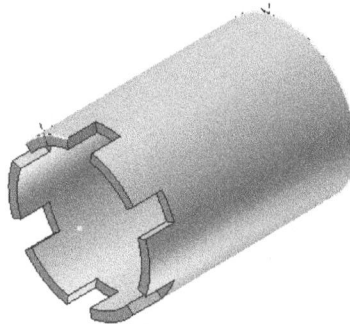

Figure 10–26

Task 2 - Create a rip feature.

1. In the *Sheet Metal* tab>Modify panel, click ▨ (Rip).

2. Select **Point to Point** in the *Rip Type* drop-down list. To define a Point to Point rip, you must select a face to rip and two points to rip between.

3. Select the cylindrical face as the *Rip Face* reference.

4. Select either one of the sketched points as the *Start Point* reference.

5. Select the other sketched point as the **End Point** reference.

6. Maintain **GapSize** as the *Gap Value* and click ▨ to ensure that the material is removed evenly from both sides of the gap.

7. Click **OK** to complete the feature. The rip displays in the model as shown in Figure 10–27.

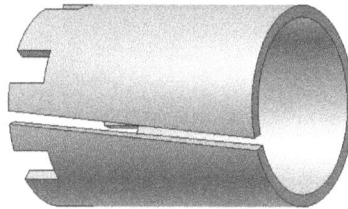

Figure 10–27

Task 3 - Create a flat pattern.

1. In the Flat Pattern panel, click ▨ (Create Flat Pattern). The model displays as shown in Figure 10–28.

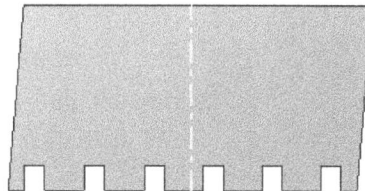

Figure 10–28

2. Save the model and close the window.

Chapter Review Questions

1. A lofted flange feature creates transitional sheet metal geometry that is blended between two profile sketches. Which of the following are true statements about lofted flanges? (Select all that apply.)

   a. Lofted flanges can be used as base or secondary features.

   b. The sketches required to define the profiles can be created before or at the same time as the lofted flange.

   c. The profiles for a lofted flange must be closed.

   d. The bend radius on each bend in the resulting geometry can be individually modified.

2. Once a Press Brake lofted flange has been created, how can you change the type to a Die Formed lofted flange.

   a. Edit the Lofted Flange feature and switch the Output option to (Die Form).

   b. Click the glyph in the model preview.

   c. Delete and recreate the Lofted Flange using (Die Form).

   d. None of the above. This is not possible.

3. Which of the following best describes what the glyph in the Lofted Flange preview enables you to do.

   a. Enables control of the resulting faceting along a bend line.

   b. Enables control of the bend radius along a bend line.

   c. Enables control of the Unfold rule along a bend line.

   d. All of the above.

4. A point can be created using the Rip dialog box so that it can be used as a reference to locate the Rip feature.

   a. True

   b. False

5. Which Rip type creates the Rip feature shown on the right in Figure 10–29?

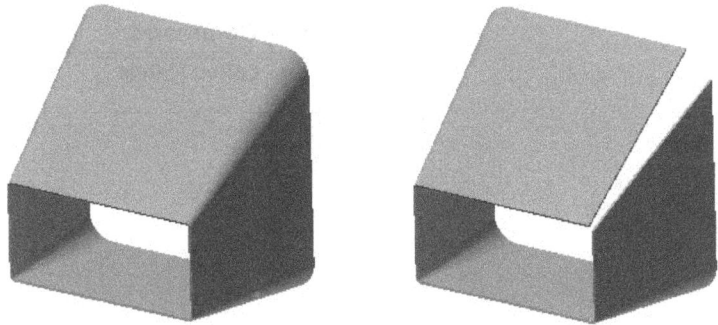

Figure 10–29

a. Single Point

b. Point to Point

c. Face Extents

d. Any of the above can be used to create this geometry.

Command Summary

Button	Command	Location
	Lofted Flange	• **Ribbon:** *Sheet Metal* tab>Create panel
	Rip	• **Ribbon:** *Sheet Metal* tab>Modify panel

Unfold and Refold

The Unfold and Refold features are available when working with folded sheet metal geometry. They enable you to unfold a model at any point in the model's design and then refold the geometry at any point thereafter.

Learning Objectives in this Chapter

- Unfold a sheet metal model by selecting a surface on the model to remain stationary while the geometry is unfolded.
- Refold unfolded geometry by using the previously selected unfold reference, or by selecting individual bends to refold the geometry.

11.1 Unfold and Refold

The Unfold and Refold features enable you to unfold a model at any point in the model's design and then refold the geometry at any point thereafter. Any features that are created between the unfolding and refolding are maintained on the model geometry as it was created when it was unfolded. For example, a sketch for a cut can be sketched and dimensioned and the cut created, all in the unfolded state. When refolded, it is positioned as required.

An additional benefit of the Unfold/Refold feature is that it enables you to unfold geometry, create additional features (e.g., stiffeners), and then refold the geometry.

On the left in Figure 11–1 a lofted flange is shown that once ripped, was unfolded. On the right in Figure 11–1, the model was unfolded, a hole feature was added, and then the model was refolded.

Features can be added when unfolded

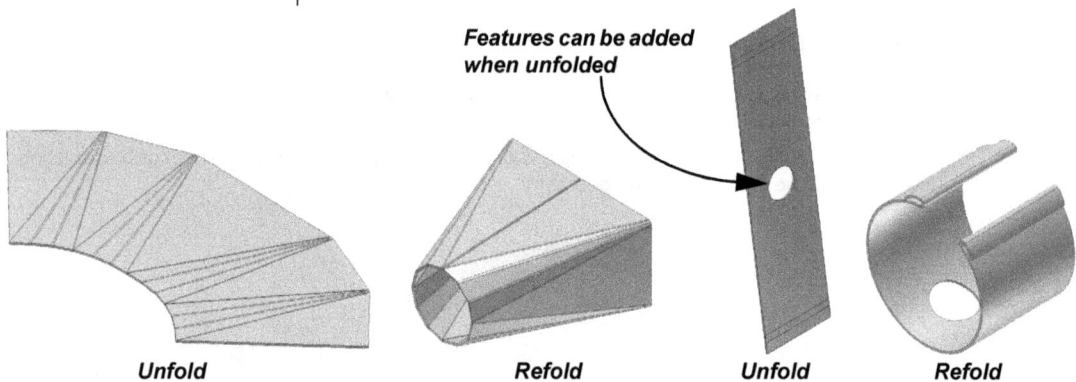

| *Unfold* | *Refold* | *Unfold* | *Refold* |

Figure 11–1

How To: Unfold a Feature

1. In the *Sheet Metal* tab>Modify panel, click (Unfold). The Unfold dialog box opens as shown in Figure 11–2.

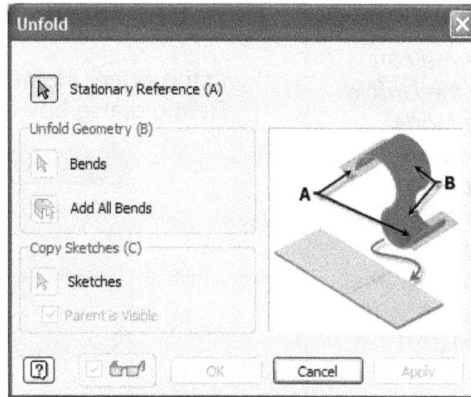

Figure 11–2

2. Define the **Stationary Reference (A)** for the model. This initial step is active by default and enables you to select a plane or face to remain stationary when bends are unfolded.
3. Define the geometry to be unfolded (B). You can unfold all bends (⬚) or selected bends (⬚). If unfolding all bends, the model immediately previews the unfolded geometry. If unfolding only selected bends, you can individually select each bend. All bends are previewed in magenta when the unfold feature is started.
4. Select any unconsumed sketches (C) to be unfolded using the options in the *Copy Sketches* area in the dialog box.

Each of the previous three steps are identified with letters (A, B, or C). Depending on the geometry in the model, the image that displays in the Unfold dialog box updates to those shown in Figure 11–3, to help identify the required references for each step.

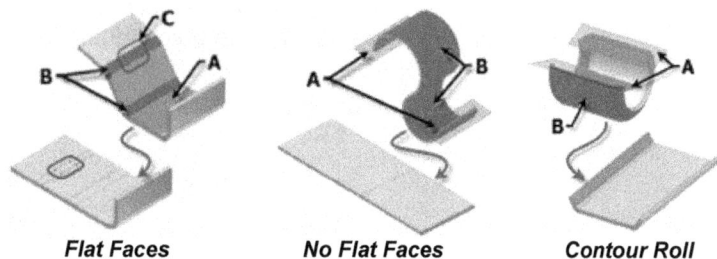

Flat Faces   *No Flat Faces*   *Contour Roll*

Figure 11–3

5. Once you have fully defined the unfold, click **OK** to complete the feature. Alternatively, you can right-click and select **OK (Enter)** or press <Enter> to complete the feature.

How To: Refold a Feature

Alternatively, you can right-click on the Unfold feature in the Model Browser and select **Refold Feature** *to refold the model. This option automatically uses the references that were selected when the model was initially unfolded.*

1. In the *Sheet Metal* tab>Modify panel, click 🔲 (Refold). The Refold dialog box opens as shown in Figure 11–4.

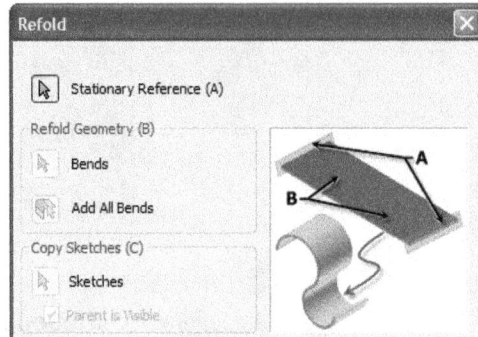

Figure 11–4

2. Define the **Stationary Reference (A)** for the model. This initial step is active by default and enables you to select a plane or face to remain stationary when the bends are refolded.
3. Define the geometry to be refolded (B). You can unfold all bends (🔲) or selected bends (🔲). If refolding all bends, the model immediately previews the refolded geometry. If refolding only selected bends, you can individually select each bend. All bends are previewed in magenta once the refold feature is started.
4. Select any unconsumed sketches (C) to be refolded using the options in the *Copy Sketches* area in the dialog box.

Each of the previous three steps are identified with letters (A, B, or C). Depending on the geometry in the model, the image that displays in the Refold dialog box updates to those shown in Figure 11–5, to help identify the required references for each step.

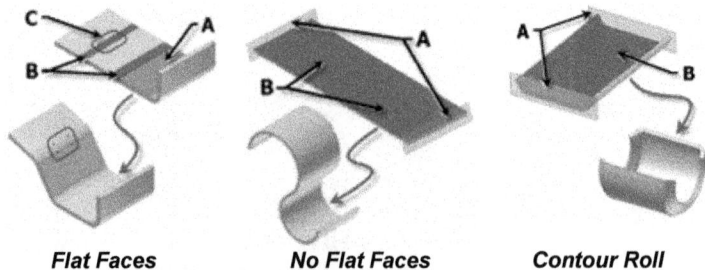

Flat Faces **No Flat Faces** **Contour Roll**

Figure 11–5

5. Once you have fully defined the refold, click **OK** to complete the feature. Alternatively, you can right-click and select **OK (Enter)** or press <Enter> to complete the feature.

Unfold vs. Flat Pattern

Unfold and flat patterns differ in that an unfold feature does not contain any of the bend and punch information that is important for manufacturing. Flat patterns are important for manufacturing and drawing creation. It is not recommended that you use an unfold feature for drawing creation.

Hint: Unfolding/Refolding Imported Sheet Metal Geometry

Imported geometry that has a zero bend radius bend can be unfolded or refolded as follows:

- For **Unfold**, select the stationary reference and the non-zero bend using the fields in the Unfold dialog box. A new face is added where the zero radius bend edge exists, as shown in Figure 11–6. The K-factor value defines the area of the face.

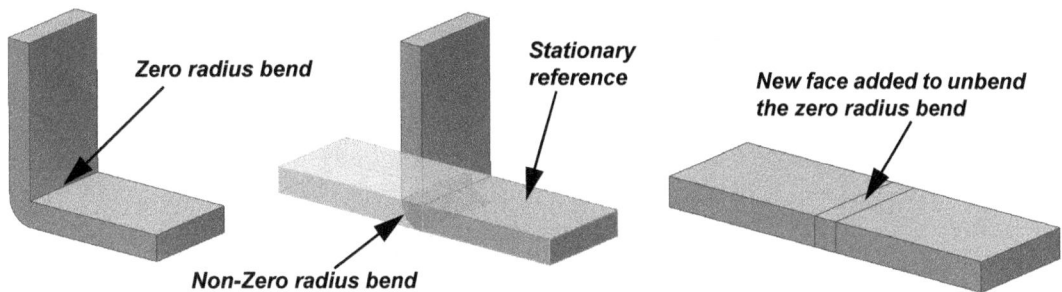

Figure 11–6

- After **Refold**, references that are created when unfolding the model remain, as shown in Figure 11–7.

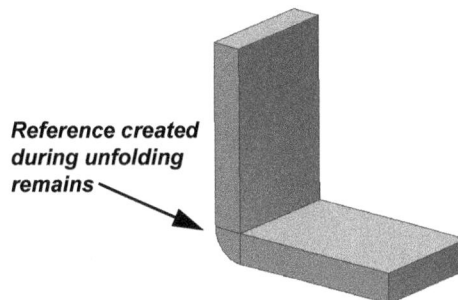

Figure 11–7

Practice 11a | Unfold/Refold

Practice Objectives

- Unfold a sheet metal model by selecting a surface on the model to stay stationary while the remaining geometry is unfolded.
- Create geometry on an unfolded sheet metal model.
- Refold unfolded geometry to display new feature geometry in the unfolded model.

In this practice, you will use the Unfold and Refold features to create a hole feature that lies on a bent surface. The completed model is shown in Figure 11–8.

Figure 11–8

Task 1 - Open a sheet metal model.

1. Open **Unfold_Refold.ipt**. A single contour flange feature is created in the model, as shown in Figure 11–9.

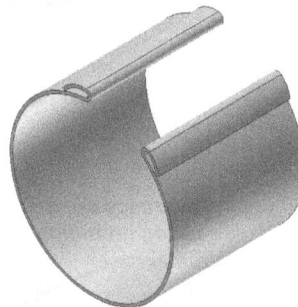

Figure 11–9

Task 2 - Unfold all bends in the model.

1. In the *Sheet Metal* tab>Modify panel, click 🖾 (Unfold). The Unfold dialog box opens as shown in Figure 11–10.

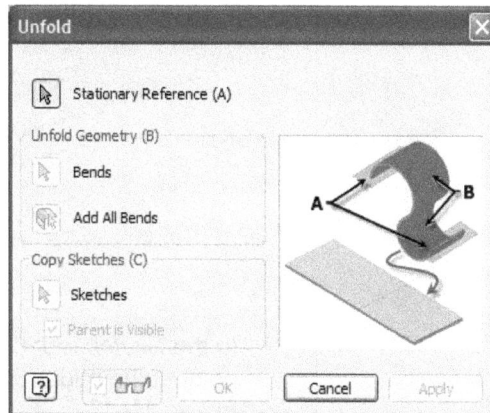

Figure 11–10

2. Select either one of the two surfaces that highlight in blue as the **Stationary Reference (A)** for the model, as shown in Figure 11–11. This surface will remain stationary when bends are unfolded.

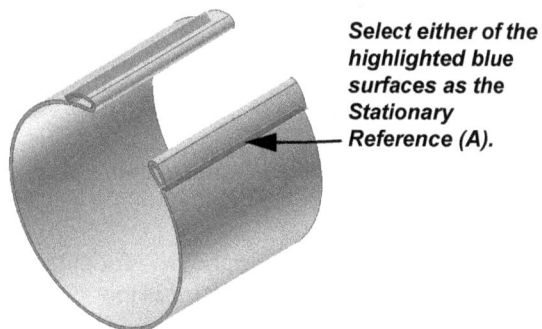

Select either of the highlighted blue surfaces as the Stationary Reference (A).

Figure 11–11

3. Click 🖾 (Add All Bends) in the *Unfold Geometry (B)* area.

4. Click **OK** to complete the feature.

Task 3 - Add a hole feature to the unfolded geometry.

1. In the Sketch panel, click ⬚ (Start 2D Sketch). Select the face shown in Figure 11–12 as the sketch plane.

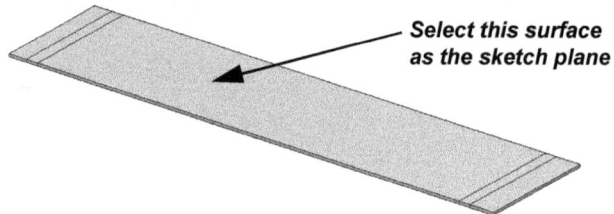

Select this surface as the sketch plane

Figure 11–12

2. In the *Sketch* tab>Draw panel, click ╎ (Point). Locate the point at the midpoint of the surface, as shown in Figure 11–13.

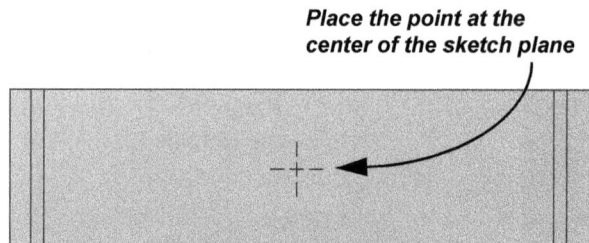

Place the point at the center of the sketch plane

Figure 11–13

3. In the *Sketch* tab>Exit panel, click ✔ (Finish Sketch).

4. In the *3D* Model tab>Modify panel, click ◉ (Hole). The standard Hole dialog box opens.

5. Select **From Sketch** as the *Placement* type, if it is not already selected. The sketched point should also be automatically selected. If not, select it.

6. Define the **From Sketch** hole as **Through All** with a **20 mm** diameter.

7. Click **OK** to complete the feature.

Task 4 - Refold the sheet metal model.

Alternatively, you can click 📋 (Refold) in the Modify panel to open the Refold dialog box and define the references for refolding.

After a refold, any features created between the unfold and refold are maintained on the model geometry, as it was created when it was unfolded.

1. In the Model Browser, right-click on the Unfold feature and select **Refold Feature**. By refolding this way, you are not required to select any references or options in the Refold dialog box. The references used to unfold are used to refold. The completed model displays as shown in Figure 11–14.

Figure 11–14

2. Save the model and close the window.

Chapter Review Questions

1. What is the difference between an Unfold and a Flat Pattern feature?

   a. The unfold and flat patterns differ in that an unfold feature contains the bend and punch information that is important for manufacturing.

   b. The unfold and flat patterns differ in that an unfold feature does not contain any of the bend and punch information that is important for manufacturing.

2. In the model shown in Figure 11–15, which surface was selected as the stationary face when the Unfold feature was added to create the model shown on the right? Both the folded and unfolded models are shown in their default views.

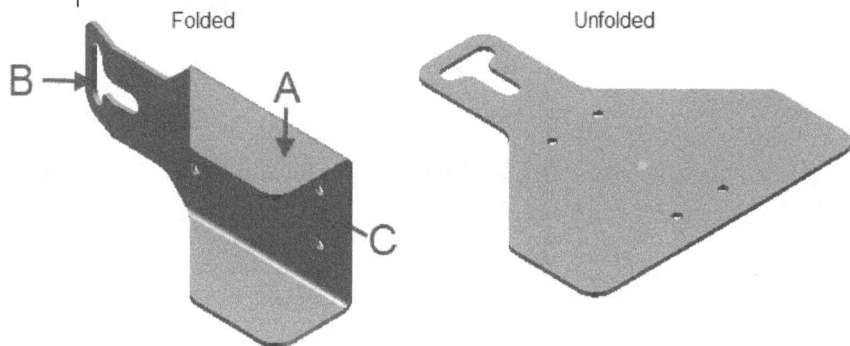

Folded   Unfolded

Figure 11–15

   a. A

   b. B

   c. C

3. When features are added between an Unfold and Refold feature, they are only displayed in the unfolded state. They are not displayed when the model is refolded.

   a. True

   b. False

4. Which of the following statements is true when using the **Refold** command? (Select all that apply.)

    a. When activating the Refold command in the Ribbon all bends in the model are refolded.

    b. When activating the Refold command in the Ribbon you can explicitly select which bends in the model to refold.

    c. When activating the Refold command by right-clicking on an existing Unfold feature and selecting Refold Feature, all bends in the model are refolded.

    d. When activating the Refold command by right-clicking on an existing Unfold feature and selecting Refold Feature, you can explicitly select which bends in the model to refold.

5. The Unfold feature must be added as the very last feature in the sheet metal model.

    a. True

    b. False

Command Summary

Button	Command	Location
	Refold	• **Ribbon:** *Sheet Metal* tab>Modify panel • (*Context Menu with a Unfold feature selected in the Model Browser.*)
	Unfold	• **Ribbon:** *Sheet Metal* tab>Modify panel

Chapter
12

Multi-Body Sheet Metal Modeling

Multi-body sheet metal modeling is a design methodology that enables you to create an entire sheet metal assembly design in a single sheet metal file. You can use a combination of sheet metal and part modeling features to create the geometry. Once modeling is complete, you can use tools to create multiple models from each solid body.

Learning Objective in this Chapter

- Create a multi-body sheet metal part file that represents multiple assembly components in a single file and then use the bodies to create individual sheet metal part files.

12.1 Multi-Body Modeling

Creating sheet metal parts using a multi-body modeling workflow enables you to create your entire assembly design in the part environment using both sheet metal and 3D modeling feature commands. The design is arranged into separate bodies in a single sheet metal part file. Figure 12–1 shows a model that has five solid bodies. **Solid3** is expanded in the Model Browser to display the features that were used to create this solid. Each of these separate bodies can then be extracted into individual parts for a new assembly.

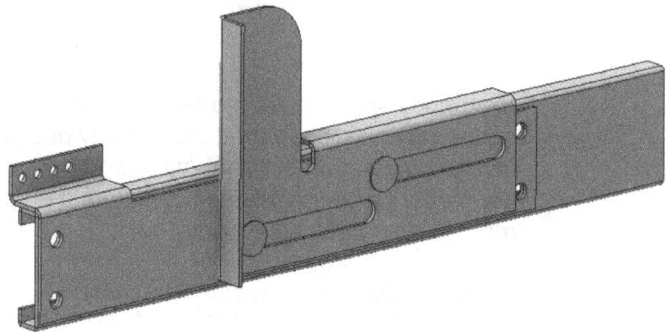

bracket_mount.ipt
Folded Model
Solid Bodies(3)
  Solid1
  Solid2
  Solid3
    Face3
    Corner Round1
    Fold3
    Cut1
    Fold4
    Fold5
View: Master
Origin
Face1
Flange1
Flange2
Face2
Fold1
Fold2
Hole1
Face3
Corner Round1

Figure 12–1

The advantages of building a file using multi-bodies include the following:

- You do not need to create an initial complex file and directory structure to design parts in the context of a top-level assembly. The entire design resides in a single file and bodies are later extracted to create parts.

- A complex part file can be better organized using separate bodies with respect to their function or position in the model.

- Relationships between bodies can be set up and broken.

- You can control the visibility of bodies as a group rather than at the individual feature level.

All sheet metal models contain a *Solid Bodies* folder in the Model Browser. This folder lists all solids in the part. For the model in Figure 12–2, the *Solid Bodies* folder contains three solids.

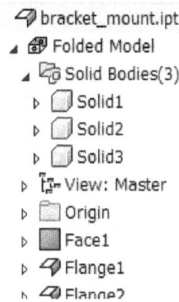

Figure 12–2

Hint: Use Sheet Metal Styles and Thickness

When designing sheet metal models using the multi-body modeling technique, it is recommended that you drive the model's thickness using the Sheet Metal Rule. This helps to ensure that when the bodies are extracted to create their own part files that the thickness values match the style of the newly created model and that the model can be flattened. If the values differ, the model cannot be unfolded.

Creating the First Solid Body

With the creation of the first feature in any sheet metal file, the first solid body is automatically created. This is because

[icon] (New Solid) is automatically selected in the feature creation dialog box, as shown in Figure 12–3. Once the base feature is created, the *Solid Bodies* folder displays in the Model Browser and the first solid body is added to the folder.

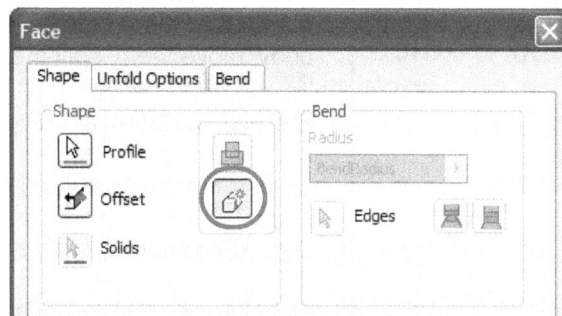

Figure 12–3

Creating Additional Solid Bodies

Once the first solid body is added to the model, each additional feature is automatically applied to it, unless a new feature is explicitly set to be created as a new solid body. To create a new solid body, create its feature as you normally would, but click ⬚ (New Solid) in the feature creation dialog box or in the mini-toolbar. Once selected, a second body is added.

Assigning Features to Solid Bodies

Once two or more solid bodies are in a model, the selection of the placement/sketch planes are important to properly locate the new feature on to the required solid body. Consider the following:

- When creating a sketched feature, it is by default added to the same solid body as that of the sketch plane. For features to be added to a different solid body, click ⬚ (Solids) in the feature dialog box and then select the required solid body.

- When creating a pick-and-place feature, it is by default added to the same solid body as the placement references. In the case of a Corner Round, for example, it is added to the same solid body as the parent feature of the placement edge. If multiple edges are selected that belong to multiple solid bodies, the feature is added to each solid body.

- When creating a sketch-based or pick-and-place feature, it is only extended through its parent solid body, even if the **Through All** depth option is selected. For features to interact with another solid body, click ⬚ (Solids) in the feature dialog box and then select additional solid bodies to be included.

Manipulating Solid Bodies

Once multiple solid bodies exist in the model, you can further manipulate them. You can redefine them as part of another solid body, move them, split them, and combine them.

Redefining/Removing Features in Solid Bodies

Once a feature is created and assigned to a solid body, you can re-assign it to another solid body or remove a solid body from interacting with the feature. To do so, redefine the original feature and click ⬚ (Solids) to activate it. You can select the new solid to apply it to or, if you want to remove a solid body from the initial selection set, press and hold <Ctrl> and select the solid body to remove.

Moving Bodies

You might need to move the various bodies in a multi-body part.

How To: Move a Solid Body

*The **Move** command is only available when working with solid bodies.*

1. In the *3D Model* tab>expanded Modify panel, click ⊕ (Move Bodies). The Move Bodies dialog box opens.
2. Select the solid bodies to move. If you need to select multiple bodies, you must click ▨ (Bodies) again after selecting the first body to select additional bodies.
3. Select a move operation using the drop-down list in the Move Bodies dialog box, as shown in Figure 12–4.

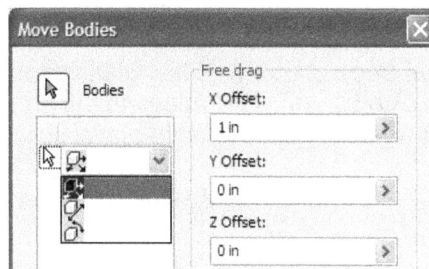

Figure 12–4

Each icon in the list enables you to move the body, as follows:

- ⊞ **(Free drag):** Enables you to enter a precise X, Y, or Z offset value, or drag the preview in any direction.

- ⬭ **(Move along ray):** Enables you to enter a precise offset value, or drag the preview offset from a selected reference.

- ↻ **(Rotate about line):** Enables you to enter a precise rotational angle value, or drag the preview around a selected axis.

4. Depending on the move operation selected, enter values and select references using the right side of the dialog box to define the movement.

5. To define a second move operation, if required, select **Click to add** and select a new move operation, as shown in Figure 12–5.

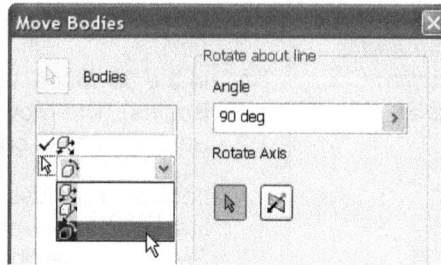

Figure 12–5

6. Continue to add move operations as required for the selected body.
7. Click **OK** to complete the feature. A Move Body feature is added to the bottom of the Model Browser, as well as into each of the Solid Bodies selected to be moved.

*To edit the Move Body feature, right-click on it and select **Edit feature**.*

Splitting Bodies

You can split a single body so that you can manipulate the resulting bodies independently.

How To: Split a Solid Body

*The **Split** command is available when working with solid bodies or Autodesk® Inventor® features.*

1. In the *3D Model* tab>Modify panel, click (Split).

2. Click (Split Solid) as the split method. The Split dialog box opens as shown in Figure 12–6.

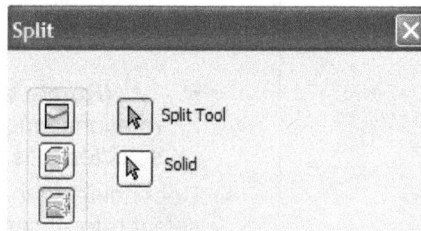

Figure 12–6

3. Select a work plane or a sketch as the *Split Tool*. The split tool defines where the split occurs.
4. Select the Solid body to split. If a sketch was selected as the split tool, the solid body to which the sketch plane belongs is automatically selected as the solid to be split. You can reselect this reference, as required.
5. Click **OK** to complete the split.

Combining Bodies

If you created two solid bodies separately during an initial design, you might decide later that they should be combined. Using the **Combine** command, you can add or remove material based on selected bodies.

How To: Combine Features

*The **Combine** command is only available when working with solid bodies.*

1. In the *3D Model* tab>Modify panel, click (Combine). The Combine dialog box opens as shown in Figure 12–7.

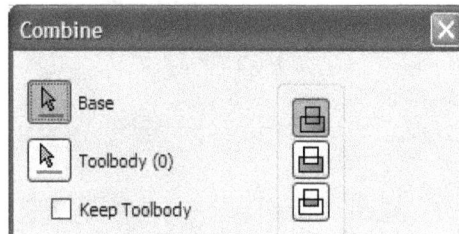

Figure 12–7

2. Select the solid body to use as the *Base* reference. The base body is the solid body on which the operation is going to be performed.

You can only select one base body, but you can select multiple toolbodies, if required.

3. Select the solid body to use as the *Toolbody* reference. The toolbody is the solid body or bodies that is going to perform the operation.
4. (Optional) To maintain the toolbody as a solid body after the operation, select **Keep Toolbody**. If you select this option, toolbody becomes invisible. This option is only available during the initial combine operation, not during the editing process.
5. Select an operation to perform on the base. The available operations include joining (), cutting (), and intersecting () the toolbody from the base.
6. Click **OK** to complete the feature. The Combine feature is listed at the bottom of the Model Browser and in the solid body used as the base reference.

Inserting Components into Parts

Using the **Derive** option, you can selectively include/exclude solid bodies (or other objects) from a source model to import it into a new or existing part file.

Creating Parts from Part Bodies

The steps for creating a part is similar to that for deriving a part.

You can extract individual bodies from a multi-body sheet metal part into separate sheet metal parts.

How To: Extract a Body to Create a New Sheet Metal Part

1. In the *Sheet Metal* tab>Flat Pattern panel, click (Make Part). The Make Part dialog box opens, as shown in Figure 12–8.

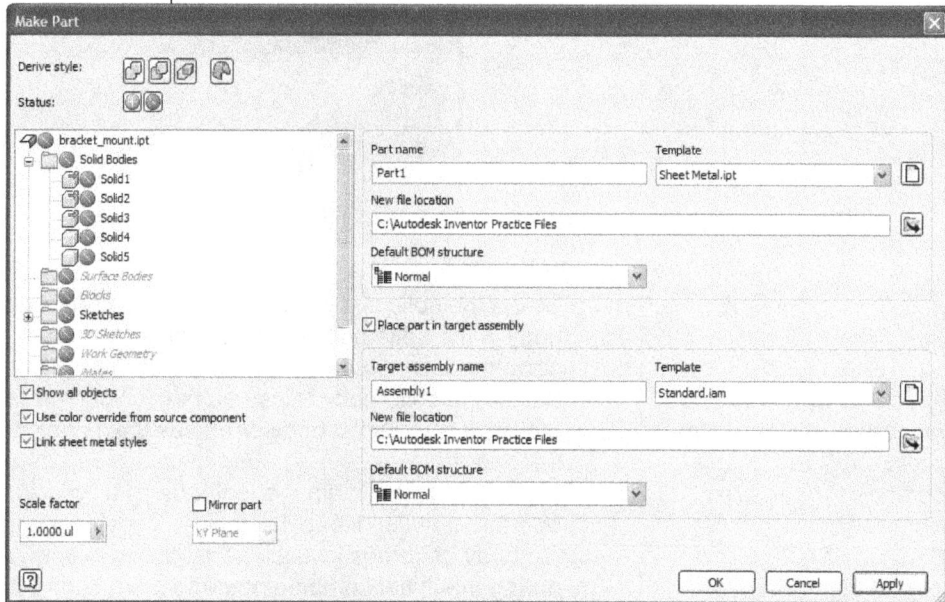

Figure 12–8

2. Select a **Derive style** icon from the top of the dialog box to define how to create the component. The icons are described as follows:

Icon	Description
	Create single solid body where seams between planar faces as removed.
	Create single solid body where seams between planar faces are kept.
	Keep each solid as an individual solid body.
	Create the body as a work surface.

*Use the **Show all objects** option to refine the tree in the Make Part dialog box to either show all objects that can be included/excluded, or to only list those headings that have applicable data in the solid body.*

3. Enable or disable which portions (e.g., solid bodies, sketches, parameters, etc.) of the model to use to create the new part by toggling the **Status** icons adjacent to the item name.

   - A yellow circle with a plus symbol (⊕) indicates that the geometry is included in the new part.

   - A gray circle with a slash symbol (⊘) indicates that the geometry is not included in the new part.

   - A circle that is half yellow and half gray (◑) indicates that some geometry in the object type is included, while some is not.

4. Define the remaining options on the right side of the Make Part dialog box to fully define the new part (e.g., part name, template to use, etc.).

5. (Optional) If you require the part to be in a new assembly, select **Place part in target assembly** and enter the assembly information.

6. Click **OK** to complete the part. Depending on the *Derive style* selected, the new part might combine the selected bodies into a single body, or keep each body separate.

The newly created part remains associative to the multi-body part, unless you explicitly break the link. In the newly created part, right-click on the source part name that has been imported and select **Break Link With Base Component**. The link can be suppressed (instead of broken) by selecting **Suppress Link With Base Component**.

Creating Components from Part Bodies

Selected bodies in a multi-body part can be extracted into separate components that are combined in a new top-level assembly.

How To: Extract Solid Bodies and Create a New Assembly from Them

1. In the *Sheet Metal* tab>Flat Pattern panel, click ⬚ (Make Components). The Make Components: Selection dialog box opens.

2. Select the solid bodies to extract in the Model Browser. All selected solid bodies are listed in the dialog box.

3. Ensure that the **Insert components in target assembly** option is selected.

4. Specify the remaining options on the right side of the Make Components: Selection dialog box to fully define the new component (e.g., target assembly name, template to use, etc.). The dialog box displays similar to that shown in Figure 12–9 once components have been selected.

*Consider using the **Make Component** command and disabling the **Insert components in target assembly** option instead of using the **Make Part** command multiple times when creating more than one component from a multi-body part.*

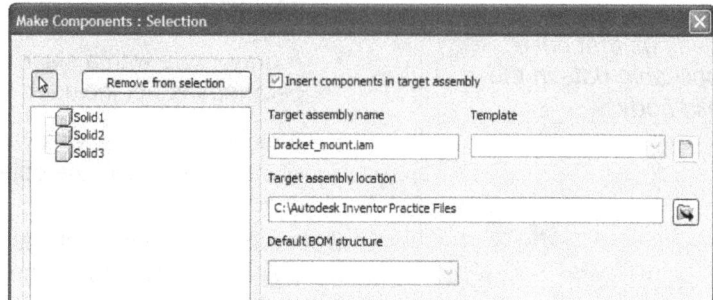

Figure 12–9

5. Click **Next**. The Make Components: Bodies dialog box opens.
6. Using the Make Components: Bodies dialog box, you can make changes to individual components that are being created as part of the assembly. You can click in each column to rename the resulting component, or change its template or BOM Structure. The dialog box opens similar to that shown in Figure 12–10.

The solid body name in the source model is used as the default name for the component.

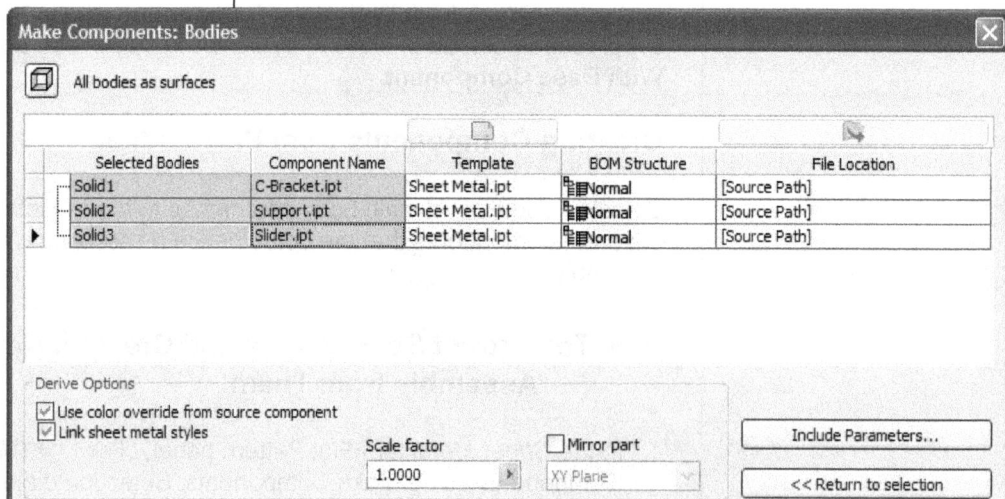

Figure 12–10

7. Set the options in the *Derive Options* area, as required.
8. Click **OK** to complete the operation.

The newly created sheet metal parts and assembly remain associative to the multi-body part unless you explicitly break the link to the parent model. To break the link, you must open each created component, then right-click on the source part name that has been imported and select **Break Link With Base Component**. The link can be suppressed instead of broken by selecting **Suppress Link With Base Component**.

Solid Body Display

To control the visibility of a solid body, right-click on the solid body and enable or disable the **Visibility** option.

Solid Body Properties

To access the properties for a solid body, right-click on the solid body name and select **Properties**. The Body Properties dialog box opens as shown in Figure 12–11.

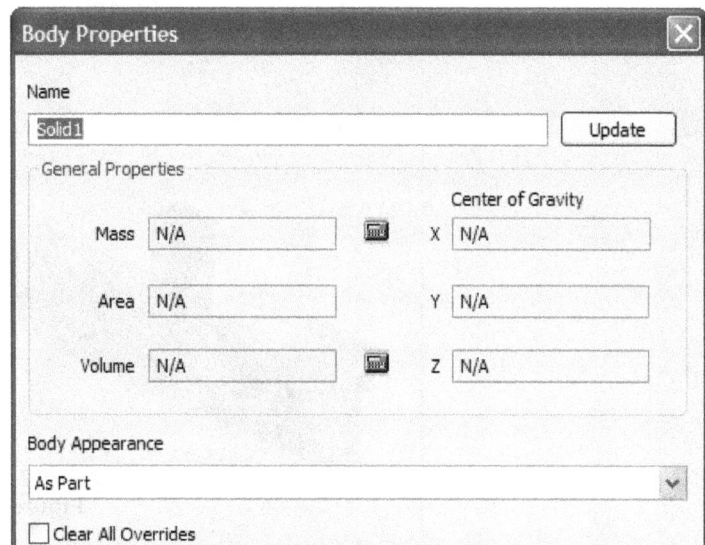

Figure 12–11

Using the Body Properties dialog box, you can do the following:

- Rename the solid body. You can also rename a solid body directly in the Model Browser.

- Update and provide the general properties for the solid body.

- Set a color style for the solid body.

*The **Clear All Overrides** option removes color overrides from individual faces contained in the solid body.*

Practice 12a | Multi-Body Sheet Metal Modeling

Practice Objectives

- Create multiple solid bodies in a single sheet metal part and modify and add features to specific bodies.
- Create a new assembly and part files by extracting solid bodies from the multi-body sheet metal part file.

In this practice, you will create a single sheet metal part file containing three solid bodies. In creating these solid bodies, you will learn to create multiple bodies in a model, add features to the bodies, and make required changes. To complete the practice you will use the multi-body model to create a top-level assembly and individual components for each body. The completed model is shown in Figure 12–12.

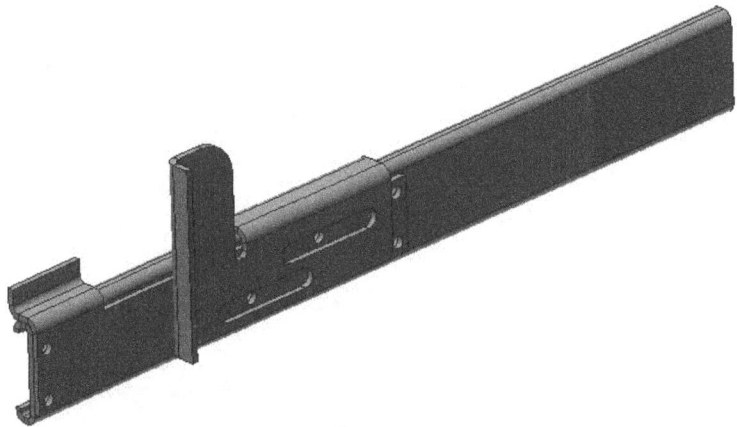

Figure 12–12

Task 1 - Modify the bend radius for the flange features.

1. Open **multibody_bracket_mount.ipt**. The model is a C-bracket and consists of a face and two flange features.

2. Zoom in on one of the ends of the model, as shown in Figure 12–13.

3. In the Model Browser, double-click on **Flange1** to open its dialog box to make a change to the feature.

Prior to the release of the Autodesk Inventor 2016 software, a zero bend radius was not possible.

4. In the *Bend Radius* field, note that the value is set to the default of **BendRadius**. Enter **0** as the new bend radius value and note how the model geometry updates, as shown in Figure 12–14.

5. In the *Bend Radius* field, enter **BendRadius/2**. Note how the model geometry updates, as shown in Figure 12–15.

Bend Radius = BendRadius

Figure 12–13

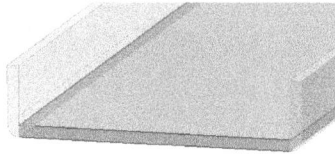

Bend Radius = 0

Figure 12–14

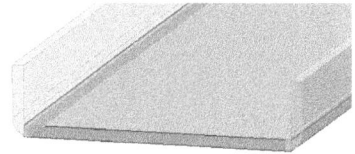

Bend Radius = BendRadius/2

Figure 12–15

6. Click **OK** to complete the change.

7. Change the *Bend Radius* value for **Flange2** to **BendRadius/2**.

Task 2 - Create a second solid body in the model to represent a new sheet metal part.

---

1. Expand the **Solid Bodies** node in the Model Browser and note that there is a single Solid Body in the model, as shown in Figure 12–16.

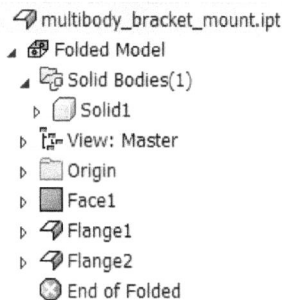

Figure 12–16

2. In the Sheet Metal tab, click (Start 2D Sketch) and select the flat face shown in Figure 12–17 as the new sketch plane.

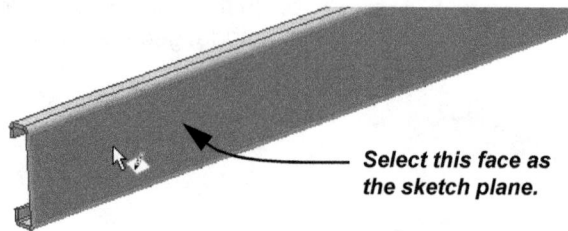

*Select this face as
the sketch plane.*

Figure 12–17

3. Prior to sketching, ensure that the orientation of the model is similar to that shown in the ViewCube in Figure 12–18. Orienting in this way ensures that the images and instructions in the following steps match.

4. Sketch and dimension the six linear entities shown in Figure 12–18. The .0625 dimension value is dimensioned to the projected edge of the bend on **Flange1**. The vertical edge on the left-hand side of the sketch is constrained to the projected Origin Center Point. Finish the sketch.

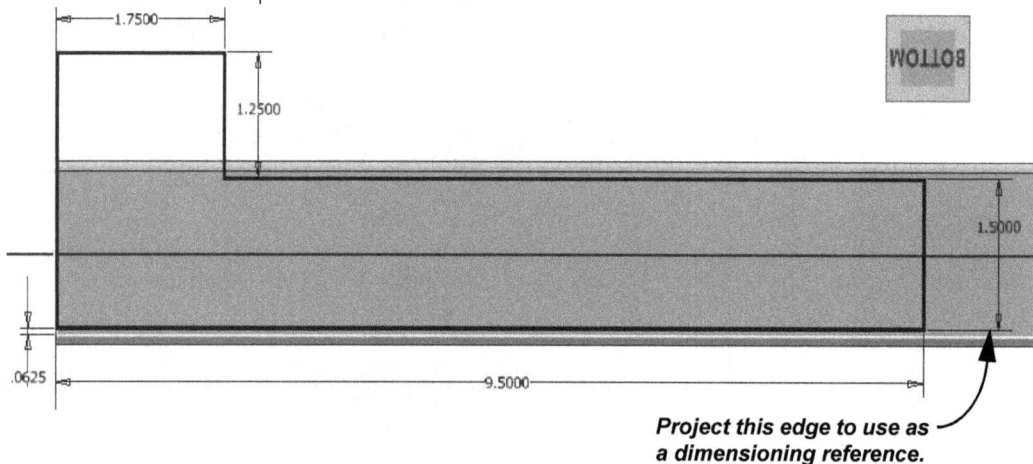

*Project this edge to use as
a dimensioning reference.*

Figure 12–18

5. In the *Sheet Metal* tab>Create panel, click (Face). The Face dialog box opens, as shown in Figure 12–19. By default, the new sketch is automatically selected as the Profile for the Face feature and a preview of the feature is displayed.

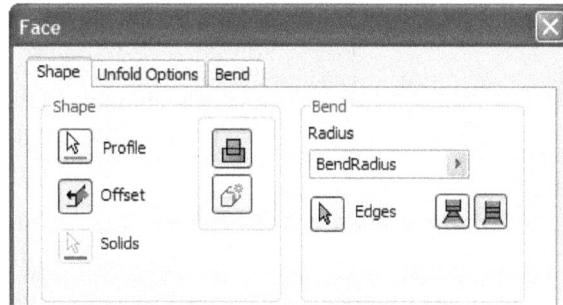

Figure 12–19

6. In the *Shape* area, click [icon] (New Solid) to create the new feature as a solid in the model.

7. Click [icon] (Offset) to flip the feature so that the Face geometry is created away from the sketch plane. This ensures that the geometry in the two features does not intersect.

8. Click **OK** to create the new feature. The new geometry should display as shown in Figure 12–20.

9. Expand the **Solid Bodies**, **Solid1**, and **Solid2** nodes in the Model Browser, as shown in Figure 12–20. Note how the new **Face2** feature is only assigned to **Solid2**, while the other features are assigned to **Solid1**. The lower portion of the Model Browser lists all of the features in the order that they were created.

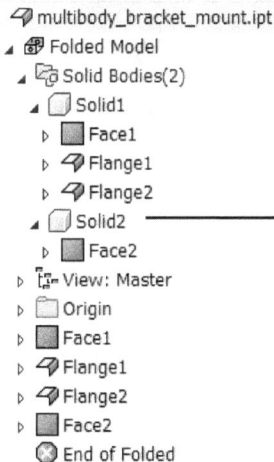

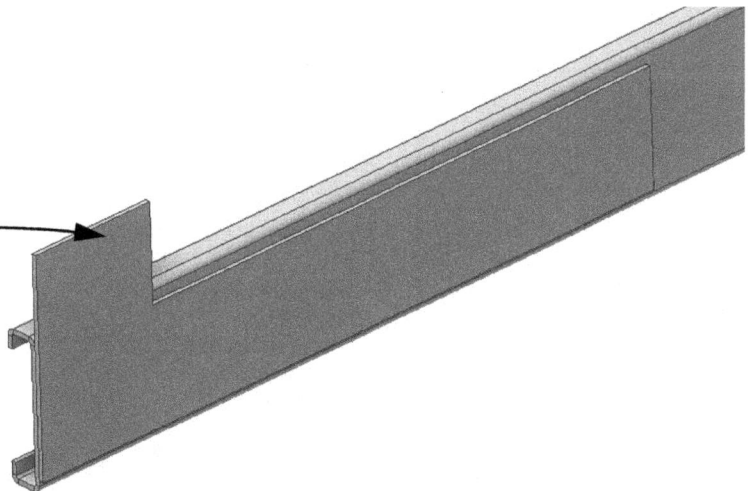

Figure 12–20

10. Create a new sketch to define the bendline for a fold. Select the new face that was created as the sketch plane and sketch and dimension the line shown in Figure 12–21. Ensure that the ends of the sketch are constrained using the **Coincident** constraint to the edges of the solid geometry.

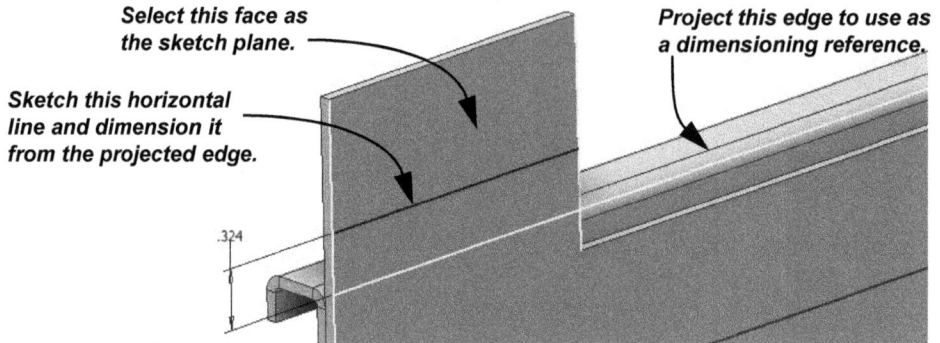

Select this face as the sketch plane.

Project this edge to use as a dimensioning reference.

Sketch this horizontal line and dimension it from the projected edge.

.324

Figure 12–21

11. Modify the offset dimension in the sketch to **.01** and complete the sketch.

12. In the *Sheet Metal* tab>Create panel, click ◿ (Fold). Select the sketched line that was just created as the Bend Line reference. Use the *Flip Controls* are required to create the fold as shown in Figure 12–22.

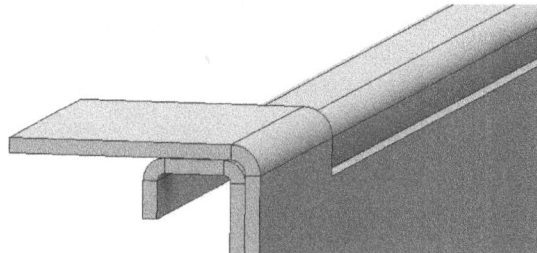

Figure 12–22

13. Create the additional fold shown in Figure 12–23.

Ensure that the bendline's sketch fully extends along the width of the geometry that will be folded.

Create this fold by sketching a bendline that is .45 in from its unbent edge.

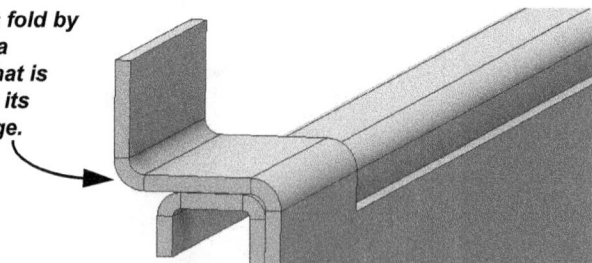

Figure 12–23

14. Create the four sketch points in a new sketch on the face of **Solid2**. Project the XY Plane and ensure that the points are symmetric about this plane. Dimension and further constrain (points align horizontally and vertically) the sketch points so that the three dimensions shown in Figure 12–24 fully constrain the sketch.

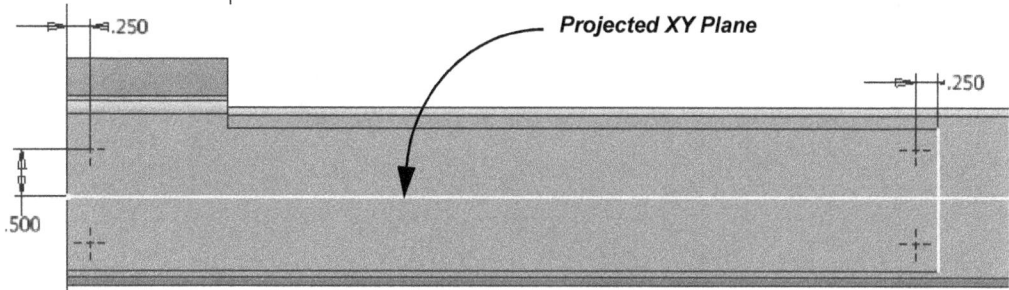

Figure 12–24

15. Finish the sketch.

16. In the *Sheet Metal* tab>Modify panel, click (Hole).

17. The four sketched points are automatically selected as references to place the holes. Enter **.25 in** as the diameter and select **Through All** as the *Termination* option. Click **OK**.

18. Spin the model and note that the holes, by default, only extrude through **Solid 2**. **Solid2** is automatically included because it is the parent of the sketch plane that was used to create the sketch points for the holes.

19. Edit **Hole1**. In the *Placement* area, select (Solids) and select **Solid1** in the Model Browser or directly in the graphics window. Click **OK**.

20. Note that the holes now extrude through both solids.

21. Expand the **Solid Bodies** node in the Model Browser and note that the **Hole1** feature is now listed in both solids.

Task 3 - Create a third solid body in the model.

1. In the *Sheet Metal* tab, click ▱ (Start 2D Sketch) and select the flat face shown in Figure 12–25 as the new sketch plane.

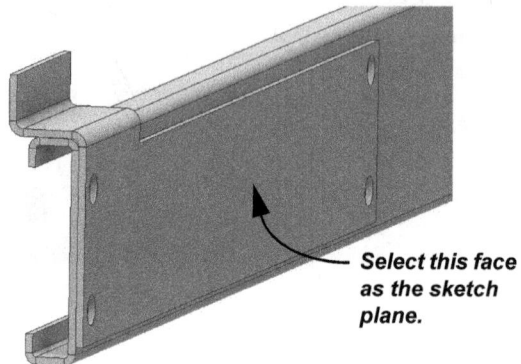

Select this face as the sketch plane.

Figure 12–25

2. Sketch and dimension the 9 entities shown in Figure 12–26. The .0625 dimension value is dimensioned to the projected edge of **Face2**. The vertical edge on the left-hand side of the sketch is constrained to the projected Origin Center Point.

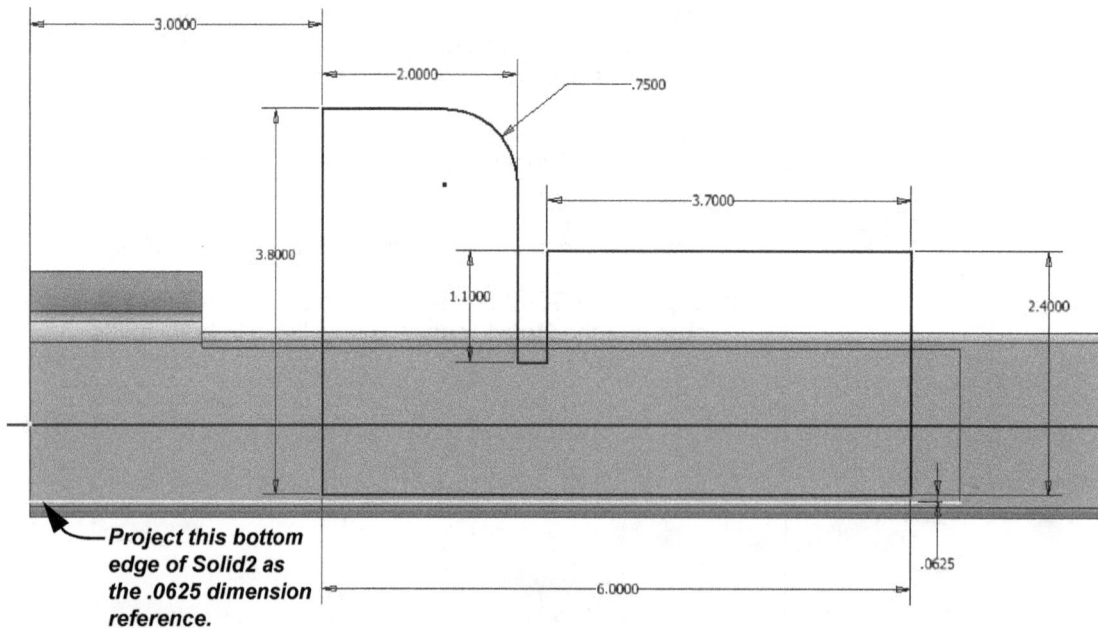

3.0000
2.0000
.7500
3.7000
3.8000
1.1000
2.4000
.0625

Project this bottom edge of Solid2 as the .0625 dimension reference.

6.0000

Figure 12–26

3. Finish the sketch.

4. In the *Sheet Metal* tab>Create panel, click ⬜ (Face). The new sketch is automatically selected as the Profile.

5. In the *Shape* area, click 🔲 (New Solid) to create the new feature as a solid in the model.

6. Click 🔲 (Offset) to flip the feature so that the Face geometry is created away from the sketch plane to ensure that the geometry does not intersect.

7. Click **OK** to create the new feature.

8. Create the fold, corner round, and slotted cut features shown in Figure 12–27. The slotted cuts can be created as either a single feature or individual features.

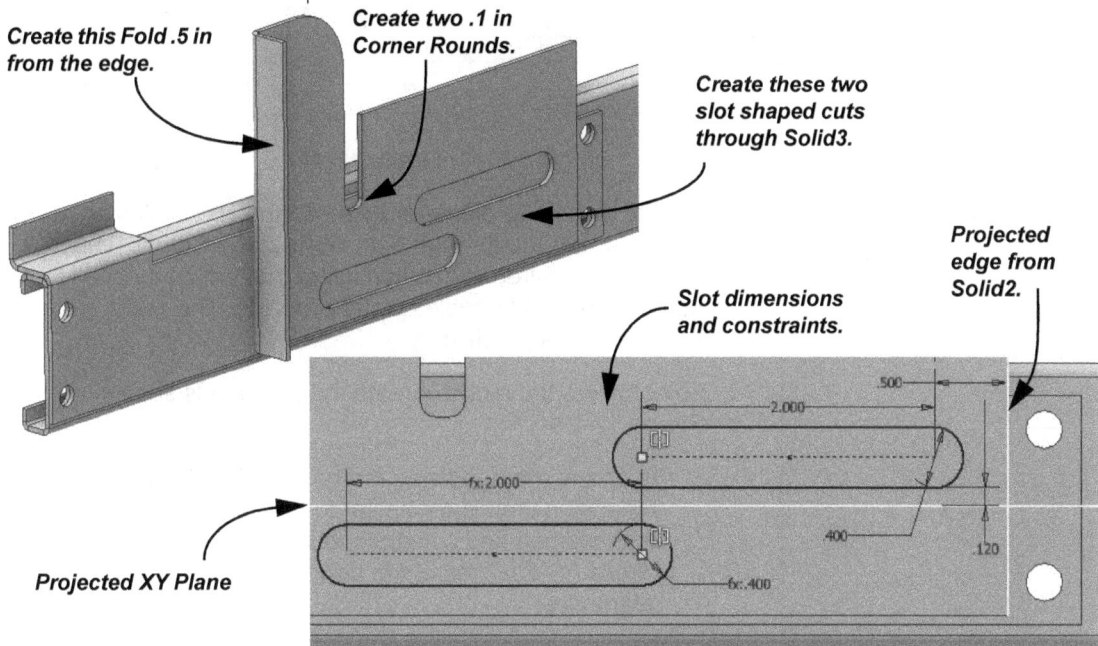

Create this Fold .5 in from the edge.

Create two .1 in Corner Rounds.

Create these two slot shaped cuts through Solid3.

Projected edge from Solid2.

Slot dimensions and constraints.

Projected XY Plane

Figure 12–27

Task 4 - Complete the model by adding holes and folds.

1. Create a new sketch on the face of **Solid2**.

2. Sketch the two points shown in Figure 12–28. Center the points vertically in the slots and dimension them horizontally from the right-hand edge of **Solid2**.

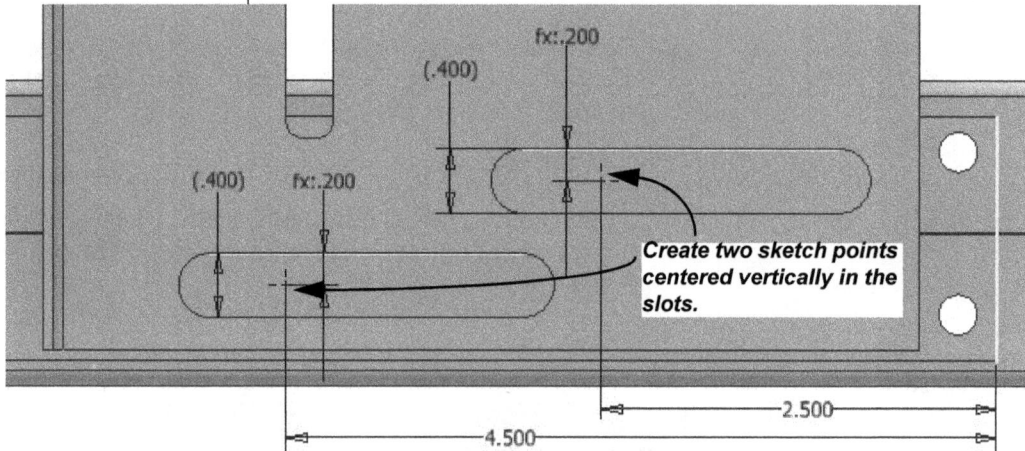

Create two sketch points centered vertically in the slots.

Figure 12–28

3. Create two **.25 in** diameter holes on the two sketch points so that they extrude through both **Solid2** and **Solid1**. These holes are required to position rivets that will connect all three components and enables **Solid3** to slide. The rivets are not created in this practice.

4. To complete the model, create the two bends shown in Figure 12–29.

   • To create the bendlines for these folds, sketch and dimension their lines similar to how the bendline was dimensioned and constrained in the fold shown in Figure 12–21. Project the bendlines in **Solid1** as references.

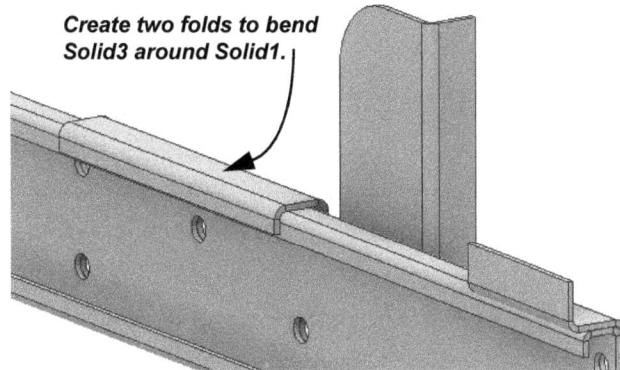

Create two folds to bend Solid3 around Solid1.

Figure 12–29

5. Save the model. If you did not successfully complete the modeling in this practice, **multi_bracket_mount_FINAL.ipt** has been provided in the practice files folder to use to continue the next task.

Task 5 - Make components from the three solid bodies.

---

1. In the *Sheet Metal* tab>Flat Pattern panel, click (Make Components). The Make Components: Selection dialog box opens.

2. Expand the **Solid Bodies** node in the Model Browser and select the three solid bodies. All selected solid bodies are listed in the dialog box, as shown in Figure 12–30.

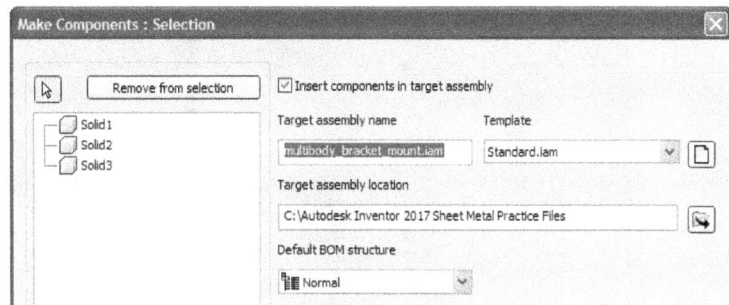

Figure 12–30

3. Ensure that the **Insert components in target assembly** option is selected so that an assembly is automatically created for this model.

4. Specify the remaining options on the right side of the Make Components: Selection dialog box.

- Assign the **Standard (in).iam** standard English assembly template.

- Ensure that the *Target assembly* location is **C:\Autodesk Inventor 2017 Sheet Metal Practice Files**.

- Accept the default assembly name and BOM structure.

5. Click **Next**. The Make Components: Bodies dialog box opens.

6. Using the Make Components: Bodies dialog box, you can make changes to individual components that are being created as part of the assembly.

- Select each cell in the *Component Name* column to rename the new components that will be created. Use the names shown in Figure 12–31.

- Select a cell in the *Template* column and select

  [🗋] at the top of the column. In the Open Template dialog box, select the *English* folder and select **Sheet Metal (in).ipt** as the default template to use. Assign this template to the other two models, as shown in Figure 12–31.

- Ensure that the **Link sheet metal styles** option is selected to ensure that the thickness is properly communicated to the new models. If this option is not selected, the sheet metal thicknesses might not match between the files and would prevent proper unfolding.

The solid body name in the source model is used as the default name for the component. As an alternative, you can also rename the solid bodies in the part file prior to making components.

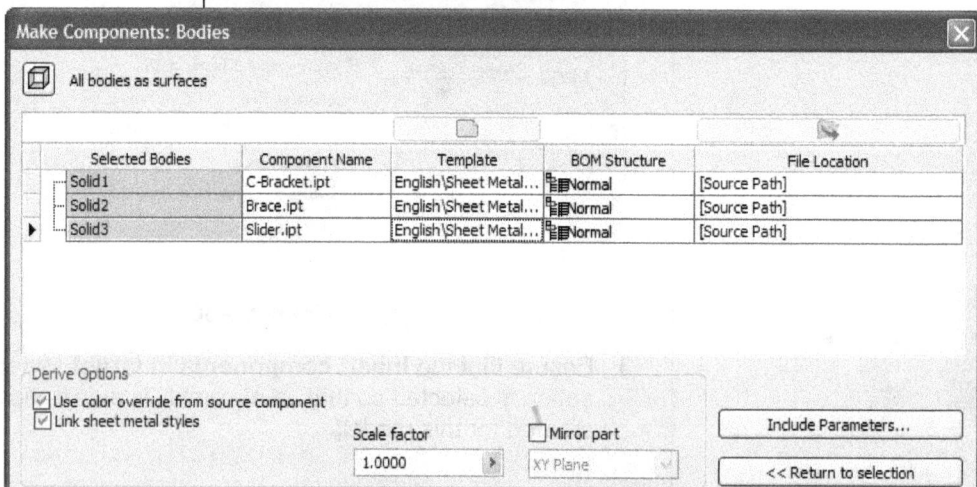

Figure 12–31

7. Click **OK** to complete the operation. A new assembly model is created, as shown in Figure 12–32.

Model ▾   ⑦

▽ ⁴ₚ Assembly View ▾ 🏘

🏠 **multibody_bracket_mount.iam**

⬜ Relationships

▷ 🖫 Representations

▷ ⬜ Origin

▷ 🕸 C_Bracket:1

▷ 🕸 Brace:1

▷ 🕸 Slider:1

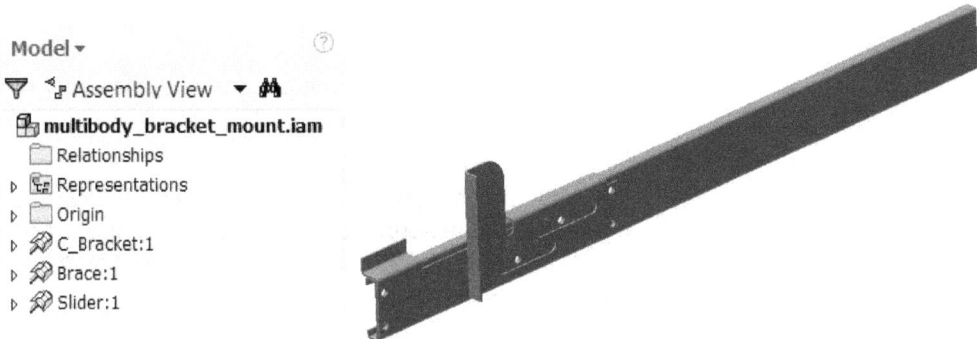

Figure 12–32

8. Save the assembly and the models that were generated from the multi-body part model.

Task 6 - Open the C-Bracket component and create a flat pattern.

1. Right-click on the C-Bracket model in the assembly Model Browser and select **Open**.

2. In the *Sheet Metal* tab>Flat Pattern panel, click 🔲 (Create Flat Pattern). The flat pattern displays.

3. Select the *multibody_bracket_mount.ipt* tab in the graphics window to return to the original multi-body sheet metal model. If you used the provided model to make the components, select the *multibody_bracket_mount_FINAL.ipt* tab instead.

4. Edit the sketch that was used to create Face1. Change the length of the sketch from **24 in** to **18 in**. Finish the sketch.

5. Return to the *C-Bracket.ipt* tab in the graphics window.

6. In the Quick Access toolbar, click (Local Update). Note that the geometry updates in the **C-Bracket.ipt** part to reflect the change in length.

Hint: Associativity

The newly created sheet metal parts and assembly remain associative to the multi-body part unless you explicitly break the link to the parent model.

To break the link, you must open each created component, right-click on the source part name that has been imported, and select **Break Link With Base Component**, as shown in Figure 12–33.

The link can be suppressed (instead of broken) by selecting **Suppress Link With Base Component**.

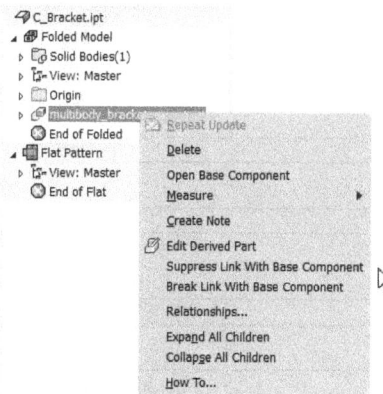

Figure 12–33

Task 7 - Change the model thickness.

1. Select the *multibody_bracket_mount.ipt* tab in the graphics window to return to the original multi-body sheet metal model. If you used the provided model to make the components, select the *multibody_bracket_mount_FINAL.ipt* tab instead.

2. In the *Sheet Metal* tab>Setup panel, click (Sheet Metal Defaults).

3. Click (Edit Sheet Metal Rule) for the Sheet Metal Rule.

4. In the Style and Standard Editor, enter **0.125 in** as the new *Thickness* value, as shown in Figure 12–34. Click **Save and Close**.

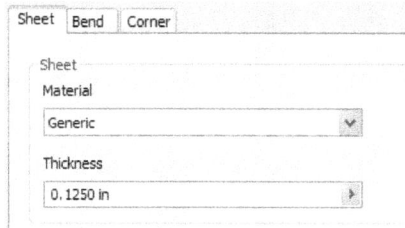

Figure 12–34

5. Click **Cancel** to close the Sheet Metal Defaults dialog box. Note that the thickness of the model is updated and that all of the geometry reflects the change.

6. Select the *multibody_bracket_mount.iam* tab in the graphics window to return to the sheet metal assembly model.

7. In the Quick Access toolbar, click (Local Update). Note that the geometry updates to the new thickness.

   - If the model fails, consider reviewing the bendlines that were created in the model and ensure that the linear sketches are fully constrained coincidentally with the edges of the model.

8. Save the model and close all windows.

Consider conducting an interference analysis in the assembly to ensure that components do not interfere. Changes can then be made in the model and all other components update to reflect the change.

Chapter Review Questions

1. Multi-body part design requires the use of an assembly. Parts are created within the context of the assembly.

    a. True

    b. False

2. Each solid body in a multi-body sheet metal model can have a different *Thickness* value.

    a. True

    b. False

3. How are the second and any subsequent solid bodies created in a model?

    a. Explicitly set a new feature to be created as a new solid body.

    b. Each new feature is automatically added as a new solid body.

    c. Use specific solid body commands in the ribbon prior to creating the feature.

    d. None of the above.

4. Which of the following buttons/options is used in the Cut dialog box to ensure that the cut extrudes through multiple solid bodies?

    a.

    b.

    c.

    d. **Through All** (extent option)

5. Which solid body manipulation option enables you to create a single solid body from two solid bodies?

    a. Union

    b. Combine

    c. Extrude

    d. Split

6. A single Corner Round feature has been added to a model that currently has three solid bodies. An edge from each of the three solid bodies is selected as placement references. Which of the following statements is true regarding the model?

   a. A fourth solid body will be added to the model.

   b. The Corner Round feature will be added to the solid body in which the first reference edge belongs.

   c. The Corner Round feature will be added to each of the three solid bodies.

   d. The Corner Round feature will cause the three solid bodies to combine into one.

7. Match the Move Body operation type in the left column with its symbol in the right column.

   Answer

   a. Rotate about line   _____

   b. Free drag   _____

   c. Move along ray   _____

8. Which of the following can be used as the split tool when splitting a solid body? (Select all that apply.)

   a. Work Plane

   b. Face

   c. Sketch

   d. Edge

9. Which of the following derive styles enables you to create a single solid body when using the **Make Part** command?

   1   2   3

   a. 1, 2, and 3

   b. 1 and 2

   c. 2 and 3

   d. 1 and 3

Command Summary

Button	Command	Location
	Combine	• **Ribbon**: *3D Model* tab>Modify panel
	Derive	• **Ribbon:** *Manage* tab>Insert panel
	Make Component	• **Ribbon:** Sheet Metal tab>Flat Pattern panel
	Make Part	• **Ribbon:** Sheet Metal tab>Flat Pattern panel
	Move Bodies	• **Ribbon:** *3D Model* tab>expanded Modify panel
	Split	• **Ribbon:** *3D Model* tab>Modify panel

Documentation and Annotation

After designing your 3D sheet metal models you need to create drawings that document and annotate them for manufacturing purposes. You can use both the folded model and the flat pattern to create drawings for manufacturing.

Learning Objectives in this Chapter

- Create a new drawing with views and annotations to communicate the manufacturing details of either the folded or flattened state of a sheet metal model.
- Display bend line and punch information in a sheet metal drawing using notes and tables to identify these items on the flat pattern view.
- Edit the bend order that was determined based on modeling to an order that meets manufacturing requirements.
- Create cosmetic centerlines to identify bends that were not modeled as part of the sheet metal geometry.

13.1 Sheet Metal Drawing Terminology

Sheet metal drawings commonly display the 2D flat pattern along with, or instead of, the orthographic and 3D isometric views of the folded model. Several terms are common to these types of flat pattern views:

- **Folded Model:** Sheet metal part with features including bends and cuts.

- **Flat Pattern:** Layout of a sheet metal part before bending. The flat pattern displays locations for cuts, punches, bends, and other features.

- **Bend Line:** Line on the flat pattern that locates the bend.

- **Bend Zone:** Pair of lines on the flat pattern that indicate the extents of the bend radius.

- **Bend Table:** Table that identifies each labeled bend.

- **Hole Table:** Table that identifies the location and diameter of each labeled hole on a drawing.

- **Punch Table:** Table identifying the location of each Punch feature.

- **Ordinate Dimensions:** Dimensions that identify the X- and/or Y-coordinate locations for features on a part. Each ordinate dimension references a specified origin location on the flat pattern.

- **As-Built Dimensions:** Dimensions that identify the sizes and/or locations of features after the folded model is completed. These are likely to be different to the flat pattern dimensions to account for the stretching and compression of areas during bending.

13.2 Creating Sheet Metal Drawings

Drawing views of sheet metal models in their final folded state are called *as-built* drawings. These types of drawings are useful because they describe the sizes and locations of the features when the model is completed. In cases where the model is to be used as part of an assembly this information can be critical for fitting parts together. Due to the nature of materials, sheet metal models deform during bending and some punching operations. Therefore, it is important to be able to create detailed information of the model in its folded state.

As-Built Drawings

Creating views of folded models with *as-built* dimensions is similar to creating drawing views of solid models. Standard orthographic views, isometric views, and custom views can easily be created. Figure 13–1 shows an example of a drawing that includes isometric and 2D views of the folded model. Most of the dimensions have been removed for clarity.

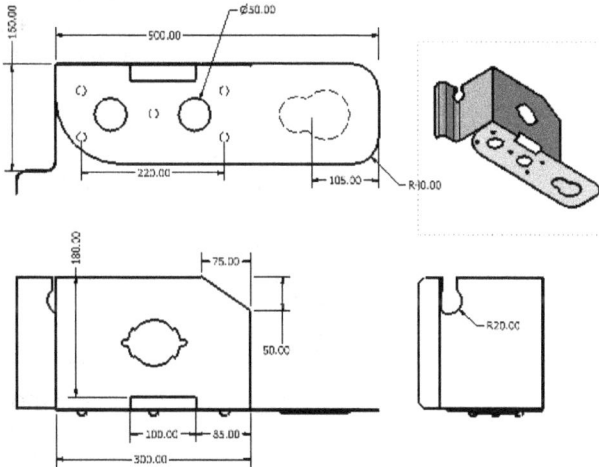

Figure 13–1

Flat Pattern Views

Flat patterns are created from the folded model. The flat pattern in the sheet metal modeling environment is in 3D and can be rotated to display the thickness of the part, or to visualize embossed and engraved features. However, the Flat Pattern views in Drawing mode are 2D representations of the 3D Flat Pattern, as shown in Figure 13–2. Rotating them does not display embossed features.

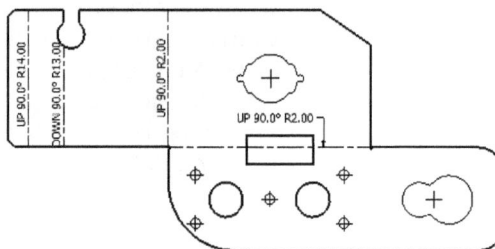

Figure 13–2

General Steps

Use the following general steps to create sheet metal drawings:

1. Create a folded model and its flat pattern.
2. Open or start a new Standard drawing.
3. Create a Folded or Flat Pattern Base view of the part.
4. Add additional views, as required.
5. Add dimensions.
6. Add annotations (Bend Notes, Bend Tables, or Punch Tables).
7. Complete the drawing.

Step 1 - Create a folded model and its flat pattern.

Design the sheet metal model including all required bends, cuts, and other features. Use the **Flat Pattern** tool to create a flat pattern and save the part file. Figure 13–3 shows a folded sheet metal model and its flat pattern.

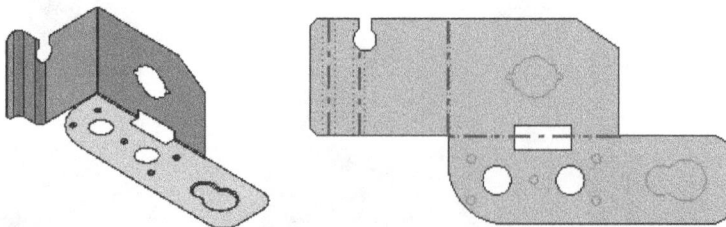

Figure 13–3

Step 2 - Open or start a new Standard drawing.

Open an existing drawing (.DWG or .IDW) file or create a new drawing file. In the New File dialog box, select a template to use for the new drawing file.

Step 3 - Create a Folded or Flat Pattern Base view of the part.

In the *Place Views* tab>Create panel, click [icon] (Base). The Drawing View dialog box opens as shown in Figure 13–4.

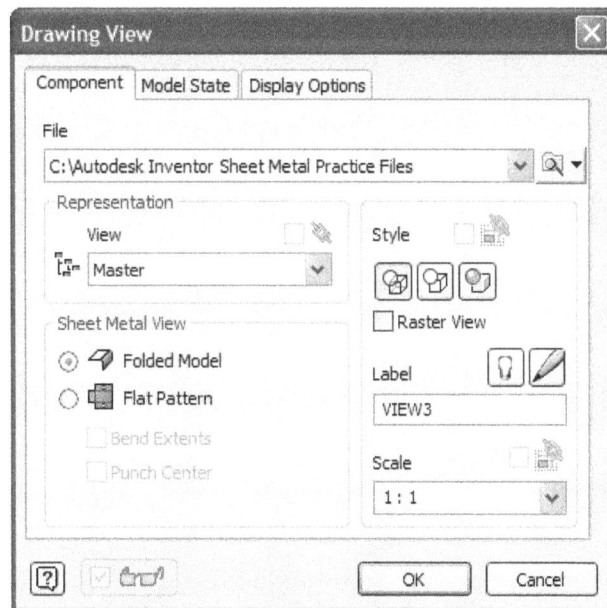

Figure 13–4

Component Tab

In the *File* area in the *Component* tab, the model that was last active is listed in the *File* area. To open an alternate model, click

[icon] (Open an existing file) to browse to the part file for which you want to create a sheet metal view.

Two *Sheet Metal View* options are available: **Folded Model** and **Flat Pattern**, as shown in Figure 13–5.

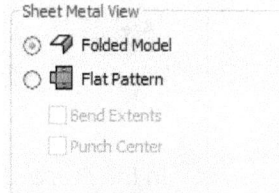

Figure 13–5

- Using the **Folded Model** option, select different orthographic, isometric, or custom view displays using the ViewCube that is displayed adjacent to the previewed view.

- Using the **Flat Pattern** option, select different rotated views using the ViewCube that is displayed adjacent to the previewed view. When **Flat Pattern** is enabled, the following additional options are available to customize the flattened view:

  - The **Bend Extents** option enables you to toggle the display of bend extents lines on or off in the view, as shown in Figure 13–6.

If you need to change the line type style for bend extents or the bend center line, use the Styles and Standards Editor in the Manage tab.

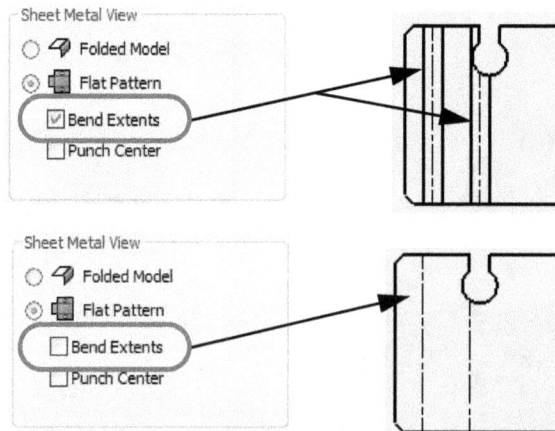

Figure 13–6

*For existing flat pattern views you can double-click on the view to edit it and toggle the **Punch Center** option on or off to control the punch center display.*

- The **Punch Center** option specifies whether the punch centers are displayed in the drawing view. Figure 13–7 shows a **Flat Pattern** with the **Punch Center** option cleared on the left and selected on the right.

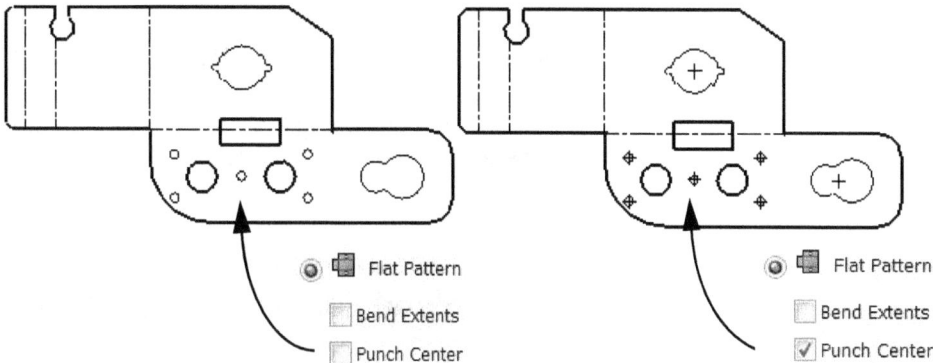

Figure 13–7

Model State Tab

In the *Member* area in the *Model State* tab (shown in Figure 13–8), you can select which member of the Sheet Metal iPart to display in the drawing if an iPart exists for the drawing model. By default, the selected iPart member is displayed based on the orientation set in the iPart table. You can also assign an orientation using the ViewCube when placing the view.

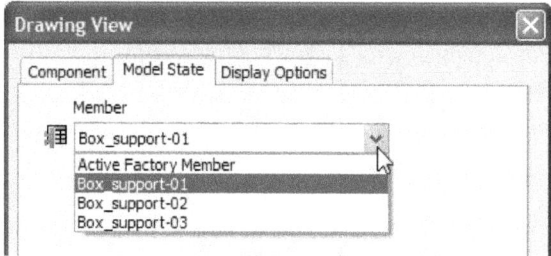

Figure 13–8

Step 4 - Add additional views, as required.

Add additional drawing views to the drawing as required. The drawing views that are available for sheet metal models are the same as those available when creating a part or assembly drawing.

Step 5 - Add dimensions.

Use standard dimensioning tools to retrieve dimensions from the sheet metal model or add dimensions, as required.

Step 6 - Add annotations (Bend Notes, Bend Tables, or Punch Tables).

Use Bend Notes, Bend Tables, and Punch Tables to add annotation to the drawing.

Step 7 - Complete the drawing.

Once you have placed the views and annotations, save the drawing file.

13.3 Bend & Punch Notes

You can add bend or punch notes to drawing views of the flat pattern. Bend notes are a type of annotation used to describe the directions, angles, and radii of bends to be made when fabricating sheet metal parts. Punch notes are also an annotation; they describe the center points of punch features. Both the **Bend** and **Punch Note** options are found in the *Annotate* tab>Feature Notes panel, as shown in Figure 13–9.

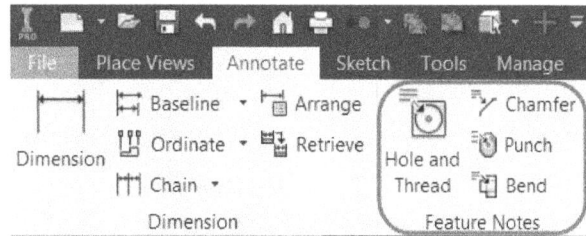

Figure 13–9

To place a bend or punch note, click ⬚ (Bend) or ⬚ (Punch) in the Feature Notes panel. Select a bend line or punch to annotate in the Flat Pattern view, as shown in Figure 13–10.

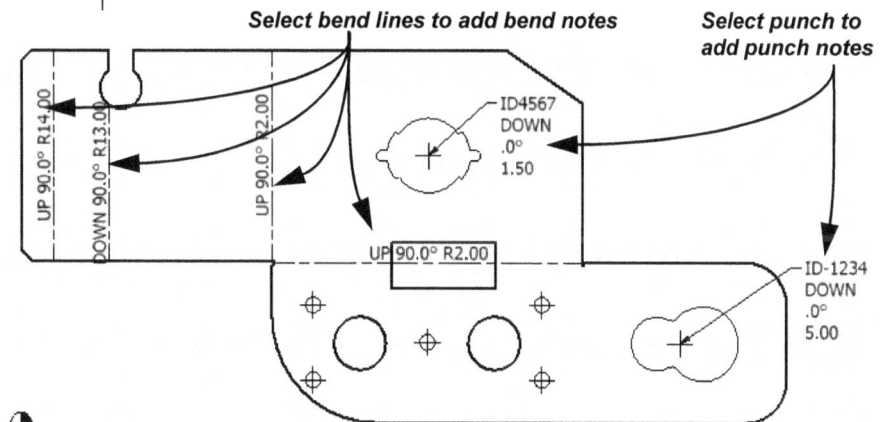

Figure 13–10

Consider using ⊞ to add a **Qty** parameter in the description for a punch note. This is done in the Edit Punch Note dialog box by right-clicking on the Punch Note and selecting **Edit Punch Note**.

By default, each note is applied at the middle of the bend line, but you can reposition them by dragging. To drag a note, hover over its text until a green dot displays on the bend line or extension line. Select the green dot and drag the text to a new position. Several options are shown in Figure 13–11.

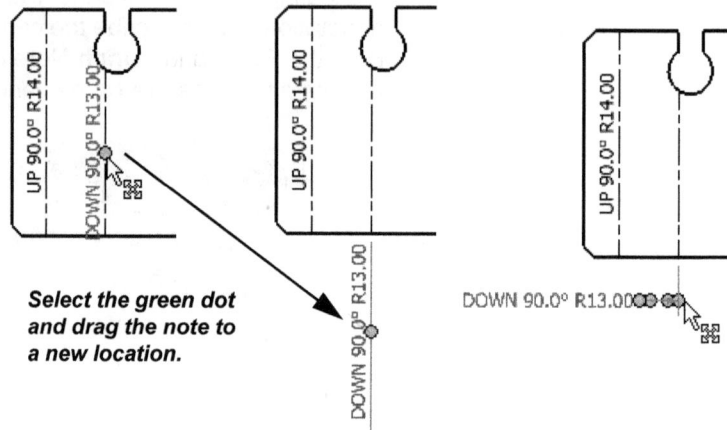

Select the green dot and drag the note to a new location.

UP 90.0° R14.00
DOWN 90.0° R13.00

UP 90.0° R14.00
DOWN 90.0° R13.00

UP 90.0° R14.00
DOWN 90.0° R13.00

Figure 13–11

13.4 Bend Tables

In some cases, adding a complete bend table is preferred over adding individual bend notes to a sheet metal drawing. Similar to bend notes, bend tables indicate the location and direction of bends to be made on the part. They place a letter or number at each bend location and place the rest of the information in a table outside the Flat Pattern view. Bend tables include bend ID, bend direction, bend angle, and bend radius. Any changes to the bends on the model automatically update in the bend table.

In the *Annotate* tab>Table panel, click ⊞ (General) to create bend tables. The Table dialog box opens as shown in Figure 13–12.

Before selecting a Flat Pattern view, the standard table information displays.

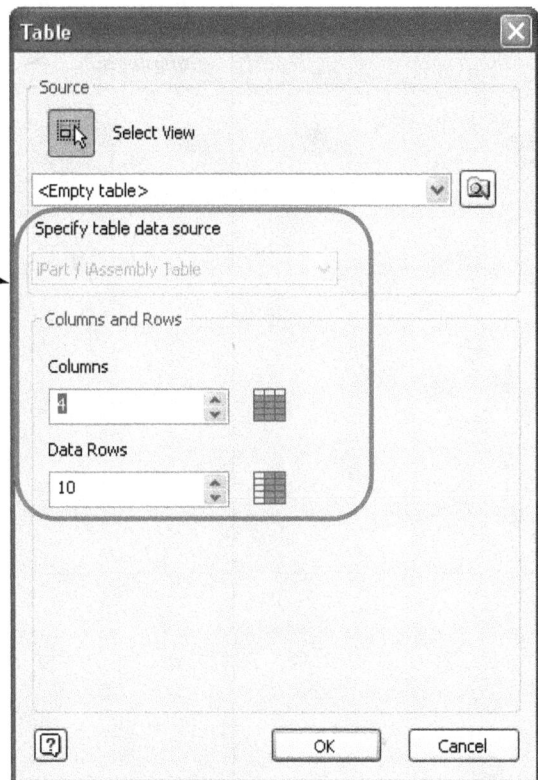

Figure 13–12

Source Options

In the *Source* area in the Table dialog box, activate ⬚ (Select View) if it is not already done and select the view to annotate. After you select a view of the flat pattern, the Table dialog box automatically updates to display as shown in Figure 13–13. You can also use ⬚ (Browse for file) to select a different sheet metal model on which to report.

After selecting a Flat Pattern view, the Bend Table information displays.

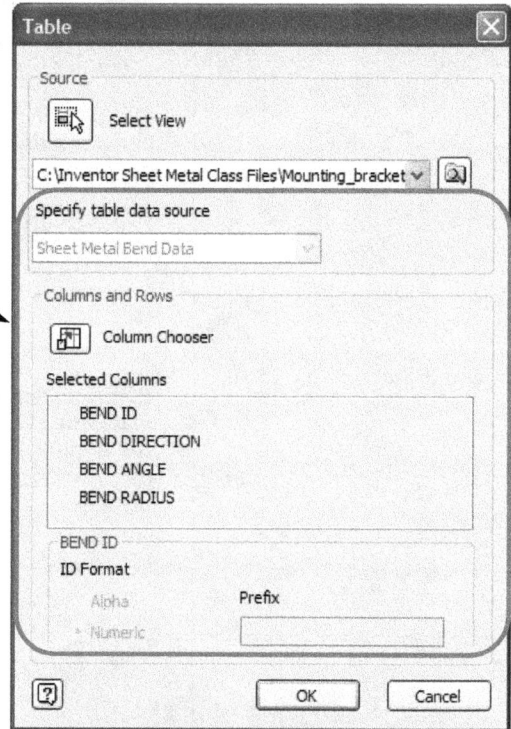

Figure 13–13

Columns and Rows

In the *Columns and Rows* area, click 🖳 (Column Chooser) to open the Table Column Chooser dialog box as shown in Figure 13–14.

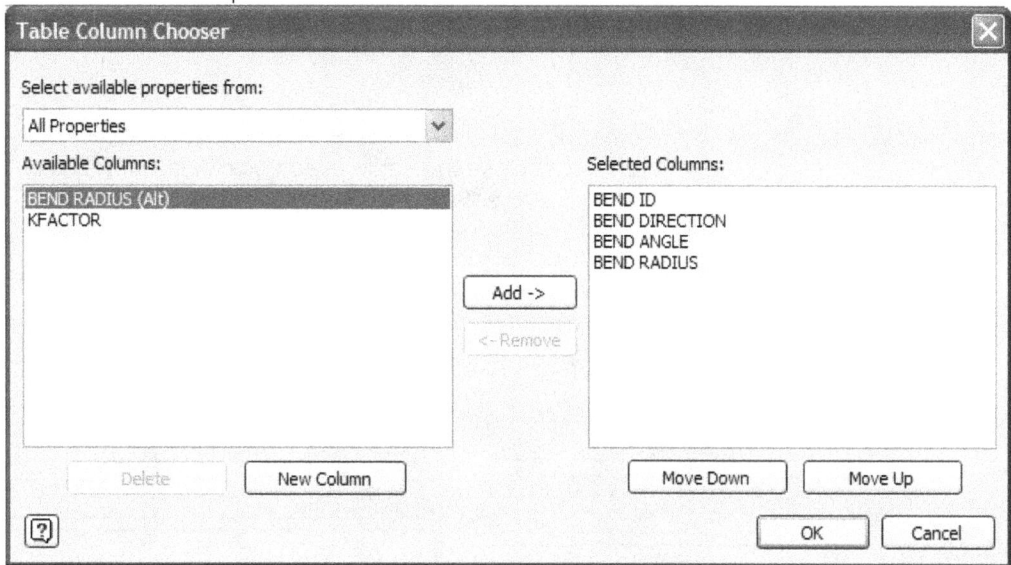

Table Column Chooser

Select available properties from:

All Properties

Available Columns:

BEND RADIUS (Alt)
KFACTOR

Add ->

<- Remove

Selected Columns:

BEND ID
BEND DIRECTION
BEND ANGLE
BEND RADIUS

Delete   New Column

Move Down   Move Up

OK   Cancel

Figure 13–14

The options in the Table Column Chooser dialog box are the same as for solid models. You can add or remove columns from the table, delete columns, create new columns, and rearrange the order of columns in the table. The default columns that display in the table are:

- **BEND ID:** An alpha-numeric label is automatically placed on each bend line when a bend table is created.

- **BEND DIRECTION:** The folding direction, either **Up** or **Down**.

- **BEND ANGLE:** The number of degrees to fold the sheet metal.

- **BEND RADIUS:** The size of the radius for each bend. Typically it is the same for all bends on a sheet metal part.

When you have finished setting up the table columns, click **OK** to close the Table Column Chooser dialog box and return to the Table dialog box.

The *Bend ID* area in the Table dialog box offers two ID Formats: **Alpha** or **Numeric**, as shown in Figure 13–15. You can also enter text in the *Prefix* field.

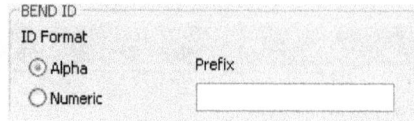

BEND ID

ID Format

⊙ Alpha   Prefix

○ Numeric

Figure 13–15

Click **OK** to close the Table dialog box. Alternatively, you can right-click and select **OK (Enter)** to complete the table.

Select a location on the drawing sheet in which to place the bend table. Figure 13–16 shows a partial view of the flat pattern and its table with numeric bend ID labels on the left, and a table with the prefix "Bend" added on the right.

Table			
BEND ID	BEND DIRECTION	BEND ANGLE	BEND RADIUS
1	UP	90	2
2	UP	90	2
3	DOWN	90	13
4	UP	90	14

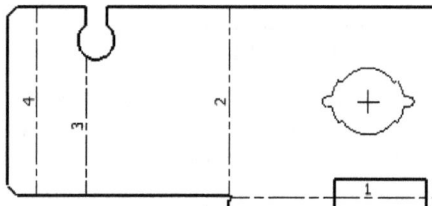

Table			
BEND ID	BEND DIRECTION	BEND ANGLE	BEND RADIUS
Bend-1	UP	90	2
Bend-2	UP	90	2
Bend-3	DOWN	90	13
Bend-4	UP	90	14

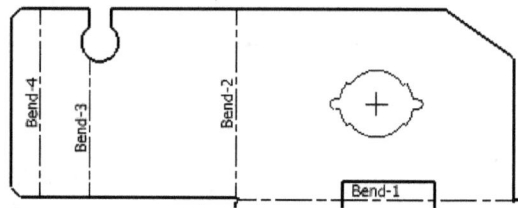

Figure 13–16

13.5 Punch Tables

Punch tables are added to a sheet metal drawing to locate the center points of Punch features and detail them in a table as opposed to using punch notes on each individual punch feature in a view. To create them, use the **Hole Table** tool with the style set to **Punch Table**.

There are three Hole Table options: **Hole Selection**, **Hole View**, and **Hole Features**, as shown in the flyout in Figure 13–17.

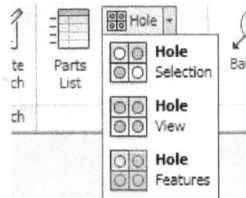

Figure 13–17

The **Hole Table** tool is the same as for solid models. The difference between hole tables and punch tables is established by changing the style in the *Annotate* tab>Format panel. Hole tables display the X- and Y-dimensions for the centers of Holes or circular Cut features. They also include a description of the diameter, depth, and other hole options, such as counterbores in solid models. Punches that are created with the **Punch** tool, are not included in standard hole tables.

Hole tables are sometimes added to sheet metal flat pattern drawings similar to drawings of solid models. Figure 13–18 shows a sample of the **Hole Selection** option for two selected Hole features. The origin indicator is located at the lower left of the flat pattern extents. Only the holes actually selected are labeled and included in the hole table.

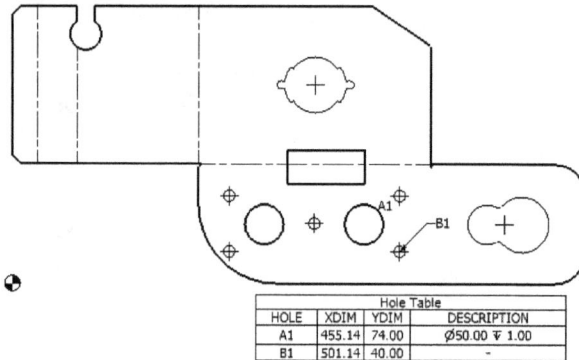

Hole Table			
HOLE	XDIM	YDIM	DESCRIPTION
A1	455.14	74.00	Ø50.00 ▼ 1.00
B1	501.14	40.00	-

Figure 13–18

Figure 13–19 shows a hole table for the flat pattern using the **Hole Features** option. In this example, all holes of the same selected feature are labeled on the flat pattern and included in the hole table.

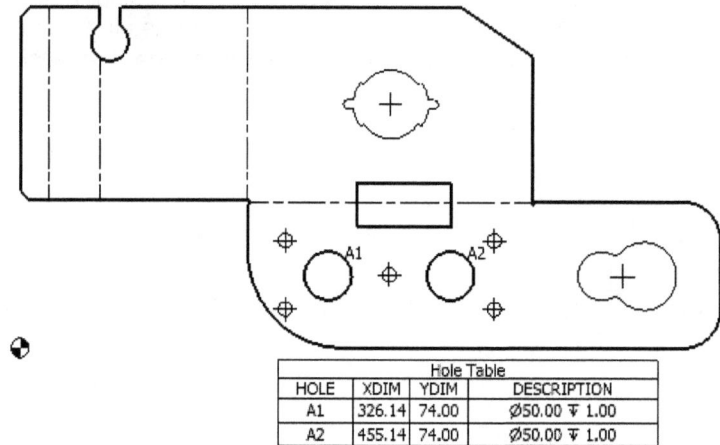

Hole Table			
HOLE	XDIM	YDIM	DESCRIPTION
A1	326.14	74.00	Ø50.00 ▼ 1.00
A2	455.14	74.00	Ø50.00 ▼ 1.00

Figure 13–19

To create a punch table for the Flat Pattern view, select **Hole View**. Next, select the view of the flat pattern. A preview of the hole table is attached to the cursor. Do not select a point on the drawing to place it yet. Instead, select the Hole Style drop-down list in the *Annotate* tab>Format panel and change the style to **Punch-Table**, as shown in Figure 13–20.

Change the style to Punch-Table —

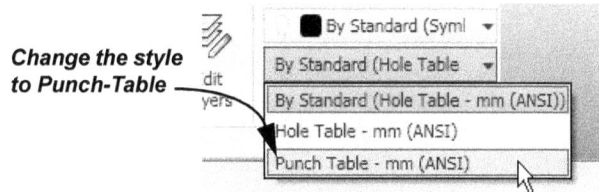

By Standard (Syml ▾

By Standard (Hole Table ▾

By Standard (Hole Table - mm (ANSI))

Hole Table - mm (ANSI)

Punch Table - mm (ANSI)

Figure 13–20

Select a location in the drawing to place the punch table, as shown in Figure 13–21. In this example all Punch features and Holes have been labeled as punches because the **Hole View** option was used. If you only want to annotate the Punch features and not the circular holes, use the **Hole Selection** tool with the style set to **Punch Table** and only select the Punches you need.

Origin indicator at lower-left extents of Flat Pattern —

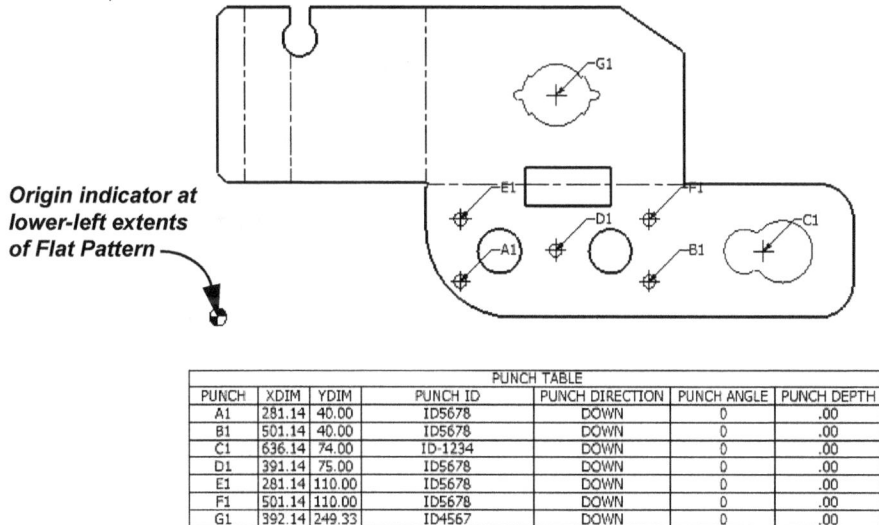

PUNCH TABLE						
PUNCH	XDIM	YDIM	PUNCH ID	PUNCH DIRECTION	PUNCH ANGLE	PUNCH DEPTH
A1	281.14	40.00	ID5678	DOWN	0	.00
B1	501.14	40.00	ID5678	DOWN	0	.00
C1	636.14	74.00	ID-1234	DOWN	0	.00
D1	391.14	75.00	ID5678	DOWN	0	.00
E1	281.14	110.00	ID5678	DOWN	0	.00
F1	501.14	110.00	ID5678	DOWN	0	.00
G1	392.14	249.33	ID4567	DOWN	0	.00

Figure 13–21

Setting the hole table style to **Punch Table** enables you to collect information about Punches on the part including: punch label, XDIM, YDIM, punch ID, punch direction, punch angle, and punch depth.

You can edit the punch table style as you would edit a hole table for solid models by double-clicking on it and changing the options in the Edit Hole Table dialog box, as shown in Figure 13–22.

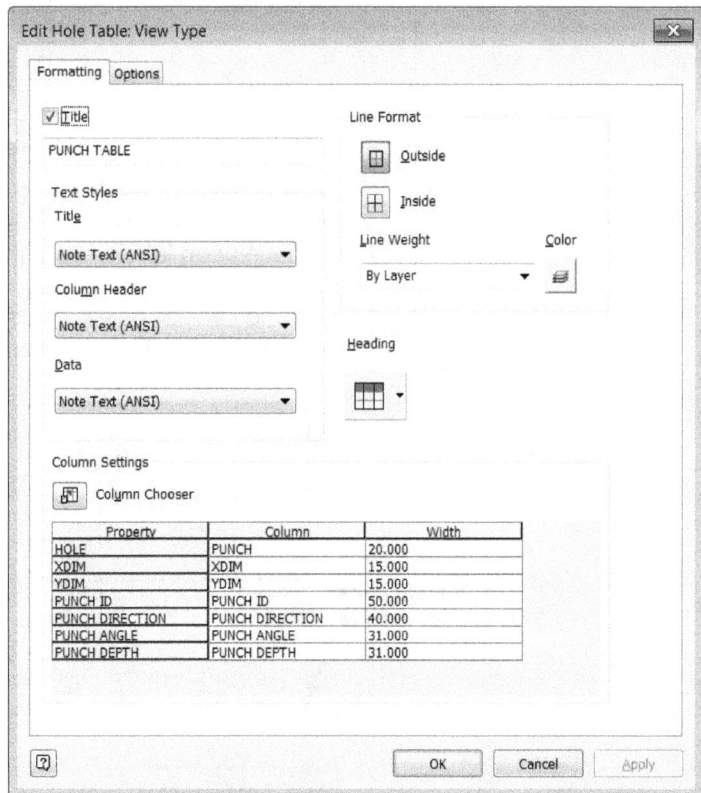

Edit Hole Table: View Type

Formatting   Options

☑ Title

PUNCH TABLE

Text Styles
Title

Note Text (ANSI)

Column Header

Note Text (ANSI)

Data

Note Text (ANSI)

Line Format

Outside

Inside

Line Weight   Color

By Layer

Heading

Column Settings

Column Chooser

Property	Column	Width
HOLE	PUNCH	20.000
XDIM	XDIM	15.000
YDIM	YDIM	15.000
PUNCH ID	PUNCH ID	50.000
PUNCH DIRECTION	PUNCH DIRECTION	40.000
PUNCH ANGLE	PUNCH ANGLE	31.000
PUNCH DEPTH	PUNCH DEPTH	31.000

OK   Cancel   Apply

Figure 13–22

13.6 Bend Order

The order in which bends are added to a model when it is created is not necessarily the same order in which the bends are added during manufacturing. Using the **Bend Order Annotation** option when in the Flat Pattern state, you can reassign the bend order to better communicate how the model is to be manufactured. You can change the bend order using any of the following:

- Directed Reorder

- Sequential Reorder

- Individual Override

Once the Flat Pattern environment is active, click (Bend Order Annotation) in the *Flat Pattern* tab>Manage panel. The current bend order is indicated by yellow numbered circles, as shown in Figure 13–23.

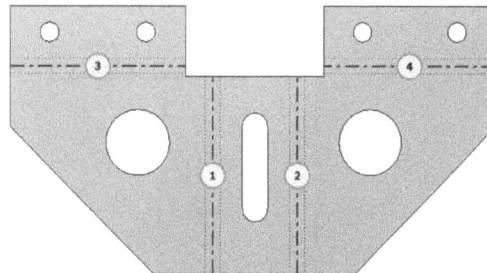

Once a bend's order is modified, it is displayed in green to indicate that the original bend order was overwritten.

Figure 13–23

Directed Reorder

For directed reorder, right-click in the graphics window and select **Directed Reorder**. Select the bend order glyph that should represent the first bend in the model. Select a second glyph to define the last bend in the model. The system automatically reorders and bends the area between the selected geometry.

Sequential Reorder

For sequential reorder, right-click in the graphics window and select **Sequential Reorder**. Select the bend order glyph that should represent the first bend in the model. Continue selecting additional glyphs to define the second and any subsequent bends. The system automatically reorders bends (if required) so that there are no duplicate bends.

Individual Override

To individually edit the bend order, select any of the current bend numbers to open the Bend Order Edit dialog box. Enter a new bend order number to change the current value. Once changed, the remaining bends are automatically reordered so that no two bends have the same bend order number. Figure 13–24 shows the Bend Order Edit dialog box for editing the bend order.

Any redefined bend orders are reflected in drawing bend tables.

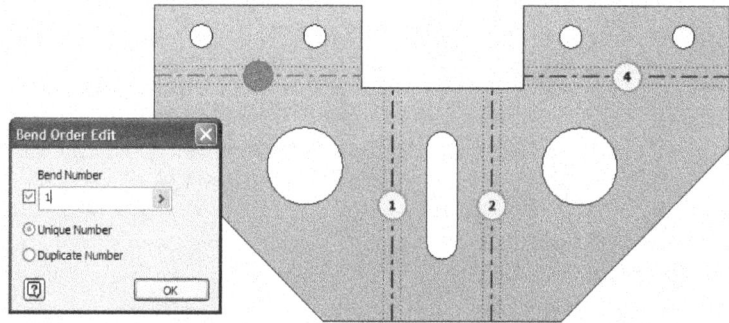

Figure 13–24

13.7 Cosmetic Centerlines

You can create a cosmetic centerline in a flat pattern to help identify where a bend is required, but not necessarily modeled with sheet metal geometry. For example, a cosmetic centerline is a useful feature to place in a model to represent stiffening creases that are produced during manufacturing. This feature enables you to convert a sketched entity to a cosmetic centerline. You must specify a bend direction and provide a value. Once created, it can be displayed in a drawing.
Figure 13–25 shows cosmetic centerlines created on a model.

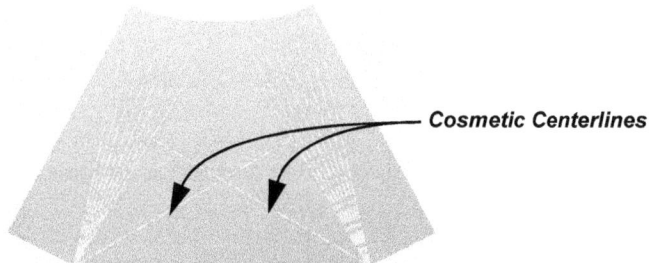

Cosmetic Centerlines

Figure 13–25

To create a cosmetic centerline, an unconsumed sketch must exist in the model that can be converted. Once a sketch exists that represents the required bend, complete the steps below.

How To: Create a Cosmetic Centerline

1. In the *Flat Pattern* tab>Create panel, click ▨ (Cosmetic Centerline). The Cosmetic Centerline dialog box opens as shown in Figure 13–26.

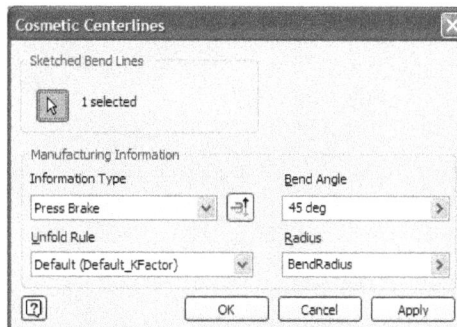

Figure 13–26

2. Select the unconsumed sketch to identify as a cosmetic centerline. Yellow bend zone lines display on the model to identify the bend.

   You can incorporate further manufacturing information on the bend by completing the *Manufacturing Information* area.

3. Define the type of bend that is to be identified for manufacturing. The types include **Press Brake** (default) and **Crease**. Once either of these are selected, the dialog box updates to provide the required entries. In addition to these options, you can select **None** to graphically identify the cosmetic centerline, but not include any additional manufacturing information.

4. Click [icon] in the *Manufacturing Information* area to toggle the bend up or down. The selected sketch displays the words **Up** or **Down** depending on its status.

5. For **Press Brake**, define the *Unfold Rule* value. The default value uses the **Default** (**Default_KFactor**) parameter value that is assigned by the Sheet Metal Rule. You can enter a different rule if required.

6. Enter a *Bend Angle* value.

7. Define the *Radius* value. The default value uses the **BendRadius** parameter value that is assigned by the Sheet Metal Rule. You can enter a different bend radius if required.

8. Once you have fully defined the cosmetic centerline, click **OK** to complete the feature. Alternatively, you can right-click and select **OK (Enter)** to complete the feature.

Practice 13a | Sheet Metal Documentation I

Practice Objectives

- Add folded and flat pattern views of a sheet metal model to a new drawing file to communicate design details.
- Identify all punches in a sheet metal model with a table and item callouts on the flat pattern view.
- Identify all bend lines in a sheet metal model with a table and item callouts on the flat pattern view.
- Display information on the direction, angle, and radius for bend lines in a flat pattern drawing view using Bend Line notes.

In this practice, you will create the sheet metal drawing shown in Figure 13–27. First, you will create views of the folded model, create a new sheet, and add a view of the flat pattern. You will then create a hole table, convert it to a punch table and add a bend table and bend notes.

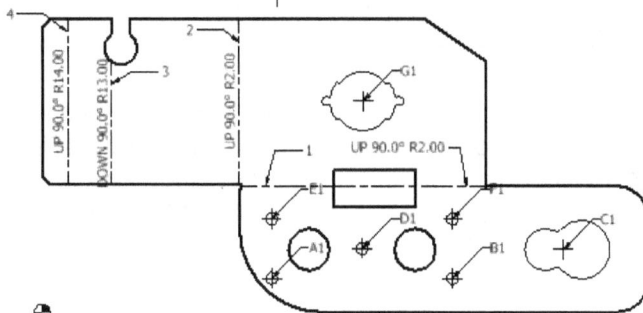

Hole Table				
HOLE	PUNCH ID	XDIM	YDIM	PUNCH DEPTH
A1	ID-5678	281.14	40.00	8.00
B1	ID-5678	501.14	40.00	8.00
C1	ID-1234	636.14	74.00	5.00
D1	ID-5678	391.14	75.00	8.00
E1	ID-5678	281.14	110.00	8.00
F1	ID-5678	501.14	110.00	8.00
G1	ID4567	392.14	249.33	1.50

Table			
BEND ID	BEND DIRECTION	BEND ANGLE	BEND RADIUS
1	UP	90	2
2	UP	90	2
3	DOWN	90	13
4	UP	90	14

Figure 13–27

Task 1 - Create a new drawing.

1. Open **Mounting_Bracket_10.ipt**. The part contains several bends, punch features, cuts, and holes as shown in Figure 13–28.

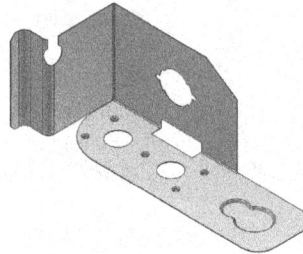

Figure 13–28

2. Create a new drawing using the **ANSI (mm).dwg** template in the *Metric* tab.

Task 2 - Create a view of the flat pattern.

1. In the *Place Views* tab>Create panel, click ▣ (Base) to create the view of the model, as shown in Figure 13–29. Ensure that **Folded Model** is selected in the *Sheet Metal View* area. Using a *Scale* of **1/2**, select **Bottom** on the ViewCube and use the rotation arrows to place the view as shown.

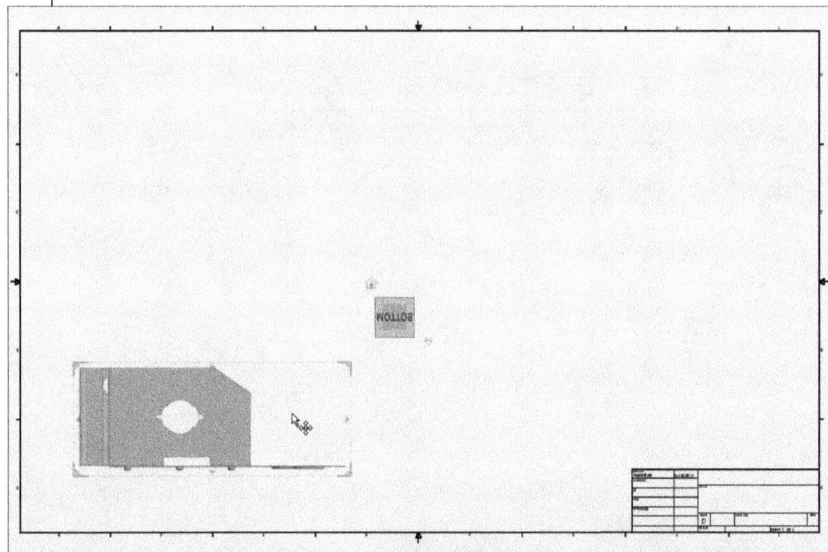

Figure 13–29

Alternatively, you can place Projected views by clicking

📑 *(Projected) (Pace Views tab>Create panel).*

2. Drag additional views from the Base view and click to place them, as shown in Figure 13–30. When all three additional views have been placed, right-click and select **OK (Enter)**.

3. Edit the isometric view and click 🖼 (Shaded).

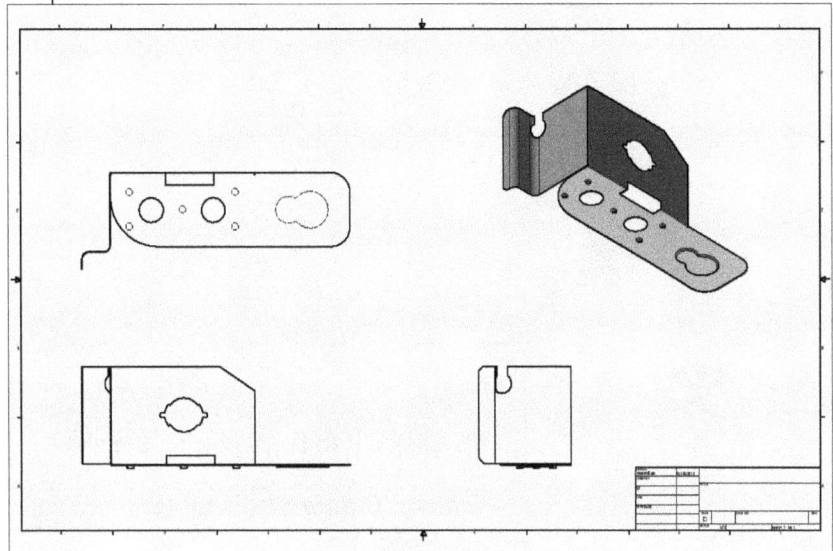

Figure 13–30

4. Save the file as **Mounting_bracket_10.dwg**.

Task 3 - Create a new sheet with a flat pattern view.

1. In the *Place Views* tab>Sheets panel, click 📄 (New Sheet).

2. In the *Place Views* tab>Create panel, click 🖼 (Base) to open the Drawing View dialog box.

3. **Mounting_Bracket_10.ipt** is listed in the File drop-down list because it is currently open. If it is not listed, browse to the *practice* files folder and select it.

4. Select **Flat Pattern** and **Punch Center** in the *Sheet Metal View* area. Use a scale of **1/4**.

5. Place the view as shown in Figure 13–31.

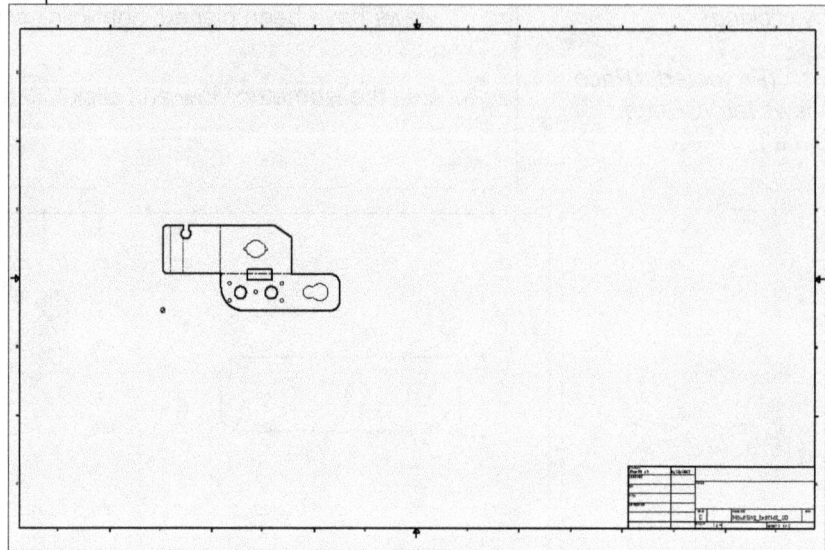

Figure 13–31

6. Click **OK** to finish placing the view.

Task 4 - Create a hole table.

1. In the *Annotate* tab>Table panel, expand the **Hole** options and click (Hole View).

2. Select the view of the flat pattern.

3. Select the intersection of the two edges as shown in Figure 13–32 as the origin. To select the intersection, hover over the endpoint of each line and move the cursor to the point where they would intersect. Dashed lines display indicating the extension of each line.

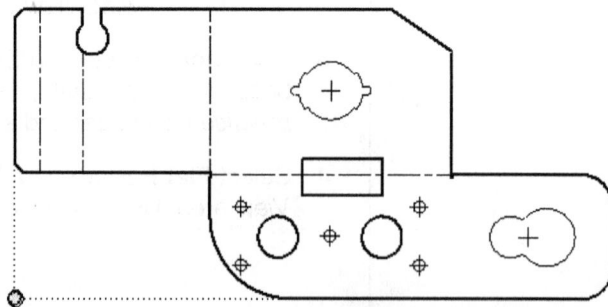

Figure 13–32

4. Place the hole table to the right of the view. Initially, the hole table only locates Hole features in the view, as shown in Figure 13–33. In the next steps, you will remove the holes from the table and add the recovered punch centers to convert the table into a punch table.

HOLE TABLE			
HOLE	XDIM	YDIM	DESCRIPTION
A1	326.14	74.00	Ø50.00 ▼ 1.00
A2	455.14	74.00	Ø50.00 ▼ 1.00

Figure 13–33

Task 5 - Convert the hole table into a punch table.

1. Select the Hole Table and select **Punch Table - mm (ANSI)** in the Style drop-down list as shown in Figure 13–34. This table style is configured in the style definition to contain recovered punch centers and properties relevant to Punch features.

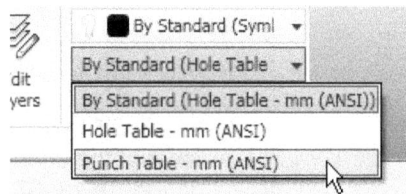

Figure 13–34

2. Right-click on **Punch Table** and select **Edit Hole Table**. The Edit Hole Table: View Type dialog box opens. Only **Recovered Punch Centers** is selected, as shown in Figure 13–35.

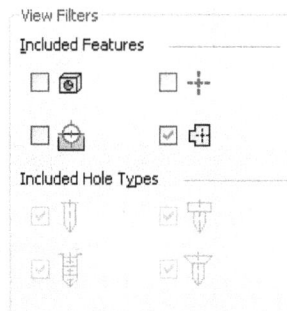

Figure 13–35

3. Select the *Formatting* tab.

4. Click ⊞ (Column Chooser) to open the Hole Table Column Chooser dialog box.

5. In the Selected Properties list, select **PUNCH DIRECTION** and click **Remove** to remove the property from the table.

6. Repeat to remove **PUNCH ANGLE** from the list.

7. Click **Move Up** and **Move Down** to reorder the properties as shown in Figure 13–36.

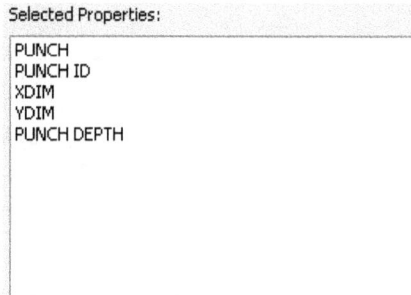

Selected Properties:

PUNCH
PUNCH ID
XDIM
YDIM
PUNCH DEPTH

Figure 13–36

8. Click **OK** to accept the property list.

9. Click **OK** in the Edit Hole Table: View Type dialog box to accept the changes to the table. The table displays as shown in Figure 13–37.

PUNCH TABLE				
PUNCH	PUNCH ID	XDIM	YDIM	PUNCH DEPTH
A1	ID-5678	281.14	40.00	8.00
B1	ID-5678	501.14	40.00	8.00
C1	ID-1234	636.14	74.00	5.00
D1	ID-5678	391.14	75.00	8.00
E1	ID-5678	281.14	110.00	8.00
F1	ID-5678	501.14	110.00	8.00
G1	ID4567	392.14	249.33	1.50

Figure 13–37

Task 6 - Create a bend table.

1. In the *Annotate* tab>Table panel, click ⊞ (General) to open the Table dialog box.

2. Select the view of the flat pattern. The Table dialog box updates as shown in Figure 13–38. This is because the view is of a flat pattern of a sheet metal part.

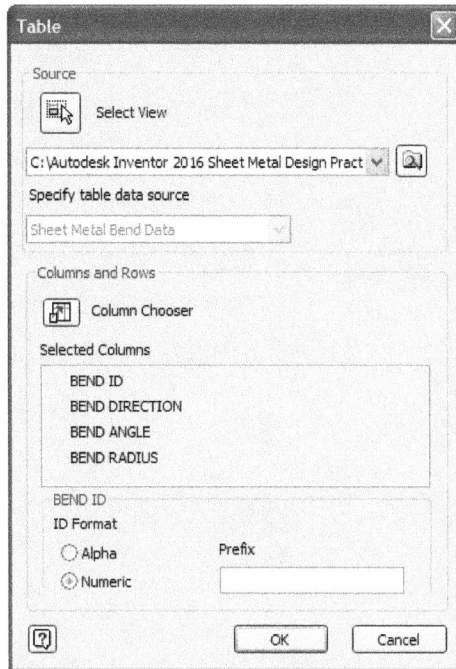

Figure 13–38

3. Click **OK** and place the table below the view as shown in Figure 13–39.

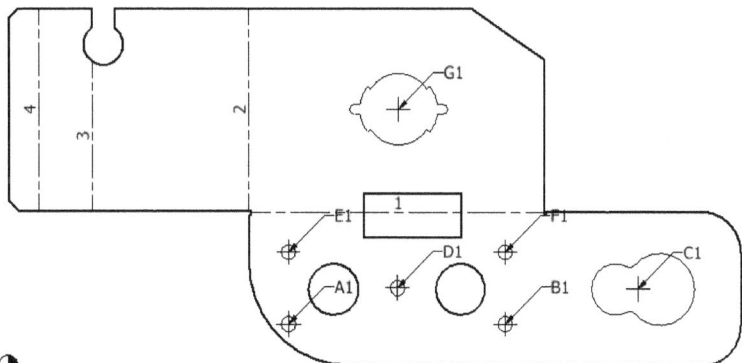

Table			
BEND ID	BEND DIRECTION	BEND ANGLE	BEND RADIUS
1	UP	90	2
2	UP	90	2
3	DOWN	90	13
4	UP	90	14

Figure 13–39

Task 7 - Add bend annotations.

1. In the *Annotate* tab>Feature Notes panel, click (Bend).

2. Window around all of the bend lines in the view. Bend notes are placed on each selected bend line.

Typically, you would display bend notes or a bend table, but not both.

3. Right-click and select **OK**.

4. Reposition the notes as required.

5. Save and close all of the files.

Practice 13b | Sheet Metal Documentation II

Practice Objectives

- Add a flat pattern view of a sheet metal model to a drawing file to communicate design details.
- Customize the display of the drawing to include bend extent lines on the flat pattern view.
- Identify all bend lines in a sheet metal model with a table and item callouts on the flat pattern view.
- Identify all punches in a sheet metal model with a table and item callouts on the flat pattern view.
- Customize the display of the punch table to combine identical punches as a single line item.
- Edit the punch representation in a sheet metal part so that the change is reflected in the flat pattern drawing view.
- Display punch information in a flat pattern drawing view using Punch notes.

In this practice, you will create the sheet metal drawing shown in Figure 13–40. You will create a view of the flat pattern and then edit the view to display the bend extent lines. Next, you will add a bend table and a punch table. Finally, you will modify the Sheet Metal Style to change the flat pattern punch representation. To complete the practice you will add punch notes to the drawing.

TABLE			
BEND ID	BEND DIRECTION	BEND ANGLE	BEND RADIUS
1	UP	60	1.5
2	UP	60	1.5
3	UP	60	1.5
4	UP	90	2.5
5	UP	90	2.5
6	UP	90	2.5
7	UP	90	2.5
8	UP	60	1.5

HOLE TABLE				
HOLE	PUNCH ID	XDIM	YDIM	PUNCH DEPTH
A	ID-5678	52.76	52.76	8.00
B	ID-7890	132.76	82.76	2.00

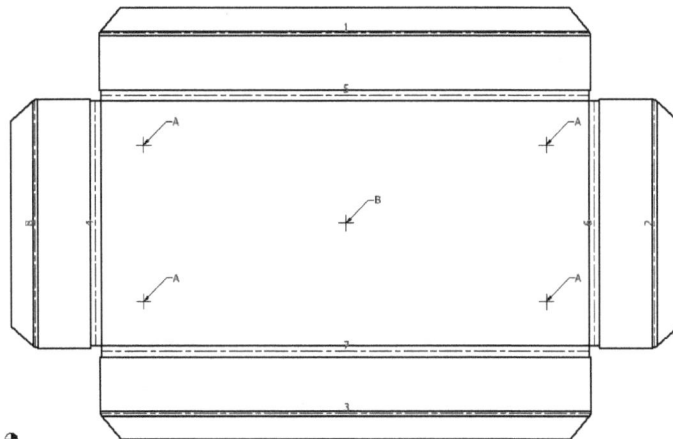

Figure 13–40

Task 1 - Create a drawing with a flat pattern view.

1. Open **Box_support.ipt**. It contains several bends, flanges, and punch features as shown in Figure 13–41.

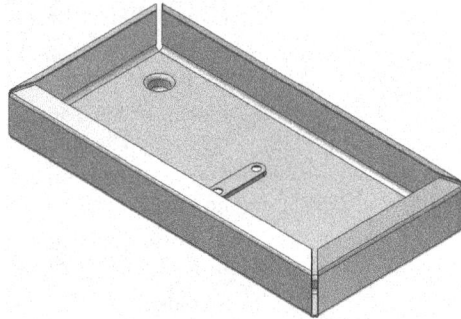

Figure 13–41

2. Create a new drawing using the **ANSI (mm).dwg** template in the *Metric* tab.

3. In the *Place Views* tab>Create panel, click (Base) to create a view of the back of the flat pattern, as shown in Figure 13–42. Select **Punch Center** and use a scale of **1:1**. Place the view near the center of the drawing sheet.

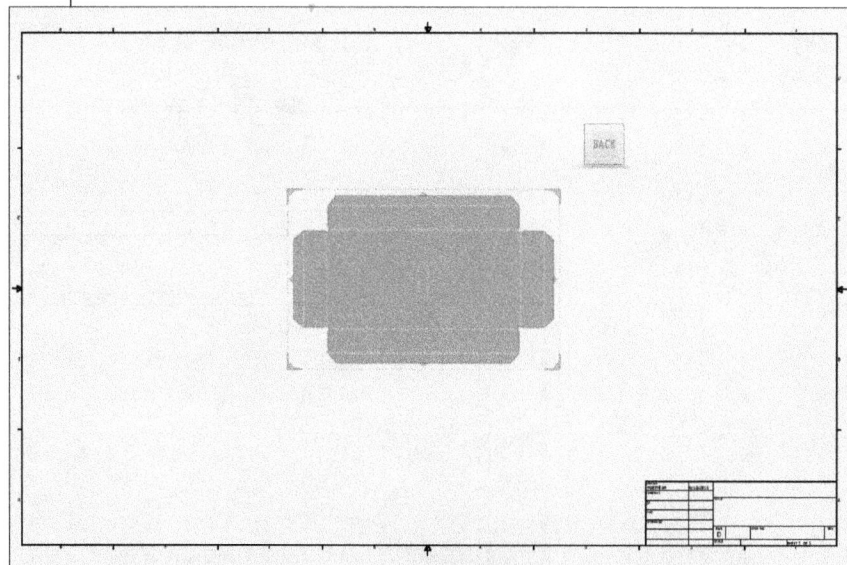

Figure 13–42

4. Save the file as **Box_support.dwg**.

5. In the Model Browser, right-click on **VIEW1** and select **Edit View**.

6. In the *Component* tab, select **Bend Extents** in the *Sheet Metal View* area. Ensure that **Punch Center** remains selected.

7. Click **OK**. The bend extent lines are displayed in the drawing view as shown in Figure 13–43.

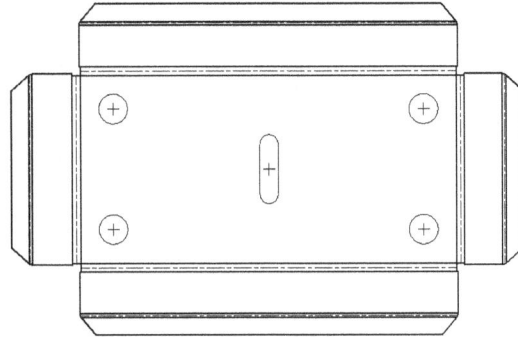

Figure 13–43

Task 2 - Create a bend table.

1. In the *Annotate* tab>Table panel, click ▦ (General Table).

2. Create a bend table with numeric bend IDs of the view. Place the table above the view, as shown in Figure 13–44.

		TABLE		
BEND ID	BEND DIRECTION	BEND ANGLE	BEND RADIUS
1	UP	60	1.5
2	UP	60	1.5
3	UP	60	1.5
4	UP	90	2.5
5	UP	90	2.5
6	UP	90	2.5
7	UP	90	2.5
8	UP	60	1.5

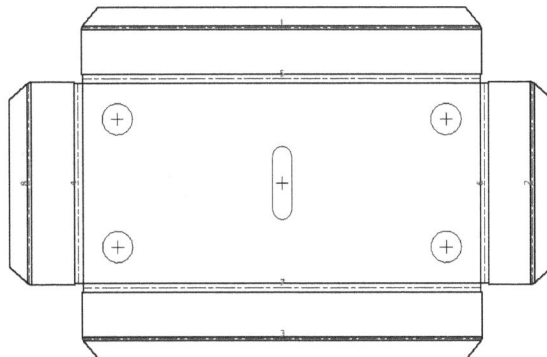

Figure 13–44

Task 3 - Create a hole table.

1. In the *Annotate* tab>Table panel, expand the **Hole** options. Click ⊞ (Hole View).

2. Select the view and place the Origin as shown in Figure 13–45.

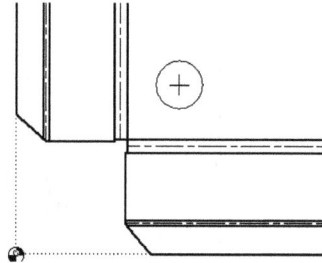

Figure 13–45

3. Place the table to the right of the bend table. The hole table does not contain data because the sheet metal part does not contain holes. You will add the punches to the table in Task 4.

Task 4 - Add punch data to the table.

1. Edit the hole table.

2. In the *Included Features* area in the *Options* tab, remove **Hole Features** and **Circular Cuts** from the table and add **Recovered Punch Centers**, as shown in Figure 13–46.

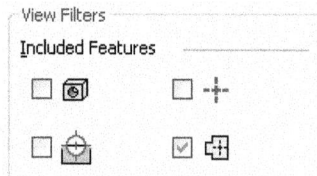

Figure 13–46

3. In the *Formatting* tab, use ⊞ (Column Chooser) to remove the **DESCRIPTION** property and add the **PUNCH ID** and **PUNCH DEPTH** properties.

4. Reorder the **PUNCH ID** so that it is listed after the **HOLE** property. The Selected Properties list displays as shown in Figure 13–47.

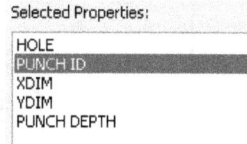

Selected Properties:

HOLE
PUNCH ID
XDIM
YDIM
PUNCH DEPTH

Figure 13–47

5. Close the Column Chooser dialog box and Edit Hole Table dialog box. The hole table displays as shown in Figure 13–48.

TABLE			
BEND ID	BEND DIRECTION	BEND ANGLE	BEND RADIUS
1	UP	60	1.5
2	UP	60	1.5
3	UP	60	1.5
4	UP	90	2.5
5	UP	90	2.5
6	UP	90	2.5
7	UP	90	2.5
8	UP	60	1.5

HOLE TABLE				
HOLE	PUNCH ID	XDIM	YDIM	PUNCH DEPTH
A1	ID-5678	52.76	52.76	8.00
B1	ID-5678	212.76	52.76	8.00
C1	ID-7890	132.76	82.76	2.00
D1	ID-5678	52.76	112.76	8.00
E1	ID-5678	212.76	112.76	8.00

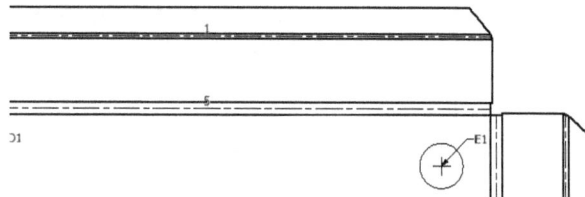

Figure 13–48

Task 5 - Rollup the punch table.

1. Right-click on the **Punch Table** and select **Edit Hole Table**.

2. Select **Rollup** in the *Row Merge Options* area, as shown in Figure 13–49.

Row Merge Options

- ○ None
  - ☑ Reformat Table on Custom Hole Match
  - ☐ Numbering
- ◉ Rollup
  - ☐ Delete Tags on Rollup
  - ☐ Secondary Tag Modifier on Rollup
- ○ Combine Notes
  - ☑ Reformat Table on Custom Hole Match
  - ☐ Numbering

Figure 13–49

3. Click **OK** to accept the changes.

4. Right-click on one of the labels for the punches in the corners and select **Match Custom Hole**, as shown in Figure 13–50.

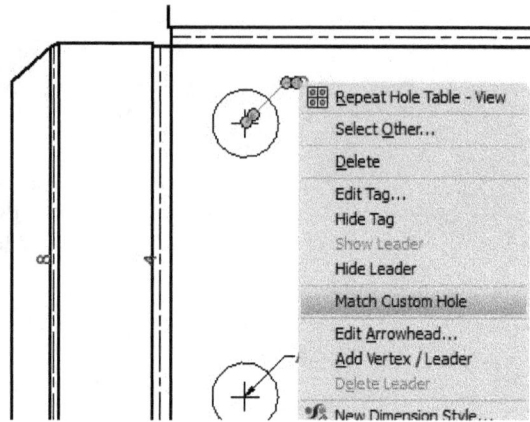

Figure 13–50

5. Select the three other labels for the punches in the corners.

6. Right-click and select **Continue**. The punch table updates with the punches rolled into one row as shown in Figure 13–51.

HOLE TABLE				
HOLE	PUNCH ID	XDIM	YDIM	PUNCH DEPTH
A	ID-5678	52.76	52.76	8.00
B	ID-7890	132.76	82.76	2.00

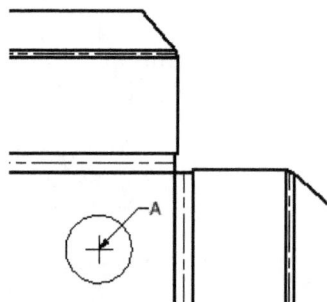

Figure 13–51

Task 6 - Change the punch representation.

1. Return to the part file.

2. Double-click on **Flat Pattern** in the Model Browser to display the flat pattern.

3. Right-click on **Flat Pattern** in the Model Browser and select **Edit Flat Pattern Definition**. Select the *Punch Representation* tab. The current Sheet Metal Rule has *Flat Pattern Punch Representation* set to **2D Sketch Representation**. This setting affects both the flat pattern in the model and any drawing views of the flat pattern.

4. Select **Center Mark Only**. Ensure that the **Ignore Individual Punch Representation Settings** checkbox is selected. Click **OK** to accept the changes. The punch representations in the flat pattern update as shown in Figure 13–52 (on the Back view).

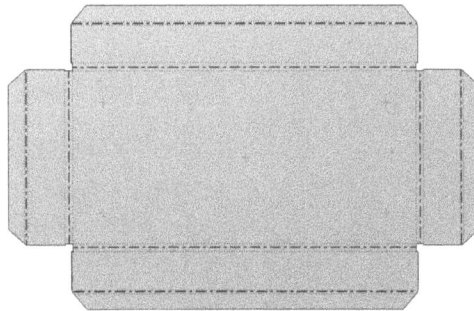

Figure 13–52

5. Return to the drawing. The punch representations in the drawing view update to only display the center marks.

Task 7 - Create a Punch Note.

As an alternative to the punch table you can also add punch notes to a drawing view. In this task you will delete the table and recreate the annotations for the punches using punch notes.

1. In the drawing, select the punch table, right-click and select **Delete**. The table and the markers in the view are removed.

2. In the *Annotate* tab>Feature Notes panel, click ⏚ (Punch).

3. Select the top left punch center mark and place the punch note, as shown in Figure 13–53. Continue to select and place punch notes for the remaining four punches in the drawing view, as shown in Figure 13–53. Right-click and select **OK**.

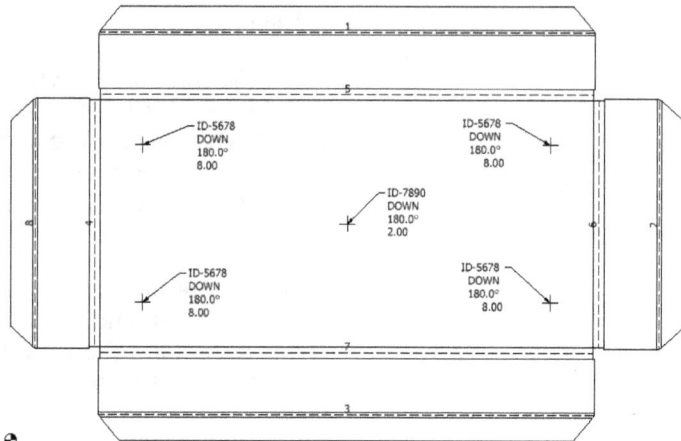

Figure 13–53

4. Right-click on the Punch Note in the top left corner and select **Edit Punch Note**.

5. Place the cursor at the beginning of the table, just before the **<ID>** parameter and click ⌗. Enter a space between the two parameters. The Edit Punch Note dialog box should display as shown in Figure 13–54.

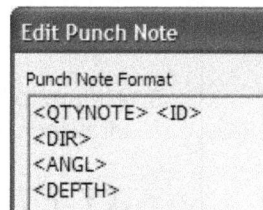

Figure 13–54

6. Click **OK**.

7. Delete the other three similar punch notes that are in the view. The drawing should display as shown in Figure 13–55.

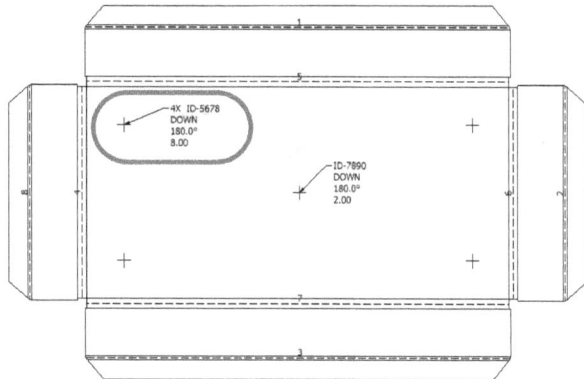

Figure 13–55

8. If time permits, return to the part model and delete one of the punch ifeature instances. The drawing should update to indicate that only three punches remain.

9. Save and close all of the files.

Practice 13c | Bend Order

Practice Objective

- Edit the original bend order and assign a custom bend order.

In this practice, you will flatten an existing part and modify the bend order, as shown in Figure 13–56.

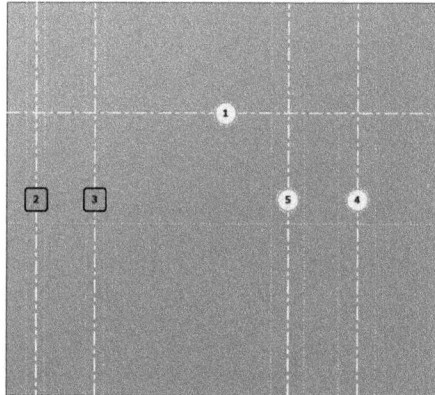

Figure 13–56

Task 1 - Edit the bend order for the sheet metal flat pattern.

1. Open **BendOrder.ipt**. The model displays as shown in Figure 13–57.

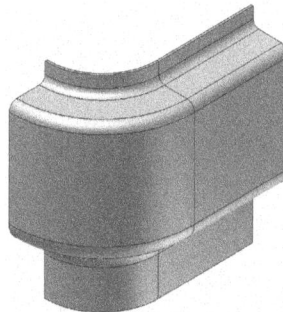

Figure 13–57

2. In the *Sheet Metal* tab>Flat Pattern panel, click ⬛ (Create Flat Pattern).

3. Once the flat pattern is active, in the Manage panel, click

   (Bend Order Annotation). The current bend order is indicated by yellow numbered circles, as shown in Figure 13–58.

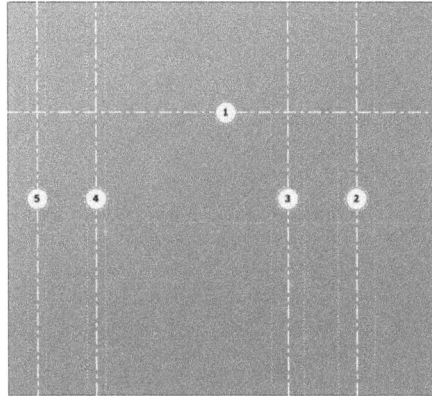

Figure 13–58

*As an alternative to individually editing the bend order of each bend, you can right-click in the main window and select either **Directed Reorder** or **Sequential Reorder**. You can use either of these options to modify the bend order.*

4. Select the bend order that is numbered **5**. The Bend Order Edit dialog box opens.

5. Select the check box next to the *Bend Number* field to enable the field. Enter **2** and click **OK**.

6. Renumber the remaining bends as required, to obtain the bend order shown in Figure 13–59. Once a bend order has been modified, it is displayed in green to indicate that the original bend order was overwritten.

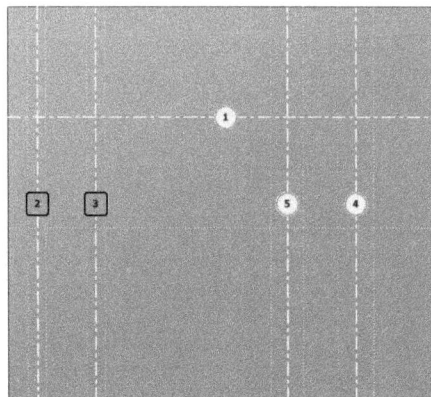

Figure 13–59

7. Save the model and close the window.

Chapter Review Questions

1. Which of the two views (A or B) shown in Figure 13–60 have the **Bend Extents** option enabled?

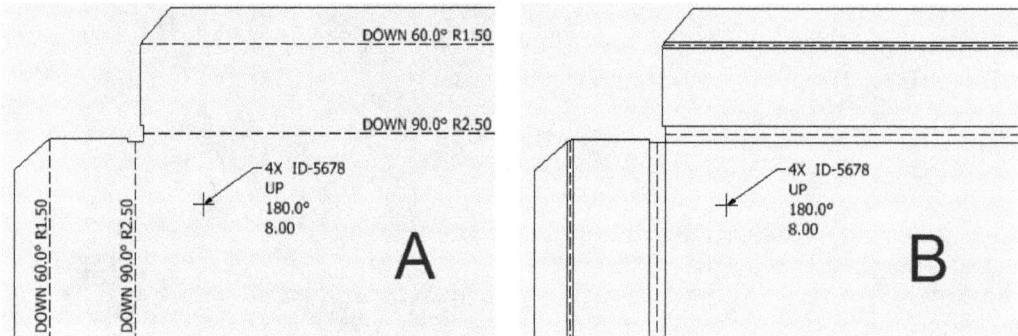

Figure 13–60

    a. A

    b. B

2. Which tab in the Drawing View dialog box enables you to select the component iPart that should be displayed if an iPart exists in the sheet metal model?

    a. *Component* tab

    b. *Model State* tab

    c. *Display Options* tab

3. Drawing views for sheet metal models can only be created using a flat pattern. You cannot create a view of the 3D folded model.

    a. True

    b. False

4. Which of the following statements are true regarding Punch notes? (Select all that apply.)

    a. To add a punch note, select individual punches in the view.

    b. To add a punch note, draw a bounding box window around punches in the view.

    c. Punch notes can be added to a folded or flat pattern view.

    d. Punch notes are added to a table and identified on the view with a punch identifier.

5. Which of the following commands is used to create a Bend table in a drawing?

   a. b.

   c. d.

6. Which of the following commands is used to create a Punch table in a drawing?

   a. b.

   c. d.

7. Which of the following are valid Bend ID formats that can be used to identify bends that are listed in a Bend table? (Select all that apply.)

   a. Alpha

   b. Numeric

   c. Alpha-Numeric

   d. Prefix

8. When editing the bend order in a model, which reorder type enables you to select each bend glyph to determine the final bend order?

   a. Directed Reorder

   b. Sequential Reorder

   c. Individual Override

9. A cosmetic centerline is simply a sketch that has been edited to display a dashed line style. There is no manufacturing information stored in the feature.

   a. True

   b. False

10. Which view best describes the tables shown in Figure 13–61?

PUNCH TABLE				
PUNCH	PUNCH ID	XDIM	YDIM	PUNCH DEPTH
A1	ID-5678	281.14	40.00	8.00
B1	ID-5678	501.14	40.00	8.00
C1	ID-1234	636.14	74.00	5.00
D1	ID-5678	391.14	75.00	8.00
E1	ID-5678	281.14	110.00	8.00
F1	ID-5678	501.14	110.00	8.00
G1	ID4567	392.14	249.33	1.50

TABLE			
BEND ID	BEND DIRECTION	BEND ANGLE	BEND RADIUS
1	UP	90	2
2	UP	90	2
3	DOWN	90	13
4	UP	90	14

Figure 13–61

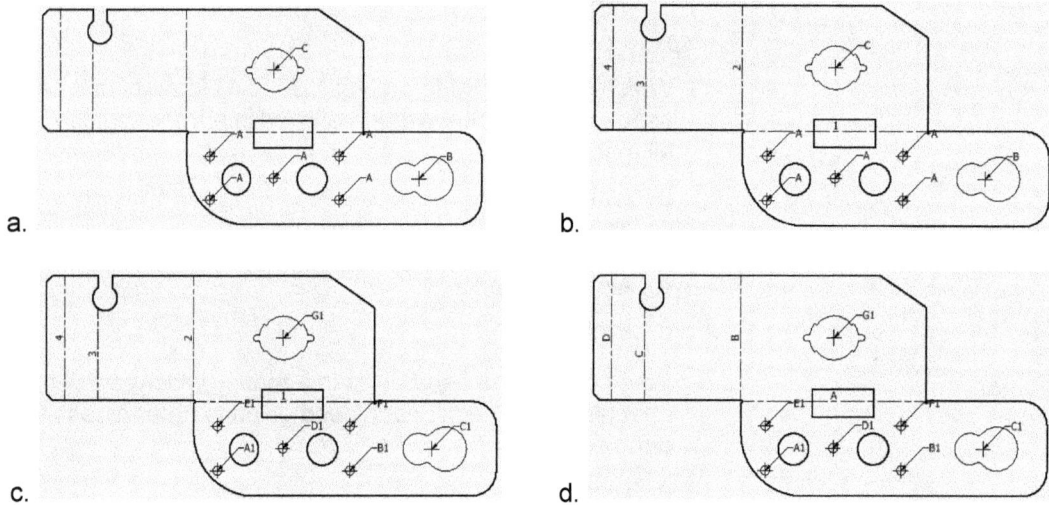

a.

b.

c.

d.

Command Summary

Button	Command	Location
	Base (view)	• **Ribbon:** *Place Views* tab>Create panel
	Bend (note)	• **Ribbon:** *Annotate* tab>Feature Notes panel
	Bend Order Annotation	• **Ribbon:** *Flat Pattern* tab>Manage panel
	Cosmetic Centerline	• **Ribbon:** *Flat Pattern* tab>Create panel
	General (table)	• **Ribbon:** *Annotate* tab>Table panel
	Hole Features (table)	• **Ribbon:** *Annotate* tab>Table panel
	Hole Selection (table)	• **Ribbon:** *Annotate* tab>Table panel
	Hole View (table)	• **Ribbon:** *Annotate* tab>Table panel
	Punch (note)	• **Ribbon:** *Annotate* tab>Feature Notes panel

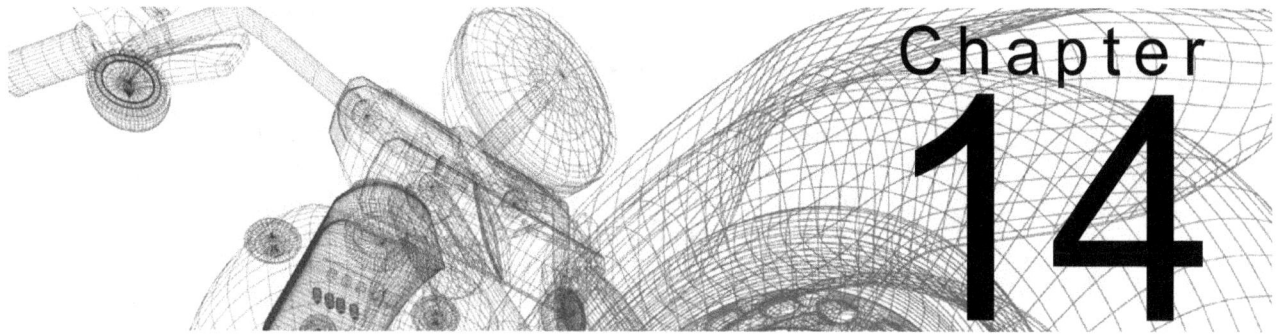

Chapter 14

Converting Parts to Sheet Metal

Some sheet metal parts can be more easily created with solid modeling tools and then converted to sheet metal. Consider the design implications before and after converting a solid model to sheet metal. For example, non-uniform thickness, fillet radii, and creation of the flat pattern's unfolding are areas that might need to be addressed.

Learning Objectives in this Chapter

- Convert an existing solid model into a sheet metal model.
- Verify the sheet metal Thickness parameter to ensure that it is equal to that of the solid model.
- Recognize how non-uniform thickness solid models can prevent sheet metal features from being successfully created once converted to a sheet metal model.
- Identify how non-rules surfaces are represented in a sheet metal flat pattern.

14.1 Converting Solid Models to Sheet Metal

For situations in which a part cannot be easily created from sheet metal, the Autodesk® Inventor® software includes a tool to convert non-sheet metal parts into sheet metal parts. For models that are fabricated from sheet metal this can be a useful tool. However, some models still need editing before or after being converted. Editing can be done with solid modeling tools or sheet metal tools depending on the types of features required for manufacturing.

Common Shapes to Convert to Sheet Metal

Two common shapes, which are easier to create as solid models and convert to sheet metal, are rolled cylindrical or conical sheet metal parts, similar to those shown in Figure 14–1. Many methods can be used to create these types of parts so that it can be converted to sheet metal. For example, a rectangular sketch that matches the thickness of the sheet metal style is revolved around a centerline or work axis. Figure 14–1 shows a 2mm thick rectangle revolved to become a cylinder and a 1mm thick rectangle revolved to become a cone.

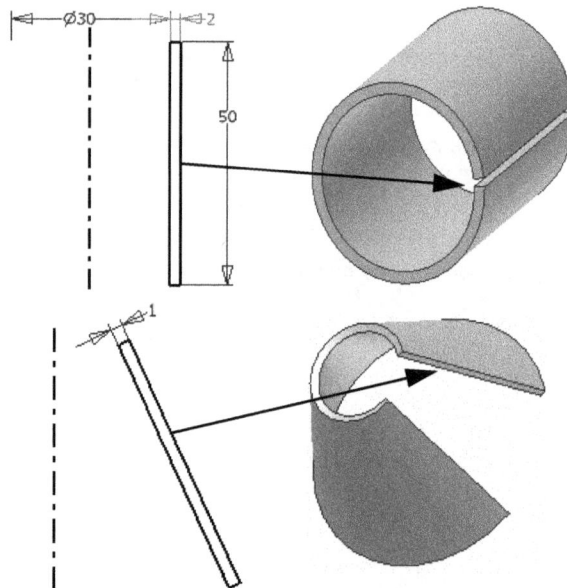

Figure 14–1

Another method of creating a rolled cylinder is to create a sketch of its circular profile and extrude it to create a cylinder as shown in Figure 14–2.

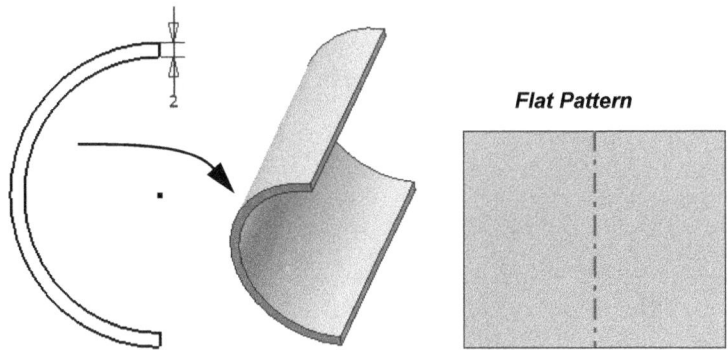

Flat Pattern

Curved profile extruded to create cylindrical part

Figure 14–2

General Steps

Use the following general steps to convert standard parts to sheet metal.

1. Create a solid model with uniform thickness.
2. Add features that cannot be created easily with sheet metal tools.
3. Convert the part to a sheet metal part.
4. Set the sheet metal style to the thickness of the part.
5. Add sheet metal features.
6. Create a flat pattern.
7. Add flat pattern cleanup (optional).

Step 1 - Create a solid model with uniform thickness.

The part that you want to convert can be simple or complex. Figure 14–3 shows a very simple cylinder created from a revolved 300 degree rectangular sketch. The sketched rectangle is dimensioned as 2mm thick.

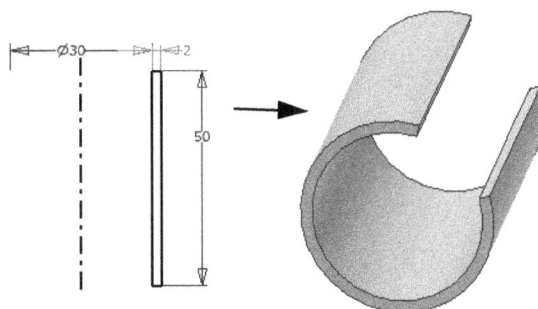

Figure 14–3

More complex solid models can also be used to convert to sheet metal. For example, Figure 14–4 shows the steps used to make a part with solid modeling tools.

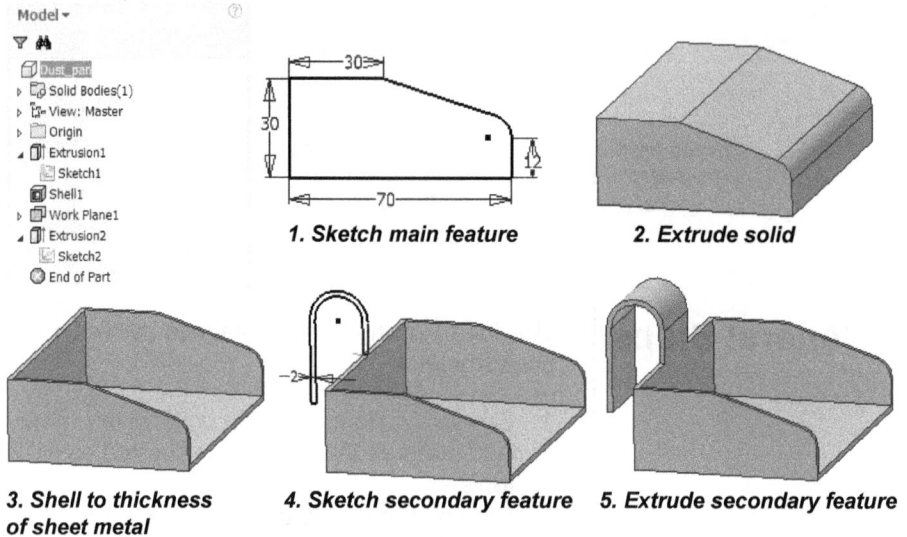

Model ▾

▽ 🛱
🗂 Dust_part
▷ 🗂 Solid Bodies(1)
▷ 🗂 View: Master
▷ 🗂 Origin
◢ 🗂 Extrusion1
　🗂 Sketch1
　🗂 Shell1
▷ 🗂 Work Plane1
◢ 🗂 Extrusion2
　🗂 Sketch2
　◯ End of Part

1. Sketch main feature

2. Extrude solid

3. Shell to thickness of sheet metal

4. Sketch secondary feature

5. Extrude secondary feature

Figure 14–4

Step 2 - Add features that cannot be created easily with sheet metal tools.

When adding features that are going to be used in a part to be converted, ensure that the pre-converted geometry is ideal for your design needs in Sheet Metal. For example, features that cannot be flattened to create a flat pattern are left as 3D. Figure 14–5 shows an example of these types of features.

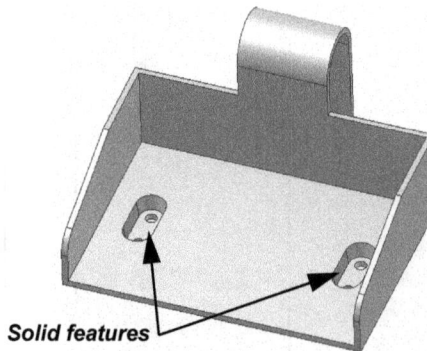

Solid features

Figure 14–5

Step 3 - Convert the part to a sheet metal part.

You might need to display the Convert panel on the Ribbon, if it is not already displayed.

*To display, expand ⊙ - and click **Convert**.*

In the *3D Model* tab>Convert panel, click 🏴 (Convert to Sheet Metal) to change a solid model to a sheet metal part. The part is immediately converted and is recognized as a folded sheet metal model in the Model Browser. Note that the model geometry does not change: the file is now just classified as a sheet metal part.

Prior to continuing in the Sheet Metal environment, you must select a base face reference. This reference is used to define the thickness of the model. Once the reference is selected, the Sheet Metal Defaults dialog box opens. The *Thickness* value is automatically updated with the measured thickness value and the **Use Thickness from Rule** option is cleared, indicating that the *Thickness* value in the rule is being overwritten with the measured value.

Figure 14–6 shows the cylinder and cone models after being converted to sheet metal. Although they have not changed, they display as folded models in the Model Browser.

*Tip: To flatten a lofted body, ensure that the number of segments in each sketch are equal. Create the loft feature, create rounds on each linear segment equal to BendRadius+Thickness , shell it using the Thickness value, and create a cut to open up the part. Once cut you can use the **Flat Pattern** option.*

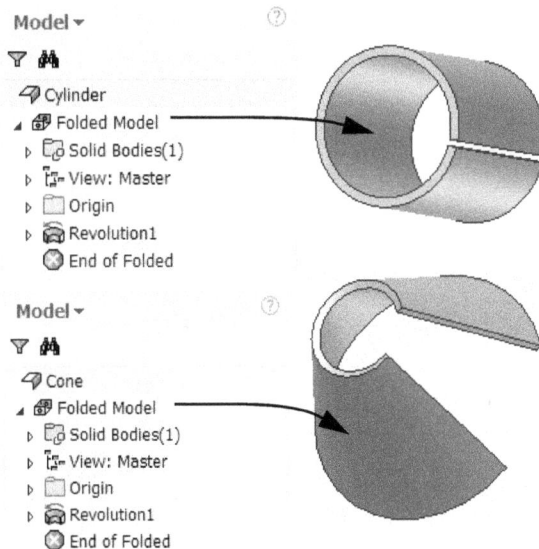

Figure 14–6

Converting Imported IGS Files

Some parts can be imported from IGES files. When a part is imported it becomes a base solid and does not list individual features, such as extrusions and holes, in the Model Browser as shown in Figure 14–7.

*When importing an IGS file, ensure that the **Solids** option is selected in the Object Filters area of the Import dialog box.*

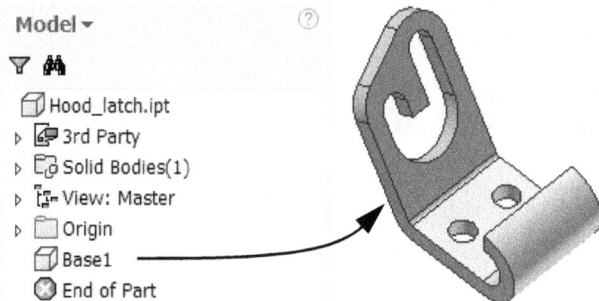

Figure 14–7

When the Sheet Metal Rule **Thickness** parameter matches the uniform thickness of the base solid you can convert it to a sheet metal part and unfold it, as shown in Figure 14–8.

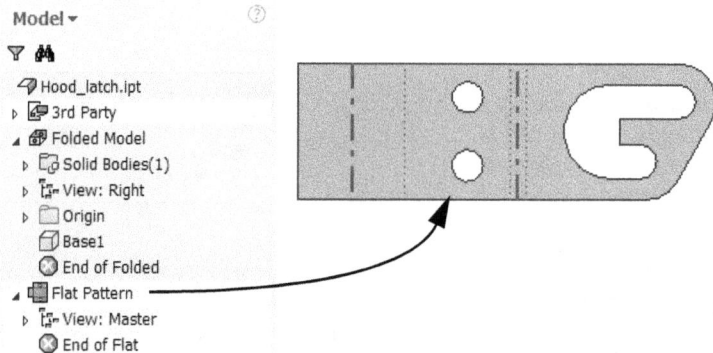

Figure 14–8

Step 4 - Set the sheet metal style to the thickness of the part.

If the *Thickness* is to be driven by the rule and not the overwritten measured value, complete the following:

1. In the *Sheet Metal* tab>Setup panel, click (Sheet Metal Defaults) to open the Sheet Metal Defaults dialog box.
2. Select **Use Thickness from Rule**.

3. Click ✎ next to the assigned Sheet Metal Rule. The Style and Standard dialog box opens.
4. Change the **Thickness** parameter value to match that of the part that you have converted, as shown in Figure 14–9.

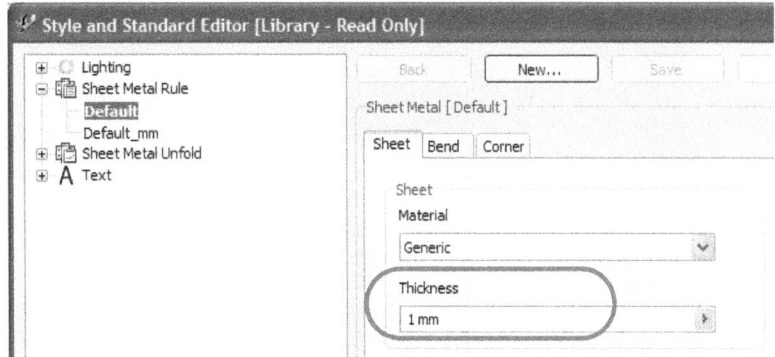

Figure 14–9

Step 5 - Add sheet metal features.

To add features to the sheet metal part, you can use both the sheet metal tools and the solid part modeling tools.

Switching Between the Part Modeling and Sheet Metal Environments

When starting a model with a standard (non-sheetmetal) template only the Part Features functionality is available. You cannot use any sheet metal tools at this point. However, after you have converted a part to sheet metal, you cab switch between the sheet metal environment and solid part modeling environment, as required. To use tools from either environment, use the *Sheet Metal* or the *3D Model* tab, as shown in Figure 14–10.

Figure 14–10

After a part is converted, appropriate sheet metal features can be added, and you can create a flat pattern.

Non-Uniform Thickness Models

To work effectively with a solid model that has been converted to sheet metal, it should have uniform thickness. Models that do not have uniform thickness still convert, but there are many limitations to how they can be modified.

For example, Figure 14–11 shows a model with uniform thickness on the left. After converting the model to sheet metal and adding Fold and Bend features, it displays as shown on the right.

Both solid and sheet metal models can be created with disconnected faces.

Original solid model with three individual extrusions

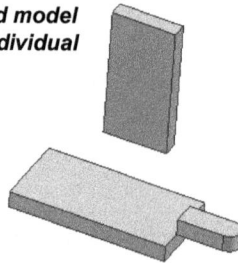

Part converted to sheet metal with Bend and Fold features added

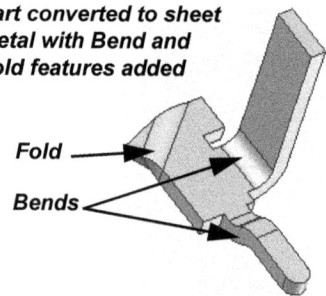

Fold

Bends

Figure 14–11

If the original part **does not** have uniform thickness, it can still be converted to sheet metal as shown in Figure 14–12. However, this would result in a model that cannot have sheet metal features added.

Original solid model with three individual extrusions that have three different thicknesses

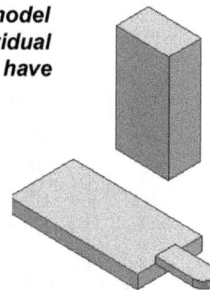

Figure 14–12

Attempting to add features between portions that do not match the **Thickness** parameter or have different thicknesses (such as Bends, Flanges, and Hems) displays the Warning shown in Figure 14–13.

Selecting edges on varying thickness areas for a Bend causes a Warning dialog box to open

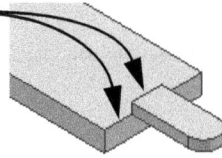

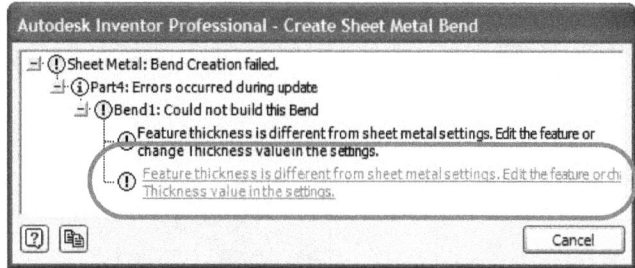

Figure 14–13

If a part has non-uniform thicknesses, setting the **Thickness** parameter to match one of the areas on the part enables you to apply sheet metal features to it. For example, in the part shown in Figure 14–14 the **Thickness** parameter matches the extrusion depth of one of the rectangular areas. Therefore, a sketched line can be added on the top plane of that extrusion and a fold can be created on that portion of the sheet metal part. If you change the **Thickness** parameter after adding a sheet metal feature, a Warning dialog box is opened and the feature fails.

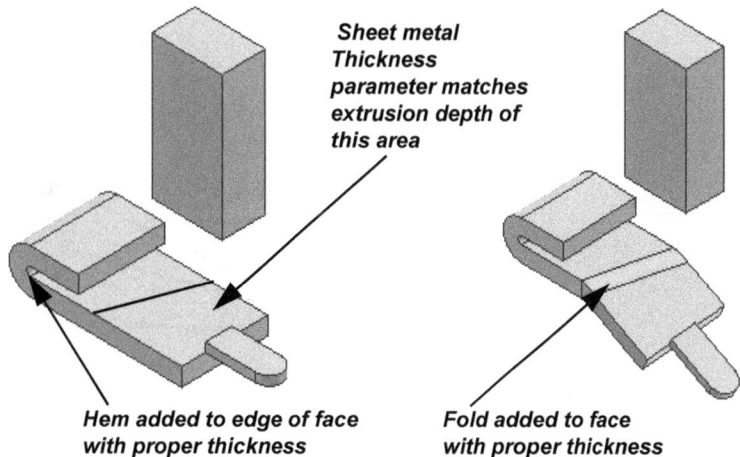

Sheet metal Thickness parameter matches extrusion depth of this area

Hem added to edge of face with proper thickness

Fold added to face with proper thickness

Figure 14–14

Hole features can be added to faces that do not match the thickness of an area on a part, as shown in Figure 14–15. By default the depth of the hole feature is set to **Thickness**. However, you can change the depth as required.

*Thickness is not deep
enough to cut through part*

| Thickness | > |

| 1 | > |

*Thickness goes through
because it is deeper
than thickness of part*

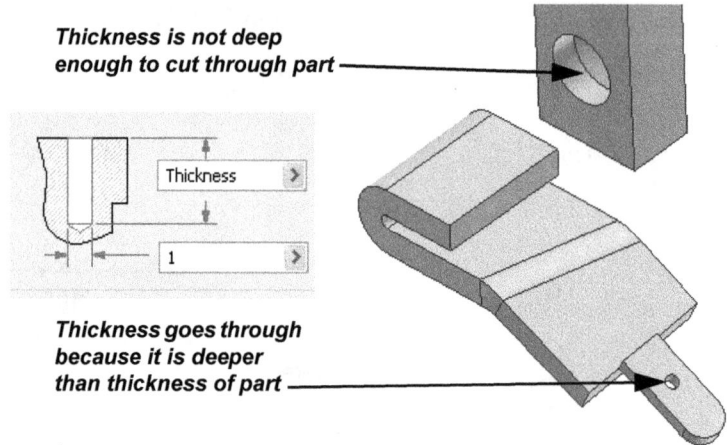

Figure 14–15

More complex shapes can also be created with solid modeling tools and converted to sheet metal. Figure 14–16 shows a solid that was created and shelled to produce a uniform thickness.

Model ▾

Part1
▷ Solid Bodies(1)
▷ View: Master
▷ Origin
▷ Extrusion1
Shell1
▷ Extrusion2
End of Part

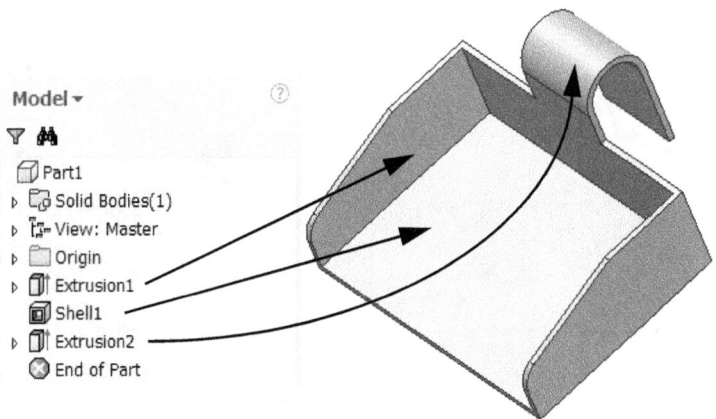

Figure 14–16

After converting the solid model shown in Figure 14–17 to a sheet metal model, the **Thickness** parameter was set to match the shell thickness. The curved extrusion was created to match the thickness of the shell.

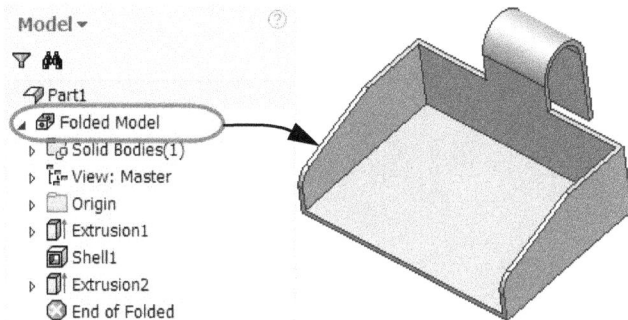

Figure 14–17

After conversion, but before creating a Flat pattern, sheet metal features (such as Bends and Corner Seam features) need to be added.

How To: Add Sheetmetal Features

1. Add Corner Seam Rip features to the edges that need to be separated when unfolding, as shown in Figure 14–18.

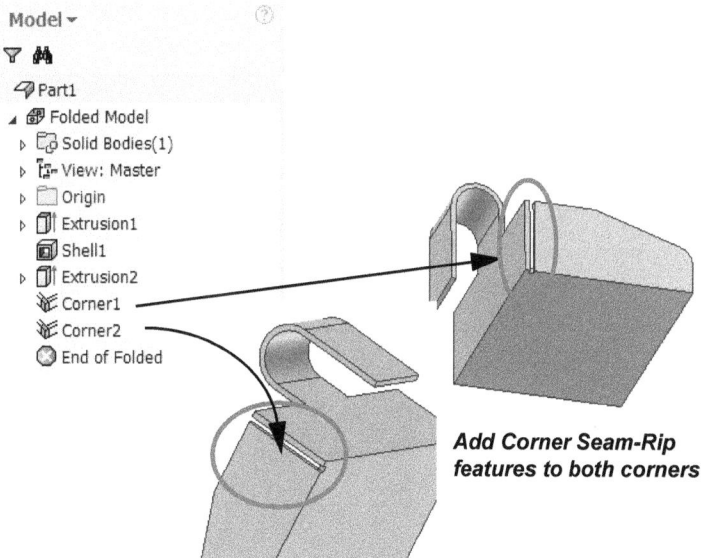

Add Corner Seam-Rip features to both corners

Figure 14–18

2. Add Bend features to corners that remain attached during unfolding, as shown in Figure 14–19.

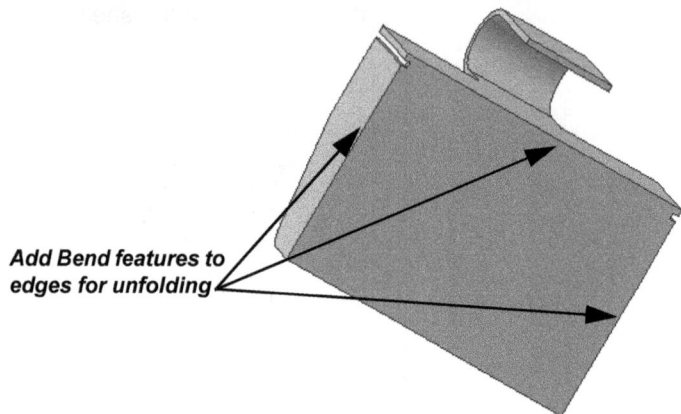

Add Bend features to edges for unfolding

Figure 14–19

The part displays as shown in Figure 14–20.

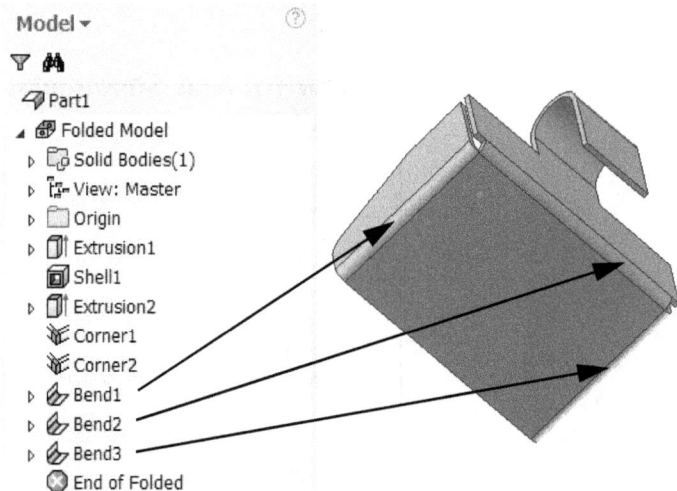

Figure 14–20

Step 6 - Create a flat pattern.

When the flat pattern is added to the model, if the default, face-up side of the sheet metal model is not appropriate, use the

⬆ (Define A-Side) command to manually define the face-up side.

In the *Sheet Metal* tab>Flat Pattern panel, click 🔲 (Create Flat Pattern) to unfold into the Flat Pattern, as shown in Figure 14–21. In this example the Flat Pattern needs to be cleaned up before the part can be fabricated.

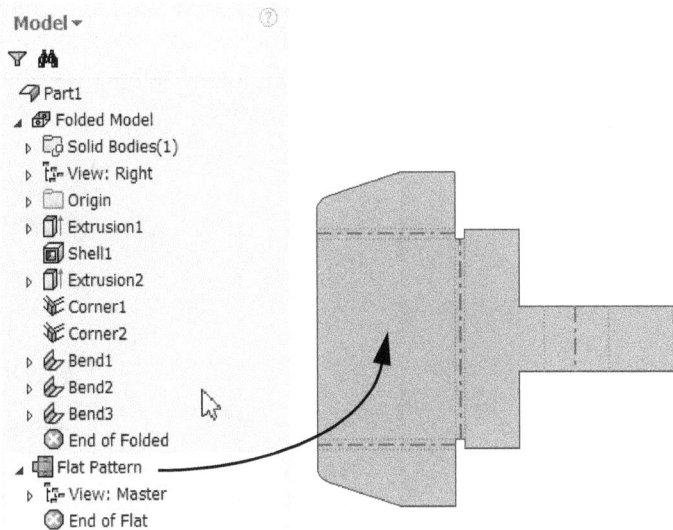

Figure 14–21

Step 7 - Add flat pattern cleanup (optional).

Depending on your needs you can add features to the Flat Pattern that would not be included on the folded model. These could include Punches, Cutouts, Corner Reliefs, Chamfers, and Fillets.

14.2 Non-Ruled Surfaces

Some parts created as solid models include non-ruled surfaces. Therefore, they are not able to be unfolded along a single axis direction. For example, a spherical shape on a part. Non-ruled geometry cannot be flattened when a flat pattern is created.

Figure 14–22 shows a flat plane with a spherical feature. The part has been shelled to a 1mm thickness to create a plane with a non-ruled feature as a louver. Creating the louver would deform the sheet metal material.

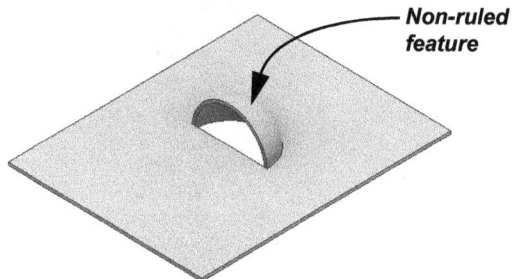

Figure 14–22

In Figure 14–23, the part has been converted to Sheet Metal. Three separate Flanges have been added.

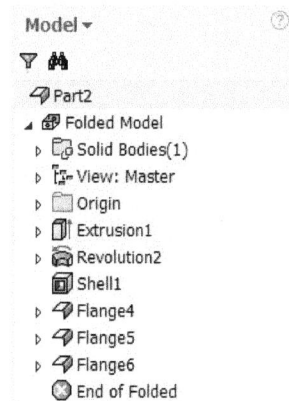

Figure 14–23

Figure 14–24 shows the Flat Pattern for the previous model. The Flanges are all unfolded; however, the Revolved feature cannot be flattened because it would require deformation in more than one direction to flatten it. This is typical for features that are pressed into a sheet metal part and deform the metal, rather than fully punching through.

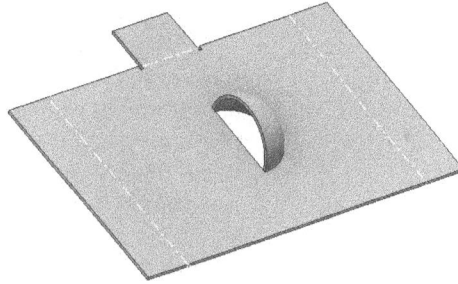

Figure 14–24

Practice 14a | Convert to Sheet Metal

Practice Objectives

- Convert an existing solid model to a sheet metal model and assign the sheet metal Thickness parameter and appropriate sheet metal features to enable flattening.
- Create a flat pattern of the new sheet metal model.

In this practice, you will convert an existing model to sheet metal and add sheet metal features to generate a flat pattern as shown in Figure 14–25. You will convert the model to sheet metal to enable the sheet metal tools and then set the **Thickness** in the Sheet Metal Rule. Next you will edit the shell features to set the shell thickness to the sheet metal **Thickness** parameter. This links the thickness of the model to the thickness in the Sheet Metal Rule. Corner rips and bends are then added enabling the model to be unfolded. Finally, you will generate the flat pattern.

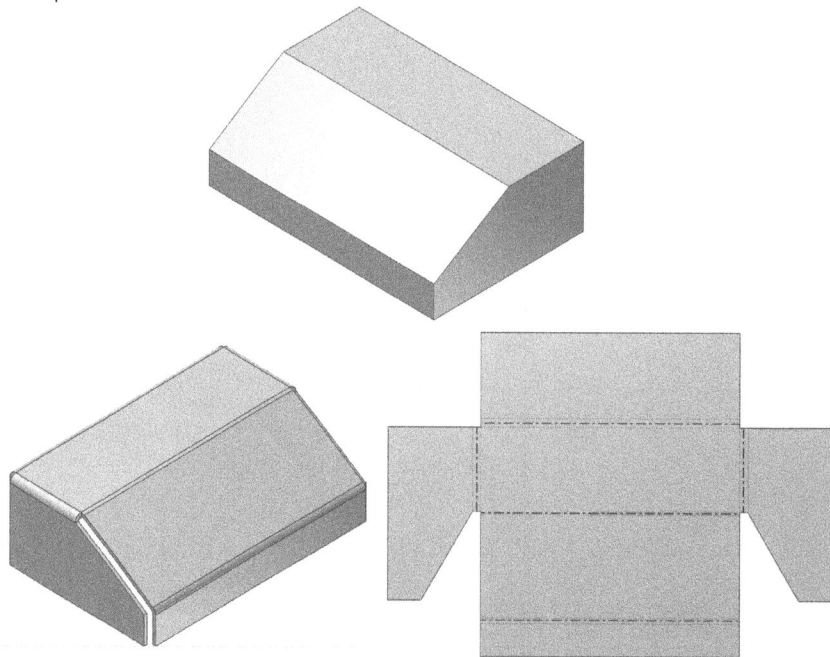

Figure 14–25

Task 1 - Convert a normal part to a sheet metal part.

1. Open **Hood_solid.ipt**. It consists of an extrusion and a shell.

2. Rotate the model to see that the face under the part is removed as part of the shell feature.

3. Edit **Shell1** to determine the shell thickness (1mm). This will be the sheet metal thickness after the part is converted to sheet metal.

4. In the *3D Model* tab>Convert panel, click ⚑ (Convert to Sheet Metal). The part is converted to a sheet metal model. The **Folded Model** node is added to the Model Browser and the Sheet Metal panel is activated.

If the Convert panel is not displayed, expand ⊙ ⁻ *and click* **Convert** *to turn it on.*

5. Select the top face as the base face reference, as shown in Figure 14–26. This face is used to measure the thickness of the model.

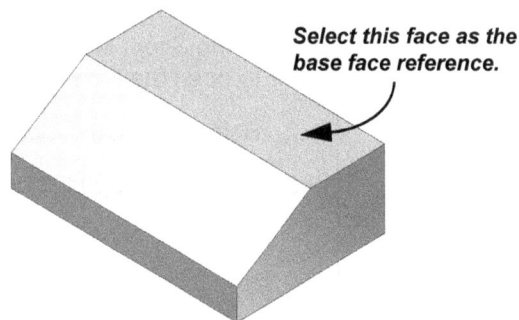

Select this face as the base face reference.

Figure 14–26

6. The Sheet Metal Defaults dialog box opens. Note that the *Thickness* value is **1.00 mm** and the **Use Thickness from Rule** option is cleared, indicating that the *Thickness* value in the rule is being overwritten with the measured value.

7. Click **OK**.

Task 2 - Modify the sheet thickness in the default rule.

1. In the *Sheet Metal* tab>Setup panel, click 🗔 (Sheet Metal Defaults). The Sheet Metal Defaults dialog box opens.

2. Click ✎ next to the assigned Sheet Metal Rule. The Style and Standard dialog box opens.

3. Change the *Thickness* to **1 mm**.

4. Click **Save and Close** to save the new thickness.

5. Select **Use Thickness from Rule** to ensure that the *Thickness* value is being driven by the default rule.

6. Click **OK** to close the Sheet Metal Defaults dialog box.

Task 3 - Modify the shell feature.

1. Edit **Shell1**.

2. Change the value in the *Thickness* field to **Thickness**.

3. Click **OK**. The shell thickness is now set to the **Thickness** parameter from the Sheet Metal Rule.

Task 4 - Open the back corners.

1. In the *Sheet Metal* tab>Modify panel, click ⍌ (Corner Seam) to open the Corner Seam dialog box.

2. Select **Rip** in the *Shape* area in the dialog box.

3. Select the edges shown in Figure 14–27.

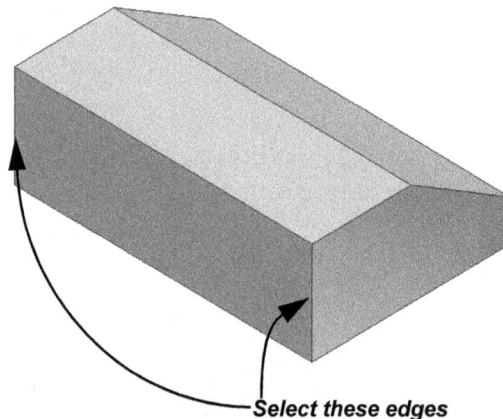

Select these edges

Figure 14–27

4. Ensure that the **Face/Edge Distance** option and 🔲 (No Overlap) are selected.

5. Click **OK**. The corners are opened as shown in Figure 14–28.

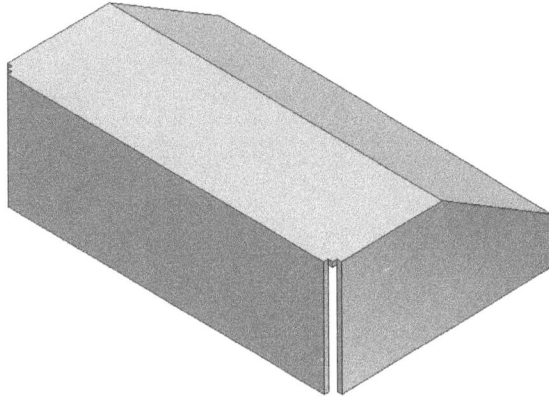

Figure 14–28

Task 5 - Add bends to existing corners.

---

1. In the *Sheet Metal* tab>Create panel, click 🔧 (Bend) to open the Bend dialog box.

2. Select the edge as shown in Figure 14–29.

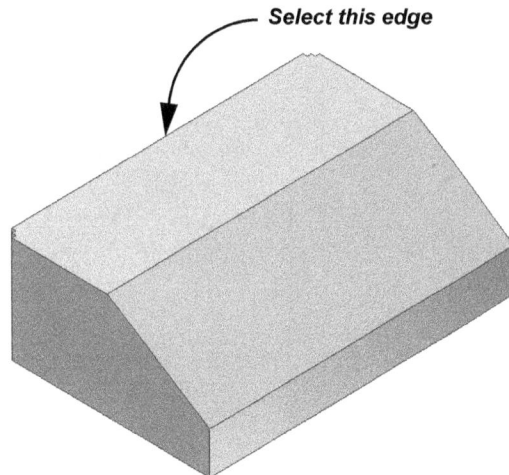

Select this edge

Figure 14–29

3. Click **Apply** to create the bend.

4. Repeat for the edges shown in Figure 14–30.

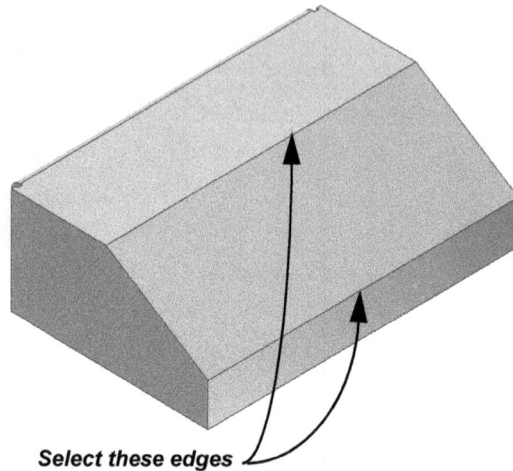

Select these edges

Figure 14–30

5. Click **Cancel** to close the Bend dialog box. The model displays as shown in Figure 14–31.

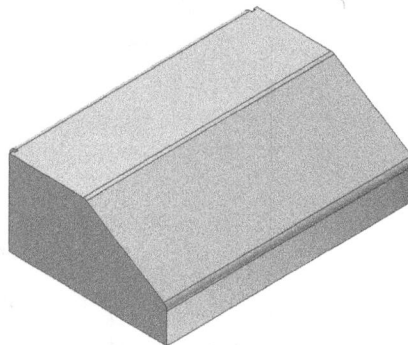

Figure 14–31

Task 6 - Open the side corners.

1. In the *Sheet Metal* tab>Modify panel, click ⌄ (Corner Seam) to open the Corner Seam dialog box.

2. Select **Rip** in the *Shape* area in the dialog box.

3. Select the four edges shown in Figure 14–32. Select two
    straight edges and two arcs. Ensure that the **Face/Edge**

    Distance option and ⬚ (No Overlap) are selected.
    Note: As of the printing of this student guide, the Autodesk
    Inventor 2017 (R1) software was unable to select all four
    entities at the same time to create the rip. You might need to
    use two rip features to properly open this corner.

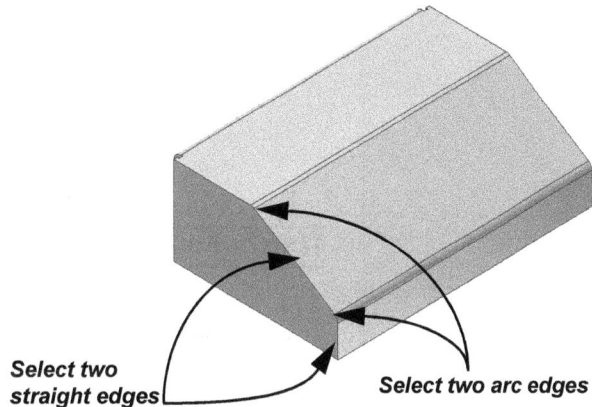

Select two
straight edges   *Select two arc edges*

Figure 14–32

4. Click **Apply** to open the corners. The model displays as
    shown in Figure 14–33.

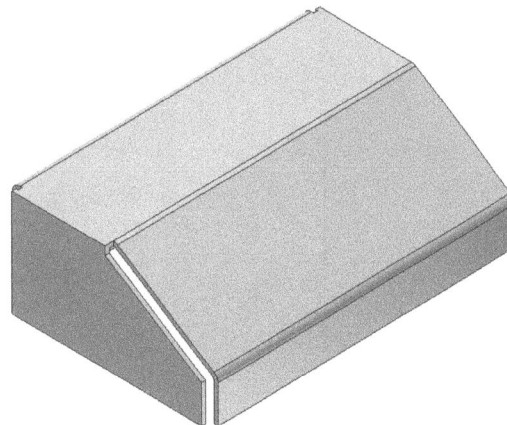

Figure 14–33

5. Repeat for the same edges on the opposite side of the part.

6. Click **Cancel** to close the Corner Seam dialog box when finished. The model displays as shown in Figure 14–34.

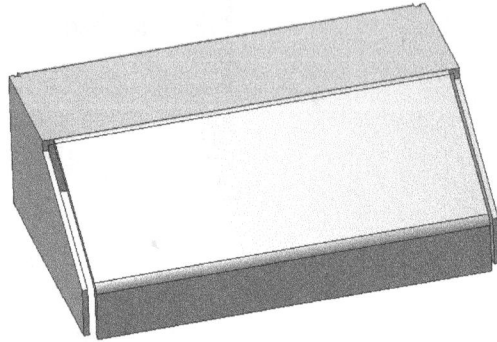

Figure 14–34

Task 7 - Add bends to the remaining corners.

1. In the *Sheet Metal* tab>Create panel, click ⌐ (Bend) to open the Bend dialog box.

2. Select the edge shown in Figure 14–35.

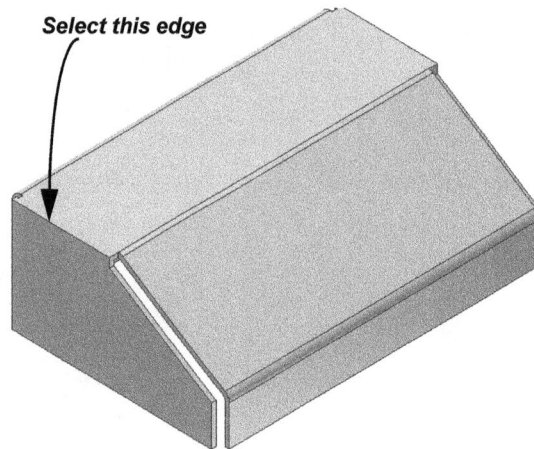

Select this edge

Figure 14–35

3. Click **Apply** to create the bend.

4. Repeat for the same edge on the opposite side of the part. Click **Cancel** to close the Bend dialog box. The model displays as shown in Figure 14–36.

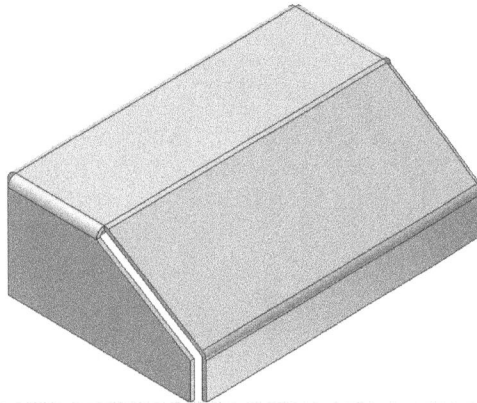

Figure 14–36

Task 8 - Create the flat pattern.

1. In the *Sheet Metal* tab>Flat Pattern panel, click ⬚ (Create Flat Pattern) to generate the flat pattern of the model. It displays as shown in Figure 14–37.

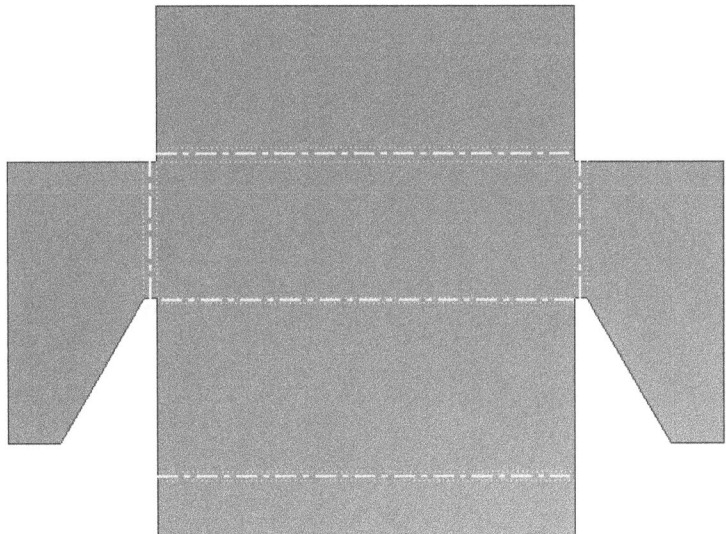

Figure 14–37

2. Return to the folded model, save, and close the file.

Practice 14b | Import IGES File

Practice Objectives

- Open an IGES file as a solid and convert it to sheet metal model.
- Create a flat pattern of the new sheet metal model.

In this practice, you will import an IGES file, convert it to a sheet metal part, and generate a flat pattern as shown in Figure 14–38. You will also modify the **Thickness** parameter in the Sheet Metal Rule to match the thickness of the part so that it can be unfolded.

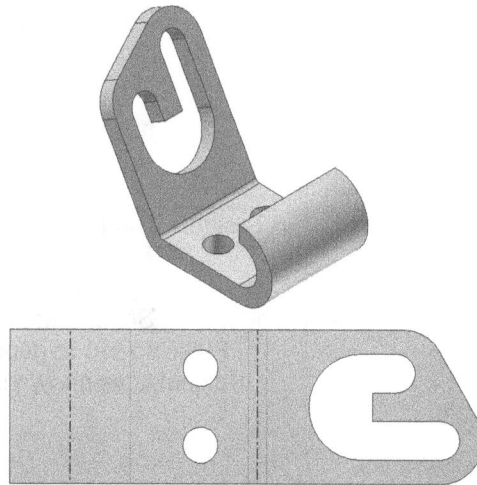

Figure 14–38

Task 1 - Import an IGES file.

1. Click in the Quick Access Toolbar to open the Open dialog box.

2. In the Files of type drop-down list, click **IGES Files (*.igs;*.ige;*iges)**.

3. Select **Hood_latch.igs** and click **Open**.

4. In the Import dialog box, ensure that the following are set:

   - Select **Solids** to import the IGES file as a solid.
   - Clear all other *Object Filters* options if any are enabled.
   - Set the units as **From Source**.
   - Maintain the remaining defaults in the dialog box.

5. Click **OK**. The IGES file is converted to a part file. No features are imported; the model is a base solid.

6. Save the file. Use the default name **Hood_latch.ipt**.

Task 2 - Convert to a sheet metal part.

1. In the *3D Model* tab>Convert panel, click ![icon] (Convert to Sheet Metal) to convert the part to a sheet metal part. The **Folded Model** node is added to the Model Browser and the Sheet Metal Features panel is activated.

2. Select one of the faces on the model as the base face reference. This reference is used to automatically measure the model's thickness. The Sheet Metal Defaults dialog box opens and indicates that the *Thickness* is **10 mm**.

3. Select **Use Thickness from Rule** to set the *Thickness* value to be driven by the rule.

4. Click ![icon] next to the assigned Sheet Metal Rule. The Style and Standard dialog box opens.

5. Change the *Thickness* to **10 mm**. The rule does not automatically get changed to the measured value, you must modify it if the rule is being used to drive thickness.

6. Click **Save and Close** to save the new thickness.

7. Click **OK** to close the Sheet Metal Defaults dialog box.

*You can also change the **Thickness** parameter in the Parameters dialog box.*

Task 3 - Generate a flat pattern.

1. In the *Sheet Metal* tab>Flat Pattern panel, click ![icon] (Create Flat Pattern) to generate the flat pattern of the model.

2. Return to the folded model, save, and close the file.

Practice 14c | Solid Model to Sheet Metal

Practice Objectives

- Create a new solid model using features that enable easy conversion to a sheet metal model.
- Convert an existing solid model to a sheet metal model and assign the sheet metal Thickness parameter.
- Create a flat pattern of the new sheet metal model.

In this practice, you will create a model using normal feature creation tools, convert the model to a sheet metal part, and generate a flat pattern as shown in Figure 14–39. You will start by opening an existing file containing the sketches required to generate the model. The model is created using two revolved features and a circular pattern. After creating the geometry, you will convert the part to a sheet metal part and set a parameter equal to the **Thickness** in the Sheet Metal Rule. The parameter you will change controls the thickness of the revolved feature, and the model updates. Finally, you will generate a flat pattern of the sheet metal part.

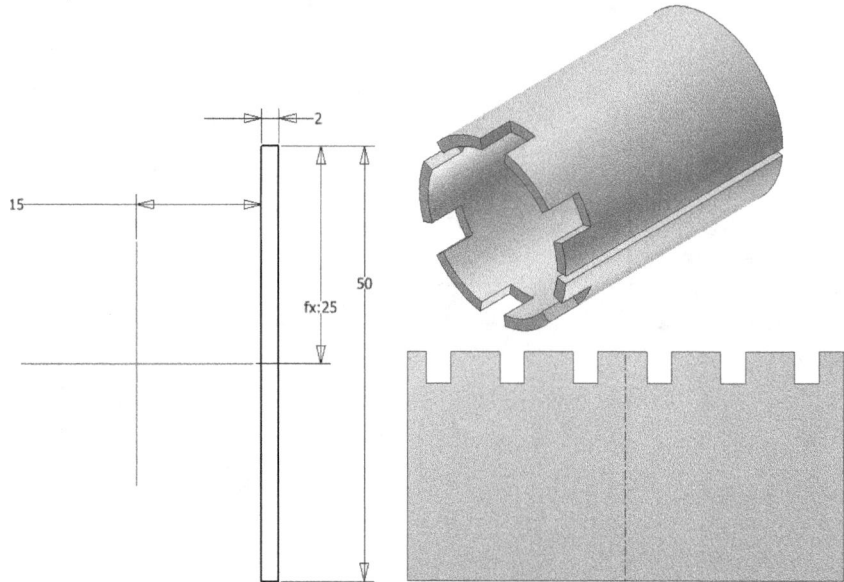

Figure 14–39

Task 1 - Create base feature.

*Change the **Files of type** menu to display Autodesk Inventor Files.*

1. Open **Cylinder.ipt**. It contains two sketches (one has the visibility toggled off) and a work plane.

2. Create a revolved feature using the profile in **Sketch1** and the Axis shown in Figure 14–40. In the Extents drop-down list, select **Angle** and enter **355 deg** as the angle to revolve.

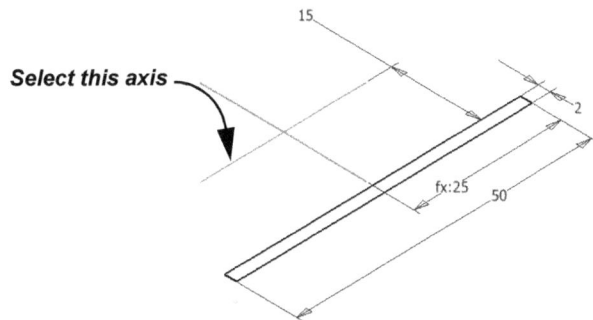

Figure 14–40

3. Complete the feature. The model displays as shown in Figure 14–41. The profile was not revolved a full 360 degrees, enabling it to be unfolded after it is converted to a sheet metal part.

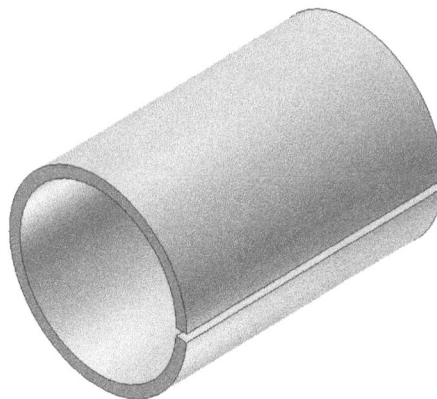

Figure 14–41

Task 2 - Create a secondary feature.

1. Toggle on the **Visibility** of **Sketch2**.

2. Create a revolved feature using the profile in **Sketch2** and the Axis shown in Figure 14–42. Set the feature type to Cut by clicking 🖨. In the Extents drop-down list, select **Angle** and enter **20 deg** as the angle to revolve. Click 🔲 to flip the direction of the cut to be created away from the gap in the cylinder.

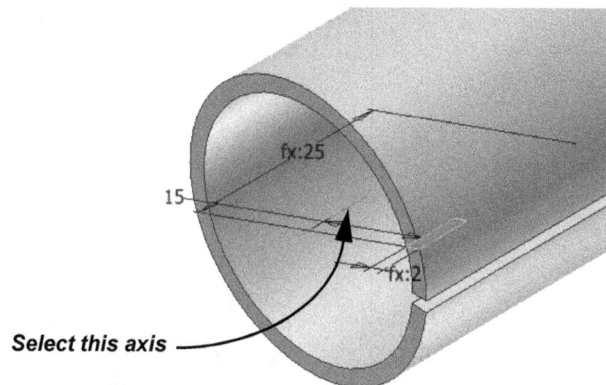

Figure 14–42

3. Complete the feature. The model displays as shown in Figure 14–43.

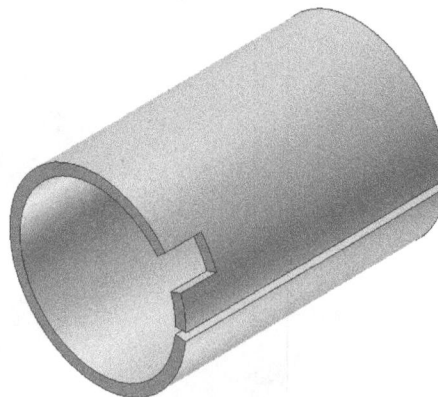

Figure 14–43

4. Create a circular pattern of the cut feature centered around the cylinder. Use **6** as the *Occurrence Count* and **360 deg** as the *Occurrence Angle*.

5. Complete the feature. The model displays as shown in Figure 14–44.

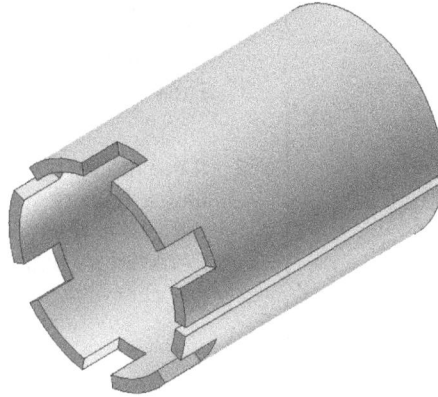

Figure 14–44

Task 3 - Convert the model to sheet metal.

---

1. In the *3D Model* tab>Convert panel, click 🏳 (Convert to Sheet Metal) to convert the part to a sheet metal part. The **Folded Model** node is added to the Model Browser and the Sheet Metal Features panel is activated.

2. Select the outside face of the cylinder as the base face reference.

3. When a model is converted, the *Thickness* is assigned by default based on the measured value and it is used instead of the *Thickness* value assigned to the rule. Currently the *Thickness* is being driven by an overwritten value of 2.00 mm that was measured on the model.

4. Select **Use Thickness from Rule**.

5. Click **OK** to close the Sheet Metal Defaults dialog box.

Task 4 - Set the thickness of the part.

1. In the *Manage* tab>Parameters panel, click f_x (Parameters) to open the Parameters dialog box.

2. Change the *Equation* of d0 to **Thickness** and click **Done**. The **d0** parameter controls the thickness of the revolved feature. It is now set to the **Thickness** from the Sheet Metal Rule.

3. If the model does not update automatically, click in the Quick Access Toolbar. The model updates to the thickness in the Sheet Metal Rule, as shown in Figure 14–45. Close the Parameters dialog box.

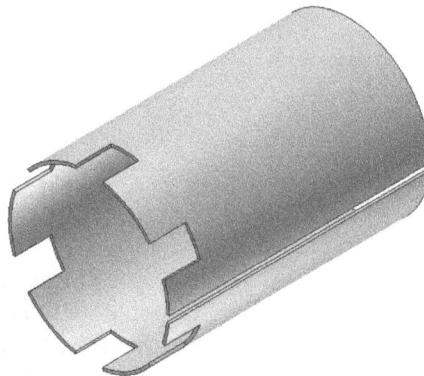

Figure 14–45

4. In the *Sheet Metal* tab>Setup panel, click (Sheet Metal Defaults). The Sheet Metal Defaults dialog box opens.

5. Click next to the assigned Sheet Metal Rule. The Style and Standard dialog box opens.

6. Change the *Thickness* to **2 mm**.

7. Save the changes and close the dialog box. The model updates as shown in Figure 14–46.

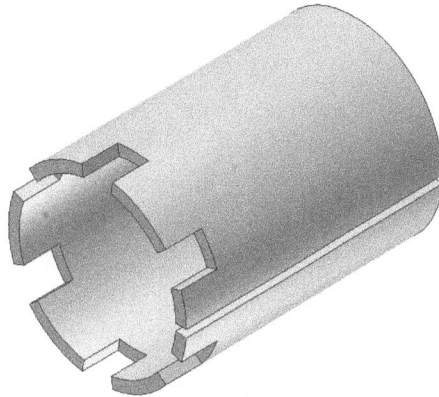

Figure 14–46

8. Close the Sheet Metal Defaults dialog box.

Task 5 - Generate a flat pattern.

1. In the *Sheet Metal* tab>Flat Pattern panel, click (Create Flat Pattern) to generate the flat pattern, as shown in Figure 14–47.

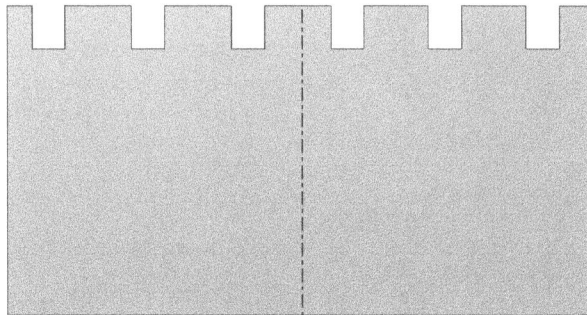

Figure 14–47

2. Return to the folded model. Save and close the file.

Chapter Review Questions

1. Which of the following best describes the situation when the **Convert to Sheet Metal** command is available?

    a. It is available in a solid part model once all features have the same *Thickness* value.

    b. It is always available on the *3D Model* tab in a solid part model.

    c. It is available on the *3D Model* tab in a sheet metal model.

    d. It is always available on the *Sheet Metal* tab in a sheet metal model.

2. Why is it important to set the **Thickness** parameter to match the uniform part thickness after converting a part to sheet metal?

    a. Without being set you cannot access the **Convert to Sheet Metal** command to convert the solid model to a sheet metal model.

    b. Because many sheet metal features, such as Bends, can only be added between faces with uniform thickness.

    c. Without being set, the commands on the *Sheet Metal* tab are unavailable.

    d. You are not required to set the **Thickness** parameter.

3. Which of the following commands can be used on a solid model that has been converted to sheet metal to enable flattening? (Select all that apply.)

    a. **Face**

    b. **Bend**

    c. **Corner Seam**

    d. **Corner Round**

4. When a Flat Pattern is created what happens to areas on a sheet metal part that require deformation for flattening?

   a. Areas that require deformation are flattened in the same way as all other sheet metal features.

   b. Areas that require deformation are not flattened. They remain 3D.

   c. The Flat Pattern feature creation cannot be added to the model.

   d. You are prompted with a dialog box that indicates you must recreate the deformed area on the model.

5. Flat Patterns in a sheet metal model are 3D and have thickness.

   a. True

   b. False

Command Summary

Button	Command	Location
	Convert to Sheet Metal	• **Ribbon:** *3D Model* tab>Convert panel
	Create Flat Pattern	• **Ribbon:** *Sheet Metal* tab>Flat Pattern panel
	Sheet Metal Defaults	• **Ribbon:** *Sheet Metal* tab>Setup panel

Sheet Metal Rules

Each Autodesk® Inventor® sheet metal part file contains one or more Sheet Metal Rules. The default rule that is initially assigned is stored in the template that is used to create the sheet metal model. Once the file is created, this rule can be changed. When you work with sheet metal part files, the current rule automatically applies specific properties to the models. For example, the active rule would apply a uniform thickness and material type for all faces in the part. If you change to a different style, the thickness and material properties for that style are automatically applied.

Learning Objectives in this Appendix

- Launch the Sheet Metal Defaults dialog box and identify the sheet metal default settings and rules that are set in the active sheet metal model.
- Access the Styles and Standards dialog box to review, activate, and manipulate the rules that are available in the active sheet metal model.
- Customize a rule's option using the Sheet, Bend, and Corner tabs in the Styles and Standards dialog box.
- Customize a sheet metal rule so that it uses a Bend Table to calculate how the dimensions of the Flat Pattern are determined when unfolded.
- Create a Bend Table by importing or entering the bend table data in the Styles and Standard editor.

A.1 Working with Sheet Metal Rules

Sheet metal rules control the default settings for a sheet metal part. Each rule sets the material type and part thickness as well as sheet, bend, and corner options.

You can change some of the rule options for individual features, such as the bend relief shape, when creating or editing the features. However, to change other settings, such as *Thickness*, you must change the defaults in the Sheet Metal Defaults dialog box, in the Style and Standard Editor, or change the parameter settings in the Parameters dialog box.

The Sheet Metal Defaults dialog box lists the current rule driving the model and any other available rules in its drop-down list, as shown in Figure A–1. To access this dialog box, in the *Sheet Metal* tab>Setup panel, click 🔲 (Sheet Metal Defaults). Using this dialog box you can click 🗹 next to the Sheet Metal Rule to open the Style and Standard Editor to edit the rule.

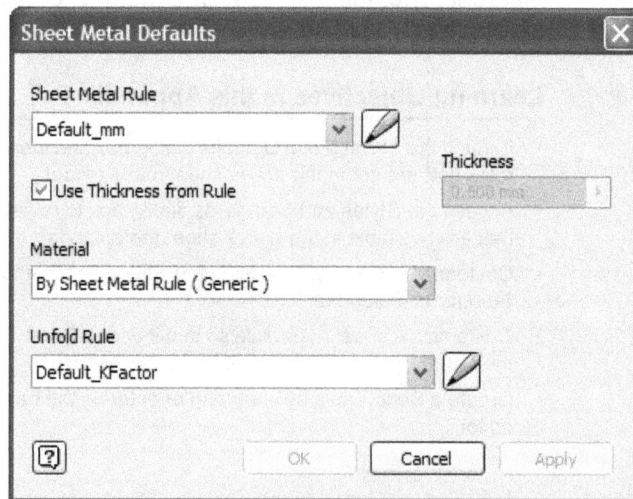

Sheet Metal Defaults

Sheet Metal Rule

Default_mm

☑ Use Thickness from Rule

Thickness

0.500 mm

Material

By Sheet Metal Rule (Generic)

Unfold Rule

Default_KFactor

OK   Cancel   Apply

Figure A–1

Rule List

The left side of the Style and Standard Editor displays all of the available rules defined in the current part (IPT) file, as shown in Figure A–2. You can select one of the styles and alter its settings in the *Sheet*, *Bend*, or *Corner* tabs.

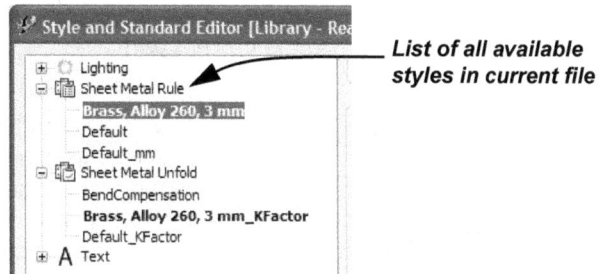

List of all available
styles in current file

Figure A–2

Setting the Active Rule

To assign a rule for a model, you can either right-click on the required rule in the Style and Standard Editor and select **Active**, or you can select the rule in the drop-down list in the Sheet Metal Defaults dialog box, as shown in Figure A–3.

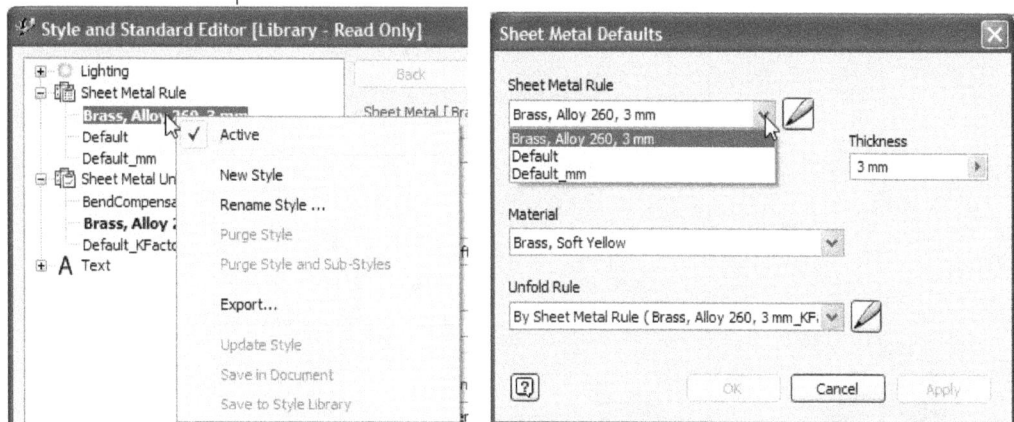

Figure A–3

Each of the standard sheet metal templates contain default rules. Although you can easily change settings in the Default styles, it is recommended that you create one or more new styles with unique parameter settings. Then you can select one of the styles to make it active and apply its settings to the part.

Because rules are saved in the individual part files, it is good practice to create and save the company standard styles in a template file stored in the Autodesk® Inventor® templates folder. Doing so means they are available for everyone to work with that template.

Modifying Existing Rules

During the design process you might need to alter an existing rule in an individual part file to change one or two of the settings. To modify a rule, select the rule name from the list in the Style and Standard Editor. Use the *Sheet*, *Bend*, or *Corner* tabs as required to change the settings. Click **Save** to apply the changes. If the style is the Active Style, the changes are applied to the current part.

Creating a New Sheet Metal Rules

To create a new rule, click **New** and enter a new name. Apply new settings as required in the *Sheet*, *Bend*, and *Corner* tabs. The default settings in these tabs are based on the rule that was selected when you clicked **New**. Click **Save**. After creating a new rule you can make it current to apply it to your part.

Deleting Sheet Metal Rules

Unused rules can be deleted from the part file in two ways. First, highlight the rule name in the list in the Style and Standard Editor, right-click, and select **Purge Style**. If a style is already in use when you try to delete it, the **Purge Style** option is not available in the menu.

A.2 Sheet, Bend, and Corner Tab Options

The three tabs in the Style and Standard Editor enable you to change settings to customize the sheet metal model's behavior during creation.

Sheet Tab

The options in the *Sheet* tab enable you to set defaults for the Sheet, Unfolding Rule, Flat Pattern Bend Angle, and Flat Pattern Punch Representations, as shown in Figure A–4.

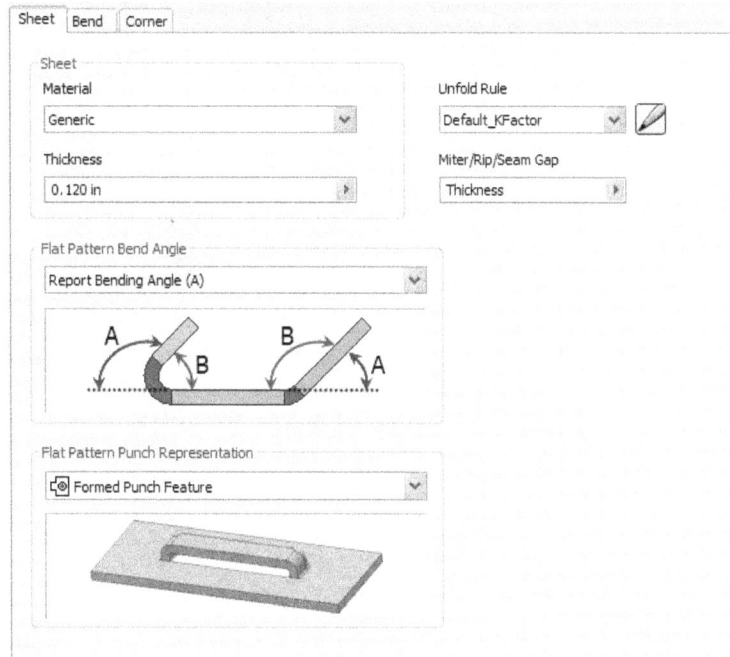

Figure A–4

Sheet Settings

Changing the Material in the Sheet Metal Defaults dialog box or iProperties dialog box overrides the setting for that part, but does not affect the rule.

Sheet settings include the *Material* type and its *Thickness* value. Select a material for the rule from a list of available types. The *Thickness* option sets the thickness of the material and populates the **Thickness** parameter for the model. You cannot change the *Thickness* value in the Parameters dialog box. In the Sheet Metal Defaults dialog box you can define whether the rule drives the *Thickness* value or whether it is driven by a value in this dialog box.

Unfold Rule

The *Unfold Rule* can be assigned using the drop-down list in this area. To create a new Unfold Rule, click [✐] next to the current Unfolding Rule. The fields enable you to edit the Unfold Method, KFactor Value, and Spline Factor. The *Unfold Method* controls how the Flat Pattern length of the part is calculated. Options include **Linear**, **Bend Table**, or **Custom Equation**, as shown in Figure A–5.

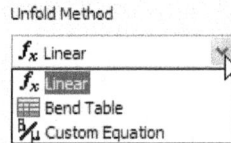

Figure A–5

- If **Linear** is specified, you assign a K factor value. When a bend is created, the inside surface of the material is compressed and the outside surface of the material is stretched. The K factor specifies the location (as a percentage of the thickness) along the thickness where the material neither stretches nor compresses, as shown in Figure A–6. This location, called the *neutral axis,* is different for different materials. Knowing its value enables the flat length of the part to be calculated. Therefore, changing the K factor affects the unfolded or flat length of the part.

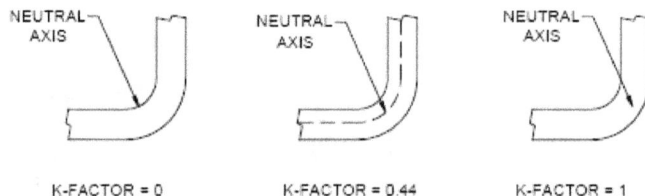

K-FACTOR = 0   K-FACTOR = 0.44   K-FACTOR = 1

Figure A–6

- If you switch the *Unfold Method* type to **Bend Table** you can define the Bend Table.

- Using the **Custom Equation** unfold method, you can define an unfold rule with a custom equation.

How To: Define a Custom Equation for an Unfold Rule

*Alternatively, you can access the Style and Standard Editor using the **Sheet Metal Defaults** option.*

1. Select the *Manage* tab>Style and Standard panel and click

   (Styles Editor).
2. Select an existing Sheet Metal Unfold rule or create a new rule.
3. Select **Custom Equation** in the Unfold Method drop-down list. The Style and Standard Editor dialog box updates as shown in Figure A–7.

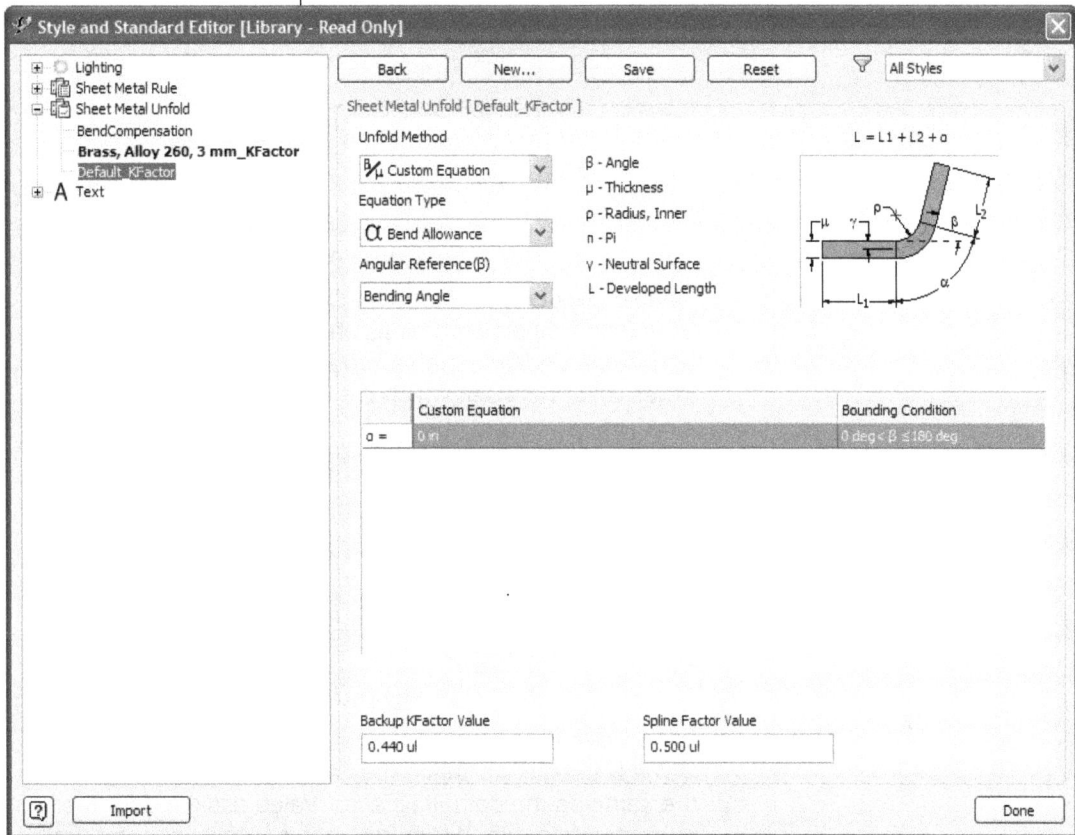

Figure A–7

*For more in-depth descriptions on the equation types, enter **Custom Unfold Equations** as the keyword search in Autodesk Inventor Help.*

4. Select an equation type: α (**Bend Allowance**), $\vee$ (**Bend Compensation**), δ (**Bend Deduction**), or $\mathcal{K}$ (**Kfactor**). The equation type determines the variable that is being solved for in the custom equation (α, $\vee$, δ, or $\mathcal{K}$).

5. Select an angular reference option: **Bending Angle** or **Open Angle**. This option specifies how the angular reference β is measured.

6. Double-click on the *Custom Equation cell* to open the Equation Edit dialog box, as shown in Figure A–8. Enter the custom equation using the variable icons along the top of the dialog box, and/or using mathematical operators, parentheses, numerics, etc., as required. Click **OK** to complete the equation.

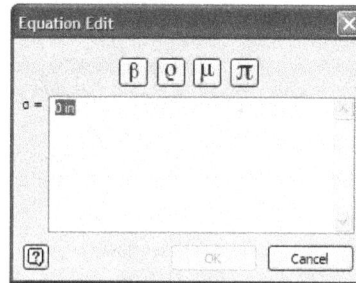

Figure A–8

7. Double-click on the *Bounding Condition cell* to open the Bounding Edit dialog box, as shown in Figure A–9. A bounding condition enables you to provide an upper and lower value between which the equation is valid.

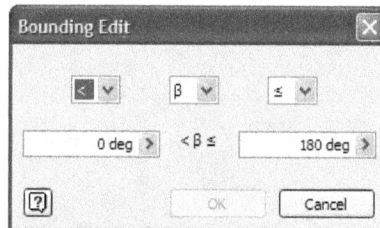

Figure A–9

8. If the *Bounding Condition* is not met, the *Backup KFactor Value* is used to calculate the flat geometry. By default, this is the same as the default KFactor Value assigned for the current unfold rule. If required, enter a new value for the *Backup KFactor Value*.

9. Modify the *Spline Factor Value*, as required. By default, the value is **0.5**. You can modify this value to affect the flattened size of contour flanges, contour rolls, and lofted flanges that have elliptical or spline segments in their profiles.

10. Once you have fully defined the custom equation, click **Save** and **Done** to close the Style and Standard Editor dialog box.

*Default sheet metal templates contain an unfold rule called **Bend Compensation** using a custom equation.*

Flat Pattern Bend Angle

The Bend Angle reporting method for a drawing can be controlled, as shown in Figure A–10.

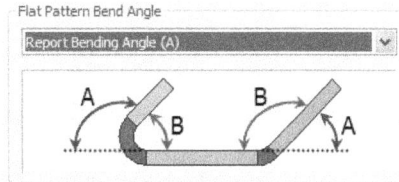

Figure A–10

The Bend Angle reporting options include the following:

- **Reporting on Bending Angle (A)**

- **Reporting on Open Angle (B)**

Selecting one or the other enables you to report a bend angle in the drawing that is measured from the inside (**Reporting on Bending Angle (A)**) or outside (**Reporting on Open Angle (B)**).

Flat Pattern Punch Representations

There are four **Flat Pattern Punch Representation** options, as shown in Figure A–11.

*The default setting can be overridden for individual parts using the **Edit Flat Pattern Definition** tool.*

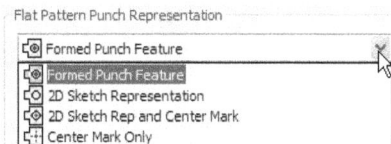

Figure A–11

The Flat Pattern Punch Representations are as follows:

- ⬛ **(Formed Punch Feature):** Displays Sheet Metal Punch iFeatures in the Flat Pattern as three-dimensional features as shown in Figure A–12.

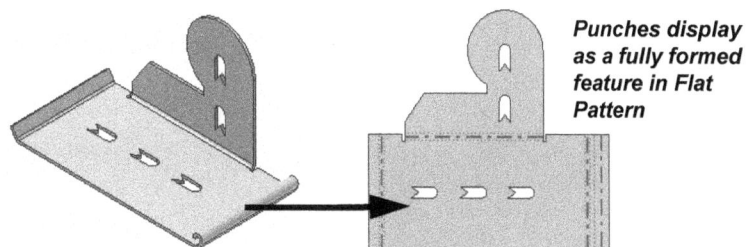

Punches display as a fully formed feature in Flat Pattern

Figure A–12

- ⬚ **(2D Sketch Representation):** Enables the display of Sheet Metal Punch iFeatures in the Flat Pattern as a 2D sketch of the feature. The 2D sketch must be defined in the Sheet Metal Punch iFeature. An example is shown in Figure A–13 using the simple rectangular sketch assigned when the iFeature was created.

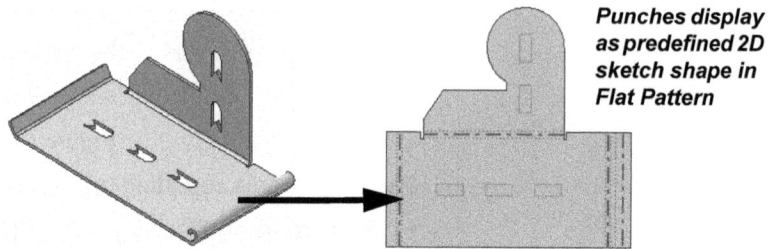

Punches display as predefined 2D sketch shape in Flat Pattern

Figure A–13

- ⬚ **(2D Sketch Rep and Center Mark):** Displays Sheet Metal Punch iFeatures in the Flat Pattern as a previously defined 2D sketch and center mark. An example is shown in Figure A–14.

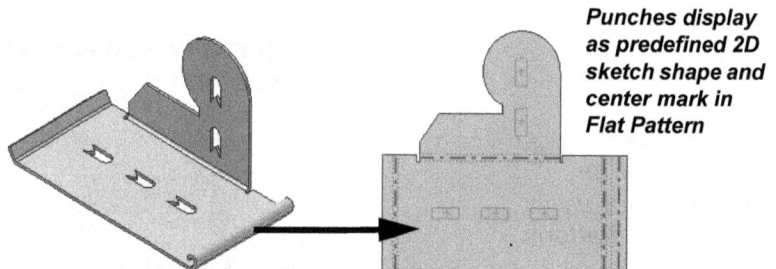

Punches display as predefined 2D sketch shape and center mark in Flat Pattern

Figure A–14

- ⬚ **(Center Mark Only):** Displays Sheet Metal Punch iFeatures in the Flat Pattern as a sketched center mark. An example is shown in Figure A–15.

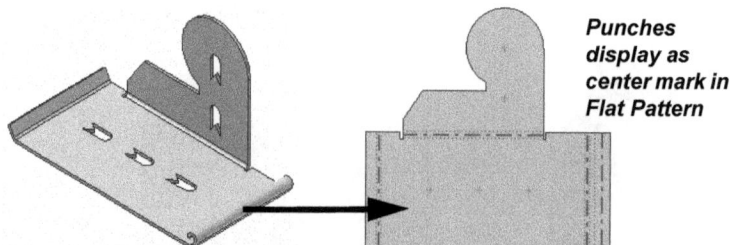

Punches display as center mark in Flat Pattern

Figure A–15

Bend Tab

The options in the *Bend* tab enable you to set the *Bend Relief*, *Bend Radius*, and *Bend Transition* settings as shown in Figure A–16.

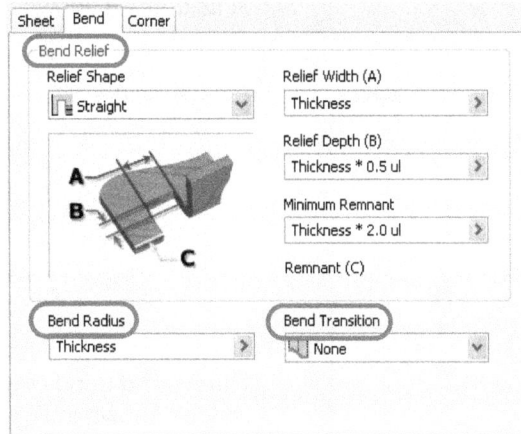

Figure A–16

Bend Relief

When a sheet metal part is bent to create a secondary feature, a small amount of material is often removed to enable clearance between the edges of the new feature and the existing feature as they are folded. This is called *Bend Relief*.

The default *Relief Shape*, *Relief* Width, and *Relief Depth* setting are assigned in the Sheet Metal Rule. These can be overridden in the *Bend* tab for individual features. The *Relief Width* and *Relief Depth* are controlled by parameter values. Figure A–17 shows the options for *Bend Relief* shapes that are supported: **Tear**, **Round**, and **Straight**.

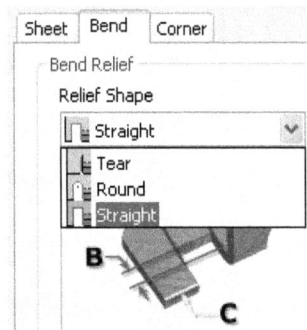

Figure A–17

The same part can often be made with any of the three bend relief shapes.

- The default bend relief shape is **Straight**. It has a square cut at its end, as shown in Figure A–18.

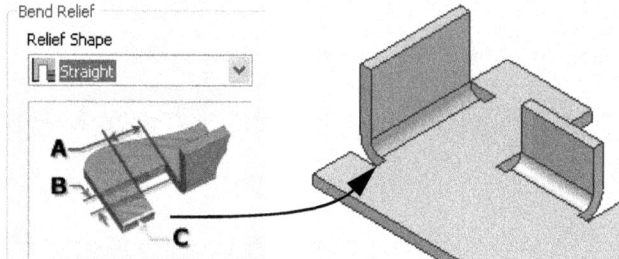

Figure A–18

- The **Round** bend relief shape has a full radius curve cut at its end, as shown in Figure A–19.

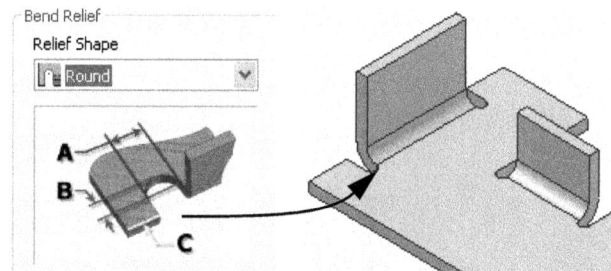

Figure A–19

- The **Tear** bend relief shape does not have any material removed. It is created by a material failure when the bend is created, as shown in Figure A–20.

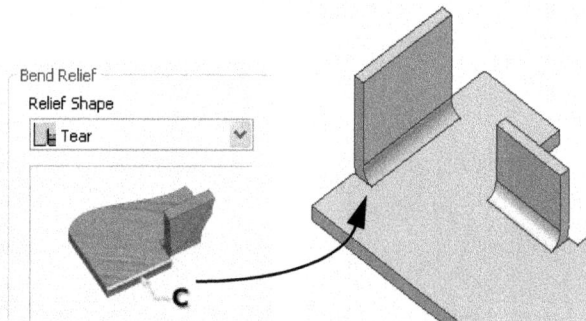

Figure A–20

Size settings for *Relief Width*, *Relief Depth*, and *Minimum Remnant* are typically dependent on the **Thickness** parameter. Figure A–21 shows how they are applied.

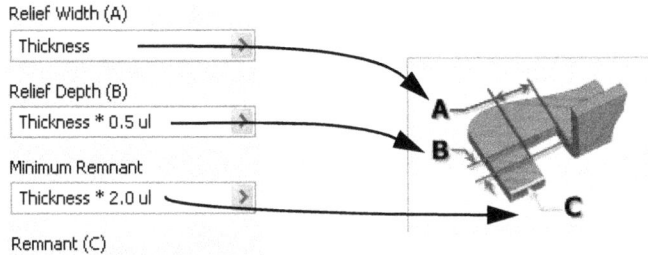

Figure A–21

Minimum Remnant

When a secondary feature is added, it might not run along the entire length of an existing edge. If the new feature is shorter than the edge, there is a distance left over between the new feature and the existing feature. This is called a *remnant*, as shown in Figure A–22.

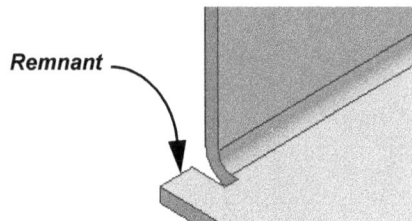

Figure A–22

If the remnant is too small, it is likely to break off or bend. The **MinimumRemnant** parameter is set so that when the remnant is less than a preset value, it is simply removed as if you had cut it off when making the part. By default, the **MinimumRemnant** is set to **Thickness *2.0 ul**, as shown in the Parameters dialog box in Figure A–23.

Parameter Name	Unit	Equation	Nominal Value
− Model Parameters			
Thickness	mm	0.25 mm	0.250000
BendRadius	mm	Thickness * 3 ul	0.750000
BendReliefWidth	mm	Thickness	0.250000
BendReliefDepth	mm	Thickness * 0.5 ul	0.125000
CornerReliefSize	mm	Thickness * 4 ul	1.000000
MinimumRemnant	mm	Thickness * 2.0 ul	0.500000

Figure A–23

In Figure A–24, a part is shown with a remnant that is larger than the required **MinimumRemnant**. Figure A–25 shows that the secondary Face has been edited and is closer to the edge of the base Face. Therefore, the **MinimumRemnant** has been cut away to avoid leaving a small area of metal sticking out.

Remnant larger than minimum required size remains 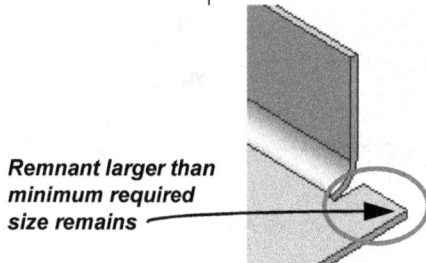   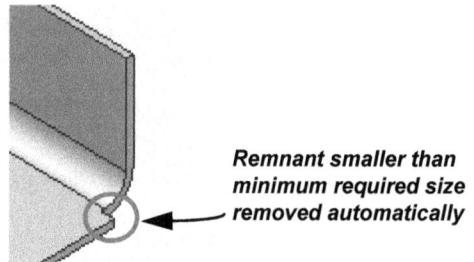 *Remnant smaller than minimum required size removed automatically*

Figure A–24   **Figure A–25**

Bend Radius

When you create a secondary face or contour flange, a Bend feature is added between the base feature and each secondary feature. This is added to accommodate fabrication of the part. For example, a sheet metal part has a defined uniform thickness. Therefore, when the flat sheet metal material is formed to create faces at angles to each other, an appropriate radius needs to be applied between the two faces. Otherwise, the part can split along a very sharp corner.

In general, the radius used for a bend is determined by the type and thickness of the material. A bend that is too sharp can cause the material to crack.

By default, the *Bend Radius* value is defined as having a value equal to the **Thickness**, as shown in Figure A–26.

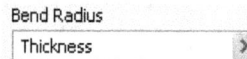

Figure A–26

If you change the *Bend Radius* value to **Thickness * 3**, it is applied to the parameter used in the *Bend* tab in the Sheet Metal Style, as shown in Figure A–27.

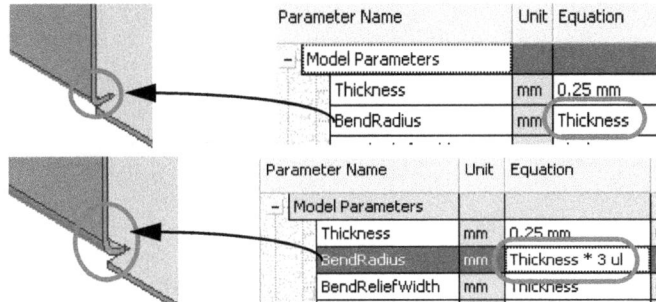

Parameter Name	Unit	Equation
− Model Parameters		
Thickness	mm	0.25 mm
BendRadius	mm	Thickness

Parameter Name	Unit	Equation
− Model Parameters		
Thickness	mm	0.25 mm
BendRadius	mm	Thickness * 3 ul
BendReliefWidth	mm	Thickness

Figure A–27

Bend Transition

Bend Transition controls the transition shape for a bend applied when a part is unfolded. This applies to parts with an angled edge that does not meet the bend at 90º, as shown in Figure A–28. It is used to represent the bend feature geometry in a flat pattern.

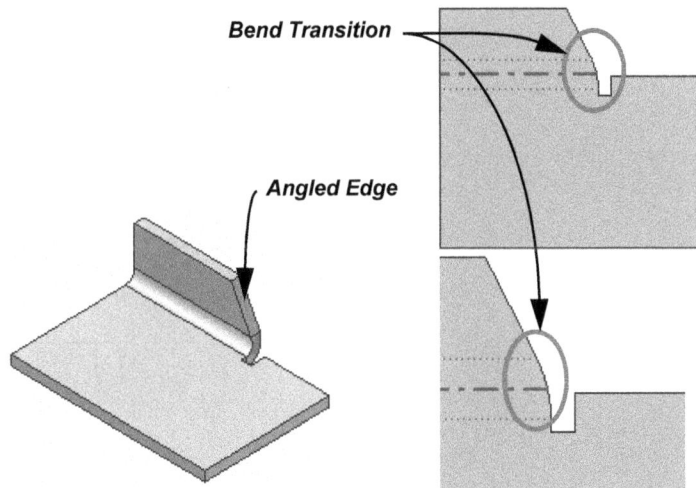

Bend Transition

Angled Edge

Figure A–28

Bend Transition shape options are shown in the drop-down list in Figure A–29.

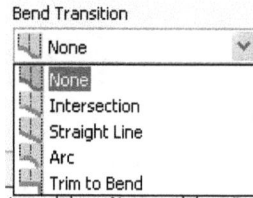

Figure A–29

- **(None):** A spline is applied between the two edges of the faces that meet at the bend feature. This type only displays in the flat pattern, as shown in Figure A–30.

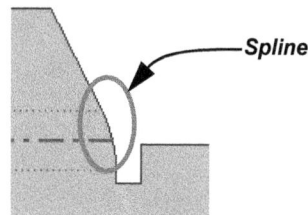

Figure A–30

- **(Intersection):** A straight line is applied from the edge of the bend zone to the edge of the bent feature. This type only displays in the flat pattern, as shown in Figure A–31.

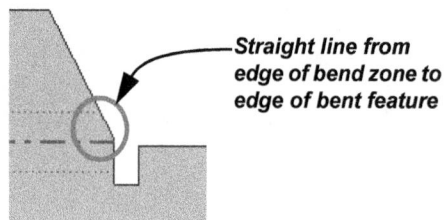

Figure A–31

- **(Straight Line):** A straight line is applied from one edge of the bend zone to the other. This can be similar to **Intersection**, depending on the shape of the model. This type only displays in the flat pattern, as shown in Figure A–32.

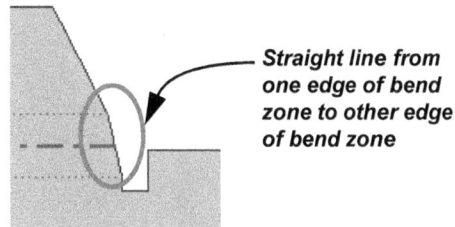

Straight line from one edge of bend zone to other edge of bend zone

Figure A–32

- **(Arc):** A radius value is required for the arc and an arc is created that is tangent to the edge of the bent feature and what would have been a straight transition. This type only displays in the flat pattern, as shown in Figure A–33.

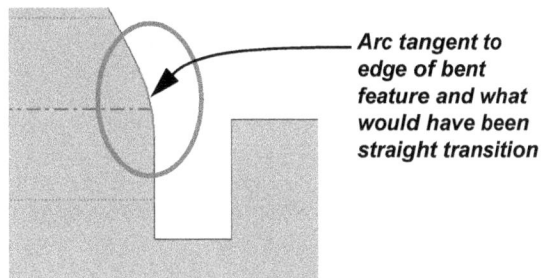

Arc tangent to edge of bent feature and what would have been straight transition

Figure A–33

- **(Trim to Bend):** A cut is applied to the bend zone, which is perpendicular to the bent feature. The Trim to Bend transition displays in the folded model as well as in the flat pattern, as shown in Figure A–34.

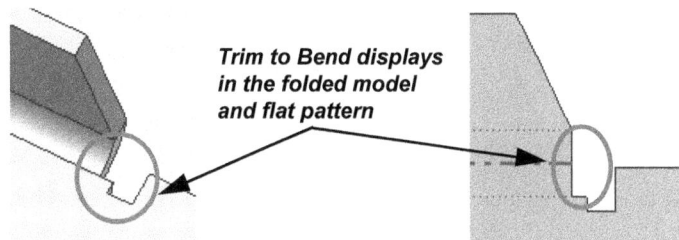

Trim to Bend displays in the folded model and flat pattern

Figure A–34

Corner Tab

When multiple Flanges are created on a flat sheet of metal where two or three bends meet, corner relief is often incorporated into the layout on the flat sheet of material before it is formed. The Corner Relief is a cut out shape that removes a small amount of material to prevent excess material at the intersection of the folded areas from intersecting and causing a bulge.

The *Corner* tab options include relief shapes and sizes for both *2 Bend Intersections* and *3 Bend Intersections,* as shown in Figure A–35.

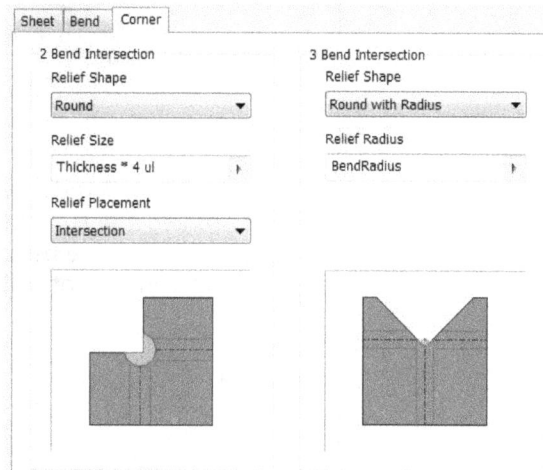

Figure A–35

Corner Relief is specified by default in the Sheet Metal Rule, but like many of the other settings they can also be modified through individual feature dialog boxes.

Corner Relief Shapes for 2 Bend Intersections

*The **Round** and **Square** Relief Shapes have additional **Relief Placement** options to control the position of the relief shape with respect to the corner.*

When an intersection occurs between two bends, one of six *Corner Relief* shapes can be applied. Each option defines the shape of the material that needs to be removed, while the sheet metal part is still flat. The six shapes are **Trim to Bend**, **Round**, **Square**, **Tear**, **Linear Weld**, and **Arc Weld**. You can override the default Corner Relief that was assigned in the Rule (**Trim to Bend**) using the *Corner* tab in the Flange dialog box (as shown in Figure A–36), or using the Sheet Metal Rule.

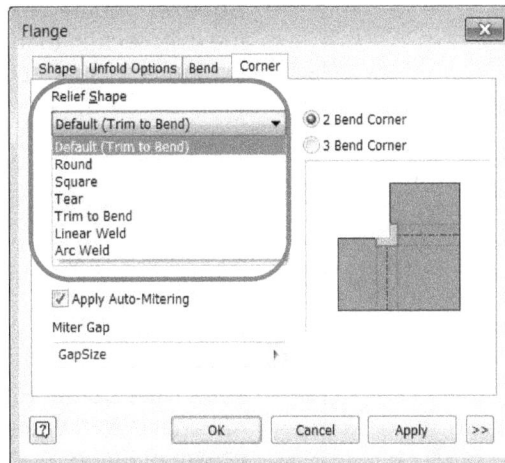

Figure A–36

- **Trim to Bend:** Default Corner Relief shape for 2 Bend Intersections (based on whether the default Rule is assigned). In the flat layout, this option is a polygonal cut out that is bounded by the bending zone lines, as shown in Figure A–37.

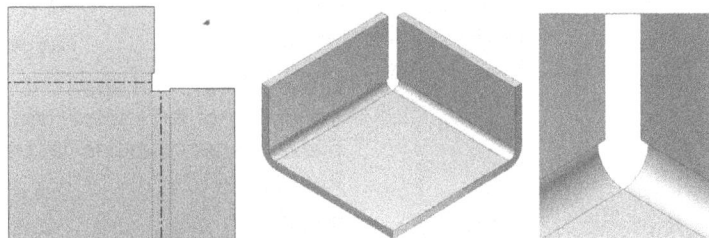

Figure A–37

- **Round:** Circular cut out Corner Relief. It can be centered at the intersection of the bend lines, as shown in the flat pattern in Figure A–38, tangent to flange edges, or positioned with its circumference on the vertex.

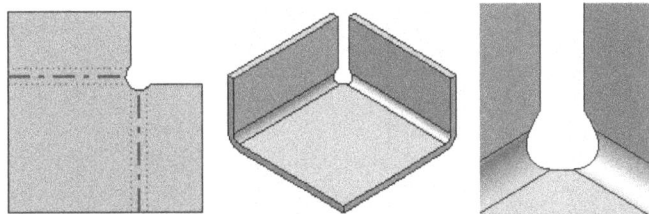

Figure A–38

- **Square:** Square cut out Corner Relief. It can be centered at the intersection of the bend lines, as shown in the flat pattern in Figure A–39, or positioned on the vertex.

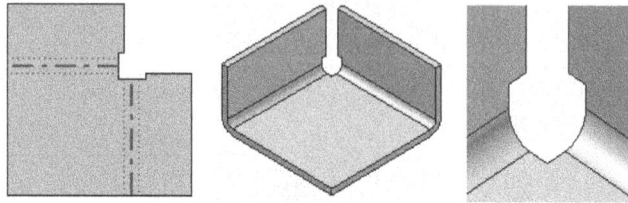

Figure A–39

- **Tear:** This Corner Relief is not a relief cut. It is simply that the material is torn at the intersection of the two bend lines, as shown in Figure A–40.

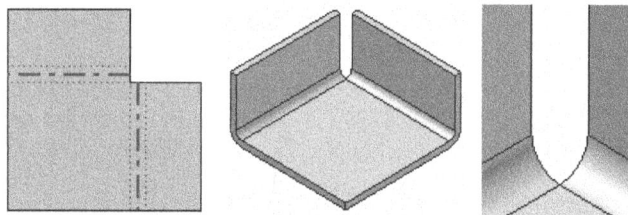

Figure A–40

- **Linear Weld:** V-shaped cut out Corner Relief. It is located at the center of the intersection of the two bend lines when the piece of sheet metal is flat before bending, as shown in Figure A–41.

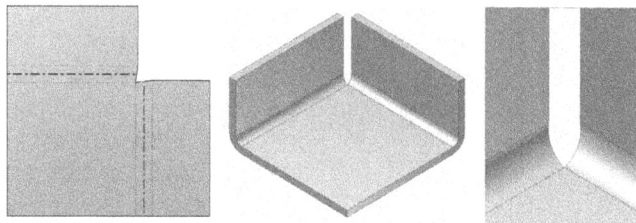

Figure A–41

- **Arc Weld:** Arc-shaped cutout Corner Relief. It is defined by curves tangent to the flange edges on the outer edge. The curves continue to a depth where the distance between the curves on each side is equal to the Miter Gap value when the piece of sheet metal is flat before bending, as shown in Figure A–42. This corner relief facilitates large radius bends.

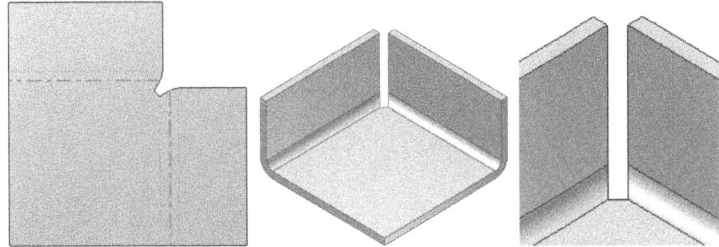

Figure A–42

Corner Relief Size

When any two Flanges or Contour Flanges meet at a two bend corner, a parameter called **CornerReliefSize** is applied. This parameter sets the space between the Flanges. **CornerReliefSize** is defined by the Sheet Metal Rule. The default setting is four times the **Thickness** parameter, as shown in Figure A–43.

Figure A–43

In Figure A–44, a part is shown with the default **CornerReliefSize** on the left and a **CornerReliefSize** on the right two times the default.

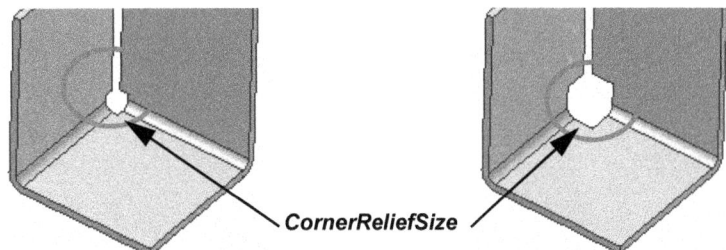

CornerReliefSize

Figure A–44

3 Bend Intersections

Where an intersection occurs between three bends, any one of four *Corner Relief* shapes can be applied to the Flat Pattern. Each is defined by the shape of the material that needs to be removed while the sheet metal part is still flat. The four shape options are: **No Replacement**, **Intersection**, **Full Round**, and **Round with Radius**, as shown in Figure A–45.

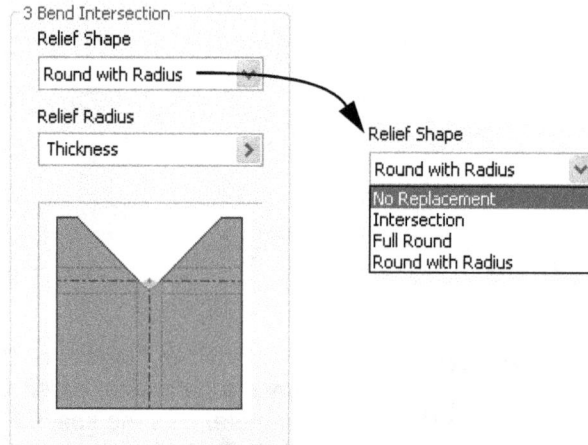

Figure A–45

Figure A–46 shows an example of a simple part with three bends meeting at a corner. The flat pattern is also shown.

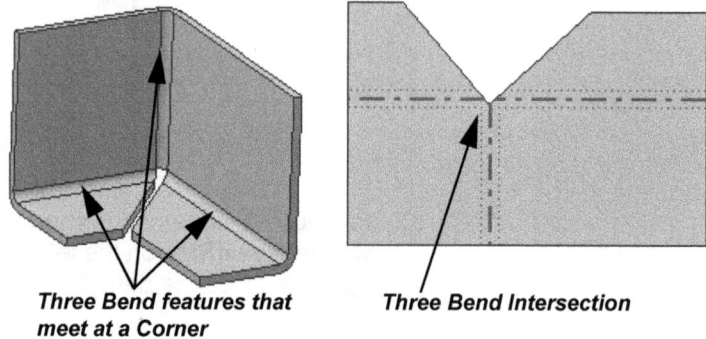

Three Bend features that meet at a Corner

Three Bend Intersection

Figure A–46

Each of the *3 Bend Intersection* relief shapes are described below:

- **No Replacement:** The true shape of the flat pattern is displayed as it was modeled in the folded part. It does not replace the geometry at the 3 Bend Intersection with a bend relief shape, as shown in Figure A–47.

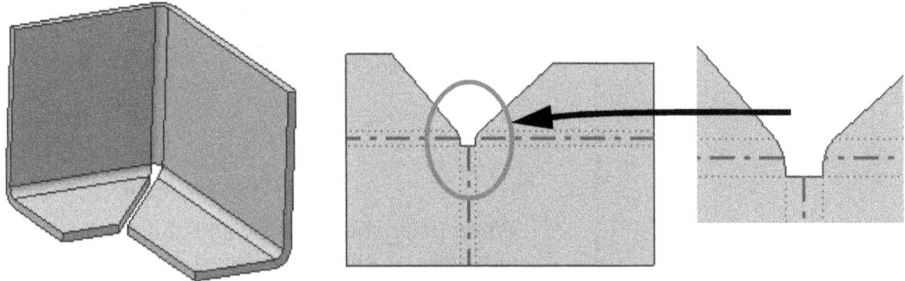

Figure A–47

- **Intersection:** A corner relief shape is created in the Flat Pattern by extending and intersecting the Flange edges, as shown in Figure A–48.

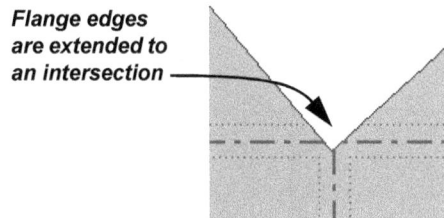

Flange edges are extended to an intersection

Figure A–48

- **Full Round:** A corner relief shape is created in the Flat Pattern by extending the Flange edges to their intersection and placing a fillet that is tangent to the bend zone tangency lines, as shown in Figure A–49. This option typically creates a larger radius than one created with the Round with Radius relief shape.

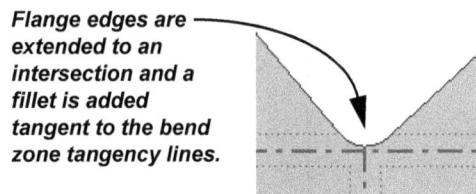

Flange edges are extended to an intersection and a fillet is added tangent to the bend zone tangency lines.

Figure A–49

- **Round with Radius:** A corner relief shape is created in the Flat Pattern by extending the Flange edges to their intersection and placing a fillet with a specified radius size, as shown in Figure A–50. The fillet radius would typically be smaller than one created with the **Full Round** option.

Flange edges are extended to an intersection and a fillet is added with a specified radius.

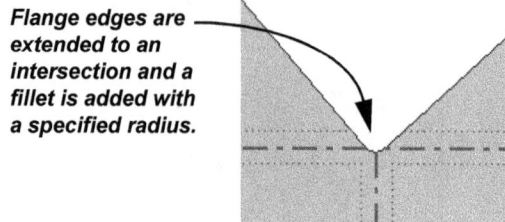

Figure A–50

When using the Round with Radius relief shape a size field is available as shown in Figure A–51. By default this is set to the **Thickness** parameter.

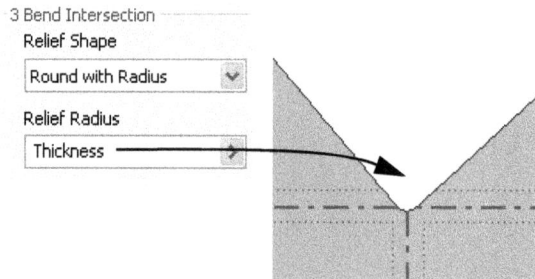

Figure A–51

A.3 Bend Tables

Bend Tables are normally used when manual measurements have been taken on a test fixture.

Materials react in different ways when bent, in terms of how much their surfaces are compressed or stretched, and the location of the neutral line. One way to approximate this behavior for a piece of material is to use the K factor. Another way is to select **Bend Table** in the *Unfold Method* area. Once done, a Bend Table is used to determine how the dimensions of the Flat Pattern are calculated for an unfolded model. A Bend Table varies the deformation of material dependent on the bend angle and bend radius.

Once the **Bend Table** option has been selected in the *Unfold Method*, the Style and Standard Editor updates as shown in Figure A–52 so that you can enter the required Bend Table information.

Figure A–52

To populate the information use one of the following:

- Manually enter the Bend Table data.

- Import a Bend Table file.

Manually Entering Bend Table Data

Select **Click here to add** in the *Thickness* area and enter the thickness value for the Bend Table. Multiple Bend Tables for various thicknesses can exist in a rule. Once a thickness has been added you can edit the table by entering values in the cells, right-click on column headers to add additional columns, and right-click on row headers to add additional rows.

Import a Bend Table File

Information for a Bend Table can be contained in a text file called a Bend Table file. It can be created with a text editor or spreadsheet. A single bend table file can contain multiple bend tables for various thicknesses.

To import data from a Bend Table file you can import a text file or copy and paste from a spreadsheet file, as follows:

- To add a new Sheet Metal Unfold style by importing a text file, click **Import** and select the .TXT file format in the Import style definition dialog box. Select and open the Bend Table file and enter a name for the table. Click **OK**. The data is imported for the number of thicknesses that are listed in the Bend Table text file.

- To copy and paste data from a spreadsheet file, select **Click here to add** in the *Thickness* area and enter the thickness value for the Bend Table you are adding. Open the Bend Table spreadsheet file and copy the cells detailing the Bend Table information for the entered thickness. Right-click on the empty *cell* in the top-left corner of the table area and select **Paste Table**.

Bend Table Format

The format for the layout of a bend table is shown in Figure A–53. Only a portion of the table is shown.

Unit of measure

Tolerance

Start of new table

Sheet thickness

Bend radii

Opening angle

```
Bend Table (mm).txt - Notepad
File  Edit  Format  View  Help
;UNITS for tolerance; thickness; bend radius and correction values
; use Autodesk Inventor standard units such as 'in' and 'mm'
/U      mm
;
;TOLERANCES valid for the whole file
;
/T1     0.000040
/T2     0.004000
/T3     0.004000
;
*** TABLE 1
;
;sheet thickness
/S      0.500000
;
;bending radii
/R          0.500000      1.000000      1.500000      2.000000      3.000
;opening angle: ---------------------- correction value x ----------
/A      1.000000      -0.069742     -0.749369     -1.380206     -1.991066
/A      5.000000      -0.023491     -0.665585     -1.259978     -1.834841
/A     10.000000       0.034323     -0.560854     -1.109693     -1.639560
/A     15.000000       0.092137     -0.456123     -0.959408     -1.444279
/A     20.000000       0.149951     -0.351392     -0.809123     -1.248998
/A     25.000000       0.207765     -0.246661     -0.658837     -1.053717
/A     30.000000       0.265579     -0.141930     -0.508552     -0.858435
/A     35.000000       0.323393     -0.037199     -0.358267     -0.663154
/A     40.000000       0.381207      0.067532     -0.207982     -0.467873
```

Figure A–53

A semicolon (;) at the beginning of a line indicates that it contains a comment.

When sending drawings to a sheet metal shop, you normally send a dimensioned drawing of the part model. The sheet metal shop usually wants to calculate the flat pattern based on their manufacturing processes.

Bend Table Information

A bend table contains the following information:

*   A new table must start with an asterisk (*).

*   **Unit of measure:** Used for the tolerance, sheet thickness, and bend radii. It is designated by a line that begins with **/U**.

*   **Sheet thickness:** Thickness of the material. It is designated by a line that begins with **/S**.

*   **Tolerance:** Specifies the tolerances for the whole file. There are three tolerances, designated **/T1**, **/T2**, and **/T3**. They designate the tolerance for sheet thickness, tolerance for minimum and maximum bending radius, and tolerance for minimum and maximum opening angle.

*   **Bend radii:** Specifies the bend radius for the part. It is designated by **/R**.

*   **Opening Angle:** The angle at which the tolerance is applied. The angle is expressed in degrees. It is designated by **/A**.

Practice A1 | Sheet Metal Styles

Practice Objectives

- Create a new sheet metal style by copying an existing style, assigning it to the model, and making changes to it.
- Compare how material thickness and unfold settings can vary the unfolded size of a model.

In this practice, you will create a new Sheet Metal Rule and modify an existing one to modify the model as shown in Figure A–54. You will determine the differences in the model by recording dimension values in the table at the end of the practice. When creating the rule, you will modify the material and thickness. You will then modify it to change the K factor, bend shape, relief width, and relief depth.

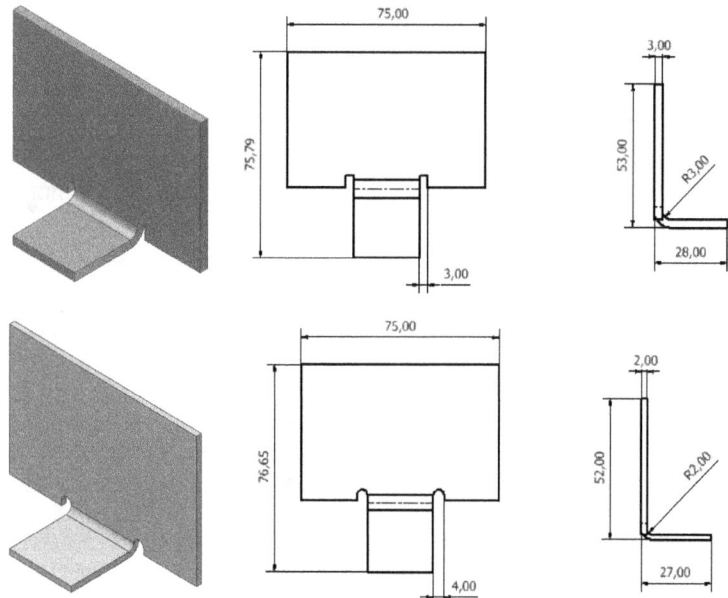

Figure A–54

Task 1 - Investigate a Sheet Metal Style.

1. Open **Styles.ipt**.

2. In the *Sheet Metal* tab>Setup panel, click (Sheet Metal Defaults) to open the Sheet Metal Defaults dialog box, as shown in Figure A–55. The current style is **Brass, Alloy 260, 3 mm**. The *Material Style* is **Brass, Soft Yellow**. The *Thickness* is driven independent of the rule and is set to **3 mm**.

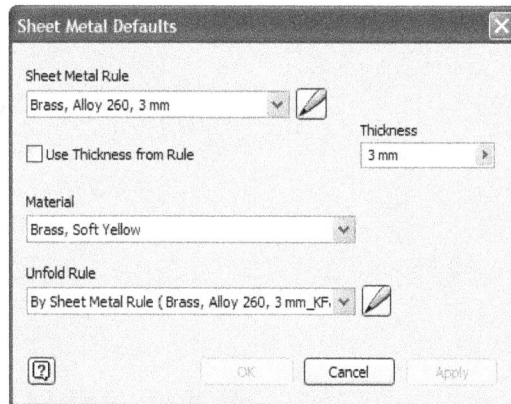

Figure A–55

3. Click next to the Sheet Metal Rule.

4. The Style and Standards dialog box opens. Select the *Bend* tab. The *Relief Shape* is **Straight** and the *Relief Width (A)* is set to **Thickness**, as shown in Figure A–56.

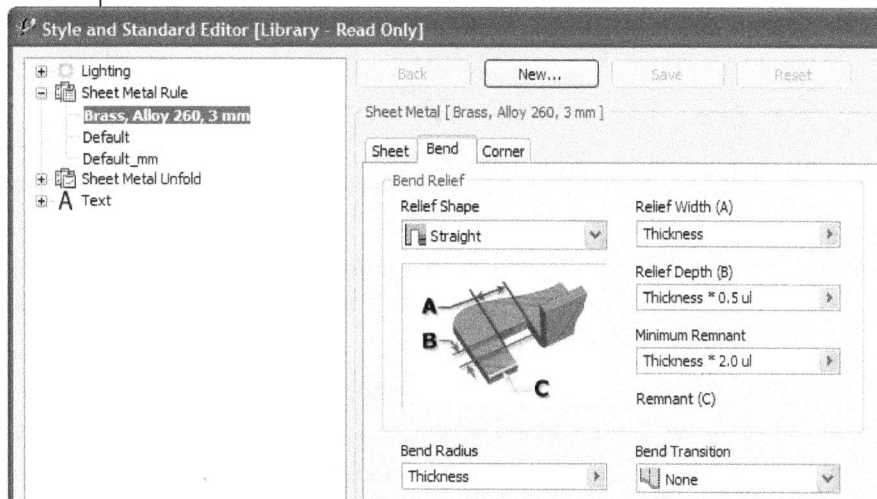

Figure A–56

5. Close both dialog boxes.

Task 2 - Open a sheet metal drawing.

1. Open the file **Styles.idw**. It contains 2D views: a view of the flat pattern and a side view of the folded model, as shown in Figure A–57.

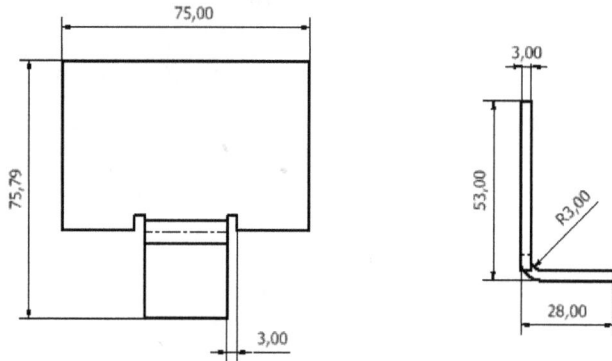

Figure A–57

2. Write the values for the dimensions in the table at the end of the practice.

Task 3 - Create a new sheet metal style.

1. Return to the file **Styles.ipt**.

2. In the *Sheet Metal* tab>Setup panel, click (Sheet Metal Defaults) to open the Sheet Metal Defaults dialog box.

3. Click next to the Sheet Metal Rule.

4. In the Style and Standard Editor dialog box, click **New**. A copy of the existing style called **Copy of Brass, Alloy 260, 3 mm** is created.

5. Change the name to **Aluminum, Alloy 6061, 2 mm** and click **OK**. The style is added to the Sheet Metal Rule list.

6. In the *Sheet* tab, change the *Material* to **Aluminum-6061** and the *Thickness* to **2 mm**.

7. Click **Save and Done** to save the changes and close the Style and Standard Editor.

8. In the *Sheet Metal Rule* drop-down list, select **Aluminum, Alloy 6061, 2 mm**. Enable the **Use Thickness from Rule** option so that the defined 2 mm *Thickness* is maintained.

9. Click **OK** to close the Sheet Metal Defaults dialog box.

10. Save the file.

11. Return to **Styles.idw**. The dimension values update with the changes to the model as shown in Figure A–58. The material thickness, bend radius, and bend relief width update with the new thickness value in the style. The change in width and length are attributed to the change in thickness. The overall width of the part does not change as is not dependent on the thickness of the material.

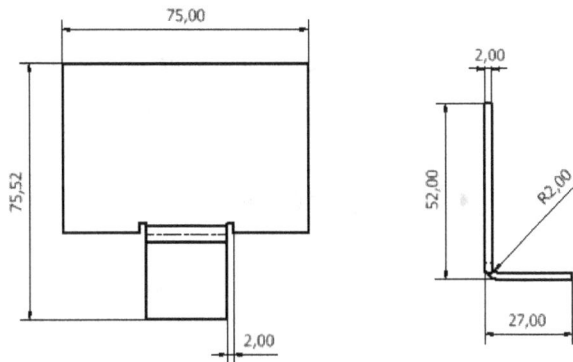

Figure A–58

12. Record the dimension values in the second column of the table at the end of the practice.

Task 4 - Modify a sheet metal style.

1. Return to **Styles.ipt**.

2. In the *Sheet Metal* tab>Setup panel, click (Sheet Metal Defaults) to open the Sheet Metal Defaults dialog box.

3. Ensure that **Aluminum, Alloy 6061, 2 mm** is set as the default Sheet Metal Rule.

4. Click next to the Sheet Metal Rule.

5. In the Style and Standard editor, click next to the Unfold Rule. The Sheet Metal Unfold settings display.

6. Click **New** to add a new Sheet Metal Unfold style. Change the name to **KFactor 0.8** and click **OK**.

7. Change the *KFactor Value* to **0.8 ul**. The Style and Standard Editor updates as shown in Figure A–59.

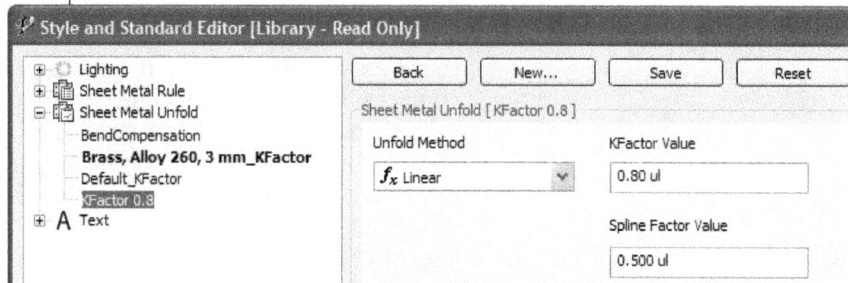

Figure A–59

8. Click **Save** at the top pf the dialog box to save the changes.

9. Select the **Aluminum, Alloy 6061, 2 mm** rule in the left column in the Style and Standard Editor.

10. Select the *Bend* tab. In the *Relief Shape* drop-down list, select **Round**.

11. Change the *Relief Width (A)* to **Thickness * 2 ul**. Change the *Relief Depth (B)* to **Thickness**. The Style and Standard Editor updates as shown in Figure A–60.

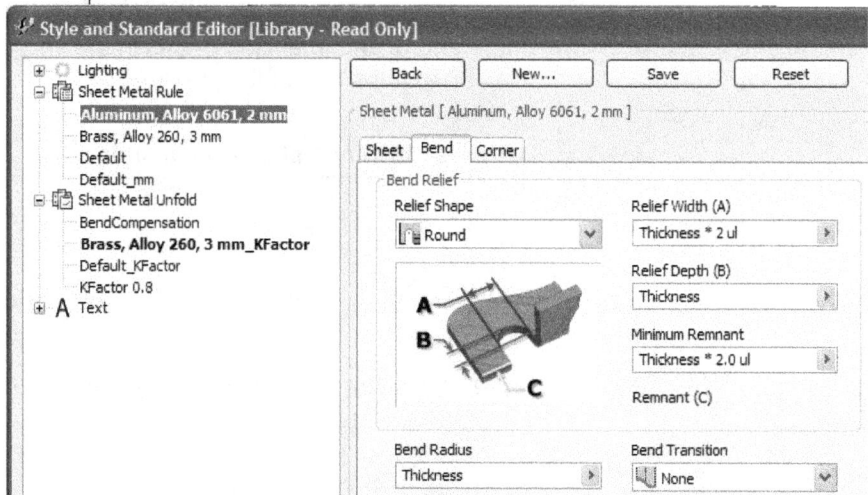

Figure A–60

12. Click **Save and Close** to close the Style and Standard Editor.

13. In the Unfold Rule drop-down list, select **KFactor 0.8**, if not already selected, and ensure that the **Aluminum, Alloy 6061, 2 mm** rule is still selected. Apply the change and close the dialog box.

14. Save the file.

15. Return to **Styles.idw**. The dimension values update with the changes to the model as shown in Figure A–61. The overall length of the part updates due to the change in the KFactor. The relief shape and size update according to the changes in the style.

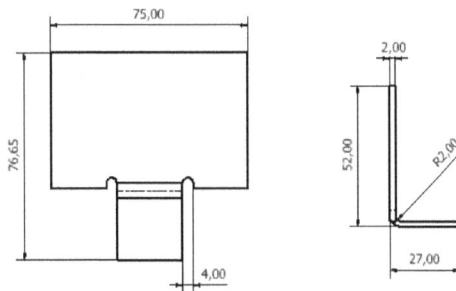

Figure A–61

16. Record the dimension values in the third column of the following table. Compare the values.

Description	Brass	Aluminum KFactor = 0.44	Aluminum KFactor = 0.8
Overall Length (Flat)			
Overall Width (Flat)			
Relief Width (Flat)			
Overall Length (Folded)			
Overall Width (Folded)			
Material Thickness			
Bend Radius (Folded)			

17. Save and close all files.

Practice A2

Bend Relief Options and Unfold Options

Practice Objectives

- Modify the Bend settings for the active sheet metal rule that is being used to drive the current sheet metal geometry.
- Modify the Unfold and Bend Relief settings for a individual feature so that they are controlled independently of the sheet metal rule.
- Review Flat pattern extent values to compare how changing the Unfold and Bend Radius settings affects the geometry.

In this practice, you will edit the Sheet Metal Rule for a part file, and override the options for a feature so that the model displays as shown in Figure A–62. You will first modify the Relief options, followed by editing the Unfold options and Bend options for an individual feature. Finally, you will modify the 3 Bend Intersection options in the rule and verify the changes in the flat pattern. You will also use Bend Extents to check the size of the flat pattern.

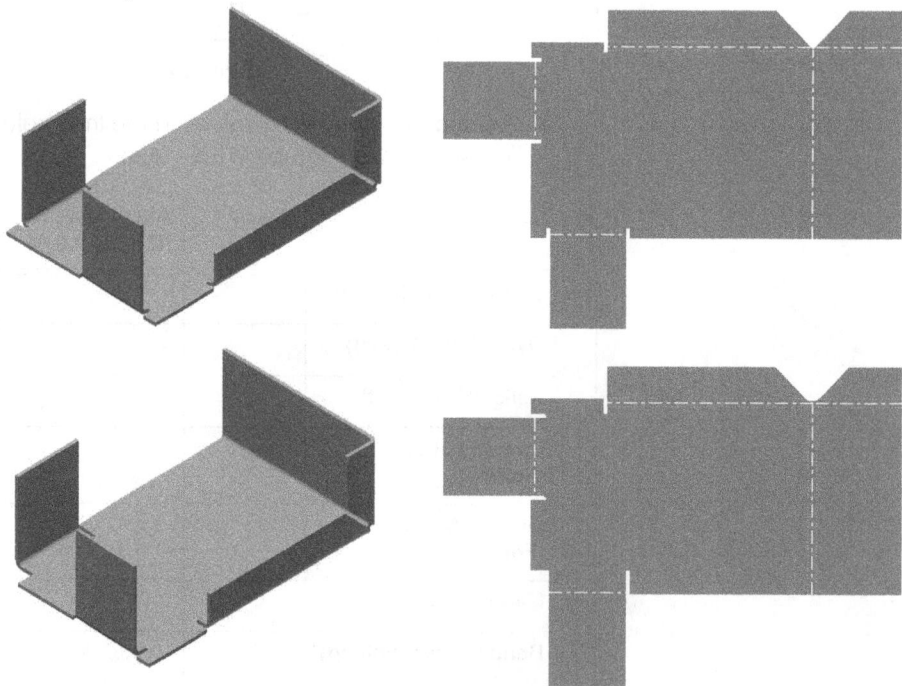

Figure A–62

Task 1 - Modify the Sheet Metal Rule.

1. Open **Options.ipt**.

2. In the *Sheet Metal* tab>Flat Pattern panel, click (Create Flat Pattern) to generate the flat pattern.

3. In the *Sheet Metal* tab>Setup panel, click (Sheet Metal Defaults) to open the Sheet Metal Defaults dialog box.

4. Click next to the Sheet Metal Rule.

5. Select the *Bend* tab.

6. Select **Round** in the *Relief Shape* drop-down list.

7. Change the *Relief Depth (B)* to **Thickness * 2 ul**.

8. Click **Save and Close** to close the Style and Standard Editor. Close the Sheet Metal Defaults dialog box. The bend reliefs shapes and depths update.

9. In the Model Browser, right-click on **Flat Pattern** and select **Extents**. The Flat Pattern Extents dialog box opens as shown in Figure A–63. Note the values and close the dialog box.

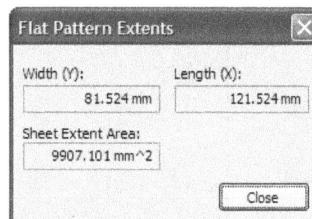

Flat Pattern Extents

Width (Y): 81.524 mm   Length (X): 121.524 mm

Sheet Extent Area: 9907.101 mm^2

Close

Figure A–63

Task 2 - Modify options on the feature level.

1. In the Model Browser, double-click on **Folded Model** to display the folded model.

2. In the Model Browser, right-click on **Flange1** and select **Edit Feature**. The Flange: Flange1 dialog box opens.

3. Select the *Unfold Options* tab.

4. Select **Default_KFactor 0.8** in the *Unfold Style* drop-down list.

5. Select the *Bend* tab.

6. Select **Straight** in the Relief Shape drop-down list, change the *Relief Depth (B)* to **BendReliefDepth * 2**, and change the *Minimum Remnant* to **5 mm**.

7. Click **OK** to accept the changes. The relief shape and depth are only updated for this feature. The remnant is also removed because its length was less than the minimum remnant for this feature as shown in Figure A–64.

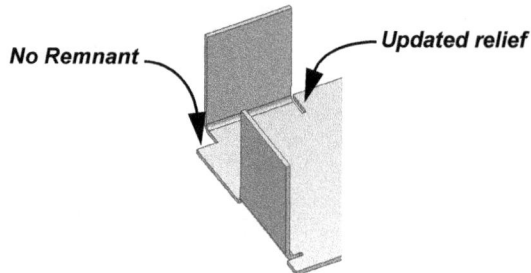

No Remnant ⟍   ⟋ *Updated relief*

Figure A–64

8. In the Model Browser, double-click on **Flat Pattern** to display the flat pattern. It has updated with the changes, as shown in Figure A–65.

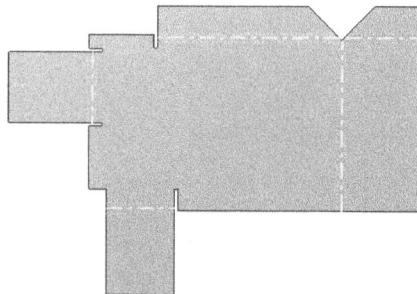

*Your orientation might vary. Consider right-clicking and selecting **Edit Flat Pattern Definition** for the Flat Pattern to reorient it, as required.*

Figure A–65

9. In the Model Browser, right-click on Flat Pattern and select **Extents**. The Flat Pattern Extents dialog box opens as shown in Figure A–66. The *Width* value has changed from 81.524 mm to 82.089 mm due to the modified K Factor.

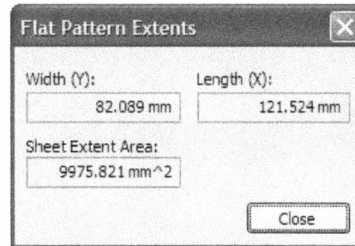

Figure A–66

10. Click **Close** to close the Flat Pattern Extents dialog box.

Task 3 - Change 3 Bend Options.

1. In the *Flat Pattern* tab>Manage panel, click (Sheet Metal Defaults) to open the Sheet Metal Defaults dialog box.

2. Click next to the Sheet Metal Rule.

3. Select the *Corner* tab.

4. In the *Relief Shape* drop-down list in the *3 Bend Intersection* area, select **Full Round**, as shown in Figure A–67.

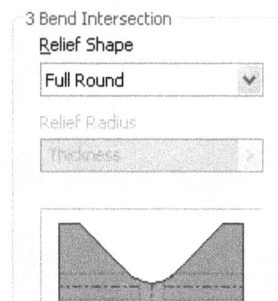

Figure A–67

5. Click **Save and Close** to close the Sheet Metal Defaults dialog box. The Flat Pattern displays as shown in Figure A–68.

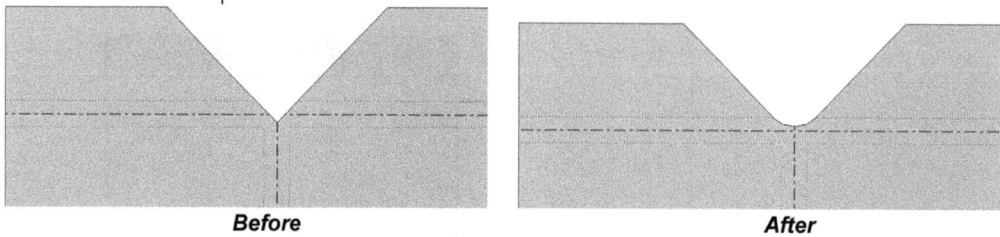

Before　　　　　　　　　　　　　　　　*After*

Figure A–68

6. In the Model Browser, double-click on **Folded Model** to display the folded model. You cannot save the file while editing the Flat Pattern.

7. Save and close the file.

Practice A3

Attaching a Bend Table

Practice Objectives

- Create a new sheet metal unfold rule that derives values based on an imported bend table.
- Create a new sheet metal unfold rule that derives values based on a bend table that is copied from a Microsoft Excel file.
- Review Flat pattern extent values to compare how changing the Unfold rule and Bend Radius value affects the geometry.

In this practice, you will change the Unfold Method to use a Bend Table. You will then modify the bend radius of a feature to use a value other then the default. To verify the changes in the model, you will use Flat Pattern Extents, as shown in Figure A–69.

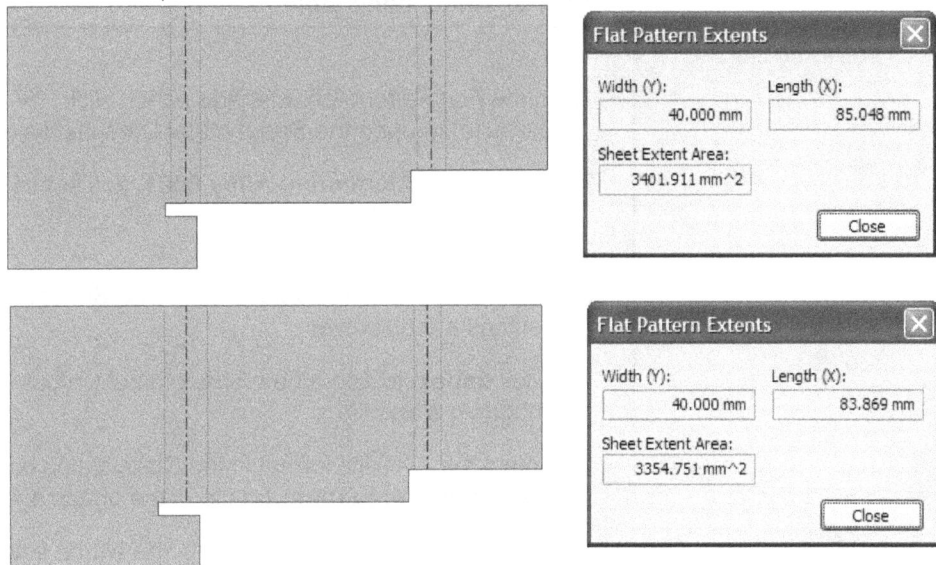

Figure A–69

Task 1 - Check the Flat Pattern Extents.

1. Open **Bendtable.ipt**.

2. In the Model Browser, double-click on **Flat Pattern** to display the flat pattern.

3. In the Model Browser, right-click on Flat Pattern and select **Extents**. The Flat Pattern Extents dialog box opens as shown in Figure A–70. Note the values for *Width* and *Length*.

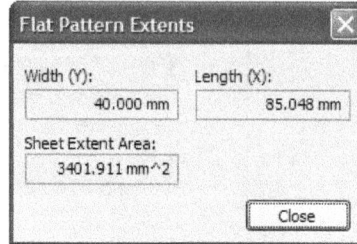

Figure A–70

4. Click **Close** to close the dialog box.

Task 2 - Add a bend table.

---

1. In the *Flat Pattern* tab>Manage panel, click (Sheet Metal Defaults) to open the Sheet Metal Defaults dialog box.

2. Ensure that **Aluminum, Alloy 6061, 2** is set as the default Sheet Metal Rule.

3. Click next to the Unfold Rule. The Sheet Metal Unfold settings are displayed.

4. Click **Import** to add a new Sheet Metal Unfold style by importing a text file.

5. Select the .TXT file format in the Open dialog box. Select and open **Bend Table (mm).txt** file in the practice files folder.

6. Enter **My Bend Table - txt file** in the *Name* field and click **OK**. The Bend Table data displays in the Style and Standard Editor. The data is imported for two thicknesses (**0.5** and **2.0**). Both of these tables existed in the .TXT file.

Alternatively you can also copy Bend Table information from an excel file. In the next steps you will create a Sheet Metal Unfold style using the excel data.

7. Select **Aluminum, Alloy 6061, 2_Kfactor** in the *Sheet Metal Unfold* area. This activates the style.

8. Click **New** to add a new unfold style.

9. Enter **My Bend Table - xls file** in the *Name* field and click **OK**. When a new style is created it duplicates the current style as the basis for the new one. If the **My Bend Table - txt file** style was active when you created the new style it would now display a populated table. It is recommended that you create new unfold styles based on styles that use the Linear Unfold Method and then add the Bend Table.

10. Select **Bend Table** in the Unfold Method drop-down list.

11. Select **millimeter (mm)** as the *Linear Unit* option.

12. Open **Bend Table (mm).xls** on your system using Excel. Scroll to row 67. The information that follows this line is for a 0.5 thickness. Copy all data in cells B70 through J107.

13. Return to the Autodesk Inventor software. Select **Click here to add** in the *Thickness* area. Enter **0.5** as the *Thickness* value, as shown in Figure A–71.

14. Right-click on the empty *cell* in the top-left corner of the table area and select **Paste Table**, as shown in Figure A–71.

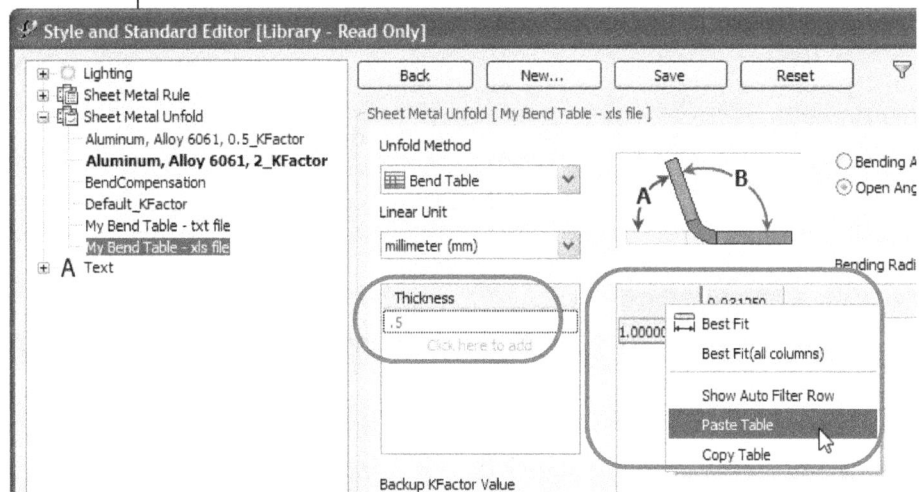

Figure A–71

15. In the Excel file, copy all data in cells B117 through J154. This is the information for the 2.0 thickness.

16. Return to the Autodesk Inventor software. Select **Click here to add** in the *Thickness* area. Enter **2.0** as the *Thickness* value. Right-click on the empty *cell* in the top-left corner of the table area and select **Paste Table**.

17. Click **Save** to save the changes.

18. Click **Save and Close** to close the Style and Standard Editor.

19. In the *Unfold Rule* drop-down list, select one of the two **My Bend Table** styles that you just created.

20. Click **OK** to assign the new Sheet Metal defaults.

21. The flat pattern becomes slightly smaller according to the values in the bend table. In the Model Browser, right-click on the **Flat Pattern** node and select **Extents**. The Flat Pattern Extents dialog box opens as shown in Figure A–72. Note the values for *Width* and *Length*.

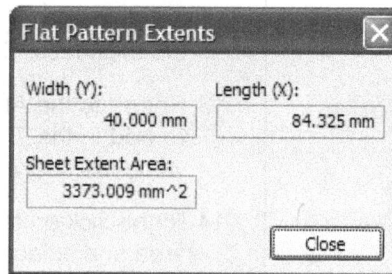

Flat Pattern Extents	☒
Width (Y):	Length (X):
40.000 mm	84.325 mm
Sheet Extent Area:	
3373.009 mm^2	
	Close

Figure A–72

22. Click **Close** to close the dialog box.

Task 3 - Modify the bend radius.

1. In the Model Browser, double-click on **Folded Model**.

2. In the Model Browser, right-click on **Face2** and select **Edit Feature**. The Face : Face2 dialog box opens.

3. Change the *Bend Radius* to **3.5 mm**. Click **OK**. The bend between **Face1** and **Face2** updates.

4. In the Model Browser, double-click on Flat Pattern to display the flat pattern. The bend extents on one bend is now larger than the bend extents on the other. This is because the bend radius is larger.

5. In the Model Browser, right-click on **Flat Pattern** node and select **Extents**. The Flat Pattern Extents dialog box opens as shown in Figure A–73. Note the values for *Width* and *Length*.

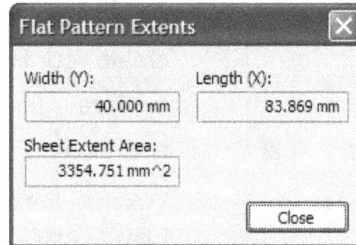

Figure A–73

6. Click **Close** to close the dialog box.

7. In the Model Browser, double-click on **Folded Model**.

8. Save and close the file.

Chapter Review Questions

1. The thickness of a new sheet metal model is determined based on the extruded distance that is entered when you create your first Face feature.

   a. True

   b. False

2. Which of the following statements are true about Sheet Metal rules? (Select all that apply.)

   a. The Sheet Metal rule must be created and assigned before creating the first sheet metal feature in the model.

   b. The Sheet Metal rule defines what the default material thickness is for the model.

   c. A sheet metal template file contains predefined rules as well as an assigned default rule.

   d. Sheet Metal rules only determine how a sheet metal model is flattened.

3. Which of the following is the active Rule (shown in Figure A–74) for the sheet metal model?

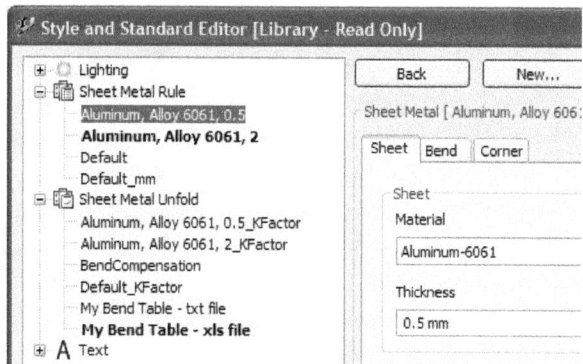

Figure A–74

   a. Aluminum, Alloy 6061, 0.5

   b. Aluminum, Alloy 6061, 2

   c. Default

   d. My Bend Table - xls file

4. Which of the following correctly explains how to change the Bend Relief shape from Straight to Round for a single Flange feature in multi-flange model?

   a. Right-click on the Flange in the Model Browser, click **Edit Feature**, select the *Bend* tab, and select **Round** in the *Relief Shape* drop-down list.

   b. In the Sheet Metal Defaults dialog box, click next to the Sheet Metal Rule, select the *Bend* tab, and select **Round** in the *Relief Shape* drop-down list.

   c. In the Manage tab, click to open the Styles and Standards editor, select the *Bend* tab, and select **Round** in the *Relief Shape* drop-down list.

   d. All of the above.

5. Which of the following can be used to define the rule for how a sheet metal model deforms when bent? (Select all that apply.)

   a. **Linear** (with a K factor)

   b. **Bend Table**

   c. **Custom Equation**

   d. **Flat Pattern Bend Angle**

Command Summary

Button	Command	Location
	Sheet Metal Defaults	• **Ribbon:** *Sheet Metal* tab>Setup panel
	Styles Editor	• **Ribbon:** *Manage* tab>Styles and Standards panel • *(Click ▨ next to the Sheet Metal Rule drop-down list in the Sheet Metal Defaults dialog box.)*

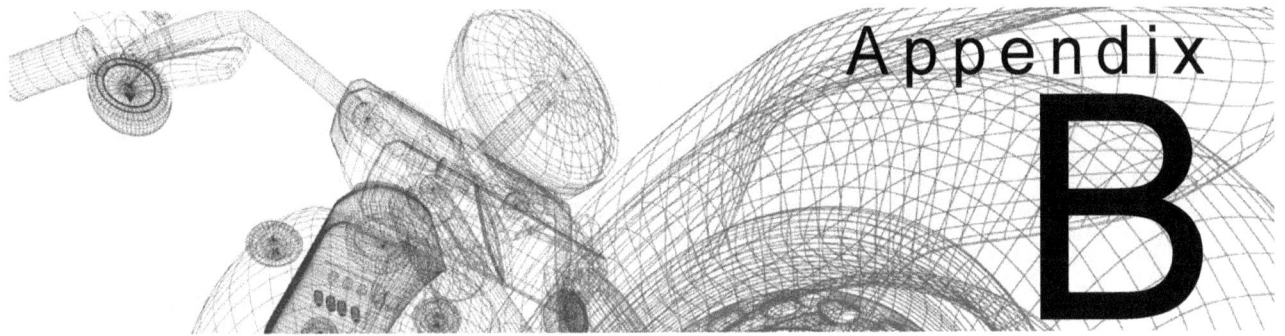

Appendix

B

Additional Practices

This appendix provides additional practices that can be used to review some of the functionality that was previously covered.

Practice B1

Create Parts

Practice Objective

- Create required sheet metal geometry using an appropriate template and sheet metal features.

Task 1 - Create the new parts.

1. Create the new part shown in Figure B–1 using the **Metric Sheet Metal (mm).ipt** template. The completed part is called **Appendix_1.ipt** in your practice files folder.

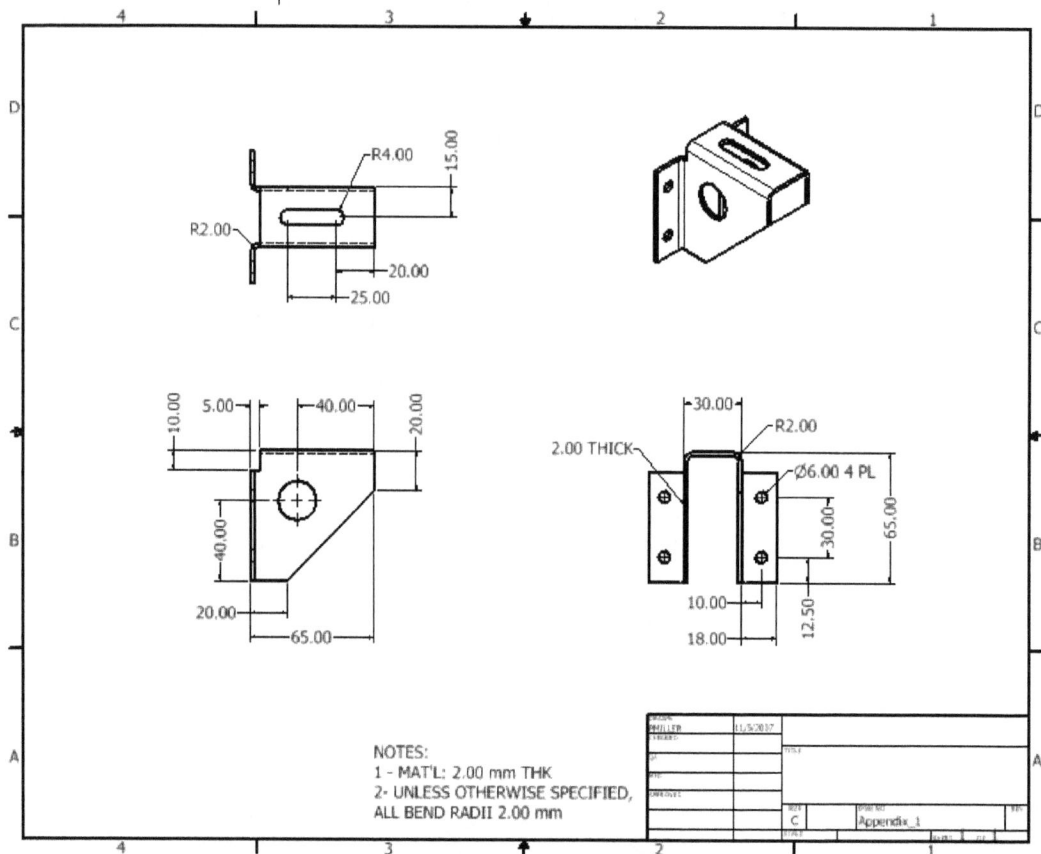

Figure B–1

NOTES:
1 - MAT'L: 2.00 mm THK
2- UNLESS OTHERWISE SPECIFIED, ALL BEND RADII 2.00 mm

2. Create the new part shown in Figure B–2 using the **Metric Sheet Metal (mm).ipt** template. The completed part is called **Appendix_2.ipt** in your practice files folder.

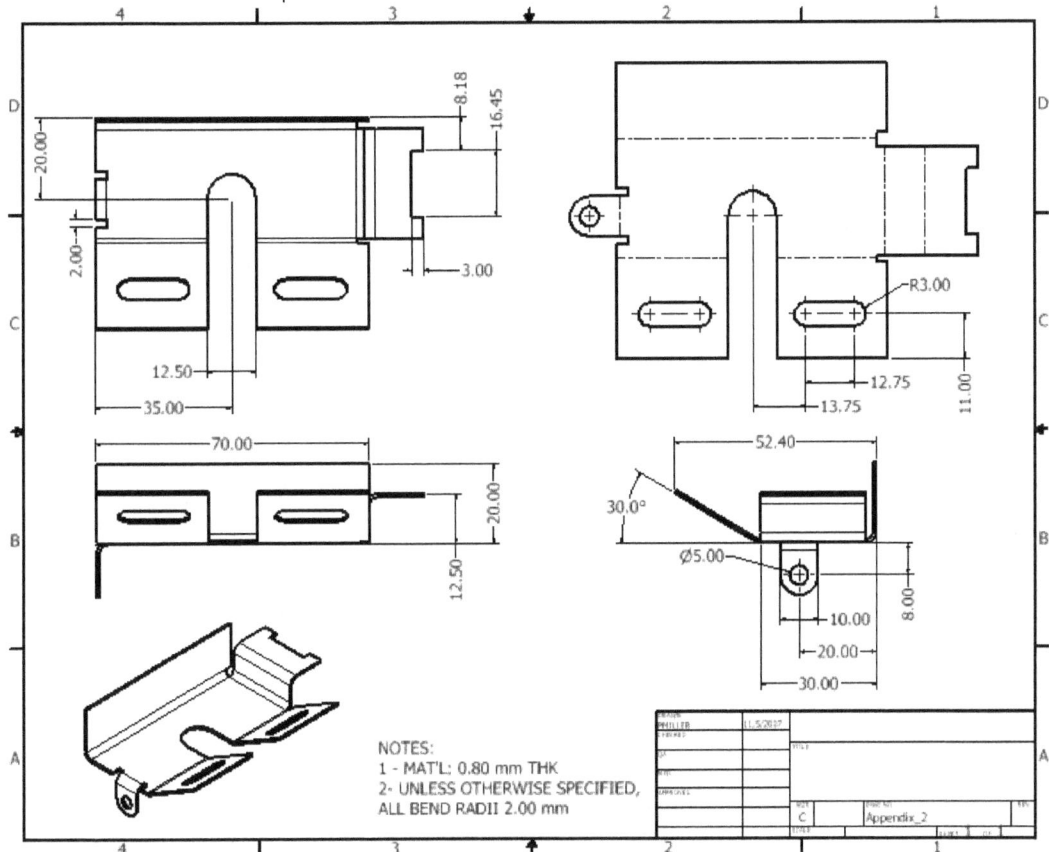

NOTES:
1 - MAT'L: 0.80 mm THK
2- UNLESS OTHERWISE SPECIFIED,
ALL BEND RADII 2.00 mm

Figure B–2

3. Create the new part shown in Figure B–3 using the **Metric Sheet Metal (mm).ipt** template. The completed part is called **Appendix_3.ipt** in your practice files folder.

R6.35   4X R6.35

16.75

6.35

63.50

31.75

30.00

50.80

6.18

56.83

6.35

101.65

126.15

A

R5.00

R2.50

9.50   10.00

NOTE: Flat Face with Rolled Hem 220 Deg.

DETAIL A
SCALE 5

NOTES:
1 - MAT'L: 2.50 mm THK
2- UNLESS OTHERWISE SPECIFIED,
ALL BEND RADII 2.50 mm

11/5/2017

C   Appendix_3

Figure B–3

4. Create the new part shown in Figure B–4 using the **Metric Sheet Metal (mm).ipt** template. The Flat Pattern is shown in Figure B–5. The completed part is called **Appendix_4.ipt** in your practice files folder.

Figure B–4

Figure B–5

5. Create the new part shown in Figure B–6 using the **Metric Sheet Metal (mm).ipt** template. The completed part is called **Appendix_5.ipt** in your practice files folder.

Figure B–6

NOTES:
1 - MAT'L: 1.27 mm THK
2 - UNLESS OTHERWISE SPECIFIED, ALL BEND RADII 1.27 mm

Autodesk Inventor
Certification Exam Objectives

The following table will help you to locate the exam objectives in the chapters of the *Autodesk® Inventor® 2017 Sheet Metal* student guide to help you prepare for the Autodesk Inventor Certified Professional exam.

Exam Topic	Exam Objective	Student Guide	Chapter & Section(s)
Advanced Modeling	Create a 3D path using the Intersection Curve and the Project to Surface commands	• Advanced Part	• 2.2
	Create a loft feature	• Advanced Part	• 5.1
		• Introduction to Solid Modeling	• 13.1, 13.2
	Create a multi-body part	• Advanced Assembly	• 4.1
		• Advanced Part	• 3.1
	Create a part using surfaces	• Advanced Part	• 8.1 to 8.7
			• 9.1 to 9.4
	Create a sweep feature	• Advanced Part	• 5.2
		• Introduction to Solid Modeling	• 12.1
	Create an iPart	• Advanced Part	• 11.1 to 11.4
	Emboss text and a profile	• Advanced Part	• A.1

Exam Topic	Exam Objective	Student Guide	Chapter & Section(s)
Assembly Modeling	Apply and use assembly constraints	• Introduction to Solid Modeling	• 16.1, 16.3
	Apply and use assembly joints	• Introduction to Solid Modeling	• 17.1
	Create a level of detail	• Advanced Assembly	• 10.1 to 10.6
	Create a part in the context of an assembly	• Introduction to Solid Modeling	• 22.1, 22.2
	Describe and use Shrinkwrap	• Advanced Assembly	• 9.1
	Create a positional representation	• Advanced Assembly	• 8.1 to 8.3
	Create components using the Design Accelerator commands	• Advanced Assembly	• 11.1 to 11.3
	Modify a bill of materials	• Introduction to Solid Modeling	• 23.2
	Find minimum distance between parts and components	• Introduction to Solid Modeling	• 19.1
	Use the frame generator command	• Advanced Assembly	• 15.1
Drawing	Edit a section view	• Introduction to Solid Modeling	• 25.3, 25.4
	Modify a style in a drawing	• Introduction to Solid Modeling	• 26.5, 26.6
	Edit a hole table	• Introduction to Solid Modeling	• 27.6
Part Modeling	Create a pattern of features	• Introduction to Solid Modeling	• 14.1, 14.2, 14.4
	Create a shell feature	• Introduction to Solid Modeling	• 9.3
	Create extrude features	• Introduction to Solid Modeling	• 2.2, 2.3 • 3.1 to 3.4 • 5.1, 5.2
	Create hole features	• Introduction to Solid Modeling	• 6.6
	Create revolve features	• Introduction to Solid Modeling	• 2.2, 2.3 • 3.1 to 3.4 • 5.1, 5.2
	Create work features	• Introduction to Solid Modeling	• 7.1 to 7.3
	Use the Project Geometry and Project Cut Edges commands	• Introduction to Solid Modeling	• 2.2 • 5.2
	Edit existing parts using Direct Edit	• Advanced Part	• 12.4

Exam Topic	Exam Objective	Student Guide	Chapter & Section(s)
Presentation Files	Animate a presentation file	• Introduction to Solid Modeling	• 20.1
Project Files	Control a project file	• Introduction to Solid Modeling	• 24.1
Sheet Metal	Create sheet metal features	• Sheet Metal	• Ch. 2 to 11 (all topics)
Sketching	Create dynamic input dimensions	• Introduction to Solid Modeling	• 2.2
	Use sketch constraints	• Introduction to Solid Modeling	• 2.2 • 3.3
	Sketch using Relax Mode	• Introduction to Solid Modeling	• 3.3
Weldments	Create a weldment	• Advanced Assembly	• 17.1 to 17.4

Index

www.ingramcontent.com/pod-product-compliance
Lightning Source LLC
Chambersburg PA
CBHW060944210326
41598CB00031B/4719